A Stern Reckoning: XXX Corps: From Gold Beach to the Seine is the story of the British Army's veteran XXX Corps, commanded by Lieutenant General Sir Brian Horrocks, that landed on Gold beach on 6 June 1944. The tale begins when its component divisions earmarked for the Normandy invasion returned to England in late 1943. Many men were not happy when they found out why they had been brought home and were quick to voice their displeasure. A large number had fought in France 1940, North Africa 1942, Tunisia and Sicily 1943 and thought they had done enough. In 1944 they commenced hard training for the new task until, in May 1944, they were moved into secure camps prior to embarkation. After storming the beaches XXX Corps entered the Bocage with its overgrown hedges, sunken lanes and fields -- a landscape perfect for defenders and a nightmare for attackers as they fought field by field and hedge by hedge in a bloody battle of attrition. Each town and village encountered had to be taken by frontal assault until ground to dust. The Germans, fiercely defending every inch of ground, made the Allies pay a high price in blood. As XXX Corps slowly advanced they left behind hundreds of gravesites in the verdant countryside. The stench of death hung on the warm summer air and hordes of black flies plagued the survivors.

Following the Bocage breakout, XXX Corps passed the hell that was Falaise and advanced to the Seine. It was here the 43rd Wessex Division would have to force a daylight crossing in small boats. German troops held the high ground on the far bank and had full observation of the crossing sites. Assault boats were riddled with bullets as they tried to force the river, but the attackers eventually reached the high ground before a savage battle ensued as the defenders were dislodged from entrenched positions. Whilst this battle raged Royal Engineer sappers commenced the construction of the David and Goliath bridges, all the time under heavy fire. More troops entered the bridgehead as the Germans brought forward Tiger tanks and infantry reinforcements before they were forced to withdraw. XXX Corps then burst out of the Seine bridgehead heading for the Reich. *A Stern Reckoning* is military history at its most dramatic and brutal viewed by a rich cast of characters who movingly relate their own experiences in great detail.

Hailing from Hull, Barrie Samuel Barnes earned a BA (hons) and an M/Phil Degree at Hull and Leeds universities, after which he gained a Post Graduate Certificate in Education. Twenty-six years in the teaching profession followed before retirement in 2007. *A Stern Reckoning* is his twelfth Book, Barrie is at present working on the second volume that follows XXX Corps progress from the Seine, where this volume leaves off, to the Reich

A Stern Reckoning

XXX Corps: From Gold Beach to the Seine

Barrie S. Barnes

Helion & Company

Helion & Company Limited
Unit 8 Amherst Business Centre
Budbrooke Road
Warwick
CV34 5WE
England
Tel. 01926 499 619
Email: info@helion.co.uk
Website: www.helion.co.uk
Twitter: @helionbooks
Visit our blog at blog.helion.co.uk

Published by Helion & Company 2023
Designed and typeset by Mach 3 Solutions (www.mach3solutions.co.uk)
Cover designed by Paul Hewitt, Battlefield Design (www.battlefield-design.co.uk)

Text © Barrie S. Barnes 2023
Images © as individually credited
Maps drawn by George Anderson © Helion & Company Ltd 2023
Special thanks to Tony Walton for providing additional editorial assistance.

Every reasonable effort has been made to trace copyright holders and to obtain their permission for the use of copyright material. The author and publisher apologize for any errors or omissions in this work and would be grateful if notified of any corrections that should be incorporated in future reprints or editions of this book.

ISBN 97-8-1804512-58-6

British Library Cataloguing-in-Publication Data.
A catalogue record for this book is available from the British Library.

All rights reserved. No part of this publication may be reproduced, stored in a retrieval system, or transmitted, in any form, or by any means, electronic, mechanical, photocopying, recording or otherwise, without the express written consent of Helion & Company Limited.

For details of other military history titles published by Helion & Company Limited contact the above address or visit our website: http://www.helion.co.uk.

We always welcome receipt of book proposals from prospective authors.

For Nick, Bob and Dave: my fellow companions on our pilgrimage to Normandy in May 2022. Thank you for your pleasant and easy company, which made it all so enjoyable. Especially to my friend Nick, who made it all possible and for driving us around to places on the Normandy coast we had not seen before. A moving journey that will never be forgotten.

Contents

List of Maps		vii
Glossary		viii
1	Operation Overlord	13
2	Back to Blighty and a New Ordeal	25
3	Away at Last	62
4	Into the Breach: King Sector, Gold Beach, 6 June 1944	94
5	Into the Breach: Jig Sector, Gold Beach, 6 June 1944	150
6	Expanding the Bridgehead: The Move Inland, 7–12 June 1944	214
7	The Deadly Bocage: June–July 1944	269
8	The Road to Mont Pinçon: July–August 1944	423
9	Breakout and Pursuit	485
10	From Falaise to the Seine	501
11	A Calvary Called Vernon, 25–27 August 1944	522
12	Out of Normandy	583

Appendices

I	Order of Battle, 50th Northumbrian Division, May/June 1944	591
II	50th Northumbrian Division Honours and Awards, 6–14 June 1944	594
III	Casualties to 50th Northumbrian Division, 6 June to 1 December 1944	601
IV	German Order of Battle, Gold Beach, 6 June 1944, 716th Static Infantry Division	602
V	Order of Battle, 7th Armoured Division, Villers Bocage, June 1944	603
VI	Order of Battle, 130th Panzer Lehr Division in the Bocage, June–July 1944	605
VII	Order of Battle, 101st SS-Panzer Battalion of the 1st SS-Panzer Division 'Leibstandarte SS Adolf Hitler' in the Bocage, June 1944	607
VIII	Biographical details of Company Sergeant Major Stanley Elton Hollis, VC, 6th Battalion Green Howards	608
IX	German reinforcement divisions which moved into the Normandy battle area between 6 and 18 June 1944	612
X	British operational codenames, 1944	613
XI	Order of Battle, 49th West Riding Division, attached to XXX Corps from 13 June–30 July 1944	614
XII	Order of Battle, 79th Armoured Division, June 1944	615

XIII	Order of Battle, 43rd Wessex Division, joined XXX Corps, 13 June 1944	616
XIV	Order of Battle, 11th Armoured Division, August 1944	618
XV	Order of Battle, 59th Staffordshire Division, joined XXX Corps, 13 June–24 July 1944 (disbanded August 1944)	619
XVI	Order of Battle, 12th SS-Panzer Division 'Hitlerjugend', Normandy, June 1944	620
XVII	Biographical details of Lieutenant General Sir Brian Horrocks, KCB, KBE, DSO, MC, LL.D	621

Bibliography	623
Index	627

List of Maps

XXX Corps landings, Gold Beach, 6 June 1944.	97
Disaster at Villers Bocage.	286
The deadly Bocage: June/July 1944.	321
The 49th West Riding Division at Fontenay-le-Pesnel, 25 June –1 July 1944.	349
The Road to Mont Pinçon, 6 August 1944.	457
From Mont Pinçon to the Noireau River, 8–16 August 1944.	488
The Falaise Pocket, the *Westheer*'s Stalingrad.	511
Assault Crossing at Vernon, 43rd Wessex Division, 25/26 August 1944.	556

Glossary

Artificial moonlight: lighting provided on land by powerful searchlights.
AVRE: Armoured Vehicle Royal Engineers. Churchill tank armed with a Petard spigot mortar that could fire a 40lb high explosive charge, nicknamed the flying dustbin. It could demolish large concrete gun emplacements very effectively.
Bangalore torpedo: metal tube packed with explosive, for blowing gaps in barbed wire entanglements.
Beach Brick: organisations that assisted the landing of men, materiel and vehicles, ensuring their smooth passage from the beaches to the troops inland.
Besa machine-gun: tank- mounted medium machine gun.
Blighty: to get a Blighty is to receive a wound that is not life-threatening but serious enough for the recipient to be sent home.
Boche: British soldiers' slang for German troops.
Bofors: 40mm Bofors gun, standard light anti-aircraft weapon.
Bomb happy: also known as shellshock; damage to the mind as a result of being under intense fire for prolonged periods.
Bought it: to be killed.
Box mine: German mine with a wooden casing that could not be found by mine detectors.
Bren Carrier: universal carrier also known as a bren-gun carrier. Light armoured British vehicle.
Bren gun: British magazine-fed light machine gun.
Brewing up: either making tea or a tank that is burning fiercely with the crew still inside.
Centaur: British tank armed with two heavy machine guns and a 95mm howitzer for demolishing concrete strongpoints.
CLY: County of London Yeomanry, tank regiment.
Compo rations: short for composite rations, field or combat rations; tinned or pre-packed meal.
Coxswain: person in charge of a boat, particularly navigation and steering.
Coy: Company.
CRA: Commander Royal Artillery.
Crab: British Sherman tank fitted with a flail to destroy barbed wire defences and make paths through minefields.
CRE: Commander Royal Engineers.
Crocodile: Churchill tank fitted with a flamethrower.
D-Day: the term is forever associated with 6 June 1944, but was originally a standard military expression for the day any operation began.

Davit: a crane-like device used on a ship for supporting, raising and lowering equipment such as boats.
DD: Duplex Drive amphibious Sherman tank; nicknamed Donald Duck tanks.
Defilade: military tactic; to use natural or artificial features as protection.
DUKW: six-wheeled Duplex Drive amphibious truck, nicknamed The Duck. Its initials come from the civilian factory categorisation of this vehicle. D: designed in 1942. U: utility. K: all-wheel drive. W: two powered rear axles.
DZ: drop zone for paratroopers, where they are expected to land.
Enfilade: military tactic. Flanking fire.
Fallschirmjaeger: German parachute troops.
Feldwebel: German NCO, translates as Field Usher.
Ferdinand: German self-propelled gun, introduced in 1943. The Panzerjager Tiger Ferdinand was massively armoured and had a powerful 88mm main gun.
FDL: Forward defensive line.
Firefly: Sherman tank fitted with a 17-pdr gun.
Flak: ground-to-air anti-aircraft fire.
Flimsy: petrol can.
FOO: Forward Observation Officer.
Funk: in a funk; temporary sadness, lack of motivation and purpose.
Funnies: nickname given to a number of specialist armoured fighting vehicles derived from tanks operated by the 79th Armoured Division on 6 June 1944, or by specialist units of the Royal Engineers. Major General Sir Percy Stanley Hobart was responsible for the development of what became known as Hobart's 'Funnies'.
Green Devils: *Fallschirmjaeger*; German airborne troops in the Second World War.
Hauptmann: Captain in German Army.
Hawker Typhoon: British rocket-firing fighter-bomber.
HE: high explosive.
Hedgehog: steel beach obstacle.
Horsa: British troop-carrying glider.
Hosing/to hose down: a phrase used when a tank saturates a building or area with heavy and constant Besa machine-gun fire.
H-Hour: the time when operations are due to start.
Hun: slang name for a German soldier.
IO: Intelligence Officer.
In the bag: to be put in the bag, or taken prisoner.
Ities (eyeties): British troops' slang for Italian soldiers.
Jabos: German slang name for Allied fighter-bombers.
Kamerad: comrade, truce or surrender word in German.
KIA: killed in action.
LAA: light anti-aircraft.
LBV: landing barge vehicle or lighter used for landing stores.
LCA: Landing Craft, Assault; small landing craft carrying 40 troops.
LCF: Landing Craft, Flak.
LCP: Landing Craft, Personnel; capable of carrying 40 troops.
LCI: Landing Craft, Infantry; capable of carrying 200 troops.

LCM: Landing Craft, Mechanised; small landing craft capable of carrying 100 troops and one tank.
LCS: Landing Craft, Support.
LCT: Landing Craft, Tank; capable of carrying up to six 40-ton tanks.
LCOCU: Landing Craft Obstacle Clearing Unit; Royal Navy divers.
LSI: Landing Ship, Infantry; capable of carrying up to 1,500 troops.
LST: Landing Ship, Tank; capable of carrying a cargo of 2,000 tons.
Luftwaffe: German Air Force.
Mae West: slang for life preserver/vest.
Matelot: from the French *matenot*; sailor.
MO: Medical Officer.
MT: Motor transport.
Mulberry Harbour: temporary portable harbours developed in the UK during the Second World War. Famously used in the Normandy landings in June 1944.
NCO: non-commissioned officers, all ranks except private below lieutenant.
Nebelwerfer: German multi-barrelled rocket launcher.
Neptune: Naval assault phase of Overlord.
OC: officer commanding.
Oerlikon gun: 60-round drum-fed 20mm cannon, mounted on naval vessels on a free-swinging pedestal with a flat armoured shield to protect the gunner.
OP: observation post.
Panzerfaust: one-shot recoilless hand-held anti-tank projectile.
Panzerschreck: the *Raketenpanzerbusche 54* was a hand-held reusable 88mm anti-tank rocket launcher, used to deadly effect in the Bocage in 1944.
Piat: Projector, Infantry, Anti-Tank; British light anti-tank weapon.
Pillbox: reinforced concrete bunker or machine-gun emplacement.
Pompadours: nickname for the 2nd Battalion the Essex Regiment, originally given in the eighteenth century to the 56th Regiment of Foot, as the shade of rose-pompadour was selected for their cuffs, lapels and collars.
Portee: military vehicle that carries an artillery piece that is not fixed to the chasse but can be easily unloaded.
POW: Prisoner of War.
Priest: 105mm self-propelled artillery mounted on a tracked chassis.
Pt: high point on a map (eg Pt 106).
RAMC: Royal Army Medical Corps.
RAP: Regimental Aid Post.
Recce: reconnaissance.
Red Devils: British airborne troops.
RHA: Royal Horse Artillery.
Rhino Ferry: barge constructed from several pontoons and equipped with outboard engines; used to transport heavy equipment and troops.
R/T: radio telegraphy.
RTR: Royal Tank Regiment.
RV: rendezvous.
Scorpion: Matilda tank fitted with a rotating flail of chains for clearing minefields.

Sortie: a raid into enemy lines.
SP: self-propelled gun.
Spandau: MG42, German general-purpose machine gun.
Stabsgefreiter: second highest rank of an enlisted German soldier.
Stand to: a time when all troops stand to their arms in case of an enemy attack, as dawn breaks or at last light.
Sten gun: British sub-machine gun.
Stonk: artillery barrage.
Tattie masher: German stick grenade.
TD: Territorial Decoration.
Tedescish: slang used by British troops for anything German.
Tetrahedron: triangular beach obstacle made of steel with a mine attached to the top; an anti-tank and anti-landing craft device used on the Normandy beaches.
The Great Swan: swift, large-scale, virtually unopposed advances over open ground.
Tiger: German super-heavy tank of 68 tons (Tiger II) armed with an 88mm gun.
Tobruk nest: defensive fighting position/earthwork constructed in a military context; first constructed by Italian engineers at Tobruk.
Tommy or Thompson gun: Thompson sub-machine gun, favoured by soldiers for its accuracy and high volume of fully automatic fire.
Tommy cooker: portable field cooker carried by British troops; also German nickname for a British tank that was blazing fiercely with the crew still inside.
TT: the formation sign of the 50th Northumbrian Division (Tyne Tees).
Unteroffizier: German Army or *Luftwaffe* equivalent of the British rank of sergeant/NCO.
Very light: pronounced 'vary'; signal flares of various colours fired from a Very pistol to illuminate the landscape or to summon up a barrage from the rear.
W/T: wireless telegraphy.
88: German heavy anti-aircraft gun used very effectively in an anti-tank role.

1

Operation Overlord

As late as November 1943, Hitler refused to believe that the Greater Reich was threatened by the opening of a second front in the west. Since Operation Barbarossa had begun, Stalin had pressed for the Allies to aid the Soviet Union by launching a counter invasion of Western Europe. On 19 August 1942, the port of Dieppe was raided by a force of 6,000 largely Canadian troops; only 2,500 of them returned to Britain. It was later claimed that the aim of this experimental raid was to assess the difficulties involved when seizing an occupied harbour for the opening of a second front. Hitler, however, saw the situation in a different light; he believed he had inflicted such a defeat on the British at Dieppe that it would deter them and their allies from launching a full-scale invasion of Europe. Furthermore, he believed his Atlantic Wall would be fully completed by the spring of 1943 and that after that date nothing could touch his coastal defences. In 1942, this assessment was borne out by the fact that the British were still suffering from the shock of defeat in 1940 and the Americans were not yet adapted to the rigours of total war. But by the autumn of 1943, the British and American air offensives against the Reich were growing in intensity and weight, Kiev had fallen to the Red Army in November and the British and American forces had gained their self-esteem as tried and tested combat troops in Egypt and then Tunisia and Sicily. In 1943, the Atlantic Wall was incomplete; in November that year, Hitler issued *Führer* Directive 51, its main ruling being to strengthen the defences on the Western Front in Europe. It stated that an Anglo-American landing was expected in mainland Europe and that all panzer and *panzergrenadier* divisions should be reinforced, but these divisions could only be redeployed on the personal order of the *Führer*. All ground forces in France and Belgium were commanded by *Generalfeldmarschall* Gerd von Rundstedt. His divisional strength stood at 46, soon to be raised to 60, 10 of these being panzer and panzer grenadier divisions.

On 19 May 1944, *Generalfeldmarschall* Erwin Rommel, as commander of *Herresgruppe B* (Army Group B) in northern France, was working hard to prepare the Normandy coast for an attack by the Allies and was looking forward to getting a couple of days leave in Germany for his wife's birthday in June:

> I telephoned the *Führer* for the first time in a couple of days. He was in the best of humours and did not spare his praise of the work we have done in the west. I now hope to get on a little faster than we have been doing. The weather is still cold and it's raining at last, the

A German labour company building a gun emplacement in Normandy. (Courtesy of M. Hearst)

British will have to be patient for a bit. I'm waiting to see whether I shall be able to get away for a couple of days in June, it's out of the question at the moment. But, unfortunately, things have not gone very well in Italy, the enemy's tremendous superiority in artillery, and even more in the air, has broken our front open.[1]

Stationed to the south of the Loire were four panzer divisions, with six more to the north. This strong, well-equipped and very mobile reserve was an essential element to the overall defensive plan, as it was not possible to reinforce the coastal front with a system of fortifications in depth at all points. The concentration of mobile armoured forces was also of importance because the other divisions stationed in the west were totally dependent for their movement upon the French railway system should they be ordered to leave their permanent bases. Supply and artillery units were mostly relying on horse-drawn transport, while the infantry manoeuvred at marching speed, making both vulnerable to the air attacks by the Allies, whose aerial superiority would severely inhibit any movement by road or rail. It was therefore of the greatest importance that the mobile panzer divisions, with their rapid off-road deployment capabilities, should be stationed near the predicted invasion areas in order to hold the line until the slower-moving infantry formations could reinforce them. The static divisions holding the coast would be protected from the Allied air raids and naval gunfire by stout concrete fortifications. These positions overlooked the beaches, which in turn were wired, mined and littered with thousands

---

1   Liddell Hart, B.H. (ed.), *The Rommel Papers* (London: Collins, 1953), p. 464.

During a quiet time, German troops relax by fooling around at a gun emplacement in Normandy, April 1944. (Author's collection)

of obstacles and booby traps made from materials that had been stripped from other areas, such as the Maginot Line and the line of Belgian forts. In theory, the idea of the Atlantic Wall was sound, and its completion would compensate for German inferiority in the air. Indeed, at the end of 1943, the Luftwaffe fielded only 300 fighters in France, and on the day of the invasion these would have to hold in check an Allied force of some 12,000 aircraft of all types. However, by the time Hitler issued Directive 51, the Atlantic Wall was far from completed.

During the quiet period when Hitler refused to believe that there was any danger in the west, German troops were more than happy to be posted to the only easy billet in their areas of operations. They ate good food and led a life of relative luxury compared to their comrades in Italy and on the Eastern Front. The work was not too hard and the dangers of actual combat seemed remote.

This was highlighted by engineer *Oberleutnant* Holger Eckhertz, of *Grenadier-Regiment 736, 716. Infanterie-Division*, who was posted to Normandy:

> It was said of the troops in France that they lived like Gods, and you know, when I joined the 716th, I realised what a lucky swine I was. The food was excellent, and it was possible to buy virtually anything you wanted on the black market. Every morning I thought of my brother in combat in Russia and I felt extremely guilty.[2]

---

2 Manuscript forwarded to author by H. Wernemann (Germany, 1990).

Grenadier Robert Voigt, serving with *Abteilung 726*, was posted to the *716. Division* and was stationed near La Riviere – later to find fame as Gold Beach – in January 1944, along with other men who had physical problems such as poor eyesight or flat feet. When he arrived, he found the morale of his comrades to be very low:

> In January I was convinced that our position was hopeless. Although there was a lot of work going on, planting obstacles and so-forth, the defences were not worth talking about. Everyone in the company knew that a good bombing would destroy everything. I felt the situation was hopeless, but when the invasion actually started, I knew that it would be a battle for survival.[3]

Soldiers are basically interested in the essentials of life, and what they have to eat every day comes top of their priorities. In Normandy, the poor official rations were not in plentiful supply and the infantry seemed to be at the bottom of the pile when it came to provisions. As soldiers have done for centuries, it was not long before the German troops began to fraternise with the locals – even though this was forbidden – and bartered spare equipment and materials for all kinds of food.

Gefreiter Werner Beibst remembered the tasty morsels he and his comrades from *Abteilung 726* of the *716. Infanterie-Division* traded from the French farmers and townsfolk:

> They had bread, milk, cider, eggs and even fresh meat, which was otherwise unavailable to us army lower ranks. In return we exchanged cigarettes, bootlaces and lamp oil, which the French couldn't get hold of at all. We would say "Fill your belly with French ham and cider, because tomorrow you may be transferred to the east, where there is only hard biscuit and snow to eat." Some of our bunkers were little storehouses of contraband food and liquor and the officers would take their share when they inspected us.[4]

Rommel took over command of *Heeresgruppe B* (Army Group B) in December 1943 and arrived to inspect the coastal defences. The cosy existence enjoyed by the troops on the Atlantic Wall was about to come to an end, Rommel being greatly displeased at the situation he found. His judgement on the troops stationed there was harsh:

> Generally speaking, the troops are not working hard enough on the construction of the defences, they just don't realise how important it is. There is still a lot to do because many a man here has been leading a soft life and hasn't thought enough about the battles that are coming. In times of peace men grow lazy and self-content.[5]

Neither was Rommel's superior, von Rundstedt, impressed with Hitler's much-vaunted Atlantic Wall, commenting:

---

3   Trigg, J., *D-Day Through German Eyes* (Gloucestershire: Amberley Publishing, 2019), p. 32.
4   Trigg, *D-Day Through German Eyes*, p. 33.
5   Liddell Hart, *The Rommel Papers*, p. 468.

Rommel inspecting the Atlantic Wall. (*The War Illustrated*, December 1944)

It had to be seen to be believed. It had no depth, little surface to it, and was sheer humbug. At best it might have proved an obstacle for 24 hours at any one point, but one day's intensive assault by a determined force was all that was needed to break any part of this line.[6]

Rommel was blunt, frank and straightforward in his dealings with his subordinates, and made an unforgettable impression on the commanders of each sector he visited. It was not long before the construction of the Atlantic Wall began in earnest as steel and wooden beach obstacles, known as 'Rommel's asparagus', began to spring up, spreading like an ugly growth along the entire coast of North-west Europe. The German defences had been designed exclusively for a landing at high tide by the British and Americans. No German commander believed that they would land at low tide, when they would have to cross a clear field of fire 800 yards deep, and for that reason the entire coastal defences had been positioned so that they covered the foreshore. *Grenadier* Robert Voigt, who was serving as an infantryman constructing the new defences on what would become known to the Allies as Gold Beach, recalled:

Before 6th June 1944 we were directly on the coast near Arromanches planting Rommel's asparagus. We did all of this at low tide when the sea retreated for several miles. We put in

6   Kershaw, R.J., *D-Day, Piercing the Atlantic Wall* (Surrey: Peter Allan Publishing, 1993), p. 22.

The Longues Battery concrete gun emplacement containing a large calibre artillery piece. Normandy, 2 June 1944. (Author's collection)

a wooden beam and then, at a distance of I'd say five yards, another beam. On top of these we attached a third beam with clamps. We attached landmines to the tips of the beams, so that at high tide the mines would be so close to the waters' surface that even a flat-bottomed boat would touch them and be destroyed. All this construction went on under great pressure because there were virtually no bunkers at our location, only dugouts. This was the time when Field Marshal Rommel said the famous words "You must stop them here on the first day, if you don't stop them here it's over." We worked in shifts around the clock, I managed to get some shut eye that night. We had built 2 and 3 storey bunk beds in a farmhouse about 500 yards from the beach.[7]

In April and May 1944, Rommel travelled extensively in Normandy, demanding of his men their utmost efforts. Any open fields inland were dotted with tall upright stakes to deter airborne landings. Hitler insisted that the coastal forces in Normandy, including the port of Cherbourg, be strengthened, and the *91. Infanterie-Division* was diverted from the Seventh Army to Normandy to play a defensive role against any assaults from the air. The American paratroopers that would drop to the rear of Utah Beach would find these defenders ready and waiting. On 9 May, Rommel visited the Cotentin Peninsula, Houlgate on the coast east of

---

7   Manuscript forwarded to author by H. Wernemann (Germany, 1989).

Merville and then moved on to Caen, where he was briefed by the senior commanders. During the afternoon of the 9th, he toured the area that would be known to the Allies as Gold, Juno and Sword beaches. The concrete casemated naval battery at Longues was visited later the same day, and the German commander ended his tour at St Lo for his evening meal.

Rommel continued to speculate as to where the British and Americans would strike, being all too aware that his enemy would do all they could to deceive the German High Command about their intentions. His thoughts on the expected invasion were forthright and practical:

> It is evident that an Anglo/American landing in the west will and must come. How and where it will come no one knows. No kind of speculation on the subject is possible. Whatever concentrations of shipping may exist, they cannot and must not be taken as evidence, or any indication that the choice has fallen on any one sector of the long Western Front from Norway to the Bay of Biscay, or on the Mediterranean: either the south coast of France, the Italian coast or the Balkans. Such concentrations can be moved or transferred at any time under the cover of bad visibility and will obviously serve as feints. At no place along our long front is an invasion impossible. By far the most important thing for the enemy will be to gain a port for landings on the largest possible scale. This alone gives a wholly special importance to the west coast ports. The enemies' entire landing operation must under no circumstances be allowed to last longer than a matter of hours, or at the most days, with the Dieppe attempt as a model. Once the landing has been defeated it will under no circumstances be repeated by the enemy.[8]

General Bernard Montgomery, commander of the Allies' 21st Army Group, knowing that Rommel, his old adversary from the Western Desert, was organising the defences of Normandy, commented:

> He is an energetic and determined commander and he has made a world of difference since he took over. He is best at the spoiling attack and his forte is disruption, he will do his level best to Dunkirk us. However, while the Allies should respect Rommel, they need not fear him. If the Allies storm ashore seeing red, imbued with infectious optimism and offensive eagerness, nothing must stop them. If we send them into battle in this way then we shall succeed.[9]

On the wet and windy morning of 4 June, Rommel left the front and returned to Germany for his wife's birthday. He also intended to ask Hitler for the transfer of two panzer divisions to the Normandy sector.

For many months before the invasion, American troops and war materiel had been pouring into England, with the US First Army and British Second Army assembled for the great undertaking. Both armies were placed under 21st Army Group under Montgomery, whose task it was to secure a bridgehead on the continent. The supreme commander of the entire operation – codenamed Overlord – was to be the American General Dwight D. Eisenhower. The exact date

---

8   Liddell Hart, *The Rommel Papers*, p. 465.
9   D'Este, C., *Eisenhower: Allied Supreme Commander* (London: Weidenfeld & Nicolson, 2002), p. 501.

Rommel consults with his commanders as he tours the Normandy front, May 1944. (Author's collection)

of the invasion was fixed by three considerations: the plan of attack, the tides and the German defences. Aerial photographs of the Normandy coastline taken that spring showed German troops and French civilians labouring constantly to build gun emplacements and mined obstacles on the beaches. The German intention was that if a landing was made at high tide, a large number of obstacles would be underwater and out of sight, but would be close enough to the surface so that even craft with a shallow keel would hit them and be destroyed. If a landing was made at low tide, the attacking troops would have to cross long stretches of open beaches, in places as deep as 800 yards, under intense German fire. Eisenhower and Montgomery settled for the latter option, and to minimise the risk to the infantry would land specialised tanks ahead of them to clear a path for the attacking troops. The landing would actually take place just after low tide so that many of the obstacles could be demolished, and the operation could continue as the tide came in.

Naval considerations demanded that the approach to the coast be made under cover of darkness. However, both naval and air forces needed an hour of daylight for the bombardment of the coastal defences. On 6 June, low tide in Normandy was one hour after dawn; on the 5th and 7th, it was still just near enough to be acceptable. These considerations fixed the time of the attack for an hour after dawn, and the date of 5 June was chosen as D-Day, with 6 and 7 June able to be used as alternatives should anything go wrong. H-Hour, the moment of landing, was to be

Troops of the German *91. Infanterie-Division* moving to Normandy, April/May 1944. (Courtesy of M. Denney)

at 0630 hours at the western end of the landing area, as the tide reached there first, and 0730 hours at the eastern extremity.

Although the German High Command now knew that the invasion was imminent, they could not agree if it would come in Normandy or the Pas-de-Calais, a difference of opinion that was in part the result of a deliberate plan of deception by the Allies. Indeed, having made their plans to launch a landing in Normandy, they did everything in their power to convince the Germans that it would come in Calais. As the troops and fleets of ships intended for the assault concentrated in southern England, dummy tanks, camps and ships were constructed in the south-east of the country. All the normal radio traffic of an army group was created in Kent, and General George S. Patton, who was well known to the German High Command from his time in North Africa and Sicily leading American forces, was brought to England to command this non-existent invasion force – given the name First United States Army Group – completing the deception of what was known as Operation Fortitude. More air reconnaissance and bombing were carried out in the Calais area than in Normandy, and the British Secret Service was also busy planting seeds of doubt in a divided German High Command. German spies that had been captured in England had their identities taken and were in turn used by British spies to send false reports to Berlin. All of this convinced the Germans that the Allies' target was indeed the Pas-de-Calais. The German intelligence services swallowed the bait: after the war, some 250 reports were found in the Nazi archives predicting where the invasion would come, and all but one were wrong.

Gefreiter Heinz Herbst, serving with the *Aufklärung Abteilung* of the *12. SS-Panzer-Division 'Hitlerjugend'*, commented on the success of the deception:

> We thought the invasion would be around Calais, but the English deceived us. Again and again, we heard on the airwaves that they seemed to be giving orders to start extensive troop movements towards the environs of Dover. We heard both the English and American orders, it was very skilled because it caused us to think that that was where the invasion would come from.[10]

Hitler refused to publically acknowledge the fact that defeat was, in the long run, inevitable, with the long-husbanded strength of two world powers set to come into action against him. However, Hitler's persona assessment of the situation, given in private, was gloomy and even gave a passing nod to the reality of the situation at one meeting of the German High Command. *General der Artillerie* Walter Warlimont, deputy chief of the operations staff of the OKW (*Oberkommando der Wehrmacht*), recalled Hitler's words as he spoke of the impending Allied landings in France:

> If we don't throw the invaders back, we can't win a static war in the long run because the material our enemies can bring in will exceed what we can send to the front. With no strategic reserves of any importance, it will be impossible to build up sufficient strength along such a line. Therefore, the enemy must be thrown back at the first attempt.[11]

Rommel was greatly concerned that the German mobile reserve would be too far from the coast to intervene when the invasion came. On 21 March, he had succeeded in convincing Hitler of the need to move the reserves nearer to the coast, but within 24 hours Hitler reversed this decision. Rommel then noted:

> My only real anxiety concerns the mobile forces. Contrary to what was decided at the conference on 21st March they have not so far been placed under my command. Some of them are dispersed over a large area well inland, which means they will arrive too late to play any part in the battle for the coast. With the heavy enemy air superiority, we can expect any large-scale movement of motorised forces to the coast will be exposed to air attacks of tremendous weight and long duration. But without rapid assistance from the armoured divisions and mobile units, our coastal divisions will be hard put to it to [resist] counter attacks coming simultaneously from the sea and from airborne troops inland. Their land front is too thinly held for that. The dispositions of combat and reserve forces should be such as to ensure that the minimum possible movement will be required to counterattack at any of the most likely points, whether in the Low Countries, in the Channel area

---

10   Miller, R., *Nothing Less than Victory* (London: Michael Joseph, 1993), p. 94.
11   Detweiler, D.S., *World War II German Military Studies* (New York: Garland, 1979), p. 551.

proper, in Normandy and Brittany, and to ensure that the greater part of the enemy troops, sea and airborne, will be destroyed by our fire during their approach.[12]

The general intention of the Allied invasion was to execute airborne landings the night before the main assault, then to land and attack on a five divisional front on the morning of D-Day, with two American and three British/Canadian divisions using an assortment of landing craft. Follow-up divisions would land on D-Day and D plus one, and after the bridgehead had been stabilised and the attacking troops were moving inland, further reinforcements would be brought ashore at the rate of more than a division each day. The purpose of the airborne landings was to protect the flanks of the main seaborne assault group – codenamed Operation Neptune – which would land with the US 4th and 1st Divisions on the right and the 50th Northumbrian, 3rd Canadian and 3rd British Divisions on the left. In addition to the numerous types of landing craft, the might of the Royal Navy and many US naval ships were to be deployed in the Channel, making for an awesome spectacle. The Allied Supreme Commander, Eisenhower, faced the daunting task ahead of him with trepidation: no commander in history had ever taken on such an awesome undertaking as that he was about to head in June 1944. He was not only responsible for coordinating the movements of the largest force ever brought together for an amphibious invasion, but knew that it had to work on the first attempt; there would be no second chance. It was literally 'death or glory'.

For months before D-Day, the great air fleets of America and Britain had ranged across the continent on strategic bombing missions. Their workload increased as D-Day drew ever closer, being now required to provide air cover for bases in the UK and to protect coastal convoys and the troops congregating in their areas of assembly.

When the assault began, they would also have to give air cover to the attacking formations. It was therefore essential that Allied fighter squadrons should maintain complete air superiority to prevent the Germans from interfering with the land and sea operations. The British army would be supplied over the beaches through minor ports and by the use of prefabricated ports. One of the latter, codenamed Mulberry, would be constructed in the area that XXX Corps would attack, between Arromanches and La Rivière, and would be towed in sections across the Channel and erected on-site.

As the countdown to D-Day continued, the misinformation the Germans were being fed was working. While the majority of indicators for the coming assault were discernible, their credibility – to those sifting through the mass of facts – was not. Rommel reflected pessimistically:

> Bearing in mind the numerical and material superiority of the enemy striking forces, their high state of training and tremendous air superiority, victory for us in a major battle on the continent seems to me a matter of grave doubt.[13]

---

12 Liddell Hart, *The Rommel Papers*, p. 469.
13 Liddell Hart, *The Rommel Papers*, p. 507.

German troops, working on the construction of coastal obstacles, run for cover as an Allied reconnaissance fighter roars overhead. (Author's collection)

Allied bombers hitting rail links and road junctions in Normandy, May 1944. (Author's collection)

2

Back to Blighty and a New Ordeal

The XXX Corps was formed in the Western Desert in September 1941 and saw service in North Africa, at 2nd Alamein, in Tunisia and Sicily. Many casualties had been taken along the way, and XXX Corps returned to England in late 1943 to refit, replenish its ranks and retrain for Operation Overlord. Inside the framework of this broad adventurous plan, the allotted task of XXX Corps would be the storming of the coastal defences between Arromanches and La Rivière, an area codenamed Gold Beach, and to penetrate as far as the ancient town of Bayeux to the west and the area of St Leger to the east. Within XXX Corps, 47 Royal Marine Commando was to come under the command of the 50th Northumbrian Division and their task would be to capture the small but essential town and harbour of Port-en-Bessin. They would land at H plus two hours and head west, taking the port from a southerly direction. In early 1944, it was obvious that the 50th Northumbrian Division did not possess enough troops to ensure success, consisting of only three brigades – 151, 69 and 231 Brigades. An extra brigade was therefore asked for and given in the form of 56 Independent Brigade. None of 56 Brigade's battalions had ever served overseas, but in the short time available to them they had been training hard as a reserve unit, working in unison with the 7th Armoured Division. Other major formations were also incorporated into the Northumbrian Division's order of battle for the coming assault: 8 Armoured Brigade, an American battalion of 150mm Priest self-propelled guns, three British artillery regiments, two anti-tank batteries and an assortment of specially fitted armoured vehicles – 'Funnies', as they were known, designed by Major General Percy Hobart – of the 79th Armoured Division, intended to overcome beach obstacles or defences, manmade or natural. As D-Day, approached the divisional strength of the 50th stood at an impressive 38,000 men.

In the Allied higher command, there was great concern about the load-bearing capacity of the landing beaches, and whether they would take the weight of tanks and other heavy vehicles. Most beaches consisted of 14 inches of sand above a layer of clay and peat. Major Logan Scott-Bowden of the Royal Engineers had the unenviable job of making a reconnaissance of the enemy-held beaches where the attack would go in. Many were very sceptical that such an operation could be done there, but Scott-Bowden was determined to prove them wrong:

> My job was beach reconnaissance, to swim ashore at night from a midget submarine or some other vessel and to carry out a reconnaissance of the beaches. Some people reckoned it would be extremely difficult to do an actual reconnaissance on an enemy held beach and

German soldiers working on the construction of beach obstacles, Normandy, March/April 1944. (Author's collection)

get away with it. We arranged a demonstration at Brancaster beach in Norfolk, which was geologically similar to the beaches in Normandy. We sailed out to sea in an LCT and swam ashore in the dark. Sentries had been posted all over the place, but we managed to crawl passed them, get our samples and take them back. Afterwards they checked all the information we had obtained and found it to be correct and I think that played a considerable part in getting permission for the reconnaissance to take place. It had been ruled by Churchill that no reconnaissance should take place without his specific authorisation.[1]

New Year's Eve 1943: "Happy New Year"

On New Year's Eve 1943, Major Scott-Bowden led a party to Normandy to gain the required information. They travelled over to France in rough weather in a motor torpedo boat, and as they approached the shoreline at Luc-sur-Mer found that the lighthouse there was working. The beam lit up the area at intervals, making the men feel very naked and vulnerable, and the rain silhouetted the houses of the village where the Germans were celebrating the New Year. Eventually, according to Scott-Bowden, samples were taken from the beach and the time came to leave:

---

1   Miller, *Nothing Less than Victory*, p. 1.

That's when the trouble really started because the breakers were quite heavy, and we were bogged down with our bandoliers and all our other kit. We had a go at getting out and were flung back to shore by the waves. We did the same again and again were flung back a second time. The prospects didn't look too good so we went out into the water as far as we could and watched the rhythm of the breakers, hoping that we could time the moment to get out. Bogged down as we were and out of our depth it was quite a feat to get through a breaker, but on our third attempt we managed it and swam like hell to make sure we weren't pitched back again. I swam out a little further than Sergeant Bruce Ogden-Smith and for a moment thought we had got separated, but then I heard him yelling, I thought maybe he'd got cramp, so I swam over to him and, this is quite true, when I got close enough I found out that all he was yelling was "Happy New Year". I think I swore at him then wished him a happy New Year. He was a good chap, a marvellous fellow. We swam out to the point we thought would be our rendezvous and started flashing our torches, always being careful we didn't get turned round in the rough seas and start flashing in the wrong direction. After what seemed to be a rather long time, we at last saw the prow of a craft coming to pick us up.[2]

The winter storms grew worse as the seasick and tired engineers headed for England with their naval escort, the little craft battling through high seas in the darkness. The trip had been a great success and was to be repeated three weeks later when the American beaches were visited by these intrepid engineers. The information gathered was of great interest to the planners of Overlord, helping when they were looking at where to land tanks and other heavy vehicles.

Operation Gambit

The Royal Navy asked for volunteers to take part in a top-secret mission that was intended to guide the invasion force to the beaches of Normandy. The only stipulation was that the men chosen had to be able to swim and that they should be single. These volunteers would be on a midget submarine, X23, that would leave the shores of England on 2 June and remain undetected off the Normandy coast, sitting on the seabed, until they were required. The submarine would be vulnerable to attack on the surface and would have to navigate its way through large minefields below the surface to get to their station. Lieutenant George Honor was chosen to command the vessel, and he recalled:

> Our part in the operation was named Operation Gambit. I looked up our occupational name in a dictionary and to our horror it said, "Pawn given away before big chess move".[3]

The volunteers trained hard aboard the cramped interior of X23 for their mission as D-Day approached, each man wondering what the future held for such a hazardous undertaking.

---

2   Miller, *Nothing Less than Victory*, p. 1.
3   Newspaper cutting forwarded to author by J. Verity (Beverley, 1991).

Vessels of all types congregating on the south coast of England, April/May 1944. (Author's collection)

The 50th Northumbrian Division comes home, November 1943, "Why us?"

In early November 1943, troop ships carrying the suntanned veterans of the 50th Northumbrian Division arrived in the Mersey estuary on a wet and misty day. Every man had been dreaming of this moment as he sweated under a blazing desert sun or in the hot vineyards of Sicily. As they set foot on land, they were greeted by American military policemen, looking smart in their pressed uniforms and white gaiters, belts and helmets, as they patrolled the dockside. Hidden speakers played music of a patriotic nature to welcome the soldiers home. The sight of the docks brought back many memories for those who had left them in 1941 when the division had set off on its adventures to an unknown land. However, many familiar faces were now missing. The first brigade to leave the shores of England in 1940, 150 Brigade, did not return; its men now lay in the ground at Gazala or were in enemy hands, having been wiped out in June 1942.

An air of tight security shrouded the arrival of the 50th Division, as Sergeant Max Hearst of the 5th Battalion East Yorkshire Regiment (5th East Yorks), 69 Brigade, recalled:

> On our way home we were told to remove all our insignia from our uniforms as no one was supposed to know we was arriving, [but] the first thing we saw as we entered Liverpool

Troops of the 50th Northumbrian Division arrive at Liverpool Docks in November 1943. (Courtesy of J. Verity)

docks was a big banner that proclaimed, "Welcome home 50th Division". Bloody marvellous, so much for secrecy! After that it was up to Scotland for training and then we got a two-week leave. If you had an Eighth Army medal you couldn't go wrong, everybody wanted to buy you a drink if you went into a pub. There were only about 90 originals left from the 5th East Yorks, some were prisoners of war, some were wounded or maimed, and many had been killed.[4]

Many soldiers returning home with the Northumbrian Division were not happy about what they had been brought home for, the D-Day landings. They felt that they had done their share – and then some – and were not shy about voicing their grievances.

Major Peter Martin, a member of the 2nd Machine-gun Battalion the Cheshire Regiment, remembered when General Douglas Graham, the 50th Northumbrian Division CO, came to

---

4   Max Hearst, interview with author (Hull, 1990).

address the officers of the division and to confirm their role for the invasion:

> All the officers had to assemble in a cinema and General Graham, who Monty used to refer to as "A gallant old war horse" and was a delightful person, stood up to address us. He said Monty had been in grave doubt as to whether the 50th or the 51st Highland Division should be one of the initial assault divisions in the invasion of Europe and, in the end, Monty had tossed a coin for it and he, General Graham, was delighted to say that 50 Div had won and would therefore have the very great honour of leading the invasion of Europe. Whereupon there was a colossal "Boo" from all around the cinema. I felt really quite sorry for General Graham, but I think the division felt it had done its bit by now and that it was time somebody else took a turn.[5]

Sergeant Max Hearst, 5th Battalion East Yorkshire Regiment. (Courtesy of Max Hearst)

Montgomery stated his reasons for wanting to use his experienced troops for the main assault:

> The army then in England lacked battle experience and had tended to become theoretical rather than practical. Officers did not understand those tricks of the battlefield which mean so much to junior leaders and which save so many lives. In the last resort the battle is won by the initiative and skill of regimental officers and men, and without these assets you fail, however good the high command. Some very experienced fighting formations had returned to England from the Mediterranean theatre at the end of the Sicily campaign. By exchanging officers between these formations and those which had never left the country, I tried to spread such battle experience as was available over the widest possible area. Again, this was unpopular, but was more readily accepted when I had explained the reason.[6]

Grousing and AWOL

Private A. Foster, 6th Battalion Durham Light Infantry (6th Durhams), had been in many bloody actions in France (1940), North Africa (1942), Tunisia and Sicily (both 1943), and did not appreciate coming home to get more of the same:

---

5 P. Martin, correspondence with author (Cheshire, 1989).
6 Montgomery, B.L., *Memoirs* (London: Collins, 1958), p. 207.

Why does it have to be us again? Some have never struck a bat. We've been to France, the Middle East and Sicily. They brought us all the way back for the landing, haven't we done our share? We didn't like that one bit.[7]

Others, like Lance Corporal George Worthington, MM, 6th Durhams, knew what taking part in such a landing would entail. He also understood that being picked for such a desperate venture was a compliment in itself, and most men took great pride in being a member of the famous 50th Northumbrian Division. Nevertheless, he recalled that few would voice this opinion in public:

General Bernard L. Montgomery. (Author's collection)

> We were not very happy about being used as the attacking troops on D-Day, but there was nothing we could do about it. Everybody was happy about coming home, but when we found out what we were coming home for it took a bit of the shine off it. The only satisfaction we got was to know that Montgomery had asked for our division because he wanted experienced troops and at least we got some leave out of it.[8]

On 16 May 1944, Lance Corporal Worthington attended an investiture ceremony at Buckingham Palace, where King George VI presented him with the Military Medal he had earned in Sicily.

Private Richard Atkinson of the 9th Battalion Durham Light Infantry (9th Durhams) remembered that most just got on with it, despite the complaints of some:

> There was a lot of moaning went on. "Not fair, not again, how about somebody else having a go",

Lance Corporal George Worthington, MM, 6th Battalion Durham Light Infantry. (Courtesy of G. Worthington)

---

7 A. Foster, correspondence with author (Durham, 1989).
8 George Worthington, manuscript forwarded to author (Durham, 1989).

things like that. But it was the usual soldiers who moaned, and we knew we had to get on with it. There's nothing we could do about it.[9]

Company Sergeant Major George Warters, from the 7th Battalion Green Howards, looked to the future with hope and felt a little aggrieved that after three years of constant action he was going to have to take part in the invasion:

> We were in the south of England on manoeuvres when Monty gathered us all together and gave us a nice speech about how we were going to have the great honour of being among the first troops ashore on D-Day. We didn't take very kindly to it at first. After three years of fighting, we reckoned we had done our fair whack, we thought we were coming back to give us a break. But Monty's way was to keep you going and going and going. We ended up in an enclosed camp near Southampton and occasionally we would be ordered down to the boats thinking this was it, but it turned out to be training practice for the real thing and we would be sent back to camp. Nobody is ever glad to be engaged in a war, but I do look back with some pride in the fact that I was there on D-Day with 50 Div.[10]

On 13 May, General Eisenhower visited the men of 151 Brigade and emphasised the importance of getting to know the American soldiers whom they would be fighting alongside. He told them of the high regard in which the 50th Northumbrian Division was held, and the speech he gave was very well received. Corporal George Richardson, 6th Durhams, recollected the event clearly:

> Ike came and started walking along our 6th Battalion line, now and then stopping and pointing at our Africa Star, saying "You should be proud of that." He had just about got to the end of the line when he said, "Aw shit, this isn't what I have come here for, I want to talk to the men." He walked over to the centre of the field and told us to move closer, not an officer or a man moved. Ike looked at our brigadier who told the commanding officers to fall us out and move over in front of him, which we did. Then the general said how proud he was to have met the men who had done so well in the Middle East. But we were now spoiling our records by fighting with the Yanks. We have a big war to win, and you have to do it alongside the Yanks not by fighting against them. He went on to say the next time we met a Yank in the pub to go up to him, shake him by the hand and offer him a drink. So, we all got on our transport and went into Cambridge that evening, [and] the Yanks must have been told the same because we all finished up the best of friends, with the Yanks paying we had a good night.[11]

Some men were so aggrieved at being picked to storm Gold Beach after all they had been through that they went absent without leave, knowing that the worst that could be done to them was a short jail term. Major John Mogg, 9th Durhams, recalled how these men were treated with leniency, as such experienced troops would be needed for the battle about to come:

9   R. Atkinson, correspondence with author (Durham, 1989).
10 G. Warters, interview with author (Hull, 1990).
11 Moses, H., *The Faithful Sixth* (Durham: County Durham Books, 1995), p. 273.

Sailors practise their anti-aircraft drills as the armada of ships gathers on the south coast. (Author's collection)

Churchill and Eisenhower, April 1944. (Author's collection)

An armoured carrier passes through a village in the south of England. (Courtesy of Reg Prothero)

The old and the bold, who had been through the whole thing since 1940, thought they were perhaps coming back to England to an easier time and not to be selected to be the first ones to be thrown into the invasion. They had been at it solidly since arriving in the desert until they came out of Sicily and had been fighting practically the whole time. The DLI of all regiments, I think I am right in saying, … had been in the thick of everything all the way through. There were quite a lot of deserters, I simply can't remember the figures, but just before we sailed an awful lot of them returned from being absent without leave. They were treated fairly leniently because we said, "Alright we need you back, you know the battalion."[12]

"Train hard and be prepared"

Once the men of the 50th Northumbrian Division realised they were to be the spearhead of XXX Corps, there was no general rejoicing. Both men and officers were experienced enough to appreciate what this meant, and it was with a fatalistic and dogged determination that the troops of the 50th faced up to their coming ordeal. As the new year dawned, so began a heavy programme of training, using live ammunition. The division had already made one seaborne landing in Sicily, and this was to be the third seaborne landing for 231 Brigade. However, because of the heavy losses sustained in the desert and Sicily, up to 50 percent of the division's manpower was relatively new and would have to be trained from scratch in this

---

12 Moses, *The Faithful Sixth*, p. 268.

XXX Corps troops training hard for the invasion, April/May 1944. (Author's collection)

kind of warfare. For two weeks, the men worked hard learning all about the skills needed when working with assault craft and the crews of the 7th Armoured Division. Each leading assault brigade – 69 and 231 – was sent to a Combined Training Centre at Inveraray in central Scotland, and during April and May four full-sized brigade exercises were held on the south coast of England at Studland Bay. This was of great value in integrating the Royal Navy and Army into one cohesive assault force. The final practice for the invasion involved all British assault forces and took place on 5 and 6 May. No major exercise took place after this, with a breathing space given in order to allow naval vessels to be refitted and to give the Army time to perform such specialist tasks as the waterproofing of vehicles for the voyage and landing.

Within this massive organisation and frantic activity was the ordinary Tommy, each with his own worries and cares about loved ones whom they were about to leave behind. At the back of the mind of every man was the thought that they may not survive the coming encounter, and they wanted to make provision for families and wives should their worst fears be realised. Private Thomas Tateson of the 7th Green Howards, 69 Brigade, was a new addition to the regiment and was surprised to be given a last chance to see his young wife:

> When I was told that I was wanted at the company office I was puzzled, since I was unaware of any transgression that could have landed me in trouble. It was the middle of May and

the 7th Battalion Green Howards had just moved to Romsey near Southampton. I was a member of the signal platoon having joined the regiment soon after its return from Africa and Sicily the previous November. To my astonishment I was told when I reported that I was to go on immediate 48 hours leave. As explanation I was told that we would be moving almost at once into the invasion assembly area. Here we would be completely isolated with no communication with our families. Consequently, a strictly limited number [of] 48-hour passes were to be allowed. The signals platoon had been allocated just one and Pronto, our signals officer, had specified that I was to be the beneficiary. Whilst elated at the news I was baffled as to why I had been given preference over the other much longer serving men than me with no suggestion of a ballot. I had time to reflect on this mystery during my tedious war-time train journey to Sheffield and believe I came up with the correct answer. For a short time previously letters home had been censored with the exception of a limited number of green envelopes, [as] the authorities recognised that men should have an opportunity of writing a few uncensored letters in which they could write to their wives and families in personal terms which they would not like to have read by their officers. It was a matter of honour and trust that no security matters would be mentioned. I had already received my limited quota when I received a letter from Olive telling me that she was pregnant again and was very upset and worried. I had to use an ordinary envelope when I replied and just hoped that it would not be opened. My letter was a very tender and emotional one and one which I would not have sent through the open post except for the urgency. Pronto never mentioned it to me, nor did the NCOs who must have surely enquired why I should be so favoured, but I feel it was because Lt Wilson, Pronto, had read the letter that he gave me one last chance to see Olive. The army was not totally without sensitivity.[13]

Private Tateson was all too aware of the risks he and his comrades ran by taking part in the invasion of France. Like all soldiers through the centuries had done before him, he went off to war wanting to make provision for his young family:

Knowing that I was very soon to be taking part in the long-awaited invasion of France, I was very conscious of the fact that there was a real possibility of my being killed. This meant leaving Olive widowed with a child not yet a year old and another on the way. It was very difficult to say what one would like to say in such circumstances, and I took the course of writing a letter which I left with Olive to be opened only in the event of my death. Apart from an expression of the happiness our lives together had brought me I wanted to convey the message that if she ever wanted to re-marry, she should know that this would have my full blessing. Even in writing I felt I had to say this in coded language which I remember even though I destroyed the letter after Olive died. We had both read it after my safe return and Olive kept it. It was a sad moment when we had to say goodbye after that last short leave and Olive was to hear no more of me from that time in May until October, when she received a printed postcard informing her that I was alive and a POW [–] this was just one week before Robert was born.[14]

---

13   T. Tateson, manuscript forwarded to author (Sheffield, 1989).
14   T. Tateson, manuscript forwarded to author (Sheffield, 1989).

New Blood: "I was absolutely terrified"

In December 1943, a draft of artillerymen of the 86th Hertfordshire Yeomanry, along with their officers, joined the ranks of the 50th Northumbrian Division. These men had seen no action as yet and were deeply impressed by the amount of medal ribbons displayed by the division's officers. Their CO, Lieutenant Colonel George Fanshawe, recalled:

> In late 1943 we were told that we were to join the 50th Tyne Tees Division who were just back from Africa and Sicily. So, we met these terrific war heroes, the more cowardly of whom had only one MC, most of them had three! I don't think we had a medal between us all, so we felt about one inch high. They were terrific and as I subsequently found on D-Day they were worth every medal they had or could ever earn. They said "We know all about the desert warfare but nothing about invasions, you teach us", well we didn't either, but after that to work with them was the greatest period of the Herts Yeos life so far.[15]

In early 1944, new men began to arrive in great numbers into the ranks of XXX Corps. The battles that had been fought in Africa and Sicily had taken a terrible toll in men and equipment, and it was essential that each unit and sub-unit was brought up to strength.

Private Peter Cuerdon joined the 1st Battalion Hampshire Regiment, 231 Brigade, and found himself among his boyhood heroes:

> I joined the 50th Northumbrian Division at the start of 1944, I was one of those unfortunates who were put into a replacement holding battalion. When we were put into the 50th Division I was terrified – absolutely petrified on arriving at the 1st Battalion Hampshire's, they were first class fighting men who had been in North Africa and Sicily, coming back to England specifically for the invasion. A lot of them were very highly trained men who knew their job. We were just twenty-year-olds when we joined this crowd which in some ways was a good thing as we had the backing of good men. I was absolutely scared stiff. We practised attacks, landings and all this sort of thing. We were taken down to Ipswich on training exercises and were off the boats then on the boats, then night exercises week after week where they fired at us with live ammunition, oh my God yes. I think Monty was keen on that sort of thing. I had no idea what we were in for, and I thought we'd go back and have a cushy time in England.[16]

Lieutenant Geoffrey Picot had enlisted in Jersey and volunteered to join the Army Pay Corps as he was short-sighted. He became a Class 3 Clerk and in May 1940 was sent to his unit in Bournemouth. He felt his new position to be the safest of any soldier in the British Army and was also excused the usual square bashing. His luck was not to last, however, and four years down the line he found himself an officer posted to the 1st Hampshires:

---

15 Newspaper cutting forwarded to author by J. Betts (Hull, 1999).
16 P. Cuerdon, manuscript forwarded to author (Hampshire, 1992).

> With four colleagues in January 1944, I joined the 1st Hampshires at Long Melford, Suffolk. John Lloyd who had been in searchlights since the start of the war regarded this as a major personal catastrophe: "Me in the second front! It's unbelievable" he used to say. Harry Wise recalled the advice his father gave him in 1939: "Don't go into the infantry my son." But he accepted his lot philosophically, what would come would come and he was ready for it. Ken Edwards thought a lot about his wife and child and brooded anxiously. Chris Needham accepted his position with good grace, he knew he was in a sticky corner, but many other people were too, and he was quietly determined to give a good account of himself. I was gloomy, I thought fate had played a scurvy trick on me and the task ahead seemed altogether beyond me. The Hampshires were back in England; I could scarcely have joined a battalion that was more battle hardened or whose record showed greater success. How on earth would I fit in with these Goliaths?[17]

Private Stanley Dwyer was a radio operator and joined the Northumbrian Division at the start of 1944. He listened with avid inerest to the tales told by the 50th's old hands in barracks at night as they fought their way up and down the desert once again:

> In October 1943 I was a wireless operator in a high-speed group in the War Office Signals based at Egham, Surrey. The section was posted en-masse to two lines of communication groups in Wimbledon. In January 1944 a number of us were posted to the 50th Divisional Signals at Long Melford, Sussex. We were living in Nissen Huts in the grounds of Long Melford Hall. The unit had just come back via Sicily and the desert and after a couple of weeks we newcomers were very conversant with the geography of the desert. Every night, when we couldn't afford to go to the pub, we were up and down the desert as the old hands gripped us with their exploits. We were told that the 50th Division was to be one of the assault divisions for the second front and the attitude was that it was going to be a very bloody affair. My attitude was that these chaps had already done two assault landings, one in Sicily and one in Italy with 231 Brigade and they were still alive. Having a father who was very badly wounded in the first Great War I realised it was different in the infantry. We found that the old hands' pet hate was Montgomery and the 51st Highland Division. They reckoned that the 51st Division took the credit for the exploits of the 50th Division. Also because of their habit of plastering their divisional sign everywhere, HD, they were called the Highway Decorators and because the 50th Division sign was TT they were known as the Town Titivators, [so it was] honours even. It was a surprise to us about Montgomery, but they were adamant that he was a rotter.[18]

Private Dwyer settled into his new unit and soon made himself at home in Sussex. But the time for action was approaching and training was going on apace, with Eisenhower coming to see the division. Dwyer continued that eventually they were moved to the south coast embarkation area:

---

17 Picot, G., *Accidental Warrior* (London: Penguin Books, 1994), p. 30.
18 S. Dwyer, manuscript forwarded to author (Wales, 1992).

Private Peter Cuerdon, 1st Battalion Hampshire Regiment. (Courtesy of P. Cuerdon)

Lieutenant Geoffrey Picot, 1st Battalion Hampshire Regiment. (Author's collection)

Guns for the invasion lined up in a Kentish field. (Courtesy of Ralph Hymer)

At Easter 1944 we were sent to the New Forest area, and we took over a Canadian camp. My job was to man a high-powered radio transmitter and receiver in a ready-made truck. There was a driver and three operators. The man in charge was also a signalman who, it was said, would never be promoted because of his unmilitary bearing, he was also slightly deaf and there was a story that was told of him that he was on the set at night during the Battle of Primosole Bridge in Sicily. The next morning, he is said to have remarked that it had been a quiet night when in fact there had been heavy shelling. Our truck was to come ashore some days after D-Day and the driver spent his time waterproofing it. For the landing we would be using a 22 set, this could be carried on the shoulders using canvas straps. We were given a box on wheels and the set was screwed onto a board running across it and the batteries were carried in the well. We spent some time pulling this cross-country to get used to them and linked up with three other similar sets.[19]

Lieutenant Picot had joined his heroes in January 1944 and held his new comrades in high regard, but was taken aback at their lack of enthusiasm for the invasion:

One day an extremely young-looking commanding officer, still in his twenties, announced: "We are going to be an assault battalion in the invasion of Europe." To my surprise nobody cheered. As a number of the officers and sergeants who had foregathered to hear this announcement had already been decorated for bravery, I thought they would be happy at the chance to win more glory, [but] not a bit of it, they were solemn, nervous and sad, as I was. So, these were not special men, they were rather like me. It was ordinary men who were going to win this war. I was told to join the mortar platoon as understudy to their commander. I noticed at once the immense respect they had for their previous commander, Frank Waters, who was now adjutant. I soon came to regard Sergeant Wetherick as the most efficient NCO I had ever met. Without any bullying or commotion, he had the 45-man platoon completely under control. I got to know members of my platoon as quickly as possible and as thoroughly as I could. Many of them accepted the fact from their previous experience that the strain of battle could prove too much for some people. I was learning fast that these were indeed ordinary men.[20]

Lieutenant John Milton of the 6th Battalion Green Howards (6th Green Howards) recalled his training:

We then started assault training at Inveraray and Hayling Island as we knew we would be an assault battalion. Eventually we were put in sealed camps, and we were not allowed out for a week or two before we went to France. All of our letters were censored so that no security was breached, but at that time we knew little of the details about what was going to happen. I wrote to my parents once only to find out later that my father had known where I was in the sealed camp as the army had stamped the envelope with the Winchester post

---

19 S. Dwyer, manuscript forwarded to author.
20 Picot, *Accidental Warrior*, p. 32.

mark. We then began to prepare for the landings and got to know more about where we were going to land.[21]

Lieutenant Stuart Hills, MC, Sherwood Rangers, took part in special tank training for the invasion amid considerable secrecy:

> Our destination for this training turned out to be the seafront at Great Yarmouth, where we took over a row of boarding houses. Here we learnt, to our considerable surprise, that we were to train on tanks which would swim! A somewhat alarming prospect as we tried to imagine tanks being launched thousands of yards from the shore and waddling in like so many overgrown ducks to attack the beaches of Europe in support of the infantry. Inevitably there were accidents. Once a driver misheard an order to form line abreast as one to deflate. The tank sank in the middle of a lake, although all the crew escaped. Unsurprisingly, there were many grumbles from men who thought: "That being a bloody sailor in a bloody tank was taking patriotism too far." I would perch precariously on my bridge at the back of the tank, which was certainly better than sitting inside it, and peered over the canvas screen. I realised fairly quickly that the screen might protect me from the salt spray, but not from a German bullet or shell.[22]

Private John Chalk had joined the 1st Hampshires in 1935 as a boy soldier, and in 1944 he was 23 years old and considered to be an old hand at all things military. He and his comrades knew that the 'Big Do' was coming, but they had no idea where it would be, apart from in France. This would be the third assault landing his unit had made, but Chalk never heard it referred to as Operation Overlord:

> Those sorts of things didn't concern us old campaigners much, we knew it was our job and that we would do it to the best of our ability. We were in a tented camp near Fawley in the New Forest and soldiers being what they were attempted to make the best of what we had. This certainly was not a lot, being under canvas in a gloomy damp forest with nothing much to do in our spare time with recurring malaria cropping up. The acute shortage of beer was one of the main bugbears. The influx of thousands of service men into the south of England was draining the pubs dry and the breweries couldn't cope with the extra demand. My cousin's wife was managing a pub in Blackfield, about two miles from the camp, [and] myself and four of my friends became privileged customers there when beer was available. We would already have a table full of beer when the doors were thrown open to admit the waiting troops. Within an hour the supplies would be sold out. We had to pay for the privilege of course by collecting and washing glasses. While at Fawley things got bigger, by that I mean not just training as a company or battalion but as a brigade, with other arms of the service involved. There was one full rehearsal at Studland Bay and another at Hayling Island involving Navy, Air Force and artillery firing over our heads. It was around this time that we were becoming familiar with all the unusual armoured vehicles we would no doubt

---

21 *WW2: People's War* <www.bbc.co.uk/ww2peopleswar> (accessed 26 December 2018).
22 Hills, S., *By Tank to Normandy* (London: Cassel, 2002), p. 142.

be working with, flail tanks for clearing mines, flame throwing tanks, swimming tanks and tanks for all sorts of jobs.[23]

Private Edward Castle, who served with the 2nd Battalion Gloucestershire Regiment, was a stretcher bearer and recalled an accidental shooting after a hard day's work:

One man[24] shot himself by accident[;] he had just come back off guard and hadn't unloaded his rifle or put the safety catch on. He threw himself down on his bed, the gun went off and he was killed. I was about a yard from him when this happened. He was the first casualty I ever dealt with, and he was next to me in the tent you see. He had dropped the rifle on the floor, and it had gone off, the bullet going through his chest and out of his back at point-blank range. There was nothing you could do for him.[25]

Demonstrations of new weapons of war were impressive, troops looking on in awe at the tremendous spectacle. Private Thomas Tateson, 7th Green Howards, remembered:

Flail Tanks, which we had not heard of previously, [were] an excellent invention[. T]he flail consisted of a rotating bar in front of the tank to which was fastened lengths of chain. These flailed the ground as the tank progressed and exploded any mines, particularly anti-personnel mines, thus clearing a path for the infantry through a minefield. There were also amphibious tanks which could erect a large hood affair above them which helped to give them buoyancy and allowed them, with the help of a propeller driven by the engine, to swim ashore from the landing craft. I had mixed feelings about the flame throwing tanks and the demonstration of the huge tongue of flame projected at a dummy pillbox was horrifying in its implications. Whilst it was quite irrational on my part, the image of men being burned to death in this ghastly manner seemed barbaric, whereas blowing their guts out with conventional weapons was more acceptable. Such is the cumulative effect of the myth of glory in battle and the images created in films, that when a man was shot, he simply drops dead. We were living in bivouacs in fields during this period and although most of the details have faded from my memory, I have a vivid recollection of the novelty of reveille being sounded over the tannoy system. I emerged from my bivouac to find a beautiful fresh May morning with grass heavy with dew and feeling that life was good. The bugle call sounded so clear, almost bell like, in the crystal-clear early morning of an English meadow.[26]

Divisional inspections took place regularly, and the 50th Northumbrian Division was visited by a number of dignitaries. The more experienced soldiers did their best to avoid the 'bull' that was associated with these events, but Private Stanley Dwyer had vivid memories of a meeting with Eisenhower:

---

23 Miller, *Nothing Less than Victory*, p. 53.
24 Private Kenneth Townsend, 2nd Battalion Gloucestershire Regiment, died on 29 May 1944, aged 18. He is buried in at St John's Church, Boldre, Hampshire.
25 E. Castle, correspondence with author (Gloucestershire, 1991).
26 T. Tateson, manuscript forwarded to author (Sheffield, 1989).

A Sherman flail tank churns up the ground as it clears a way through the wire and minefields for the advancing infantry. (Author's collection)

About this time there was a series of inspections, the first one being by the King. The only ones on parade, from divisional signals, were us and the replacements as the old hands had skived off. Our colonel was most embarrassed when the King said to him: "Where are my men of the Eighth Army, I came to see them." A similar thing happened when Montgomery came, I was on cookhouse fatigues, so I missed him. For Eisenhower it was different again, everyone wanted to go. We broke ranks at his invitation and sat in front of his jeep with his curvaceous driver standing behind him. He told a story about two soldiers looking out of a window as he went by, "I wouldn't like his job" said one. "Why not" asked the other. "No promotion" he answered. This went down very well, also his description of the perks of the job [–] he described his driver by waving his arms to show her curves. If there was a serious side to it, I can't remember, but we all went back happy.[27]

Stories of insubordination and discontent abounded at this time, and Dwyer and his comrades heard of a number of incidents concerning the 50th Division:

It was about this time that stories were heard of lorries marked with: 'No leave – no second front' and the CSM who marched his company to the station, dismissed them and said he was going home. A friend of mine, when we were at Long Melford, had gone on seven days leave and had decided to make it fourteen and when he returned, he was told to report to

27 S. Dwyer, correspondence with author (Wales, 1992).

Scotland Yard, and they would tell him where to go. He was told to join the others from his mob in the cells till morning and said it was full of 50th Division men, including Majors.[28]

The time for the invasion was approaching fast, and all units would soon find themselves in camps near the south coast that were locked down and subject to the tightest of security. These camps stretched for miles along the roadsides, and from the inside they resembled prisoner of war facilities. Many men found them oppressive, which in turn led to tension and at times disorder in the coming weeks. The fields around the camp areas were choked with artillery and ammunition dumps, while the roads leading to the south coast were clogged up with trucks and tanks, all heading to the ports. At the ports, large ships waited at anchor to receive their cargoes of men and machinery; the logistics of this enormous task was a staggering achievement.

Company Sergeant Major Stanley Hollis, 6th Green Howards, recalled the miserable time spent in training before his unit moved south:

> We did our training for the invasion in Inveraray, Scotland, we knew exactly how to do it and what to do. We had done it before in Sicily, but we still did additional training. It was miserable in January and February and cold. However, we got over it and came down to the south coast to prepare for the invasion. We were put behind the wire in Winchester, briefed, and told exactly what we were going to do and how we were going to do it.[29]

Major Alexander Edward Craven Bredin, 1st Battalion Dorsetshire Regiment, was now part of the 50th Northumbrian Division. He was involved in combined operations training in early March, where the troops were instructed on the kinds of obstacles that they would encounter on the Normandy beaches and the latest mechanical methods to overcome them:

> We moved to the Combined Training Centre at Inveraray, Scotland. It had been decided on a high level that the 50th Division were to take the place of another formation in the assault and 231 Brigade would be, for the third time, an assault brigade, and so it was. Time was limited, so our course at Inveraray was considered to be short and rather rushed through, it was just as well as we had been through that sort of thing twice before. We started with lectures and craft training, followed by dry-shod exercises on 17th March. More ambitious waterborne exercises followed, the last, carried out on the 22nd of March, was a brigade exercise, designed to approximate roughly to our operational task.[30]

Private Walter Scott, RAMC (Royal Army Medical Corps), had been moved about the country during recent months. He had had enough of drilling and polishing kit when the order came for a move:

> I eventually ended up in a camp in Newhaven, handy for the docks. It seemed like the whole army was there and we could guess why. We played football and had visits from entertainers including Jack Warner, later to be known as Dixon of Dock Green. Other

---

28   S. Dwyer, correspondence with author (Wales, 1992).
29   Morgan, M., *D-Day Hero CSM Stanley Hollis VC* (Gloucestershire: Sutton Publishing, 2004), p. 59.
30   P. Cuerdon, manuscript forwarded to author (Hampshire, 1991).

Civilians go about their everyday business as long lines of tanks, trucks and guns wait their turn to file onto the docks. (Author's collection)

entertainers told some of the bluest jokes I've ever heard, [and] when they'd finished a Salvation Army cornetist got up and played Silent Night, there was a moment's silence then the hall exploded into thunderous applause. That was what we wanted to send us off. We were about to risk our life; we were worth more than blue jokes and we knew it.[31]

Private Thomas Tateson returned from his short leave and went back to the 7th Green Howards to find a flurry of activity as his comrades prepared for the coming assault. His unit was visited by General Montgomery, who left a lasting impression on this young soldier about to go into battle:

It was during this period that I came face to face with Field Marshall Montgomery. We were all assembled in a large open space to be shown some of the advanced weapons to be used in the invasion. As a preliminary we were drawn up for inspection by Monty and as there were many hundreds, possibly thousands there, this was of course a brisk but lengthy affair. When he got to where I was, he stopped and looked at me [–] when this happens the soldier involved is supposed to look straight ahead but curiosity caused me to look into his eyes. They were steely blue, and he gave me a searching, appraising and challenging look which seemed to me to last for a long time so that I thought he was about to speak to me. However, he must have decided that I was not really worthy of his attention, and he passed on. The

31 *WW2: People's War* <www.bbc.co.uk/ww2peopleswar> (accessed 15 February 2019).

inspection over he took up his familiar position on top of some army vehicle and called on us to gather round. In an informal manner he then told us in his characteristic way that we were going to land in France, knock Gerry for six and finish the war off. There was absolutely no doubt about it as it was all planned and organised. We would just go in, do the job and that was that. From this distance in time and after seeing all the comic impersonations of Monty, this probably sounds corny stuff, but in fact there was something so tremendously impressive, almost hypnotic in his performance that it did inspire us with confidence which in retrospect was not at all justified. It was the sheer matter of fact certainty of his message that was so much more effective than the high flown Harfleur type of effort.[32]

Some men keyed up for battle needed an outlet for their pent-up energy and would often take their grievances out on Army property with a level of violence and aggression that was totally unexpected. Sergeant George Mackenzie, Royal Engineers, wrote of one such incident:

All leave and short passes are cancelled, curse it. Nearly all the vehicles are waterproofed now and what a sight they look, all pipes and paste. We have no work to do and not much recreation either but can't blame the authorities this time as they are doing their best. Most of the time is spent discussing our chances of survival, sometimes with confidence, sometimes with blood curdling pessimism. The boys are on the rampage, can't bottle one's emotions after three or four years of nomadic existence. Windows are being smashed and every crash of glass is loudly cheered. They are making their way now to the officers' quarters, a shower of bricks and cans, or whatever is handiest, goes crashing through the windows. The officers discreetly file out the back door, apparently none of them wish to be the senior rank around. Personally, I kept well out of the way as I don't wish to get in the way of a flying missile. Their destructive appetite apparently quenched; at midnight all is quiet. Morning shows what has become a common sight, only this mess wasn't caused by bombing. The following night it is the NAFFI's turn for a bashing.[33]

Into secure camps

Private Denis Bowen of the 5th East Yorks had not been in the Army long when his unit was posted to a secure camp at Canning Town, East London, where the troops lived under canvas on a bomb site. The camp was not fully completed, and Bowen recounted that the men found themselves erecting the barbed wire perimeter fence:

It was quite a curious place, because surrounding the camp were civilian houses and the local Londoners were saying: "You'll be going abroad soon" but there was no mention of the invasion. One evening we were paraded and were told we were all confined to camp, no one would be allowed out. Sentries were posted all around the camp patrolling the perimeter to keep us in. It didn't particularly bother me as I found a way I could get out so I could go to

32 T. Tateson, manuscript forwarded to author (Sheffield, 1989).
33 G. Mackenzie, correspondence with author (Exeter, 1989).

Mealtime for troops in their enclosed camp. (Author's collection)

the cinema and then get back in. It didn't make a lot of difference because I didn't have any secret information or anything. I got out through a hole in the wire like lots of other people did too. We weren't stupid enough to go off and do something silly. We'd go to the cinema and then go straight back. In fact, the sentries would see us, but they turned a blind eye, they were soldiers like ourselves. When the camp was sealed there was no further contact with the civilians, they weren't even allowed to come up to the barbed wire. That was really the thing that upset us more than being told we were confined to camp. A lot of men used to go to people's houses for a cup of tea or something and that was suddenly stopped. There wasn't any bother as the troops who were there were well behaved rather than well disciplined. They weren't particularly smart, boots polished, foot stamping soldiers, but they were well behaved. We remained within the barbed wire the whole time and I found that period absolutely boring. The cry in the camp as you walked down to the NAFFI and saw a sentry on the other side of the wire was "let me out". It was funny because on the day when we were leaving the camp to go down to the boats somebody in line called out "let me in".[34]

Edward William Broadbent, a crewman on an LCT (Landing Craft, Tank), looked upon the days before the invasion as a sort of holiday and spent his time pleasantly practicing on his assault bike and taking part in a little training. Unlike the infantry, he was not kept at it for hours each day:

---

34   J. Betts, manuscript forwarded to author (Hull, 1988).

It was summertime at its best and our evenings were spent in Southampton, where the servicemen outnumbered the civilians by seven to one. The walk back to camp from Southampton was a pleasant one, my mates and I would stroll back talking of home, parents, wives and sweethearts, and of the day that must surely dawn soon. Around May 10th a drastic move took place, the camps were sealed, and our training was over. The days that followed were strange to be sure, barbed wire skirted the camp and there were armed guards too. We received no mail but were still allowed to write home subject to strict censorship. There was little or nothing to do except for the army cinema shows which were daily. The boys spent many hours playing cards or Housey-Housey in the NAFFI. Some of us read books, any old thing to kill time, for we knew the day must be close at hand.[35]

Lance Corporal Kenneth Tout, serving with the Sherwood Rangers, remembered being sat behind thick barbed wire entanglements. The tanks of his unit were placed in a parking area and the men were allocated large bell-tents to reside in. A concert party was organised for incoming troops in an open marquee. The performers worked in shifts, the last one being at 2230 hours. Soldiers sat on chairs in front of the bare platform, squatted in the long grass or smoked as they leant against trees, Tout recalled:

At 22:30 p.m. [*sic*] a pianist in a dinner jacket and a girl with bare legs and wearing a frilly, fairy skirt climbs onto the platform and go into their routine. This is the very essence of romance, hundreds of soldiers spending their last night in England before sailing for the hazardous shores of Normandy, many of those soldiers destined never to return, never to see another English girl. Many, like me, without formal female attachments, yet full of dreams of a someday love affair. Above us the fulsome moon illuminates the glades of the woods. Moonbeams sparkle on distant strands of barbed wire. On the bare stage a tiny, frail but spirited girl with a tearful contralto voice sings the songs of home, love and parting and of a future return. She sings something about "But if you can keep her heart, even when you're far apart, then that's not the moon, that's love my son". Under the D-Day moon the masses of soldiers claim encore after encore as they sway with the singer's movements and think of wives, sweethearts and romances not yet born.[36]

Private Frank Rosier, 2nd Gloucesters, found that there was little to do in his secure camp, so sports matches were organised. Here, Frank got his first taste of American racist attitudes:

We started playing rugby to keep ourselves amused as we weren't doing much, inter-company rugby and football challenges. Inside our camp were some black Americans cooking our food who used to watch us playing. They said, "We'll beat you at your own game, then you try and beat us at basketball." So, we played them at rugby and actually beat them, but they got their own back and beat us at basketball. Then came the order that we

---

35 E.W. Broadbent, correspondence with author (Lancashire, 1992).
36 Tout, K., *Tanks, Advance!* (London: Robert Hale Ltd, 1987), pp. 19–20.

were not to play with the black Yanks as the white Yanks had objected. As a cosmopolitan cockney used to playing with black children, Indian children, Chinese or whatever as a kid, it was part of my life, and I couldn't believe my ears. I was 18 and I thought that's stupid, I still can't believe it today.[37]

Private A. Vince, 2nd Battalion Essex Regiment (2nd Essex), found the training hard as he waited for news of the move to France:

On 25th March we moved by train to Inveraray to undergo ten days training at the Combined Training Centre. The countryside was beautiful and the training interesting though arduous. We played with all the known forms of landing craft. 4th April found us back in the south of England, this time in the area of Christchurch, with less than two months to put the finishing touches to our preparations. Here was the final sort out of men and materials and the continuance of our battle training. We hardened our feet by tramping 100 miles through the Hampshire countryside in seven days. Here we carried out more invasion exercises when a sad accident occurred when Major Norman Ayres[38] and six other ranks were drowned whilst wading out to re-embark on our invasion barges. For some months now leave had been stopped and on 19th May we had to relinquish our last bit of freedom when we went behind barbed wire in Camp B 3 near Beaulieu in Hampshire. This was to be our home under canvas for exactly 15 days before embarkation, 15 days of boredom.[39]

Pte William Evans, serving with the 2nd Battalion South Wales Borderers, thinking about the likelihood of being killed in the invasion, decided he must see his family at all costs one last time:

After a few days at Christchurch, we moved to Beaulieu and the sealed camp. Like many others I remember this as being like a prison with rain teeming down and living in tents with duckboards to walk on. At some stage I went over the wire, absent without leave, and got back home to South-Wales in order to say goodbye to my family just in case I didn't survive the invasion. By the time I got home the local policeman had visited and was looking for me. I went and saw him and promised to be on the early train back. No punitive action was taken on my return, probably because any punishment at that stage would have meant replacing a rifleman.[40]

However, not all officers were keen on men leaving of their own accord at such a time, and thought the punishment for them should be much harsher. Sergeant Richard Philips, 2nd South Wales Borderers, commented:

---

37 Bailey, R., *Forgotten Voices of D-Day* (London: Ebury Press, 2010), pp. 63–64.
38 Major Norman Ayres, 2nd Battalion Essex Regiment, was drowned on 4 May 1944, aged 29. He is buried in the City of London Cemetery and Crematorium, Manor Park.
39 A. Vince, manuscript forwarded to author (Essex, 1989).
40 W. Evans, correspondence with author (Wales, 1987).

General Montgomery addressing the troops. (Author's collection)

> Some men did get out of the camps and there was hell to pay. The CO addressed the battalion, and he was saying how dangerous this was and that those who did get out should have been hanged. This was Lt Colonel Craddock who was a bit of a fire eater.[41]

One day, Private Denis Bowen was on pay parade and found he was being paid in French notes called 'invasion money'; he now knew he would be off to France. His unit had been told that they would be used as reinforcements for other formations that had suffered casualties during the invasion:

> We were taken from the camp in a mixed draft with men from other units, mostly infantry, but some were engineers. We were marched down to either the West India or East India Dock where we got onto an old troop ship and sailed down the Thames and out to sea. The ship dropped anchor and we just laid there. Then small drafts began to be taken off the boat and taken away, we didn't know where. Craft would come along side and men would scramble down the side and get into them. One man actually took off, jumped over the side of the boat and swam off to the breakwater amid great cheers. I never heard of anybody else doing that or of anyone making a deliberate attempt to get away by pretending to be sick or self-inflicting a wound. I did later in Normandy, but not on the boat. Then came the time when myself and three or four other lads were taken down and put into a boat and

---

41　R. Philips, manuscript forwarded to author (Cheshire, 1991).

we found ourselves being put onto a landing craft with landing craft assault on the side, it was then I knew for sure I was going to be part of the invasion with the 5th Battalion East Yorkshire Regiment. The company commander greeted us and said: "I'm sending you to Sergeant Mayhew's and Corporal Stevenson's platoon." All these men had been my heroes and Corporal Stevenson, who'd been in the desert and done the invasion of Sicily, it was nothing to him the fact that he was doing another invasion, although he wasn't right keen on it. They were still feeling a bit jaundiced about it, it was resentment rather than objection. I was very pleased to be going into action with men who were skilled fighting men, they weren't particularly slick on things like daily rifle cleaning, but they were seasoned troops who knew what it was all about. Their usual phrase was: "Stick by me kid and I'll see you alright." There was no question of anybody attempting to be heroes, all they were interested in was keeping their heads down, getting the war over and getting back home.[42]

Embarkation: "I hope we don't lose too many of the old faces"

As the invasion time grew ever closer, the troops of XXX Corps found themselves preparing for the final move out of their camps. Lieutenant Colonel Cosmo Nevill, CO of the 2nd Battalion Devonshire Regiment, was with his battalion in their secure camp on 29 May when orders were received that they were to move out for embarkation:

> At 10:30 a.m. on the morning of the 31st of May the battalion assault group, complete with all representatives of the supporting arms, fell in for the last time. The move in MT from the camp to Southampton went without a hitch. We were driven straight to the quay alongside which HMS *Glenroy* was lying ready to receive us. Tea was served to all ranks in the shed while the adjutant handed the many forms and detailed lists to the embarkation staff. Embarkation was completed in record time; each serial, or landing craft load of men, was received on board by our Assistant Military Liaison Officer, and by the ship's Master at Arms. A royal marine acted as guide, who not only led the serial to their correct deck, but also showed each commander the quickest way to the landing craft assault allotted to him. The efficiency with which the troops were received and stowed on board demonstrated the value of the close liaison which had been established with the officers and ratings of HMS *Glenroy*.[43]

Private Stanley Dwyer, with the 50th Divisional Signals, moved with his unit to Winchester and then on to Southampton, where they found their transport waiting to take them across the Channel:

> We had one last night out in the pubs of Lyndhurst and moved to our destination the next day. It was surrounded by barbed wire and guarded by the Americans, in fact they ran the camp though the food was British. We lived in tents and unusually there was a large

---

42 D. Bowen, manuscript forwarded to author (Shropshire, 1991).
43 Saunders, T., *The Battle for the Bocage, Normandy 1944* (Barnsley: Pen & Sword, 2021), p. 19.

canvas container of ice-cold water outside. At the end of May we were trucked down to Southampton where we went through an empty shed to a ship in dock, the SS *Crossbow*. Our barrow and wireless went into the hold, and we found our berths which were wire beds in tiers of four. I was on top underneath the galley which was very hot during the day. The time was spent chatting and playing cards, there was very little talk, as far as I can recollect, of why we were there. I suppose everyone was occupied with their own thoughts. The weather had been calm and the days sunny, but on the Sunday before D-Day the weather changed. I remember this very well because it was the day the RC chaplain came aboard to say mass and to give general absolution. I remember being very fervent that day.[44]

Colonel Stanley Christopherson, DSO, MC, a squadron commander with the, Sherwood Rangers, was among the last to embark:

The weather at the beginning of June was extremely cold and unpleasant, and we all kept wondering whether there would be a postponement. Sometimes I hoped there would be, a kind of urge to put off the evil hour, and at other times I had a longing to get cracking and to get the thing started. The answer was not long in coming. In the afternoon of June 4th, the word came and quickly spread around the camp. We gathered our possessions, loaded what petrol, ammunition and food we immediately needed onto our tanks and consigned the rest to the lorries of B Echelon. Then we moved in column out of the gate and down to the quay, where the LCT was waiting for us.[45]

Private Ralph Martin of the Gloucestershire Regiment watched events with interest:

We spent nearly five days in the Solent swinging on the anchor chain with each tide. All we could see were boats of all descriptions filling the Solent in all directions and turning in unison. It was a wonderful sight to see so many boats gathered together not so many miles from the German high command. During the night we up anchored and moved out into the English Channel round the Isle of Wight and moved west, almost I think to the Scilly Isles, where we joined many other ships to form a massive convoy. Imagine the amount of clear water needed to turn a convoy of such magnitude, the convoy was several miles wide and many miles long. Think of the work of the minesweepers as they ensured that such an amount of water was cleared of mines.[46]

Major George L. Wood, DSO, MC and Bar, of the 6th Durhams noted that his men seemed in fine fettle now they knew that the invasion was on and very close at hand. It was with mixed emotions that he marched his men out of their camp, and as he did so he looked at the faces of the old hands who had survived so much. His thoughts drifted away to his wife and child at home, wondering what they would be doing on this day:

---

44 S. Dwyer, correspondence with author (Wales, 1992).
45 Holland (ed.), J., *An Englishman at War: The Wartime Diaries of Stanley Christopherson DSO MC, 1939–1945* (London: Penguin, 2020), p. 74.
46 *WW2: People's War* <www.bbc.co.uk/ww2peopleswar> (accessed 15 February 2019).

We had a visit from Anthony Eden [the Foreign Secretary], a most pleasant and cheerful man and a great personality. He was most interested in our past history as he has a family connection with this battalion. He walked around our camp, very interesting to note how easily he conversed with the men, they all seemed to enjoy his conversation and are all smiles. Our brigade commander, R.H. Senior, DSO, talked to the men this morning and as he spoke, confident in manner, direct gaze, a little touch of humour and lastly "Good luck and God speed to every one of you", one could read in the faces of the men, their admiration for him, their complete trust in his leadership and their growing confidence in the so-called second front. They know it will be successful, Monty said so. Their only doubt: "I wonder how I shall come through all this?" We marched out of our camp this morning and embussed beside the gates. There is a small boy standing just outside, he attracts the attention of all eyes. On his jersey he is wearing our regimental and divisional sign the double TT and on his chest is pinned the ribbon of the Africa Star with Eighth Army clasp. I find myself thinking whether any of our men feel as proud of their Africa Stars as this little boy so obviously does, if so, they certainly don't show it, but then they always hide away their true feelings and it's not always easy to know what the men are thinking. However, they are all cheerful this morning, smiling and whistling, waving and calling to the girls as we pass them en route for the docks. People wave from their windows or stand on the pavement and wave. Somehow one has the feeling that they know that this is it, some are very cheerful and shout: "Good Luck, get it over quickly." Others look sad, with some silently weeping. Perhaps they have a husband, son or sweetheart whom they know will be on this move also. My thoughts are very mixed, what a grand set of men, hope we don't lose too many of the old faces this time, already they've seen and done so much. They know what it's all about, what to expect as they have done it before and have no false illusions. War is not a pleasant pastime; besides we cannot possibly expect such an easy landing as we had in Sicily. The English countryside is at its best [and] is so lovely, [but] how long will it be before we see it again? I believe this thought is in everyone's minds and I wonder what my wife is doing at this moment [–] it's such a nice day, I expect she is taking the baby for a walk. Lord how heavy and irksome all this equipment feels, Christmas tree order the troops call it. However, we can't do without any of it, it's all essential. I suppose we sail tonight, I have never been sea-sick before, hope we have a smooth crossing.[47]

In the first days of June, this mass of men and machines began to slowly stir, as if a great monster had been disturbed from its slumber. Sealed camps emptied and men in their thousands formed columns of unbroken lines that stretched deep into the countryside, the sounds of their crunching boots and roaring transports echoing throughout the night as they passed village after village on their way to the ports of embarkation. Those residing in the south of England watched events unfold with interest and lined the route like mourners at a funeral. Many of them recalled similar scenes from 30 years before when the fathers of these men trooped down the same roads to fight in the Great War.

---

47 *The Silver Bugle, Journal of the Light Infantry* (Durham, autumn 1984), p. 34.

Able Seaman Jack Tear, a member of the Royal Marines Armoured Support Regiment, Royal Navy, left his camp in Hampshire in a column of open-top trucks, heading for his landing craft at Stoke's Bay:

> The roads were crowded with vehicles crawling along bumper to bumper. Whenever we stopped, local people, who had guessed what was happening, greeted us with: "God Bless" and "Good Luck" and gave each of us a rose saying: "Here's a little piece of England to take with you." It was very emotional. On the LCT the tanks had already been chained to the deck of the craft when we got aboard. Discomfort and apprehension made sleep impossible on the night of the 4th of June and we set off at about 08:00 a.m. on the 5th to take our place in the invasion fleet.[48]

Private Anthony Atcherley of the 2nd South Wales Borderers, 56 Brigade Signals, wrote home on 4 June:

Major George L. Wood, DSO, MC and Bar, 6th Battalion Durham Light Infantry. (Courtesy of Ralph Hymer)

> I wrote what might be my last letter home to my mother. On 4th June we drove the short distance to the harbour and embarked. We were on quite a small landing craft with enough room for a number of vehicles. On board we reported to a lieutenant of the Glosters, a quiet and cheerful man who did all he could to keep us calm. On one occasion he forlornly reflected that it was Sunday, and that people would be out in London in Kew Gardens enjoying themselves. With a genuine beach assault map, he showed us that we were to land in Normandy between the villages of Le Hamel and La Riviere about eight miles east of Bayeux which we were to take. Of course, we all knew about the famous tapestry from our schooldays and now Operation Overlord was going to put William's conquest into reverse.[49]

Private Ernest Harvey, 6th Durhams, remembered the generosity of the troops to the older civilians as they left for the docks:

> The main thing I can remember was when we were in all these three-ton trucks going down to the docks. All the money that blokes had on them they were giving it to any old pensioner. If the lorry had to stop and a pensioner happened to walk by, they would call

---

48 *WW2: People's War* <www.bbc.co.uk/ww2peopleswar> (accessed 7 March 2019).
49 A. Atcherley, correspondence with author (Carnarvon, 1990).

them over and give any spare English money they had to them. They knew it was no good to them where they were going, and I think the people of Southampton must have done very well out of it.[50]

A Henley-on-Thames housewife has left an anonymous account of the departure of an artillery unit that had been stationed in the park opposite her house. Her family had got to know them well and many were considered friends:

> It was a warm, quiet and peaceful evening, my children were tucked up in bed and I leaned for a few moments out of the window thinking how far away the war seemed, when, very quietly at first, I heard the sound of "Eternal Father Strong to Save" coming from the camp. It became louder as more voices joined in the singing. It was so moving, and my eyes filled with tears. That night we heard the rumble of midnight traffic. The next day – nothing.[51]

Impressionable young boys looked on as large numbers of troops, guns and tanks gathered in their area. Brian Selman was 10 years old in 1944, his family having been evacuated to Poole, and he found himself at the centre of this great accumulation of military hardware:

> I went to school for half days in a building shared with a local school whose pupils clearly resented our presence. One day Poole Park was packed with British army vehicles parked side by side under the trees. Some evenings I and two or three other boys would secretly cycle down to Sandbanks where we would slip through the coastal defences and barbed wire for a quick swim. We always posted one of our number to watch the sky over the sea off Bournemouth for hit and run raiders who occasionally flew in low over the sea and swung low along the beach looking for targets to machine-gun.[52]

Nurse Violet Bingley, who served with the St John's Ambulance, was an industrial nurse working in a factory at the Royal Victoria Docks at Silvertown in East London:

> For several days my twin sister and myself watched the invasion craft arriving just outside the docks. During those few days, when troops were stationed near the docks, I spoke to many of them and understood the fear of those who were young like myself. One Sunday we were on our way home from church when we saw the start of the movement of troops to the docks. Hundreds of vehicles containing vast numbers of soldiers, some singing, most guessing where they were going and putting a brave face on things. Some, like my husband, were very young indeed and frankly worried. As each vehicle turned from Barking Road into the docks volunteers were stopping with collecting boxes to provide every soldier with five Woodbines and a bar of chocolate. As one truck passed the soldiers inside sang 'Two little girls in blue' to my sister and me. We were both in our uniforms. Even today I still get a lump in my throat when I hear that song.[53]

50 E. Harvey, conversation with author (Durham, 1991).
51 Kershaw, *D-Day, Piercing the Atlantic Wall*, p. 44.
52 *WW2: People's War* <www.bbc.co.uk/ww2peopleswar> (accessed 26 December 2018).
53 P. Baily, manuscript forwarded to author (London, 1989).

A Valentine tank moves down the main street of a south coast town on its way to the docks.
(Courtesy of Jim Betts)

Sidney Booth, a police constable in Portsmouth, was part of the security force trying to keep the troops and people in order:

> My job was to keep people away from Southsea Common on the seafront, as it was a prohibited area. No one was allowed there unless they had a lawful excuse and if any stray person started to walk across there, we used to escort them back to the road. When the troops started moving off our job with the military police was to follow the convoys of vehicles and make sure the troops didn't throw out any letters or make any form of communication as they went along. Some of them were throwing out letters for people to post, things like that, which was taboo.[54]

Mrs Marjory Box lived in Holbury, Hampshire, and had a number of soldiers billeted across the road from her house. They were not supposed to talk to civilians, but their officers never enforced this rule. The officers had given the men a barrel of beer on their last night before leaving England and asked the people living close by if they would bake for them, providing all the necessary ingredients and a great deal more. Marjory recalled that the civilians were invited to the party that night:

---

54 S. Booth, correspondence with author (Canada, 1989).

Troops of the Green Howards board their transport. (Author's collection)

We had a lovely time, the men were singing and drinking and, unbeknown to me, adding rum to my husband's mug of beer. He got very merry and what a time I had getting him upstairs to bed. When my husband does have one too many, which is not very often, he starts to laugh and that night everything to him was hilarious. There I was trying to get him to bed, the soldiers were outside shouting "Do you want any help" and suchlike. We and about three other couples were up at dawn to see them go. We waved till they were out of sight, me with tears streaming down my face. They left before I could make them a cake and I knew they had found this way of just giving us some very rare rations. I often wonder how many of them came back.[55]

The naval force that was to carry XXX Corps across the English Channel, protect them and land them on the beaches was known as Force G. At the beginning of June, the corps headquarters was established on board its HQ ship in Southampton Docks. The various brigade groups waited in their separate camps and were made ready for their move by sorting them into craft loads. The greater part of Force G took on their cargoes of men and machines at Southampton, and by the evening of 3 June the entire compliment of XXX Corps was afloat in the Solent, with some lying alongside in Southampton. D-Day was originally planned for 5 June, but bad

---

55 M. Box, manuscript forwarded to author (London, 1988).

weather forced a postponement. Eventually, it was decided that it was now or never and that the assault would take place on 6 June come what may.

Major George Chambers of the 8th Durhams was on the quayside waiting to get aboard:

> I was standing on the quay, as we were going over on an American landing craft infantry, and who should come along but Winston Churchill, Ernie Bevin, Field Marshal Smuts and I can't remember who else, Churchill with his big cigar. He passed by with tears running down his cheeks. "God bless you boys" he kept repeating and walked on smoking his cigar. Which didn't improve our morale, we thought "My God what are we up to, what are we in for."[56]

Royal Navy Marine Edward William was part of a three-man crew on an LCI (Landing Craft, Infantry) which was to pick up troops of the Durham Light Infantry:

> We sailed to Southampton and embarked all of our troops, all Geordies, plus a great pile of bicycles. We did not guess that this was the real thing at the time and thought it was just another rehearsal. When we anchored near the Isle of Wight it dawned on us when the ship was sealed. The men on board quickly settled down and began playing cards for French money.[57]

Private Thomas Tateson marched with his company of the 7th Green Howards to Southampton Docks and boarded an American ship called the *Empire Mace*:

> Slung from the davits were two tiers of landing craft infantry, 14 in all. These could be loaded with men while still on the davits before being lowered into the water. This was a distinct improvement on the scrambling nets which we had used in training on Loch Fynne while training at Inveraray, Scotland. We slept in hammocks and the days of waiting were spent in eating, sleeping, physical training and studying aerial photographs. These photographs were updated daily and showed all the German defences, gun emplacements and buildings on the sector allocated to us. One of the features just off the shoreline showed up as a white oval ring and in explaining our planned assault and progress this was referred to as the lavatory seat. We expected to sail on the 4th of June but there was a postponement due to heavy storms in the Channel. Meantime there were hundreds of ships as far as the eye could see assembled in the Solent, it was quite incredible that there was no sign of the Luftwaffe, not even a single spotter plane. On Monday the 5th of June there was an announcement over the ship's tanoy system that we would be sailing that evening for the shores of France. What had seemed somewhat unreal, almost as though we were engaged in training manoeuvres, now became a reality.[58]

Doctor Christopher Bartley, RAMC, checked all his medical equipment had been loaded onto the American LCT he found himself on:

---

56 G. Chambers, correspondence with author (Northumberland, 1991).
57 E. Williams, manuscript forwarded to author (Southampton, 1992).
58 T. Tateson, manuscript forwarded to author (Sheffield, 1989).

Troops heading for the docks to board their transports. (Author's collection)

We were on an American LCT anchored at Southampton. This vessel, a sort of roll-on roll-off ferry with a lift to the upper deck like an aircraft carrier, was already fully loaded with a miscellaneous collection of vehicles. Deep at the rear of the vehicle hold was our theatre tent containing all our main medical equipment. The units on the craft were from 231 Brigade to which we were being temporarily attached as a sort of seaborne field ambulance and we realised we were being prepared for a beach landing. There were about 300 men on board, [and] we were informed we would be unloading our vehicles by Rhino Ferry onto a strip of beach referred to as Jig Gold. Our emotional tension was not lessened by a 24-hour delay because of bad weather. Real fear was subdued by our growing confidence in the mighty organisation we saw assembled around us.[59]

Private A. Vince looked on with his fellow 2nd Essex men as the weather deteriorated:

On 3rd June the battalion embarked at Lymington onto a Landing Craft Infantry. These craft are capable of taking just short of 200 men. Anxiously we watched the sky as the wind increased and we hurriedly made quickly available our bags [for] vomiting and enquired for anti-sea sickness pills. That night we tied up in Southampton docks and learned that the operation had been postponed for 24 hours. However, we were on the ships, and on the ships we were forced to stay.[60]

---

59 *WW2: People's War* <www.bbc.co.uk/ww2peopleswar> (accessed 5 March 2019).
60 A. Vince, manuscript forwarded to author (Essex, 1989).

Private Denis Bowen waited patiently on his rolling ship with his 5th East Yorks comrades and was quite pleased when the postponement of the operation was announced:

> We passed the time playing cards and having singsongs and that sort of thing. Each night as dusk fell it was surprising how quiet the ship went. There were a couple of lads who had mouth organs and they would play, and the song would eventually be all round the ship. Everybody tried to get up on deck and join the singing and in the morning we sang Beautiful Dreamer. I realised I was going to be part of something that was going to be big and when you stood on the deck and looked around you couldn't see anything else but ships, north, south, east and west. Some had barrage balloons flying above them. I don't know what I expected but I felt quite safe among these experienced soldiers who had spent three years in almost continuous action, I was absolutely certain that they would carry me through. It wasn't boring on the ship, we had a proper routine of getting up in the morning, going for breakfast in a cafeteria system where you went through with a metal tray with indentations for the food. Then you would have a muster parade. We had to wear white life jackets all the time and if you went to the toilet you had to take it with you. It was on the Sunday when they suddenly appeared with blackboards and photographs and things. It was a mass briefing, and all the men were paraded on deck. He told us it was going to be a difficult job but that the beaches would be well softened up by naval gunfire and that most of the beaches would be cleared of mines. We were told there would be some German snipers still firing at you but don't expect any German armour or any German heavy artillery. This was rather pooh-poohed by the men who had been in action before, but I suppose I believed it. We went to bed and when we got up the next day expecting to go, the rumour went round that it had all been cancelled and that we were going back home as someone else was going to do the job: thank God. But of course, when we went to bed that night, we were told that tomorrow morning there would be an early reveille because we were going ashore. That was it, I didn't sleep that night, I didn't know of course what it was all about and how horrific it was going to be. The men who had done it before already knew what it was going to be like, so it was nothing to them.[61]

Some men who had seen action in the North Africa and Sicily campaigns were under no illusions as to what the coming battle would mean. Major Peter Martin, 2nd Machine-gun Battalion the Cheshire Regiment, commented:

> I can remember again that unreal feeling that one had before leaving for the invasion of Sicily. Everything was totally normal, and the countryside there was gorgeous. If my guess was right, in a few days' time, we would be going into an absolute charnel house.[62]

In the early hours of 5 June 1944, this great seaborne force began to move out of the west Solent, and throughout the night of 5/6 June headed across the Channel towards the enemy-held Normandy beaches. Everything had been planned down to the last detail: 5,333 ships and

---

61 Miller, *Nothing Less than Victory*, p. 133.
62 P. Martin, correspondence with author (Cheshire, 1988).

landing craft were now in the Channel, supported by 9,210 aircraft, all taking part in the most complicated large-scale military operation ever attempted. But the individual soldier only knew of events taking place within sight of the craft he was on; no one could see so many ships or aircraft, each man only aware of the fear, hopes and resolution within himself. It is from this point of view that the only true impression of the looming momentous events can be given. This was to be a soldiers' battle. The plans had been completed and explained with meticulous care to the men involved, but once the order was given for the assault to begin, the generals could only sit back and wait as the troops – from the rank of colonel downwards – put their plans into operation and launched Operation Overlord.

Sat in the coastguard station on the top of St Alban's Head near Swanage in Dorset, Percy Wallace looked out to sea and witnessed a sight no man had ever seen before:

> I looked down on the landing craft and could see the troops in battledress on board. Beyond them line after line of tank landing craft side by side were escorted by motor launches. Then came the armed trawlers, the ocean-going tugs and behind them echelons of minesweepers. Out to sea destroyers and frigates took up their stations. On the horizon, coming up from the west beyond Portland, the battleships and heavy cruisers waited. Throughout the day of the 5th of June, the ships weighed anchor and by dusk the sea was empty once again. Then the sound of aircraft in the sky. I said to my wife "This is it." Later when we were going to bed, we looked at one another for a moment and I said quietly "A lot of men are going to die tonight, we should pray for them."[63]

On the other side of the Channel, nervous German soldiers looked out to sea through the gloom. The weather was bad, giving them confidence that the invasion could not possibly come in such a storm. *Leutnant* Arthur Jahnke was inspecting positions dug-in along the crest of a sand dune, with a lookout scanning the horizon through his binocular scissor telescope. Jahnke asked, "Anything?" "No *Herr Leutnant* no news." Jahnke stepped up to look through the telescope, scanning the beach and out to sea. The night was black, and rainclouds were shrouding the moon. He commented:

> They won't come in this weather, rough sea, poor visibility, with force 5/6 wind and rain likely to get heavier. Most probably we won't even get our usual air raids. There is little prospect of short-term changes in the weather during the next few days. That means that the various conditions of tide, moon and the general weather situation necessary for a landing here in Northern France will not coincide again until the second half of June.[64]

---

63 P. Cuerdon, manuscript forwarded to author (Hampshire, 1990).
64 Carell, P., *Invasion – They're Coming!* (London: Harrap and Co., 1962), p. 4.

3

Away at Last

Early on 5 June 1944, the sea was rough in the Channel and the wind was howling. At 0700 hours, officers opened their sealed orders and learned the names of their objectives for the next day. Two hours later, the vast assortment of vessels that had been anchored in the Solent cast off their moorings and made for their assembly areas to the south of the Isle of Wight. Force G was to land on Gold Beach, Force S on Sword Beach and Force J on Juno Beach. The American ships advanced from the west to join them: Force U would land on Utah Beach and Force O on Omaha Beach. The high seas meant it took most of the day to manoeuvre over 2,000 vessels into position, but as darkness fell on 5 June the leading ships passed by the buoys that marked the safe channels – that had been swept for mines – leading to the beaches of Normandy. So far, no German aircraft had appeared near the vast convoy that comprised Operation Neptune, the greatest amphibious operation in history.

The midget submarine X23, which had been on the seabed a mile off the Normandy coast since 2 June, surfaced on the 5th only to be informed that the operation had been postponed. Once again it descended to the seabed and waited in the gloomy silence. In the early hours of 6 June, the order finally came through verifying that the great invasion fleet was approaching. X23 thus surfaced again and activated the beacon that would guide the landing craft and amphibious DD (Duplex Drive) tanks ashore. The submarine's efforts were a great success, thanks to which the majority of landing craft beached in the correct areas.

On board an American craft anchored in an English port on the south coast, a war correspondent watched in awe as the vast flotilla moved out to sea:

> These tightly packed ships represent only one of the rivers of men and machines that all along the coast are pouring out into the sea. Four years ago, almost to the day, the tide of war had flooded from the east into the French Channel ports before swirling back on Paris and beyond. Now the tide has turned and in this suspended moment of history the first mighty wave is gathering before it crashes down on the enemy beaches. The near observer gets no more than a fleeting, awesome glimpse of it that a solitary swimmer would have of a great breaker in an angry sea.[1]

---

1   Stafford, D., *Ten Days to D-Day. Countdown to the Liberation of Europe* (London: Little, Brown, 2003), p. 258.

Troops aboard their Landing Craft, Tank waiting to move out into the Solent. (Author's collection)

"We are making history"

Private Eric Broadhead, of the 9th Durhams, felt tense on LCI 501 as he waited for events to unfold on the night of 5 June:

> We had fun whistling at the wrens on the dockside which seemed to relieve the tension for a short while. At 21:00 p.m. we were issued with seasickness pills, and we now knew that by morning we should be in less peaceful waters. That evening 501 weighed anchor and slid slowly down the river into sailing position. We sat on the decks looking towards the shore still calling to any female that could be spied, but behind these joking habits much deeper thoughts passed through the minds of everyone on board. As darkness fell we went below decks and lay in our bunks fully clothed. Outside the wind was howling even more as we headed out to sea. I dozed off before we really turned on to full steam, only to be awoken by a horrible sickly feeling inside. 501 was rolling in every imaginal [*sic*] direction, the

seasickness pills had failed to work and there was only one thing to do, that was to lie still, which was dreadful and only served to make me feel worse. At 05:00 a.m. I made a supreme effort and crawled on deck and the lovely fresh air was worth a million pounds. The scene was unforgettable as over a vast expanse of the Channel there were ships of every type, from small MTBs to HMS *Rodney* and her escort. Overhead was an array of the immense power of the RAF as it roared through the skies heading for France. The sea was rolling, and the morning light revealed a picture that could not be forgotten. I was on deck for less than half an hour and looking at the sea only served to send me back to lie on my bunk.[2]

Captain William J. Arnold of the 6th Durhams recalled that he sailed from Southampton in rough seas:

I had been many thousands of miles on troop ships but had been unable to overcome my seasickness, so the crossing was a misery for me personally. We, the officers, tried to persuade the men to get some sleep, but for the same reason we could not sleep, and neither could they. The conversations that went on that night were many and varied. As we were second flight and not assault troops most people seemed to be wondering whether the leading troops would have cleared the beach and established some kind of bridgehead. We were not equipped for close combat bearing only personal arms, in my case it was a simple 38 Webley revolver.[3]

Lieutenant Colonel Stanley Christopherson of the Sherwood Rangers sat uncomfortably aboard his LCT:

We talked quietly among ourselves and tried to catch a few moments of sleep, but the tension and growing sense of excitement and anticipation made this impossible. The night was cold and the sea still quite choppy as the flat bottomed LCT lost any protection from the English coast and began to slide about on the surface of the waves in mid-Channel. Many of us still felt seasick, despite the pills we had been issued to counter this, and we had by now been so long at sea that our sense of disorientation had grown. Mugs of hot soup were passed around and these gave us a momentary warmth. All of us were looking forward to the moment when we could leave the ships and the sea behind us and get back onto dry land. Indeed, that anticipation overcame any accompanying nervousness about the prospect of going into action.[4]

Company Sergeant Major William Brown, of the 8th Durhams, remembered the miserable time the troops had through seasickness:

Morale was getting pretty low as people were getting sick and spewing. The smell below decks was vile and men were trying to lie in their bunks with their equipment on. The handiest things were the spew bags because you could use them then throw them over the

---

2   Manuscript forwarded to author by E. Broadhead (Durham, 1992).
3   Newspaper cutting forwarded to author by W. Ridley (Durham, 1992).
4   Holland (ed.), *An Englishman at War: The War Diaries of Stanley Christopherson*, p. 34.

side. I was so nervous I hadn't eaten much in two days so there wasn't anything to come up. The orderly corporal came up as I was leaning over the side of the ship and I said, "Good morning, where's the parade state", the book with all the company details. He said "Here's the bloody parade state" as he threw it over the side. He continues "This is our fourth bloody do and I wish I was off this bastard." We would have gone into the water anywhere rather than be sick.[5]

Private Thomas Tateson, 7th Green Howards, recalled being restless and strangely detached as his transport ship headed for the French coast:

No one slept much that night, 5th June 1944, many of us being up on deck watching the flashes from the French coast where our bombers were attacking the coastal batteries. I remember thinking that I should be frightened and that instead I seemed to be detached and observing myself as though I were in a film. The feeling of unreality, the subconscious thought that this can't be really happening to me, was in some way a calming influence. Reveille was sounded at 03:15 a.m. on 6th June and we hastily went for breakfast. This being an American ship the galley was equipped with multi-course indented trays which I had not previously encountered. In one indentation was porridge and in another, what must have been surely the most unsuitable meals that could have been devised, we were served with minced liver. We were to see this for a second time after we had been at sea in the small assault landing craft for a few hours. We were also given a rum ration and for many years after the war I could not stand the smell of rum, in spite of the thoughtfully provided vomit bags and the fresh sea-air. There was a pervading stench of retched liver and rum in the boats as we headed for our encounter with Gerry. At 04:20 a.m. we began getting into the assault craft and by 05:30 a.m. we had left the ship and we made our way to the shore.[6]

Sapper C.R. Wampach, serving with the Royal Engineers, was due to land with 231 Brigade and begin clearing a way through the minefields for the infantry:

One officer said to me "We are making history" and as the landing craft tossed in its anchorage many a thought came into my head. I thought of my family, what would we encounter on the other side and would I be able to control my fear. Could I do the job I was trained for? The adrenaline was pumping as the engine of the craft roared into life and we moved out of Southampton Water into the Channel.[7]

Private Jack Heath, with the 20th Flotilla Combined Operations, sailed through heavy seas in an LCT, which was full of armour and infantry:

We sailed across the English Channel through a lighted path that had been swept through the minefields and the crossing was very rough. Especially as the craft had a flat bottom and only drew three feet forward and five feet aft, not ideal for a rough crossing. Those poor soldiers

5   W. Brown, interview with author (Durham, 1992).
6   Manuscript forwarded to author by T. Tateson (Sheffield, 1989).
7   Manuscript forwarded to author by Brian Cook (Carnegie Heritage Centre, Hull, 2016).

A German machine-gun crew scan the horizon from their concrete emplacement on Gold Beach. (Courtesy of P. Cuerdon)

were by this time looking very green and sick and were praying to get off the LCT as soon as possible. The tank drivers were sitting at their controls wearing a Davis Safety Harness.[8]

Private Stanley Dwyer, a radio operator with the 50th Divisional Signals, watched in silence as the heavily laden men of the 1st Dorsets clambered down nets into their landing craft that were waiting for them at the sides of the larger ships, moving up and down on the swell:

> On Monday night we upped anchor and were up and away, there was little sleep that night, 5th June, and most of us were up by 03:00 a.m. There was a constant drone of aircraft overhead and when it got light we could see the planes. At about 05:30 a.m. the tannoy barked something about landing craft being manned. The infantry, Dorsets, were climbing into them where they lay lashed to the sides, their faces were startlingly white, and all the blood had left them. There was mostly complete silence broken only by one of them shouting goodbye to a friend.[9]

Trooper Kenneth Mayo, Sherwood Rangers, was a veteran of the Eighth Army in North Africa. Within weeks of his return to England, he was thrown in at the deep end and began training with the top secret Sherman DD tanks that would have to swim ashore during the landings in Normandy:

8   *WW2: People's War* <www.bbc.co.uk/ww2peopleswar> (accessed 27 May 2019).
9   Manuscript forwarded to author by S. Dwyer (Wales, 1992).

The regiment moved to Norfolk and to Fritton Lake to prepare for the assault and by May we were in the New Forrest [*sic*] for final training with our brand-new tanks. We loaded on board our LCT in Southampton Harbour on 2nd June. I shall always remember our sailing from the Solent in rough seas at midnight on 5th June, many of us couldn't sleep and were violently sick. As dawn broke we were amongst a vast armada of ships and crafts of all sizes.[10]

Lance Corporal Frank A. Wright, 47 Royal Marine Commando, looked out over the Solent in awe at the sight that met his eyes:

I've never seen a sight like it before or since, the Solent was jam packed with ships. Our mother ship, the *Princess Josephine Charlotte*, was moored off Key Haven, and looking northeast towards Portsmouth was ship after ship of every imaginable type in a magnificent show of strength. Surely the invasion couldn't fail, could it?[11]

Royal Navy Sub Lieutenant Walter Marshall had already been to France in a mini submarine with a small special reconnaissance patrol whose job it was to assess the strength of the beach obstacles facing the landing areas of 231 Brigade. The patrol went out on 3 June and returned to Portsmouth on the 5th:

The infantry was massing ready for the following morning's invasion. There was such tension on their faces, and I felt sorry for them, many of them were just young lads straight out of training in England. I scrounged together sweets and cigarettes from the men at the base and threw them at those young soldiers. I was only 20 myself but I was a veteran by then, which made me feel older.[12]

Wireless Operator Austin Baker, with the 4/7th Royal Dragoon Guards, worried about his chances of survival in the coming operation, having been through so much already:

We eventually sailed off down the Solent at midday. Major Baker called the 4/7th chaps into the captain's cabin, which was about the size of a double bed, and told us where we were headed. It turned out to be a little place between Caen and Arromanches called La Riviere. Our particular stretch of the beach was known as King Red beach and our rendezvous was at the village of Ver-sur-Mer. Major B read out messages from Eisenhower and Montgomery and told us that he personally thought we should all be very honoured to be in on this affair. I think most of us felt that we could have stood the disgrace of being left out of it.[13]

Private Maurice Wells, 2nd Gloucesters, was aboard his transport ship on the night of 5 June when he and his comrades received a great shock:

---

10   Bowman, M.W., *Air War D-Day. Gold, Juno and Sword* (Barnsley: Pen & Sword, 2013), pp. 22-23.
11   *47 Commando.org* <www.47commando.org.uk> (accessed 15 October 2018).
12   W. Marshall, correspondence with author (London, 1993).
13   Miller, *Nothing Less than Victory*, p. 161.

> During the night there was an almighty loud scraping all along the side of the ship and we all thought "What the hell was that?" A sailor said nonchalantly "Don't worry it's only a mine." If it had gone off none of us would have survived below decks, it was bloody frightening. It was rough on our ship, the sea that is, you got whatever sleep you could get but it was very uncomfortable.[14]

Captain Roger Bell, serving with the Westminster Dragoons, was the commander of a flail tank, one of the 'Funnies'. Hard training meant he was well prepared for the tasks that would be demanded of him and his men as his LCT got under way on the morning of 5 June:

> As we passed the Isle of Wight the weather was rough, and it took the shine off the party feeling that had prevailed up until now. Most of the 30 men on board were seasick, in spite of the Hyoscine pills they had taken. There was very little to do and as we looked out over the wet Bulwarks, we could see the other landing craft of the flotilla. As dusk began to fall that evening, I felt no apprehension or fear for what was coming in the morning. I had never been in a battle or seen a dead man. Darkness fell and our craft plunged onwards. What I did feel was a tremendous elation at taking part in such a great adventure. It never crossed my mind that the invasion might fail, I had read Monty's personal message and he said he had complete confidence, and so that was that. As night fell I encouraged the men to sleep on the steel decks. There was only one other army officer on board apart from myself; the skipper of the LCT had to be on the bridge all night and he offered us his cabin. At midnight, two thirds of the way across the channel, with a clear conscience and not a worry in the world, I fell fast asleep.[15]

Doctor Christopher Bartley, RAMC, sat aboard his LCT with men from 231 Brigade. They were about a mile out from Gold Beach when a naval launch came near:

> A naval launch was thumping its way through the choppy seas in bursts of spray as it approached. A notice was given out over the tannoy that a naval chaplain had come aboard and would shortly celebrate Holy Communion on the foredeck, all were invited to attend. When I decided to join in I was astounded to find that I had been beaten to it by well over 200 others. Immediately in front of the chaplain, who wore a white surplice over his uniform, was a table covered with a white cloth anchored down by pieces of assorted weaponry, on which was a silver cross and chalice. The bread and wine were shared out and men returned to their places of waiting, a little subdued perhaps but with a new degree of calmness.[16]

Private A. Vince would soon suffer the effects of the rolling sea as his LCI moved out of Southampton Water with his fellows from the 2nd Essex:

---

14 *WW2: People's War* <www.bbc.co.uk/ww2peopleswar> (accessed 13 December 2010).
15 Manuscript forwarded to author by R. Bell (London, 1987).
16 *WW2: People's War* <www.bbc.co.uk/ww2peopleswar> (accessed 5 March 2019).

Enormous Landing Craft, Tanks, loaded with men and machines, at anchor off the south coast, all ready for the move to Normandy. (Author's collection)

> In the late evening of 5thJune we cast off and slowly moved down Southampton Water to take our positions in the greatest mass of shipping ever known in this world. To us on board it seemed that had the opposition been able to bomb they would have had almost a dry land target, so closely packed was the invasion fleet. Darkness fell before we reached the open sea and below decks we drank our tins of self-heating soup and cocoa and played a little pontoon or housey-housey before trying to get a few hours' sleep before the great day. We slept well that night without a worry, but the morning light of 6th June found us very shaken by the pitching and rolling of our ship.[17]

Corporal Anthony Coglan, of the 9th Durhams, found it very hard to get any rest on the eve of D-Day:

> Sleep during the night was limited as we were all keyed up for what was to be the biggest invasion in history. But of course, the sleeping arrangements were really primitive. I tried

---

17 Manuscript forwarded to author by A. Vince (Essex, 1989).

sleeping on the toolbox of the Bren-carrier but as it was only four feet long and one foot wide, I was unsuccessful. Next, I tried sleeping in the driver's seat, but it was not made with that in mind, all in all it was a pretty uncomfortable time.[18]

Lieutenant Colonel C. MacDonald, 2nd-in-command (2 i/c) of the 6th Green Howards, looked out at the gathering armada:

> The invasion fleet formed up off Spithead was an incredible sight. The sea was a forest of ships of all shapes and sizes and not an enemy plane got near us. What a difference from when we left France in 1940. Eventually, after 24 hours postponement, we set sail at night. It was a fast little ship, but the sea was vicious, really vicious, with heavy swells and huge waves. In fact it seemed as if the sea was doing all it could to make our invasion as difficult as possible, we got no sleep. During the night messages were received of ships in difficulties having to turn back to England.[19]

Some found the heavy seas made boarding the landing craft a trial, as recounted by Lieutenant David Holdsworth, 2nd Devons:

> Clambering down the side of the ship hand over hand, gripping a suspended rope, was for me a particularly unpleasant and frightening experience. I had no head for heights, and I hated the sea. Without the military paraphernalia which we carried it would have been bad enough, it was like playing a game of Russian roulette. Rifles, pouches, bayonet scabbards, each took their part in offering the chance of a speedy death by getting caught in the ropes or on someone else. To further complicate our individual balancing acts the rope net, which we held onto so grimly, had a nasty habit of swaying against the movement of the ship and becoming more slippery the nearer we got to the assault craft which was bobbing around like a cork on the sea below us.[20]

Major Antony R.C. Mott was on board HMS *Arquebus* with his men of the 1st Hampshire when they were ordered to move:

> We were called up over the blower "Serial 2042 to No4 boat station, port side, now". I led my boatload, consisting mainly of Coy HQ and an assault rifle section, up to our LCA [Landing Craft, Assault]. All our heavy kit had been pre-loaded and needed only a quick check before we could report all was well. We said our final goodbyes and good lucks before we were lowered into a lumpy sea, everything was ominously quiet.[21]

Lieutenant Colonel Cosmo Nevill, 2nd Devons, recalled a restless night, an unappetizing breakfast and the sight of the distant battle:

---

18 Moses, H., *The Gateshead Gurkhas* (Durham: County Durham Books, 2001), p. 271.
19 Manuscript forwarded to author by F.W. Vickers (ex-6th Green Howards) (Barnsley, 1992).
20 Manuscript forwarded to author by Brian Cook (Carnegie Heritage Centre, Hull, 2016).
21 Saunders, T., *Gold Beach – Jig* (Barnsley: Pen & Sword, 2002), p. 48.

Few of us slept well that night and at about 03:30 a.m. we were roused for breakfast which consisted of almost cold liver and onions and a lukewarm mug of tea. The outlines of the neighbouring ships could be seen, all moving at a steady 12 knots. In the distance there were signs of the battle, star shells and incendiary bullets were constantly flashing in the sky, but we were too far away for the sound of battle to be heard. At dawn we anchored seven and a half miles from the coast and a never-ending procession of LCTs and all types of naval craft passed us, whose job it was to prepare the way for the landing of the infantry.[22]

"There must be an easier way of earning a living"

Lance Sergeant Ken Rutherford, with the 5th East Yorks, was a veteran of the 50th Northumbrian Division and had served in its ranks since 1939, seeing action in many theatres of war. Thoughts of his own mortality came to mind in the early hours of D-Day:

Lieutenant David Holdsworth, 2nd Battalion Devonshire Regiment. (Author's collection)

> Once we had got into the landing craft the sea was rough and it threw us about like a toy boat, a few were sick, but not a lot. In our craft it was very cramped but at least we could sit back. I started to think what I would be doing this time tomorrow as we'd been through so many actions since 1940 and I began to wonder whether my chances of surviving this one was good or bad.[23]

Sergeant S. Wills, 2nd Devons, celebrated his sixth wedding anniversary on 6 June 1944, though not in the circumstances he would have liked:

> Few of us slept well that night and at about 03:30 a.m. we were roused for breakfast which consisted of cold liver and onions and a lukewarm mug of tea. Then we assembled into our pre-determined positions to be loaded into our landing craft. My landing craft being first off had to cruise round and round the mother ship until all the other landing craft were lowered from the davits. The officers and men used the scrambling nets to get from the decks into their allotted landing craft. On board my landing craft was the CO and part of battalion HQ, the MO [Medical Officer], some stretcher bearers, a few supporting

22 Manuscript forwarded to author by P. Cuerdon (Hampshire, 1994).
23 K. Rutherford, interview with author (Hull, 1992).

Troops of the Green Howards clamber down rope nets into their landing craft. (Author's collection)

arms personnel, as well as the CO's jeep and the RAP [Regimental Aid Post] jeep. The choppy sea caused a little seasickness, helped I suppose by fear. Sitting in front of me was a stretcher bearer called Wally Hodkin who was using a bucket because he had diarrhoea and was at the same time being sick into a bucket in front of him. The smell was frightful and combined with the action of a very choppy sea several others became seasick, me too eventually. Once our assault craft were loaded and assembled in flight order we set off for the shore which could now be seen a few miles away. Most of the seasickness seemed to terminate then for there was so much of interest going on around us. There seemed to be within sight hundreds of small and large assault craft and behind us dozens of larger mother ships, some lowering assault craft into the sea, and countless naval ships. A sneaky little thought crept into my mind which was "How's this for a wedding anniversary?" June 6th, 1944, was the sixth anniversary of my marriage and I felt I had more fireworks for its celebration than any other living person.[24]

24 Manuscript forwarded to author by S. Wills (Devon, 1989).

Bombardier Jack Styan, Battle Axe Coy, Royal Artillery, could not help but be apprehensive as to what the future held in store for him. However, such thoughts were somewhat outweighed by the sight of the great naval flotilla that was on the move and gathered all around him:

> There was this massive movement of ships of all sizes ploughing through the rough seas, it looked to me as though you could walk from one boat to another right across the Channel and step off in France, it was so massive. It was a sight I wouldn't like to have missed and yet I was there but didn't want to be, we were all just scared stiff as we approached the shore.[25]

RAF Pilot Officer James Kyle, DFM, flying with 197 Typhoon Squadron, took off from a south coast airfield and was faced with a fantastic view of the Solent:

Bombardier Jack Styan, Battle Axe Coy, Royal Artillery. (Courtesy of J. Styan)

> Immediately the wheels of my aircraft left the ground I was confronted with an almost unbelievable panorama of ships of all sizes and shapes grouped closely together for as far as the eye could see. The armada-like stream of naval traffic in the Solent and across the Channel was maintained over the whole hundred miles to the French coast. The Isle of Wight was surrounded and looked as though it was being towed out to sea. What a spectacle it was! Flying low over this continuous stream of ships, the sea looked rough and I spared a thought for those poor devils below me.[26]

Private Denis Bowen, 5th East Yorks, was fearfully sick in the landing craft along with many others as the sea tossed the tiny vessel about like a cork. All they wanted was to get onto the beach and feel firm ground beneath their feet:

> Reveille was about three thirty or four a.m. time, I washed and shaved and had breakfast and as we came out of the dining room, we were given two 24-hour ration packs containing the usual thing, oatmeal biscuits, tea, sugar and powdered milk. On the mother ship a high percentage of people, though not all, was sick, yes, I was sick. Every day as soon as I had my breakfast I'd go straight out and throw it up in the scuppers. Some of the Royal Navy personnel had said to me whatever you do don't go without food, if you have to be sick let your stomach have something to be sick with. People were saying "I'll be bloody glad to get off this boat" even though it meant landing on the beach. It was even worse when we got into

---

25 J. Styan, correspondence with author (Middlebrough, 1990).
26 *WW2: People's War* <www.bbc.co.uk/ww2peopleswar> (accessed 5 March 2019).

A German sentry on the Normandy coast looks out to sea for any sign of the invasion, 1 June 1944. (Courtesy of H. Wernemann)

the assault landing craft, we had quite a bit of trouble getting on the assault craft because the sea was extremely rough. We got down the netting hanging at the side of the ship and the ship was rolling with the landing craft bouncing up in the air and crashing back down again, probably six to twelve feet. You had to time it so that you could step from the netting onto the landing craft when it came up on a wave. I was fortunate, the thing came up and I stepped off and then went down with it. There were quite a few men who got hurt, mistimed the jump and fell quite heavily, they never got ashore at all. They were taken straight back onto the ship with broken limbs or dislocated shoulders. It took about 20 or 30 minutes to fill the LCA, we set off and had to circle round and round just waiting for the others to fill up. They had RN speedboats with loud hailers, and you could hear all the orders coming over, you know, "4986 follow me". Everybody was bellowing and shouting orders to get us into position. Then we started heading in, of course I didn't see anything then because we were down in the boat, it had high sides. You could have climbed up the sides to have a look, but nobody did. The big naval barrage had started by then, it seemed to me that every ship in the Channel was firing onto the beach. The landing craft was flat bottomed and because of the rough sea it was lifting up in the air and banging back down. Everybody was spewing over everybody else. I was keen to get off that damned thing although I knew I was going into action. I didn't see it as me, an individual fighting, I merely felt I was a little tiny person

Rommel chats with the crew of a self-propelled gun, Normandy, 1 June 1944.
(Courtesy of H. Wernemann)

in the middle of a whacking great event that was about to happen. In my mind all that was happening was that I was on this boat, I was sick along with all the other people, the front of the craft was going to go down, I was going to get off and I was going to run up the beach. I didn't think anything about firing my weapon or that the enemy would be firing at me. The front was going to go down and I would get off and say, "Thank God".[27]

Sergeant Bert Davies, of the 6th Durhams, recalled a very uncomfortable crossing:

We were all issued with two sea-sick tablets, and I thought I'll not take mine yet. As soon as we set off I watched other people being sea-sick one after the other. I thought I'd best take mine and was sea-sick within ten minutes. The pills did no good at all as I should have taken them an hour before. The sea was very rough. The boat would rear up right to the top of a wave and then the wave would disappear, the boat then slapped onto the sea just like a bomb dropping into the water. I was darned pleased when we got to the other side.[28]

Private Robert S. McDowall, 5th East Yorks, sat in his crowded landing craft feeling sick as the Normandy coast approached:

There must have been about 20 of us in the small rectangular assault craft, all sitting uncomfortably on the low raised woodwork which served as seats. We wore gas capes to

---

27 Manuscript forwarded to author by D. Bowen (Shropshire, 1989).
28 Moses, *The Faithful Sixth*, p. 277.

protect us from the flying spray and clutched our vomit bags, which were only too soon having to be put to use as our tiny craft made its way through mountainous seas. Many of those who had had occasion to use these bags attempted to throw them into the sea, but the wind merely blew them into the faces of the soldiers behind them. As the light began to dawn it became clear what was going on. To our left and right were the rest of the little landing craft steering towards the shore, while away behind us lay the ships which had brought us over. Warships were shelling the shore, which was as yet scarcely visible, and rocket ships sent their missiles into the air with terrific roars. Above us flights of bombers droned their way towards the land ahead of us while we ploughed forward below, miserably sea-sick and not feeling the slightest bit like attacking anything or anybody. Slowly the land showed up clearer and closer and spouts of water rose from the sea around us as the Germans returned the warships' fire. Suddenly it seemed to be fully light, and we could clearly discern the shore in front of us. "There's the lighthouse" shouted Lt Lowe, second in command of our company, "and it's still standing." I remember I felt just a trifle discouraged that all our bombing and shelling had failed to destroy it.[29]

Thoughts turned to home for Able Seaman Jack Tear, of the Royal Marines Armoured Support Group, who was on an LCT that was being battered by the rough seas:

What a bloody journey that was, there was a heavy swell, and our flat-bottomed craft went rhythmically up and down. Occasionally it would catch the top of a wave on its way down and shudder as though it might break in two. We had all made our last will and testament two weeks earlier. Now between bouts of nausea most of us wrote last letters home just in case.[30]

Major David Warren, with the 1st Hampshires, had every confidence that this operation would be a success:

What we all felt, and I think this is the most astonishing thing about the Normandy landings, is that everyone was 100% confident that whatever happened to me, anyone else or the Hampshires, it was going to be successful. There was no question of thinking it might not be and I think everybody was quite glad to get on with it because it was the green light for the end of the war, or so it seemed at the time. We had the advantage of having marvellous models of where we were going to land, and so before we got aboard the ship we were able to brief everybody about the enemy positions, the models were very good indeed and showed all the intelligence about the enemy, their positions and anything else that was going to be relevant. We knew a great deal about the beach on which we were going to land. Going in I suddenly realised that with the bombardment there was such a lot of smoke, fire and dust that it was difficult to see where we exactly had to land; we knew where we wanted to land but to pick it out was difficult.[31]

---

29 Manuscript forwarded to author by Brian Cook (Carnegie Heritage Centre, Hull, 2017).
30 *WW2: People's War* <www.bbc.co.uk/ww2peopleswar> (accessed 7 March 2019).
31 D. Warren, correspondence with author (Hampshire, 1990).

Troops of the 50th Northumbrian Division look tense as they head for the Normandy coast in their Landing Craft, Assault. (Courtesy of Norman Hardy)

Captain Roger Bell, a flail tank commander with the Westminster Dragoons, woke up at dawn on 6 June to see the same grey turbulent sea, but it was now full of ships of all shapes and sizes, with the bombardment in full swing:

> I had been cynical when General Hobart had talked of the honour of being among the first to land, [but] now I began to see what he meant. It was the first time we had seen a fleet ready for action and the first time we had any real impression of the fantastic size and power of the force which had been assembled. As we steamed through the lines of warships towards the shoreline of France we did feel proud. The men aboard the LCT finished their breakfast, after which they packed away their personal equipment and washed and shaved. Everyone was happy now that the crossing was nearly over and looked forward to standing on land again. The chains and chocks holding the tanks in position were cleared and from the tank turret I looked across in the direction of Gold Beach. We were going to land at the eastern end near La Riviere. We pressed forward under the arc of the gunfire from the warships behind us but had not seen any activity from the German batteries as

yet. The smoke from the bombardment hid the hills and hung over the village, but as we drew nearer the beach could be seen clearly, it looked deserted, as if nobody had set foot on it for years.[32]

Lance Corporal Frank Wright recalled the tension in his fellow members of 47 Royal Marine Commando as they prepared to close in on the beaches:

> We moved to about ten miles offshore about five in the morning and all the troops assembled at their stations on the boat deck. We had blackened our faces with grease paint and as it was pitch dark anyway, we shuffled sheepishly around trying to get in the correct order barely able to see one another. Nobody said much, the tension was getting to everybody. Finally, we got it right and began jumping into the LCA. We were very heavily loaded, and I was the reluctant bearer of the troop Bangalore Torpedo. The LCA was lowered into the water, engines revved, and we steered away from the *PJC* [*Princess Josephine Charlotte*] under our own power. The first thing I did was to unhook the toggles of my assault jacket, [as] if I ended up in the water with this weight I would go straight to the bottom.[33]

Company Sergeant Major Stanley Hollis, 6th Green Howards, mentioned the difficulty the men had getting into the LCA burdened with all their equipment:

> We had to go down scrambling nets into the landing craft. The sea was rough, and the landing craft was going up and down, it was awkward getting down with our equipment: big Bren pouches sticking out and rifle and Sten butts. I remember thinking to myself when going down the nets "There must be an easier way of earning a living". However, we got into the craft, about 18 or 20 men in a boat, and at this stage I would like to mention that one of the passengers said as he took his place in the boat, that he would rather be anywhere else than there at that time. We cast off from the ship and circled round and round in circles until the whole company was afloat and then we set off.[34]

Lieutenant Colonel Robin W.S. Hastings, CO of the 6th Green Howards, watched his men negotiating the scrambling nets before following them:

> These great nets hung from the side of the merchant ship, down which we had to scramble, carrying all sorts of equipment which seemed especially designed to catch in the nets. The sea was going up and down to no uncertain tune and the sides of the ship were heaving, the craft being tossed in every direction below us. Having achieved this apparently impossible task we circled for three-quarters of an hour in rough water before setting off.[35]

Corporal Frank Cosgrove sat in his LCT on the approach and played cards with his mates in 47 Royal Marine Commando:

---

32 Manuscript forwarded to author by R. Bell (London, 1987).
33 *47 Commando.org* <www.47commando.org.uk> (accessed 23 January 2019).
34 *Middlesbrough Evening Gazette* cutting sent to the author by R. Walker (Scarborough, 1991).
35 Morgan, M., *D-Day Hero CSM Stanley Hollis VC* (Gloucestershire: Sutton Publishing, 2004), p. 75.

Troops of 47 Royal Marine Commando in their Landing Craft, Assault looking wet and tense. (Courtesy of F. Cosgrove)

> Nerves [took] a hold then and we were pretty quiet for a bit. Different people act in different ways. Four of us played cards, for hours and hours we played cards and it's pretty cramped in an LCA. There's not much room to move around and I think we nearly wore those cards out.[36]

Sergeant Kenneth Lakeman, serving with the Royal Corps of Signals, had to keep an eye on the men in his command as feelings were running high and nerves were frayed:

> Andrews was a great big fellow, six feet tall, fifteen or sixteen stone, but he had this jumpiness about him, and he was wandering around this limited space of this LCT. There were huge packing cases and boxes there with serial numbers on them, he prised one of these open and he changed colour. It was full of white crosses: "God" he said "I don't mind going to my death but to take my own cross." He was visibly upset. Being in charge I rollicked him for this because it was upsetting the rest of the crew. My driver mechanic, a wonderful bloke called Fred Mincher, he would take the mickey sometimes, and he said: "Well of course Andy it's probably got your name and number on it." Well that nearly started a fight

---

36   F. Cosgrove, correspondence with author (Hartlepool, 1991).

so I had to calm them down. That's the sort of edginess that was going on at the time and you can understand it.[37]

Great fleets of bombers had been smothering the German defences with high explosive for some time, and at 0510 hours the massive naval force assembled off the coast of northern France began its bombardment of carefully selected targets. At an appointed time, each enemy position underwent its ordeal by fire: bombs fell on them and naval guns rained shells upon them, followed by a hail of shells and rockets from smaller craft. This huge battering ram from the air and sea heralded the arrival of the 50th Northumbrian Division on Gold Beach as it crept towards the Normandy coast.

Private A. Vince, 2nd Essex, was impressed by the invasion fleet he saw as he headed for the shore through a very rough sea:

> It was a miserable cloudy sky overhead as our convoy crawled towards the shore. Clouds of smoke could be seen billowing upwards from the land and battleships, cruisers, destroyers and rocket firing craft were still pouring their fire into the coastal defences. Occasionally a sea mine would float past and as the morning progressed we struggled into our equipment as best we could on the crowded decks. We put on water-proof trousers and discarded them immediately, for we would never have got ashore in such cumbersome garments, laden as we were.[38]

Lieutenant Colonel MacDonald, 2 i/c 6th Green Howards, heard large numbers of aircraft roaring overhead all night on 5/6 June:

> Soon flashes were visible from the Normandy coastline, a cheering sight. The sea was so rough and visibility so poor that our little ship was ordered to lead the Landing Craft Assault to a point where identification of the coastline was unmistakeable. Just before dawn on 6th June there was so much activity from our armada that for a few foolish minutes I think I believed it would be a walk over. It seemed like everything was being hurled at the coastline and beyond and the naval bombardment was fantastic to behold.[39]

Pte Richard Atkinson, 9th Durhams, who had fought in Africa and Sicily and twice been wounded, began to think of his own chances of survival once they hit the beach:

> There were the usual pre-battle nerves, and you were frightened there's no doubt about it. There was a funny feeling inside your stomach and that. You didn't know what to expect and by this stage, the war was getting along, and you would say "Well I've been pushing my luck quite a lot". All these thoughts were running through your mind. We may not have said that to each other, but they were there. You weren't the happy soul that you should have been and kept saying to yourself "My number must be on one now". Being wounded twice before you say to yourself "Next time will I be so lucky?" You're shaking and saying

---

37 Manuscript forwarded to author by K. Lakeman (London, 1987).
38 Manuscript forwarded to author by A. Vince (Essex, 1989).
39 W.F. Vickers, correspondence with author (Barnsley, 1991).

prayers. I saw men that were as scared as I was, and I was very scared. But you still went on and were not going to let your mates see you were scared.[40]

Sapper Ralph Rayner, with 82nd Assault Squadron, Royal Engineers, sat in an LCT as dawn broke and was astounded by what he saw around him:

> The view of the convoy was a sight to behold and one that I shall never forget. There were ships and landing craft in all directions for as far as we could see. We eventually found ourselves at the front of the column heading for Gold Beach. As our formation moved closer to the coast the heavy warships suddenly opened fire and this bombardment continued [until] just before touch down, then the barrage moved forward to areas beyond the beach. Combined with the explosions of German incoming shells the noise was deafening, [and] a number of our own craft were hit causing many casualties.[41]

As Lieutenant A.A.M. Gregson of the 147th Field Regiment, Essex Yeomanry, Royal Artillery, neared the landing area it was his job to give supporting fire to the infantry with a troop of Priest self-propelled guns on his LCT while out at sea:

> There was France, a low misty outline far ahead. I wondered for the hundredth time how I was to measure the range when our barrage was to commence. Where the hell had that Fairmile patrol boat, that was to indicate the range, got to? The No1s were busy preparing the guns, the ammunition on deck was being unboxed, muzzle and gun covers stowed and camouflage nets rolled back. The coastline grew clearer and larger, and the coastal details became visible. All was peaceful, just the throb of the engines, the hiss of water and the smell of diesel fumes from our funnel. Our infantry in LCIs must have been about a thousand yards ahead of us but we could barely see them. Our barrage time was approaching but without an accurate range to the beach I could not fire our barrage close ahead of the infantry. So I added 2,000 yards to the estimated range for safety. I ordered "Fire!" The noise and concussion of four big guns so close together was terrific. Wreaths of smoke appeared on the beaches and inland. We repeated the five rounds [of] gunfire again and again until the paint began to blister on the gun barrels. Our last rounds of deck ammunition were fired just as H Hour struck.[42]

Meanwhile, Sergeant Major Jack Brown, also of the 147th Field Regiment, approached the beach with his unit and the 25-pdrs on his landing craft opened fire:

> We started firing about six [o'clock] when we were about 3,000 yards offshore. Everybody opened up, the noise was horrific, and it was ear shattering. It was bad enough with our people firing but there were rocket things on either side, there were capital ships, destroyers dashing backwards and forwards. We'd never experienced anything like it. That running shoot made the guns too hot to handle for the blokes, grease was running out of the breach

---

40 Bailey, *Forgotten Voices of D-Day*, pp. 247–48.
41 R. Rayner, correspondence with author (Durham, 1993).
42 Lund, P. and Ludlam, H., *I Was in the War of the Landing Craft* (London: Foulsham, 1976), p. 166.

Troops of the Royal Marine Commando, packed tightly into their landing craft, head for the Normandy coast. (Author's collection)

blocks and cartridge cases were being thrown over the side. We didn't have time to be afraid and you don't get time to think.[43]

Petty Officer Reginald S.F. Coaker was off Gold Beach aboard the destroyer HMS *Urania* and in the vanguard of the attack:

No sooner had we opened fire on our target on the beach, the pill box, and knocked it out, then almost simultaneously came in a wave of rocket firing Typhoons and bombers and the whole beach seemed to erupt and was covered in sand and smoke. And in next to no time where we had been right out at the forefront of the attack, we were then seeing soldiers going by us in these landing craft. The whole thing was so totally well organised. Wheeling overhead the whole time were groups of our Spitfires and Hurricanes, perfect air cover.[44]

As Sub Lieutenant Jack Harper, Royal Navy, guided his LCT to Gold Beach, the tanks and self-propelled guns aboard were to give supporting fire and to target strongpoints on the shore while the infantry approached:

---

43 J. Brown, correspondence with author (Essex, 1987).
44 Manuscript forwarded to author by J. Betts (Hull, 1991).

American aircraft bombing the Normandy coast, June 1944. (Author's collection)

Visibility was bad, in addition to which you had the early morning mist and the smoke from numerous explosions drifting inland. The sea was pretty rough, and we had on board two fair sized tanks, four self-propelled guns that were rather like a tank but with a very large gun fitted, and a few lorries and jeeps. When we were near the coast there was a great lighthouse on top of a cliff at a place called Ver-sur-Mer. For about 30 minutes, on the approach, we bombarded the positions around the lighthouse with these huge guns. The blessed guns had sent shattering vibrations right through the ship. The cook came up to me and said, "Excuse me sir but we haven't got a single cup or plate left in the galley." The whole ship's crockery had been reduced to a pile of chippings. My cabin had also been wrecked.[45]

Unfortunately for those about to land, the air assault on Gold Beach was not effective, most of the fire intended for the beach strongpoints having landed well behind the shoreline. This caused serious problems for the attacking troops.

45 G. Curry, correspondence with author (Sussex, 1990).

Telegraphist George Lester was on board the frigate HMS *Kingsmill* off Gold Beach on the morning of D-Day:

> The *Flores*, a Dutch gunboat, was part of the opening bombardment. Being of much shallower draft she came up and anchored herself not more than a hundred yards away from us and was belting away with all of her guns. You could feel every reverberation right through our ship as she fired.[46]

Trooper Kenneth Mayo, among the Sherwood Rangers with orders to support the 1st Hampshires, prepared to launch his DD tank into the sea as the barrage raged around him:

> The Naval bombardment started, shells and rockets screamed overhead with RAF fighter bombers adding to the din. The whole coast that lay ahead of us was a pall of smoke and exploding missiles. We approached Gold Beach and due to rough seas closed to within 1,000 yards to launch at approximately 07:20 a.m. Action stations were called, and all crews were in their places. I had netted in the radio and our supporting canvas superstructure was inflated. The LCT ramp was lowered, and we launched into a very choppy sea and then shells, and other incoming fire, started to reach us but missed. I saw two Sherman flail tanks brewing up on the beach and wondered about our reception. We finally grounded on the beach, deflated the canvas sides and hey presto we were ashore.[47]

The secret DD tanks had been designed to leave their craft some distance offshore and to swim under their own power to Gold Beach. However, the rough seas prevented this and they were landed in the conventional manner. Centaur tanks were mounted in pairs in their landing craft, but were mostly delayed or could not cope with the rough weather and had to turn back; only two arrived on time at Gold Beach. The assault went in on time for the attacking infantry brigades, who bore the brunt of the hardest fighting that day: 231 Brigade on the right and 69 Brigade on the left, plus supporting arms. Shortly before the infantry landed on Gold Beach, the sappers of 280 Field Company, Royal Engineers, landed in 69 Brigade's sector, and those of 73 Field Company, Royal Engineers, in 231 Brigade's sector. These would also receive assistance from B Squadron tanks of the Westminster Dragoons and the 82nd Assault Squadron Royal Engineers to break through the beach defences. These Beach Clearance Parties had the unenviable task of clearing lanes through the hundreds of deadly obstacles that lined the beach, with the aid of AVRE (Armoured Vehicle Royal Engineers) Churchill tanks, some of Hobart's 'Funnies'. This was to be performed under a hail of fire from German weapons that had survived the softening up process that still roared over the heads of the engineers and their support tanks as they struggled ashore late because of the rough seas.

---

46 Bailey, *Forgotten Voices of D-Day*, p. 187.
47 Bowman, *Air War D-Day*, p. 23.

First on the beach

Major Leslie O. Clayton, who commanded 280 Field Coy, Royal Engineers, remembered the day well and spoke with pride about the performance of the 153 men under his command:

> At 07:30 a.m. five minutes before H Hour, our craft beached in line in heavy seas and the AVRE tanks immediately started to proceed ashore. All preparations had been completed beforehand for the last tank to tow our folding boats onto the beach, but in practise this method of getting ashore proved a dismal failure. All rehearsals had been carried out in reasonably calm seas and it had always been presumed that these conditions would prevail during the assault. The actual conditions however were quite the reverse to calm, and the folding boats were found to be incapable of standing the buffeting they received in the heavy seas. Most of them either broke in two or capsized, discharging their contents into fairly deep water. All ranks rose to the occasion magnificently, they waded ashore and without further ado commenced clearing the obstacles. Owing to the heavy seas and following winds the water had advanced further up the beach than had been anticipated, but here the value of long periods of drill and rehearsal became apparent as 200-yard gaps were completely cleared of all enemy underwater obstacles before the tide made further work impossible. The Naval frogmen of the Landing Craft Obstacle Clearance Unit did magnificent work during this period, and even when the tide was at its highest, they still continued towing obstacles and helping in the removal of drowned vehicles. During the whole of this initial period heavy enemy fire was encountered owing to the lack of protection on the flanks. The beaches were being raked by machine-gun fire, a number of mortars were also in action and an 88mm was still firing along the beach from an emplacement in the sea wall at La Riviere. Despite this no man faltered in his task and when the tide made further work impossible, and the roll was called, it was found that eight men had been killed and 25 wounded. The LCOCU had one man killed and four wounded.[48]

Lieutenant Richard Peart also landed with 280 Field Coy, Royal Engineers, and was to be awarded the Military Cross for his actions that morning:

> There were three landing craft, on the centre craft was me, 27 sappers and one Churchill tank fitted with a petard mortar where the gun used to be. The craft on my left had in it my platoon sergeant, 25 sappers and one armoured bulldozer. The craft on my right contained one fellow officer, 26 sappers and one Covenanter flail tank. The Churchill tank was fitted with a 6in mortar which could penetrate, with its high explosive bombs, up to 14 feet thick reinforced concrete. The tank carried five such bombs, which were very sensitive, [and] also carried large quantities of high explosives for our later use. Our plan was that as soon as we had cleared a small gap wide enough the flail tank would go up the beach to clear a single path through the landmines for the Churchill to go up to blast the sea wall. This went fine until the Churchill approached the sea wall. Unbeknown to us the Germans had cunningly built a gun emplacement behind the end of the sea wall that could fire along the beach with

---

48 Manuscript forwarded to author by L.O. Clayton (Canterbury, 1989).

Royal Naval frogmen of the Landing Craft Obstacle Clearance Unit. These brave men were among the first on the beach before the main landings and carried out their difficult task while under intense fire. (Author's collection)

an 88mm gun. This hit the Churchill tank a full broadside and there was a brilliant green flash. I am no way exaggerating but that tank with five sappers inside completely vanished all but for the engines and turret. They were all blown so high in the air that when they dropped to earth they hit the beach so hard that they were all buried in the soft sand, and nothing could be seen of the tank or the five sappers. I felt violently sick, and my heart sank to my boots. The commander of the flail tank had detached the flail onto the beach and seeing what had happened to the Churchill he took his tank up close to the sea wall, put his gun muzzle into the slit of the German emplacement and fired twice, completely destroying the Germans.[49]

Leading Seaman Walter Blanchard, a Royal Naval diver with the LCOCU, landed on Gold Beach in the early hours of 6 June:

I was ashore before four in the morning, and I immediately started work. There was a diver working below me and I had what was known as snorkel gear if I needed it, but I

---

49 Manuscript forwarded to author R. Peart (Cornwall, 1988).

Aerial view of the Normandy landing. (Author's collection)

worked virtually on the surface. There's a pier at Arromanches and I was working to the seaward side of that, our craft was tied up under it and I went about my business. We had to be able to blow our charges, but not before the bombardment started. The bombardment duly started, and we duly started blowing our charges. The Germans would mistake them, we hoped, for the bombardment coming in, but we didn't succeed in doing all of it. The Germans had done all sorts of things; they had left a lot of pre-war beach kiosks and things like that on the promenades, left them all in position. Only of course they looked like kiosks, but they were really pill-boxes, either painted to look like they were before or heavily reinforced. And they did indeed open fire as soon as the landing craft appeared and dropped their ramps. I engaged what looked like a kiosk where I'd seen what I took to be a heavy machine-gun muzzle emerging from the slot. I had it covered and fired straight into it. I managed to subdue whatever was going on there, by which time the infantry landing craft were near the beach.[50]

Major Richard Gosling, Forward Observation Officer with the 147th Field Regiment, Essex Yeomanry, Royal Artillery, started to wade ashore, and as he did so the guns of his unit fired a creeping barrage overhead:

> As we got nearer and nearer we could see flashes from German guns, [and] we heard what I thought was a swarm of bees, [but] it wasn't, it was German machine-guns firing on fixed lines over our heads. We got through the deep water and then we could see the German machine-gun bullets furrowing the sand. We were supporting the Hampshires, I was with Colonel Nelson-Smith, and we started to run across the wet sand. We could see the sand dunes 50 yards in front of us and one or two people were shot as we ran. Suddenly there was a great bang just behind me and I felt my legs kicked away from under me and I was lying on the wet sand. Poor old Nelson-Smith, who was next to me, had his arm shot through at the elbow.[51]

Private Jack Heath, of 20th Flotilla Combined Operations, saw the shore getting closer as his Landing Craft, Tank was about to hit Gold Beach:

> As we approached the beach we dropped our kedge anchor[52] and ran into the shore and made a dry landing. We dropped the door and the ramp extensions and away went our tanks. We also had on board with us a group of Royal Navy signallers. Their leading hand jumped ashore, and the poor lad landed on a mine. The rest of the party wouldn't go ashore until the skipper threatened them with his pistol. All this time our craft was slowly edging down the beach with the tide, so we lifted the doors free so we could winch back our kedge cable. By now we were facing a German gun emplacement with an 88mm which depressed its muzzle to fire on us. He must have depressed too far because we could see the shells hitting the sand. I thought: "This is it lads, the next one is ours", but someone must have smiled on us because a self-propelled gun from the next craft to us rolled off, swung his gun and fired, hitting the 88mm right on top of his gun shield taking the crew with it. All the time there were shells, mortar bombs and small arms fire all around, a proper hell hole. There were lots more LCAs landing on the beach, but many never made it. We were just coming free of the beach when there was an almighty bang, [and] the bows went up in the air. We had hit a mine and the boat settled on the sand. We were in a proper pickle and were left high and dry with not a hope of getting off.[53]

Sapper Ralph Rayner, serving with the 82nd Assault Squadron, Royal Engineers, drove his armoured bulldozer off an LCT and onto the beach:

---

50 W. Blanchard, correspondence with author (London, 1989).
51 Bailey, *Forgotten Voices of D-Day*, p. 251.
52 Kedge anchor: a secondary anchor located in the bow; used to move a ship by means of a line attached to a small anchor dropped at the distance and direction required.
53 *WW2: People's War* <www.bbc.co.uk/ww2peopleswar> (accessed 27 May 2019).

Exposed sappers, under fire from air bursts, trying to clear obstacles on the beach. (*The War Illustrated*, December 1944)

> My job on reaching dry land was to immediately join up with a team of sappers and a unit of Royal Navy commando divers. Our task was to clear all the beach obstacles, most of which contained explosives and were under water at high tide. As my bulldozer crept out of the water two RE tanks, AVRE, immediately in front of me were both hit by German shellfire, and each simultaneously burst into flames. I saw only one survivor leap clear before each tank exploded.[54]

Lieutenant Richard Peart and the men of 280 Field Coy, Royal Engineers, continued their hazardous task of clearing the beach of obstacles for the infantry and tanks:

> My sappers were all busy. They were dressed in part battle order with a difference, they had two pouches on their chest with an additional haversack instead of a water bottle. These contained ten made up charges of plastic explosive in the pouches on either side of the haversack, on the left hip haversack they carried Bangalore matches and insulating tape and in the right hip haversack ten made up fuses and detonators. These sappers were walking bombs and I am very proud to tell you that not one sapper funked his duty by failing to wade ashore, even though they could have remained on the tank landing craft. Their task was to fit the plastic high explosive on the centre of the hedgehogs, steel obstacles, prime them up then stand with right hand raised, and when all was ready I blew a loud blast on my special whistle, they then withdrew to the water's edge and laid flat on the sand. Then there was a loud bang, and the first row of obstacles was gone.[55]

54 *WW2: People's War* <www.bbc.co.uk/ww2peopleswar> (accessed 7 March 2019).
55 Manuscript forwarded to author by R. Peart (Cornwall, 1988).

Lieutenant Ian Wilson, 73rd Field Regiment, Royal Engineers, recounted a feeling of grim determination:

> All I can remember is this great feeling of confidence and seeing the run in to the point we were heading for, a tremendous surge you know, and the sea was very rough. The British army had waited for four years to get back to France. I was still at school at the time of Dunkirk, but we were going back to France and no way was anybody going to kick us out again. I remember working on the beach when an LCT near us discharged its DD tanks into the sea; these were tanks that were supposed to swim ashore under their own steam. One after the other they just disappeared from view below the waves.[56]

Able Seaman Stanley Hook beached with a fully loaded Landing Craft, Tank:

> When we went in the noise was horrific, I've never heard noise like it. They gave us a rocket firing ship for protection and this ship was laying down a covering fire of rockets. I always remember seeing two American fighters, they just flew into this lot and exploded. Bodies were now beginning to float in on the tide and there was thick smoke everywhere. The Germans had built scaffolding at the water's edge with mines like huge milk bottles painted black on the ends of poles. We manoeuvred our vessel in between two of these. The sandy beach was mined and at the top was a convex sea wall that had to be got over. The door went down and the first tank, a flail, made a road up to the convex sea wall. The second tank off had a huge bridge built onto the front of it, he went up this cleared stretch of sand and manoeuvred the thing into position. Then the bridge was detonated off and he slowly climbed the sea wall to the top.[57]

Lieutenant Peart and his men then cleared the second and third rows of hedgehogs, and bulldozers moved in to clear away the debris. After this was done, mines were cleared and a gap of 250 yards from the low water to high water lines was completed for the assaulting infantry to pass through. Their task done, the engineers regrouped under the relative shelter of the sea wall, but the Germans now knew where they were and gave them no respite. Peart continued:

> The Germans rained mortar bombs on us and three of my sappers were instantly killed. I ordered my sergeant to disperse the sappers along the beach digging fox holes with their steel helmets, making sure to spread out in fighting positions in case the Germans counter attacked. I thought that if not all the Germans in the gun emplacement were killed they would still be able to fire along the beach and kill my men, so I stealthily crept into the entrance of the gun emplacement when the gun suddenly moved and I froze. To my relief it was one of the dead German gunners collapsing and falling against the gun. Now the main forces were pouring through the gap. I had been wounded three times, first in the head, secondly in the knee and thirdly when a land-mine was set off by our own bulldozer which upon turning around had just touched the edge of the mine with its track and set it off. The

---

56 I. Wilson, correspondence with author (Wolverhampton, 1992).
57 *WW2: People's War* <www.bbc.co.uk/ww2peopleswar> (accessed 27 May 2019).

driver had been told to stay still while I spoke to my sergeant to answer his questions, but he thought he could turn around. I put my arm up to protect my face but a large piece of metal casing from the mine penetrated my chest. With lots of bleeding from my head and chest I was quite a mess.[58]

An RAMC sergeant arrived and started to dress Lieutenant Peart's wounds. A label was attached to his battledress and the sergeant told him: "It's Blighty for you sir." Peart argued that he must stay with his men, but the sergeant was adamant and told him if he did not go to hospital he would get gangrene from the red painted metal that the Germans used to make the mine. Peart was duly taken to hospital; his war was over.

Able Seaman Edward Williams, 47 Royal Marine Commando, piloted his LCI loaded with men towards the beach:

We were travelling to the beach for what seemed like a lifetime. I kept looking around, but it was too dark to see much, and the sea was very rough. There was a terrific noise and every ship in the ocean seemed to open up at once. Each time one of the big shells went over us the craft lifted up. The poor infantry lads were suffering from seasickness and were itching to get onto dry land. We landed and let the troops off the craft then we headed back to the troopships to load up with more men and then went back to the beach. We got a great cheer from the big ships' crews each time we passed them.[59]

Captain Frederick Parham, commander of the cruiser HMS *Belfast*, moved to his firing position off Gold Beach and found navigating a path through the numerous smaller craft around him very difficult:

The final approach to our bombardment position was hair-raising in a narrow-swept channel with strong cross tides. We were almost always under helm, dodging myriads of landing craft whom we had to overtake in order to open fire on prearranged targets well before the landing craft went to touch down.[60]

Pilot Officer James Kyle of 197 Typhoon Squadron roared over the armada of ships and landing craft as the French coast came into view:

As we approached the French coast we saw the morning sky ablaze with rocket salvos and a bombardment from the mightiest naval Armada ever assembled in the history of warfare. We could feel the drama that was unfolding below us that day. The massive number of shells exploding on the boiling and blazing beaches seemed remote and unreal as we crossed the coast inbound at about 500 feet.[61]

---

58 R. Peart, correspondence with author (Cornwall, 1988).
59 E. Williams, correspondence with author (Tunbridge Wells, 1992).
60 Thompson, J., *Victory in Europe* (London: Sidgwick & Jackson, 1994), p. 53.
61 *WW2: People's War* <www.bbc.co.uk/ww2peopleswar> (accessed 5 March 2019).

Troops of 231 Brigade head for the shore in their LCI. (Courtesy of Peter Cuerdon)

With the assault from both the air and the sea roaring and crashing over their heads, the naval force carrying the 50th Northumbrian Division moved slowly towards the coast of Normandy. The uncomfortable night passage across the cold, rough Channel, and the seasickness that made life so miserable for many, was about to end. Shellfire thudded around the little landing craft as the men huddled down in the hope that nothing would drop into theirs. The light of dawn had revealed the Normandy coast appearing before them, shrouded in smoke and fire. The infantry were now about to fulfil their classic role as the spearhead of the operation. Warships fired steadily at targets as yet invisible to the troops, while overhead all manner of aircraft roared and thundered. The infantry in their landing craft were thrown around by the heavy seas while bigger rocket-firing craft hurled salvoes of missiles over their heads at the beach defences. Tanks and self-propelled guns in their larger landing craft move towards the shore steadily, firing their guns as they did so. The Duplex Drive tanks, designed to leave their craft some distance from the shore ahead of the infantry, could not be launched because of the poor weather. It was decided that they would instead be taken to the beach and landed conventionally, providing essential support for the infantry by then already ashore. The assault went in on time and the men of the 50th Division sat staring at the front of their landing craft as they waited for the moment when the ramp went down and each man's destiny would be decided.

Royal Navy Sub Lieutenant Roderick Braybrooke, commanding an LCT, watched events as they neared the beach:

> We sort of fanned out into a line and of course there were the obvious problems of boats not quite sure of where they were as opposed to where they should be. It was a question of really finding a space and getting in. There were LSTs, LCTs and assault craft going in at the same time and there was a lot of mortar fire coming at us from the shore. They'd got

the range too as they were dropping mortar shells in a line. If you were lucky one exploded to the left of you and the next one to the right of you. If you were unlucky, it landed right on top of you. I remember one boat loaded with about 20 or 30 army fellows, an infantry landing thing, an open boat with a door that lets down. They were just getting ready to go ashore and a mortar shell just landed on top of them, little boats like that just sort of disappeared.[62]

Major Iain Norman Macleod had been appointed 50th Northumbrian Division Assistant Quartermaster General, an unexpected promotion brought about because many of his immediate superiors had burned themselves out during the planning phase of Operation Overlord. He got up early on 6 June and went on deck to see what was happening:

The coast of Normandy was taking shape through the haze. Then, as full light began to come, one could see ships and planes. It was a sight so paralysing that tears came to my eyes. It was as if every ship that had ever been launched was there, even as if the sea had yielded up her wrecks. It was as if every plane that had ever been made was there and so it seemed in fantasy as if the dead crews were there too. There had never been since time began such a rendezvous of fighting men and there will never be again. I remember reciting, not in scorn but out of sheer delight at being part of that great company in such a place 'And gentlemen in England now abed…'.[63]

At 0630 hours on 6 June, *Generalfeldmarschall* Erwin Rommel, at his home in Herrlingen, Germany, where he had been celebrating his wife's birthday, was woken by a call from *Generalleutnant* Hans Speidel, his chief of staff, at La Roch-Guyon near Paris. Speidel informed Rommel that reports of a huge invasion fleet anchored off Normandy had been confirmed and told him of the retaliatory measures taken so far. Rommel cancelled his visit to Hitler and was driven back to France with all speed. However, he would not arrive at his headquarters until nightfall on that fateful day.

---

62 R. Braybrooke, correspondence with author (Coventry, 1989).
63 Bastable, J., *Voices from D-Day* (Newton Abbot: David and Charles, 2004), p. 157.

4

Into the Breach: King Sector, Gold Beach, 6 June 1944

"They're coming!"

The seas had been whipped up by high winds, and waves 5ft high sent white-topped breakers crashing onto the beach. The wind was so strong that the tide was being forced inshore a good 30 minutes ahead of its predicted time. On 50th Northumbrian Division's front, 16 craft, each carrying two Centaur tanks, should have been landed to give valuable support to the infantry on the beach. Yet only two of these craft arrived, some being delayed and others having to turn back because of the rough seas.

Grenadier Heinrich Runder manned a defensive position with his comrades covering an observation post and an anti-tank gun. The walls of the trench he was in were shored up with logs sunk into the sand. Runder had been in action before, being wounded in the head in Tunisia, and was not looking forward to going into action again. But in the early hours of 6 June, he looked out to sea and saw hundreds of ships on the horizon:

> A vast number of ships, absolutely vast, I can tell you that my throat went dry, painfully dry, and my hands began to shake. I wasn't the only man to be affected that way, one of our very young lads began to retch as if he was going to be sick. It was the effects of pure fear.[1]

In a coastal artillery command post, *Major* Werner Pluskat looked out to sea and saw this huge armada filling the sea to the horizon. He immediately called the German divisional intelligence officer, Block, and told him: "There must be 10,000 ships out there, it is unbelievable, fantastic." Block questioned this report, as he did not believe the Allies had that many ships. Pluskat replied, "For Christ's sake come and see for yourself", and because his view of events continued to be questioned he added, "To hell with you" and threw down the phone. Pluskat left a vivid account through German eyes of the first moments of the assault just before the troops hit the beach:

> We saw planes approaching from the sea and they began bombing the beaches. The bombing continued for a solid 40 minutes and there were thunderous explosions all around

---

1   Manuscript forwarded to author by H. Wernemann (Germany, 1989).

us. We watched absolutely petrified as the armada approached steadily and relentlessly, it was an unforgettable sight. I don't think I have ever seen anything so well organised and disciplined. At 05:30 a.m. the fleet out at sea began manoeuvring in front of us and I realised that the battleships were preparing to fire. I telephoned Block and asked for permission to fire but was told we were short of ammunition and must not fire until the troops were nearing the beaches. To my horror I could see the guns of the British fleet being elevated as they swung slowly round to point in our direction. A lilac-coloured flare was fired and the bombardment from the sea began. The shells screamed over like a thousand express trains, and all seemed to be converging onto our position.[2]

The command bunker was hit by one of the first shells to land; the impact shook the emplacement, and the men inside were thrown to the ground. After the explosion, the interior was filled with dust, dirt and pieces of concrete. The bombardment continued, shell after shell hitting the outer concrete casing. The dazed men sat inside as the bunker shook and heaved under the terrible onslaught. By 0700 hours, all communications had been cut except for one underground cable to the rear. This phone kept ringing, the officers at the other end of the line demanding to know the exact location where the shells were falling, to which a harassed and distraught *Major* Pluskat screamed: "For God's sake they're falling all over the place, what do you expect me to do, go out and measure the holes with a ruler?"

A vision of hell

Leutnant Arthur Jahnke sat in a reinforced wooden position that had been sunk into the sand just behind the anti-tank wall. Looking out over a hazy grey sea, he could hear the drone of British bombers in the distance. Sure enough, a wave of twin-engine bombers flew from the sea towards the coast to the south in impeccable fly-past formation. Jahnke looked on in horror as the first wave broke formation and flew down the coast towards his position. Looking through his binoculars, he saw the bomb doors swing open and the bombs come tumbling out:

> An infernal roar, flashes like lightning, smoke and stench. That lot dropped this side of the macadamized road, [but] already the next wave was coming in, more crashes and bursts, far side of the road this time. The next stick was on the near side and the screech seemed to come down louder and louder on our dug-out. Covered in sand, [I thought I] must get out of this shallow crater, no cover here. Among the bomb bursts I could hear crackling and popping like a fireworks display. The ammunition bunkers were going up! It looked as though God and the world had forsaken us; what's happened to our airmen and what is our artillery up to?[3]

Heinrich Runder also watched as flights of British and American bombers and fighters flew overhead. A lone Messerschmitt appeared, shot over the beach at high speed and then disappeared. Fighter bombers then attacked Runder's position and naval gunfire exploded all around

---

2   Manuscript forwarded to author by H. Wernemann (Germany, 1989).
3   Manuscript forwarded to author by H. Wernemann (Germany, 1987).

him. Rockets from the fighters screamed down and detonated with a roar, throwing out a liquid fire that burned very bright and stuck to everything, setting alight men and bunkers.

Gefreiter Stephan Heinevez was in his concrete bunker when the rockets struck outside the gun port:

> The explosion was completely blinding, I saw fragments of burning material pour in through the aperture, these fragments expanded and burned with a fire that would simply not go out and it covered the gun-crew. There was complete panic and disorder. The men near the gun were consumed in these white flames, uniforms peeled off in scorched pieces and their bare skin was set alight by the fire. Someone threw open the steel door of the bunker and I hurled myself at it. I made the mistake of looking back into the bunker, [and] I can tell you that the interior was a vision of hell, an obscene sight that remains with me even now.[4]

Lieutenant R.B. Davies, Royal Navy, commanded LCT 647, which carried AVRE tanks that were to land on Gold Beach ahead of the infantry and begin clearing obstacles before the main assault arrived on King Sector:

> No opposition as yet on the approach, then suddenly hundreds of flashes right along the sand-dunes. "Here it comes" I thought "coast batteries opening up at the last moment." But nothing came and I realised that the flashes were the explosions of our rockets. Then the exodus of a mechanised Noah's Ark began. Flail tanks, armoured trucks with impossible gadgets, metal monstrosities of all types. The pride of the REME designed to clear beach mines and other defences for the infantry coming in behind us. The first tank moved out, amazing, unbelievable, not a shot was fired. All was quiet on the beach for a minute or two but for the British bombardment with nobody on the beach but one tank. An explosion as the waterproofing was disposed of. Her flails started and then black smoke came from the tank as she was hit and caught fire.[5]

Tanks of the Westminster Dragoons and the flails and other 'Funnies' of the 82nd Assault Squadron, Royal Engineers, landed from their LCT at La Rivière before the main assault and, according to one anonymous eyewitness, almost immediately came under fire:

> We were still several thousand yards off the shore when a signal came through that we were ten minutes ahead of time. Our whole force halted, and we were able to study our battlefield. Suddenly a gun of the Mont Fleury Battery opened fire and landed a shell within 100 yards of the lead LCT. The gun was straight away engaged by one of our LCGs, a landing craft carrying two 4.7-inch guns, which drew in very close to the shore. The enemy gun soon stopped firing. By this time the bombardment was in full swing.[6]

All the tanks got onto the beach and began to head towards the sea wall, but the German 88mm gun which was positioned behind 17in of concrete had been missed by the bombardment and was still in action. The same eyewitness said two AVREs were hit by it and burst into flames:

---

4   Trigg, *D-Day Through German Eyes*, p. 72.
5   Kershaw, *D-Day, Piercing the Atlantic Wall*, pp. 148–49.
6   *Westminster Dragoons* <www.westminsterdragoons.co.uk> (accessed November 2019).

Into the Breach: King Sector, Gold Beach, 6 June 1944 97

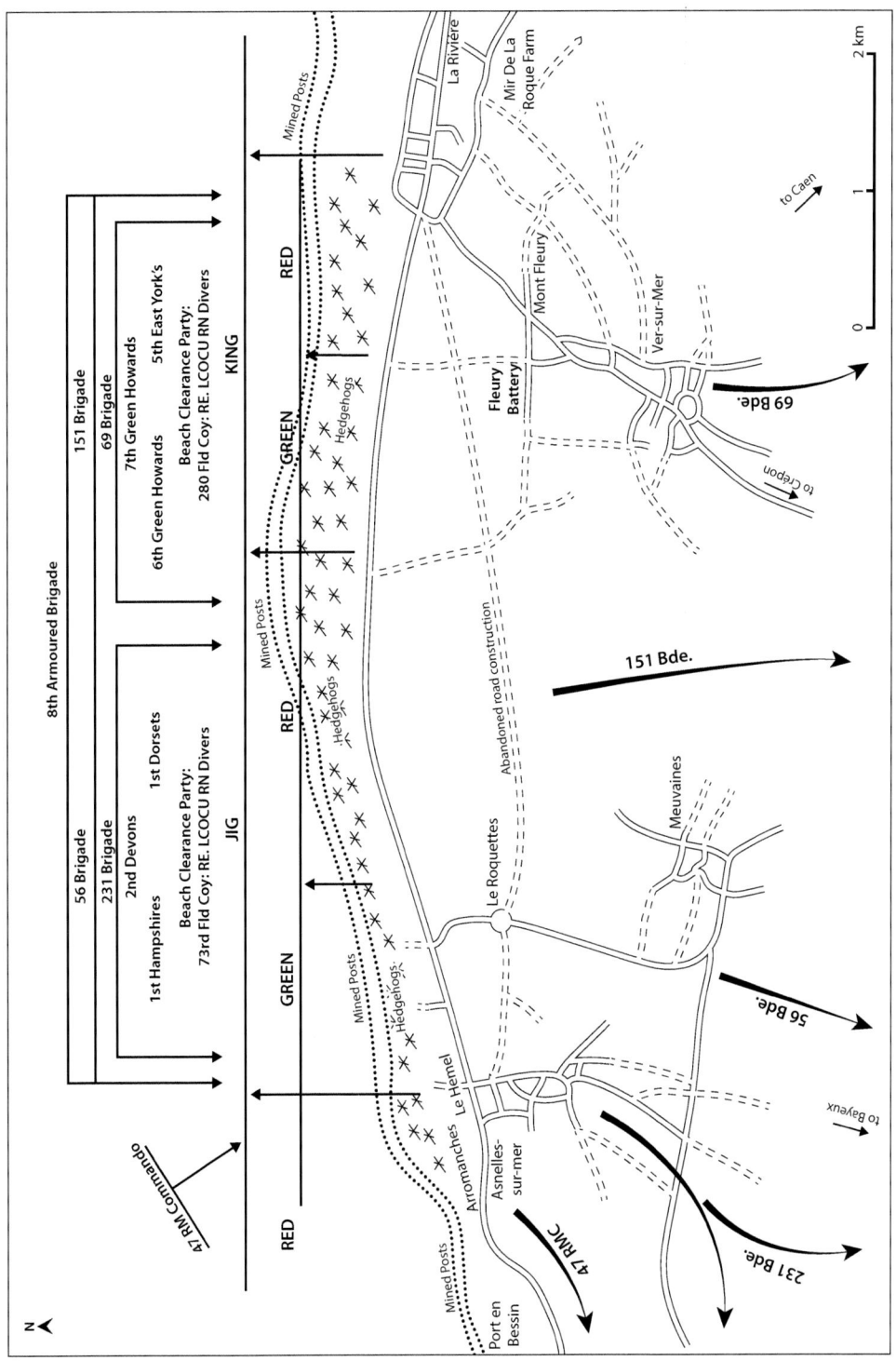

XXX Corps landings, Gold Beach, 6 June 1944.

Captain Bell saw the tanks being hit and realised at once where the fire was coming from. Turning his tank so he could return fire at the concrete bunker he sat for a moment in the line of fire at a range of 150 yards, the 88 could have knocked him out at 1,500 yards. His tank was standing in the open beach with no cover as he brought the gunner onto the target. He fired five shots and the fifth shot entered straight through the aperture, silencing the gun. Had this 88 remained in action there is no doubt that it would have had a very serious, or even disastrous, effect on the landing of 69 Brigade.[7]

Grenadier Heinrich Severloh, serving in a German shore battery, was asleep in his bunker as the assault came in:

> The battery commander woke us up and had a message: "It's starting!" I had been expecting this for a long time as we were aware that the invasion would eventually come. The noise got louder and louder as the heavy bombers pass over our heads. Their loads come whistling and crashing down and everything starts to shake. But the bombers miss their targets, we are not hit. Not one shot is being fired by us as we are under strict orders to wait until the enemy soldiers have left their landing craft and are in knee-deep water.[8]

SS-Obersturmführer Peter Hansmann, of the *12. SS-Panzer-Division 'Hitlerjugend'*, watched the assault begin from a cliff top near Arromanches, from where he had a clear view of the whole of the Gold Beach sector:

> Fast boats with high white foaming bow waves, landing boats that spat out brown balls of soldiers onto the beach. I also saw fountains of white water rise up in the landing sectors, probably from our coastal batteries. Then I could clearly see and hear the muzzle flashes of German MG42s [heavy machine gun, nicknamed 'Hitler's Buzz Saw' due to its rapid rate of fire]. This meant therefore our coastal defences had not been completely overrun. The British troops wore flat helmets and whole companies were slowly tramping ashore through the dunes in our direction. Smoke passed over us and at times covered the entire bay.[9]

Hansmann looked on in awe as whole troops of tanks made their way up the beach and into the dunes without stopping. Among their number were strange-looking tanks which he did not recognise:

> I clearly saw tanks that were pushing long dozer buckets ahead of them. Were they building a coastal road already? Unflinchingly, further tanks surfaced directly from the sea, is there such a thing? At first one saw the cupola and then they surfaced like some monster from the deep. Nothing appeared to hinder them, is there no 88mm flak there?[10]

---

7   *Westminster Dragoons* <www.westminsterdragoons.co.uk> (accessed November 2019).
8   Manuscript forwarded to author by H. Wernemann (Germany, 1989).
9   Manuscript forwarded to author by H. Wernemann (Germany, 1989).
10 Manuscript forwarded to author by H. Wernemann (Germany, 1989).

Able Seaman Ian Michie served on the cruiser HMS *Orion* as it bombarded the battery at Ver-sur-Mer. The crew was called to action stations at 0400 hours on 6 June, and it was reported to them that targets inland were getting a very heavy battering from the RAF:

> We moved slowly down the swept channel towards our bombardment position. The commander reported that the sweepers had made a much wider channel than was expected and we'd have room to manoeuvre, audible sighs of relief. At 05:00 a.m. *Orion* was the first cruiser to open fire, good old *Orion*, always first there. Our shooting was very good and direct hits were soon being recorded. We scored 13 direct hits on the battery before shifting target. The other cruisers were all ripping away, and the *Belfast* was firing tracer.[11]

Able Seaman Ronald Scott, serving as a Radar Operator aboard the minesweeper HMS *Ready*, wrote home to his parents of his experiences on 6 June:

> Five mighty cruisers were silhouetted against the streaks of light where the sun would soon rise. I don't think I have ever seen anything so impressive, it thrilled me through and through. Slowly the vessels nearest to us brought their powerful guns around and then Boom! Boom! and then two resounding crashes. Then all the other ships opened fire and it became one series of ear-splitting salvos one after the other. In the half light of dawn, our task completed, we were free to steam up and down having a good look at everything. There was a terrific bombardment at one end of the bridgehead and when we got there we found two battleships firing away for all they were worth. We were right up close to one, so close we could even hear the sigh of the shells as they left those massive guns.[12]

Though the larger German batteries remained virtually invulnerable, and some artillery positions had been recently moved, the overall effect of the naval and air bombardment was to temporarily silence most of the fixed batteries. This was achieved as the leading ships came into range of the German guns, and any battery that did recover and begin firing again was at once engaged by naval forces until they again fell silent. The cruisers operated much closer inshore than the bigger warships, and could target pillboxes, redoubts and even machine-gun posts. This second wave of the naval assault made sure the first troops and tanks ashore would not be seriously held up by the prepared German positions.

69 Brigade, King Sector, Gold Beach

As the leading landing craft assault neared the shoreline, beach obstacles – consisting of iron stakes with mines or shells fixed to them – could be seen clearly above the water level. These would prove to be a great hazard to craft landing later, as the tide was rising fast.

As the ships of Force K continued with their lethal assault, the various types of landing craft crashed into the shingle, their doors came down and the troops rushed out onto the beach,

---

11   Newspaper cutting sent to author by H. Thompson (Beverley, 1994).
12   Bowman, *Air War D-Day*, p. 30.

between the Dorsets on the right and La Rivière on the left. Leading 69 Brigade into the attack was the 5th East Yorks on the left flank, known as King Red, and the 6th Green Howards on the right flank, King Green, in the general area of La Rivière and Ver-sur-Mer. The third battalion of 69 Brigade, the 7th Green Howards, was to land and pass through the beachhead at 0815 hours and take the German battery at Ver-sur-Mer. If the attack was successful, 151 Brigade would follow up behind 69 Brigade and complete the final stage of the assault.

5th Battalion East Yorkshire Regiment

As Private Jack Danby, 5th East Yorks, rushed out of his landing craft, he noticed to his surprise that there were men already working on the beach before the infantry had landed:

> There were frogmen and engineers on the beach already ahead of us, clearing away as many of the mined metal obstacles as they could to make things easier for us landing craft troops. They were up to their armpits in cold, rough water with mortar bombs exploding all around them, working to defuse intricate mechanisms, getting rid of bombs and booby traps, knowing that failure could mean disaster for dozens of men. Those engineer soldiers and naval frogmen were the most courageous of all and they deserved more recognition than ever they were given.[13]

The men of the 5th East Yorks ran into a hail of fire being directed at them from the western part of La Rivière, but without hesitation headed up the beach. The left-hand company met the heaviest opposition as the bombardment had missed an area that stretched the length of the village, from where the enemy put down a heavy fire with all the weapons at their disposal. An 88mm gun was situated in a bunker and had a field of fire directly along the beach, supported by machine-gun emplacements. When the leading craft hit the beach, this murderous fire was directed onto them as the troops moved up the beach. Some craft ran onto beach obstacles before they reached land and the men had to swim ashore, being under fire as they did so from the German sea wall positions and the houses beyond.

Sergeant Max Hearst was among the first men from the 5th East Yorks to run ashore:

> When we hit the beach it was door down, out and run like hell. I was the seventh man on the right-hand side, and I was carrying a Bren-gun. I was supposed to get down and give covering fire. When the barge hit we ran out into deep water, two people in front of me totally disappeared. I went in up to my chest and waded out. I was running up the beach behind Major Harrison when he jumped up in the air, landed and kept on running. When we got the sea wall we were under crossfire from mortars and what have you. He said, "I'm hit", he had a bullet through his heel. As he couldn't walk he told me to go back down to the water's edge and to give his compliments to Captain White and tell him to bring his platoon forward. This Captain White was laid at the waters' edge, so I had to go down the bloody beach again to get him. On the way back I picked up a number of wounded and

---

13   J. Danby, correspondence with author (Hull, 1989).

Troops under fire land on a beach congested with wrecked tanks, vehicles and landing craft. (Author's collection)

helped them to the safety of the sea wall. I heard a bloke shouting [for a] stretcher bearer, so I ran over, it was a kid I knew well but he was hardly recognisable, a mine had exploded in his face, and it was like a black football. I got him to the sea wall, but he died later. Jerry was throwing hand-grenades over the sea wall, and they were bouncing off the shoulders of the men that couldn't move, we had a hell of a lot of casualties that way. We were pinned down and couldn't get over or around the sea wall. First Chalky White went over the wall with pistol in hand and down he went.[14] There was this bloody great gun firing and this RSM got on the backs of a couple of blokes and lobbed grenades through the gun aperture and went through, if anyone was still alive he finished them off. He then came out of a doorway on the top of the bunker still firing his Sten-gun and as he was firing he shouts: "Right lads, get over."[15]

Private R.S. McDowall, 5th East Yorks, found himself up to his chest in water as he left his landing craft:

Almost before we realised it the marines were preparing to let down the front door of the landing craft and we prepared to disembark. At first the marines were anxious to get rid of

---

14   Captain James Helier White, South Lancashire Regiment, attached to 5th Battalion East Yorkshire Regiment, was killed in action on 6 June 1944, aged 35. He is buried in Bayeux War Cemetery, France.
15   Max Hearst, interview with author (Hull, 1991).

An aerial view of Gold Beach, 6 June 1944. (Author's collection)

us and to get to hell out of it, they were going to release us farther from the shoreline than was practicable. Lt Lowe persuaded them to take us in a bit closer in case we found ourselves in deep water that was too deep for us to wade through. A marine promptly let down the door and jumped off to test the depth. He had barely done so however when the first men were off the craft and ploughing through the water towards the shore. When my turn came, before me was about 40 yards of heaving sea reaching to my chest and ahead a slowly rising beach covered with round flat stones. The lighthouse and some buildings stood facing the sea on a road about 300 yards inland. To my left other landing craft were disgorging their loads and a tank was blazing and exploding, while further to my left was the sea wall, pill-boxes and the village of La Riviere. I was now wading through two feet of water and was making surprisingly swift progress. I reached the shore and could walk without the water dragging at my legs at last. I found the rest of the company laid flat on the ground behind a sand-dune when all at once a tank close to my left blew up and scattered fragments of metal flew over my head. Meanwhile shells from our warships still screamed inland.[16]

16 Manuscript forwarded to author by Brian Cook (Carnegie Heritage Centre, Hull, 2017).

German gunners inside the Ver-sur-Mer Battery, May 1944. (Author's collection)

Midshipman John Lund was heading for Gold Beach on an LCT, on which were two Oerlikon guns that would give supporting fire to the infantry as they landed:

> A number of 88mm shells missed us as we made the run-in, they came from a pillbox on our port bow. Above and beyond this could be seen seaside boarding houses from which a large amount of small arms fire was coming. Unfortunately, the gunner on the port Oerlikon was an inexperienced youngster who was more than a little disconcerted about the small arms fire going in his direction. The starboard gunner, Able Seaman Franks, walked over to the port Oerlikon, strapped himself into it and proceeded to pour four pans of ammo into the pillbox. This put the 88mm out of action fortunately as it could have clobbered our first tank as soon as the ramp door was dropped, making it impossible for the remainder of the tanks to disembark. It was found afterwards that the Oerlikon gun shield had been hit three times and the gun's ready use locker had been pierced twice. Able Seaman Franks received the DSM for his brave action.[17]

---

17 Lund and Ludlam, *I Was in the War of the Landing Craft*, p. 135.

The unlucky troops that were dropped into deep water had to struggle ashore as best they could. Many never survived this ordeal and were dragged under by their heavy kit or run down as more landing craft headed for the beach. (Author's collection)

Private Archibald Cairns, with 50 Div Royal Signals, was hit as he ran up the beach:

> When the ramp went down, I could see spurts of sand on the beach where mortar bombs were landing and the road at the top of the beach seemed a long way off. I was destined to get no further than halfway to the road as some Germans dropped a bomb nearby which wounded me in the right leg and also damaged the set. It was only a flesh wound but nasty enough, [and] I made it to the top where my friend summoned the MO who dressed my wound. The excitement turned to apprehension as the mortar bombs kept falling. I lay there for a long time among other wounded, some far worse than me, and some German prisoners.[18]

Carter Barber was an American film cameraman who had been sent to record the historic moment on Gold Beach as the Allies returned to Europe. He described the scene as the 5th East Yorks and the 6th Green Howards landed:

> The way we took those barges onto the beach was like a review at first, you couldn't see the heads of the troops over their sides, just the coxswain's helmet showing from the stern. As we came in, we saw the first bunch of men as it was getting light, and the scene quickly changed from one of an even line of landing craft knifing through the water in orderly rows towards the beach to a scene of carnage. One boat took a direct hit from the shore and disintegrated. There were no survivors, and I couldn't even see the dismembered parts of the troops come down after they had been blown sky high. The noise was terrific on the beach. When we saw an LCT get hit and rushed to her aid, I noticed plenty of men already floating face down in the water.[19]

18 A. Cairns, correspondence with author (Newcastle, 1991).
19 Newspaper cutting sent to author by F.W. Vickers (Barnsley, 1992).

Into the Breach: King Sector, Gold Beach, 6 June 1944   105

A flail tank smashes its way through barbed wire and mines as it advances up the beach.
(Author's collection)

Gefreiter Erich Behrendsen had been wounded in the initial bombardment of Gold Beach and watched the British troops landing from his bunker. Contact had been lost with the other companies of the *716. Infanterie-Division*, the wires having been severed in the rain of bombs and rockets that fell all around him. He barked orders at the man behind the heavy machine gun near him:

> Open fire! The machine-gun hammered away and swept the sand. Higher I said and the burst caught a bunch of Tommies running alongside a tank. They heeled over like trees, shouted and flung themselves on the ground. Now a field gun was firing along the beach, its first shell struck the water. A landing craft drove straight into the next one. There was an explosion, flames and smoke as the boat slewed round, hit the beach broadside on and it turned over. Burning bodies were rolling in the sand. But those accursed tanks that were coming all the way from deep water could not be halted. They crept on and on like tortoises. Others carried enormous reels with chains and steel balls, damn them![20]

Trooper Charles Baldwin, with the 4/7th Royal Dragoon Guards, drove his Sherman flail tank through the water as he headed for the beach, watching the infantry and sappers ahead of him falling victim to Spandau fire:

> As the German machine-gun fire hit them, they were flung about clutching various parts of their body and jolting like rag dolls. Then they sank out of sight into the water. I often wondered if any of those unfortunate men survived the landing. Even if slightly wounded the weight of their equipment dragged them under.[21]

Trooper Ronald Mole, a gunner/wireless operator with 4/7th Royal Dragoon Guards, landed on Gold Beach with the 5th East Yorks in his Sherman tank to support the infantry:

---

20   Carell, *Invasion – They're Coming!*, p. 94.
21   Manuscript forwarded to author by R. Protheroe (Leeds, 1991).

Anything that moved we were giving it a burst and there was an AVRE, it was a Churchill fitted with what they called a petard and had a shortish barrel that fired a 40-pound charge of dynamite, a real block buster. This thing came up and passed us and I was watching it go in front. It had gone something like 50 yards up the beach when suddenly there was a flash and 60 tons of metal just disappeared in front of our eyes, and then came down a sprocket and a piece of track as flames licked the sand. A whole Churchill tank had literally disappeared, there must have been a ton of dynamite on board, and this had been hit by an 88. We were given a brief to attend to a house reinforced with a pillbox that was spraying the beach and the poor old infantry were really catching it. So, we were firing into this thing with high explosive and not making any headway so we switched to armour piercing, the idea being that if I could make a hole and put a HE round through the hole that would be it. My tank commander had the turret flap open and was standing behind me looking through his periscope. He stuck his head above the turret to get a better view and he was dead. He was shot right between the eyes and his elbow hit me on the neck as he fell, his other elbow hit the gun and his knees got me in the kidneys. My immediate reaction, in my innocence, was to wonder where that came from, and I leaned back to climb out to have a look. Fortunately, my chum, an ex-Nottingham City policeman, told me not to be a bloody fool. I was as green as grass, he saved my life.[22]

Lieutenant Basil Heaton, of the 86th Field Regiment, Herts Yeomanry, Royal Artillery, landed to the rear of 69 Brigade:

I was the junior officer in a troop of self-propelled guns. Our role was to bombard the beaches from the sea on the run-in shoot and then go ashore behind the first wave of infantry. We opened fire at 06:50 a.m. closing on the shore at a rate of 200 yards per minute and landed at 08:05 a.m. in support of 69th Infantry Brigade. We landed just below the Ver-sur-Mer lighthouse and in front of the dreaded Mont Fleury Battery. The 5th East Yorks took the lighthouse and by 09:00 a.m. our guns were clear of the beach. We were all very young.[23]

Gunner Frank Davies, 73rd Anti-tank Regiment, Royal Artillery, headed for the shore aboard a Rhino ferry – a barge constructed from several pontoons – with four Sherman tanks and a 3-ton lorry:

The Sherman chassis were mounted with American three-inch naval guns, which, according to Battery Sergeant Major Silver, could effectively fire round corners. There was a driver and another man who kept repeating at intervals "We'll all get killed". The Rhino craft we were on was driven by two outboard motors mounted on the rear corners, [and] these were steered by switching the motors on and off as required. Progress to the beach was slow and we had time to study the amazing scene. To the left, right and behind were hundreds of ships, many of them sporting a barrage balloon which shimmered in the bright

---

22 Manuscript forwarded to author by R. Mole (Norwich, 1989).
23 Manuscript forwarded to author by B. Heaton (Colchester, 1994).

sun. There were multi rocket firing ships on the right and left of us. We couldn't see the one protecting us from behind, but it put the fear of hell up us at intervals as the rockets screamed overhead.[24]

Gunner Davies could see the cruiser HMS *Ajax* to his right, firing at German gun emplacements in support of the Americans on Omaha Beach. When Gold Beach came into view, it was a mass of carriers, flail tanks, bridging tanks and other vehicles, some of them knocked out and burning amid the chaos, emitting great columns of black oily smoke. Davies recalled that shells burst all along the beach and the whole area was dotted with infantry:

> Suddenly we were looking to our left-hand outboard motor area which seemed to be out of commission, we realised we were out of control and had become a lethal threat to the ships around us. The remaining outboard motor operator was soon doing a magnificent job using the cross-tide as the missing engine. Our hearts were in our mouths as our pilot, with great skill, weaved in and out and around the ships. I remember noticing open mouthed faces looking down at us as we missed ships by yards. We grounded on the correct beach, Gold, a splendid effort worthy of a VC I thought.[25]

As Private Jack Danby hit the beach with his 5th East Yorks comrades, they ran into heavy small-arms fire from buildings on the seafront:

> We reached the shore directly opposite a high sea wall and ahead was a line of fortified buildings. Pre-bombing by the RAF had put a lot of the Nazis out of action, but they were still lively along our section of seafront. There was small arms fire from every building. Barbed wire was strung all along the sea wall and it was a very formidable obstacle. Tucked in under the sea wall we were out of range of small arms fire, but mortar fire exploding on the beach could get at us. We managed to cut some of the wire and cleared a narrow path up a concrete ramp. When we had crossed the promenade behind the wire, we were able to get into the shallow communications trenches which the Germans had made around the buildings. From there we could shoot into the window spaces left in the fortified houses.[26]

Lieutenant H.M. Irwin, Royal Naval Volunteer Reserve, commanded a Landing Craft, Assault that was heading for Gold Beach, full of men of the 5th East Yorks. As he hit the beach, the ramp was dropped and Irwin had a grandstand view of the battle as it unfolded before him:

> I watched through the visor slit as one tank drove ashore and moved up the beach, its mine-exploding flails whirring. Two mines were exploded, then the tank exploded in smoke and flames as it took a direct hit from a German gun emplacement. I saw no survivors. A second tank also took a direct hit and then a third moved in and silenced the gun. Bullets were spattering our craft from a machine-gun post to the east of our landfall. 20 minutes had elapsed since the first assault troops of the 5th Battalion East Yorkshire Regiment had

---

24 Manuscript forwarded to author by F. Davies (Clacton, 1989).
25 Manuscript forwarded to author by F. Davies (Clacton, 1989).
26 Danby, correspondence with author (Hull, 1989).

landed and rushed up the beach, many of them to their deaths. They were met by machine-gun fire and shells, and I watched shocked as one man fell and then stumbled into cover never to rise again. I was only 150 yards away from the infantry assault.[27]

When CSM Laurie Whittle, 5th East Yorks, landed on Gold Beach, he had to take ashore with him an unwanted guest:

> As we went ashore enemy fire was still sweeping the beach and men were being killed or wounded all around. Strangely the enemy fire was of little concern to me as I was busily trying to avoid being strangled and drowned by a fellow soldier. During the night crossing of the Channel, he decided he could not face the coming battle and shot himself through the left foot. After receiving medical attention, he was brought before the CO on a charge, the CO ruled that he would have to go ashore and that I would guard him at all times to ensure that he did so. I was ordered to get him ashore and dump him on the beach, then to hand him over to the medical people for further treatment. All went well until the moment we jumped off the landing craft into the sea. I was supporting him with both of his arms wrapped around my neck, [but] as soon as the salt water got into his wound he started to struggle and dragged us both under the water, that was when I knew the real meaning of fear.[28]

Fortunately, CSM Whittle was able to control the situation and stumbled out of the water onto the beach, dragging the terrified soldier behind him. When he placed him with the medics, he turned his attention to the scene on the beach before him, which was now being swept by shell and machine-gun fire:

> The view at dawn on that morning is still imprinted on my mind. The sea all around was covered with shipping of every sort and size, above us flew hundreds of planes on bombing missions, shells were exploding among the ships and the navy was bombarding strong-points. The coastline was obscured by low clouds of smoke from the explosions of countless shells, bombs and rockets and the fires that they caused. Above all of this could be heard the penetrating sound of gunfire and small arms fire.[29]

When Private Jack Craddock landed at La Rivière, most of the 5th East Yorks men on his craft were suffering from seasickness and were glad to get onto dry land:

> We ran up the beach and my friend, Sapper Bill Lacey, whose job it was to clear mines, was just ahead of me. A sniper got him, and I remember having to walk past him and assure him that he would be alright and that the stretcher bearers would be along soon. Sadly, I was told later that he died shortly after being hit.[30]

27 H.M. Irwin, correspondence with author (Leeds, 1993).
28 L. Whittle, interview with author (Hull, 1991).
29 Whittle, interview with author (Hull, 1991).
30 J. Craddock, correspondence with author (Beverley, 1989).

Landing craft circle around as they wait for others that are leaving the mother ship.
(Courtesy of L. Whittle)

Private Roy Walker, 5th East Yorks, drove his waterproofed Universal Carrier into the sea some distance from the shore and eventually landed in the same area as CSM Whittle. He was involved in an incident that would be photographed and turn out to be one of the iconic images of the D-Day landings:

> Our Bren-carriers were waterproofed with sides which we fitted ourselves. We made sure we did a good job because we were supposed to float ashore. Once we had left the landing craft it worked fine as we were dropped off quite a distance from the shore, [but] I had to keep my foot down hard on the accelerator so that the water didn't get into the exhaust. Luck was on my side once again and I made it, landing on time at H Hour. A lot of the poor devils never got ashore, they were mowed down by machine-guns, snipers and shell-fire, their bodies were just floating in the water. I had a motor bike tied on the back of my carrier and its driver was sat in the back of the carrier. He had his hand over the side of the carrier as he looked through the plates while I looked through the visor. Shortly after we hit the beach his thumb was shot clean off, so I bandaged his hand with a field dressing, I used his as well, but the blood was still pouring out. I chased along the beach in my carrier, from Gold to Juno Beach, and was stopped by a beach-master who bawled at me: "What the bloody hell are you doing! You're attracting enemy fire" because I was going like hell in my carrier and the German gunners followed us along the beach. I told him what had happened, and I had to walk with my mate down to the waters' edge where a first aid post was being set up. As I walked back to my carrier somebody took a photo which was later in all the daily papers. On the way back to Gold Beach I picked up a Canadian officer whose ship had been sunk. I gave him the other lad's rifle and he said: "That's great, I can't wait to get at those bastards."[31]

---

31 Manuscript forwarded to author by R. Walker (Scarborough, 1990).

One of the most iconic pictures taken on D-Day on Juno Beach. Private Roy Walker, 5th Battalion East Yorkshire Regiment, can be seen bottom left. (Courtesy of R. Walker)

Corporal Goodman Tyson, who landed on Gold Beach with the 5th East Yorks, recalled the frightening chaos he and his comrades were faced with:

> I had no time to think about being sea-sick, especially when I saw the coast, there was all hell let loose then. We were a bit frightened really because we didn't know what to expect, we'd been bunged up so much about this Atlantic Wall that we all wondered what it would be like. On the landing craft we couldn't see over the sides unless we stood up, but we all knew enough to keep our heads down, no point in tempting fate. The sailors driving dropped the doors as soon as we hit the sand. I was a section commander at the front, and we were the first off. There were quite a few shell bursts near our landing craft and the sailor was shouting at the top of his voice: "Get off the bloody thing, get off!", he wanted to be out of it and go back for more men. The shellfire and machine-gun fire coming from the sea wall was concentrated on the beach and we had orders to get off it as quickly as possible. We went hell for leather up that beach but a few of the lads were hit, fell and were left behind.[32]

---

32 G. Tyson, correspondence with author (Bridlington, 1989).

A flail tank that never made it onto the shore burns furiously as troops leave their LCIs. (Courtesy of R. Walker)

When Sub Lieutenant Jack Gaster, Royal Naval Reserve, a Beach-master with 47 Royal Marine Commando, landed in King Sector, Gold Beach, he realised he was in the wrong place:

> We could hear the deafening bombardment long before we reached our holding area. I watched as the heavy guns of the Monitor *Roberts* fired shells weighing a ton apiece over the landing area, [and] it was possible to watch their flight over the beach. As we came in, we could see the wreckage of damaged landing craft where they had hit beach obstacles that had mines attached to them as we approached the landing site. It then struck me that we were coming in on the wrong beach as far as J Commando was concerned. This was King Beach in the Courselles area. As soon as we cleared the LST I arranged with the beach-master for a lift with an LCM Mk1 to ferry us along to the beach at Le Hamel. I was upset to see quite a few bodies of young soldiers in the shallow waters off King Beach; they had never made it ashore.[33]

The troops taking shelter against the sea wall were suffering heavy casualties from enemy mortar-fire and hand grenades, but it was suicide to remain there. It was not long before a breach was made that enabled the troops to burst out from the beach. Private Leonard Chapman, 5th East Yorks, remembered the horrors he saw all around him:

> Eventually, miles off the French coast we were lowered over the side into assault craft, on to a sea that tossed the tiny craft about like corks. Men were so sea-sick that they were praying

33 J. Gaster, correspondence with author (Hampshire, 1990).

Stretcher-bearers and wounded take cover from enemy fire behind a knocked-out AVRE Petard on Gold Beach. (Author's collection)

to get ashore. As they staggered out of the landing craft machine-guns mowed them down and the dead floated ashore buoyantly supported by their packs. The troops on our left flank made it to the sea wall and were pinned there. Nearby a tank was manoeuvring for a position to attack a pillbox which was preventing our advance. Trapped in the sprocket at the rear of the track was the body of a soldier in full kit and great coat. As the tank changed gear from forward to reverse the soldier's body went up and down like a ragdoll. Close to my feet was a body with no face, just ears and a little bit of flesh at each side blanched white by the salt water. As we crouched there, helpless to move, an occasional German soldier crawled to the sea wall and dropped a hand-grenade over the edge. Near the end of the wall was a mass of barbed wire which we managed to cut and clamber off the beach.[34]

One platoon of the East Yorkshires, supported by an amphibious tank, forced their way over the sea wall through a thick belt of barbed wire and began to clear the machine-gun positions in the houses facing the beach.

Sergeant Max Hearst recalled the moment he and his comrades from the 5th East Yorks got over the sea wall and made for their first objective, Mont Fleury, supported by amphibious tanks and AVREs. Once this had been achieved, the troops worked their way around the back of La Rivière and began clearing the houses. The village was clear of enemy troops by 0900 hours, 42 prisoners having been taken and many Germans killed:

---

34 L. Chapman, correspondence with author (Leeds, 1990).

When we eventually got over the top of the sea wall, we advanced onto our first objective which was a gun emplacement, Mont Fleury, and a tower used for observation. The men in the forward platoon went into the lower parts of the tower when our self-propelled guns, AVREs, opened fire and blew it down with our men still in it. We moved through a corn field in extended order to the rear of La Riviere, when Sergeant Major Bert Greener shouted to me: "Hey Hearst, fan out that way with your Bren gun as there's somebody over there." I yelled out: "Come out you bastard!" All I heard was *Kamerad, Kamerad*. I moved up to see who it was and found a German soldier with two or three dead Germans around him and he was sat behind a Spandau machine-gun holding his arm. I said "On your feet" and was none too gentle as I dragged him up. He let go of his forearm which hung limply at his side attached only by a piece of skin and one of the lads said "Nobody can fix that" so I nicked it off with a knife and threw it away. We dressed what was left of the stump and away he went down to the beach.[35]

The Mont Fleury Battery

Private Denis Bowen, 5th East Yorks, recalled being stuck behind the sea wall as more and more reinforcements came up the beach, forcing the first troops to move over the wall. As they went along the road to the battery at Mont Fleury and behind La Rivière, the old hands began firing into the smoke and dust that had been thrown up concealing the enemy:

I couldn't see the enemy, but as we ran across the road we fired from the hip in their general direction. We got across to the other side which was a wet area, and the sergeants were shouting: "Don't hang about, keep going forward" and that's the first time I started to see the German soldiers. They had trenches and pillboxes; some were already putting their hands up but, in the excitement, they were the ones who got shot. You never think of taking prisoners when somebody is shooting at you and then you see people coming out and putting their hands up. All you see is a man in an enemy uniform and although you don't lay on the sights, take aim and shoot, you just blindly fire in their direction. I can remember firing and seeing people fall. Some of the German soldiers were within 50 yards of us, running to get into their positions. If one got up and ran everybody fired at him and of course he'd just go down in a lump. Some of our men were being hurt as well.[36]

6th Battalion Green Howards

On the brigade right flank, the 6th Green Howards had landed several hundred yards west of their intended position. At 0737 hours, the leading companies of the 6th Battalion waded ashore. Some unfortunate men landed in deeper water and were drowned before they could reach dry land. The first troops ashore advanced up a deserted beach as the naval barrage roared

---

35   Max Hearst, interview with author (Hull, 1989).
36   Manuscript forwarded to author by F.W. Vickers (Barnsley, 1991).

Scattered equipment and dead soldiers of the 5th Battalion East Yorkshire Regiment lie in front of a German bunker after the battle has moved on. (Courtesy of R. Walker)

over their heads, but when they had advanced about 200 yards machine guns and mortars opened fire on them with great accuracy. Major R.J.L. Jackson, 6th Green Howards, recalled:

> The beach was completely deserted as we approached, and I remember being puzzled by the comparative silence. Of course, the naval bombardment was now landing far ahead, and we could see some of the big shells passing over us, but the absence of any direct fire at us was strange and the lack of any opposition became eerie. Suddenly they threw everything at us. The mortars took us first and I was hit badly in the leg. My radio operator and regimental policeman were both killed outright by the same explosion, but the radio was intact enabling me to keep in contact and assist with troop movements for a bit and the waves of infantry passed over me. Then I realised that the tide was coming in, it was the worst moment of the war for me, I could not move, and no one was there to drag me beyond the high-water mark. The water came swirling in until it covered my dead companions and then it lapped against my legs and reached my chest. It was a clear sunny day, but the sea was icy cold. I knew I was badly wounded but not mortally and it seemed absurd to die like that in inches of water. But then the sergeant of regimental police, from my hometown, came along the beach and saw me in time, [and] he carried me to a sand dune where I lay all day.[37]

---

37 Manuscript forwarded to author by R. Walker (Scarborough, 1992).

Major Claude MacDonald Hull, MC and Bar, 2 i/c 6th Green Howards, travelled on the main communications ship, but because of the rough seas and poor visibility was ordered to lead the landing craft assault to a point where identification of the coastline features was unmistakeable:

> Just before first light there was so much activity from our armada that for a few foolish moments I think I believed it would be a walk over. Everything was being hurled at the coastline and beyond. The naval bombardment was fantastic and as dawn broke it was still on. Naval bombardment, RAF aircraft strafing the beaches and rocket ships hurling their rockets, of what seemed to be a continuous stream of fire. The floating 25 pounders were at it too. Not since Alamein and Mareth had we seen such firepower. The Landing Craft Assault began forming up in this terrible sea. All that could be seen were these tiny craft being tossed up and down this way and that, like little pieces of uncontrolled cork. None of the men inside were visible. We moved in and the little craft followed, sometimes up in the air on the crest of some huge wave and more often than not disappearing altogether, leaving one with the terrible thought that they would never reappear again. The nearer we came to the coast the bigger our little ship seemed to become and down below us the LCAs struggled on. At last, our ship stopped with the Normandy coast clearly visible in detail. The LCAs in good formation roared past us, their flat bottoms slapping the sea as they bounced towards the coast.[38]

Lieutenant Stuart Hills, MC, a DD tank commander with the Sherwood Rangers, moved towards Gold Beach in heavy seas in an LCT. As the ramp went down, he found himself with 700 yards to go before they hit dry land, but his tank was destined never to make it:

> We were the front tank on the LCT and were poised at the top of the ramp. A shell slammed into the water just in front of us, then one on the side of the ramp and another on the starboard beam. Sergeant Sidway and Bill Enderby were wounded, and it was surely only a matter of time before a shell hit us. I gave the order: Go, go, go! Geoff Storey moved into gear, and we lumbered slowly down the ramp and into the sea. Geoff engaged the propellers, and we were on our way. I was still standing on my bridge position on the back of the tank feeling terribly exposed while peering over the canvas screen. The sea was rough and the struts holding the screen were hard pressed to do their job, possibly the screen itself had been damaged by one of the shells. At any rate without it we wouldn't be able to stay afloat for long. We had gone about 70 yards in the water towards the beach when it became clear that something was seriously wrong, and it certainly wasn't the canvas screen. The tank was shipping water from the bottom in the driver's compartment, Geoff Storey was already knee deep in water. Arthur Reddish slipped into the co-driver's compartment and engaged the bilge pump, it worked but the damage below must have been huge as soon water was pouring from the driver's compartment on to the deck. Whatever the cause we were without doubt sinking and sinking fast.[39]

---

38 *Hull Daily Mail* newspaper cutting sent to author by M. Hearst (Hull, 1993).
39 Hills, *By Tank to Normandy*, p. 79.

A massive German concrete gun emplacement armed with a large-calibre artillery piece. (Author's collection)

Lieutenant Hills surmised that the damage had been caused by one of the shells which had landed so close that it had damaged the metal plates beneath the tank. There was no effective armour here, and that part of the vehicle had been exposed as the tank waited on the ramp:

> I gave the order to bail out and Corporal Footitt had the presence of mind to pull the ripcord to inflate our yellow dinghy. Sam Kirman, our only non-swimmer, put it over the side. The tank was now virtually awash, and we didn't have long. I frantically scrambled about inside the turret to retrieve my map case but without success. Trying to work quickly and calmly in a sinking tank is hard at any time and, with shells dropping close by, it was harder still. Everything became tangled up, so I gave it up as a bad job, ripped off my earphones, jumped out of the turret and fell into the dinghy. All of our personal possessions went to the bottom of the sea with the tank.[40]

Captain Stanley Green approached the shore with the first wave, his Royal Artillery battery firing their 25-pdrs at the shore defences over the heads of the 6th Green Howards' landing craft:

---

40   Hills, *By Tank to Normandy*, p. 79.

Into the Breach: King Sector, Gold Beach, 6 June 1944   117

German troops rush to their battle stations as the invasion fleet approaches. (Courtesy of W. Gilson)

As we started up the engines of our self-propelled guns, I saw one of the nearby craft drop its ramp, the leading tank started off and down it went like a stone. The tide was low enough to expose teller mines fixed to stakes, there was a lot of fire from big guns inland, mortar fire and machine-gun fire from pillboxes on the foreshore. On the beach we were confronted with a barbed-wire barricade with notices hanging on it that said 'Achtung Minen'. The REs [Royal Engineers] busted a way through with Bangalore torpedoes and as I had landed in a Bren-carrier with a driver and two signallers the driver turned sharply for the opening and because of the stony nature of the beach the track of our carrier came off. There we were stranded; all of our equipment and clothing was on the carrier and shells and mortars were dropping all around us. I was looking for enemy positions, assessing possible dangers such as mines and booby traps, also keeping up with the Green Howards for who it was my responsibility to give artillery support.[41]

Telegraphist Harry Siggins, aboard HMS *Ajax* off Gold Beach, was in possession of grid and map references and waited to be contacted by spotters on the beach or spotter planes. His job

---

41   *WW2: People's War* <www.bbc.co.uk/ww2peopleswar> (accessed 11 September 2018).

was to pass on the locations of enemy positions to the gunnery officers so the ship's heavy guns could give supporting fire to the advancing infantry:

> A spotting pilot contacted me and as we talked to each other in very plain language, I distinctly recall that amongst the first of our targets were enemy pillboxes. He said: "Enemy pillbox grid reference so and so." I passed this on and we fired first of all a ranging salvo. The pilot came back with a correction: "You're too high, come back 50." I passed that on and back he came: "Now up 20." I passed that on, and the correction was put on the guns, we fired another salvo. An excited voice came over the air: "That's it, that's it, give them the lot, give them the lot" and the whole four turrets [of] 18-inch guns belched out fire. He then shouted: "They're coming out and running, keep firing, keep firing, that's it" and so it went on. This was my D-Day, seven miles offshore picking off individual targets. The day wore on and eventually I got relieved. I always remember the hot mugs of tea and corned beef sandwiches that tasted like chicken.[42]

Corporal Francis William Vickers, MM, 6th Green Howards, was in the thick of the action from the start:

> Lots of the lads were seasick, I stood up all the way, watching the shore getting nearer, if I had sat down I knew I would be seasick. The battleship HMS *Warspite*, cruisers and destroyers were firing salvoes at the beach and there was plenty of replying fire coming from the shore as well. There were ships firing rockets toward the shore and several landing craft were hit by enemy fire as we neared the beach. When our landing craft was far enough in the ramp went down. I was sixth in line getting ready to jump out. My mate Sergeant Rufty Hill[43] jumped off the craft with two other privates, [but] they disappeared under the assault craft as where they had jumped was a deep bomb crater and with the weight of all the extra gear they carried, and perhaps the assault craft coming down on them, the three of them drowned. By the time the rest of us jumped out the landing craft had moved slowly forward over the bomb hole. The water was just over my knees, and I was soon up the beach and got down behind a ledge of higher ground. Looking around and along the beach I realised it was obvious we had landed 80 to 100 yards to the left of where we were supposed to have landed. A flail tank landed to our left and as it went up and over this high ground it was hit and blew up. One of its wheels came spinning along the beach just missing 18 Platoon's sergeant, George Authwaite; he had got a bullet in his thigh and was laid on the beach and was hit again as we who were left moved inland.[44]

In the same landing craft as Corporal Vickers was Company Sergeant Major Stanley Hollis, 6th Green Howards,[45] who was standing at the front and received a nasty wound that would plague him for years:

---

42 Manuscript forwarded to author by S. Power (Newcastle, 1990).
43 Lance Sergeant William Allan Hill, known as Rufty to his friends, 6th Battalion Green Howards, was killed on 6 June 1944, aged 22. He is buried in Bayeux War Cemetery, France.
44 Manuscript forwarded to author by F.W. Vickers (Barnsley, 1992).
45 Company Sergeant Major Stanley Hollis would be awarded the Victoria Cross for his actions on 6 June 1944.

Corporal Francis William Vickers, MM, 6th Battalion Green Howards. (Courtesy of F.W. Vickers)

Lance Sergeant William Allan Hill, 6th Battalion Green Howards, KIA 6 June 1944. (Courtesy of Paul Cheall)

It was then that I got the most painful wound I had in the whole war, I lifted the stripped Lewis gun off the gunwale, and it was white hot, I got a bloody great blister across my hand, as thick as my finger. We charged about waist deep into the water and the man in front of me, Sgt William Allan Hill, who had been a very good soldier all throughout the war, a real fighting man, dropped into a shell hole under the water. He couldn't come up with all the stuff he was carrying, and the landing craft went over him, the propellers cut him to bits. As we were coming over the beach a tank blew up and its escape hatch bowled along the beach right through the company like a top but never touched anyone, if it had it would have been curtains. We dashed over the beach, a lot of our boys had been seasick, and they were only too glad to get out of those boats. We ran up to the top of the beach and along a ridge. There were heaps of rolled wire. An Irishman alongside me saw two or three birds sat on this wire. Mullaly[46] said to me: "No bloody wonder they are there, sergeant major, there's no room in the air for them."[47]

---

46 Private Joseph Mullaly, 6th Battalion Green Howards, was killed on 6 June 1944, aged 28. He is buried in Bayeux War Cemetery, France.
47 Morgan, *D-Day Hero CSM Stanley Hollis VC*, pp. 60–61.

As the men struggled out of the water they were met by heavy mortar and machine-gun fire from pillboxes on the sea front. Major Frederick Harvey Honeyman led his company into the attack, and with the help of a tank of 4/7th Royal Dragoon Guards crushed the resistance. The advanced sections were then held up at the sea wall, where the enemy dropped grenades on them. By this time Major Honeyman had been wounded in the arm and leg, but despite this he restored the impetus of the attack by leading his men over the wall and into the enemy positions. Two of his NCOs, Lance Sergeant H. Prenty and Lance Corporal A. Joyce, followed their officer and leapt over the wall and charged into the enemy bunkers, firing their Sten guns from the hip and throwing grenades before them until the Germans were all dead or had surrendered. This act cleared the beach of small-arms fire. The bravery shown by these three men was rewarded with Major Honeyman getting the Military Cross, and Prenty and Joyce the Military Medal. Honeyman was fated to be killed at Cristot just five days later. The success they achieved was immediately exploited, the following troops forcing through a track exit from the beach and after some difficulty capturing the Ver-sur-Mer battery, which was, however, found to be out of action. Nevertheless, 50 prisoners were taken.

Off the beach and the advance inland

Lieutenant John Milton, of the 6th Green Howards, unexpectedly found himself heading the full battalion as they moved off the beach:

> The sea was very rough and not everybody had a good landing as some of the landing craft hit mines, the men on them were stranded in deep water and drowned. My platoon was lucky, I was off the landing craft first and charged up the beach to be faced with signs that said there were mines all along it. We followed a flail tank towards our objective which was a house with a circular drive, where I believe Stanley Hollis saved the lives of my platoon by taking out a pillbox. Then my company took the lead which meant I was leading the whole battalion which was rather daunting as I had no battle experience, [and] I was leading a battalion of men who had far more battle practice than me.[48]

CSM Hollis advanced behind Lieutenant Milton and noticed a pillbox had been passed unnoticed and would be able to fire into the backs of Milton and his men and onto the troops still advancing up the beach. Hollis, realising what needed to be done, moved to the attack with his company commander, Major Ronald Lofthouse:

> I saw where the fire was coming from and Major Lofthouse said to me: "There's a pill-box up there Sergeant Major." Well, when he said that I saw it and it was very well camouflaged, I saw these guns moving around in the slits. I got my Sten-gun and I rushed at it, spraying it hosepipe fashion. They fired back but they missed. How a Spandau firing 700 rounds a minute missed me I don't know. I jumped on top of the pillbox, bent down and then I threw in a grenade through the aperture, I went round the back and went inside,

---

48 *WW2: People's War* <www.bbc.co.uk/ww2peopleswar> (accessed 11 September 2018).

two of the Germans were dead and I wounded the rest. There were 16 or 17 of them. I also cleared a lot of Germans from a trench behind the pillbox, taking 35 prisoners that morning. We found out later that this was the command post for the Mont Fleury Battery.[49]

Lieutenant Colonel Robin W.S. Hastings, MC, CO of the 6th Green Howards, landed with A Company and witnessed the heroics of CSM Hollis:

By the time we landed there should have been nothing left, but A Company found quite a lot of people firing at them and had casualties crossing the beach. They got across it but found machine-gun fire sweeping the beach from one pillbox and also mortar bombs landed among them. They got up under the sea wall and huddled, as men will under fire. It was the sort of moment when an operation can so easily bog down however careful the planning. The initiative of individuals is the deciding factor. Two NCOs, who were renowned for being in all kinds of hot water, broke the deadlock, they threw grenades over the sea wall and rushed after them, turning their tommy guns on the defenders. It was after leaving the beach that one of those incidents occurred which make the difference to success or otherwise. Stan Hollis, the sergeant major of D Company, suddenly saw a pillbox 20 yards in front of him and behind the leading platoons, from which automatic fire was coming. Without hesitation he simply charged it and shot the inhabitants. How he survived is hard to imagine as one bullet grazed his eyebrow and took a clip out of his ear. His instant reaction cleared the hill and was the first of many actions that day which gained him a Victoria Cross.[50]

Company Sergeant Major Stanley Hollis, VC, 6th Battalion Green Howards. (Author's collection)

Many individual actions that day cleared the way for the move off the beach and inland. Corporal Francis William Vickers, 6th Green Howards, saw one platoon in difficulties and, without thought of personal danger, moved to the attack:

I knocked out a Spandau machine-gun post which was about 100 yards up the beach and was firing across our front at 18 Platoon on our right. I was able to get right up-close firing my Bren-gun from the hip, killing two and taking six prisoners. I took them towards where 18 Platoon had been moving up in a ditch by the side of the road that ran inland

---

49 Newspaper cutting sent to author by W.F. Vickers (Barnsley, 1992).
50 Manuscript forwarded to author by F.W. Vickers (Barnsley, 1993).

from the beach, six of the lads of 18 Platoon were sat or laid there, they had been hit in the legs. I remember two of their names: Eric Charlish from Bedale in Yorkshire and Jack Walton from Middlesbrough. I saw them both after the war; Walton lost a leg as a result of his wounds. I took the six prisoners out to the beach and handed them over to a naval beach officer. One of them had an Africa Corps sign around the bottom of his sleeve and I shook hands with him and wished him well. I went back and joined my platoon, [but] all the company officers, with the exception of the company commander, had been killed or wounded, as well as sergeants, lance sergeants and corporals.[51]

CSM Hollis now took command of 16 Platoon as the officer had been wounded on the beach. As he passed through a village, Major Lofthouse gave each platoon a house to clear along the road. Hollis and 16 Platoon entered the garden of one house:

We came to the gate and the house was locked so I broke the door down. I went up the stairs into the various bedrooms, I burst into one of the bedrooms and there was a small boy about 10 or 11 years old and I just saw him disappear round a corner. He is now the owner of the farm. He must have been pretty frightened as I was covered in blood, he must have been terrified. I'm convinced he thought I was going to kill him. Anyway, there was nothing in the house, so I came down again. I decided to have a look to see if there was anything round the back of the house. This was where I was the most frightened I ever was in my life. I looked round this wall corner and straight away a bullet knocked a lump of stone off the wall.[52]

Lance Corporal Alan Carter, 6th Green Howards, recalled:

We went on up the road and we came to the first house. There was movement inside, we stopped and got ready to sling a grenade in. All of a sudden an old French woman came out. She was pointing out to sea and tears were rolling down her cheeks. I knew what she was asking, she was saying: "Is this the real thing, is this liberation?" I nodded my head then her old man appeared with a bottle, and it warmed us up because we were wet through.[53]

On the right of 69 Brigade's front, things were progressing nicely, the 6th Green Howards having taken the Meuvaines Ridge over a mile inland and continuing the attack in a southerly direction.

7th Battalion Green Howards, "The main road to Hell"

Lieutenant Colonel P.H. Richardson, commanding the reserve battalion, 7th Green Howards, landed 400 yards to the right of the unit's intended position at 0815 hours after the main landing. He could see the troops of the 6th Battalion already in action as they moved off the beach. As the 7th landed, all was confusion on the beach as tanks, self-propelled guns, AVREs,

---

51   Manuscript forwarded to author by F.W. Vickers (Barnsley, 1993).
52   Morgan, *D-Day Hero CSM Stanley Hollis VC*, p. 64.
53   A. Carter, correspondence with author (Sheffield, 1990).

carriers and jeeps, intermingled with hundreds of troops, crowded in on the narrow strip of mud and sand between the enemy minefields and the water's edge. The long grasses just off the beach were ablaze, giving off clouds of acrid smoke and shielding the view beyond. Some vehicles and tanks had been hit and were on fire, adding more clouds of smoke to the chaos. Landing craft that had already visited the beach crowded onto the shingle a second time, taking wounded men on board that the hard-pressed-stretcher bearers were carrying from the forward areas as mortar bombs thudded around them. German prisoners, some wounded, were being guarded at the top of the beach, waiting to be taken away by sea.

Private Thomas Tateson, with the 7th Green Howards, recalled the difficult landing as his craft was disabled:

> The assault landing craft carried about 30 men tightly packed. They were low lying flattish boats, and we were seated so that our heads were below the level of the gunwale. We were ordered to keep our heads down as we approached the coast to avoid enemy fire. However, our landing craft was disabled by an underwater mine or other obstacle, [and] it became impossible to steer. One of the other LCAs was brought alongside and although it was fully loaded with a similar number of men, we had to abandon our boat and clamber aboard. The new craft was now grossly overloaded as well as being exposed to enemy fire. From my new position I was able to see more of the action and one image which remains with me is of the rocket ships sending off large numbers of rockets with each volley at an angle of 45 degrees. Although there is of course no recoil from a rocket, there was to me an optical illusion of the ships and barges moving backwards as each flight of rockets was fired.[54]

Sergeant Jock Mackenzie, Royal Signals, was feeling decidedly seasick as the LCA carrying his unit moved in for the landing in rough seas:

> Our little LCA was being tossed about all over the place, we were packed in like sardines and all standing. I was thinking that at any moment now we could capsize. I suppose those that were being sick didn't care very much. About 100 yards from the beach the bloke in charge of the LCA called out: "Sorry lads but this is the best I can do, mind how you go off the ramp as it might crush your feet." Well off we went, bedroll on our shoulders, kit on our back, rifle slung around our necks and fingers crossed. The water struck us cold at first, but I soon forgot that in frantic efforts to keep on my feet. The sand underfoot was like a quagmire and as you put one foot down you had the devil's job to get it out. When you did it was a miracle if you could keep your balance. Although the water probably wasn't four feet deep, the shell holes and bomb craters made it eight feet deep in places. The beach itself was a shambles: guns, tanks, landing craft and scores of vehicles were either floating around, stuck in the sand or were burnt out. Houses and factories just inland were bombed or burned, [and] rows of bodies covered with greatcoats or blankets lay on the sand. Jerry prisoners, insolent as ever, were marching down to the beach as we staggered up it. It looked just like the main road to Hell.[55]

---

54 Manuscript forwarded to author by T. Tateson (Sheffield, 1991).
55 J. Mackenzie, correspondence with author (Guilford, 1988).

Private Frederick Aycliffe of the Royal Electrical and Mechanical Engineers (REME) landed with the 7th Green Howards, his Universal Carrier floating ashore but having to avoid hitting vehicles and dead men:

> Our carrier followed the others down into the water, levelled out and began to make its way to dry land. We had to avoid many knocked out vehicles and blackened bodies floating face downwards in the water. The beach in front of us was crowded and we came to rest in about two feet of water awaiting our turn to get into the taped off lanes.[56]

The main purpose of the 7th Battalion was now to get away from this unhealthy spot as quickly as possible, and they walked along the beach through acrid clouds of smoke to their intended position. Once there, they found the road leading inland to Ver-sur-Mer, setting off along it to the accompanying sound of gunfire.

Company Sergeant Major Jack Verity came ashore with the 7th Green Howards and acted as landing officer:

> We dropped into the water up to our chests on account of these obstacles in the water that stopped the landing craft getting close to the beach; they were dug into the sand below the water. The sailors would only take us so far because if the ramp hit an obstacle they would blow up. One thing I'll never forget when I was in the water was the terrific strength of the currents between my legs – one or two of the lads were caught and slipped by. On the beach a fella said: "Keep walking about mate, there are snipers about." I was waiting for the rest of the battalion, and I found I was the only landing officer where I was. I looked out to sea and saw that flipping lot. It was out of this world to see all those boats and the battleships firing over us. I didn't see any enemy aircraft, but we didn't half get some muck thrown back at us from Jerry.[57]

Company Sergeant Major George Warters felt his landing with the 7th Green Howards was easy compared to the first wave of troops that had come ashore on Gold Beach:

> The crossing was alright but when we had to get into the flat-bottomed craft, we were all sick as dogs. It was dark when we set off for the beach, but it was light when we arrived and all hell had been let loose, I've never heard such a noise. We were lucky as where we landed it was fairly easy. We had our friends in the 6th Battalion on one flank and the 5th East Yorkshires on the other. They had a very rough time of it, but we were able to press straight through. We had been told not to expect to fight on the beach and we got across it quickly as we had been trained to. We lost a few men going up the gradual rise of the beach and others in the water. The barbed wire had been cleared and we moved steadily inland with the tanks. We had expected more opposition, but we were lucky. Later when we had been in action for quite a while there was no particular feeling other than whether or not we should see tomorrow. The officers told us things were going well and that was good news.[58]

---

56 F. Aycliffe, correspondence with author (Richmond, 1992).
57 J. Verity, interview with author (Beverley, 1989).
58 Newspaper cutting sent to the author by J. Betts (Hull, 1992).

Following the lanes to the exits

Private Frederick Aycliffe, REME, followed the men of the 7th Green Howards off the beach when his carrier came under fire:

> We slowly made our way to the exit, carefully avoiding other vehicles that were stuck in the soft sand and soil. We had just reached the exit between two houses when enemy shells started coming in. We moved up a single-track lane off the beach which was quite steep with walls on each side. As we reached level ground at the top the column came to a standstill owing to a vehicle in front having a track blown off by a mine. We were stuck there quite a while and most of us climbed out to put our feet on firm ground. I was standing with our driver, Cpl Johnson, Nobby Clark, Pte Merrikin and the driver of the carrier in front. There was a blinding flash followed by a terrific explosion and we were all blown off our feet. I remember hitting the ground with the others falling on top of me. Nobby Clark was screaming for help with a gash in his thigh, Cpl Johnson was wounded in the chest and seemed to be unconscious. I could not get up until some help came and moved Pte Merrikin who had been killed instantly, one side of his face was blown away.[59] On getting to my feet, I was grateful to find that my only injuries were temporary deafness and concussion.[60]

As the 50th Northumbrian Division streamed through the sand dunes, German reconnaissance units were sending panicky reports back to the formations outside the main battle area. SS-*Obersturmführer* Peter Hansmann, of the *12. SS-Panzer-Division 'Hitlerjugend'*, radioed to his superiors:

> Over 400 ships with a wall of barrage balloons along the whole 30km stretch towards the Orne Estuary. The British are streaming ashore unhindered, including heavy equipment. Eleven heavy tanks identified, coastal defences knocked out and overrun. Infantry in battalion strength moving south towards Bayeux. Enemy naval gunfire is engaging Bayeux and approach roads. Fighters are strafing cliff strong points. I will recce towards Creully, out.[61]

Private Thomas Tateson moved inland with his company of the 7th Green Howards and for the first time met some French civilians:

> Once we located this road, we marched along it and I recall our first meeting with French civilians in a small hamlet, which was probably La Riviere or Mont Fleury. I remember a hill curving left with houses on the right, from which people came out to greet us and to offer us drinks of cider. We gave the children sweets in return.[62]

---

59 Private Harry Merrikin, 5th Battalion East Yorkshire Regiment, was killed on 6 June 1944, aged 33. He is buried in Bayeux War Cemetery, France.
60 Neillands, R. and Norman, R., *D-Day 1944, Voices from Normandy* (London: Cassel, 1993), p. 215.
61 Manuscript forwarded to author by H. Wernemann (Germany, 1989).
62 Manuscript forwarded to author by T. Tateson (Sheffield, 1991).

The follow-up brigades land on Gold Beach. (Author's collection)

The advance inland: CSM Stanley Hollis, 6th Battalion Green Howards

The 6th Green Howards then advanced towards Crepon, with the 5th East Yorks following. CSM Stanley Hollis was passing through the village of Crepon with his men at 1100 hours when he cautiously peered up a country lane to make sure it was clear of the enemy. Hollis observed:

> I saw two dogs standing near a gap in a hedge, they were dancing about, wagging their tails and jumping up and down. I knew full well we were the forward troops, so I knew they were no mates of ours that were there. On closer inspection I saw a field gun, so I went back and told the company commander what I had seen. He told me he would see what we could do about it, but before I went back I told 8 men of 16 Platoon to dash out and engage whatever was in the hedge. Just open up with Bren guns and shoot the hedge up I said. Well, they ran out and immediately they were killed stone dead. I thought there's not much future here and I reported back to the company commander. I said I would go back with a Piat and try to knock it out and I and two Bren gunners got into a big patch of rhubarb at the back of a farmhouse. We got to the forward edge of the rhubarb patch, I poked the Piat gun through and had a shot, well as usual with me I missed. The Jerry gun opened up and blew the farmhouse down, there was sticks, stones and masonry flying all over the place, and the company commander said we were to bypass it.[63]

---

63   *Middlesbrough Evening News* cutting sent to author by J. Verity (Beverley, 1989).

The 6th Green Howards advanced, leaving the gun position to others who had the firepower to deal with the enemy artillery piece. After pressing forward approximately a short distance, Hollis was informed that the two Bren-gunners were still in the rhubarb patch near the farm:

> We had advance about a quarter of a mile when someone said that two of our Bren-gunners had been left behind. They were pinned down and couldn't get out, so I went back with a Bren gun and waited behind a wall until there was a lull in the firing. I ran straight across the farmyard and sprayed the hedge with the Bren gun, that quietened them down and I was able to shout to the lads to get out and come back and join me. Which they were able to do, and we re-joined the company.[64]

Later in the day, CSM Hollis was at a crossroads and led the remnants of his platoon down a sunken lane, when they came under fire from a Spandau machine-gun post. Hollis realised at once that this German position needed to be taken out if the advance was not to be held up, so moved to the attack:

> It was pouring down with rain and the lane was in a hell of a mess having been churned up by tanks. Going forward we heard a lot of banging on both sides. On one side of the lane we were getting casualties from small arms fire. I laid down and I could see two Germans who were getting up and firing a burst down that side of the lane and then getting down. I watched them for a few seconds which seemed like a long time. I got the idea of how they were firing, and I decided that the next time they stopped I would have a go at them. When they did I ran forward and threw a grenade, it didn't explode but it made them duck down. I ran in before they had chance to get their wits about them and shot them both dead. You know I had the feeling all that day that I wouldn't be killed.[65]

For his outstanding initiative, leadership and bravery throughout D-Day, CSM Hollis was awarded the Victoria Cross.

The East Yorkshires, having suffered considerable casualties in the initial fighting, had been forced to reorganise into three companies at Ver-sur-Mer. Private Norman Cohen, 50 Div Signals, was inside his communications vehicle at Ver-sur-Mer when he decided to get out to have a drink. As he half-opened the door, he remembered he had left his tin mug behind and turned to get it:

> As I closed the door a bullet hit it. I contacted communications HQ and told them that someone was firing at me. Some minutes later the phone rang, and I was told to open the back door again. I replied "Not fucking likely" and got a flea in my ear from the voice on the phone which turned out to be a major no less. "That's an order, do it now!" he said. I carefully levered the door open when immediately another bullet hit the truck followed by a staccato burst of machine-gun fire from another direction. It turned out to be a Frenchwoman who objected to our having broken up her romance with a German soldier

---

64 *Middlesbrough Evening News* cutting sent to author by J. Verity (Beverley, 1989).
65 *Middlebrough Evening News* cutting sent to author by J. Verity (Beverley, 1989).

and she was attempting to extract her revenge. She was spotted hiding up a tree and when she fired a second time our troops fired back and got her.[66]

Creully: 7th Battalion Green Howards

By 1230 hours, the 7th Green Howards had reached Crepon and were faced with opposition in the form of sniping and small-arms fire. The advance continued to progress, and by 1500 hours the battalion had seized the bridge over the River Seulles at Creully. Lieutenant David Trasenster, 4/7th Royal Dragoon Guards, was supporting the advance of 69 Brigade in his Sherman tank (called Winchester) as they moved into Creully:

> Winchester was hit for the first time by an armour piercing round, knocking off our spare bogey, eight foot of Willet's aerial and the troop pennant, also a chunk of armour was gouged out near my head. Another enemy tank missed us by 100 yards as we were approaching the river bridge over the Seulles at Creully. By putting down smoke bombs, one of which miraculously landed on the bridge, we got to cover and our supporting infantry, 7 Green Howards, cleared the houses rapidly.[67]

This bridge was of vital importance as it was situated on the main axis of the Allied advance to the south. The bridge over the Seulles was found not to be mined, so the troops and tanks passed over it in the direction of Fresnay-le-Crotteur. As they approached the narrow road over the bridge at Creully, a German staff car approached at great speed from the west and was stopped by a stream of machine-gun fire, sending it slithering into a ditch. It was found to contain a dead German medical officer whose luck had just run out. A Panther tank appeared on the far side of the bridge, but quickly withdrew when it saw the approaching British armour. Feeling very vulnerable, the Sherman tanks of the 4/7th Royal Dragoon Guards crossed the bridge in single file. It was with an intense feeling of relief that the first squadron emerged from the village and moved out into open country.

A gentle warm summer breeze sent ripples through the ripe cornfields and gently disturbed the leaves on the trees on what had become a clear sunny afternoon. The tank crews of A Squadron, 4/7th Royal Dragoon Guards, were confronted with this scene of undisturbed tranquillity as they pressed on beyond Creully. This was good tank country, containing long open views with occasional hedges and woods. The squadron commander ordered his men to push on at speed: "Shake out into two-up formation. 1st Troop left, 2nd Troop right, 3rd and 4th behind. Now let's go!"[68]

Lieutenant Trasenster recalled the move they made through Creully:

> My troop Corporal and I drove through the eerily deserted streets. Passing through Creully the squadron advanced towards a ridge, then we really hit trouble; nine tanks were knocked out in about as many minutes from an anti-tank gun ahead.[69]

---

66 N. Cohen, interview with author (Wrexham, 1993).
67 Manuscript forwarded to author by G. Ford (Essex, 1991).
68 Stirling, J.D.P., *The First and the Last, The Story of the 4/7th Royal Dragoon Guards 1939–1945* (London: Art and Educational Publishers, 1946), p. 152.
69 Manuscript forwarded to author by G. Ford (Essex, 1991).

As the tanks of the 4/7th Royal Dragoon Guards advance over a ridge, they ran into heavy opposition from anti-tank guns of the German *352. Infanterie-Division*. The two tanks to the right were hit and exploded in sheets of flame with the crews still inside. Each tank gave off clouds of dense, acrid smoke that billowed over the battlefield. The squadron commander, Captain Jack d'Avigdor-Goldsmid, realised that the forward tanks were completely exposed to the German anti-tank crews and ordered the squadron to make for cover behind a line of trees some 400 yards distant. Tanks of the 3rd Troop had heard the warnings coming over the air, but had no idea of what was going on in the forward positions. Slowly, the tanks in the rear edged their way forward to get a better view of events, with the burning tanks of 2nd Troop coming into view in the middle of a field. As one of the tanks nosed its way through the trees, it received a direct hit and chunks of steel flew off the turret. The tank instantly became an inferno.

Lieutenant Trasenster recalled the chaotic scene as the advancing British forces, as well as receiving German fire, were also hit by the big guns of HMS *Orion* when it sent large-calibre shells over that landed on them rather than the intended German defenders:

> HMS *Orion* opened fire with several broadsides. Any tank crews that were out of their tanks and the poor infantry were massacred. Ten of the regiment were killed and 16 wounded. The regiment had penetrated about six miles inland at the cost of 19 tanks and 24 casualties. Reg Cox saw the tank his brother was driving explode 20 yards in front of us.[70] Lipscombe's tank was brewed up and all the crew were wounded.[71]

Private Thomas Tateson, with the 7th Green Howards, watched aghast as the tanks were hit one after another, he assumed by German gunfire:

> Although my recollections from here on are disjointed and fragmentary, I recall with horror how I felt at the time during an episode involving tanks. One tank came out of cover to advance across an open field on our left. It received a direct hit and immediately went up in a sheet of flame, nobody had any chance of getting out. A second tank then broke cover and advanced in the same way, presumably hoping to identify the source of the enemy fire and to silence it. Almost at once it was hit and similarly became a flaming inferno. Yet a third tank was then sent out only to meet the same fate. The German self-propelled guns, tanks and anti-tank guns were so easily hidden in this close country that it was pretty well impossible to locate them, and three tank crews were sacrificed in vain.[72]

Then a flash followed by a wisp of smoke was spotted in the distance, and some of the remaining tanks opened fire on the source, hoping to knock out the offending anti-tank gun. However, the area around the tanks of the 4/7th Royal Dragoon Guards then erupted as what were believed to be enemy shells landed amongst them, making them rock on their bogeys. Several tanks were hit and many infantry killed. Only later was it discovered that this barrage was in fact British naval gunfire from HMS *Orion*.

---

70 Trooper Ronald Cox, A Squadron, 4/7th Royal Dragoon Guards, was killed in action on 6 June 1944, aged 21. He is buried in Bayeux War Cemetery, France.
71 Manuscript forwarded to author by G. Ford (Essex, 1991).
72 Manuscript forwarded to author by T. Tateson (Sheffield, 1991).

British Churchill tanks move inland to support the infantry. (Author's collection)

Private George Nicholson and his 7th Green Howards comrades were prevented from advancing by heavy German machine-gun and artillery fire:

> One very accurate Spandau position had us pinned down at a crossroad, [then] a tank moved up and it only fired one shot but that was enough. When we got to the Jerry position there was one bloke who was a right mess. It had turned him inside out. The other bloke looked as if he hadn't been touched except for his brains hanging out of his skull. But the other bloke had been absolutely filleted by the look of him, poor bastard.[73]

Tanks and infantry were forcing the Germans to retire when the salvo of heavy naval shells landed amongst them, forcing the leading companies of the 7th Green Howards to withdraw. After reorganising, the companies moved forward to the village of Coulombs, their final objective being the radio transmitter there, which was heavily fortified and surrounded by minefields. With dusk falling and the approach to the village bereft of cover, the 7th Battalion reached the minefield and came under fire from the radio station. The troops then withdrew for the night to a position just north of Coulombs.

73 G. Nicholson, correspondence with author (Bradford, 1988).

CSM Jack Verity of the 7th Green Howards remembered the heavy fighting his unit had as they pressed on to their objective:

> Christ it was rough going, we came under fire from our own side at one point when naval gunfire fell short and landed on us. We were quite far forward, and I wondered if some silly bugger had identified us as Germans and called down a big stonk [military slang for an artillery bombardment]. There were blazing tanks in front of us and all this mortar and small arms fire dropping amongst us. My mate Stan was sat on the ground holding his stomach, when I asked him what was wrong he said he'd been hit and was waiting for the medics. There were quite a few casualties laid about. By then dark[ness] was falling and we were still under fire, [so] we settled down till morning. Not that it was a quiet night, tracer rounds flew everywhere, and fires seemed to be burning all around us.[74]

Private Tateson later reflected on events towards the end of the day on 6 June:

> Progress on this first day was very rapid but my recollections are scanty. An incident which has remained very clear however occurred later on in the day after we had covered several miles. Without warning a salvo of gunfire landed right in the middle of the troops to our immediate left followed by a second shortly afterwards. From messages we could hear being passed on the radio I learned that no-one knew who was responsible, except that it was coming from behind us. When the third salvo landed with the most enormous crack my signals training deserted me and I sent an unauthorised message: "Stop this fucking barrage!" By complete coincidence, but to the flattery of my ego, the firing ceased. We later learned that it came from the navy lying offshore, they did not realise that we had advanced so far.[75]

The 6th Green Howards were continuing their advance on the right flank of the 7th Battalion, and just before 1500 hours were on the high ground near Villiers-le-Sec, a mile to the north-west of Creully. Corporal Francis William Vickers was back in the thick of the action inland with the 6th Battalion and had been lucky so far:

> As we moved inland, we took a lot of casualties from sniper fire, one I remember was John Thomas Jackson from Middlebrough,[76] he was an old regular soldier who had served in India on the Northwest Frontier with our 2nd Battalion. By now our ranks were getting thin so I teamed up with another Bren-gunner called B. Charles Elmer and on account of his initials he was nicknamed Before Christ. As we went up this track we heard this gun firing from the other side of the hedge, just then a Sherman tank came up behind us, there was an officer standing in the turret, so we asked him to put a couple of shots into the gun position over this hedge. He asked us if it was an 88, we told him we didn't know, he then spoke into the wireless he had on his chest and the tank turned round and went back the

---

74 Interview with author, J. Verity (Beverley, 1989).
75 Manuscript forwarded to author by T. Tateson (Sheffield, 1991).
76 Corporal John Thomas Jackson, 6th Battalion Green Howards, died of wounds on 9 June 1944, aged 33. He is buried in Bayeux War Cemetery, France.

Dead German troops line a Normandy hedgerow. (Courtesy of M. Hearst)

way it came. That was the first tank I saw that day and the last. Charlie went around the gate at the back of where the gun pit was, and I put my Bren through the hedge. Charlie, or Before Christ, opened up with his Bren and I fired a full magazine into the gun pit.[77]

Lieutenant John Milton, with the 6th Green Howards, reached the village of Crépon later in the day after numerous skirmishes, and was instructed to keep advancing:

The most notable things were the small fields and all the cattle that had been killed by the shelling. I am sure that the great noise of the shelling that day is what is to blame for my need for a hearing-aid now. By the sides of the road there were many dead bodies and wounded who were crying out for water. We were ordered not to stop as there was a danger that they were hostile, or could be, and also the troops further back would take care of the wounded. I think that by the end of the day we were one of the furthest forward battalions of D-Day. That night I asked a butcher in my platoon if he could cut some steaks from the dead cows in the field, so we had steak for supper on D-Day.[78]

---

77 Manuscript forwarded to author by F.W. Vickers (Barnsley, 1993).
78 *WW2: People's War* <www.bbc.co.uk/ww2peopleswar> (accessed 28 February 2019).

Corporal Vickers, having returned to fight with the 6th Green Howards after delivering his prisoners to the beach, finally had his luck run out:

> Charlie and I brewed up a dixie of tea from the 24-hour packs we had been issued with. Then some of our lads came up the track and we moved inland. As we came out into open ground and onto a road a barrage of mortar bombs landed among us, I don't remember much after that. When I came to I was on a stretcher near the beach and had shrapnel wounds in my upper arm.[79]

The 5th East Yorks, following up from Ver-sur-Mer, pressed on through the 6th Green Howards, who sat tight for the time being on their commanding position. The East Yorkshires advanced through heavy mortar and small-arms fire into corn fields, driving the enemy before them. The Germans were soundly beaten, and the 5th Battalion went on without pause in the direction of St Gabriel as large numbers of prisoners began to file down the dusty roads towards the beaches.

Keeping moving inland

The 5th East Yorks arrived at St Gabriel and was at once ordered to keep moving through and take possession of Brecy, north-west of Coulombs. Sergeant Max Hearst, with the 5th East Yorkshires, was not pleased to be given no respite before being pushed into the next fight:

> We had lost a lot of men by the time we reached St Gabriel but when we got there, expecting a short rest, we were sent forward straight away, only to be expected I suppose but we were so tired by then, some of the younger ones were falling asleep while advancing or whenever we stopped for a short while. It was a hard slog with constant moves one after the other. There were some woods on our left and we came under heavy small-arms fire, but before nightfall we had reached our objective.[80]

The men were kept on the move constantly and dug-in at every opportunity, only to be ordered forward again and again in a relentless advance. Private Denis Bowen recalled the intense pressure all of the 5th Battalion felt:

> We always got the same command when the line needed straightening: "Dig in! Dig in!" which means scratch a hole in the ground to get into. You don't have to be told after the first time, you realise that if you dig a hole and get into it, you'll survive. Then along came the NCOs: "Get forward! Get forward!" And you get out of your little mucky hole and advance. The one thing you do is that when you find a French shovel, which has a bigger head than ours, you keep it because with that you can dig down a lot quicker. Life or death depends on you getting into a bit of bullet-proof cover by digging. By the afternoon some of the men were beginning to talk about food, [but] I hadn't even had a drink of water yet. I

---

79 Manuscript forwarded to author by F.W. Vickers (Barnsley, 1993).
80 M. Hearst, interview with author (Hull, 1990).

German prisoners on Gold Beach. (Author's collection)

never stopped and just seemed to be constantly running forward, digging in again, running forward and firing, firing.[81]

Lieutenant Philip Bransom wrote of some help the 5th East Yorks received from a French policeman:

> As we were advancing down a street a Gendarme of all things appeared on a bicycle pedalling furiously towards us and waving his hands, obviously trying to indicate to us that the Germans were still in the village. I remember him clattering to the ground with the next burst of fire from a Spandau. It was a brave effort of his to try and give us some warning.[82]

Lieutenant Bransom noticed the stoic way men coped with continuously being in action:

> We approached a German position moving along the relative safety of a sunken road on the side of this meadow and eventually came to a gate which we had to pass in front of. It was obvious that if any enemy were holding positions near the gate that it would be pinpointed

---

81 D. Bowen, correspondence with author (Shropshire, 1992).
82 P. Bransom, correspondence with author (Durham, 1993).

by at least one of the German gunners. Nevertheless, we had to get past it, and we used the normal technique of a group of chaps running by the gate quickly, to be followed by another group. As the third group went by a Spandau opened up. In my unit there was a big Yorkshire contingent of men from Hull and one of their qualities is that they have a kind of stoicism mixed with a strange kind of humour. One lance corporal in the third group went by the gate, he was caught by the gunfire, he came bouncing back clutching his backside and cursing that the buggers had shot him in the arse. Immediately there was a temporary halt while his mates pulled his trousers down – his wound was pouring with blood. They were trying to put a field dressing on it, God knows where, when his friend had a good look at his wound and announced with some triumph "It's alright, they've missed them", [meaning] his testicles, as if that made everything right.[83]

Denis Bowen found himself near a farmhouse when the order went out to prepare for a counter-attack:

We had dug-in near a little farm by the side of a duck pond. I remember the sergeant racing round saying: "This will be your arc of fire, watch out because Jerry will come back, don't think it's all over he'll be back for us", so we Stood-To. I was completely petrified that these Germans would come storming back after we had been shooting and killing them all day and would attempt to shoot and kill us. But the men of the 5th East Yorks stood fast, they were good old sticks.[84]

The 6th Green Howards joined in the attack from the right flank at 2130 hours, supported by the machine guns of the 2nd Battalion Cheshire Regiment and the self-propelled guns of the 86th Field Regiment, Royal Artillery. Brecy was cleared of enemy troops, and it was here the brigade commander called a halt on the night of 6 June. Members of 69 Brigade had fought many actions in the villages, hedgerows and corn fields of Normandy and were a mile short of the St Leger area, their planned objective, but the weary troops had fought their way 7 miles inland and had at last penetrated the much-vaunted Atlantic Wall.

Nightfall

Private Frederick Aycliffe recalled the final stage of the advance of the 5th East Yorks on D-Day:

It was early evening before we reached a road that wasn't under shellfire, and we were able to move forward about four miles. We moved past farms that were burning and scores of German prisoners that were being escorted to the rear. As night fell the gunfire lessened and we moved across a field to take cover in an area surrounded by trees. With darkness falling, tree roots everywhere and everyone wanting to get their heads down, most of us gave up digging and took a blanket and crawled under the vehicles. So ended a very long day.[85]

83 P. Bransom, correspondence with author (Durham, 1993).
84 D. Bowen, correspondence with author (Shropshire, 1991).
85 F. Aycliffe, conversation with author (Richmond, 1991).

Private Norman Cohen, of 50 Div Signals, also reflected on the end of a tiring day:

> I fell asleep exhausted, bivvying next to our wireless truck. I was woken next day at 06:00 a.m. to take over as duty wireless operator. I was fully dressed and only had to put my boots on and report for duty. When I went outside, I saw very close to our tent, much too close for comfort, a German plane that had crashed in the field next to us during the night. In my exhausted state I had slept right through the crash and heard absolutely nothing.[86]

151 Durham Brigade

Members of 151 Brigade were due to land as follow-up troops on Gold Beach behind 69 Brigade at 1100 hours, and at 0900 hours the French coast came into view for them. News was received by the Durhams that the leading brigades were off the beaches and moving slowly inland. As the landing craft carrying the brigade made their way to the shore, an amazing sight met their incredulous eyes. Huge numbers of ships stood out to sea as landing craft in their hundreds continually disgorged their cargoes of men and materiel onto the shore. Meanwhile, destroyers and frigates fired at selected targets as they weaved in between the larger vessels. Many of the various kinds of landing craft that had taken 69 Brigade to the beach could still be seen on the shoreline with their ramps down. Some lay at odd, ungainly angles, having been hit and destroyed by enemy gunfire, struck beach obstacles and been blown up or damaged in the heavy seas.

For most of 151 Brigade, the landing was going to be a wet one. However, Major George L. Wood, of the 6th Durhams, recalled a rare dry landing:

> We touch down and the craft shudders as she touches the bottom. Down come the ramps into the water and Ron Simpson steps off, he is a big strong chap but that's no use as the sea sweeps him away. He just manages to grab the rail in time to pull himself back on. One of the crew starts swimming for the shore with a line as it's only a few yards away. But he doesn't seem to be making any headway. At last, he makes the beach but has lost the lifeline and then the ship's captain shouts to us to stand clear and up come the ramps. He is going to put out to sea and come in again at a different place. Another half-hour passes and we are getting terribly late. A small motorboat goes past us towards the shore, it's the brigade commander who spots us, smiles and waves. In we go again only this time the ramp comes down on dry ground and off we walked without getting out feet wet.[87]

Private Jim Radcliffe spoke of his landing with the 9th Durhams:

> We sailed past cruisers, HMS *Belfast* and HMS *Orion*, while they were firing broadsides and the blast from their guns was flattening the waves in front of them. As we got close to the shore we could see wrecked vehicles in the water, we hit the beach and it still looked a

---

86   N. Cohen, interview with author (Wrexham, 1993).
87   Manuscript forwarded to author by R. Pope (Durham, 1991).

A view of Gold Beach after the first assault troops had moved inland. Troops, tanks, men and materiel constantly poured into the ever-expanding bridgehead. (Author's collection)

fair way to dry land. The skipper yelled to the men controlling the ramps to hold on as he would try to get us a bit closer, which he did bless him. Once ashore the battalion had to make for an assembly area a little way inland.[88]

Private Eric Broadhead, also with the 9th Battalion, was ordered off his LCI into 4 feet of very cold and turbulent water:

> We scrambled along 501's deck with naval personnel shouting at us: "Get ashore". Ships were everywhere, it was like a traffic jam. Down the ramps we went and then came ten horrible yards between ship and shore with water in between. Still dizzy from seasickness we went over the side into water four feet deep; each man let out a gasp as the cold water swirled around him. We struggled ashore and it was the hardest ten yards I ever did, but I was mighty grateful to be off 501 and her terrible motion. One thing I remember was that the cold water brought me round like a footballer's magic sponge. When we got ashore we regrouped as a battalion. I saw my first German soldier as the lads who beat us ashore were bringing him in as a prisoner.[89]

Major John H. Mogg, 9th Durhams, recalled the effect that shellfire had on him and his men as they approached the shore:

---

88 *WW2: People's War* <www.bbc.co.uk/ww2peopleswar> (accessed 4 January 2019).
89 E. Broadhead, correspondence with author (Durham, 1991).

The first two shells which landed in the water fairly near to our boat destroyed any signs of seasickness on us. The soldiers wanted to go like mad to get out of it. We had to jump into about three feet of water and wade ashore and there were lots of obstacles which we had to climb over. The only casualty we had was when we lost the signals sergeant, he jumped off the craft into an enormous great shell hole filled with water and he went down and never came up again. That was the only casualty we had on the beaches.[90]

Captain A.E. Hooper, also of the 9th Battalion, found himself in deep water, but to his surprise he floated:

They issued us with some oil-skinned trousers which came up to our chests. When they dropped the ramp, I was standing on top of the ramp when we hit a mine, it exploded and blew the ramp up. I got a hell of a shock in my feet, but apart from that it didn't affect me. I never thought, as I stepped off the ramp, that the explosion of the mine had made a hole in the sand, [but] when I got into the water I couldn't touch the bottom. I started to float as the air in the trousers was compressed up to my chest where the trousers were tied tight with string. As I began to get buoyant I was going over when the pressure of the water burst the trousers and let me down again.[91]

Private Reg Pope had served in the 9th Durhams since 1939, seeing action with them in Belgium, France, North Africa, Tunisia and Sicily. He now found himself seconded to the 2nd Machine-gun Battalion the Cheshire Regiment and landed on Gold Beach with 151 Brigade supporting his old battalion:

The crossing was rough and, on the run up to the beach, the ramp went down, and we were dropped into water that came up to our chests. I couldn't swim and was more worried about drowning than getting shot. I landed on Gold Beach with 151 Brigade and had been in so many major actions by now that I had no real expectation of surviving this lot. The scene on the beach was terrible, pure pandemonium. The Yorkshire lads had been given a hard time and their dead were laid about everywhere. When we saw all these destroyers and battleships blasting away, we thought it's going to be a cakewalk. They'd been pounding the shore for hours before we went in you know, I thought there can't be much left. But as we moved inland, they were there alright.[92]

Sergeant Bert Davies waded ashore with the 6th Durhams and was deeply impressed by what he saw on the beach and out to sea:

Once ashore I turned around and looked out to sea. Bloody hell, I thought, I couldn't understand how the Germans must have felt. There was thousands of ships and you thought you were a part of something really big. This was a change for us, we were dishing it out and they had to accept it. We knew they were more frightened than us. Once we got off the

---

90 Moses, *The Gateshead Gurkhas*, p. 272.
91 A.E. Hooper, correspondence with author (Newcastle, 1991).
92 R. Pope, interview with author (Durham, 1991).

A medic of the Durham Light Infantry tends to wounded German soldiers. (Courtesy of W. Ridley)

> beach I had another look round and what a terrific sight. Aircraft above, countless ships, some with barrage balloons above them, all these heavy ships firing away. Tanks were being unloaded onto the beach at a very early stage, that was a good sign. Flail tanks had soon left the beach and flailed a path through the minefields for us. Once we were through the minefields we had to spread out. The sooner you got off the beach and inland the better.[93]

Private Richard Atkinson, with the 9th Durhams, stepped onto a crowded beach where a very stressed beach master was trying to keep things moving: "Get off my bloody beach," he screamed at the Durhams. "We don't want to be on your bloody beach," shouted back Atkinson as he moved on. A Lieutenant Williams also waded ashore with the 9th Durhams and could see signs of the struggle that had taken place there:

> In a matter of minutes my chaps were ashore and shedding their waders, a ghastly garment that went over your equipment and completely waterproofed the wearer up to the chest. While my chaps were splashing ashore I found time to scan the beaches. 69 Brigade had not found it so easy. I saw the water lapping at the muzzle of a submerged anti-tank gun. The wheels of an armoured car, completely turned over, spinning lazily as the tide struck them. There was a landing craft infantry down by the shore to the left of me and there were other signs of resistance at the water's edge. It struck me suddenly as I looked about that all this noise and violence which was in the air had Jerry on the receiving end. Even as I

---

93 B. Davies, correspondence with author (Durham, 1989).

Troops inspecting a knocked-out German bunker on Gold Beach after the battle had moved inland. (Author's collection)

thought, I saw a mortar bomb fall near a group of naval ratings, [and] two of them lay down as though they were very tired.[94]

Lieutenant Bert Jalland, 8th Durhams, was keyed up for the landing, but as he stepped off his LCI things went drastically wrong:

> The LCIs started going round in tight circles and moved towards the beach circling in that way and eventually, when they were within striking distance, peeled off one at a time to ram their prows into the beach. Then the next LCI would come in next to it and ram in their prows and it worked like a charm. The prow of our boat hit the shingle and an American sailor lowered the ramp and I knew exactly what to do, walk down the gangway onto the beach and get off it as quickly as possible because a lot of shelling was expected. I went down the ramp, manfully I hope, and stepped into the water. I don't know how deep it was, but it was deeper than I was, and I went straight to the bottom on my hands and knees. I was aware of the fact that the prow of this LCI I was under kept smashing

---

94 Moses, *The Gateshead Gurkhas*, p. 273.

into the shingle right next to me and I could see it smashing my arms or legs or me if I got anywhere near it. I had these waders full of water and I couldn't do a thing, [and] my first act was to get rid of the folding bicycle I was carrying, I threw it away. I managed to tear off the waders and I also unfastened my webbing and slipped that off. I eventually landed on Hitler's fortress on my hands and knees having crawled up the beach wet through, very frightened and completely unarmed.[95]

The rubber waders with which the troops had been issued were not popular with the men who had to wear them. Company Sergeant Major William Brown of the 8th Durhams commented on them:

The water filled the gas trousers we had been issued when we waded ashore. We could feel it sloshing around inside of them and we stood on the beach like a bunch of bloody idiots with our trousers full of water.[96]

An anonymous account by an officer of the 9th Durhams describes the scene as the Durhams moved inland off the beach:

About 800 yards from where our craft was due to beach I could see a Sherman tank fitted with flails crashing its way through a minefield on a green slope just off the beach. It looked like a giant crab as it crawled forward and there was, every now and then, a burst of flame as it flailed a mine. Further to the right I could see orderly lines of men filing out of the beach landing craft and then converging into thicker lines as they made for the pre-arranged beach exits. From that distance they resembled a nice orderly football crowd until into their midst fell one or two mortar bombs and the resemblance ended. Yet the flow of men was in no way halted or dispersed. They looked, as indeed they were, inexorable and irresistible.[97]

The 8th Durhams moved off the beaches heading inland, and at 1345 hours was ordered to advance with the 6th and 9th Battalions in the direction of Bayeux. Company Sergeant Major William Brown of the 8th Battalion watched his men struggling with the bicycles they had been ordered to carry which were making progress difficult, and thought of an ingenious way to get rid of them:

When we were finally off the beach we met up in a hide where we had a self-inflicted wound in D Company. I heard the rifle shot. It was an old fellow of 40, he was a bundle of nerves and had shot himself in the hand. I said: "You've shot yourself you bastard." He said: "I'm sorry sergeant major but I can't go on." "It's alright," I said. "Leave your rifle there and get yourself back, if anybody asks you've been hit in the hand." I wasn't going to court-martial him. From our hide we moved off on our bicycles trying to keep up with the battalion pace. We'd used the bikes to get to the hide and they'd been useful but cycling at a marching pace was pretty hard work. When we stopped I attracted the attention of a

---

95 Newspaper cutting sent to author by W. Ridley (Durham, 1991).
96 W. Brown, correspondence with author (Durham, 1989).
97 Rissik, D., *The DLI at War* (Durham: DLI, Brancepeth Castle, 1953), p. 241.

A flame-throwing Crocodile tank was a terrifying, if effective, weapon of war. (Author's collection)

passing tank commander and asked him to do me a favour. "What do you want?" he asked. "Run over them bloody bikes, aye run them over with your tank." He just ran them over and squashed them. I said to my officer: "The bikes have gone sir and the bloody tanks have run over them." He said: "Oh well, if you haven't got a bike you haven't got a bike."[98]

Major George L. Wood, 6th Durhams, had taken over command of the battalion after his commanding officer, Lieutenant Colonel A.E. Green, had been taken to hospital suffering from malaria. Major Wood has left a vivid account of the move inland by his battalion:

> The ill effects of the sea crossing were soon shaken off as we advanced to the battalion assembly area near Ver-sur-Mer. The battalion was assembled and ready to move off by 14:00 p.m. A Squadron 4/7th Royal Dragoon Guards, under Major Bell, was with us and took part in the advance during the next two days. The mobile column under Major Thomlinson moved off at 15:00 p.m. two hours behind the time planned. Movement was slow because of the congestion of troops and material on and near the main roads and the difficulties of driving Shermans through narrow village streets. Some enemy pockets were met near Villers-le-Sec but quick action by Lt Kirk, in command of the vanguard, drove the enemy from their position. During the whole of the move forward we encountered no enemy artillery fire and were held up by only small pockets which were soon beaten up.[99]

The 6th Durhams reached their first objective at Esquay-sur-Seulles by 2000 hours, where they waited for orders regarding their next move. When they arrived, the battalion was told to stop at Esquay and dig in for the night. Major Wood saw the battalion's first trophy of war at Esquay:

---

98 W. Brown, correspondence with author (Durham, 1989).
99 Clay, E.W., *The Path of the 50th* (Aldershot: Gale and Polden, 1950), pp. 246–47.

We had our first spoils of war at Esquay in the form of a Ford car, proudly driven into the battalion area by Major Kirby, officer commanding C Company. Two days later its German camouflage disappeared and the emblem TT60 was put in bold letters on the body. The car lasted throughout our part in the French campaign. We also took our first prisoners here, mostly foreigners of 642 Ost Battalion [troops conscripted by the *Wehrmacht* from conquered territories in Eastern Europe], who had no desire to fight and seemed quite content to be marched back under escort.[100]

Lieutenant T.M. Kirk, 6th Durhams, moved through open country but found the going difficult because of the hedgerows and congestion:

When we got to Villers-le-Sec we met a few pockets of resistance but when we turned our not inconsiderable fire power onto them they quickly retired. I found the greatest difficulty in stopping the tanks once they had started firing as they were both blind and deaf. I tried rapping on the turret with my pistol, [but] it did not have much effect. We reached Esquay-sur-Seulles and pushed on to the main Bayeux–Caen Road, where the tanks indulged in an orgy of destruction knocking down telegraph poles. It was now 20:00 p.m. so we stopped there and dug in.[101]

Captain David Fenner, a veteran of many actions since 1940, landed with the 6th Durhams in the follow-up waves. They did not meet heavy opposition, but it was obvious from the scenes around them as they left the beach that the lead units had been involved in some hard fighting that was still going on further inland:

We beached successfully, the bow gangways were lowered, and we waded ashore in about four feet of water. Beach Masters, RN and Army Landing Officers, met us and urged us on our way. We moved left along the beach past a smashed strongpoint and its dead crew, up a gap in the minefield and into the village. Progress was slow because the Yorkshire brigade was fighting just to our front and dealing with any enemy opposition. Also, we were heavily laden with 200 rounds of ball ammunition, a pick or shovel, 24-hour ration pack and lightweight folding bicycles. We followed up behind the Yorkshiremen past the detritus of the battlefield. I met two friends with whom I had a wild party in Cairo the previous spring after the division had returned from Tunisia. They told me about the fighting on the beach [but] they were both killed in the next few days. I did not know it at the time, but we were in the area where the first and only VC of the day had been won by CSM Hollis of the Yorkshire Regiment.[102]

Bayeux in sight

Major Peter Martin, 2nd Machine-gun Battalion the Cheshire Regiment, supporting 151 Brigade, was under the impression that Bayeux had been liberated:

---

100 Clay, *The Path of the 50th*, p. 247.
101 Moses, *The Faithful Sixth*, p. 280.
102 Manuscript forwarded to author by I.R. English (Durham, 1990).

We landed on time and walked up to our assembly area behind Ver-sur-Mer and met our transport, everything was going to plan. There was a little sniping and the odd mortar bomb. I could hear 231 Brigade battling it out in the Arromanches area. We sat around in the assembly area until about 14:00 p.m. when two columns from 6th and 9th DLI pushed forward to the line of the Caen/Bayeux Road without any opposition. We were due to RV [rendezvous] just north of St Leger. All was quiet and I went to the RV and from there to the Caen/Bayeux Road. I said to my jeep driver: "Shall we just potter down to Bayeux and liberate it." He thought this was a good idea and I thought it must be in our hands by now, [but] on the outskirts a Frenchman whistled at us and pointed down the road: "Boche – Boche". We did a quick turn and were driving back the way we had come when we were machine-gunned by an American fighter. We had to dive for the ditch but one of our tyres was holed. We returned to brigade HQ after the quickest wheel change outside a Grand Prix meeting.[103]

Private Atkinson, with the 9th Durhams, knew that the liberators were not always seen as conquering heroes, most civilians having lived quietly with their German overlords and gone about their agricultural activities as they had from time immemorial. Many troops did receive a hearty welcome from the populace, but others could see in the people's faces a fear of what was about to take place as they found themselves and their families in an active battle-zone. Atkinson reflected:

The civilians didn't want you there. They weren't too happy because you only brought with you death and destruction. The Germans treated them well because they were feeding the Germans and the food was going back to Germany. It was a beautiful area with lush farming land. In the fields all their cows were dead with their legs up in the air and all livestock had been killed. They didn't want us there because we'd killed all their stuff and we were pinching their wine. The Germans hadn't done anything like that so there was no love lost at this stage [–] we wrecked their houses and killed all their livestock so it's not surprising.[104]

Lieutenant Bert Jalland, of the 8th Durhams, was given little intimation of what was happening or where he was going, but recalled the charming Normandy countryside:

My recollection of the countryside that day is that it was pleasantly rolling land with numerous hedgerows and trees. There were scattered farmhouses and other buildings and fields with ripening crops. There was plenty of cattle but few people, as most inhabitants had fled the bombardment or were in hiding where they hoped they would be safe. It must have been a ghastly day for them. In the main we did not know what was happening, information was not getting down to the companies. We had to rely on news given to us by passing dispatch riders or tank crews as we came into contact with them. We met a few of the enemy on the first day, those we captured were gunners or infantry in German uniforms who claimed that they were Russians. They were obviously shocked by the ferocity of the

---

103 Thompson, *Victory in Europe*, p. 70.
104 Moses, *The Gateshead Gurkhas*, p. 275.

bombing and bombardment, but they received very little sympathy from our troops, who regarded them as traitors to the Allied cause.[105]

Trooper A. Wilson of the Royal Artillery had suffered a terrible landing that had been hampered by strong tidal movements and enemy fire. He was glad to get out of the beach area and to move inland:

> Eventually a way was cleared off the beach and the battery half-track moved inland as I walked along behind it with the rest of the command post staff. It crawled along a narrow lane that the engineers were sweeping for mines. Then we came to fields and hedges and two poor stone cottages, [and] here we met our first Frenchmen. These two grey stubbled old men kissed us on both cheeks and jabbered away in the Normandy dialect. The road ahead was crowded with vehicles and infantry moving inland, it was quite a sight.[106]

Lieutenant Eric Hooper, 9th Durhams, plodding along the road inland, was moved by the plight of two civilians he and his men came across:

> I'll tell you of one incident that made me feel very sad. On our route we came across a farmhouse that had been shelled and when we got there we met an old lady and a nun. The old lady was very distraught and in the conversation I found out that her two grandchildren were buried in the ruins. They wanted us to try and get them out. But we couldn't as we were under strict orders to be at a certain point at a certain time and we had to move on and leave them. That was very upsetting for me.[107]

The brigade plan had the 9th Durhams advancing on the right flank, the 6th Battalion on the left flank and the 8th Durhams following in reserve. A troop of Sherman tanks was in support. By 1400 hours they were on the move, a mobile column from each battalion heading the advance, and were taking their first casualties from incoming shellfire. All three battalions settled down for the night to the south-east of Sommervieu, where the 9th Battalion had cleared the village.

Private Jim Radcliffe waited with his mortar team in the 9th Battalion assembly area, ready for the inevitable move forward, when they came under friendly fire:

> The three-inch mortars left the assembly area and were told to occupy a small ridge before the 21st Panzer Division took it. We thought this was hilarious as we had met these buggers before and knew they would drive straight through us. Anyway, we set off and had been going along this road for a few minutes when half a dozen Typhoons started bombing and strafing the road a few hundred yard ahead of us. The last plane was just coming in for his two-penny worth when he saw our column. He turned and came straight down at us with his cannons blazing and he dropped a couple of bombs, but luckily for us they landed in the soft earth in the fields.[108]

---

105 Manuscript forwarded to author by W. Ridley (Durham, 1992).
106 Manuscript forwarded to author by A. Wilson (Gateshead, 1989).
107 E. Hooper, conversation with author (Durham, 1987).
108 *WW2: People's War* <www.bbc.co.uk/ww2peopleswar> (accessed 5 March 2019).

146   A Stern Reckoning

Gold Beach British Cemetery, 9 June 1944. (Author's collection)

Private Eric Broadhead was in the same column as Jim Radcliffe:

> We reached the high ground without incident and from here one had a perfect view of the bay with its vast array of ships of all shapes and sizes. Not long after this we came under fire in earnest for the first time. Strangely enough it wasn't enemy fire. We pushed along the lane all keyed up and expecting almost anything except what happened. Overhead came a flight of fighter planes coming from the Channel and heading over France, RAF fighters. As they zoomed overhead they peeled off one by one and machine-gunned the column. This was far from pleasant, and we dived in all directions as lumps of dirt were flying everywhere. It was over as quick as it had started, and we pushed on with nerves that had been somewhat stirred. It was later that we learned we had not come through without loss and a little cross sprang up in Normandy.[109]

Lieutenant T.M. Kirk recalled a similar occasion when the 6th Durhams came under friendly fire:

> A squadron of American Thunderbolts, fighters, appeared and started to circle around. "Good old air cover," I said, "but I'll just put up some recognition signals." Well, that did it, immediately one of their number dived down and opened up on us with his machine-guns. Naturally we all hit the deck, which was just as well as our worthy ally hit the back of my carrier and set off a box of 77 grenades which showered burning phosphorous all around the vehicle. By now my carrier was burning furiously and before we could put it out the swine came back. We had a slight lull then back came our intrepid aviators. We were well hidden in a deep ditch, but it was still most unpleasant, although made humorous by my

---

109 Manuscript forwarded to author by E. Broadhead (Durham, 1991).

Into the Breach: King Sector, Gold Beach, 6 June 1944   147

Rocket-firing Typhoons of the Royal Air Force attacked any German vehicles that moved on the roads of Normandy, and sometimes their own side too. (Courtesy of M. Hadley)

driver Marsh who thought 'Gazala' the best carrier in the battalion and was furious at her ignominious end. His comments on the Yankee Air Force were weird and wonderful.[110]

As night fell, the men of 69 Brigade and their supporting arms settled down in their positions and took stock of the situation: many familiar faces were missing, and they all knew this was just the beginning of their ordeal. They thanked their good fortune that they had been spared, hoping that their luck would continue to hold in the future. Private Reginald Rome of the 9th Durhams recalled:

> My personal reflections at the time were that here I was sitting in a slit trench enjoying a cigarette in the fields of Normandy. Not long ago I had been enjoying a hot meal in the New Forest back in Blighty. Today when I read the histories of D-Day and look at the photographs which have been published, I think to myself, Christ I was lucky.[111]

---

110 Moses, *The Faithful Sixth*, p. 280.
111 Manuscript forwarded to author by N. Hardy (Hull, 1989).

Sapper Harvey Smith, 82nd Assault Squadron, Royal Engineers, had landed on Gold Beach with the AVREs in the second wave amid shot and shell. He remembered the after-effects of battle he witnessed:

> We made our way to the rendezvous with 82nd Squadron in an orchard south of Ver-sur-Mer. I was asked by an officer to go and take a look at a monastery which had been used as a barracks by the enemy. The mess still had all the pictures of Hitler on the wall. The tables were littered as though it had been suddenly vacated and in the entrance-hall was a dead body. I went to turn it over to identify it and an officer shouted: "Don't touch that, it's probably booby-trapped." That night I slept under the stars.[112]

Gunner Frank Davies, of the 73rd Anti-tank Regiment, Royal Artillery, was greatly relieved to be on dry land, and as his unit settled down for the night he found he was left alone in the dark while his comrades patrolled the area:

A sniper of the 5th Battalion East Yorkshire Regiment cleans his rifle as his young comrade sleeps. (Author's collection)

> We scurried off into the well-worn tracks of the tanks which had gone ahead of us and saw a British Tommy flattened out in the right-hand track, a sight that made us feel very hard towards the Germans, which was probably a good thing at the time. We passed German prisoners who had been told to make for the beach and a number of them had French girls still hanging on to their arms. Light was fading and we leaguered in a large pit. The officer and the other men went off on a recce leaving me alone with four M10s, one Bren-gun carrier and of course my own Sten-gun. When they had left a lone aircraft passed overhead, which I could only just make out, and an eerie silence followed which seemed to last a very long time. I was relieved when they all arrived back. I asked Lt Brown how long they had been out and was told 20 minutes – it was the longest 20 minutes I have ever known.[113]

---

112 H. Smith, correspondence with author (Chester, 1991).
113 F. Davies, correspondence with author (Stockport, 1989).

Trooper Joe Minogue of the Westminster Dragoons settled down for what he hoped would be an uneventful evening when he was confronted by an unusual sight:

> Our colonel, Blair-Oliphant, came striding along wearing white overalls, looking like an itinerant house painter who had stumbled into the act by mistake. He had hitched a ride in one of the regiments' recovery vehicles and was now asking us what had happened to our tank commander. Then, with a brief word of praise to the crew he strode off again. That night was a lively one when two German fighters began to strafe the many ships lying off the invasion beaches, which put up such a barrage of anti-aircraft fire that the night was lit up by tracers at the end of an exceptionally long day. After we were relieved we slept like the dead after surviving a truly memorable day, just glad in fact to be alive.[114]

CSM Jack Verity of the 7th Green Howards breathed a sigh of relief as the light faded and took care to make sure his men were all fed and bedded down, with sentries posted:

> I picked men for sentry duty who were to be relieved regularly, as we were all dead on our feet. Many didn't bother to eat but laid down where they were and immediately fell into a deep sleep. Shellfire could still be heard but at least it wasn't falling on us for a change. We had some of the East Yorks lads with us who had got lost, I told them to get their heads down and find their unit in the morning. The landing was over, and we had survived, but there were many familiar faces missing. I don't remember falling asleep that night, I was just grateful to be alive and to still be in one piece.[115]

By midnight on 6 June, the Allied armies were established on the continent. Not all named objectives had been taken, but in most cases the Allies had cause for satisfaction and great hopes for the future with the situation they were in. The invasion had tested the units involved and vindicated the meticulous planning that had gone into it. By securing the beachhead, the hopes of the Allied commanders had been fulfilled, with more than 156,000 British, American and Canadian troops ashore. Now would come the break-out. Montgomery had won the first round, but all veterans knew that the Germans would recover and come on again. Rommel had returned from Germany, ensuring that the next round would be a hard-fought one.

An anonymous German soldier who had survived the initial part of the invasion wrote a letter home to his wife in Germany:

> On the morning of the 6th of June, we saw the full might of the English and Americans. At sea, close inshore, the fleet was drawn up, limitless ships small and great as if on parade, a grandiose spectacle. No-one who did not see it could have believed it. The whistling of the shells and shattering explosions around us create the worst kind of music. Our unit has suffered terribly but you and the children will be glad to know I survived.[116]

The unsent letter was found on his body later in the campaign.

---

114 Neillands and Norman, *D-Day 1944, Voices from Normandy*, pp. 228–29.
115 J. Verity, interview with author (Beverley, 1991).
116 Mayo, J., *D-Day Minute by Minute* (London: Short Books, 2014), p. 221.

5

Into the Breach: Jig Sector, Gold Beach, 6 June 1944

231 Brigade

The men of 231 Brigade were to land on a 900-yard stretch of Gold Beach named Jig Sector, which was to the east of Le Hamel, and establish themselves on the high ground overlooking Arromanches. This town was the biggest in the divisional area of operations and was to be the site for the Mulberry harbour, which would play such an important role in supplying and replenishing the British armies in Normandy. Once off the beach, the brigade was to capture Ryes, Arromanches and the important battery at Longues. Meanwhile, 47 Royal Marine Commando, who were under the command of 231 Brigade for the operation, would capture Port-en-Bessin. In reserve, 56 Brigade would beach after the initial landing to reinforce the bridgehead and advance towards Bayeux.

1st Battalion Hampshire Regiment

SS-Oberstürmfuhrer Peter Hansmann, of the *12. SS-Panzer-Division 'Hitlerjugend'*, had been ordered to Arromanches on a reconnaissance mission to ascertain what exactly was going on along the coastal strip in that sector. He arrived there in his heavily camouflaged half-track as it became light, his vehicle soaking wet because of the early-morning mist. The areas he passed through were a hive of activity as German troops dug in, and the sounds of battle from the British airborne attacks in the rear could be heard clearly. His reconnaissance detachment met heavy oncoming traffic as they reached the coast, which assured them that the British had not landed here yet. Eventually, disturbing news reached Hansmann of heavy fighting on the beach at Arromanches. It was not long before he saw burning buildings and large explosions on the coast. To gain a better view of events, he drove to the high ground at Magny-en-Bessin. From a farmhouse there, he had a view of the whole Arromanches inlet:

> Over there heavy artillery fire was coming down. Fountains of earth as big as houses rose up and collapsed in on themselves. To the east stretched a seemingly limitless dark grey mass, the sea, endlessly to the horizon, but slightly lighter than water. I looked through binoculars and now I could make out the individual silhouettes of ships. In the foreground

Into the Breach: Jig Sector, Gold Beach, 6 June 1944 151

A large-calibre German gun in its thick concrete casemate, Normandy, May 1944. (Author's collection)

and beyond, up to the horizon, ships, masts and command bridges. In the background flashes blinked at irregular intervals but incessantly: naval artillery. Between the beach and the dark grey ship armada was a murky grey sea. White stripes were apparent within this shadowy mass of water, stretching along an endless front of ships extending from the cliffs at Arromanches to the horizon east of the Orne Estuary, all coming towards us![1]

SS-Obersturmführer Peter Hansmann, *12. SS-Panzer-Division 'Hitlerjugend'*, observing the landing of 231 Brigade at Arromanches. (Courtesy of H. Wernemann)

1 Kershaw, *D-Day, Piercing the Atlantic Wall*, p. 165.

Grenadier Robert Voigt of *Regiment 726*, was heading for the cliffs at Arromanches when he became caught up in carpet bombing by the RAF. Having survived this, he continued to his destination and as he approached he could hear the sounds of battle ahead. Looking out to sea, he gained his first sight of the Allied fleet:

> Somewhere I heard a voice shouting: "Enemy landing craft approaching!" I had a good view from the top of the cliffs and looked out at the ocean. What I saw scared the devil out of me. Even though the weather was so bad we could see a huge number of ships. Ships as far as the eye could see, an entire fleet, and I thought "Oh my God, we're finished."[2]

The beach in Jig Sector was pounded by the fire of destroyers and a great collection of other craft arrayed before the shore, pouring high explosive shells from the water line to the vegetation line. Behind this mass of firepower came the landing craft carrying the infantry of 1st Hampshires on the right flank and 1st Dorsets on the left flank. At the allotted time, the infantry and tanks stormed ashore, finding their progress held up at the beachhead because of the terrible fire from mortars, machine guns in pillboxes and 88mm guns further inland. This heavy opposition was partly due to the fact that RAF bombers had missed their mark, leaving strongpoints still intact. The Hampshires collected on the beach and found themselves pinned down as casualties began to mount.

Lieutenant David Render sat on his Sherman tank as the LCT carrying him and the other Sherwood Rangers tank crews made its way towards Gold Beach:

> The LCT continued to plough through the heaving ocean to the ever-closing line of sandy beach. We had passed the planned launching point of 6,000 yards but still pressed on as the distance to the shore reduced and the sporadic fire of German ranging shells began to bracket us. Estimating that the fast-running tide and heavy sea state threatened to swamp the DDs, the skippers of the LCT flotillas had consulted with the tank squadron commanders and decided to launch the swimming tanks as close in as possible to increase their chances of making it to the beach. As the distance to the shore shortened the accuracy and concentration of the enemy fire increased. Thick angry columns of white water shot up in the sea and mortar bombs sent up fountains of soaking spray as the yards between the tightly packed vessels and the land continued to count down. Through the waves splashing over the bow ramps commanders could make out the square features of seafront villas on the shoreline and the grey squat outline of pillboxes that were marked by the jagged muzzle flashes of their machine-guns. The pitter-patter of small arms fire striking our metal superstructure was audible above the din.[3]

Sapper C.R. Wampach, Royal Engineers, sat in an LCT as it made its way to the beach to land with the first wave. Looking around him, he was amazed at the sight that met his eyes and assailed his senses:

---

2   Manuscript forwarded to author by H. Wernemann (Germany, 1989).
3   Render, D., *Tank Action, An armoured Troop Commander's War 1944/45* (London: Weidenfeld & Nicolson, 2016), pp. 15–16.

The Channel was a mass of ships, hundreds of landing craft, destroyers, cruisers and battleships. Overhead hundreds of bombers were making for the French coast. At about 03:00 a.m. the main barrage against the coastal defences opened up and the noise was deafening. Destroyers pounded away with their 6-inch guns while 16-inch salvos from the battleships poured death and destruction onto the German gun emplacements. There were also dozens of rocket-firing ships which fired 50 rockets at a time. As soon as we landed our objective was Port-en-Bessin which would be the other end of the pipeline. The first to land were the assault engineers of 32 Armoured Engineer Regiment whose job was to clear the minefields and mark safe lanes for the infantry. Everyone had to keep moving as remaining on the beach was a death trap.[4]

Private Lewis Richards, MM, 50 Div Signals, accompanied Brigadier Alexander Stanier, CO 231 Brigade:

As dawn was breaking, I could hear formations of heavy bombers passing overhead, [and] slowly visibility improved. At first I could see only the ships near us, then the outline of the coast came into view and finally line upon line of ships of all sizes and shapes, from the sleek and lean destroyers and cruisers to the squat and cumbersome landing craft. The smaller assault craft had been lowered from their parent ships and were circling around. The coastline was now receiving the attentions of the Royal Navy and squadrons of planes and was soon covered by a pall of thick smoke. The cruiser HMS *Orion* was firing broadsides only a few hundred yards from our LCA. My brother was on this ship, but little did he know that I was so near yet so far from him. As we approached the coast we were shelled and as I looked over the side of the craft my eyes met a sight that I shall never forget. The shore was about 80 yards away and the beach seemed to be crowded with tanks and carriers, but not one appeared to be moving, although one or two were burning. Between the shore and our craft were rows of formidable looking obstructions, there were long poles about seven inches thick embedded in the sand at an angle pointing out to sea with mines attached. I saw five or six men clinging to what looked like a telegraph pole, they were being tossed about unmercifully by the sea and the wash of various craft attempting to land added to their discomfort. On the approach I was behind a jeep when I was shaken by a violent explosion. My steel helmet evidently got tired of waiting and jumped overboard deciding to fend for itself. In a flash I realised we had hit a mine and my hope of a dry landing faded into the background. I was more concerned about the depth of the water in front of us. A message came over the set which I duly wrote down and acknowledged. On looking up to see who I could hand it to I was alarmed to discover that I was alone, the remainder of the party I observed through the open end of the craft were strung out in a line in the water making for the shore. The nearest person was quite some distance from me, the water was up to his chest. I intimated to all stations in code that I was about to land.[5]

---

4   Manuscript forwarded to author by Brian Cook (Carnegie Heritage Centre, Hull, 2017).
5   Manuscript forwarded to author by D. Harrison (Hampshire, 2014).

HMS *Rodney* bombarding the Normandy coast, 6 June 1944. (Author's collection)

Private Richards did not know it, but not all people had left the craft. They were out of sight in a Universal Carrier, and when Richards heard voices, he climbed on to the front of the vehicle and looked inside:

> I saw Cpl Davidson and Cpl Gunning who were making a wounded officer comfortable. The latter's hand was smashed when the mine had exploded; the officer had been blown overboard and hoisted back in almost immediately. Cpl Davison said he would drive the carrier onto the beach, and I volunteered to stay on the front and give him steering instructions as he was unable to see from the driving seat. He started the engine, and we began to move as I stood on the front with my back to the carrier. As we moved down the ramp the carrier hit the side of the landing craft and I felt myself falling sideways. I didn't realise what was happening and found myself being dragged through the water alongside the carrier. My fingers hurt like hell as I was pulled along, but I knew I would lose my tow ashore if I released my grip. Cpl Davidson stopped the carrier in shallow water, and I was able to stand up. He said he thought I was dead and could hardly believe it when I told him what had happened. Two mines on poles were only inches away from the carrier.[6]

6   Manuscript forwarded to author by D. Harrison (Hampshire, 2014).

David Render stood on the observation platform at the rear of his Sherman tank, trying to catch a glimpse of the shoreline the LCT carrying him was headed for:

> The small shapes of beach front buildings beyond the bow ramp could just be seen, erupting in flashes and blasting sand and smoke as the naval bombardment continued to strike the enemy defences. The powerful pulsing throb of the LCT's racing diesel engines and the smoky rumble of the tank engines combined with the terrific ear-splitting roar of the ships' gunfire to make a constant wall of noise. Fear gnawed at stomachs, long since emptied by the ceaseless vomiting and retching, as men wondered silently about what awaited them on the shore.[7]

Lieutenant David Render, Sherwood Rangers, Nottinghamshire Yeomanry, Royal Armoured Corps. (Author's collection)

Signaller Kenneth Rees followed the Hampshires onto the beach:

> Our signals vehicle was not well waterproofed enough and spluttered to a halt before we reached the shore. The officer on board was being about as typically nonchalant as a British officer could be, sitting on top of the vehicle viewing the scene through binoculars as if on holiday, despite our efforts to pull him down. We landed just opposite a huge pillbox. I remember a particular feeling of pathos at seeing the seemingly unmarked body of a British soldier with every stitch of his clothing, including his boots, blown off by blast, lying face down in the sand.[8]

Private Peter Cuerdon, of the 1st Hampshires, thought it was relatively quiet as he headed inshore from the mother ship. But this soon changed when the barrage began. He found himself in an unreal world as he stepped onto the beach amid a hail of incoming fire:

> About three or four in the morning we were pretty far out, and you could just see the outline of France. Do you know what went through my mind? I always thought I was going to see millions of Germans standing along the beach and firing at us, but it was a quiet morning until it all started. It was the most impressive thing when the battleships, destroyers and cruisers started up their barrage, the rocket-firing assault craft were the most impressive sending volleys of 50 rockets at a time screaming overhead. To hear all that

---

7   Render, *Tank Action*, p. 13.
8   K. Rees, correspondence with author (Kidderminster, 1994).

noise going on made us think that it's going to be alright as there will be nothing left. The noise was colossal, but we didn't have time to think about it as we were too busy. While we put condoms on the ends of our rifles to keep the water and sand out, shells were whistling over us, and I used to wonder where that one was going. The impression one gets is of a sort of dream world. The fire coming from the beach was terrific and we could hear it hitting our craft and see it hitting the water. We were hit and the sailors couldn't lower the ramp, so we lost our carrier and had to wade ashore. We ran like hell up the beach and dozens of men were hit as we did so, [and] some drowned as they couldn't swim. To see my first man killed was a ghastly sight, it rather upsets one. We ran up to these dunes and sheltered in the tall grass and held there waiting for some officers to turn up. We were joined by a young Lt and there was firing all around us, machine-guns, snipers and mortars, it was terrible and put the fear of God up you. It's difficult to describe the fighting as it was so chaotic; we rambled on ahead and got down every now and again. The officers were damned good though, I admired them, we lost quite a few and they weren't much older than myself.[9]

Gunner Frank Topping, 147th Field Regiment, Essex Yeomanry, Royal Artillery, hit the beach in an LCT, and on impact the ramp dropped down:

A few yards from the beach we hit bottom and the ramp flopped down with a great crash. I thought we had hit one of the submerged mines, so I ducked, caught my waterproof trousers on a tank projection and ripped the suit. This meant that when I jumped into the sea, I touched bottom as my suit filled with water. The others had difficulty in standing up as their suits were filled with air. We managed to get rid of an obstacle and the tanks landed without mishap. Soaked to the skin I ran up the beach to my tank, intent on climbing into the turret to get out of the way of mortar shells and sniper bullets. Just as I reached it a shell exploded alongside me and I felt a blow between my shoulder blades. I was sure I had bought it, but the co-driver leaned down and picked up a lump of dried mud off my back. Apart from subsequent bruises I wasn't even scratched.[10]

Private I.G. Holley, 1st Hampshires, having been in action before in the Middle East, felt like an old soldier as he tried to tell the new replacements what it was like. The tension grew as his landing craft headed for the beach amid a crescendo of noise, the men bracing themselves:

Brakey, one of our reinforcements, was not yet 19 and was very apprehensive about going on his first operation, [so] I tried to reassure him. In our LCA there was a small keg of rum and a couple of bottles of whiskey put there by some unknown person, I never found out who it was. Probably with the intention, good or bad, that we might need a little Dutch courage. One drink was enough for me in the hope that it would settle a queasy stomach caused by the flat-bottomed boat tossing about in the swell. On board we had a naval Sub-Lt who, either from the magnitude of the event or from the esprit de corps obtained from the rum, felt impelled to stand up and give forth a little speech on the great thing we assault troops

---

9 Manuscript forwarded to author by P. Cuerdon (Hampshire, 1993).
10 Neillands and Norman, *D-Day 1944, Voices from Normandy*, p. 212.

were about to do. Overhead there was the continuous whizz of naval shells homing in on their targets to soften them up for us. We were soon within range of the mortars, a weapon we had come to respect, and we could hear the sharp crackle of machine-gun fire. We had the word to get ready and tension was at its peak when the ramp went down. I was with the second in command and he went out with me close behind him. We were in the sea up to the tops of our thighs floundering ashore with the other assault platoons to the left and right. Mortar bombs and shells were erupting in the sand, and I could hear clearly the burp-burp of Jerry Spandau machine-guns through the din. There were no shouts, only the occasional cry as men were hit and went down.[11]

Corporal Fred Cooper admitted to being apprehensive as he landed with the 1st Hampshires:

On the approach we could see big landing craft firing broadsides of rockets, all we could hear was the loud whoosh-whoosh as they flew over us. I had butterflies and yes, we were afraid, who wasn't.[12]

Gunner James W.A. Bright, 147th Field Regiment, Essex Yeomanry, Royal Artillery, was shaken by what he saw as he made the final run in to Gold Beach in an LCT:

It was that final approach to the beach that I shall never forget, and it is as vivid to me now as it was then, when the full reality of war occurred. The German return fire was increasing and next ahead of us was a landing craft packed with infantry which received a direct hit. Because of the strict timing and spacing of vessels following us we could not stop or slow down, neither could we move to the right or left because of the lines of craft going in with us. We just ploughed on through the wreckage and those men struggling in the water. A few minutes either way and it could have been our craft that was hit.[13]

Gunner James W.A. Bright, 147th Field Regiment, Essex Yeomanry, Royal Artillery. (Author's collection)

Company Sergeant Major Jack Brown, also with the 147th Field Regiment,

---

11 Manuscript forwarded to author by I.G. Holley (Croydon, 1990).
12 F. Cooper, interview with author (Cleveland, 1992).
13 *WW2: People's War* <www.bbc.co.uk/ww2peopleswar> (accessed 28 February 2019).

remembered the distress of the infantry who were struggling ashore in deep water and his own feelings of helplessness in being unable to help them as his Landing Craft, Tank forged ahead to the beach:

> One thing I will never forget is seeing these poor chaps in the sea, these infantry blokes were only being kept afloat by their lifebelts. We had to get to the beach and there was no way our landing craft could avoid them, we just went through them, just passed them by. I don't know what happened to them, but we couldn't help the poor souls. We were getting closer and closer to the beach and had just finished firing our 25 pounders when we were hit. Lt Gregson had gone forward with the navy bloke to supervise the ramp going down when there was a violent explosion and the LCT shuddered. A shell had hit the ramp and wounded him and at least three of the navy people. Everybody struggled to get the ramp down, but it was jammed, and we drifted with the tide while they tried to fix the ramp.[14]

The tanks of 79th Armoured Division landed before the infantry. The 'Funnies', as they were called, were specialist armour from the 82nd Assault Squadron, Royal Engineers, and B Squadron, Westminster Dragoons.

Trooper Austin Baker, 4/7th Royal Dragoon Guards, Royal Armoured Corps, had a strange feeling of fear over what lay ahead as he and his comrades viewed the coast of France for the first time. As his LCT drew closer to the shore, it moved past large troopships which lay at anchor having already sent in their infantry landing craft:

> There were several cruisers firing broadside after broadside inland. We passed within a hundred yards of one which I remember was the *Belfast*, [and] the noise of her guns was ear-splitting. There was a big battleship firing in the distance, the *Rodney*, so the skipper announced over the loud hailer. Two squadrons of rocket-firing Typhoons roared over us after the 88[mm gun] which we knew was on the beach, [but] they didn't get it. The 88 knocked out two Churchill tanks before we arrived, [but] was itself knocked out by a flail tank. We saw a terrific explosion on the shore which was presumably one of the Churchills going up. There were destroyers right in close to the beach firing like mad, they must have

Trooper Austin Baker, 4/7th Royal Dragoon Guards, Royal Armoured Corps. (Author's collection)

14   *WW2: People's War* <www.bbc.co.uk/ww2peopleswar> (accessed 28 February 2019).

been almost aground. LCTs carrying batteries of rocket-firing guns and self-propelled guns added to the general din. Smoke hung over everything and we could just see the flashes of exploding shells on land.[15]

When Trooper Baker and his comrades were about half a mile from the shore, a naval motor-boat drifted past with a dead sailor lying across the foredeck. This was the first dead man Baker had seen, but it would not be the last. Some 200 yards from the beach, great spouts of water erupted near the LCT. The beach was now plainly in view, and it was black with men and machines, numerous LCTs discharging their cargoes amid the rough sea:

> I saw several lorries turn over in the breakers as our LCT went in and the bows touched the bottom. Before the ramp could be lowered our craft was swung round by the force of the current and the skipper had to back her out again among the infantry who were wading ashore up to their necks in water. We went in a second time and there was a terrific crash and the LCT jerked backwards, it had hit a mine. Number one, who had been standing in the bows, had been blown into the air. I think he broke a couple of ribs, but he got up and carried on directing the lowering of the ramp. Captain Collins' scout car was first down the ramp, [and] it was immediately hit and knocked out by a shell. The rest of our vehicles got safely ashore. My memories of the beach are very confused, and I remember noticing a number of DD tanks still there, but I couldn't see whose they were.[16]

Trooper Norman Smith, 5th Battalion Royal Tank Regiment, waited in his Cromwell tank with the engine running:

> We drove off down the ramp and into the drink, [but] it was far too deep. The first wave tore through all the ropes holding our bedding on the back of the tank, the second swamped the specially built air-intake chute. The engine stopped and we had water over the whole of the hull, and it was lashing around in the turret. Knocker Knight, our tank commander, leapt down into the water, opened up the flaps and pulled Ian, our driver, and Billy Cotton, our co-driver, out. A few yards away a vehicle hit a mine and men and debris were blown into the air. Shells were still coming over and there were many marine commandos lying dead on the beach.[17]

Captain John Leytham, a member of the 82nd Assault Squadron, Royal Engineers, landed with the Hampshires near Le Hamel. His commanding officer, Major Harold Elphinstone,[18] was killed, so Leytham was ordered to take control:

> The waiting is probably the worst time before any set piece operation such as Overlord. For myself it was not so much the fear of death, though that in itself is not an attractive

---

15 Manuscript forwarded to author by Brian Cook (Carnegie Heritage Centre, Hull, 2017).
16 Manuscript forwarded to author by Brian Cook (Carnegie Heritage Centre, Hull, 2017).
17 *WW2: People's War* <www.bbc.co.uk/ww2peopleswar> (accessed 26 September 2020).
18 Major Harold George Almond Elphinstone, Commander of 82nd Assault Squadron, Royal Engineers, was killed on 6 June 1944, aged 34. He is buried in Bayeux War Cemetery, France.

prospect, but more the fear of possible mutilation. Far worse than either of these possibilities was the uncertainty as to how one will react to one's baptism of fire. This operation was to be the most traumatic experience of my life.[19]

Sergeant John Bosworth, 25th Beach Recovery Company, REME, sat in his D8 armoured bulldozer looking through the observation visor as his landing craft hit the beach and shuddered as though it had been hit. A large house up the beach came into view, then smoke covered everything as a sailor waved Bosworth down the ramp. He was 200 yards from the shore and in 4 feet of water which gradually receded as he moved towards the beach. He then felt a sharp pain in his right hand, which he put down to him banging it due to his own clumsiness. The beach guide took him to the seawall, where he paused:

> To my left was a Sherman tank which was half-way up the wall and firing its gun. Between me and the tank was a sand-bagged emplacement with corrugated sheeting on top and some soldiers looking out from a hole between the bags. I switched off the engine and climbed out of the D8 to unwind the winch rope and carry out de-waterproofing when an explosion went off near the seawall which blew sand all over the place. "Come in here you silly bugger," shouted someone from the emplacement, "Jerries are dropping hand-grenades from up top."[20]

Bosworth was soon under cover, and in the emplacement he found six soldiers who had been ashore about an hour before him. They could not locate the RE section to which they had been attached and had built this shelter. They had liberated three bottles of rum and were eating compo rations, and a corporal told him they were waiting there until something happened. Bosworth replied: "I thought something had!" By now, Bosworth could see other landing craft disgorging their loads onto the beach:

> I could see other D8s ashore and thought it was time I showed myself, but a naval Beach Master said we should stay and clear the entry points as soon as the wall was breached. He then gave us a large tot of rum from a stone jar and, taking off my left-hand glove, I noticed there was blood where something had stuck in the palm of my hand. The officer said I should get it fixed up and pointed me to a forward aid post nearby. He said: "Take my dog with you, the walk will do her good and I can't leave here yet." I put on my steel helmet, got hold of the dog's lead and went to the FAP [First Aid Post] where the MO [Medical Officer] was up to his neck in wounded troops. He looked like a butcher with blood stains all over his white gown. "Take that bloody dog out of here," he said. "Whose is it?" I told him it belonged to the beach master and needed a walk. He looked at my hand and said: "That's an easy one, sergeant take out the shrapnel and sew him up, don't forget the injection." I got hold of the dog and went back to the beach master who was now questioning some prisoners: "Bloody Russians," he said. "Thanks for walking my dog and take it easy, have another rum."[21]

19 J. Leytham, correspondence with author (Swindon, 1994).
20 Miller, *Nothing Less than Victory* p. 359.
21 Miller, *Nothing Less than Victory*, p. 359.

Trooper Joe Minogue, a gunner on a flail tank with the Westminster Dragoons, knew he had to get his tank off the LCT as quickly as possible and begin flailing:

> We had to keep going until we reached the road and then turn right to the village of le Hamel. We saw the first couple of tanks get off and then the third. We were the fourth tank off the landing craft and were very apprehensive about being in the water. I think the driver of the tank was a bit more apprehensive than the rest of us because he blew part of the waterproofing off a little before he should have done, and we thought we'd been hit. I only had a forward view, but I could see the three tanks in front of us were not doing too well. The first AVRE tank had stopped because its commander had been killed. The second AVRE tank had been a bit close to him and had slewed to the right and hit a clay patch and been bogged down. The flail tank behind him was hit in the side and I saw the crew busily scrambling out. At that moment the tank commander hit me on the head with his microphone, which was his signal to do a 360-degree traverse of the gun turret to break the waterproofing around the turret ring. This gave me a fantastic view of the whole thing and as the turret came back towards the sea I could see the infantry beginning to come ashore. It was all a bit unreal, but it was a sobering sight as the Hampshires left their smaller infantry landing craft. Men were dropping while still in shallow water, to be dragged forward by their mates and left on the sand. All the while their comrades ran on in a purposeful steady jog trot which betrayed no sign of panic.[22]

Sergeant Stanley Clark, of the 1st Hampshires, was feeling miserable as his landing craft headed for the shore:

> It gradually got lighter and when we were about three miles from the shore the naval ships started their own bombardment. It took our minds off our own miserable conditions and made us feel a lot happier knowing that the enemy was on the receiving end of that lot. As we got nearer to the shore the enemy added his own fire in our direction. A hell of a lot of stuff was falling around us and some other landing craft took hits.[23]

Lieutenant Raymond Ellis, 82nd Assault Squadron, Royal Engineers, landed in his LCT with the Hampshires on Gold Beach. He had under his command three AVREs and two flail tanks, and was tasked with getting a lane cleared through the minefields for the infantry:

> The skipper drove the LCT hard onto the sand, the ramp lowered, and we went ashore without difficulty and blew off the waterproofing air inlet extensions and drove up the beach. We had to steer between barbed wire, tetrahedra and wooden poles with mines on facing out to sea. The peat clay composition of the beach caused us little trouble, [but] enemy shells were falling fast by this time as the leading AVREs, roughly in line abreast, reached the top of the beach near low sand-hills. I sent forward the first flail tank into the minefield to beat and explode the mines with its revolving chains. Many of the Hampshires

---

22 Manuscript forwarded to author by Brian Cook (Carnegie Heritage Centre, Hull, 2016).
23 S. Clark, conversation with author (Kent, 1995).

A dead German soldier lies outside the bunker he defended. (Courtesy of J. Styan)

were now waiting to get through the minefield. I regret to say many were killed and were lying blazing on fire, a rather horrifying sight. The shrapnel from exploding shells had ignited the mortar ammunition they were carrying on their backs. The noise of shells landing was terrific, many landing within 10 to 15 yards, they made a crunch not a bang.[24]

In a giant concrete casemate at Le Hamel, a captured Polish 77mm anti-tank gun was situated, the fire from which would be a problem to landing craft and tanks as they tried to get ashore and across the beach.

Tank commander Lieutenant David Render moved in toward the beach in an LCT and noticed that some vessels were opening their bow doors very early, whereas others were pushing past him and continuing to the beach. His craft opened its bow doors and his tank moved slowly into the sea. The Sherwood Rangers tank crews stood on the tank decks and braced themselves against the canvas sides of the flotation screen to help keep it firm as they entered the water. Accurate shellfire fell close to them, and some of the men standing were hit by shrapnel. Now the enemy had got the range it became a distinctly unhealthy place to linger. Tanks and flotation screens that had been hit by shrapnel bobbed in the water and finally sank, eight tanks of the

---

24 Manuscript forwarded to author by P. Cuerdon (Hampshire, 1991).

Sherwood Rangers disappearing below the waves, but most of the crews had time to escape in their flimsy dinghies. However, things would become much worse for those that made it to the beach, as Render recalled:

> The disintegration of the planned order of arrival caused by the shellfire and sea conditions meant that some of Hobart's Funnies were landing ahead of the intimate battle-tank support. A Sherman flail tank was already wading ashore through the surf in front of modified Churchill tanks belonging to the engineers. Clearing the water to its track line it blew off its waterproofing and engaged the drive to the large metal rotating drum extending from the front of the tank. The heavy ball chains fixed to the drum beat the ground in front of the tank in a flashing blur of metal, sand and exploding mines. The tank's driver selected a gear, eased the clutch and the flail started to move forward up the beach to begin clearing the first of several lanes through the minefields. As it moved beyond the waterline of the incoming tide it broke into the left-hand arc of fire of a concrete encased gun situated on the edge of Le Hamel. When its first target nosed into view the 77mm fired with a resounding high velocity crack and seconds later the flail was a burning wreck of flames and belching thick black oily smoke. The Le Hamel gun had claimed its first victim. One of the DDs from B Squadron was grinding up the shingle of the beach, water pouring from the running gear as the tank drove clear of the sea and stopped to disengage its propellers and drop its canvas screen. The tank was engaged by a burst of heavy machine-gun fire from a German position among the grass topped sand dunes. The next moment there was a blinding flash as the tank was hit by a 77mm round that set fire to the vehicle's spare fuel and the collapsing screen of canvas. Sergeant Bill Digby heard the troop commander reporting frantically on the radio that his tank was on fire until the voice stopped abruptly in mid-sentence and the net went dead.[25]

Brigadier Alexander Stanier, DSO, MC, commanding 231 Brigade, recalled the well-placed position of the 77mm gun at Le Hamel:

> The air strikes not only missed Le Hamel but most importantly it had missed the pillbox at the eastern end which caused us all the

Brigadier Alexander Stanier, DSO, MC, CO of 231 Brigade. (Author's collection)

25 Render, *Tank Action*, p. 17.

trouble. It was completely defiladed from the sea by massive concrete walls, and it had a magnificent enfilade shoot along the entire beach. Its low profile, and the way it blended into the background, meant that it was not bombarded from the sea.[26]

When Lieutenant Michael Trasenster, 4/7th Royal Dragoon Guards, landed on Gold Beach, he still felt as though his Sherman was rolling with the motion of the waves:

> On landing the tank seemed to continue to roll and pitch from the motion one had got used to from the rough LCT crossing of the Channel. D-Day had a certain unreality that I found not too conducive to the sort of fear we felt later. It seemed like an unpleasant dream, and one took part almost as an observer rather than a participant.[27]

Sergeant Stanley Clark, 1st Hampshires, felt his landing craft hit the bottom quite a way from the beach, but his luck held:

> We grounded quite a way out and waves were sweeping in as the ramp went down. The craft didn't stay grounded because one wave would sweep us in and the back surge would drag us out, then back again and so on, mostly at a nasty angle to the beach. A lot of men were lost as the craft came down on them while they were in the water, knocking them down and going straight over them. The officer near me was knocked over by a wave so I followed him and gave him a hand up. Fortunately for both of us a big wave literally picked us up and carried us to the shore.[28]

Sergeant James Bellows, serving with the Signals Platoon of the 1st Hampshires, landed in an LCT that contained, apart from its tanks, part of the battalion headquarters, three armoured engineer vehicles and two reconnaissance vehicles:

> One of the crocodiles [flame-throwing Churchill tanks] was first off and went straight under, all you could see was the snorkel and the top of the turret so the water must have been 10 feet deep. One recce vehicle was next, it turned right [and] went straight out to sea and we never saw it again. The next recce vehicle turned left and got ashore safely. The armoured bulldozer went straight down. One wheel on the trailer caught the chain on the ramp tipping the trailer over into the water, men fell off and the trailer floated away. One of my signallers had been bomb happy since Italy and was huddled under his gas-cape shaking like a jelly. The naval officer commanding our craft said he was returning to England for repairs, and nothing would persuade him to change his mind. I hailed a nearby LCA, and he came up to the ramp. We loaded our stores and the brigade link set on its trolley. I left the bomb happy signaller behind. The LCA pulled up, the ramp went down, and a sailor said we were among mines. I told them they would be alright, but they pulled back. An LCT was approaching with its ramp already down, we hailed her and transferred.[29]

---

26   Manuscript forwarded to author by P. Cuerdon (Hampshire, 1991).
27   M. Trasenster, correspondence with author (1990).
28   S. Clark, correspondence with author (Kent, 1993).
29   Thompson, *Victory in Europe*, p. 68.

Into the Breach: Jig Sector, Gold Beach, 6 June 1944   165

A knocked-out Sherman tank at the water's edge on Gold Beach, 6 June 1944. (Author's collection)

Bellows thought his LCT had grounded in deep water, but his officer was confident they were in the shallows:

> We grounded and the ramp went down, we were a hell of a way from the shore and the waves were still passing us, I thought they were pretty bloody high for shallow water. I said: "We are not in shallow water here, we're in deep water." All sorts of things were going off around us at this time, but we were in our own little world. This Sub-Lt said: "We've grounded" and we started arguing about the depth of the water. He called for a rod, and he put it in the water and said: "Four foot six." I said: "You must be bloody joking, we're in deep water and stuck on an obstacle." He said: "No we're not, I'm in charge of this ship and I'm captain", stupid sod. So I went to my chaps and told them to be prepared for a bloody wet landing.[30]

30 Arthur, M., *Forgotten Voices of the Second World War* (London: Ebury Press, 2004), p. 312.

Captain Alastair Morrison, 4/7th Royal Dragoon Guards, watched as the tank in front of him shuddered to a halt and a great black plume of smoke shot out of the turret, rising into the air in a long column. Only one crew member escaped. Morrison recalled:

> This was unexpected, and while I was watching it another tank stopped and exactly the same thing happened. We had no idea until then that a Sherman could blow up this way. Michael Trasenster likened this period to a very unpleasant dream: "You feel you are a spectator the whole time," he said. "The whole thing is such a shock to the system." This was enhanced by an unwarranted trust in our armour against battle-field hazards and isolation caused by being deaf to most external noise from wearing radio headsets and the general noise of a tank.[31]

Captain Alastair Morrison, 4/7th Royal Dragoons Guards, Royal Armoured Corps. (Author's collection)

Meanwhile, David Render watched as the 77mm Polish gun at Le Hamel continued to take a heavy toll of the advancing tanks of the Sherwood Rangers:

> With no time to stop and find out what had happened to his fellow B Squadron crewmates, Digby pressed on up the beach until the almighty clang of an armour piercing shell brought his Sherman to an abrupt stop. The AP round came into the turret slicing through three inches of armoured steel, wounded the gunner and took off Digby's[32] legs above the knee before ricocheting off the inside of the tank and hitting another crew member in the foot. The grotesquely injured commander collapsed onto the turret floor in an agony of mangled limbs and blood. Despite being hit there was no fire, and the vehicle was drivable. With presence of mind, born from survival, the driver threw the tank into reverse and backed down the beach out of the line of fire.[33]

Private I.G. Holley, of the 1st Hampshires, saw a signaller crawling on his hands and knees in the water, who still had on his headphones and was trailing his radio behind him. Holley thought he had been hit:

> I learned later that he'd had a relapse of malaria and had no idea what he was doing. The beach was filled with half-bent running figures and we knew from experience that the

---

31 Manuscript forwarded to author by T. Hewson (Dudley, 1990).
32 Corporal William Digby, Sherwood Rangers, Nottinghamshire Yeomanry, Royal Armoured Corps, died of his wounds on 8 June 1944, aged 22. He is buried in Bayeux War Cemetery, France.
33 Render, *Tank Action*, p. 18.

safest place was to get as near to Jerry as we could. A near one blasted sand over me and my set went dead, it was riddled with shrapnel. A sweet rancid smell was everywhere, it was the smell of burnt explosives, torn flesh and ruptured earth. High up on the beach a flail tank was knocked out. I saw B Company HQ group take cover behind it as a shell scored a direct hit on them. They were gone in a blast of smoke out of which came cartwheeling through the air the torn shrieking body of a stretcher bearer, with the red cross on his arm clearly visible.[34]

Stanley Clark ran up the beach as his 1st Hampshires comrades fell around him:

Our instructions were to get off the beach as quickly as possible and to stop for nothing. We didn't need telling twice and set off at a run through the flak that was coming in our direction. I remember going up the beach through the hedgehog defensive obstacles set in the sand, each one with a mine fixed to the seaward side. As I ran Cpl Bill Winter, MM, was on my left and he was wounded within half-an-hour, on my right was Pte Monty Bishop. Bullets were flying everywhere, but strangely with the noise of the bombardment, the wind and the sea you couldn't hear them. You didn't realise anyone had been hit until you reached the sand dunes and when I looked back I saw our men lying, some wounded some dead, on the beach.[35]

Having fallen asleep on the approach to Gold Beach, carrier driver Private Reginald Shickle, of the 2nd Machine-gun Battalion the Cheshire Regiment, woke to hear a naval officer making an address over the tannoy:

I was woken up by: "Now hear this, now hear this." I must have dozed off, but how I don't know, for the noise was tremendous. It came from the battleships all around us and the shells and rockets that were being fired towards the beach. 200 yards, 100 yards then crash, and our craft came to a shuddering halt amid a loud explosion. A jeep that should have been first off was no more, [and] in its place was a gaping hole in the deck. The ramp went down and with the engine of my carrier roaring I rammed it into first gear, let off the brakes and shot over the hole into the sea. Its tracks gripped the beach and we moved slowly forward. An eternity, then fresh air. On the shore Haggerty, one of my crew, was looking dumbly down at his leg. His foot had been blown off; this was our first casualty.[36]

As casualties mounted, Corporal Fred Cooper was forced to take command of his section of the 1st Hampshires:

Our section sergeant was killed by a sniper, but I didn't have the nerve to look at his body. We had to get off the beach and I knew I had to take over. On finding my Bren-gunner dead I told another man to pick it up even though he wasn't keen, so I ordered him to do

---

34 Manuscript forwarded to author by I.G. Holley (Croydon, 1990).
35 Manuscript forwarded to author by S. Clark (Kent, 1993).
36 R. Shickle, correspondence with author (Basingstoke, 1991).

so. I noticed four Germans going into some kind of dug out, so I threw in two Bakelite grenades after them. I didn't stop to see the results.[37]

Major Richard B. Gosling, 147th Field Regiment, Essex Yeomanry, Royal Artillery, who landed with the Hampshires, recounted the heavy opposition:

> A swarm of angry bees buzzed just above our heads, [and] our Hampshire comrades were war experienced and recognised it as German heavy machine-gun fire and ran forward. In front of us the sand furrowed and spurted from Spandaus firing down the beach in enfilade on fixed lines from Le Hamel. The colonel shouted at us to lie down but the wet sand was unattractive, so we sprinted for the cover of the dunes 50 yards ahead. Some mortar bombs and 88mm shells were falling and one landed just behind the CO and I, smashing one of his arms and filling my leg with shell fragments. We made it to the dunes and threw ourselves into a depression in the sand. Bombs and shells continued to fall and machine-gun fire swarmed through the reeds above our heads. We lay very flat and still and after a few minutes German fire seemed to have switched down to the beach to engage another flight of landing craft. I crawled up the dune to peer over the other side and was horrified to see a German 20 yards away, I fired my revolver in his general direction and slid back. A Hampshire corporal lying near me, already wounded, knelt up to look over the dune and was at once shot through the chest by a sniper.[38]

Private James Aldred, 1st Hampshires, got to the sea wall on Gold Beach and was ordered over it. As he did so, the Germans opened up with terrific Spandau fire that cut down his comrades, and he escaped only because he slipped accidentally as the burst of fire came:

> My major and three other men came forward and he hollered out: "Follow me." I followed. Suddenly, I thought I'd been hit and keeled over. I was paralysed down one side. I dropped my rifle and crawled along, as I looked up there was a blast and the left eye of my glasses shattered. I rolled over on my back and found my spare pair of glasses in my pouch and put them on. I looked up and was able to read a sign that said '*Achtung Minen*'. I was crawling through a minefield. I took my bayonet and was prodding the ground as I was creeping along. I lost all track of time.[39]

Trooper Kenneth Mayo, Sherwood Rangers, hit the beach with the Hampshires:

> The infantry of the 1st Hampshires were taking all possible cover on the beach from the withering fire from the pillboxes and the 88s on the high ground, which knocked out the tank on our right. It was a terrible sight to see the crew gunned down as they bailed out from the blazing vehicle. We then returned the fire from the pillboxes with success. At last, the sappers taped off the exits from the beach and we all began to move off through the sand-dunes. When about 50 yards into our lane there was a loud explosion, [as] we hit

---

37 F. Cooper, interview with author (Cleveland, 1992).
38 Saunders, *Gold Beach – Jig*, p. 75.
39 *WW2: People's War* <www.bbc.co.uk/ww2peopleswar> (accessed 1 December 2020).

a mine which damaged our nearside track, we were immobile. This didn't prevent us from using our firepower to hit the many targets which presented themselves, in support of the advance and to try to winkle out the snipers who were proving a real menace.[40]

The Hampshires moved across the open beach in a hurricane of flying steel and were unable to make a swift penetration of the defences. Machine-gun and mortar fire swept the bridgehead and artillery fire cracked overhead, smashing into tanks and landing craft alike. As the Hampshires pressed forward into this fusillade, they found their way barred by deep minefields fronting the German defences, every inch of which was covered by enemy fire. At 0900 hours, two companies passed through a gap on the eastern side of Le Hamel and attacked Asnelles from the rear. The flail tanks that had survived the initial attack did sterling work clearing paths through the wire and mines for the infantry, though not without cost.

Private James Aldred, 1st Hampshires, came close to death on more than one occasion. He was left stunned by the experience of being in battle and started to hallucinate:

> My brain was numbed and all I could hear was the sounds of bullets flying past. I looked up and saw a figure in white beckoning me to come closer, I thought it was St Peter. I must have been delirious as right in front of me was this figure. My mind was focussed on it and wanted to go towards it. When I finally crossed the minefield the figure had gone but it gave me the strength to live. I lay down and heard voices, I looked up, they were Germans, I gave them my name, rank and number, as was required of prisoners of war. A voice said: "Tommy, we are prisoners and are here to pick up the wounded."[41]

The German prisoners picked up Private Aldred and cradled him in a greatcoat, caring for him as they carried him off the battlefield. As a result of his injuries, he lost one lung and some ribs, but survived the war.

Grenadier Walter Hubbne, in his bunker as the British DD tanks landed, watched these strange-looking monsters advance towards him while firing their guns:

> On the command we opened fire, then saw lots of strange looking tanks coming off the boats and I thought: "My God, if they get to us, we are finished." Some of the tanks sank in the sea but others rolled up the beach and we could not stop them. But we heard our anti-tank guns firing and three of the tanks were destroyed. The others were shooting at us and all kinds of debris was flying about. I felt something hit my forehead and blood flowed so I wrapped a handkerchief around my head. There was a horrible crash and the bunker filled with smoke. I fell down and saw bodies and thought it was the end. Then the *Feldwebel* came and helped me up and together we started firing again with an undamaged machine-gun, [then] after a while we heard a lot of noise behind us and realised that the enemy tanks and infantry were in our rear. Suddenly there was a lot more noise and the whole bunker collapsed [–] a tank had come up and fired a heavy charge that destroyed everything.[42]

---

40 Bowman, *Air War D-Day*, p. 23.
41 *WW2: People's War* <www.bbc.co.uk/ww2peopleswar> (accessed 1 December 2020).
42 Manuscript forwarded to author by Brian Cook (Carnegie Heritage Centre, Hull, 2016).

Lieutenant Anthony Barraclough, 82nd Assault Squadron, Royal Engineers, pressed forward into the sand dunes when his tank hit a mine:

> When we landed, I was leading a line of flail tanks clearing a path through the enemy minefields. As we went up the beach my tank hit a mine and there was a hell of a bang. Although the tank was disabled no-one was hurt and the tank behind me took up the lead and went over the top of a sand-dune directly ahead. What none of us knew, and what we couldn't see from our tanks, was that beyond the dune was a culvert which the Germans had flooded. The tank drove straight into the culvert and sank. Two of the crew drowned but the rest escaped only to be cut down by mortar fire. There was only one thing I could do, so I built a bridge on top of the submerged tank from rubble while under continuous mortar fire. I spent my 21st birthday in the early part of the invasion.[43]

This was a crucial moment in the battle for Jig Sector, as the CO of the Hampshires, Lieutenant Colonel Harold David Nelson-Smith, MC, had been wounded and the Hampshires' command group was paralysed. The second-in-command, Major Arthur Martin, was summoned to take charge of the brigade, but no sooner had he extricated himself from the battle to join headquarters than he was himself killed.[44] Some time elapsed before Major David Warren was contacted and ordered to take command. However, the company commanders still leading their troops did not wait for orders, but led their men on towards their objectives.

Sergeant James Bellows of the 1st Hampshires got to the road beyond the beach and saw a touching scene among the carnage:

> Just off the beach there were two or three little cottages and opposite these there was a road that led to the beach. One of our men had been killed here and his mates had just dug a hole, put him in and covered him up with soil. The reason they had done this was that if they hadn't it was more than probable he would have been run over by tanks and carriers. It was a humanitarian gesture you might say. Out of one of these cottages came an old lady, goodness knows how old she was, and her skirts were touching the ground. She hobbled across the road carrying a posy of flowers which she placed on the grave. She knelt down, said a prayer, got up and made the sign of the cross and then walked back to her cottage. It was one of the most moving sights I think I saw in the war.[45]

1st Battalion Dorsetshire Regiment

On the left flank of the Hampshire Regiment, the 1st Dorsets landed to the east of Jig Sector, Gold Beach. Their landing was to be relatively easy compared to the Hampshires. They had minefields to negotiate, but the Germans relied on the presence of a marsh to deter a landing and so the area was lightly held. B Company of the 1st Battalion landed at 0737 hours and was

---

43 Manuscript forwarded to author by A. Barraclough (Herts, 1988).
44 Major Arthur Charles Woolcott Martin, DSO, Dorsetshire Regiment, attached to 1st Hampshire Regiment, died on 6 June 1944, aged 27. He is buried in Ryes War Cemetery, Bazenville, France.
45 J. Bellows, correspondence with author (Yorkshire, 1990).

unlucky to be in the area where most German troops were concentrated, coming under heavy and concentrated fire from the defenders. Private Ted Vigour, of the 1st Dorsets, was with B Company when they hit the beach:

> We felt great fear and tension as we jumped out of the LCI under heavy fire. One of our lads fell face down in the water but nobody stopped. I rushed up the sand and shingle with bullets whizzing passed me and actually reached the top of the beach. I heard yells and screams behind me on each side which sounded bad, but our medics soon tended to the wounded. I lay head down in a state of funk with the remaining lads falling down around me in the same state, but we grinned in relief to be alive. The noise was terrific, and we heard some Jerry machine-guns not far away. A lieutenant and a sergeant came up and urged us on, so we crawled off the beach a little way and lost two more men. There was green grass and debris and a lot of mist and smoke. When I glanced back I was amazed at the sight of the invasion fleet, it made me feel we couldn't lose.[46]

The Dorsets were pinned down on their section of the beach and were unable to move forward to cut a path through the wire and minefields. To their front stood two pillboxes and well-hidden machine-gun posts. Behind them, the beach was being swept by heavy fire coming from Le Hamel. The Dorsets now knew that the only hope of survival was to get off the beach.

Private Kenneth McFarlane, 1st Dorsets, noticed a flurry of activity as dawn broke on 6 June. Sat in his Bren-carrier, he had a limited view but could plainly see fleets of planes flying overhead:

> Then at last we started a square run for the beach. Suddenly there was a big bang from the stern, and we started to go in at an acute angle. The first carrier drove off on an angle and turned turtle. Our landing craft drifted a few feet then the boat marshal waved me to go out. I stood up on my seat and said that the tank was supposed to go next. He said: "Bollocks, get out now." So I shut my eyes and eased off the ramp with my heart in my mouth. As the next bit had been practised so often, I carried on as though in a drill, over the sand, through the gap, onto the beach road, turn right, forward a few yards and wait for my anti-tank gun crew to join me. This they did eventually and my sergeant, Lofty Dawson, said: "Get the waterproofing off." While I did this he joined the crew in a ditch. I asked Lofty what the puffs of smoke were all over the sky. "Airbursts," he said. What are they for, I asked, and when he said they were shrapnel shells I shrank as low as I could to finish the job without being too big a target. My D-Day was a very long day. I had no watch, but time seemed to stand still.[47]

Private Frank Wiltshire was part of a 1st Dorsets mortar crew and only 22 years old when he landed on Gold Beach:

---

46 Saunders, *Gold Beach – Jig*, p. 76.
47 Manuscript forwarded to author by P. Cuerdon (Hampshire, 1992).

Troops take cover from heavy machine-gun fire before advancing up the beach. (Author's collection)

> I jumped from the LCA straight into about seven feet of water. I was number one on the mortar team and I had to jettison the base plate of my mortar as it weighed over 50 pounds and it would have kept me under. After wading ashore, I made a dash across the sand to reach the bank. Eventually we managed to assemble one mortar out of the six, the other five were lost. I got the mortar in a firing position, but the barrel was full of sand and water because somebody had dragged it along the beach. After seeing my friends killed and injured around me I thought it would be my turn soon. I managed to get off the beach after a couple of hours; the bloodshed was terrible, and the Germans were tough fighters.[48]

An officer of the 1st Dorsets left an anonymous account of the carnage he witnessed:

> We had to move across the sand at some speed, most of us had seen men shot before but nothing like the damage caused by Spandau fire and 88s. Men were blown apart and in the case of machine-gun fire men were hit a dozen times at once, [with] not a chance for them to live. We had been trained in almost all aspects of war and actually knew what to expect.

---

48 P. Cuerdon, correspondence with author (Hampshire, 1992).

However, it was not enough to prepare you for this kind of carnage. I took a few minutes on the beach to comprehend, adjust and then to move forward.[49]

Hobart's 'Funnies' to the rescue

Specialist armour came to the assistance of the Dorsets, with flail tanks smashing a way through the minefields and wire obstacles. However, the engineers were hampered by the soft marshy ground and heavy clay. Trooper John Wilson, Royal Artillery, had the job of working in a team that laid down steel matting over the waterlogged ground and sand which would prevent the following vehicles from being bogged down, yet things did not go to plan:

> I was one of the roly-poly team whose job it was to drag out onto the shore a huge roll of matting and wire-mesh. The roly-poly was about eight feet in diameter with an axle to which ropes were attached. Most of us stripped down to our vest, pants and gym shoes for this task. We hit two mines as we were going in but that didn't stop us, although our ramp was damaged and the officer standing on it killed. We grounded on a sandbank and the first man off was a commando sergeant in full kit who disappeared like a stone into six feet of water. We grasped the ropes of the roly-poly and plunged down the ramp into the icy water. The roly-poly was quite unmanageable in the rough water and the swell dragged us away toward some mines. We let go of the ropes and swam and scrambled ashore. All I had on was my PT shorts, I had lost my shoes and vest in the struggle. George Chapman in the Bren-carrier was the first vehicle off the LCT; it floated for a moment and drifted onto a mine and sank. George dived overboard and swam ashore. Our survey jeep came off the LCT and went down like a stone, it being so overloaded. The MO's jeep followed and met a similar fate – we pulled out a half-drowned driver. The rising tide helped the LCT lift off the sandbank and it moved inshore, squashing the two jeeps flat. The battery half-track made it and was going up the beach with me running behind it, my gear was on it and when it stopped I struggled into my clothes. The beach was strewn with wreckage and a tank blazed nearby. There were bundles of blankets, bodies and bits of bodies. One poor bloke near me had been cut in half by a shell and his lower part had collapsed in a bloody heap in the sand. Several shells burst overhead, and shrapnel spattered on the beach as machine-gun bullets were kicking up the sand.[50]

Trooper Edward Lawrenson, B Squadron, Westminster Dragoons, moved forward in his flail tank once they had beached. Dodging between the beach obstacles, he headed for the thick wire before the sand dunes, with other tanks going before him:

> We flogged through the heavy barbed-wire and into the minefield while another flail tank turned right heading for Le Hamel. My tank hit a mine which blew off the front bogey assembly and later we found the front driving sprocket had been hit by an AP

---

49 Newspaper cutting forwarded to author by J. Styan (Hull, 1991).
50 Manuscript forwarded to author by J. Wilson (Blackburn, 1990).

Stretcher-bearers worked ceaselessly caring for the wounded, often under fire. (Courtesy of P. Cuerdon)

[armour-piercing] round. Over 40 percent of our chains had been blown off and the explosion had damaged the radio, so I was sent back through the minefield to find Major Elphinstone who commanded our beaching party.[51] He had been killed and the beach was now under heavy fire from strongpoints in Le Hamel.[52]

Tank Commander Charles Wilmot, of the 24th Lancers, landed with his crew at Arromanches:

As we went over the Channel the Navy were running up and down the beaches with their rocket ships firing salvoes. When we got to the beaches the Beach Master shepherded us off the LST and then we moved up the beach. We had a little bit of an explosive charge to unseal the equipment and after that we could operate the guns. The beaches were all

---

51 Major Harold George Almond Elphinstone, 82nd Assault Squadron, Royal Engineers, was killed in action on 6 June 1944, aged 34. He is buried in Bayeux War Cemetery, France.
52 E. Lawrenson, correspondence with author (Brentwood, 1993).

mined, and we had to follow the white tapes showing where they had been cleared, but the worst thing was the snipers. Anyway, I didn't last long as an 8-pound mortar bomb came over and hit the tank turret; of course we got blown to the bottom of it. It was all down to sympathetic detonation, which means that the power with which we were hit set the ammunition off around the tank. There was a round up the spout and the pressure set that off as well. I was in the way of the recoil which came back and smashed my arm up. We managed to crawl out and the medical people were soon with us in a half-track. We were taken down the beach where all the medical units were and put in a compound. Later I ended up on a hospital ship, there were quite a few Germans aboard – two of them refused to be treated and died.[53]

Trooper Joe Minogue of the Westminster Dragoons drove his flail tank into the sand dunes:

We had reached the high-water mark and began to flail, and I remember hitting the first mine on the first rise of the sand dunes. How many mines we flailed I have no idea but when we reached the road the tank commander told us that the tank behind was doing well and was following us along. We turned right when we reached the road and at the first corner there was a dead German there, it was like something from a film, he was young, huddled up and hatless, or rather his helmet had fallen off. He was very blonde, and it seemed so stupid in a way that there should be a blonde dead German on the very first corner.[54]

Private Lewis Richards, of the 50 Div Signals, moved off the beach with 231 Brigade's CO, Brigadier Stanier, and found the route inland blocked:

There was a big crater holding everything up and blocking the coast road. It was being filled in by Royal Engineers using their heavy equipment. The beach parties and tank crews were waiting patiently to get forward. Soon after the tanks rumbled past and men from 47 Royal Marine Commando came along. They had lost a lot of their equipment after a rough landing and busied themselves getting re-armed by picking up discarded British and German weapons and ammunition. Then they moved off.[55]

Private Lewis Richards, MM, 50th Divisional Signals. (Author's collection)

Major Richard Gosling, of the 147 Field Regiment, Essex Yeomanry, was wounded as the troops made it to the sand dunes:

---

53 C. Wilmot, correspondence with author (Tunbridge, 1991).
54 Newspaper cutting forwarded to author by R. Protheroe (Hull, 1993).
55 Manuscript forwarded to author by D. Harrison (Bristol, 2014).

> Just behind the sand-dunes there was a pillbox which the German troops had used as sleeping quarters. It had been turned into a little first-aid post for us and we crawled into it, smelly as it was. The remains of their breakfast lay on the table still, plus some red wine. There was a letter from a French girl to one of the Germans. It said *"Hans Cheri"*, Dear Hans, *"Je vous attendrais"*, I will meet you, *"Derriere le pillbox"*, behind the pillbox, *"A six heures du soir le six juin"*, at 6pm on 6th June. It was signed Madeleine. We all looked out for her to come along but Madeleine never did.[56]

Joe Minogue had flogged a path through the sand dunes with his flail tank and watched with satisfaction as troops and vehicles came streaming through:

> We were sitting by the track smoking and looking out to sea. A stream of vehicles was now using the lane we had cleared through the mines. At that moment we felt proud that all the training we had undergone had been worthwhile and that the faith of the commander of 79th Armoured Division, Major General Percy Hobart, in his beloved Funnies had been justified. While we were having a smoke Neville Duell was scrabbling about idly in the loose flailed earth: "What's this then," he asked in alarm. It was a German box mine which the flail had missed, it was armed with the wooden wedge that drove into a trip wire showing red side up. We shouted a warning, got back into the tank and Sgt Hardy turned the tank round and we went back to detonate the mine. This done we resumed our interrupted smoke. I watched in horror as the driver of a Ben-gun carrier got down to pick up some object in his path which turned out to be an anti-personnel mine that blew off his hands. His screams, as his hands were blown off, put all the other noise in the shade.[57]

By 0900 hours, the Hampshires and Dorsets had moved off the beach and began attacking Asnelles from the rear. The village fell by noon, and in the streets civilians walked about as though they were watching the making of a movie. The CO of the Hampshires had been wounded and his second-in-command killed, and all units involved suffered heavy casualties.

2nd Battalion Devonshire Regiment

The reserve battalion of 231 Brigade, the 2nd Devons, landed at 0815 hours on a beach still being swept by enemy fire. Obstacles on the beach, both above and below water, were still intact and Le Hamel had not yet been taken yet. Lance Corporal Norman Travett, of the 2nd Devons, recalled the stiff opposition they found as they came ashore:

> When we beached we had to jump into the water, and it came up to waist height. While I was wading ashore I lost a couple of friends as the beach had been bombed beforehand and left great craters below the water that we could not see. Some poor buggers actually walked into these craters and were drowned as the weight of their packs pulled them under. There

---

56 *WW2: People's War* <www.bbc.co.uk/ww2peopleswar> (accessed 20 June 2014).
57 Manuscript forwarded to author by Brian Cook (Carnegie Heritage Centre, Hull, 2016).

was quite a number of dead bodies in the water but not necessarily from my own regiment because we went in second flight. I think the Dorsets were in front of us, then it was the Devons. But prior to that the engineers had been in to demolish mines on poles to make way for the tanks to get ashore – that must have taken some guts. We managed to get ashore, and we had to run up the beach, which seemed to take a long time until we reached the wall. I could see bullets splashing in the water and in the sand beside us. We got what shelter we could under the cover of the wall because there was considerable fire coming from pillboxes on our right. It was a low wall and I think it formed part of the road that ran along the top of the beach. There were lots of soldiers with me and everyone was trying to get as much cover as they could.[58]

Private David Powis, of the 2nd Devons, felt his landing craft suddenly come to a grinding halt as the ramp went down. Men ran off it into the tracer bullets that flew all around, and even into the craft:

We stepped of the craft and hit the water and went down and down and down; would we ever stop this long underwater descent? When our feet eventually touched the bottom of the exceptionally deep channel, we automatically bent our knees and pushed upwards. A brief intake of fresh air refilled our lungs and down we went again. The weight of our equipment should have taken us to the bottom much quicker but the air in our Mae West life belts was impeding our descent. A strong sense of relief came when on our next descent we were able to push upwards sooner than before. Again and again we were able to break the surface a little easier for air, our feet were at last more frequently contacting the sea bed. At long last our heads were at a level where we could get an occasional glimpse of what lay ahead. We had survived that ordeal without discarding a thing, including rifle and folding bicycles.[59]

Private George Laity, a Piat gunner with the 2nd Devons, was apprehensive as he approached the shore:

I wondered what we would be in for when we hit the beach. As we got nearer shells began to burst around the landing craft and we beached at half-tide with iron obstacles still sticking out of the water. The noise, the infantry, the little LCAs, all was confusion and bewilderment. German 88s started pounding the beach and my company was pinned down, it seemed endless.[60]

Private Reginald Burge, also with the 2nd Devons, landed in a waterproof carrier that was loaded to the hilt with armament:

My carrier had false sides to enable it to float and was filled with .303 ammunition, mortar bombs, petrol in jerry cans and a roll of wattle fencing tied to the front. As we approached

---

58 N. Travett, correspondence with author (Yorkshire, 1989).
59 Saunders, *Gold Beach – Jig*, p. 35.
60 G. Laity, correspondence with author (Essex, 1991).

Priest self-propelled guns coming ashore with the second wave. (Author's collection)

the beach the tide was so strong that we drifted over to the next sector and landed broadside against obstacles which had mines attached to the tops. The ramp was lowered, and we could see the bodies of the commandos who had gone ahead of us. I drove off, turned left and reached the beach safely, although two other carriers were drowned in deep water. We pushed on up the beach amid the chaos and noise of the Naval bombardment and the rocket barrage. We were ordered to keep going forward and we made our way down the country roads. As we turned onto a main road we hit a mine on the grass verge which knocked out the front bogey, [but] nobody was injured so we shortened the track and drove on. How we got off the beach I'll never know [–], why wasn't I one of those killed? We pushed on until evening when we re-grouped at Le Hamel.[61]

Lieutenant Frank Pearson, 2nd Devons, was just 20 years old but had already twice been wounded and had contracted malaria before D-Day, from which he was still recovering:

I would not have missed D-Day for anything. My past experiences in Italy and Sicily had made me a realist and I thought our chances of survival were small. Near the beach the noise was tremendous with everything banging away. Our LCA grounded on a sandbank but came off again and drifted ashore. We waded onto the beach and up to the high-water mark without any casualties. One or two tanks near us had been knocked out and beside

---

61 Paper cutting forwarded to author by N. Hardy (Hull, 1991).

one lay a Tommy without a head. It is strange to remember such details after all this time, but they stay at the back of your mind like old photographs. The tide was now coming in fast, bringing with it more troops, and the beach got smaller as their numbers grew. It seemed to me as if the whole of the 50th Division was pinned down on this beach and likely to remain so. Then the breakthrough came when one of the Funnies climbed the seawall and began to flail a path across the minefield. We peered over the wall holding our breath and watched it flail a path through. It seemed as if most of 231 Brigade and forward elements of the 50th Division followed in the wake of that one flail tank. Perhaps it wasn't like that, but that's how it seemed to me.[62]

Lieutenant Colonel Stanley Christopherson, Squadron Commander with the Sherwood Rangers, was to support the Devons with his DD tanks when they landed on Gold Beach:

When we were about a mile from land, all crews were mounted and tank engines running in preparation for the landing. The craft had to be steered through numerous underwater obstacles, just visible above the water, but also had to avoid other LCTs struggling with the same difficulty and all converging on the same point; it was a formidable task for the craft commander. We did however ram an obstruction, an iron stake, fortunately not capped with a mine, which prevented further forward movement, but caused no extensive damage. It took a little time to extricate ourselves; we had to reverse and make a complete turn, and our nose pointed once again towards England, I had a sneaking desire to continue in that direction. About 100 yards from the shore the craft commander gave the order: "Full speed ahead" and drove his craft at the shore, when the bows touched down the ramp was released with a crash, down which each tank slowly and painfully made its way through a few feet of water onto the shore. As I landed, I noticed Bill Enderby, wounded in the arm, and in obvious pain, slowly making his way onto a tank landing craft, which was just about to reverse and return to England with other wounded on board. I waved to him and continued to extricate my way up the beach, which was littered with a variety of army equipment, including knocked out tanks, and pitted with deep bomb holes, which made progress difficult.[63]

Sergeant William Edward Wills of the 2nd Devons was walking up the beach looking for a way off when he heard a familiar voice:

As I walked along the beach trying to locate the track up which it had been intended the vehicles should drive to the de-waterproofing area, I heard a voice say: "Hello Wills, get me a blanket if you can." There was this bedraggled figure half sitting, half lying against the sand dunes. He had a Devon Regiment shoulder badge and a major's crown. I looked hard at his badly smashed face and was eventually able to recognise Major Howard who commanded C Company. Looking around the beach the only blankets to be seen were draped very regimentally around the haversacks on the backs of the military policemen,

---

62 F. Pearson, correspondence with author (Hampshire, 1992).
63 Holland (ed.), J., *An Englishman at War, the Wartime Diaries of Stanley Christopherson, DSO, MC, TD 1939–45* (London: Penguin, 2014), pp. 380–81.

who were sign-posting the various beach areas. As I walked by one, he dropped suddenly and lay very still except for twitching in his hands. A bullet had gone straight through his tin hat from back to front and taken some of his brains with it. There was nothing I could do for him, so I removed his neatly folded blanket and took it back to Major Howard.[64]

Lance Corporal Norman Travett crouched for cover behind the low sea wall with other men of the 2nd Devons, along with officers and senior NCOs. He knew the people in charge and held them in high esteem:

> Some of our leaders were fearless. The average chap like me found as much cover as he could, but these people would say: "Come on we can get out of here it'll be alright." The rest of us thought twice about it. People were being killed all around because shelling was still coming from inland onto the beach. We could not possibly advance until these pillboxes had been destroyed. We lay there in our wet trousers with water oozing out of our boots for what seemed ages. Eventually the most troublesome pillbox was silenced. That was when I saw my first dead German, a gruesome sight. Those poor chaps had probably been called up for service like us and had no wish to be where they were. They didn't stand a chance, not here, they just, well, what could they do?[65]

When Lieutenant Colonel C.A.R. Nevill, the 2nd Devons' CO, landed he found a scene of mayhem. Tanks were hit and burst into flames, smothering the beach in black choking smoke, while tracer bullets criss-crossed the beach and mortar bombs thudded into the sand. He found a pillbox directly to his front:

> The gun had fortunately been knocked out and a number of dead German soldiers lay beside it. We expected to see a nice clear beach with all the correct signs neatly arrayed pointing the way to our assembly areas. A very different picture greeted us, the beach was covered by a swarm of troops lying flat on their faces, ostrich like, trying to make as small targets of themselves as possible. All was not well.[66]

Lieutenant Colonel C.A.R. Nevill DSO, CO of 2nd Battalion Devonshire Regiment. (Courtesy of S. Chalk)

64 Manuscript forwarded to author by Brian Cook (Carnegie Heritage Centre, Hull, 2016). Major M.W. Howard survived the war.
65 N. Travett, correspondence with author (Yorkshire, 1989).
66 Saunders, *Gold Beach – Jig*, p. 89.

Off the beach and moving inland

Sergeant Wills never forgot the harrowing scene he witnessed as he made his way off the beach:

> At this stage I felt no fear, only discomfort and disgust at losing my kit, my weapon and my jeep. Making my way off the beach I saw many dead men and quite a few stretcher bearers carrying wounded off the beach, and I could see order was coming into the activities of all on the beach. Then I saw one incident which upset me more than a little. An amphibious tank came out of the sea, paused and then made its way along the beach with its canvas screen still up. A sapper went to move across its path about ten yards in front of it when he was hit by a bullet. The tank driver obviously could not see him and drove on, one track passed over the pelvis and buttocks of the fallen man, killing him.[67]

Private George Laity moved off the beach with his 2nd Devons comrades and found himself in a surreal world:

> We moved inland with no real idea of time; it was then I saw my first dead German laying in the road. I remember seeing dead cows in the fields, blown up like barrage balloons, they were laid on their sides with their legs sticking out.[68]

Lieutenant John Absalom, 25th Light Anti-aircraft Regiment, Royal Artillery, who pulled out with his unit from the confusion of the beachhead towards Ryes, recalled a nice sunny day as he travelled up a straight treeless road. However, he thought how exposed they were and worried about the possibility of an air attack or being shelled by the enemy as they came into view. The silence lulled the convoy into a sense of false security, and seeing no troops in front of them they assumed the advance had gone so far ahead that they needed to keep moving forward to catch up with the lead elements:

> I wasn't battle-wise, or I would have realised the danger of everything being so quiet. We were very lucky and reached our destination at Creully without any trouble. We met the remainder of the troop and our HQ moved into a narrow sunken lane parallel to the road to the bridge at Creully 200 yards distant. The lane had high banks and was well concealed by trees and all was still quiet. Glancing up I saw to my horror what appeared to be a company of German soldiers doubling towards Creully. Fortunately, they didn't notice us, but the sunny afternoon country feeling was shattered. We then realised we had run through our own forward areas into enemy held territory.[69]

Lieutenant Absalom, armed only with a Sten gun, decided that discretion was the better part of valour. He did not challenge the passage of the German troops, who seemed too preoccupied to notice him. When they had moved on, the general panic of forming an all-round defence began. Bren guns, ammunition and rifles were still stored under piles of kit, and nobody knew

---

67 Manuscript forwarded to author by Brian Cook (Carnegie Heritage Centre, Hull, 2016).
68 Bailey, *Forgotten Voices of D-Day*, p. 203.
69 *WW2: People's War* <www.bbc.co.uk/ww2peopleswar> (accessed 15 March 2019).

Formations of Allied aircraft bombed targets inland as troops struggled to establish the bridgehead. (Courtesy of I.R. English)

where their weapons were in the general confusion. It was then that solid shot and machine-gun fire, coming from the direction of the beach, started hitting the tops of the trees around them:

> As I seemed to be in charge, I decide we would remain on the defensive unless directly attacked. As I patrolled up a track I saw a pair of boots and some field grey trousers sticking out from behind a bush and for some reason I didn't fire. I kicked one foot and ordered him to surrender with my finger on the Sten-gun trigger, and to my amazement out of the bush came a grey-haired old Frenchman. How close he came to getting a full Sten magazine he'll never know, [but] I told him to go home and to change his trousers and I think he got the message as he was gone like a rocket. I peered through the hedge but there was nothing in sight, so collecting the Bren crew I made them take up a position that would protect our rear. Then we saw three Germans with a Spandau doubling across the field in full view, unaware of the danger. After a couple of bursts from the Bren they went down. Having collected the Spandau and ammunition we checked that the wounded Germans were not armed and got them back to the road where we stopped an ambulance heading for Ryes. The driver reluctantly stopped and was hopping about as we loaded on the wounded Germans. I enquired what the problem was and he replied: "There are three bloody great Tigers half a mile back at the crossroads" and with that he left at high speed.[70]

---

70   *WW2: People's War* <www.bbc.co.uk/ww2peopleswar> (accessed 15 March 2019).

47 Royal Marine Commando

Landing at 1000 hours, just behind 231 Brigade, 47 Royal Marine Commando was tasked with passing through the troops on the beach and then to move on to seize their objective, the harbour and town of Port-en-Bessin, before linking up with the Americans on Omaha Beach. Their commander, Lieutenant Colonel Cecil Farndale Phillips, was ordered to avoid contact with the enemy where possible and to press on with all haste to their objective. During the run in to the beach, four LCAs carrying commandos were sunk when they hit beach obstacles with mines attached, and another seven suffered some form of damage from incoming fire. The men on them lost all their weapons and wireless sets. They had landed at Le Hamel in the correct place, only to find the beach still under fire, with one landing craft hit by a shell and sunk. Such was the confusion that Phillips lost contact with his men and Major O'Donnell started to gather together any he could find and take them to the prearranged rendezvous at Buhot. By this time, 73 other ranks and five officers were missing. The commandos now had to make a forced march through enemy-held territory, carrying all their weapons, ammunition and supplies, with the prospect that at the end of it they would have to fight a very stiff battle to take Port-en-Bessin.

Able Seaman Alexander Hutton, 47 Commando, watched as landing craft were hit and men were thrown into the water during the landing:

> I was sorry to see some of the lads aboard as the sea was still rough and a lot were seasick. As we got nearer to the beach the noise of gunfire from the big ships was overwhelming and seeing men struggling in the water as their craft had been hit was very frightening.[71]

Corporal Gordon W. Tye was caught in a deluge of enemy fire as his 47 Commando LCA approached the beach:

> Few of our boats got ashore, they all got shelled and holed. There were things like railway tracks buried in the sand and when it was high tide the craft just ran onto them. Water was pouring into our craft everywhere. We had a rough time getting onto the shore and I reckon we lost about 100 men on the beaches, most of them were drowned. It wasn't until we'd been ashore for some time that we realised that we'd lost our troop commander, Lt Batty,[72] and a lot of other officers. We were fired on all day long by snipers and mortars, I've got to give them their due the Germans were good mortar men, they could put their mortar bombs on a sixpence. If one of your own soldiers gets shot, they just go down and you

Corporal Gordon W. Tye, 47 Royal Marine Commando. (Courtesy of H. Forth)

---

71 Newspaper cutting forwarded to author by R. Walker (Scarborough, 1990).
72 Lieutenant Denis St John Batty, 47 Royal Marine Commando, was killed on 6 June 1944, aged 20. He is buried in Bayeux War Cemetery, France.

think to yourself well that's that and there's nothing you can do about it. It happened many a time, the man next to me would get shot and killed, they are your friends, your mates, but you have got to keep going, you can't stay.[73]

Lieutenant John Forfar, MC, a Medical Officer with 47 Commando, watched the carnage as the commandos headed for the shore in their small LCAs:

> Far from the shore one LCA was hit and sank, 12 of the marines were killed or drowned, 11 were seriously injured but reached the shore. As the other LCAs moved in they had to cross a wide band of obstacles constructed of steel girders, many of which were tipped with mines. Unfortunately, the state of the tide was such that many of the obstacles were only just covered as 47 RMC moved in and the LCAs passing over them were in great danger of being impaled on a steel girder and exploding mine. Four other LCAs were impaled in this way and sank, of the remaining 9 LCAs 7 were damaged and only 2 were able to return to the mother ship. The orders were that incoming craft were not to stop to rescue men in the water. As a consequence, wounded men would have had to struggle in the water and in their wounded state some were drowned. Others were caught in a coastal current which swept them far from the landing beach.[74]

Able Seaman George Amos was in one 47 Commando LCA when it was hit:

> On the run in the sickness was appalling, my memory is of sitting there, hands green with bile, when suddenly there was an almighty bang as our landing craft was hit. You felt it right through your body. I was carrying a Thompson machine-gun and a Bangalore torpedo, but when you're loaded up you can't swim so you get rid of your equipment. I came ashore with nothing.[75]

Major Paddy Donnell, 2 i/c 47 Royal Marine Commando, disembarked on Jig Green, but the landing was a terrible shambles and the surviving commandos found themselves spread over a frontage of some 1,500 yards:

> About this time a 75mm battery on the high ground above Le Hamel opened accurate fire on the LCAs. The CO ordered a turn to port and all craft, in some disorder, began running east, parallel to the beach. At least one craft was hit and sunk, and it soon became a case of every craft for itself. The beach was crowded with all types of vehicles and equipment, mostly wrecked or swamped. Each craft picked its own landing place. Very few had a dry landing, most grounding well offshore, in some cases on obstacles in water so deep that the only way ashore was to dump equipment and swim. At least one craft ran onto a mine and had its bows blown off, [and] of the 14 craft that started out only two returned to the LSI mother ship. As planned, we moved west in boat groups along the road that ran parallel to the beach towards the RV which was the Church in Le Hamel. The CO, four officers and

---

73 Bowman, *Air War D-Day*, p. 42.
74 *Telegraph* newspaper cutting forwarded to author by B. Harrison (Manchester, 1990).
75 *Telegraph* newspaper cutting forwarded to author by B. Harrison (Manchester, 1990).

73 other ranks were missing. Practically all the Bangalores and three-inch mortar bombs had been sunk. X and B Troops were reasonably dry and equipped, A Troop was complete but had lost most of their weapons. Q and Y Troop had each lost a craft load and there was only one Vickers and one three-inch mortar out of four each, the latter was without a sight. HQ was almost complete, but all the wireless sets were doubtful starters.[76]

Lance Corporal Frank Wright felt very nervous as his landing craft headed for the beach with his 47 Commando comrades. No-one said much, and he did not feel confident of achieving success in his mission:

> As we neared the beach enemy fire came our way. I heard an almighty explosion about 30 yards to our right on the starboard side, an LCA had taken a direct hit, and I could feel the vibration through to my boots as a huge column of debris and smoke rose into the air until it became a great spreading tree over 100 feet high. Two irregular black shapes, men, rocketed straight upwards through the smoke, they turned slowly over and over before plummeting downwards. I felt sick and cold. As we were hitting the beach another landing craft only 50 yards away hit a mine and sank. As the ramp went down I was thinking "I'm not ready for this" but then we were out into only a few inches of water. Nobody seemed to be shooting at me but in front was a burning tank and as I ran past, I noticed one of the tank crew lying dead by it curled up on the sand on his left side in an attitude of sleep. His knees were drawn up and his arms folded across his chest, his head was bent forward so that his face was turned towards me. But where his face should have been there was a bloody pulp, a featureless red mask.[77]

Captain William Frank Niemann Gregory-Smith, DSO and bar, DSC and bar, Royal Navy, landed on Gold Beach, where he was beach master to 47 Commando. He was met by a scene of carnage:

> A number of badly wounded men were clinging weakly to beach obstacles against which the flood tide was brutally battering them. Closer inshore several dead men were lying in the shallows, their bodies rolling back and forth as the waves advanced and receded over them. High up the beach were little mounds, which looked from a distance like piles of sand, which proved to be khaki clad casualties from the initial assault. Of the living there was no sign. The several hundred men who had just landed had vanished into the dunes as if the sand had swallowed them. Only the rattle of small arms fire gave them away. To my right the battle for the dunes was continuing, although it was barely audible amid the general noise of aircraft, naval guns and shouting men.[78]

Able Seaman Ken Green, 47 Commando, was lucky and landed on time:

> We hit the beach and down came the ramp, and the officer and myself got off by jumping over the side, which was good thinking for coming out the front was risky. One poor chap

---

76 Newspaper cutting forwarded to author by P.G. Kendrick (Nottingham, 1988).
77 F. Wright, interview with author (Yorkshire, 1991).
78 Lee, D., *Beachhead Assault* (London: Greenhill Books, 2004), p. 147.

was hit and badly wounded and asked us to pull him out of the sea. He was in such a bad state, an 88mm shell had exploded near him. The officer said: "Should I shoot him?" but I said no let's pull him onto the beach. We left him there, but I don't think he lived very long. We had a long walk to meet up with the rest of the commandos but there were sand dunes, thank God, and these gave us plenty of cover.[79]

Lieutenant John Winter was part of the flotilla of 14 landing craft containing men of 47 Commando that headed for the beach in line astern. The craft of his commanding officer, Lieutenant Colonel Phillips, was swept to one side and found itself parallel to the beach, presenting a good target for the Germans. Meanwhile, Winter's war was about to end:

Our landing craft made their way in heavy seas through an area packed with un-cleared mined beach obstacles. As we landed the beach was heavily congested, five LCAs sank, and five were damaged or capsized causing many casualties. My landing craft hit a mine and I was knocked unconscious for a while. When I awoke I found myself in the water with a broken leg and arm and I attempted to swim ashore but ended up going round in circles. A sergeant saw me and despite the awfulness of the situation he said: "You won't get anywhere fast like that sir, you had better think of something better." I eventually made it ashore where Marine Woodgate, my medical orderly, met me with the words: "I thought you might like a cup of tea sir." I can tell you that no cup of tea ever tasted better. The doc could do little for us wounded as he had only a few orderlies and they had lost all their medical equipment when their landing craft sank. It took me three days to reach a hospital in England.[80]

Medical Officer Lieutenant John Forfar assessed the situation on the beach:

Mustering on the beach the commando had already lost 28 killed, 21 wounded and 27 missing. As LCAs sank many weapons and much other equipment had been lost. Reduced to 340 men the commando was under fire and passed through the first line of enemy front-line defences to embark on a 12-mile march through enemy held territory, several enemy positions were overcome and in these encounters some of the commando's lost weaponry was made good.[81]

Sergeant J. Gardner landed with 47 Commando and heard amongst the mayhem a comment that made him smile, but not for long:

We ended up having to swim ashore looking like drowned rats. We were under heavy machine-gun fire all the time as we moved up the beach. It was at this point I heard some wag say: "Perhaps we are intruding as this seems to be a private beach."[82]

---

79 Manuscript forwarded to author by Brian Cook (Carnegie Heritage Centre, Hull, 2016).
80 J. Winter, correspondence with author (Thetford, 1994).
81 *Telegraph* newspaper article forwarded to author by B. Harrison (Manchester, 1990).
82 J. Gardner, interview with author (Hull, 1989).

47 Royal Marine Commando Beach Group. (Author's collection)

Lieutenant Jack Gaster, Royal Naval Reserve, J Commando, beach master to 47 Commando, described the scene as he landed on Gold Beach:

> The Landing Craft Obstacle Clearing Units were busy doing their dangerous work making the beach safe for the landing craft who were coming ashore in an endless stream, to disgorge their military hardware onto the beaches. In the meantime, the Royal Engineers beach recovery tanks and bulldozers were clearing the hedge-hog obstacles away from the beaching areas. Other tanks fitted with flails were busy clearing a path through the minefield that lay to the right of the beach.[83]

Commandos who had lost their equipment re-armed themselves with weapons the Germans had left behind, and as they fought their way forward to the assembly area they found it was being held by a company of German troops of *Regiment 726* of *716. Infanterie-Division*. The attack on this position cost the commandos a further 40 casualties before it fell. The now rather badly depleted commandos advanced quickly to the small village of Escures to the south of Port-en-Bessin and occupied it by last light on 6 June.

Private David Powis, 2nd Devons, watched as the commandos struggled ashore and advanced up the beach to pass through his unit:

83 Lee, *Beachhead Assault*, p. 151.

A drenched and dripping commando unit now joined us at the side of the road. They were almost completely unarmed and looked a very sad sight. They explained that they had come in on the high tide and that their landing craft had hit the ramps or bottle mines, so they were forced to throw off their equipment and swim ashore. Having armed themselves with whatever they could from dead soldiers, they welcomed anything we could spare in the way of armaments and ammunition. I gave them one of my two 50-round bandoliers of rifle ammunition, a grenade and two magazines for the Bren-gun. The commandos went along the road, furnishing themselves with small arms and ammunition from the German and British soldiers now lying dead there. They filtered through the leading Devon company, engaging the Germans with their captured and borrowed weapons.[84]

Royal Marine Sergeant Frank Miller was on a Landing Craft, Flak manning twin Oerlikon guns, providing close support for the troops on the beach, who directed his fire by a system of signals:

A lamp flashed on the beach followed by coloured smoke. We closed and raked gun emplacements and machine-gun nests with pom-pom and Oerlikon fire until we got another signal: "Thanks!" It was impossible to hear orders over the noise of explosions and gunfire, so orders were passed by messenger. "Check firing" was by a thump on the back of the gunner. The air was filled with the smoke of battle and cordite, plus the din of light and heavy gunfire.[85]

Marine medic Lance Corporal P.G. Kendrick, MM, moved inland with 47 Commando, the fighting along the way being hard and costly:

Our task was to land and to break out of the beach, heading towards Port-en-Bessin. Captain Walton, our officer, took us through to a junction on the coast road and told us to dig-in. As we did so we exposed a German telephone junction which must have connected all the enemy military telephones, [so] we blew it up. Later as we advanced we had some skirmishes with German units. A machine-gun opened up on us, killing and wounding some of the lads. One of the wounded was in pain [and] cried out for me, and as I tended to the lad I realised I couldn't do all the necessary first aid in a prone position. I stood up and the machine-gun opened up again. I could see and hear the bullets hitting the hedgerow near me but as they came closer the gun must have lifted. Although the firing continued the bullets were flying over my head. We put in a flank attack and captured the machine-gun crew. The German gunner had a right shoulder injury and I had to treat him. When I had finished he hugged me.[86]

Captain Gregory-Smith marvelled at the lack of enemy aircraft overhead as his unit travelled to Port-en-Bessin:

---

84 Manuscript forwarded to author by Brian Cook (Carnegie Heritage Centre, Hull, 2016).
85 F. Miller, conversation with author (Hull, 1991).
86 P.G. Kendrick, correspondence with author (Nottingham, 1989).

> Sometime after midnight, after confirming that the wounded were being smoothly evacuated, I scraped a hole in the ground. During the past 22 hours I had been in and out of the water and had eaten only a bar of chocolate. I was cold, wet and hungry, and badly in need of alcoholic refreshment. But having none I lay shivering in my foxhole.[87]

Lieutenant John Forfar pressed on along his given route, feeling exhausted after the days exertions, and as darkness fell the Medical Officer stopped to bed down for the night. His next objective was in sight, but he and the men were too exhausted to worry about it and soon fell asleep:

> What a day it had been, the commando stopped for the night on a hill near Escures where we looked down on Port-en-Bessin.[88]

That night the commandos licked their wounds, counted their losses and prepared for the next bloody round as they tried to take Port-en-Bessin at dawn on 7 June. They looked down into the town and port, and with heavy hearts the young officers settled their men down for the night and posted sentries. All had been done that could be, and with the dawn would come a new trial by fire.

56 Independent Infantry Brigade

There were three regular battalions of infantry in 56 Independent Infantry Brigade: the 2nd Essex, 2nd Gloucesters and 2nd South Wales Borderers. The brigade was formed in March 1944, its men being inexperienced in the latest battle techniques as they had all been on home service since 1940. Nevertheless, they landed on Gold Beach behind 231 Brigade and followed up the assault brigades through scenes of destruction and death.

Private A. Vince of the 2nd Essex recalled their landing:

> As we approached the beach the sea held much evidence of tragedies already enacted, [with] wrecked landing craft and vehicles, disabled tanks and floating items of equipment. The leading craft grounded, the ramps went down, and the men streamed ashore. Some into water only knee deep, others up to their necks.[89]

Sergeant Dick Philips, 2nd South Wales Borderers, was dismayed by what met his eyes as he stepped onto the beach:

> The sea was quite rough, and the landing craft had wide bows which made things worse. As we landed I remember seeing these young chaps dead in the water, lying in the surf, with the Star of Africa ribbon on their chests. There was a lot of shelling still going on and it was all a bit hairy. I said to the driver to get behind a knocked-out tank, but our jeep sank

---

87 Newspaper cutting forwarded to author by R. Walker (Scarborough, 1990).
88 *Telegraph* newspaper article forwarded to author by B. Harrison (Manchester, 1990).
89 Manuscript forwarded to author by A. Vince (Essex, 1989).

and we had to leave it. Captain Talmadge and I grabbed hold of the battalion signs and took them towards the rendezvous area. As we were leaving the beach there was one poor chappie going up a bank and a shell exploded at his feet in the sand. We saw his body flying through the air towards us, [but] we were lucky and got away with it.[90]

Private Leslie Holden, 2nd Essex, was one of a party of four who had been chosen to act as an advanced party that would land before the main body of 56 Brigade and guide each unit off the beach as it landed through the lanes cleared in the minefields:

> We had to liaise with the sappers and mark the routes they were clearing through the minefields with white tape. This information we would then convey by wireless to the incoming craft. We erected regimental banners for quick recognition by incoming troops to assist in the rapid movement of troops off the beaches through the gaps that had been cleared. It was almost mid-day when I saw what I had been waiting for, LCIs spilling out men of the 2nd Battalion the Essex Regiment. They waded ashore and marched up the beach in single file led by their colonel. It was my duty, and honour, to welcome my colonel and fellow Pompadours and relay to them their marching orders. I said: "Black route is open sir!" Colonel Higson slapped me on the back and said: "Well done, stay on the beach, recover your jeep and re-join us in due course."[91]

Private Bill Evans, 2nd South Wales Borderers, disembarked quite a distance from the shore and found himself in deep water:

> With other silly Welsh buggers, I landed at Le Hamel on Gold Beach in an LCI. The ramp went down only to see it disappear at right angles to the deck. "Landing aborted" was the cry. "Use the gangway at the left side." We looked towards the chaos on shore when the officer shouts: "You, you and you, take one of those ashore with you", pointing towards the deck where five folding bicycles lay. Not believing what I was hearing, the voice said: "Come on, snap to it", and we began our ascent into eight feet of water. Seeing little Smithy's pack disappear in front of me and then his helmet going out of sight I took a deep breath. My immediate thought was "Christ he's going to drown" so I let go of the guide rope one of the American crew had taken ashore and tied it to some object and grabbed Smithy by the back of his collar and lifted him up out of the water. Then it was my turn to fail to touch the bottom, so another deep breath and I was under. I have no idea how any of us made it to the shore, only God knows. I made it to the road and that voice shouted again: "That way", pointing up this road, then: "Evans, give that bike to my batman", thereby denying me of a nice little ride to our rendezvous. I had to footslog it, diving in ditches, as shells and mortars were still coming over.[92]

Major Philip Barrass, of the 2nd Essex, landed amid a scene of some chaos:

---

90   *WW2: People's War* <bbc.co.uk/ww2peopleswar> (accessed 13 December 2020).
91   L. Holden, manuscript forwarded to author (Essex, 1994).
92   W. Evans, correspondence with author (Wales, 1989).

Into the Breach: Jig Sector, Gold Beach, 6 June 1944 191

Members of the 2nd Battalion Essex Regiment leaving their Landing Craft, Tank to land on Gold Beach, 6 June 1944. (Author's collection)

An aerial view of Gold Beach; the assaulting brigades have moved off the beach and a line of lorries can be seen moving inland along the road. (Courtesy of R. Walker)

> We all beached on different landing craft. I was with my company and half of somebody else's company, but that half company had to marry up with its other half coming off another LCI. There was quite a bit of re-organising to be done before we all got into our proper groups ready to advance. I remember that A Company started off first on bicycles and carriers. They went on ahead and the rest of us followed. St Sulpice was the place we were aiming for, which was about five miles inland towards Bayeux. We weren't really sure where the enemy was, so we travelled in battle formation. We went up this dusty road moving in file on either side.[93]

Trooper Kenneth Mayo had driven his Sherman of the Sherwood Rangers over a mine as he was about to exit the beach, and was waiting for it to be repaired in the marked lane:

> I heard on my radio that our forward units were heading for Le Hamel and then on to Bayeux. Orders were given for us to sit tight and await the fitters, so we closed down and gave what help we could on the beach. There was considerable congestion. Late in the afternoon we were standing by our tank discussing the damaged track when an armoured bulldozer came towards us widening the beach exit. When it was a few feet from us there was an almighty explosion. All went black and I was flung through the air into a minefield. I crawled towards the shouts of the crew, they bandaged me the best they could and took me to the nearest Field Dressing Station. I spent a very restless night in the open wrapped in a blanket with Jerry strafing the area.[94]

Major F.D. Goode, commanding D Company of the 2nd Gloucesters, recalled one strange scene as he moved off the beach:

> We ran in, grounded, and the navy let down the gangways. I took the first one to port and wearing waterproof trousers ran down the gangway to be the first of the regiment to land in Normandy. Alas I stepped into five feet of water, tripped over some obstacle and fell flat. Scrambling to my feet I saw I was about three feet from a very ugly looking sea mine which I avoided and waded ashore, kicking off the useless trousers. There seemed to be quite a lot of noise and there was still some small arms fire. I concentrated on following the taped gap to my left through the dunes, marked by a wrecked Sherman flail tank. Keeping to the middle of this I was followed by a mixed bag of troops all anxious to get off the beaches which were a target area. We were now in the area of the main German beach defences which had been heavily plastered by the navy and RAF. Pillboxes and blockhouses were shattered, and I have a clear recollection of one embrasure out of which a German officer had tried to climb. As it was hit it had descended on him, squashing his top half flat, leaving his legs with a well-polished pair of boots protruding. I went through the dunes and stopped for a while to look at my map, but we were off it, so my best bet was to find the lateral road and turn right in the direction of Le Hamel.[95]

---

93 Manuscript forwarded to author by P. Cuerdon (Hampshire, 1992).
94 Bowman, *Air War D-Day*, p. 23.
95 F.D. Goode, correspondence with author (Worcester, 1993).

After leaving his landing craft, Private Vince, of the 2nd Essex, moved up the beach:

> We crossed the short stretch of shingle and clambered over the low sea wall. To our left the transport was having a much more difficult time; mines were encountered in great numbers and the few clear lanes were blocked by bogged down or drowned lorries and tanks. According to plan we formed up in boat loads and moved off to the pre-arranged assembly area near Ryes. On the rising ground to our left, we could see a long line of Shermans forming up and we gasped as we saw that they were parked almost head to tail. As we marched along we saw and heard the noise of battle as German beach defences continued to hold out, but our orders were to get inland, so we pushed on past batches of prisoners, on we went through minefields already gapped. Large numbers of dead and wounded from both sides littered the road. The road itself was now being shelled by 75s at close range. When we reached the assembly area in a small wood, which was not entirely cleared, the odd sniper was still operating, [and] we dug-in for the first time.[96]

Lieutenant Nicholas Summerville, 2nd South Wales Borderers, remembered the first casualty he saw as he cycled forward:

> We set off straight through the smoke like a cycling club. There was a German 88mm firing from up on the Meuvaines Ridge down at us. We just pedalled on because our job was not to stop but to get through somehow or other. I looked round and found this thing had fired solid shot over me, it had found a chap behind me who still pedalled on without a head for a short while before he crashed into a ditch, which was rather worrying. He was the first casualty I saw, and I had a sick feeling about it. But the obvious thing to do was to get on as fast as we could.[97]

Major Goode led his men of the 2nd Gloucesters inland, where he came under fire and met an old friend:

> We had cleared the dunes and came to a field. It seemed quite peaceful for a while, but ahead of us, barring our route, was a minefield, protected by wire and signed '*Achtung Minen*'. We were now off the maps and did not like the idea of walking across a minefield. There was no time to clear a way through so this was a risk that must be taken. My mixed bag of troops was as unenthusiastic as I was. However, at that moment a cow wandered across the field unhurt, so we hoped it was a dummy minefield and we ran across unscathed. The road we moved along was very flat with no cover at all, so we lay down flat and hoped for the best. At that moment the enemy started shelling with 88mm guns and they had the road ranged to perfection. There was soon news of our first casualties further up the road. My second-in-command, Butch Holgate, was lying next to me and consoled me with the thought that here at least he would not get an income tax demand. Shells burst fairly close by and one within a few yards. We then moved on to our next halt on the road to Ryes. Just

---

96 Manuscript forwarded to author by A. Vince (Essex, 1989).
97 Kershaw, *D-Day, Piercing the Atlantic Wall*, p. 152.

off the road here there was a stout stone wall surrounding an orchard which gave us good cover and we waited for further orders. At this moment a gunner major came up riding a bicycle that was far too small for him. I recognised him as John Gaye,[98] who had been in my house at Bradfield. John and I chatted for a moment or two and he cycled on. He was moving up to spot for the guns.[99]

Private Harry Pinnegar, 2nd Gloucesters, moved to the agreed rendezvous in an orchard, only to find the place occupied by the enemy:

> Our instruction was to get on our bikes as soon as possible and rendezvous in an orchard. Well, we got to the orchard alright minus a lot of men that were wounded and one thing and another. There happened to be German tanks nearby and I don't think they had refuelled yet as we had surprised them. Unfortunately for us the biggest weapon we had was a Piat anti-tank gun. There was no artillery, no tanks and no heavy vehicles, all we had was infantrymen. One of our boys hit the track of one tank with his Piat which knocked off the track and put the tank out of action. This jammed up the exit for the other tanks to get out of the wood. They were driving round and round looking for a way out and we were riding on them waiting for them to open a hatch so that we could drop in a phosphorous or a 36 hand-grenade [Mills bomb].[100]

Private Frank Rosier's patrol of the 2nd Gloucesters spotted a group of Germans heading straight for them:

> They looked like big helmets on matchstick legs, they were just boys. Our officer said: "Open fire" and someone said: "Sir they're children". "Never mind that," he said, "their bullets will kill you just the same." We opened fire and afterwards I went up to them, [and] some of the wounded spat at us as they lay there. They were 14 years old at most.[101]

Most tank commanders liked to have their heads out of the turret to get a clear view of their surroundings, but Lieutenant Colonel Stanley Christopherson, leading a squadron of the Sherwood Rangers in support of the 2nd Essex, knew this was a dangerous activity, having already lost his commanding officer and others to German snipers. The Rangers arrived at their rendezvous but found no sign of the Essex colonel in charge. To take his tank down narrow lanes packed with German infantry was not a good idea, so Christopherson left his 2 i/c, Keith Douglas, in command and set off on a horse to find the relevant Essex officers:

> Never in my wildest dreams did I ever anticipate that D-Day would find me dashing along the lanes of Normandy endeavouring, not very successfully, to control a very frightened horse with one hand, gripping a map case in the other, and wearing a tin hat and

---

98 Major John Chester Gaye, 102nd Northumberland Hussars Anti-tank Regiment, Royal Artillery, was killed on 30 July 1944, aged 29. He is buried in Hottot-le-Bagues War Cemetery, France.
99 F.D. Goode, correspondence with author (Gloucester, 1993).
100 Correspondence with H. Pinnegar (Oxford, 1992).
101 Bastable, *Voices from D-Day*, p. 298.

black overalls. The Essex colonel was somewhat startled when I eventually found him and reported that my squadron was ready to support his battalion in the next phase of the attack.[102]

Major Goode recalled the violence of the rocket-firing Typhoons that supported the advancing troops of the 2nd Gloucesters:

> The shelling had eased off as we moved along the road in the direction of Le Hamel, where we turned inland in the direction of Ryes and Bayeux. By this time the rain had ceased, the sun had come out and it was going to be a warm day. The enemy were holding the hedge of the opposite side of the field some 150 yards away. At this point I took time to change my shirt and vest for dry ones from my pack as I was soaked with sea water and sweat. We heard the roar of the engines of aircraft as they swept over us at nearly ground level. They released their rockets behind our position, and we could hear these swishing over our heads. The whole line of the hedge opposite burst into flame with a thunderous bang and we clambered through our hedge and advanced through dead cattle. There did not seem to be any firing from the direction of the enemy and when we arrived at their position it was deserted. There were a number of dead Germans lying about and there was a sickly smell of death in the air.[103]

As the last light of 6 June began to fade, the lead elements of 56 Brigade stopped short of Bayeux, where they dug in. Private A. Vince of the 2nd Essex recounted:

> During the night, patrols went out to look at the anti-tank ditch surrounding Bayeux. In the gathering dusk we looked at the spires of the cathedral and it seemed as though the city was undefended. The returning patrols confirmed this impression. However, it would have been a brave or foolish man who would have suggested that we could take Bayeux without a shot being fired.[104]

Major Philip Barrass of the 2nd Essex also saw the spires of Bayeux as patrols edged towards the town, probing for the enemy:

> The CO sent out patrols to find out what was going on. It was getting dark, [and] when they came back they said that the Germans were still there. They didn't know in what strength, but they had been fired upon. It was decided that there was not much point in trying to launch an attack that night. We would do it in the morning in daylight. Our objective had been Bayeux but not necessarily on D-Day itself, I think we'd been given latitude to D-plus 1. One of the things I can remember clearly seeing before it got dark was the spires of Bayeux Cathedral enchantingly sticking up over the trees.[105]

---

102 Holland (ed.), *An Englishman at War*, p. 383.
103 F.D. Goode, correspondence with author (Worcester, 1993).
104 Manuscript forwarded to author by A. Vince Essex 1989.
105 P. Cuerdon, correspondence with author (Hampshire, 1992).

Troops waiting for the order to advance. (Author's collection)

A German machine-gun position near Bayeux. (Author's collection)

The British had assumed that all civilians would have been evacuated from the battle area, but many had stayed in their homes. Audrey Genget was a young French girl aching to see her liberators after the thunderous barrage that had done so much damage –, her local church had taken a direct hit and the people of her little village were doing their best to quell the flames. She lived in a small village on the high ground above Arromanches and was excited to witness such events. In her diary, she refers to the Germans as 'tenants' as she watched the German forces retreat:

> Suddenly a big gun was fired from the sea and the smaller cannon of the Boches were answering, there can be no doubt that a big battle is commencing, we dare not move and we put cotton wool in our ears. The noise was terrific, and we wondered how it would all end. The hours seemed very long but after a while the firing ceased and we heard our front door open and a voice calling out: "It is finished, we are free, and the English are at the crossroads." Out tenants came out of their trench in the garden next door and GL arrives, everyone is well at his house, and he tells us of the great English victory. He says we should go and look at the sea. We got ready in spite of being very upset and afraid and got to the Villa St Come, [and] from there what a sight met our eyes! For as far as we could see there were ships of all kinds and sizes and above floated big balloons, silvery in the sun. Big bombers were passing and re-passing in the sky. It is a marvellous and unforgettable sight, a very consoling sight for the suffering of the last few hours. As we watched we could see tanks and armoured cars passing on the road to Asnelles, there is so much to see, and all is so interesting. Finally, we go back home leaving the people to show the way to the English soldiers. What a noise everywhere and a smell of burning! We return to our rooms and from the window we see a file of tanks passing through the fields opposite on their way to Bayeux. Are we dreaming? Is it all really true?[106]

The fighting on Gold Beach had cost the 50th Northumbrian Division some 1,000 casualties in killed, wounded and missing. This total would have been much higher was it not for the brave men of General Hobart's 79th Armoured Division with their 'Funnies' that had proved so crucial. Many of them had gone into action for the first time in these strange, modified machines of war, but thanks to their efforts in helping to breach the Atlantic Wall, the infantry was able to get through before the Germans had time to recover.

231 Brigade at Le Hamel

The coastal village of Le Hamel was 231 Brigade's next important objective on 6 June. Defended by four platoons of the German *352. Infanterie-Division* who had recently been moved into the area, the village had been fortified and consisted of numerous machine-gun pillboxes and weapon pits. In the east of the village was a Polish 77mm anti-tank gun and three pillboxes covering the exit from the beach, plus many communication trenches and concrete shelters. Houses in the village had been turned into strongpoints, with their windows bricked up. The

---

106 Bastable, *Voices from D-Day*, p. 172.

hospital/sanatorium, had been made into a formidable strongpoint and would prove a tough nut to crack in the coming battle. On the seafront, houses and walls had been demolished to give a clear field of fire for the machine-gun posts that were situated along its length. The houses to the western end of the seafront were bricked up for defence, with a concrete casemate built into the sea wall.

Lieutenant David Render of the Sherwood Rangers knew of the danger of the Polish 77mm gun at Le Hamel and looked on as the beach was becoming overcrowded as more landing craft disgorged their human and mechanical cargoes onto the narrow strip. Captain Arthur Warburton, Forward Observation Officer for the 147th Field Regiment, Essex Yeomanry, Royal Artillery, watched as a few tanks made it to the sand dunes, whereas others dared not move into the field of fire of the 77mm anti-tank gun. Warburton needed to get his Sherman inland so he could call down the fire of the Sexton self-propelled guns he was spotting for. His luck ran out as he travelled along the road at the top of Gold Beach with German infantry fleeing before him. The 77mm gun then came into view and a shell crashed into his Sherman, bringing it to an abrupt halt. Feeling very angry, Warburton contacted the only Sexton to have got ashore so far, commanded by Sergeant Robert Palmer, 147 Field Regiment, Essex Yeomanry, Royal Artillery, and demanded that it destroy the offending 77mm gun. Palmer knew he would have to act quickly and raced his vehicle up the beach to the concrete emplacement.

Render then saw the self-propelled gun do its work:

> The first round glanced off the top right-hand corner of the bunker with a crack and a shower of steel and concrete fragments. Another round was already in the breech as Palmer shouted adjustments. The second round went straight through the embrasure and detonated inside the bunker. Minutes later what remained of the gun crew staggered out of the back of the bunker with their hands up.[107]

After much confusion and chaos, the troops of 231 Brigade left the sand dunes and headed for the village of Le Hamel, where the 1st Hampshires found themselves held up by heavy enemy fire. The troops holding Les Roquettes gave them covering fire as the Hampshires advanced, using hedgerows and ditches for cover. Wireless communication was lost and casualties began to mount, but the men were in a savage mood and out for revenge. Major Antony Mott of the 1st Hampshires recalled the deadly sniper and Spandau fire coming from Le Hamel:

> Lt Lionel Bawden[108] was hit early on and killed instantly. The platoon sergeant, Sgt Smith, a tough man, was also hit and wounded. This left them rather helpless so I called on Graham Elliot to get 11 Platoon on in any way he could covering themselves. At this point mortar bombs started pitching among us though the troops thought they were mines.[109]

Sergeant Stanley Chalk, 1st Hampshires, crouched low to avoid the vicious fire coming from Le Hamel:

---

107 Render, *Tank Action*, p. 21.
108 Lieutenant Lionel Arthur Bawden, 1st Battalion Hampshire Regiment, was killed in action on 6 June 1944, aged 27. He is buried in Bayeux War Cemetery, France.
109 P. Cuerdon, correspondence with author (Hampshire, 1993).

Petard AVRE tanks advance up a Normandy lane to support the Hampshires. (Author's collection)

In the dunes we went down into a kneeling position to get our breath back. Another platoon to our right was trying to sort out a pillbox that was giving us trouble. I noticed that Monty was leaning heavily on my right shoulder, and I thought that like me he was puffed and pleased to have someone to lean on. But when we got orders to move forward and I got up, he just fell forward onto the sand – he was dead.[110] A bullet coming

Sergeant Stanley Chalk, 1st Battalion Hampshire Regiment. (Author's collection)

110 Private Montague Bishop, 1st Battalion Hampshire Regiment, was killed in action on 6 June 1944, aged 30. He is buried in Bayeux War Cemetery, France.

from the sanatorium or houses on the seafront at Le Hamel just to our right must have hit Monty while we waited to move off.[111]

The Germans hurled grenades at the Hampshires from a below-ground system of trenches. German patrols were sent down the road to Le Hamel to locate other British platoons, and as they approached the village British tanks were seen moving towards them. There was a sharp crack and one tank burst into flames, followed by two more. The men on foot now realised that there was an anti-tank gun emplacement up ahead of them so turned back, looking for another route into the village. Private Lewis Richards, 50 Div Signals, ducked as sniper fire came from Le Hamel. He could see that nothing was going to plan:

> A recce patrol went up to Le Hamel to investigate the situation and we made our way along the road past an enemy pillbox with a dead German sitting outside its entrance. The pillbox had been hit by a shell or a rocket taking with it many of our infantry. The bodies were lined up along the road covered by gas capes and ground sheets, and the wounded were being stretchered back to the beach. Our progress was very slow.[112]

Private Frank Topping, 147th Field Regiment, Essex Yeomanry, Royal Artillery, was a radio operator in a Sherman as he moved with other tanks towards Le Hamel:

> We moved towards the small hamlet of Le Hamel, and I was beginning to feel that I had had enough excitement for one morning, but sadly it was not to be. An anti-tank gun opened up from down the road and we received an armour piercing shell in the engine which arrived with a metallic crash. We all bailed out and lay with the infantry at the side of the road. Shortly after that, two more tanks were knocked out.[113]

The German *Infanterie Regiment 915* had been marching west to the American airborne landings on the Cotentin Peninsula but was diverted from this objective and told to turn around and head for the area east of Bayeux. They arrived there later on 6 June, but by then it was impossible to influence events in the area. It was left to local commanders to mount their own limited counter-attacks against the British forces. Montgomery's plan to dissipate German reserve forces seemed to be working. Nevertheless, at this juncture, the success of the landing in Jig Sector was by no means certain in spite of the British superiority in men and materiel.

Major David Warren, DSO, MC, who had been given command of the 1st Hampshires, at once withdrew two of his companies as he could see that any attempt to advance along the beach and the narrow stretch of dunes would expose his troops to concentrated machine-gun fire and even heavier casualties. These troops were redirected to the outer eastern perimeter of Le Hamel using a route inland. The Hampshires advanced along a track that took them through Les Roquettes and on to their objectives. All the fields in the area were signposted as minefields for at least a mile inland. These minefields had not been reported by the intelligence services, and it

---

111 S. Chalk, correspondence with author (Kent, 1992).
112 L. Richards, conversation with author (Wantage, 1991).
113 F. Topping, correspondence with author (Gwent, 1992).

was noted that some of the signs displayed had white backgrounds while others were yellow. It was discovered much later that those with a white background were quite safe.

The advance was not to prove easy, as RAF fighters overhead mistook the advancing Hampshires for the enemy. Private Tony Coglan, 1st Hampshires, recalled:

> About an hour or so into our journey we saw six fighter aircraft, our own thank goodness, coming over. They were flying abreast and the one nearest us didn't seem to like the look of us. He peeled off from the group and dropped his bombs on the end of our column which wrote off a truck, and then proceeded to machine-gun the whole column. I could see the spatter of the bullets as they passed about two or three feet from my face.[114]

By late morning of 6 June, four companies of 231 Brigade were still fighting to take Le Hamel – three from the Hampshire Regiment and one from the 2nd Devons. The lack of specialist armour held up the infantry, who found it hard to break into the village. C Company, 2nd Devons, was held up by a strongpoint that pinned them down, and every move was stopped by heavy machine-gun fire. Although only 30 yards away from the Germans, they did not have the firepower to take out the position. A sniper kept picking off men and was an ever-present danger to anyone who showed themselves. Corporal Jock Russel, 2nd Devons, warned an officer not to expose himself:

> At that point Major Duke[115] ran through the fire and into the ditch that held me and three or four others and asked what was holding us up. I told him and, holding his binoculars, he immediately crawled out of the ditch to see for himself. I shouted twice to him to get down, knowing the sniper would be watching, but it was too late. A bullet hit him in the head and blood poured out of his mouth, he was killed instantly. C Company lost some good men at Le Hamel but the most tragic was Major Duke.[116]

The route being followed by the Hampshires brought them to Asnelles, where Major Warren tried to reorganise his companies. Having done so as best he could, an advance was ordered along the Asnelles–Le Hamel road, where they were to give covering fire to B Company, who would make an assault on the enemy positions around the sanatorium and the seafront bunker. The 2nd Devons, who were still in the dunes and in the houses on the eastern outskirts of Le Hamel, aided this assault by keeping a number of the enemy pinned down in the opposite direction to the Hampshires' attack. Sherman tanks of the Sherwood Rangers then started to arrive in Asnelles, and as they moved forward made good targets for the inland-facing German anti-tank guns. The German crews held their fire until the tanks reached a crossroad, as Major Warren recounted:

> There was a terrific explosion and a tank burst into flames. One member of the crew managed to get out and reported that the gun was loaded and that the flames might fire

---

114 Manuscript forwarded to author by Brian Cook (Carnegie Heritage Centre, Hull).
115 Major Hugh Victor Duke, MC and Bar, MID, 2nd Battalion Devonshire Regiment, was killed in action at Le Hamel on 6 June 1944, aged 25. He is buried in Bayeux War Cemetery, France.
116 Saunders, *Gold Beach – Jig*, p. 90.

Troops and tanks press on from the beaches through a French village. (Courtesy of P. Cuerdon)

the shell in the barrel at any moment. This was most disconcerting as it pointed directly at Battalion Headquarters.[117]

The Hampshires' advance, which began at 1345 hours, took them more than an hour as they constantly pushed back the determined troops of the German *352. Infanterie-Division*. Those that were defending Le Hamel proved to be far superior to the coastal units of the *716. Infanterie-Division*. The fighting in the east of Le Hamel was bloody. Most of the German fire was coming from the sanatorium, and the Hampshires found themselves held up when only 50 yards away. By good fortune, an AVRE of the Sherwood Rangers that had driven from Asnelles then appeared and the Hampshires launched a series of probing attacks on the sanatorium, using back gardens and trees as cover. Prisoners soon began to be taken and the AVRE fired its Petard into the building, causing the whole structure to shake.

Sergeant Stanley Clark of the 1st Hampshires recalled:

> The sanatorium was a main defensive position in the area and should have been taken out by a low-level air strike just before we landed, but because of low cloud none of the concrete-busting bombs found their target and the place was still bristling with guns of all types.[118]

---

117 Saunders, *Gold Beach – Jig*, p. 93.
118 S. Clark, correspondence with author (Kent, 1994).

Self-propelled gun commander Sergeant Robert Palmer moved down a track towards Le Hamel and saw an officer waving his arms about:

> He came over to where we were, and I leaned over the side of the turret and spoke to him. He said: "Down there, you see those two big posh looking houses, well they've been heavily fortified and they're making a nuisance of themselves. They've already knocked out about six Bren-gun carriers and killed a lot of our ground troops, so please deal with them." When we got to within 50 yards away, within easy range, I could see they were not ordinary houses at all. All around the windows was piled up with concrete they'd added to the original building. I could see movement in the upstairs right window of the first one, so I said to the gun layer: "Put one into the upstairs right window." He fired and the first shot exploded on impact. Within seconds a whole pile of people, 10 maybe 12, came running out of the side door of the ground floor with their hands up. The infantry boys of the Hampshires collected them up as prisoners.[119]

Company Sergeant Major H.W. Bowers, 1st Hampshires, had been complaining that the boots he had on were killing him and looked forward to getting a nice pair of soft German boots. When the landing craft beached, the ramp went down and he and his comrades dashed up the beach:

> Terrific fire was coming from our right from a pillbox we didn't know was there. We decided to attack it and at this moment a wireless message came through for the company commander to return and take over the remnants of the battalion. Off he went with a runner leaving me and the wireless operator there, who at that moment was killed, leaving me alone and not feeling so happy. I decided it was impossible for me to attack the pillbox on my own and I tried to return to my original position. On the way I found the commanding officer badly wounded. He said: "Hello Bowers, you still living?" I said: "Yes, just about sir" and explained the position to him. He said: "OK, you carry on." I thought Christ! he must think I can take on the whole German army. However, I edged back a bit to get through the wire and I picked up a couple of naval commandos, who in their humorous way asked if they could come along for a bit of fun. We crawled through the minefield and across a couple of fields, eliminating the Germans that were in the slit trenches there and eventually reached the sanatorium building, the end of which was the pillbox. I put the commandos into a firing position and crawled into the sanatorium and so down onto the top of the pillbox. The Germans immediately put out a white flag. I thought to hell with you after all this trouble and I slipped in a 36 Mills grenade. After the explosion a few seconds passed, and they came running out with their hands up shouting: "Russkis-Russkis!" I was not interested in their bloody nationality. All I was interested in was those nice soft boots they were wearing, and it was my intention that a size eight pair of them would belong to me in the very near future.[120]

---

119 Manuscript forwarded to author by R. Palmer (Essex, 1990).
120 Manuscript forwarded to author by L. Anthony (Southampton, 1990).

A soldier of the Hampshire Regiment being given a glass of Calvados by grateful French civilians. (Author's collection)

Major David Warren moved his men of the 1st Hampshires through the sand dunes and off the beach to subdue the fire that was making things so hard for the attacking infantry in the beachhead:

> Despite the fire coming at us we managed to make our way off the beach, and we had got through the minefields and barbed wire when I met a tank, an AVRE, a Royal Engineers assault tank that had been especially equipped. This particular one had a mortar like gun on it called a Petard which fired a large bomb. I waved him down and spoke to the commander, I told him to support our attack on Le Hamel. The tank rumbled forward and fired a bomb into the buildings that had been giving us so much trouble. As the building collapsed, we assaulted it and went into the ruins, [and] it was silenced. That was a great relief to all concerned because there was a lot of landing craft having difficulties getting onto the beach.[121]

Major Peter Selerie of the Sherwood Rangers saw where the main enemy fire was coming from and looked on as the AVREs were called into action:

---

121 Imperial War Museum 12962.

> It appeared that the main enemy fire was coming from a large many storied house, so I ordered the Churchill AVRE forward to demolish the house with its Petard. Maximum covering fire was given by the Sherman tanks. The Petard fired and something like a small flying dustbin hit the house just above the front door. After the explosion it collapsed like a deck of cards spilling the defenders with their machine-guns, anti-tank weapons and an avalanche of bricks, into the courtyard.[122]

The Hampshires rushed into the sanatorium after an AVRE had given it five shots from its Petard and found badly shaken Germans with no fight left in them. These men had fought to the last and could do no more. The German forces in the east of Le Hamel had held out until 1600 hours and had cost the Hampshires dearly in killed and wounded. It was not until the Polish 77mm gun and the sanatorium had been cleared that the Hampshires moved on to assault the west of Le Hamel. This part of the town was fortified by houses that had been turned into strongpoints, protected by wire and minefields. The destroyers out to sea were waiting for calls to fire from the Hampshires, but had received none since the commander of 231 Brigade and his number two had become casualties. The ships dared not fire throughout the morning or early afternoon as no-one knew the exact positions of 231 Brigade's companies, though the explosions in the village showed they were in Le Hamel. By late afternoon, contact with the ships offshore had been made but no naval barrage was called for as the Hampshires were by then in the village fighting to take it. More of Hobart's 'Funnies' were now off the beach and out of the sand dunes, moving forward to aid the Hampshire in the taking of Le Hamel. The houses here were so strongly fortified that it was impossible for the Hampshires to take them alone and unsupported; they were extremely tired and had been in action for 12 hours, suffering many casualties. The AVREs that had moved up in support showed their combat effectiveness in this situation as they blasted their way through the village, with the Hampshires following them and clearing one house at a time. Private Ron Eastman of the 1st Hampshires remembered it as: "Bloody awful; after losing so many comrades, I just did what I was told. I didn't expect to survive."

Corporal Fred Cooper had lost his senior NCO and Bren-gunner and had been forced to take command of his section. As they approached Le Hamel, he took stock of the situation and reported his casualties to his company commander:

> I took what was left of my section on a recce along this road that led into this small place. We didn't know if there were any Jerries in the houses we passed but just in case we lobbed grenades through the bedroom windows. As we passed through and round a bend in front of us there was a German pillbox. We approached but were not fired on. Then this tall German officer came out with his hands up followed by another man. A massive dog also came out and was coming for me, I raised my Sten to fire, but the officer called it back. I escorted them to Company HQ, and I found out later that the dog was kept as a trophy of war by the Hampshires. The dog was given the name of Fritz and became the Hampshires' regimental mascot back in England.[123]

---

122 Newspaper cutting forwarded to author by P. Cuerdon (Hampshire, 1991).
123 F. Cooper, interview with author (Cleveland, 1992).

Dog captured by the Hampshires. It would later be named Fritz and adopted as the regimental mascot. (Author's collection)

A three-man forward observation patrol watches for any movement by the enemy. (Courtesy of F. Chalk)

Arromanches

Elements of 231 Brigade moved in a southerly direction to Arromanches and bypassed the west of Le Hamel, which prevented the German defenders from withdrawing; they had been told that the British would kill any man who surrendered, so they fought on until they were forced out of their positions thanks to the firepower of the AVREs. Out to sea, the Landing Craft, Flak greatly assisted the Hampshires by firing heavy barrages into the houses on the seafront. An account of the effects of these bombardments was been left by a young German soldier, *Grenadier* Agnussen, who was manning one of the reinforced houses as the Hampshires attacked:

> The noise was tremendous when the enemy opened fire and I saw two of their strange tanks knocked out by our anti-tank guns. We fired through what had been large windows which we had boarded and sand-bagged, firing our weapons through the small holes at the Tommies. We had an excellent and wide field of fire and made a very strong impression on the British who were forced to go to ground and made no way forward against us. Our *Feldwebel* and *Stabsgefreiter* were manning machine-guns, but we began to feel that we would not survive as the heavy bombardment continued.[124]

As more British tanks arrived on the scene, the German defenders were running out of ammunition. Many troops holding the fortified houses had been killed or wounded, and the cries of the injured were pitiful to hear as they could not be evacuated from the battle area. The German NCOs harried their men to hold fast and told them that the *21. Panzer-Division* was on the way to relieve them. *Grenadier* Agnussen remembered the terrible fire coming from the Petards:

> The battle seemed to go on and on and soon half our men were casualties and we had nothing left to eat at all. I received a splinter in the arm and had to lie down while Hans bandaged it up with a paper roll. Then I returned to my position in time to see two British tanks armed with heavy mortars opposite our position. The noise was indescribable as they fired great bombs at us. All hell broke loose, and the building began to collapse. We were forced out. Our ordeal ended when the *Hauptmann* waved a small piece of white cloth and Tommy came forward; we threw out our weapons, which were now useless, and helped remove the wounded. The bodies of our comrades had to wait.[125]

The infantry cleared the wreckage of Le Hamel slowly and methodically, and it was not until 2000 hours that the last building was secured. The battle for Le Hamel was a fine display of the crushing firepower of the AVRE tanks. During the naval and air barrage earlier in the assault, most of the village's defensive positions had been missed, allowing the German defenders to be ready when 231 Brigade began their attack.

As the fight to secure Le Hamel was raging through the day, other elements of 231 Brigade were pushing passed Le Hamel and fighting enemy strongholds that barred the approaches

---

124 Manuscript forwarded to author by H. Wernemann (Germany, 1987).
125 Manuscript forwarded to author by H. Wernemann (Germany, 1987).

A British soldier searching for snipers in Le Hamel. (Author's collection)

to Arromanches. On a plateau to the east of Arromanches stood a radar station defended by entrenched German infantry, part of a dense network of similar facilities that were situated along the Atlantic, Channel and North Sea coasts. The Arromanches radar station was surrounded by dense belts of barbed-wire, nearly 20ft in depth, with a liberal sprinkling of mines. Numerous machine-gun posts surrounded it and covered the shore and inland areas. For 15 minutes, the station was bombarded by the Royal Navy from the sea and the 147th Field Regiment, Essex Yeomanry, Royal Artillery on land. As the Hampshires advanced towards it, accompanied by a troop of tanks from the Sherwood Rangers, numerous prisoners were taken and a few Germans escaped into Arromanches, but many had been killed. The infantry moved into the position and cleared the bunkers and trenches. One perk for the troops was that they found the enemy canteen and ration store fully stocked and untouched. This dominating ridge, and the fire coming from it, had delayed the advancing infantry of 231 Brigade, but the fight for its possession had been nothing like the protracted bloodbath at Le Hamel, thanks in the main to the properly directed and coordinated shellfire from the navy and artillery.

German troops resisting the assault in the streets of Arromanches. (Author's collection)

The cliffs to the east of Arromanches were the next objective for the Hampshires, including two pillboxes, a field gun on the cliff top and numerous machine-gun positions situated in a complicated trench system. These positions were shelled heavily, after which the surviving stunned garrison gave up without resistance. From this advantageous position, the Hampshires could now look down the steep slopes into Arromanches itself. During the initial bombardment prior to the invasion, Arromanches had been left relatively unscathed as the port and town was to be used as the main entry point for the landing of men and materiel, and a Mulberry Harbour would be built here. Before the Hampshires could enter Arromanches, they would first have to take out a position on the western cliff, where German snipers were active, but reinforcements were moving forward to assist the Hampshires. Again, naval firepower was brought to bear and the position was overcome with very little resistance: 20 prisoners were taken and the Hampshires suffered no casualties.

Arromanches was liberated soon after. Major Mott recalled the move into the town:

> We were to meet some tanks in case we needed help, but they never arrived, so we went in from the south without them. Arromanches was full of French people, [and] flowers came out plus tricolours and the Union Jack.[126]

126 Saunders, *Gold Beach – Jig*, p. 130.

Accounts of the liberation of Arromanches vary, depending on the area being described. Some troops report the civilians wandering about as the Germans were being rounded up, just watching events with interest and getting in the way. Some troops had an easy time, but others were fired upon and faced the task of liquidating the surviving Spandau teams, many of which put up determined opposition. But by 2100 hours, the town was securely in the hands of 231 Brigade. On that day alone, the Hampshires suffered the loss of five officers killed and 11 wounded. Casualties among the other ranks were 166 killed and wounded.

Royal Artillery driver Ted Gibbs advanced with his unit into the battle area, but never got over the terrible sights he and his comrades saw:

> What brought it home to me was the dead, and the way that they were just left there. I just couldn't get over that at all really. They had just been left with a helmet laid on their body and were only partly covered up. There would be a rifle by the side of them with some kind of make-shift cross. The smell of dead men, horses and cows was terrible. You would go into a field where there would be the bodies of bloated cows and horses on their backs all over the place. The smell was sweet and peculiar. We came across some British infantry who had been in a farmhouse and had met the Germans head on, there was German and British dead lying all over the place, so there must have been some bitter fighting here. Three men who had been hastily buried hadn't been completely covered over and they had just thrown some dirt over them. That did us in straight away as we'd never seen anything like it at all.[127]

Private R. Gladman of the 1st Hampshires was very young, part of a draft to make up for the casualties incurred. As he tramped forward through the dusty battlefield, he saw some disturbing sights:

> There were many make-shift shallow graves containing German soldiers. Their bayonets had been fixed to their rifles and thrust through their bodies with helmets hanging above. Boots and other body parts were showing above the ground. Later we passed two British soldiers who had been killed lying in a crawling position; a padre was there, he had placed a gas cape over their bodies. As we passed by the sunlight reflected on their boot studs and there were flies buzzing about all over.[128]

Lieutenant Edward Wright of the 1st Hampshires remembered:

> We went through Arromanches as most of the Germans who had been there had now gone. We pressed on beyond Arromanches to our allotted areas and by the evening of 6th June we arrived in the approximate area where we were supposed to form a defensive ring around the bridgehead. There had to be a certain amount of reorganisation because the battalion had suffered quite a lot of casualties[129]

---

127 Manuscript forwarded to author by J. Styan (Middlesbrough, 1992).
128 R. Gladman, correspondence with author (Hampshire, 1993).
129 *WW2: People's War* <www.bbc.co.uk/ww2peopleswar> (accessed 27 May 2019).

As Lieutenant Wright's platoon dug in, darkness was falling and he was surprised to hear raised angry voices:

> Where my platoon's positions were, on the outskirts of Arromanches, there were some nice villas, [and] we were instructed to dig-in which we proceeded to do. I was busy digging when from one section position I heard raised voices in argument and a female voice saying: "I demand to speak to the officer I charge." I was very surprised to hear this and went over to see what was going on. I found there a lady who declared she was English and I'm sure she was. She pointed an accusing finger at me and said: "Your men are digging up my flower beds and making a whole mess of the place, it's quite unnecessary and I demand that they stop." I was put out by this momentarily and I thought back to the stories we heard about the German invasion of the Low Countries when they were said to have employed paratrooper saboteurs dressed as nuns. I wondered for a moment if this was a similar situation, but it obviously wasn't. She was very smartly dressed and very insistent. I thought I must put a stop to this and told her very curtly that I was not going to have any of this nonsense, and I asked her if her house had a cellar. She said it had so I said to her: "Well if you don't want to be shot go down there and stay there until I tell you if you can come out." She was very incensed but off she went down to her cellar and that was the last I saw of her.[130]

Trooper Keith Ewing, of B Squadron, Sherwood Rangers, was with the Hampshires as they settled down in their positions for the night. The fear of counterattack by German tanks seemed very real to the men guarding the bridgehead:

> We supported the Hampshires, and the colonel of that regiment asked our colonel if our tanks could stay behind them in the line for the night. Our colonel explained to him that it was out of the question as normally all the tanks laagered up at the rear during the night because there was no cover in the line. After some discussion he agreed to leave one squadron. The squadrons went back and settled down for the night and we drew lots for who would go back up the line and of course B Squadron lost the toss. So we went back into the line and it was most unnerving because we were sticking out like a sore thumb. There was this huge tank sticking out there in the dark and we couldn't see a thing. We spent a most uncomfortable night.[131]

With the capture of Arromanches, 231 Brigade had taken nearly all of its given objectives, and had done so against the seasoned troops of the German *252. Infanterie-Division*, whose fighting qualities had contributed to the near disaster on Omaha Beach. Now that 56 Brigade continued its advance south towards Bayeux, 231 Brigade could focus its attention to the west and the battery at Longues-sur-Mer. This battery fired over 100 rounds on D-Day and was bombed and shelled but to no avail. The German gunners had targeted HMS *Bulolo*, the HQ ship for Gold Beach, which had to retreat out of range. They began firing on Gold Beach at 0605 hours on the

---

130 *WW2: People's War* <www.bbc.co.uk/ww2peopleswar> (accessed 27 May 2019).
131 131 *WW2: People's War* <www.bbc.co.uk/ww2peopleswar> (accessed 26 May 2019).

Troops of the Hampshires being welcomed by French children. (Author's collection)

Troops of the 1st Battalion Hampshire Regiment in positions overlooking the port of Arromanches. (Author's collection)

morning of the landings. For the British to link up with the Americans, it was essential that the Longues-sur-Mer Battery and Port-en-Bessin were taken.

Meanwhile, Private Lewis Richards, 50 Div Signals, had time to reflect on the historic event he had just taken part in as he settled down for the night:

> I arrived back from the last visit of the day in time to do Stand-to. In the darkness, and for the first time, I saw German planes attacking our shipping. The flak didn't give them a pleasant welcome and two were shot down in flames. My clothes had dried on me during the day, and I slept with them on. Before going to sleep the events of the day passed through my mind and I could not help thinking that at last we could say the war was entering its final phase.[132]

Sergeant Reginald William Webb, a Crocodile tank commander with the Sherwood Rangers, had found some bottles of wine for his crew, but found sleeping a problem because of all the anti-aircraft batteries nearby:

> What one reads about D-Day night is that there wasn't much air activity, but we thought there was a decent lot. We'd been two or three nights without much sleep and the ack-ack guns I recall were near us with some Borfors [sic] and they were banging away and creating one hell of a racket. My crew always say, but I don't remember the truth of this, I went up to the officer in charge of the Borfors and asked him not to make so much noise because we couldn't get to sleep. I think we found some booze and I might have had a couple of drinks.[133]

Trooper Reginald Mole, 4/7th Royal Dragoon Guards, prepared to settle down for the night, but before he could think of eating or sleeping there was still work to be done so that his Sherman would be battle-ready should the need arise:

> It had been a heck of a long day and before we bedded down for the night, we had to scrub the gun, load up with about 80 gallons of diesel, [and] replenish the 75 shells and boxes of Browning machine-gun bullets. If you were a wireless operator you had to do wireless watch for an hour. Others had to do an hour's guard duty. Obviously we couldn't make fires and I was so grateful to Mr Heinz and his products and his self-heating soup. This was a can with a little recess, and you dug out the middle which revealed a little fuse. You touched that with a lighted cigarette and within 30 seconds you had a hot drink. The biscuits we were given had surely been made of concrete, but we made bully and jam sandwiches.[134]

The troops and supporting tanks of the 50th Northumbrian Division had pushed 6 miles inland by the end of D-Day, with 56 Brigade already sending patrols to probe the outskirts of Bayeux, which they would occupy the next day. The important feature of St Leger was now tantalizingly within reach.

---

132 L. Richards, correspondence with author (Royston, 1991).
133 Newspaper cutting sent to the author by W. Ridley (Durham, 1992).
134 Bailey, *Forgotten Voices of D-Day*, p. 356.

6

Expanding the Bridgehead: The Move Inland, 7–12 June 1944

By first light on 7 June, the Allied armies were tentatively established on the continent. Not all objectives had been achieved, but the success of the landing and the grip established ashore already taken gave grounds for satisfaction, with the prospect of greater gains ahead as the bridgehead was expanded and the beaches linked up. The battery at Longue-sur-Mer was captured without a fight at midday on 7 June by C Coy, 2nd Devons, and 184 German troops were marched into captivity.

The seaborne assault was now over, and the land campaign had begun. On the right, the Americans had recovered from a difficult landing, in the centre XXX Corps had achieved most of its objectives with the clearing of Bayeux on the morning of 7 June, and on the left the British and Canadian 3rd Divisions were firmly implanted on French soil, but Caen had not yet been taken. On the extreme left flank, British airborne troops had secured a bridgehead over the Orne and occupied villages to the east of the bridge being held. The situation the Germans now found themselves in was critical, though not totally hopeless; the invasion had been a success, but there can be little doubt that the Germans had planned for such a contingency. The next obvious step for them was to contain the bridgehead through the speedy deployment of armoured reserves in order to counter-attack the invaders and drive them back into the sea.

For the Allies, it was a matter of expanding the foothold already gained as rapidly as possible and bringing in troops and materiel by sea at a greater rate every day. Driver Charles Wales, 633rd Coy, Royal Army Service Corps, was off Gold Beach on the evening of 6 June, but did not land until D-plus 1:

> On approaching the shore there was a Beach-master equipped with a bat in each hand, signalling us to a position ashore between the underwater obstacles and some wrecked landing craft. All our DUKWs, amphibious vehicles, had been pre-loaded with cargoes before leaving England; mine had flame-thrower liquid stored in cylinders. We'd be carrying supplies ashore and then six stretcher casualties, from the Casualty Clearing Stations, we took back to an LST offshore. An LST could accommodate three DUKWs inside, bow to stern. After unloading the stretcher cases we would back out and go to a designated ship to load up again and then back to shore with more supplies. We operated from Jig Sector of Gold for 80% of the time. There was a wide concrete slope from the road down to the beach and Beach Control was at the foot of this slope. A nearby field was used

Tanks come ashore into the ever-expanding bridgehead. (Author's collection)

as a taxi rank; you had to park around the perimeter and as vehicles were called for, we all moved around the field like a line of taxis.[1]

The weather now came to the assistance of the Germans as high seas began to batter the invasion fleet, making the work of the Royal Navy and Beach Groups extremely difficult and at times impossible. For days, the landing of supplies was held up, but eventually the storm passed and the build-up continued, gathering pace as it did so. The Germans, however, had their own problems: as they tried to move their reserves of men and armour to the coast, a hurricane of destruction was rained down upon them by the marauding aircraft of the Allied air forces. *SS-Sturmmann* Jochen Leykauff, *12. SS-Panzer-Division 'Hitlerjugend'*, waiting in his assembly area, commented on the Allied air activity:

> There were great swarms of bombers that daily droned their way overhead, unloading their blessings on us and they had us worried. Above all else one kept an eye out for the low-level fighters. But then, certainly, our own fighters would come? Or so we thought.[2]

Unteroffizier Hans Rudolph Thiel, of *Panzergrenadier-Regiment 125*, had been working hard planting anti-glider posts north of Caen on 5 June and was resting with his comrades that night. However, the noises they heard in the distance disturbed their sleep:

---

1 C. Wales, correspondence with author (Yorkshire, 1993).
2 Manuscript forwarded to author by H. Wernemann (Germany, 1989).

> Our platoon commander allowed us to catch up on the sleep we missed last night as well as we can. At high altitude above us one enemy bomber squadron after the other flies into the hinterland, and from there we can hear a terrible thundering. Even I can't conceal a sense of unease. After the relative calm of the last few weeks, I turn my thoughts to the massive bombardments of the hinterland. Something is going to come down on us and soon.[3]

The German troops inland, if they were lucky enough not to be in the main target areas of the British bombers, sat tight in their positions and listened to the aircraft droning overhead and the detonations of their bombs. *Leutnant* Martin Poppel, with the *1. Fallschirmjäger-Division*, rose from his slumber and looked up into the sky:

> Vast numbers of enemy bombers reappear, bringing death and fire into the French hinterland. Naturally their targets are the railway junctions, strategic concentration points and channels of communication, as well as our advancing armoured units. They know well enough that if they can eliminate our reinforcements they should be able to achieve their objectives without massive casualties. As for our own pilots they are nowhere to be seen. Enormous explosions can be heard in the north and north-east, which must be coming from the Allied naval heavy artillery. We can also hear the noise of battle coming from that direction.[4]

The *Luftwaffe* commander in the coastal area gloomily commented on the situation:

> Ground installations being systematically smashed, especially all fighter airfields. Enemy carpet-bombing raids on transport installations intense. Ratio of air strength generally 1 to 20, during major operations 1 to 40. Own fighter operations now only conditionally possible. Effective fighter and reconnaissance operations entirely ruled out in the invasion area.[5]

Death from the skies

In the early hours of 6 June, the *130. Panzer-Division*, better known as the *Panzer-Lehr-Division*, was ordered to begin its advance to the battle front. As they prepared for the move, their commander, *Generalleutnant* Fritz Bayerlein, drove over to *7. Armee* Headquarters at Le Mans. The division had been kept waiting and Bayerlein was told upon his arrival by *Generaloberst* Friedrich Dollmann, in command of *7. Armee*, that he should begin the move at 1700 hours in daylight. Bayerlein argued that his division should only advance at night to avoid being attacked by Allied air forces, but was overruled by his superiors. Bayerlein was an experienced senior officer, having been Rommel's chief of staff in the North African campaigns. He had come to realise that the main danger to large movements of troops and vehicles was from the air. The clear summer skies over northern France were alive with British fighter-bombers, and on the day of the move by the *Panzer-Lehr-Division* Bayerlein proposed to give the go ahead after nightfall, but again his request was over-ruled. In view of the threat from the air and the destroyed roads and

---

3   Manuscript forwarded to author by H Wernemann (Germany, 1989).
4   Poppel, M., *Heaven and Hell, the Diary of a German Paratrooper* (Kent: Spellmount, 1988), p. 179.
5   Carrel, P., *Invasion – They're Coming* (London: Harrap and Co, 1962), p. 187.

bridges from the Allied aerial campaign, Bayerlein pointed out the average speed at which his division could move would be at best just 5 miles per hour. Nevertheless, Dollmann insisted that his orders be put into operation. An angry Bayerlein returned to his divisional area and changed the direction of approach where he could. As the units started their move to the Normandy front, Bayerlein was driving in front of the middle column with two staff cars and two headquarters signal vans. It was not long before the first Allied fighter-bombers appeared, and after the first attacks the German columns became dangerously strung out. Soon, all of Bayerlein's grim forecasts came to fruition. Bayerlein himself painted a graphic picture of events:

> We were moving along all five routes of advance. Naturally we had been spotted by enemy air reconnaissance and before long the bombers were hovering above the roads, smashing crossroads, villages and towns in our line of advance and pouncing on the long columns of vehicles. At 23:00 p.m. [sic] we drove through one town and the place was lit up by flares hanging above it like candles on a Christmas tree. Heavy bombs were crashing down on the houses which were already burning. At 02:00 a.m. [sic] the scene was as bright as day with fires and explosions.[6]

The little town was quaking under a ceaseless barrage of bombs. Bayerlein's group reached as far as the southern outskirts, but it was impossible to get any further. Behind them the roads were blocked, and the battlegroup was trapped in this cauldron of fire. Pungent smoke and dust were so thick that visibility was nil, great clouds of sparks being blown around the vehicles. Overhead, the British bombers continued to rain death upon the town and surrounding areas. It was hard to breathe for the engineers who struggled to clear the roads, but eventually a way through was made and the column moved on. *Hauptmann* Alexandre Hartdegen, Bayerlein's orderly officer, recalled the drive through this nightmare scene:

> This drive showed us clearly what the regiments had been through on their move. Dozens of wrecked vehicles, now no more than steel skeletons, lay by the roadside burning and smouldering. The sector from Caumont to Villers Bocage was a road of death. Burnt out trucks, bombed field kitchens and gun tractors still smouldering with dead bodies strewn alongside. We had just reached Hill 238 and were bowling along the road when we saw three fighter bombers in the dawn sky. They had evidently spotted us for they were streaking along the line of the road at low altitude straight at us. The brakes screeched and, as a dozen times earlier that day, General Bayerlein let himself drop into a roadside ditch out of the moving car. Cpl Kartheus also managed to get out of the car just before the aircraft cannon spat out their first shells. In an instant the BMW staff car was ablaze. The next plane streaked right along the ditch, [and] the 20mm shells burst immediately in front of my concrete culvert. The Corporal had just called out to Bayerlein: "Crawl away from the car Herr General, get away from it" [but] then he was silent. Our staff car was a gutted heap of metal on the road, Corporal Kartheus lay dead in the ditch. As if by a miracle General Bayerlein got away with a few cuts and shrapnel wounds.[7]

---

6   Carell, *Invasion – They're Coming*, p. 115.
7   Carell, *Invasion – They're Coming!*, p. 116.

Despite this carnage, by 7 June the German armoured reserves were on the move, some being close to or already in the battle-zone. Before Caen, the *21. Panzer-Division* defied all Allied attempts to take the ancient Norman city, their tanks and infantry fighting stubbornly for every field and hedgerow. The *Panzer-Lehr-Division* travelled from Chartres, attacked by Allied fighters and bombers all the way. During the 90-mile journey they had lost 130 trucks, 84 self-propelled guns and five tanks. Bayerlein commented: "These were serious losses for a division not yet in action."

An anonymous German officer of the *Panzer-Lehr* left an account of the carnage the Allied air attacks caused:

> Our motorised columns were coiling along the road towards the invasion beaches. Then something happened that left us in a daze. Spurts of fire flicked along the column with splashes of dust on the road. Everyone was piling out of their vehicles and scuttling to the neighbouring fields, several vehicles were already in flames. This attack ceased as suddenly as it had crashed upon us 15 minutes before. The men started to drift back to the column again, pale and shaky and wondering how they had survived this fiery rain of bullets. This had been our first experience with the *Jabos*, fighter-bombers. The column march had now been completely disrupted and every man was on his own to pull out of this blazing column as best he could. It was none too soon because an hour later the whole thing started all over again, only much worse this time. When this attack was over the length of the road was strewn with splintered anti-tank guns, the pride of our division, flaming motors and charred dead men and implements of war.[8]

Hauptmann Alexander Hartdegen of the *Panzer-Lehr-Division* described the terror he felt as the Allied aerial forces attacked his exposed column:

> Unless one has been through these fighter-bomber attacks you cannot know what the invasion meant. You lie there helpless in a roadside ditch or in a furrow in a field, or under a hedge pressed to the ground, your face in the dirt, and then it comes toward you roaring. There it is diving at you and now you hear the whine of the bullets, now you are for it. You feel like crawling under the ground and then the bird has gone. But it comes back twice, three times. Not until they have wiped out everything in view will they leave. Even if you survive it's no more than a temporary reprieve. Ten such attacks in succession are a real foretaste of hell.[9]

Sturmmann Karl Heinz Decker, who fought with the *12. SS-Panzer-Division 'Hitlerjugend'*, recalled the British fighter-bombers always being in the skies as they searched for and hunted down their prey:

> *Jabo* activity made it virtually impossible to move about during the daytime, so we always moved at night. We moved every night to another position. It was horrendous in

---

8   Manuscript forwarded to author by H. Wernemann (Germany, 1988).
9   Manuscript forwarded to author by H. Wernemann (Germany, 1989).

Rocket-firing Typhoons left a trail of death and destruction in their wake as they attacked the defenceless German columns. (Author's collection)

the daytime; you just couldn't move at all. I was walking by the edge of a field early one morning; there was a lot of enemy air activity. I was on my own, but even so these fighter-bombers came down after me. They attacked me even though I was on my own. Let me tell you I jumped into the woods at the side of the field pretty damn quick. The sky was full of planes, all Allied, and they shot at everything that moved.[10]

Rommel watched events unfold with trepidation as the movement of his troops became ever-more problematic:

The enemy has total command of the air over the battle area up to a point some 60 miles behind the front. During the day practically our entire traffic, on roads, tracks and open country, is pinned down by powerful fighter bomber and bomber formations, with the result that the movement of troops on the battlefield is almost completely paralysed, while the enemy can manoeuvre freely. Even the movement of minor formations on the battle-field, artillery going into position, tanks forming up etc, is instantly attacked from the air with devastating effect.[11]

---

10 Manuscript forwarded to author by H. Wernemann (Germany, 1989).
11 Liddell Hart, *The Rommel Papers*, pp. 476–77.

A German convoy blazes in the road after being attacked by British Typhoon fighter-bombers.
(Courtesy of M. Perkins)

To the south and west of the 50th Northumbrian Division was the *12. SS-Panzer-Division 'Hitlerjugend'*, whose nightmare trek of over 100 kilometres to the Normandy coast had been a terrible ordeal, losing 22 men killed and 60 wounded, plus numerous vehicles wrecked.

SS-Sturmmann Helmuth Pock grew anxious about the constant air raids as his regiment of the *12. SS-Panzer-Division 'Hitlerjugend'* drove past the blackened and burning debris of previous attacks along the road:

> One shot-up half-track had the rear hatch open and from it protruded the leg and lower torso of a soldier and what looked like a knee. As we drove slowly past it became apparent that the top half of the corpse had been completely roasted. Perhaps he had already been mercifully dispatched by a bullet. The fighters are about again cleaning up the roads. We are among the houses, partially protected and camouflaged. Movement descended into a series of stop-start races from one area of overhead cover to another before the fighter-bombers reappeared. Outside the village a few vehicles must have been surprised by the aircraft because the machines dived down without pause and badly aimed bursts are smacking into the walls and streets as far back as us here.[12]

Pock and his comrades were not always submissive victims when the raids came down upon them, reverting to their training drills by putting up a heavy flak fire from the sections not under direct attack:

> I took up my weapon, loaded it, and began to track the daring fighters' flight from cover. Now they have disappeared into the sun, and one cannot locate them. But in came the first, engines howling, at great speed. The cone of fire detonated on the road, a low-level strafing. I took aim just like in the training manuals and the burst is away. Meanwhile all

---

12 Manuscript forwarded to author by H. Wernemann (Germany, 1989).

around the others have opened fire on the fighter: "Not one of these buggers is smoking at all," exclaimed one fellow near me. And he seemed to be right, for although our fire was generally accurate, we were not able to shoot a single one down.[13]

Hauptmann Helmut Ritgen, a *Panzer* commander with the *Panzer-Lehr*, wrote in his memoirs:

> Even today memories of this march still evoke nightmares for those of us who took part. The division's columns had hardly got under way when they were spotted by enemy reconnaissance aircraft and attacked shortly afterwards by *Jabos* with rockets and bombs. They flew in clear skies, spotted the columns, attacked, then called on other *Jabos* to replace them. Soon mushroom clouds of black smoke from vehicles on fire would appear. The advance was slowed by every attack and the speed of the advance was slowed even further still by bombs dropped on roads, towns and bridges.[14]

Generalleutnant Heinrich von Lüttwitz, commander of the *2. SS-Panzer-Division 'Das Reich'*, found his division's move to Normandy from southern France hampered by the dreaded *Jabos*:

> Suddenly the Allied fighter bombers swoop out of the sky. They came down in their hundreds firing rockets at the concentrated tanks and vehicles. We could do nothing against them, and we could make no further progress. The next day ground we had taken we were forced to give up and the division was back where it started, having lost 30 tanks and 800 men.[15]

The officers in command of the columns of reinforcements realised that their movements had to be postponed and all vehicles were swiftly hidden in woods, dense bushes and among farm buildings. No one dared move in daylight, and after their experience of Allied airpower travelled only at night, and even then by sticking to back roads which had high bushes and hedges. The German divisions moving to the Normandy front were originally planned to be used in an armoured counter-attack, but they eventually had to go over to the defensive just to hold the line. There was now no possibility of driving the invaders back into the sea.

Group Captain Scott, an RAF Typhoon pilot, remembered the system he and his fellow pilots evolved when attacking enemy columns. A reconnaissance squadron would spot a convoy on the move and radio its position to the operations room, describing the type of column and the number of fighters required for the attack. Each pilot would attack in relays, giving the Germans on the ground the illusion of being attacked by swarms of fighters, turning around and attacking again. Many Germans complained that the sky was full of *Jabos*, which not only attacked them without mercy but also destroyed roads and bridges, further slowing down progress. Scott recalled the terror he inflicted on the enemy with gusto:

> The convoy's first vehicle was a large half-track. In my haste to cripple it and seal off the road I let fly all eight rockets in a single salvo. I missed but hit the truck behind, it was

---

13 Manuscript forwarded to author by H. Wernemann (Germany, 1989).
14 Trigg, *D-Day Through German Eyes*, pp. 170–71.
15 Ellis, J., *Brute Force* (London: Andre Deutsch, 1990), p. 367.

thrown into the air along with several bodies and fell back on its side. Two other trucks piled into it, there was no escape. Typhoons were already attacking in deadly swoops at the other end of the column and within seconds the whole stretch of road was bursting and blazing under streams of rocket and cannon fire. Ammunition wagons exploded like multi-coloured volcanoes. A large, long barrelled tank standing in a field just off the road was hit by a rocket and overturned in a ditch. Several teams of horses stampeded and careered wildly across the fields dragging their broken wagons behind them. Others fell in tangled kicking heaps or were caught up in the fences or hedges. It was an awesome sight: flames, smoke, bursting rockets and showers of coloured tracer. When we went in on an attack I honestly don't think we had any feelings about it. We were young and you tended to enjoy things. Over the years you tend to forget the horrible things and shooting up a whole lot of troops on the ground was fun. It was very impersonal.[16]

Another RAF Typhoon pilot, an unnamed New Zealand officer who took part in many low-level attacks on the Germans in Normandy, painted a stunning picture of the ground he flew over:

Swirling clouds of yellow dust hung over the busy roads beneath us and further to the south-east the battered city of Caen flickered and smouldered under a huge mushroom of pink and black smoke. Southwards, in the region of Villers Bocage, a furious gun battle was taking place and to the west thin streams of coloured tracer spouted into the sky before falling away in chains of red-hot clusters. In the more open country, the fields were strewn with the bloated carcasses of hundreds of tan and white cattle. Shell craters, bomb holes and burnt-out tanks littered this tortured countryside.[17]

Fellow RAF Typhoon pilot John Thompson found the fighter-bombers were difficult to handle, even for experienced fliers like him:

Let me give you an example, a Hurricane's motor was about 1,300 horsepower, the motor in the Typhoon was 2,400 horsepower. It was a big monster of a fighter. A Hurricane weighed about two and a half tons, a Typhoon weighed seven tons. It was a big aircraft. We would dive in at sixty degrees to around two or three thousand feet, fire our rockets, fire our cannon, and then when you get too close to the ground you would start to pull out.[18]

Luftwaffe chief *Reichsmarschall* Hermann Goering had promised 1,000 fighters to destroy the Allied forces, but on the day of the landings only 36 German aircraft are recorded as being in operation over Normandy; 31 of them were shot down, with the remaining five limping home damaged. There was a huge numerical imbalance between the two air forces as the Allies moved inland; against 170 available German fighters, the Allies fielded 4,029, giving them complete aerial superiority. The skies thus belonged to the Allies, and the German troops on the ground were left looking in vain for support from the *Luftwaffe*. The few German aircraft formations

---

16   Kershaw, *D-Day, Piercing the Atlantic Wall*, p. 197.
17   Hastings, M., *Overlord: D-Day and the Battle for Normandy 1944* (London: Michael Joseph, 1984), p. 356.
18   J. Thompson, correspondence with author (Retford, 1996).

that could be spared were moved to France from every other front – 300 fighters came from Russia, while 15 squadrons were moved from the Reich, leaving the skies over Germany clear for marauding Allied bombers. This left many of the German pilots feeling bitter. They had heard Goering's pledge and had believed it, and the troops on the ground suspected that while they were fighting for their lives, the *Luftwaffe* sat in the comfort of their bases. The truth was that hundreds of German pilots did take part in the Normandy battles, trying hard to counter the vastly superior numbers of Allied planes, which outnumbered them 20:1. Indeed, in the two weeks after the D-Day landings, 594 German pilots were shot down.

Luftwaffe fighter pilot Alfred Wagner had believed Goering's promise to be true, and in a mood of confidence shot down seven Allied planes before he succumbed to the inevitable and was himself brought down:

> We were being attacked by three or four Allied planes at one time, so much for Luftwaffe superiority. I was hit from behind and saw flashes sparking from part of my wings, the wings were shredded. I felt a stab in my right foot, it must have been an explosive shell and my foot was shredded too. My plane started to burn, and I had to get out, I ejected the cockpit hatch but couldn't push myself out properly because my right foot was useless. I eventually managed to push myself out with my arms but as I did my right arm struck the bodywork and a bone broke. The air battles in France took place quite close to the ground and my parachute had only just enough time to open.[19]

Wagner survived but lost his right leg below the knee, along with one of his toes and the middle bone of his left foot. Fellow pilot Wolfgang Fischer had taken part in a raid on Gold Beach on 6 June, and a day later was over the same area when he too was shot down:

> Pieces of shrapnel tore into the fuselage and engine cowling, and I knew instinctively that this was it. Hauling back the stick I pointed the nose of my Focke-Wulf skywards. I needed to gain altitude, not only to escape the tracer being hosed up at me, but also to give myself sufficient height to bail out. We had flown a wide arc out to sea before mounting our attack and now, fortunately, a stiff offshore breeze was carrying me to the coastline. I found myself reflecting on my predicament [while] descending helplessly towards the Normandy invasion beaches.[20]

Beyond the Seine, the *2. SS-Panzer-Division 'Das Reich'* was a hive of activity as it prepared to continue its move to the battle area. From the Loire in the south, the *17. SS-Panzergrenadier-Division* advanced to meet the British, and before the 50th Northumbrian Division's front was the *Panzer-Lehr*. The latter formation's name translates literally as 'Demonstration Division', and little was known at the time of its fighting capabilities. But as the troops of XXX Corps were about to find out, *Panzer-Lehr* was to become a deadly, ruthless and skilful opponent until its destruction in later battles.

---

19   Carruthers, B., *Voices of the Luftwaffe* (Berkshire: Archive Media Publishing Ltd, 2011).
20   Fischer, W., *Luftwaffe Pilot* (Oxford: Casemate Publishing, 2010), p. 87.

Panzer IV tanks of the *12. SS-Panzer-Division 'Hitlerjugend'* move to the Normandy battlefront. (Author's collection)

For the next two-and-a-half months, the British would have to keep up a relentless pressure on the Germans in order to gain ground and maintain the initiative in preparation for a breakout beyond the Seine. Montgomery claimed it was his intention that his forces would make a series of offensives to draw in the German armour. These armoured forces would be allowed no respite, and through aggressive action would be drawn into the battle piecemeal as they arrived at the front to plug holes in Hitler's depleted defences. This, Montgomery claimed, would allow the Americans on the right to clear the Cotentin Peninsula, take Cherbourg and thrust to the south in a *blitzkrieg*-style advance. By engaging the German army south and west of the Seine, Montgomery sought their destruction once and for all. Hitler had allowed Montgomery to fight the battle on his own terms, thus ensuring the British general would be successful in his aims. The biggest and most decisive battle of the Second World War in the west was about to begin.

General Miles Dempsey, commander of the British Second Army, recalled a conference with Montgomery when maps were spread out across the floor with officers crawling over them:

Monty stressed the fact that after the immediate reserves had been drawn in all German reserves would arrive at the battle front from the east and south-east, thus, to get across to the American sector of the bridgehead, they would have to pass across the British front around Caen. It was my job to make sure they didn't move across and that they were kept fully occupied fighting us in the Caen sector.[21]

Lieutenant Colonel Robin Hastings, MC, commander of the 6th Green Howards, commented on the type of troops he was up against in the Normandy Bocage countryside:

> The German forces we met in the last fortnight had been very different from those of the coastal divisions. They came mainly from the 12th SS Panzer Division Hitler Jugend and the 130th Panzer Lehr Division. They were on the whole very young men who had been brought up as Nazis and were prepared to die rather than surrender, [so] these were determined fighters.[22]

The early capture of Villers Bocage, a major part of the Second Army plan, was considered to be of great tactical importance. Twenty miles inland from the beaches, Villers Bocage was a centre of communications for the enemy and its retention was essential in the German plan to contain the Allied bridgehead. The town itself was on high ground at the junction of five important roads. Higher features overlooked this Norman town, and these would have special significance in the coming weeks for the men of XXX Corps as they struggled to take the area. To the north-east was Point 213, which stood on a ridge 2,000 yards in length. To the east stood Points 140 and 158, and to the west was Tracy Bocage. This Bocage countryside was closer than anything the men of XXX Corps had experienced before, with its numerous high hills and deep valleys. Tall thick hedgerows surrounded each small field, and these were flanked by ditches and narrow meandering roads and tracks. These natural features made the work of the tanks extremely difficult, while for the infantry, fighting in such terrain was to prove a nightmare. Gunner Cecil Newton, 4/7th Royal Dragoon Guards, found this strange new landscape hard to master:

Lieutenant Colonel Robin Hastings, MC, 6th Battalion Green Howards. (Author's collection)

---

21 Ellis, *Brute Force*, p. 373.
22 R. Hastings, correspondence with author (Ripon, 1991).

Wounded men of 69 Brigade being taken to a first aid post near the front. (Courtesy of R. Walker)

> The terrain of the Bocage was new to us, very different from the type of desert warfare we had been used to; there were no open spaces to be found here. No-one knew about it beforehand, nobody told us what to expect, [so] these close deep lanes with high hedges came as a great shock to us all.[23]

The battle was now to be fought out in this tightly packed Bocage countryside at close quarters. Initially, the German troops, with their experience of fighting in Russia, had the advantage, but the Allied soldiers soon mastered the battle techniques needed to wage war in this new terrain. With the failure to take Villers Bocage on D-Day, XXX Corps settled down to a lengthy and bitter period of fighting. Every hedge and field had to be fought for and then held against a very skilful, ruthless and determined enemy, who had the additional motive of knowing that if he failed to contain the Allies, devastating warfare would be taken to the very heart of the Reich.

On the morning of 7 June, XXX Corps consolidated its gains and counted the cost. For some units there were still objectives to be taken, and many actions were being fought by the troops at the front.

---

23   C. Newton, correspondence with author (Cheshire, 1994).

7th Battalion Green Howards, attack on the radio station on the Coulombs–Loucelles road, 7 June

Early on 7 June, the objective for the 7th Green Howards was to be a radio station housed in a farm a few hundred yards west of the Coulombs–Loucelles road. These buildings were heavily fortified and surrounded by strong minefields and wire. The open plateau on which this position stood gave no cover to the attacking infantry as they approached. The 7th Battalion had moved up to the enemy minefields late on 6 June and been fired upon from the station itself. At this time, the 7th Battalion were well in advance of the remainder of 69 Brigade and settled down for the night on 6 June north of Coulombs. Lieutenant Colonel Richardson, commander of the 7th Green Howards, made his plans for the assault, which was to take place at 0530 hours on 7 June. Although the ground surrounding the position was very open, there was a valley to the west which offered a limited amount of cover for the advancing troops. A and B Companies in support were to occupy the valley with the intention of cutting off the enemy's retreat and to give covering fire to the main assault. C Company would be the assault company and would be supported by the fire of artillery, mortars, machine guns and a squadron of tanks from the 4/7th Royal Dragoon Guards. Having no natural cover, the task given to the men of C Company was not an easy one.

Private Thomas Tateson, of A Company, 7th Green Howards, was ordered forward on a recce patrol before the main assault began:

> I was awakened at 04:00 a.m. after two hours sleep and ordered to accompany an NCO on a forward patrol to establish whether the wireless station had been abandoned. We approached through a cornfield in the semi-dark and got to within perhaps 100 yards when we saw smoke rising. I reported this over the radio and immediately there was a burst of Spandau fire from the building. We went to ground and although I have no recollection of the return journey, we must have got back by crawling through the corn.[24]

An inadequate smokescreen was laid down, and under its partial cover the engineers began to clear a path through the German minefield in broad daylight for the infantry to advance through. As small-arms fire from the radio station cut down one engineer after another, Private Tateson watched events unfold, in awe of the engineers who attempted to clear a path through the minefield:

> Our Sergeant, Potterton, realising that somehow we must make progress, then went forward on his own without a detector, laying a tape behind him to establish a safe path. If he didn't suffer the same fate as the three engineers before him we had a fair chance of following him through without further casualties. We could only watch him with increasing apprehension as he edged his way forward, and having seen the gruesome results of the previous effort, admire his cold-blooded courage. The tension was almost unbearable and was only slightly reduced when he reached the far side of the minefield and started to return along his taped path. This again he negotiated safely and then led us safely back through. After the first

---

24 T. Tateson, interview with author (Sheffield, 1991).

A tense moment as British infantry await the order to advance. (Author's collection)

section had got through, he again returned and led his other section through. His actions in the minefield demanded cool courage without the stimulation of violent action.[25]

Sergeant W. Potterton was awarded the Military Medal for these courageous acts, although Tateson thought a VC would have been more appropriate.

The attack was launched on schedule at 0530 hours, one section of C Company reaching the entrance to the radio station but being driven back with casualties. Tanks of the 4/7th Royal Dragoon Guards then moved forward, firing solid shot at the station as the machine gunners of the 2nd Cheshires kept up a steady fire throughout. Under cover of this deluge, the men of C Company stormed the eastern entrance to the station as A Company broke through the defences on the western side. More than 50 Germans gave themselves up.

Private Tateson took part in the assault with A Company:

> My personal recollection of entering the gateway to the radio station was of passing the body of one of our men who had been killed in the first attack which had been repulsed. He was lying in the gateway with his guts literally blown out and the remains of his drawers cellular adhering to them. I thought how sordid war really was and how the glory of battle is such a wicked lie. I have a recollection of coming across an abandoned machine-gun post with a dead German soldier lying there covered in a blanket. I turned back a corner of the blanket that was covering the dead man's head; there was no blood on his face but there

---

25 T. Tateson, interview with author (Sheffield, 1991).

Wounded German soldiers surrendering. (Author's collection)

was a very small hole in the middle of his forehead. Foolishly I stood there gazing at him and thinking that somewhere in Germany his relatives still had to be told that he no longer existed. His face was of a narrow triangular type with a small mouth, and his hair was dark and lank. That picture of his face remains clear in my mind after all those years. I covered his face again and moved on with a feeling of shame for having intruded.[26]

Once the men had taken the position, it was seen that the radio station and surrounding buildings had been converted into a veritable fortress. Communication trenches criss-crossed the whole position, and barrack rooms were found in the rear. By noon, the battalion had consolidated their position astride a crossroads a few hundred yards past the radio station.

Tateson looked for souvenirs with his comrades and reflected on the day:

> We explored the buildings gingerly in case of booby traps amongst the mass of radio equipment and connecting wires. I acquired a Luger pistol which one of our officers in turn acquired from me a few days later when I rashly tried firing it into the ground. In the

---

26 T. Tateson, interview with author (Sheffield, 1991).

German prisoners being escorted to the beach look on as General Montgomery passes in his jeep. (Courtesy of M. Hearst)

ditch surrounding the station I came across the body of a German soldier lying beside his wrecked Spandau machine gun and realised that it was positioned to cover my approach route through the corn when on that two-man patrol earlier that morning. Whether or not he was the one who fired that burst at us I don't know, but it was certainly the point from which the fire had come. It seemed to me then that this event had happened days ago, although in fact it was not much more than six hours previously. This was the late morning of Tuesday 7th June and I had had a total of three hours' sleep since the morning of Sunday June 5th, a period of about forty-six hours.[27]

56 Independent Brigade at Bayeux, 7–9 June

Patrols from 56 Brigade had confirmed by the morning of 7 June that the city of Bayeux had been virtually evacuated by German troops and their administrative echelons. The 2nd Essex and 2nd South Wales Borderers, with the support of the tanks of the Sherwood Rangers, liberated the town later that morning without any major problems.

27 T. Tateson, interview with author (Sheffield, 1991).

Lance Corporal Arthur Dyer, 56 Brigade Signals, 2nd Gloucesters, set off for Bayeux in his M14 armoured half-track radio vehicle at 0830 hours:

> A [Universal] carrier went ahead until it was out of view, and we pulled up to negotiate a trip wire across the road. This done we moved forward at speed and ran into a lot of bumps in the road. Our driver George steered his way through the maze just in case they were mines and by a miracle we missed each one. A carrier behind us hit one and it turned out they were mines; the signals officer was seriously hurt. We carried on ahead looking for the leading carrier and stopped short of a corner and the driver went to investigate. He returned and said there were Jerries just around the corner. We had taken the wrong road and arrived in Bayeux before our troops.[28]

Private A. Vince of the 2nd Essex recalled some of the events of that day:

> At 11:00 a.m. on 7th June A Company went in supported by tanks of the Sherwood Rangers. Only a little sniping in the streets developed and the offenders were quickly liquidated. By 13:00 p.m. the town was secure. The companies deployed defensively, and the inhabitants sufficiently recovered from the shock to commence looting the German QM [Quartermaster] stores. Now we received our first introduction to Calvados, that fiery spirit resulting from distilling cider and named after the department of France from which it originates.[29]

Lieutenant Colonel Stanley Christopherson, Squadron Commander with the Sherwood Rangers, was in the first troop to enter the town:

> We were most relieved to find that except for isolated strong points in the town and the odd sniper no other Germans were to be found, which prevented any damage to the beautiful and historic buildings. We were given a most enthusiastic and spontaneous reception by the inhabitants who appeared genuinely delighted to welcome us and demonstrated their joy by throwing flowers at the tanks and distributing cider and food among the men.[30]

Unknown to the British, the switchboard of the German LXXXIV Corps Headquarters was still being manned in Bayeux by a young German woman in the Telephone Auxiliary. A German officer by the name of Hayn rang the exchange asking for the intelligence officer, only to be told: "*Herr Major*, British tanks are now passing the soldiers club. They are right in the middle of the town." A speechless *Major* Hayn replied: "How on earth do you know? Is there no-one left at headquarters?" "All staff officers have joined the fighting. British armoured forces have broken through our main front line and are attacking the town. I'm the last one here and now the Tommies are driving past the building outside. You can hear for yourself *Herr Major*," the woman then said, holding the receiver outside the window. "It could only be the 50th

---

28 Letter to author from A. Dyer (Gloucester, 1991).
29 Manuscript forwarded to author by A. Vince (Essex, 1990).
30 Beevor, A., *D-Day, The Battle for Normandy* (London: Penguin, 2010), p. 175.

Division I'm afraid, I've got to ring off now, I'll disappear through the orchards at the back." Then the line went dead.[31]

In an Official Dispatch from Bayeux, war correspondent William Downs commented on the situation in the town:

> The streets are lined with men, women, children and a lot of dogs. The women and children smile while the men look grimly on and wave. People have dug out their tricolour flags and the whole town is spotted with British flags from goodness knows where. Whenever we stop our jeep a crowd gathers, young boys are all over it. But it cannot be called a riotous welcome, it is a welcome with reservations and the reservations are only a mile away. The boom of the German guns and machine-guns that still can be heard are reminders to these people, who have lived under the Hun for four years, that liberation takes some getting used to and it has to be made to stick. Somehow you can't blame them for these reservations. Meanwhile the people are making us welcome and genuinely want us to stay. Our armour and goodwill are slowly convincing them that this is not another Dunkirk. The peculiar thing about this battle is that the French civilians are doing their best to ignore it.[32]

Sergeant Gordon Duffin, 2nd Gloucesters, was amazed to see Bayeux fill up with all kinds of troops, some of them straight from England. The troops who had been doing the fighting since D-Day were in a poor state, with torn uniforms covered in dust and mud. They received comments from some of the smartly dressed new arrivals that were not welcome:

> Bunting was being put up all over the place and the town was packed with servicemen. They were all smart and gleaming, then there was us straight out of a slit-trench. We sat down outside the municipal baths and dozed off until I received a kick. It was a guardsman making fun of us; they were all done up to the nines. One said: "Glosters, I have heard about county regiments, but I didn't know they were so filthy." Another Gloster said to me: "Shoot the bugger Duff." The Bren-gun was cocked and aimed when a time-served Sergeant from the Guards apologised for his men and diffused the situation. He gave them a very serious talking to, after which he explained to the Glosters that the guardsmen were green and had only just landed.[33]

Private Vince recalled the 2nd Essex passing through Bayeux:

> That night we reached the little feature south of Le Loup Hors without incident and dug-in either side of the main road to the south. In the late evening we had our first meal in France, small though it was. A German motorcycle combination drove slap into our lines and after a sharp engagement two of the three passengers were taken prisoner and the third liquidated more decisively. A German press correspondent also drove into C Company's area and was most surprised to find he could not return. In the late evening of 9th June we were relieved and spent a wet night in the fields near Bayeux before coming under command of

---

31 Carell, *Invasion – They're Coming* pp. 133–34.
32 Newspaper cutting forwarded to author by W. Ridley (Durham, 1992).
33 Manuscript forwarded to author by D. Eshelby (Birmingham, 1994).

French civilians welcome their liberators. (Author's collection)

the 7th Armoured Division on the following day. Before first light we were off again and by midday we had put several miles between ourselves and Bayeux.[34]

For all the celebrations, there was a darker side to the liberation of Bayeux that would be repeated in numerous cities, towns and villages as the invasion progressed through northern France. Collaborators were hunted down by the resistance and other townsfolk in a frenzy of hatred. Women who had taken German lovers were ritually humiliated by being stripped in public and having their heads shaved. Other more serious collaborators would be taken out into the woods and never seen again.

War correspondent William Downs watched events unfold:

> The people of Bayeux seized leading collaborators, men and women, who had helped the Germans. The chief of them was forced to march through the town while the populace

---

34   Manuscript forwarded to author by A. Vince (Essex, 1991).

A disturbing scene of humiliated shaven-headed French women who were said to have fraternised with German soldiers. (Author's collection)

lashed him with whips and sticks. There is a deep and intense bitterness among the French, more profound than anything we have experienced in Britain. Wherever our troops arrive they find Frenchmen who ask only for a chance to enlist and hit back at the Germans.[35]

At this point of the campaign, 56 Brigade left the 50th Northumbrian Division to become part of the 7th Armoured Division.

47 Royal Marine Commando, Operation Aubery: the attack on Port-en-Bessin, 7–8 June

The men of 47 Royal Marine Commando had emerged as one of the elite commando units by June 1944, and the task they were allocated would prove to be a tough nut to crack. Their objective of Port-en-Bessin was situated in the middle of a 15-mile gap between the British on Gold Beach and the Americans on Omaha Beach. The early capture of this town was considered of vital importance to the security of the right flank of XXX Corps, and it was essential that the US 1st Division be linked up with at the earliest opportunity.

---

35 Newspaper cutting forwarded to author by W. Ridley (Durham, 1991).

The main defences of Port-en-Bessin were on 61-metre-high cliffs known as the western and eastern features, situated on either side of the low ground in which Port-en Bessin-lay. On the Bayeux road, to the south of the port, was an entrenched German concrete position with defences that stretched into the harbour area. A prisoner had told the commandos that the troops holding the port were infantrymen of *1. Kompanie* of the *1. Bataillon, Grenadier Regiment 726*, and that their battalion headquarters were close by. To make matters worse, the sniper school of the *352. Infanterie-Division* was close at hand in La Fosse-de-Saucy, and there was no sign as yet of the Americans from Omaha. As dawn broke on 7 June, 47 Commando sent out patrols to try and make contact with the Americans; unknown to the British, the Americans had met with great opposition on their beach and the timetable was now running badly behind schedule.

The original plan of attacking the cliff-top positions and avoiding the town was now thought to be impractical and was abandoned. Instead, 47 Commando CO Lieutenant Colonel Phillips launched his men into the streets of the town itself, where they were to clear the buildings and port before attacking the cliff-top defences to the east and west.

The marines' wireless sets that had been lost or damaged in the landings had not been repaired by the morning of 7 June, but despite this they entered the port and began fighting their way forward house by house. The defensive position on the Bayeux road was attacked and fell after a brief fight, with many prisoners being taken. During the afternoon, the cruiser HMS *Emerald* and rocket-firing Typhoons bombarded the cliff-top strongpoints and the 25-pdr guns of 147th Field Regiment, Essex Yeomanry, Royal Artillery, fired high explosive and smoke from positions near Le Hamel. This massive concentration of firepower from the 147th was directed with extreme accuracy by a Forward Observation Officer who had joined the commandos' most advanced positions. He was awarded the Military Cross for his work that day. This was followed by an attack by the commandos which captured the base of the western heights.

With the air full of choking, acrid smoke, Captain David Walton of 47 Royal Marine Commando raised himself up and gave the order to fix bayonets. Lance Corporal Frank Wright recalled:

> Our target had been transformed into a miniature volcano. I clicked my bayonet onto my rifle and thought "I must be dreaming; this isn't really happening; I'll wake up in a minute." We were then running and shouting and in moments had reached the foot of the mound, miraculously still alive. Our faces were blackened, and we pushed into the concrete entrance as mad as hell. We went into a large bunker and found cowering inside 20 Germans, white faced and hands in the air. They were shaking uncontrollably at the sight of these ferocious looking madmen.[36]

The Germans now launched a series of counter-attacks and overran the commando rear headquarters. Another attack across the Escures–Port-en-Bessin road cut off the troops defending Escures. The commandos were now reduced to 280 men in the port and ammunition was running low. Trucks of 522 Company, Royal Army Service Corps, braved enemy tank and machine-gun fire and arrived at the commandos' positions at a crucial moment in the battle. Captain Brian

---

36   Collier, R., *D-Day, June 6th, 1944* (London: Cassel, 1992), p. 137.

Lindon, RASC, who led his vehicles to the position the commandos were holding, bringing them badly needed water, food and ammunition, commented:

> We passed through the leading elements of the 2nd Devons in the area of Longues, who warned us that the enemy was dead ahead. We carried on intending to contact the commando near Escures at point 72. The enemy were on our flanks, and they poured small arms fire onto us as we passed, the vehicles were hit several times but kept going. We succeeded in our task and returned to our own lines in one piece.[37]

The importance of support units in actions of this kind are often overlooked, but it is clear that without the actions of this brave RASC officer and his men, 47 Commando would not have been able to overcome the German garrison of Port-en-Bessin. Captain Lindon was awarded the Military Cross for his courage and leadership.

Private Stanley Arthur Coo, RASC, 69 Brigade, was the driver for Brigadier James Hargest,[38] who had served with distinction with the New Zealand forces in the First World War and was now an observer during the invasion. Following in the wake of 47 Commando as they headed for Port-en-Bessin, Private Coo remembered what they encountered on their journey:

> We'd heard about these guns that had been finished off by the aeroplanes and we went down the coast road and came across the site. There was four of these big gun emplacements, huge places they were, damned great guns pointing out to sea. They'd had a lot of bomber raids, I don't know how many, they had blasted the hell out of the whole district. You couldn't see a piece of ground that was there prior to the bombing, every bomb hole was overlapping the next bomb hole. These concrete encasements weren't even scratched yet all the crews were dead, the whole lot of them were killed by concussion. The guns were just as good as the day they were put in there and it hadn't even scratched the bleeding concrete.[39]

The commandos now resumed their attacks on individual strongpoints in the harbour, gradually clearing these positions but at a great cost in lives. They found themselves moving down narrow streets and passing stone buildings that needed clearing; the street fighting was of a very confusing and slow, laborious nature. All the while, two German flak ships in the harbour kept up a steady but murderous fire on the attackers. A Troop bypassed the street fighting and launched their attack up a slope to the west of the town, mines and wire barred their way and the bunkers they encountered had to be cleared one by one. By 2030 hours, however, over 100 Germans had surrendered.

---

37 Newspaper cutting forwarded to author by C. Spandler (Hull, 1992).
38 Brigadier James Hargest, CBE, DSO and Bar, MC, MID, Chevalier la Legion D'Honneur and the Greek Military Cross 1st Class, New Zealand Forces, was killed on 12 August 1944, aged 53. He is buried in Hottot-le-Bagues War Cemetery, France.
39 *WW2: People's War* <www.bbc.co.uk/ww2peopleswar> (accessed 12 October 2019).

Private Stanley Arthur Coo, Royal Army Service Corps. (Author's collection)

Brigadier James Hargest, CBE, DSO and Bar, MC. (Author's collection)

The Eastern Feature

The enemy's eastern cliff-top positions dominated the town, and probing attacks up the hill through mines and barbed wire were driven back with heavy loss of life. A reconnaissance patrol was organised by Captain Terence Frederick Cousins in the direction of the feature, and a cliff path was discovered that led to the positions on the top. The flak ships in the harbour made matters worse, firing onto the marines' probing attacks up the cliff.

Lieutenant John Forfar, MC, a Medical Officer with 47 Royal Marine Commando, watched the attack on the eastern feature as a tragedy unfolded:

> A Troop was then detailed to attack the feature and as the marines moved up the open slope rifle and machine-gun fire was directed at them, and grenades were thrown down on them. The slope was also mined and had a number of hidden positions with flame-throwers. Using their field craft to good effect the men advanced more than half-way up the slope when disaster struck. The intelligence given to the commando was that the harbour was empty of any armed ships, but just before D-Day two flak ships had moved into the harbour and had a direct view of the slope. They opened fire and killed 12 and wounded 17, more than half of the troop, [and] within a few minutes the troop had to withdraw.[40]

---

40 *WW2: People's War* <www.bbc.co.uk/ww2peopleswar> (accessed 29 December 2015).

Major Patrick Donnell of B Troop then led an attack on the flak ships under cover of the fire of his men in houses in the town.[41] Further help was at hand when two destroyers, one of them the Polish ship *Krakowiak*, shelled the flak ships, sinking one; the other duly surrendered.

Lieutenant Colonel Neville, 2nd Devons, was informed that 47 Commando was having a hard time in the port, a number of their ammunition carriers having broken down and the forward troops consequently running out of ammunition again. Support arrived in the form of carriers of the 2nd Devons from Longues-sur-Mer that were loaded with ammunition. They advanced into the commandos' positions and soon became involved in the fighting on the outskirts of the port. Private Jim Wilson, 2nd Devons, recalled the incident:

> We came down a hill past a small chateau that the platoon commander expected to be defended, but there were no Germans in sight. My sergeant thought they may be the ones that tried to ambush us earlier on. Further down the hill to Bessin we got more Spandau fire from the high ground into the open top of the carrier which didn't give us much cover. We fired back with Brens, but later when we went up the hill, we saw the Spandaus were in concrete Tobruk nests, so we probably wasted our time. We were under fire from Bessin all night, but we got some Jerries who were trying to get out of the town and up our side of the hill to join the Spandau boys.[42]

As the Devons advanced, the nature of the countryside became noticeably different to troops that had previously been fighting in villages and towns. Sergeant William Baker, 2nd Devons, recalled the nature of the land around Port-en-Bessin:

> After we got past the built-up areas and houses, we came into what we call close country. It was all hedgerows and fields with high banks around them, not open warfare like we trained for quite a bit, it wasn't like that at all. We had to stalk the hedges and dare not go out into open fields if we could help it. Jerry had these Spandau machine-guns perched in little out of the way corners ready to spray us with fire.[43]

As darkness fell on 7 June, it was looking doubtful if the German positions on the clifftop could be taken that night. Captain Cousins led a party of four commando officers and 25 other ranks up the eastern feature without being detected, and as soon as the troops reached the position on the heights they went into action and penetrated the defences. The enemy was taken by surprise and thrown into confusion as the commandos attacked them from the rear. The German commander was captured in his bunker and was persuaded to lead the commandos through the minefields and to summon the remainder of the garrison to surrender, which they did. Dugouts and trenches riddled the top of the feature, and the final mopping up was to be a grindingly slow process. A concrete bunker on the cliff top was attacked by Captain Cousins and four of his men. The bunker fell but all the men attacking it were wounded and Cousins was killed by a grenade.

---

41 Major Patrick Donnell was awarded the Distinguished Service Order for the action at Port-en-Bessin.
42 Saunders, T., *Commandos and Rangers: D-Day Operations* (Barnsley: Pen & Sword, 2012), p. 124.
43 *WW2: People's War* <www.bbc.co.uk/ww2peopleswar> (accessed 1 June 2019).

Private Peter Forbes of 47 Commando remembered:

> The Germans were entrenched on the high ground on either side of the port, and we moved down under fire to the outskirts of the town to flush out the Germans who were occupying the houses. We followed through to A Troop who were starting to clear out the heights on the other side of the canal; this was a hazardous business because of the pillbox on the top, which gave the Germans cover while they continued to keep us under fire. Captain Cousins asked for volunteers to try and take the pillbox out. It proved very risky. Captain Cousins took with him a bag full of explosives to blast the German strongpoints. Unfortunately he didn't survive the attack.[44]

Lieutenant Forfar, 47 Commando, recalled how the group came under heavy fire as it ascended the hill. Captain Cousins sent his men into some unoccupied trenches nearby, and taking with him a small group consisting of Marines Delap, Howe and Madden, he moved through a gap in the wire and rushed a bunker, shooting as they went. Grenades were thrown at them and as one exploded, Cousins fell forward, killed outright. Madden was wounded in the head and Delap was concussed.[45]

Private Arthur Delap, 47 Commando, later spoke of the attack on the bunker led by Captain Cousins:

> When the grenades went off in front of you it was terrible. There were big flashes in front of your eyes, no pain, but my ears were ringing a lot from the noise. I was deaf and concussed for a few seconds. Then I started shooting again and after that they put up their white hankies and surrendered, [but] Cpt Cousins lay dead next to me.[46]

Private Fred Wildman, 47 Commando, also took part in the attack on the eastern feature:

> The Germans had had enough and started to surrender. Q Troop wheeled to the right on reaching the cliff top and charged along the top firing from the hip, and very soon began taking prisoners. It was by now about 2300 hours and the eastern feature was effectively ours.[47]

Private Arthur Delap, 47 Royal Marine Commando. (Courtesy of N. Hardy)

Medic Lance Corporal P. G. Kendrick and his comrades were taken by surprise as an enemy vehicle came into view:

---

44 P. Forbes, ccorrespondence with author (Frome, 1994).
45 Manuscript forwarded to author by Brian Cook (Carnegie Heritage Centre, Hull, 2016).
46 *Telegraph* newspaper cutting forwarded to author by B. Harrison (Manchester, 1990).
47 F. Wildman, conversation with author (Stevenage, 1989).

German prisoners taken at Port-en-Bessin. (Author's collection)

A scout car with six Germans in it suddenly rounded a bend in the road and we dealt with them – none survived our ambush. Soon after we heard a horse galloping down the lane and as it came into view we saw it had a German rider on it. Sergeant Hooper stepped into the lane and fired his Tommy gun. The horse galloped off with the dead body still on its back. We approached a small village and found an elderly woman crying by the roadside. I could see the old lady was wounded in the arm, so I tended to her and wanted to get her to the safety of a house. While I was trying to get her to understand that she should be in bed she slapped my face and I realised that she had completely misunderstood. I had no choice but to give her a morphine injection and move on. After so many years I can almost hear the noise of the gunfire, see the sky blackened with planes and out to sea see hundreds of ships around us as far as the eye could see.[48]

---

48   P.G. Kendrick, correspondence with author (Nottingham, 1989).

Port-en-Bessin after the battle. (Author's collection)

The Western Feature and the fall of Port-en-Bessin

The momentum of the attack was now in full swing, even though the commandos were outnumbered by the Germans by four to one. The fearsome commandos fought their way up the western feature, storming through concrete emplacements, barbed wire and minefields. Under cover of the artillery barrage, Captain Walton led his 47 Commando troop along hedges until they were in a position where they could launch an assault into the enemy trenches and bunkers. The sight of the black-faced, howling commandos was enough to persuade the Germans the game was up; weapons were discarded, and hands went up before the attackers could get to work. One by one, the enemy positions fell and before dawn on 8 June the feature was in the hands of British troops.

Corporal George Amos, 47 Commando, was taken prisoner as his comrades attacked. He was only too aware of Hitler's directive that any commandos captured should be taken outside and shot out of hand:

> When they captured me I was tending my wounded sergeant and the Germans thought I might be a medic. By that stage I'd worked out that everyone was going to be shot except medics, so when they asked me to deal with their wounded I pretended to know what I was doing. Later they gave me a cup of acorn coffee and I went to sleep. Next thing I knew I was being woken up and the whole German garrison was surrendering.[49]

---

49   *Telegraph* newspaper cutting forwarded to author by B. Harrison (Manchester, 1990).

Captain Peter Winter, 47 Commando, watched as Corporal Amos came down the hill with his prisoners:

> Corporal Amos fell the Germans into three ranks and with a large white flag marched them down the hill and that was that. Except that when he got to the bottom of the hill, his troop commander said: "Amos, where have you been?" Looking closely at him and ignoring the ranks of his prisoners, he added: "You haven't had a shave!"[50]

Captain Terence Frederick Cousins, 47 Royal Marine Commando. (Author's collection)

This convinced the remaining Germans on the western feature that further resistance was futile and they all surrendered. At 0400 hours, the commandos reoccupied Escures and on 8 June the German garrison at Port-en-Bessin surrendered, the garrison commander and 300 men marching into captivity. By then, 47 Royal Marine Commando consisted of just 200 men and officers. Captain Cousins[51] was recommended for the Victoria Cross because of his leadership, initiative and bravery during the battle, but was denied this honour, much to the disgust of his men and brother officers.

As the fighting subsided at Port-en-Bessin, Private Stanley Coo, RASC, arrived with Brigadier James Hargest:

> We went into this port the marines had captured, they were all hanging about, and we stood there talking to them. The old man wandered off with an officer and had a conflab with him. I was sat on a wall and all of a sudden blinking bullets kept hitting the house just behind me and I thought: "Where the hell's that coming from." I couldn't make it out, so I got my rifle out of the jeep and I'm having a look round as bullets are still whistling past. The Brigadier came back and said: "Having a shot Coo?" I said: "I can't see any bugger to shoot at sir." We never did find out where they came from[;] anyway we went back to this officer, and he had this bloke sat alongside him with his hand bandaged. The Brigadier said: "Have you been wounded?" The officer said: "Self-inflicted, he'd shot his finger off." He was under close arrest [–] nobody took any notice of him, [so] I gave him this bottle of rum, he must have drunk half of it.[52]

---

50   Saunders, *Commandos and Rangers*, p. 121.
51   Captain Terence Frederick Cousins, 47 Royal Marine Commando, was killed on 7 June 1944, aged 22. He is buried in Bayeux War Cemetery, France. A memorial, with portrait picture of Captain Cousins, was unveiled at Port-en-Bessin in 2009.
52   *WW2: People's War* <www.bbc.co.uk/ww2peopleswar> (accessed 12 October 2016).

During the battle for Port-en-Bessin, 47 Commando suffered 116 casualties, with 46 killed and 70 wounded. A memorial now stands on the cliff top to the men who fought there. At 2100 hours on 8 June, patrols of 47 Commando and the 2nd Devons made contact with the American 1st Division in the village of Escures, meaning the beaches were finally linked up to form a single Allied bridgehead.

As soon as the fighting for the port ended, the Beach Commandos of the Royal Navy entered the harbour and set up their headquarters. The work of making sure the port was in a fit state to land large stores of food and ammunition then began in earnest, including on the PLUTO pipeline (Pipeline Under The Ocean) that was to deliver the bulk of the enormous quantities of fuel required by the Allied forces. The first pipeline to bring fuel from tankers moored off the coast came ashore at Port-en-Bessin on D-plus 19. Other supplies came ashore here in the conventional manner, the port playing a major part in supplying the British Army long after the fighting had moved on to the borders of Germany itself.

The joint post: 6th Battalion Durham Light Infantry, 7–8 June

On 7 June, the Durhams and Green Howards of 69 Brigade were ordered to hold a joint post at the vulnerable junction between 151 and 69 Brigades, where the road from Ducy-Sainte-Marguerite met the minor road which ran south-east from Condé in the valley of the River Seulles. Their purpose was to stop the Germans infiltrating their lines by moving up the River Seulles. It was not an area that would be easy to defend, and matters were made worse because 69 Brigade was delayed getting there, being held up by enemy action at St Leger.

Captain David Fenner, of D Company, 6th Durhams, had sent out patrols the night before to see if the area was occupied by the enemy, and after first light on 7 June his column moved forward and was soon on its objective. The armour and artillery took up the positions that had been selected off the map back in England before embarkation, and while these movements were going on the troops of the 6th Durhams were attacked by Typhoon fighter-bombers as they advanced. This friendly fire knocked out one carrier, but the crew, who were old hands, bailed out before the strike. Captain Fenner recalled:

> We displayed our recognition signals of yellow smoke and fluorescent panels; no further attacks took place. We were behind the bomb line on the Tilly/Caen road and should have been safe from attack from our own aircraft. We picked up some prisoners, including some flak troops and Tartars. The latter were small Mongol-featured Russians; ex-POWs recruited into the German army. Shortly after this the battalion came marching up to the position. Each company headed for its map selected position. A screen of machine-guns of the 2nd Cheshires was deployed for local protection and the battalion began to dig in. It was as smoothly done as one would expect from a well-managed battle-experienced battalion.[53]

---

53   Manuscript forwarded to author by D. Fenner (Durham, 1990).

British troops look for enemy snipers before advancing. (Courtesy of R. Hymer)

Fenner knew that 69 Brigade had been one of the assault brigades, and unlike his unit had experienced some hard fighting on D-Day. Taking this into account, he expected them to be late arriving. Subsequent events proved this assumption to be correct:

> We heard some firing as the carriers had ambushed two German motor-cycle combinations who had driven into the left flank of the battalion positions. The left flank was open because 69 Brigade was still fighting its way forward. Two rifle sections of 18 Platoon dug-in astride the railway line on the bridge which crossed the road. Passing under the arch of the bridge to the left was a small farmhouse and yard, [and] here the carrier section was deployed. Back under the bridge was a bank between the railway embankment and the road. In the gap between the two, HQ was set up. About 100 yards to the north up the road a copse known as Strip Wood joined the road and it was here that the six-pounder anti-tank gun was positioned to be able to deal with any tank coming up the road under the bridge.[54]

Fenner placed his men on a viaduct and in various buildings in the locality, and as he did so German troops began an attempt to reconnoitre the area:

> While this was going on there was some shooting on the carrier sections side of the bridge. They had killed a young SS man, a panzer grenadier, but another had got away. I

---

54 Manuscript forwarded to author by D. Fenner (Durham, 1990).

Troops of the 6th Battalion Durham Light Infantry take cover in open ground. (Courtesy of J.H. Clark)

concluded that this could have been a two-man reconnaissance patrol out to examine our layout and everyone was warned to keep a good look out. Then a Frenchman from a farm just south of our position came to us and reported a party of Germans had passed west to east through his farm. Yet again our little force was alerted. [There was] an outbreak of firing from the direction of the six-pounder anti-tank gun position, [and] two or three men ran past the HQ in the direction of the carrier section under the bridge. These were in fact the six-pounder crew survivors. I stepped from behind the bank into the road and charging down the road towards us was a bunch of angry Germans. I jumped back behind the bank as we all began firing through the hedge that topped the bank. A furious firefight developed at very close quarters. One of our number was hit but we seemed to have succeeded in checking the German attack temporarily. I yelled for the carrier section to come and support us, and I lobbed one of the 69 plastic grenades I had in my pouch over the bank.[55]

The Germans stopped firing and retreated the way they had come, followed by the Durhams' carrier section, which had moved up in support. Captain Fenner ran past an abandoned machine pistol and a pair of binoculars and assumed they had belonged to the German commander who had been hit. Fenner and his men then pursued the enemy:

55 Moses, *The Faithful Sixth*, p. 282.

> At the entrance to the wood, we ran into another firefight at close range, probably a covering party to secure the withdrawal of the assaulting force. We took three more casualties including the brave carrier section commander, Cpl King,[56] who was killed. As these Germans ran back to the wood, they were shot up by 18 Platoon from their position on top of the railway bridge. We found the six-pounder intact, and we also found the six-pounder commander. He had been walking up the line of the wood when he surprised the Germans coming the other way. They shot him down and sprayed him with bullets as they ran past after the other gunners. He was badly shot up but was able to walk. We found one wounded and two dead Germans. The German patrol was skilfully handled as the young SS men pressed home their attack. The whole affair could only have lasted a few minutes, but it was pretty savage while it happened.[57]

At 0900 hours on 8 June, the joint post was reoccupied and came under fire from a German armoured car when another enemy attack was launched but beaten off. At 1100 hours, a second enemy assault was launched which was far heavier than the others, the Durhams in danger of being overrun as the enemy infiltrated their flanks. Lieutenant T.M. Kirk saw the situation and decided to withdraw, covered by artillery and mortar fire. Meanwhile, Corporal George S. Richardson sat in his slit trench with 24 of his comrades, the dead still lying about as there had been no time to bury them. As midday approached, a battle was being fought to his right all along the viaduct:

> I started sending broadcasts back giving a running commentary, numbers of Germans and the action we were taking. Jerry was slowly closing in, and we could see we were going to be overrun. I said I could bring artillery fire down on this position and the Lt gave me the map reference, I gave the signal: "Murder" and an eight-figure map reference. "Three minutes" he told Sergeant Cooper. "Get the men ready to run back" [–] which they were all too willing to do as soon as he shouted, "Up and go". I turned the dials off our station, put a bullet through the top and bottom of the radio to put it out of commission and ran like hell for about 100 yards, [to where] there was a hedge with a ditch behind it. It took five to six minutes for the artillery to open fire, about 24 25-pounders ranged on one position [–] they all came down and shattered the whole of the wooded area.[58]

Corporal Richardson was Mentioned in Despatches for his part in this action.

As the carriers made their way back to the battalion positions over an open hillside, they came under heavy fire. The carrier that Private Davidson was driving stalled, and under the eyes of the German gunners he calmly dismounted and cranked the starting handle until the engine once again burst into life. He then returned the starting handle to its normal position and drove off unscathed. Three men were reported missing. Two of them had been taken prisoner,

---

56 Corporal Leslie John King was killed on 7 June 1944, aged 24, and is buried in Bayeux War Cemetery, France.
57 Moses, *The Faithful Sixth*, p. 282.
58 Moses, *The Faithful Sixth*, p. 283.

Privates Evan Hayton[59] and William Barlow.[60] Their captors took them to the grounds of the Chateau d'Audrieu near Condé where, along with 24 Canadian prisoners, they were executed on 8 June by troops of the *12. SS-Panzer-Division 'Hitlerjugend'*, an act witnessed by the family living in the chateau. The truth of their fate was not confirmed until 1994.

8 Armoured Brigade mixed column, St Pierre and Point 103, 7–12 June

The 50th Northumbrian Division was ordered to gather a strong mobile column, consisting of 8 Armoured Brigade: tanks of the Sherwood Rangers, 4/7th Dragoon Guards and 24th Lancers. They were joined by self-propelled guns of the 147th Field Regiment, Essex Yeomanry, Royal Artillery, the 1st Dorsets in vehicles, the 61st Reconnaissance Regiment in armoured cars and carriers, the 288th Anti-Tank Battery of the Northumberland Hussars, one company of the 2nd Machine-gun Battalion the Cheshire Regiment, a Royal Engineers reconnaissance party, a detachment of the 168th Light Field Ambulance and 86th Field Regiment Royal Artillery. At 2300 hours on 7 June, this force was ordered to concentrate in the area of Brecy and be ready for action at first light on the 8th. The route of the column would take it to the south into the heart of the Bocage country and along meandering wooded lanes leading past Point 103 north-east of Tilly-sur-Seulles. It was then to pass through the village of St Pierre, cross the River Seulles and then move due south to force a passage into Villers Bocage.

Corporal George S. Richardson, MiD, 6th Battalion Durham Light Infantry. (Courtesy of R. Pope)

Lieutenant Colonel Stanley Christopherson of the Sherwood Rangers remembered the move forward to Point 103:

> The regiment was ordered to make a right hook and occupy some high ground known as Point 103, which overlooked the villages of St Pierre and Fontenay. We encountered en route anti-tank guns, which we bypassed, and snipers as usual compelled all tank commanders to keep their heads down. We arrived at our destination without a casualty, except for Victor Verner, one of my troop commanders, who was hit in the head by a sniper and eventually

---

59 Private Evan Hayton, 6th Battalion Durham Light Infantry, was murdered on 8 June 1944, aged 20. He is buried in Beny-sur-Mer Canadian War Cemetery, France.
60 Private William Henry Barlow, 6th Battalion Durham Light Infantry, was murdered on 8 June 1944, aged 21. He is buried in Hottot-le-Bagues War Cemetery, France.

A mixed column preparing to move off. (Author's collection)

died from his wound.[61] He had fought with us in North Africa and at all times in battle nothing ever disturbed him: his imperturbability and quiet efficiency inspired confidence in those under his command. His death was a grave loss to the squadron.[62]

Brigadier Hugh John Bernard Cracroft, CO of 8 Armoured Brigade, commented on the inclusion of the 1st Dorsets in the operation:

> As my motorised battalion, 12 KRRC [King's Royal Rifle Corps], had been excluded from the earlier landing craft loading tables, a battalion from 231 Brigade, 1st Dorsets, was allotted to me for this role and quite magnificently did they carry it out, although they had never worked with armour before, and the nearest they came to a motorised battalion in the matter of equipment, was to have a Company equipped with cycles. Their CO, Lt Colonel Norrie, joined my Tac HQ on the morning of the 8th and not long afterward the remainder of the battalion moved into the assembly area at Rucqueville, where they came under my command. The country on this line was very thick and very built up, and it was apparent that

---

61 Lieutenant Laurence Hubert Verner, Nottinghamshire Yeomanry, Sherwood Rangers, Royal Armoured Corps, died of wounds on 9 June 1944, aged 38. He is buried in Ryes War Cemetery, Bazenville, France.
62 Holland (ed.), An *Englishman at War*, p. 389.

we should need considerable infantry support to get the tanks through it. I thought at this time that there was probably only a thin crust of German resistance and that if I could once break through there would be no further organised resistance. How wrong can one be?[63]

Major Peter Martin, 2nd Machine-gun Battalion the Cheshire Regiment, received orders at 2330 hours on 7 June that his unit was to assemble with the armoured column at first light the following morning:

I was quite certain that if an armoured column had set off on the afternoon of D-Day there would have been absolutely nothing to stop it; but having been held up for 36 hours it was too much to expect an easy drive to Villers Bocage. We assembled but didn't set off until 10:00 a.m. As we advanced, we found the whole complex of hamlets that make up the village of Audrieu was where the 1st Dorsets were fighting hard.[64]

The 1000 hours start time of 8 Armoured Brigade on the 8th was hampered by German anti-tank fire coming from the east, which was dealt with by the Dorsets in Loucelles. However, stiff opposition was also encountered on the line of the railway between Loucelles and Bas-d'Audrieu. B and C Companies, 1st Dorsets, moved to outflank the enemy holding the villages south of the railway, and because this was done quite late in the day it meant the defenders would have to be winkled out of Audrieu that same night. The Dorsets' battalion history describes it as "a very ticklish business". They faced elements of the *Panzer-Lehr-Division*.

Major Philip Henry Kerman Brownrigg, of the 61st Reconnaissance Regiment, moved forward with the brief to draw fire, retreat and report back enemy positions:

The move forward was peaceful at first, but after about a mile A Squadron was held up by isolated parties of the enemy and lots of snipers. We were being pressed by brigade to get on: "Use your big friends, tanks, and push on" kept coming over the air to me on the rear link radio.[65]

Tank commander Lieutenant David Render, Sherwood Rangers, advanced with his unit and found little opposition as they headed for Point 103:

The regiment's route took them through the village of Audrieu. Little notice was taken of the imposing chateau situated on the southern side of the village as they pressed on to Point 103. Follow up units of the brigade would later make the grisly discovery that it was the place of execution for 45 Canadian prisoners of war. It was later established that they were shot out of hand by soldiers of the 12th SS Panzer Division Hitler Jugend prior to withdrawing from the chateau at the approach of the British armour. A callous wanton act, it was a harbinger of the savage nature of the fighting that lay ahead.[66]

---

63 National Archives WO171/613.
64 Arthur, *Forgotten Voices of the Second World War*, p. 328.
65 Saunders, T., *The Battle for the Bocage, Normandy 1944* (Barnsley: Pen & Sword, 2021), pp.58–59. Major Brownrigg would be awarded the DSO in February 1945.
66 Render, *Tank Action*, p. 51.

Men of the 1st Battalion Dorsetshire Regiment get a lift forward on the Sherman tanks of 8 Armoured Brigade. (Author's collection)

The fight for Audrieu continued into the night, the streets lit up by the flashes from exploding grenades and the rattle of small-arms fire as the Dorsets cleared one house at a time. Many prisoners were taken, among them a number of *SS-Panzergrenadiers*.

It was not until late on 8 June that troops from the 1st Dorsets were in position between St Pierre and Tilly and on Point 103 to the south of Audrieu. Troop commander Lieutenant George Ames, Sherwood Rangers, was not in action long before he was injured:

> We were just south of Tilly-sur-Seulles in a village called St Pierre on a hill called Pt 103. Our range was about 4,000 yards from the enemy, we had quite a good view from our position and were having a satisfactory shoot over a hedge. I was told to go back for more ammunition, [and] I sent one tank at a time. My troop sergeant had gone back and returned with his ammunition and the troop corporal had done the same. Then I went back, got my ammunition and was on my way back to Hill 103 when I ran headlong into a battle with troops who had a 17-pounder gun, a [Sherman] Firefly tank, which was commanded by one of my colleagues. I blundered into the fight, and he was rather cross because I was spoiling his battle as it were. He was waving at me to get the hell out of it. In the confusion my tank ran into a French apple tree and as it came down it slammed one of the tank hatches down onto my hand completely smashing it up. Although there was quite a bit of fire still flying about at the time we got out of the tank and I think I drank half a bottle of whisky and I felt a little better then, more able to cope. The rest of my hand was an awful mess, but my

driver and co-driver were marvellous. They pushed my fingers back into position and then took me back to the regimental aid station.[67]

The whole column was now being urged to press forward to the important Point 103, and early on 9 June A Company of the 1st Dorsets entered Le-Haut-d'Audrieu and linked up with C and D Companies in Audrieu itself. The whole battalion now occupied a line of villages from Le-Haut-d'Audrieu to Bas-d'Audrieu. Meanwhile, 8 Armoured Brigade had taken point 103.

Major Peter Martin, 2nd Machine-gun Battalion the Cheshire Regiment, recalled:

> Shortly after mid-night I was ordered to report to the Brigadier, [and] he told me that a squadron of tanks had reached Point 103, a dominant feature south of Le-Haute-d'Audrieu and the southernmost hamlet. My company moved across country to join them and what a nightmare journey we had through enemy held territory. By 02:30 a.m. we were up on Point 103.[68]

At first light on 9 June, German tanks approached Point 103 from the south and engaged the British tanks. Two Shermans immediately received direct hits and burst into flames, sending columns of black smoke into the sky. Other British tanks were also hit, and the remainder withdrew down a reverse slope, leaving the Cheshires totally isolated. Major Martin watched as the German tanks stood fast in hull-down positions preparing to shell Point 103:

> They were only about 200 yards away and they proceeded to soften up our positions with high explosive shells which caused many casualties. On several occasions the powerful Tigers would cruise too far forward with their turrets open, and our machine-gunners would open fire on them to make them close down. The situation was precarious because if the enemy put in a determined counterattack from the south, he would be right on top of us before encountering our tanks and anti-tank guns. We were very cheered when soon after mid-day recce parties from the 1st Dorsets arrived to say that Audrieu was being cleared and that the whole battalion would soon be coming up to join us.[69]

Captain Michael Howden, Sherwood Rangers, moved his Sherman tank out from the protection of tree cover to get a better shot at his tormentors. As he did so, his tank received a hit on the front, where the armour was thickest:

> The tank stopped abruptly, and I told the crew to get out. Everyone managed to clamber out without getting hit, after Stan Cox, as gunner, had righted the turret to twelve o'clock, straight ahead, so that the driver and co-driver could get out of their hatches at the front. Cox was last out and was sliding down the back of the tank when he realised he still had his headphones on. As he stopped to take them off he jumped off the tank and it was hit again on the left-hand side; he caught the blast and bits of shrapnel. He lay there fully conscious feeling curiously numb. The rest of the crew had run to the woods for cover but returned

67 *WW2: People's War* <www.bbc.co.uk/ww2peopleswar> (accessed 26 May 2019).
68 Arthur, Forgotten *Voices of the Second World War*, p. 328.
69 Arthur, *Forgotten Voices of the Second World War*, p. 328.

to drag him clear. Another hit on the tank caused huge angry flames to shoot out of every hatch, followed by thick black oily smoke that billowed across the battlefield.[70]

According to Lieutenant Colonel Stanley Christopherson of the Sherwood Rangers, Point 103 was not a healthy place to be on 9 June:

> Point 103 seemed to be the main target of German mortar and shellfire. Enemy tanks had also appeared on the scene. Although trees on Point 103 gave some cover from view, it was quite impossible for the tanks to find a hull-down position, and each time they came forward to engage from the top of the hill they became a sitting target for the German tanks in the village, especially for one which cleverly and continually ran up and down a deep lane in the valley that afforded natural cover and in which alternative fire positions were plentiful. However, after watching his movements carefully, Sergeant Dring eventually scored five direct hits with his 17 pounder and blew him up, [but] not before he had caused us some damage. Michael Howden, Sergeant Rush and Sergeant Houghton all had their tanks knocked out, but they and their crews bailed out without injury, except that Mike's stammer prevented any kind of speech for half an hour and his complexion, which at the best of times was devoid of colour, was even whiter than snow. Peter Pepler[71] from B Squadron was killed by a piece of shrapnel as he was entering his tank. Keith Douglas,[72] my second in command, was hit in the head by a piece of mortar shell as he was running along a ditch towards his tank and killed instantly. The countryside was extremely difficult and unpleasant for tanks, and the enemy, with tanks and infantry, were infiltrating constantly.[73]

The column had advanced more than 6,000 yards through very difficult countryside and brought the infantry of the 50th Northumbrian Division to the vital road centre of Tilly. Their arrival stirred up a veritable hornet's nest as two German divisions had arrived in strength in the area: *Panzer-Lehr* and the *12. SS-Panzer-Division 'Hitlerjugend'*. The 8 Armoured Brigade column had the 8th Durhams added to their compliment on 9 June, the battalion moving to the right of the Dorsets at 0650 hours along the Bayeux–Caen road and approaching to within a mile of St Leger. Here, the Durhams were joined by the tanks of the 24th Lancers, along with self-propelled guns and anti-tank crews with their guns. At 0930 hours, the column set off with many of the infantry riding on the tanks, others following on bicycles but finding these were of little use as the column did not use the roads but travelled over the rolling fields. Once established, the next task was to take St Pierre, as the advance could not continue until this was completed.

---

70 Manuscript forwarded to author by M. Howden (Stow-on-on-the-Wold, 1990).
71 Lieutenant Peter Pepler, Nottinghamshire Yeomanry, Sherwood Rangers, Royal Armoured Corps, was killed on 9 June 1944, aged 24. He is buried in Tilly-sur-Seulles War Cemetery, France
72 Captain Keith Castellain Douglas, 2nd Derbyshire Yeomanry, attached to Nottinghamshire Yeomanry, Sherwood Rangers, Royal Armoured Corps, was killed on 9 June 1944, aged 24s. He is buried in Tilly-sur-Seulles War Cemetery, France. He was born in Tunbridge Wells in 1920 and won a scholarship to go to Oxford to study. His talent for poetry was recognized early in his career, and his first published poem appeared when he was only 16 years old. He wrote the book *From Alamein to Zem Zem*, which was due to be published before D-Day. He commented prophetically in a letter home: "I cannot afford to wait, because of military engagements that may be the end of me." The book was eventually published in 1979.
73 Holland (ed.), *An Englishman at War*, p. 390.

69 Brigade at Cristot and Point 103, 11 June 1944: 6th Battalion Green Howards

Sunday 11 June was a day of torrential rain. Lieutenant Colonel Robin Hastings, MC, 6th Green Howards, was summoned by the commander of 69 Brigade to make sure his battalion was ready for a move at 1400 hours to take part in an as-yet-unspecified task. The 8 Armoured Brigade mixed column had earlier advanced south towards Tilly-sur-Seulles. A reconnaissance had been made which had led them to a hill south of the village of Cristot, and with a company of Sherman tanks of the 4/7th Royal Dragoon Guards they had been able to almost reach the top, encountering only minimal resistance, this in countryside where vision was limited to the next field ahead. They concluded that if this hill could be held by infantry, the flank of 8 Armoured Brigade's mixed column would be secured. This was the task that Lieutenant Colonel Hastings and his troops would be required to do at very short notice. The basic concept was simple, but speed was of the essence. Hastings had little time to prepare and no time to make a reconnaissance of the area he was to attack. He thought it a reckless thrust into the unknown, but earlier reports were hopeful that the Germans were not present in force. The main worry was the close countryside, with woods and small fields surrounded by high banks and thick hedges; a journey through this terrain for over half a mile could prove very difficult. A few resolute defenders armed with hand-held anti-tank weapons could hold up a whole brigade, as had already been demonstrated on numerous occasions. Support tank crews felt very vulnerable in this type of countryside, for although their main armaments had a good range, the tanks themselves were hemmed in on their flanks with high banks and thick hedges which they found very difficult to penetrate. Even if they broke through these obstacles, the moment they appeared they were at once a target for the tank-killer crews of the *Panzer-Lehr-Division*.

Brigadier Cracroft, CO of 8 Armoured Brigade, wrote:

> In the morning, in preparation for this attack, I ordered 4/7th DG [Royal Dragoon Guards] to carry out a reconnaissance in force. B Squadron reached the village and saw a great many infantry but met no organised resistance. The probability is that they disorganised an enemy counterattack as it was forming up; but also, that the enemy were forewarned of the impending attack.[74]

The 6th Green Howards were given orders to advance and occupy Point 103 near Cristot. Support for the assault was to be given by the tanks of 4/7th Royal Dragoon Guards, the artillery of the Essex Yeomanry and 90th Field Regiment, Royal Artillery, and the machine guns of the 2nd Cheshire. By 1430 hours, the 6th Green Howards were on the move, passing through Duoy-St-Marguerite, and by 1600 hours had got beyond Audrieu. The advance so far had gone off without incident, but the nerves of the men were taut as they scrambled through hedges, never knowing if the Germans would be on the other side waiting for them with a murderous hail of Spandau fire. The lack of preparation for this operation had meant a dearth of information on any enemy positions, so there could be no artillery plan and therefore no registered targets. Fire support would depend on the Forward Observation Officers of the Royal Artillery who accompanied the troops as they advanced.

---

74 National archives WO 171/613.

The German reconnaissance troops of the *SS-Hitlerjugend Aufklärung Bataillon* were in position and waiting, and at 1800 hours they watched the tanks of the 4/7th Royal Dragoon Guards pass by where they lay before opening a withering fire on the men of B Company, 6th Green Howards, inflicting heavy casualties. The company commander, Major J.M. Young,[75] walked about the battlefield rallying his men in full view of the enemy with a reckless disregard for his own safety until he was wounded. Captain R.C. Mitchell[76] was killed along with many others. Lieutenant P.C. Bawcombe[77] was commanding the right forward platoon of B Company when it came under heavy machine-gun fire from very short range. He rallied his men and advanced 300 yards in the face of fierce fire, and receiving the news that his company commander and second in command had become casualties, Bawcombe took charge of the company and led them forward.

Lieutenant Colonel Hastings looked on as the Germans opened fire on B Company on the right flank, and saw Lieutenant Bawcombe rallying his men in the open:

> This company had very heavy casualties, but largely owing to the efforts of Coy Commander, who walked about the fields in full view of the enemy with total disregard for his own safety, they pushed on until the company commander, the 2nd in command and several senior NCOs had become casualties.[78]

Although company runner Private James Leary had been hit in the left leg, he continued with his hazardous work, time and time again crossing the ground that was being swept by Spandau and mortar fire. When Major Young was wounded, he went to him and pulled him into cover and dressed his wounds. He then carried his orders back to the hard-pressed platoons to continue the attack. Upon trying to get back to his own platoon for the final assault, Leary[79] found he could now barely walk as the pain was so bad. An officer saw his distress and ordered him to retire to the Regimental Aid Post (RAP). Numerous such acts of courage were performed that day, many unwitnessed, the men slowly moving forward until they were pinned down, killed or wounded.

Company Sergeant Major Stanley Hollis, 6th Green Howards, was in a slit trench with his comrades when they saw a wounded German soldier near them in the uniform of the SS. One of the men roughly pulled the wounded man into the trench, only to find he was a young boy, no older than 14 or 15 years. In a quiet moment, the Green Howards took pity on the young man, dressed his wounds and shared their food and water with him. The young German took advantage of the relaxed situation and grabbed a gun from one of the British soldiers, shooting one of them dead. Hollis reacted instantly, grabbed his Sten gun and shot the boy dead. Years

---

75 Major J.M. Young was awarded the Military Cross for his actions at Cristot on 11 June 1944.
76 Captain Ralph Charles Mitchell, 6th Battalion Green Howards, was killed on 11 June 1944, aged 24. He is buried in Bayeux War Cemetery, France.
77 Lieutenant P.C. Bawcombe was awarded the Military Cross for his example to his men and his qualities of leadership at Cristot on 11 June 1944.
78 National archives WO 223/31.
79 For his devotion to duty, Private James Leary was awarded the Military Medal for the action of 11 June 1944.

after the war had ended, this moment would haunt the dreams of Hollis, the memory of it keeping coming back to him.

Meanwhile, C Company on the left was pinned down by particularly heavy fire coming from the orchards near Cristot. The company commander, Captain R.C. Chambers,[80] was killed, along with CSM T. Ferguson[81] and Lieutenant K.B.I. Rynning,[82] while a Lieutenant G.A. Kenny was wounded. Amid a heavy crossfire, the company was trapped in the middle of a cornfield. German snipers in the trees took a steady toll of men, and additional enemy fire was taken from farm buildings in the area. Lieutenant Colonel Hastings now appeared on the scene and ordered A Company to attack around the right flank of B Company, outflanking the farm buildings in their front:

> D Company forced their way up the axis supported by tanks, took 25/30 prisoners of war in Les Hauts-Vents and joined up with A Company. This helped C Company to get on and capture the White Farm. The position was now that the Bn was together, one field short of its objective with heavy MG and anti-tank gunfire in front.[83]

Captain J.B.E. Franklin, 2 i/c of C Company, then took over and went forward to find a confused situation:

> I found the fighting very confused with Spandaus and Bren guns firing in every direction. And since the company commander and the CSM had both been killed the platoons had lost cohesion and were fighting individual battles. Fortunately, at this time, A Company's attack came in and cleared the area of the farm buildings. Largely owing to the leadership of Major Honeyman, A Company got to within one field of its objective.[84]

At this point, the supporting tanks of B Squadron, 4/7th Royal Dragoon Guards, entered Cristot and came under heavy anti-tank fire. The squadron leader's tank and others were hit and destroyed, the crews either killed or taken prisoner as they bailed out. The reconnaissance battalion of the *Hitlerjugend* was waiting in well-prepared positions, the British Shermans picked off one by one by guns they never saw as they advanced down the main street of Cristot.

Having forced their way forward, A and B Companies linked up with the surviving tanks of C Squadron, 4/7th Royal Dragoon Guards, taking 30 prisoners in the process. C Company was then able to continue their advance and reorganise close to the farm buildings near Point 103. German and British dead and blazing tanks littered the ground as at least 20 prisoners were herded to the rear, Green Howards historian W.A.T. Synge describing them as "tough and

---

80 Captain Raymond Charles Chambers, Company Commander, 6th Battalion Green Howards, was killed on 11 June 1944, aged 30. He is buried in Bayeux War Cemetery, France.
81 Company Sergeant Major Thomas Ferguson, 6th Battalion Green Howards, was killed on 11 June 1944, aged 34. He is buried in Bayeux War Cemetery, France.
82 Lieutenant K.B.I. Rynning's death is reported in the regimental history on pages 304 and 305, but he is not listed as a war casualty by the Commonwealth War Graves Commission. In the regimental history he is reported to be a Norwegian officer, but I could not trace him.
83 National Archives WO 223/31.
84 Synge, W.A.T., *The Story of the Green Howards, 1939–1945* (Richmond: The Green Howards, 1952), p. 304.

Some of the German soldiers taken prisoner were very young and many of the Tommies were shocked when they realised that they were fighting mere boys. (Author's collection)

arrogant Nazis". With losses in the battalion having been very heavy, and Lieutenant Colonel Hastings sent for the support weapons to be brought forward.

A report then came through that the tanks and infantry of *SS-Panzer-Regiment 130* had broken through the positions held by 8 Armoured Brigade on the right flank and were now in very close proximity to the 6th Battalion's axis of advance. Hastings ordered an immediate withdrawal, but Major Frederick Honeyman[85] told his commanding officer that a party of men with Company Sergeant Major G.E. Calvert was unable to withdraw because of the heavy fire being directed on their position, and asked for permission to go forward and get them. As he moved carefully forward, Honeyman looked through a hedge to locate his men and a sniper shot him through the head. A tragic loss of a well-liked and outstanding company commander, his death was deeply felt. About an hour later, CSM Calvert[86] led his platoon to safety after three hours of desperate fighting. Calvert brought up the rear of his party while carrying a wounded man himself. He commented on Major Honeyman's loss: "None of us will ever forget Major Honeyman, he was a fine chap and gave his life for his comrades."[87] Honeyman's batman, Thomas Harris, said of his officer: "He was not only my company commander, but also my best friend and he treated me more like a brother. At the most unfortunate moment he sent me back out of the way and considered my safety before his own."[88]

The 6th Green Howards then withdrew in good order, getting most of the wounded away on the tanks of the 4/7th Royal Dragoon Guards, although the more seriously wounded were made comfortable and left in enemy hands. At 2300 hours, the battalion arrived at a position between Point 103 and Audrieu, where they dug in. Over 250 casualties had been taken at Cristot, many of them NCOs and officers, and 90 percent of the leading tank squadrons had been lost. As the evening wore on, Hastings could hear the sounds of heavy fighting going on from the area

---

85 Major Frederick Harvey Honeyman, MC, 6th Battalion Green Howards, was killed on 11 June 1944. He was originally buried in Le Haute-Audrieu War Cemetery, but was moved to Bayeux War Cemetery, France, on 7 May 1945.
86 Company Sergeant Major G.E. Calvert was awarded the Distinguished Conduct Medal for his leadership, courage and example at Cristot on 11 June 1944.
87 G.E. Calvert, correspondence with author (Sheffield, 1994).
88 T. Harris, correspondence with author (Barnsley, 1996).

Major Frederick Harvey Honeyman, MC, 6th Battalion Green Howards. (Author's collection)

Company Sergeant Major G. Calvert, 6th Battalion Green Howards, being presented with the DCM by General Montgomery. (Author's collection)

of Point 103, thought to be a German counter-attack. Early on the morning of 12 June, the battalion withdrew again to a position north of the railway line south-west of Loucelles. The attack had been bogged down, with the tanks unable to move forward. Hastings had lost so many men and officers that he had no choice but to call off the attack. They had shot their bolt, and if brigade headquarters wanted to hold the summit of Point 103, they would have to send in a fresh battalion. Padre Henry Lovegrove[89] worked tirelessly tending the wounded and dying all day and night, even when under fire showing little regard for his own safety. A worse day for the 6th Green Howards could not be imagined; their casualties numbered nearly 250 within a few hours' fighting, with nothing to show for it. Hastings commented on the action:

> The contact battle was merging into static warfare. Those are difficult and expensive moments. Certainly, the enemy were not deeply entrenched but were using the natural cover and protection of hedgerow and ditch. In this thick leafy country, the advantage is with the defender who can stay still and hold their fire until the last moment. By the 11th of June the enemy was recovering from his first shock and was fighting to the death. It was too late to plunge into deep un-recced country with insufficient knowledge of the strength or disposition of the enemy.[90]

---

89 Padre Henry Lovegrove was awarded the Military Cross for his bravery and devotion to duty at Cristot on 11 June 1944.
90 Saunders, *Gold Beach – Jig*, pp. 94–95.

7th Battalion Green Howards

On 11 June, the 7th Green Howards were established in positions between St Leger and Ste-Croix-Grand-Tonne. Outposts were further forward and in contact with the Canadians north of Bronay. Orders were received early on 11 June that the 7th Battalion was to be prepared to advance on Cristot. The troops and their supports were marshalled, and at 1430 hours they crossed the start line on the Bayeux–Caen road. To the west of Bronay was a railway embankment, which was to be taken by B and D Companies, while the village of Bronay was to be attacked by A and C Companies. As B Company attacked, they came under intense machine-gun fire from the start and men began to fall. Members of the company found themselves pinned down and unable to progress. Twice they regrouped and attempted to advance, but the volume of fire drove them back each time. B Company was eventually withdrawn at 1030 hours on 12 June, such was the level of their losses, leaving their dead and wounded scattered around the embankment. Lieutenant P.H. Ruddock made two brave but unsuccessful attempts to rescue Private Maurice William Caris,[91] who lay wounded in no-man's land. D Company tried to resume the attack, but suffered the same fate as B Company and was eventually withdrawn.

Battalion commander Lieutenant Colonel P.H. Richardson accompanied A and D Companies to the high ground north-east of Bronay, where he established mortar and artillery observation posts to enable supporting fire to be accurately pinpointed in support of the attacking companies. Around Bronay, the enemy lay hidden in wrecked buildings and dug-in positions that were totally invisible to the attackers; it was only when the leading platoons of A and D Companies approached the outskirts of Bronay that they came to life. At close range, the Green Howards were cut down in a hail of concentrated machine-gun fire. The fire was so heavy and prolonged that a smokescreen had to be put down to allow the survivors of the attacking companies to be withdrawn. By midnight, the whole battalion had been pulled back to a wooded area to the north of Bronay. It had been a disastrous day for the 7th Green Howards, with nothing to show for the heavy casualties taken.

Lieutenant David Render, Sherwood Rangers, passed through Cristot, on his way to Point 103, after the village had finally fallen. He has left a vivid account of the terrible scene that met his eyes:

> As we headed for Point 103 via Cristot in the early hours of the morning, I noticed how great rings of corn in the surrounding fields had been scythed flat by artillery fire. The odd burned-out Sherman, forlorn and broken, made grim milestones to mark our progress. The fields on the outskirts of Cristot, where the attack by the Green Howards had been stopped short, were still full of their dead bodies putrefying in the summer heat, adding to the all too familiar stench of rotting cattle. In the village itself the wax like dead of both British and Germans were mingled together in the gardens and side roads. We steered to avoid a cadaver stretched out in the small winding high street and passed a handcart full of corpses with a German soldier dead in the traces. The passing scene had a sobering effect on the crew, and we drove on in silence as we made our macabre progression through the village.

---

91   Private Maurice William Caris, 7th Green Howards, was killed at Bronay on 11 June 1944, aged 29. His body was never found, and he is remembered on the Bayeux Memorial to the Missing, France.

Though our hatches were closed down the men could see enough of the carnage through their periscopes, and the smell of death pervaded my open hatch. The scenes we witnessed in those few hundred yards were testimony that there is no glory in war. We were relieved to put that charnel house of Cristot behind us.[92]

8th Battalion Durham Light Infantry, St Pierre, 9–12 June

At 1745 hours on 9 June, the 8th Durhams moved to the attack, and as they did so shells from the self-propelled guns of 147th Field Regiment, Essex Yeomanry, Royal Artillery, shrieked overhead, striking the village of St Pierre with earth-shattering detonations.

Unteroffizier Petrov, *Panzer-Lehr-Division*, recalled the devastating effect of the British barrage on the St Pierre sector:

> We put in our attack, and we had three self-propelled guns under command. As we attacked the village the British artillery opened up and amid the explosions there was much confusion. That certainly was not much fun for us. Then there came an attack by the English. We were forced to pull back and after a long search under fire we eventually found our vehicles, half-tracks, but the enemy planes found us, and heavy artillery fire came down on us yet again. We retreated in short bounds back to our Regimental HQ awaiting further orders. Shall I have to go forward again? Thank God we are staying here overnight.[93]

The 8th Durhams captured St Pierre under a supporting barrage of high explosive and smoke, suffering many casualties in the process. The troops facing them were the *1. Bataillon, Panzer-Lehr-Regiment 901*. The Germans had waited until two of the forward companies were about to enter the village before opening up with Spandau and mortar fire. Taking numerous casualties, the Durhams pressed forward until they were practically on top of the Germans, vicious close-quarters fighting breaking out in the gardens and orchards of the village.

Corporal Frederick Spencer was only 19 years old at the time and had good reason to remember only too well those days in early June with the 8th Durhams:

> We advanced in extended order in front of a squadron of Sherman tanks of the 24th Lancers and I don't know which was more disconcerting, the sniper fire from the front or the replies from the tanks' guns in the rear that flew over our heads. The tanks passed through us and about 400 yards to our front came under fire from 88mm guns. I saw at least three blow up, followed by the machine-gunning of the poor bloody crews as they tried to escape.[94]

The battle was short and brutal, and in the shock of the assault the Germans withdrew before these dogged north-country men. With the area littered with the dead and wounded of both sides, the Durhams swiftly dug in. Very light flares indicating victory soared up into the sky, whereupon the other companies of the 8th Durhams moved into the area. Officers ran from

---

92 Render, *Tank Action*, p. 95.
93 *The Observation Post* <www.theobservationpost.com> (accessed 1 June 2019).
94 F. Spencer, correspondence with author (Durham, 1993).

Two wounded soldiers of the 8th Battalion Durham Light Infantry share a cigarette at St Pierre. (Author's collection)

position to position, preparing the defence for the inevitable counter-attack as the enemy swept the area with a steady stream of machine-gun and mortar fire.

Major Ian English, MC and Two Bars, 8th Durhams, wrote of the situation:

> Although the Germans had been driven out of the village, they stubbornly kept up steady and accurate mortar fire upon us, and one or two of their machine-gun posts still holding out in front of C and D Companies made it extremely dangerous to move about in these two company areas.[95]

Corporal Frederick Spencer, also of the 8th Durhams, added:

> During the next few hours, we sat it out exposed to airbursts, moaning-minnies [*Nebelwerfer* multiple rocket launchers], snipers and mortar fire. At night it was standing patrols in the valley on our right flank to prevent infiltration by German patrols. The worst hazard was getting back to the safety of our slit trenches before first light. Our positions were on a forward-facing slope, and we were harassed each day by a German self-propelled gun which came forward to fire at us at very close range.[96]

---

95 Lewis, P.J. and English, I.R., *The 8th Battalion Durham Light Infantry 1939–1945* (Newcastle: J. & P. Bealls, 1949), p. 247.
96 F. Spencer, correspondence with author (Durham, 1993).

The 288th Anti-tank Battery, Royal Artillery, moved into St Pierre to support the infantry of the Durhams as enemy tanks were known to be in the area. The Germans counter-attacked at 0700 hours on 10 June. To the front of the Durhams' infantry positions, artillery Forward Observation Officers spotted for the gunners in the rear; two of these brave men were killed as the German infantry poured into the town, followed by tanks, overrunning the Durhams' forward positions. Heavy shelling and mortar fire fell on the Durhams, and any man who survived fled to the rear and relative safety, but most positions held. C Company, 8th Durhams, had been quickly overrun, and as German armour appeared in the area the tanks of the 24th Lancers withdrew in the face of the attack to Point 103. D Company, 8th Durhams, came under heavy pressure from the advancing *panzergrenadiers*, one section being wiped out completely in a fierce melee. A young Bren-gunner named Private Protano remained at his post and kept up a withering fire on the Germans until they were driven off and the position reoccupied. The gunners of the 288th Anti-tank Regiment were also ordered to pull back, but some refused to do so and continued to man their guns. Sergeant G. Downs and Lance Bombadier R. Gilmour sat behind their 6-pdr gun as the battle moved towards them, and when a German tank appeared they opened fire and knocked it out; if it had got into the remaining infantry positions it could have been a disaster, and the sight of a burning enemy tank must have raised the spirits of the hard-pressed Durhams. St Pierre was now partially overrun, and a Ferdinand self-propelled gun was brought forward to aid the *panzergrenadiers* in their quest to eject the Durhams. Downs and Gilmour immediately went into action and scored hits on the gun, knocking it out. For their courageous actions in the face of the enemy, Downs was awarded the Distinguished Conduct Medal and Gilmour the Military Medal. To their left, another anti-tank gun was in action manned by Sergeant A. Heaton and Gunner T. Beresford. They saw two tanks approaching, knocking out the first one and forcing the other to withdraw. Heaton and Beresford were both awarded the Military Medal for their actions that day. Lieutenant R.L. Bramfeld, Royal Artillery, stayed forward throughout the action to spot for the gunners and was awarded the Military Cross.

Corporal Frederick Spencer spent a most uncomfortable time with his 8th Durhams comrades under fire from snipers and mortar bombs. Some German snipers had tied themselves to the trees they were in, and it was not long before they were seen dangling from the branches as a result of accurate retaliatory fire. Spencer recounted:

> As dawn was breaking a sentry pointed out some 50 men 150 yards to our right front. The mortar and machine-gun fire increased as their infantry advanced. Crouching in our holes we replied with rifle and Bren-gun fire, and the enemy ran out of the field into a hidden sunken road. They tried repeatedly to get at us, but we drove them back. A little later we heard the creaking of tank tracks, and my heart sank. A Tiger rumbled up the sunken road and stopped at a gap in the hedge about 150 yards away. The tank fired several shells into the bank behind our line then moved on and engaged the section to my right. I could hear screams coming from that direction after which the tank moved away, and we were attacked by infantry again. I fired my Bren into them and forced them back into the sunken road. During this engagement our two company snipers saw a man with a machine gun and another with a mortar creeping along a ditch towards my section and shot them both dead. Later I found in the sunken road a large number of dead Germans.[97]

---

97   F. Spencer, interview with author (Durham, 1994).

Well-concealed German anti-tank gunners in the Norman Bocage. (Author's collection)

The 8th Durhams were joined by the tanks of the 24th Lancers from Point 103. The first British tank to enter St Pierre was hit and burned furiously, blocking the road. Two other tanks were struck as they tried to negotiate the surrounding fields, the rest seeking cover in orchards and hedgerows. Still the German tanks and infantry pressed forward into the Durhams' positions, taking heavy casualties as they did so, but by noon they had shot their bolt and withdrew, leaving behind their dead, wounded and blazing tank hulks.

Private John Harold Clarke remembered the stiff resistance the 8th Durhams faced:

> The Germans were that strong we couldn't get any further forward; they were shooting us up right and left all the time. These poor sods in the tanks took a real beating and mortar bombs and shells fell all around us. Our own casualties were really heavy. Later we were getting fresh troops all the time to make up our numbers, but these were young lads with no experience – what chance did they stand in this?[98]

The noise of the battle rose to a terrifying climax as the day wore on, the thunder of guns and mortars mingling with the sharp crack of machine guns and rifles. However, by 1130 hours the

---

98 J.H. Clarke, interview with author (Durham, 1991).

A German gun team prepare their *Nebelwerfer* multi-barrelled mortar for action. (Author's collection)

worst of the crisis had passed for the Durhams, and British tanks were now in the village. The badly mauled Durhams then took stock of their situation. The most-forward positions had been abandoned and in the afternoon a platoon of infantry and a troop of tanks moved back into the village to deal with any enemy pockets still holding out. By 1400 hours, communication between the companies of the Durhams was restored as they reorganised to the east of St Pierre, but the village was now a no-man's land.

On 11 June, the Regimental Headquarters of the Sherwood Rangers was situated in a small enclosed farmyard to the north of St Pierre, while officers and the HQ of the 8th Durhams were located in an adjacent building. Lieutenant David Render of the Sherwood Rangers recorded the tragedy that unfolded when the farmyard was hit by German shellfire:

> The group had been talking and broke up and the assembled officers were walking in the cobbled courtyard when the first shell struck. The courtyard was no bigger than the size of an enlarged tennis court so the impact of the 105mm projectile in this confined space was devastating. With splintered cobbles adding to its lethal effect, jagged edged shrapnel and sharp broken flint scythed into the group of officers killing our CO,[99] his adjutant[100] and

---

99 Acting Colonel Major M.H. Laycock, MC. Nottinghamshire Yeomanry, Royal Armoured Corps, was killed on 11 June 1944, and is buried in Tilly-sur-Seulles War Cemetery, France.
100 Captain and Adjutant George Arthur Jones, Nottinghamshire Yeomanry, Royal Armoured Corps, was killed on 11 June 1944, aged 24, and is buried in Tilly-sur-Seulles War Cemetery, France.

his intelligence officer[101] and wounding three more. In an instant the heart of the Sherwood Rangers had been cut down in a storm of steel and stone.[102]

All through the day on 11 June, the remnants of the 8th Durhams sat tight in their positions, then at 1900 hours a storm of accurate artillery and mortar fire swept over the village once again. Under cover of this inferno, the tanks and *panzergrenadiers* of the *12. SS-Panzer-Division 'Hitlerjugend'* approached from the east and south-east. Part of this attacking forced bypassed St Pierre, making for the Dorsets on Point 103, and for a time the 8th Durhams were completely surrounded. In response, 69 Brigade attempted to move forward at this point to relieve the Dorsets on Point 103 but ran headlong into the German infantry taking part in the counter-attack already underway.

Private Jack Craddock, of the 5th East Yorks, had just begun to dig-in when his platoon came under fire from the attacking German formations:

> Our platoon commander ordered us to dig-in at the centre of a large cornfield. Having started the digging, Jerry commenced firing at us from concealed positions on our flanks with Spandau machine guns. Lt Sykes[103] was hit in the chest immediately and died. I was caught with a bullet in the left side which bounced off a rib and went through a lung then came out; my war was over.[104]

Sergeant Max Hearst, 5th East Yorks, dug-in not far from Craddock, and as he crouched in the shallow hole he had made he came under heavy mortar and machine-gun fire from the attacking Germans:

> All of a sudden there was a hell of an explosion, and I could hear men shouting and screaming. The noise from all the explosions was terrifying and we could see brewed-up tanks giving off clouds of thick black smoke that rose into the air. Dust and debris flew everywhere. We knew German armour was not far away and we couldn't get through to the Devons, who must have been getting it worse than us. My mate was hit in both legs by mortar fragments and was given morphia for the pain. We could not return fire and were pinned down in the open.[105]

Private Denis Bowen had seen many actions with the 5th East Yorks since 1940 and all through the North African and Sicily campaigns. He began to think deeply about the sights he saw around him, and one in particular made him very uneasy:

> We were off again and there was a company in front of us and our job was to go through them and continue the advance. When we got to them, they had come under heavy fire and

---

101 Intelligence Officer Lieutenant Alfred Laurence Head, Nottinghamshire Yeomanry, Royal Armoured Corps, was killed on 11 June 1944, aged 29, and is buried in Tilly-sur-Seulles War Cemetery, France.
102 Render, *Tank War*, p. 54.
103 Lieutenant John Laverack Sykes, 5th Battalion East Yorkshire Regiment, was killed on 11 June 1944, aged 26, and is buried in Hottot-les-Bagues War Cemetery, France.
104 J. Craddock, correspondence with author (Yorkshire, 1993).
105 M. Hearst, interview with author (Hull, 1993).

Recently decorated young *Panzergrenadiere* of the *12. SS-Panzer-Division 'Hitlerjugend'*.
(Courtesy of N. Hardy)

there was one man tending a wounded soldier. As I walked past them this lad said to me: "Will you help me?" I said: "What's wrong?" He said: "Will you look at him?" I looked at this soldier that was laid out and said: "Well he's dead." He had four or five shots in him and a couple in the head, he was obviously dead. I remember the other lad saying: "He can't be, he can't be dead, I promised his mother I'd look after him." Then, oh God, it struck me that there was something wrong with war, I could quite happily have put my rifle down. I can only presume that when they joined up his mother wouldn't let him go but his friend assured her he would be alright with him and there he was dead. That's the only time I had any hesitation about fighting and killing.[106]

Lieutenant David Render withdrew with his Sherwood Rangers unit to higher ground, leaving several of their knocked out Shermans in St Pierre and on the lower slopes of Point 103:

The enemy attack was supported by heavy artillery fire, but the British response was heavier. The combined fire of several artillery field regiments and the large calibre guns of the naval battleships off the coast raked the advancing Germans and decimated their ranks.[107]

---

106 *WW2: People's War* <www.bbc.co.uk/ww2peopleswar> (accessed 20 June 2019).
107 Render, *Tank Action*, p. 56.

Major Peter Martin, 2nd Machine-gun Battalion the Cheshire Regiment, commented on the fighting around Point 103:

> The battle for Point 103 raged on for two days and eventually the enemy began to close in. Shermans were blazing everywhere, and I was hailed by the CO of the 24th Lancers who was sitting on the ground with his arm in a sling. He handed me a rifle saying: "Put a round in the breech, at least I'll take one of them with me." I thought "My God it's as bad as that." Shortly afterwards all firing ceased. It had been the final attempt by the enemy before pulling out and leaving St Pierre.[108]

The Tigers of the *12. SS-Panzer-Division 'Hitlerjugend'* launched a ferocious attack on the positions held by the Dorsets and 8 Armoured Brigade, and a bitter struggle ensued with heavy casualties to both sides. The 88mm shells from the Tigers exploded in the trees above the defenders as tanks and infantry fought it out. The men who fought in this area subsequently christened Point 103 'Tiger Hill'.

David Render sat amid the chaos in his Sherman as the German armour looked for a weak point to be exploited:

> Point 103 became an increasingly dangerous place as the German reaction began to take form. Enemy tanks probed the slope from the lower ground and artillery and mortar fire began to fall on the exposed British positions. In an ideal tactical situation, a tank seeks to engage the enemy from a hull-down position behind a solid piece of ground, high enough to shield its hull but low enough for it to fire over. The forward incline provided the Sherwood Rangers with little opportunity for concealment or protection, and they suffered for it, losing three Shermans on their second day of occupation. I still wince at the memory of the shattering crack of the high velocity projectiles as they gouged out big furrows in the ground around us. All tank crews had a horror of being burned alive in their vehicles. The padre later recorded that Douglas had shared the premonition of his death with him. It reflected on the fatalism held by many who had survived the fighting in North Africa and considered that a fresh campaign in Europe put them on borrowed time.[109]

Trooper Fred Ebb, of the 61st Reconnaissance Regiment, found himself rounded up with a rag-tag group of anybody who could be found to cover the men of the Dorsets, who were forced to pull back from the forward positions under the violence of the German assault:

> The day was pretty chaotic. The sergeant major came round and collected half a dozen of us to give covering fire to some Dorsets who were withdrawing. There was me, the sergeant major, the squadron cook, the squadron clerk; that was the sort of detachment he gathered up. We took up some positions at the bottom of a ditch with intermittent trees along it. After we'd been there about an hour a troop of tanks pulled up right behind us, spreading out along this ditch line. These Shermans with short barrels opened fire. They got picked

---

108 Arthur, *Forgotten Voices of the Second World War*, p. 330.
109 Render, *Tank Action*, p. 53.

off one after the other, almost as fast as Jerry could reload his gun. One of them was only a matter of feet behind us when we heard a dull thud and two of our lads got hit by splinters. Two seconds after, I've never seen five blokes come out of a tank as quick in all my life, just like a jack in the box. As the last man came out, a flame 20 feet high shot out after him. Not long after that we saw some movement and these Dorsets ran across a field towards us.[110]

The battle continued with increasing ferocity until at 2230 hours the *Panzer-Lehr-Division* withdrew from St Pierre, leaving behind a scene of utter desolation and carnage. Prisoners were gathered and the Durhams still had a precarious hold on St Pierre, while the Dorsets and 8 Armoured Brigade still held Tiger Hill.

On the night of 11 June, Lieutenant Render made his way to the area where the other Shermans were parked up in an orchard:

A fleeting moon shone through the scudding clouds, its radiance illuminating the tank's outline against the inky darkness that had descended over the area. The sounds of shallow snoring, coming from beneath the black shape of the stretched tarpaulin slanting down from the tank's side, confirmed the presence of the crew as I approached. I laid out my bedroll and crawled in beside the sleeping bodies. The crump of artillery and mortar fire sounded in the distance and bright flashes briefly lit up the sky. I settled down to try to get some sleep.[111]

Also settling down for the night was Trooper Fred Ebb of the 61st Reconnaissance Regiment, who recounted one tragic incident:

Our squadron pulled up around the edge of a field; we used to call it going into harbour. We parked the vehicles in such a way that they would give us as much shelter as possible. There was one unfortunate incident when some troops had been out on a fighting patrol. At that time, we had a complicated system of passwords that changed at 01:00 a.m. every day and these people should have been back hours ago. They didn't have the new password and when they were challenged couldn't give the correct response. Our lads thought it was a Jerry patrol and opened fire on them, killing one or two.[112]

On 12 June, the 8th Durhams were ordered to withdraw from the St Pierre area as they now occupied a dangerous salient, leaving with only half the number of men who had gone in. Major Ian English of the 8th Durhams commented:

Everyone was now extremely tired, and the effective strength of the battalion was about half of what it had been three days previously when the 8th first entered St Pierre. A short rest out of the line sounded very attractive. On the other hand, to give up the village after such a gallant struggle seemed poor recompense for the effort and great sacrifice which had been made in order to hold it. It was decided to regroup, the battalion was to withdraw and

---

110 F. Ebb, interview with author (Swindon, 1991).
111 Render, *Tank Action*, p. 56.
112 F. Ebb, interview with author (Swindon, 1991).

revert to the command of 151 Brigade in reserve. It was a great shame that the village had to be evacuated.[113]

The 5th East Yorks relieved the Dorsets on Point 103. The attacks made by the infantry and tanks of the *Panzer-Lehr-Division* and *12. SS-Panzer-Division 'Hitlerjugend'* was evidence of the strong build-up of German forces around the bridgehead. Although the British were in command of the battlefield, it was evident that the Germans were increasing their strength around Tilly-sur-Seulles every day. A decision was taken that the column should advance no further but should sit tight and hold the ground it had taken. This in itself was no easy task, as enemy infantry probed constantly looking for a weak link to exploit.

113 Manuscript forwarded to author by I.R. English (Durham, 1994).

7

The Deadly Bocage: June–July 1944

As the spearhead of the 50th Northumbrian Division's advance ground to a halt, it was given new objectives for the next round of fighting: the capture of Tilly-sur-Seulles, Hottot and Villers Bocage. On the right of the 50th Division, the 7th Armoured Division – including the infantry of 56 Independent Brigade – concentrated for their next move to the village of Hottot, which would be remembered by the troops of XXX Corps for the stubborn resistance by SS formations as they fought to take it. Hottot lies to the south-west of Tilly-sur-Seulles on rising terrain on the main Tilly-sur-Seulles–Caumont road, which at that time was in use by the Germans as one of their main lateral routes. The attack on Hottot was intended to be a preliminary action before a further attack upon Villers Bocage.

As this was happening, *General der Panzertruppe* Geyr von Schweppenburg's *Panzergruppe West* was heading for Normandy with the intention – somewhat optimistically – of splitting asunder the Allied invasion front with a great armoured thrust. The German *7. Armee*'s war diary of 10 June observed:

> Precise military calculations were rendered largely academic by the violence of the Allied air attacks.[1]

The headquarters of *Panzergruppe West* was located by British fighter-bombers and devastatingly attacked on 10 June, wiping out its whole senior headquarters staff, with the exception of Geyr himself. These were senior commanders whom Rommel could not afford to lose during such a time of crisis.

At first light on 10 June, the tanks and other formations of 7th Armoured Division began their advance. They were slowed down by parties of enemy troops armed with anti-tank weapons; the infantry tasked with eliminating them finding it difficult because the terrain made concealment so easy for the Germans. Adding to the problems facing the 7th Armoured were German armoured half-tracks reinforcing the anti-tank units.

Lieutenant David Render was a rookie compared to the old hands of the Sherwood Rangers that manned his tank, but was having to learn fast if he was to survive:

---

1   Belfield, E. and Essame, H., *The Battle for Normandy* (London: Purnell, 1965), p. 85.

German troops get a lift forward on a StuG III assault gun. (Author's collection)

In this close-knit countryside death could be lurking in every sunken lane or waiting behind every hedge line. Terrain features could conceal an anti-tank gun, an enemy tank or German infantry equipped with a *Panzerfaust*, ready to rip the thinly protected crew compartment of a Sherman asunder with an explosive shaped charge warhead or an armour piercing projectile. These were the new rules of the game and they had taken the old North Africa hands by surprise.[2]

A succession of tank commanders were picked off by snipers as they tried to look out of the turret in order to guide their tank forward or pinpoint enemy positions. Lieutenant John Cloudsley-Thompson, of the 4th Battalion County of London Yeomanry, knew it was impossible for tank commanders to wear steel helmets for protection:

> There were a lot of snipers about and it was very close country. You had to use earphones when you were commanding the tank because you had to have your head out of the turret. Well, the trouble with the Cromwell was that if you were wearing these earphones you couldn't wear a tin hat, we had to wear our berets. We sat in a field while C Squadron skirmished in front. They lost a troop, temporarily under the command of the infantry, and it was sent down a narrow lane. It was a fatal place to go as there was no room to manoeuvre

2   Render, *Tank Action*, p. 86.

A tank-killer unit of the *Panzer-Lehr-Division* about to move off, armed with multiple *Panzerfausts*. (Author's collection)

and every tank was knocked out. I saw these tanks sometime later and the body of a driver, his legs burned to nothing, was still in one and there were graves by all the others. They talked about Shermans being Ronsons, a well-known cigarette lighter. Well, Cromwells could burn pretty quickly if they were hit.³

Trooper Austin Baker, 4/7th Royal Dragoon Guards, recalled the tactics used by the Germans as they ambushed the British advance at every opportunity:

This set piece attack with infantry was planned just as in the textbooks, to have tanks leading, followed by the infantry who would in turn be followed by more tanks. This arrangement proved to be a dismal failure. Jerry laid low until the first tanks had passed

---

3   Williams, A., *D-Day to Berlin* (London: Hodder & Stoughton, 2004), pp. 97–98.

and then opened up on the poor infantry with Spandaus. Then they would set upon the cut-off tanks that had been in the lead.[4]

The countryside through which the British armour and infantry was moving was a natural chequerboard of fields, each marked with high banks topped with ancient thick hedges, ditches running along the length of the fields. The landscape was dotted with villages, the tall towers of medieval churches being used as observation platforms by the Germans. Large farmhouses, with a cellar for shelter, surrounded each village; they had been constructed for defence in medieval times. All this formed a unique combination of man-made and natural defence systems for the enemy. The Bocage countryside was a formidable aid to the German forces, who made excellent use of it as the British pressed forward. Whoever held the Bocage was in a very strong position, and the attacking force would have to take heavy casualties to capture each small part of it. *Panzergrenadier* Rolf de Boeser mentioned the benefits for the defending forces of being in such terrain:

> The roads were covered on both sides by high bushes, and you ended up with these sort of ditches on either side, which were overgrown. These ditches were quite deep, one or two metres, sometimes a bit more. They were great protection for us; we would just fall into them. If they fired at us the rounds would just pass overhead. Or there were these sunken lanes. Many of them you couldn't see into from above because the trees covered them, it was like a tunnel.[5]

The situation became worse as the 50th Northumbrian Division became bogged down in the attack in the Tilly-sur-Seulles area. The nature of the terrain favoured the formidable troops of the *Panzer-Lehr*, who were adept at fighting with their Panther tanks and also used short-range weapons such as the *Panzerfaust* to deadly effect in this close countryside.

Sergeant Charles Benford remembered the confusion as he pressed on into the Bocage with the carriers of the 2nd Essex:

> We came round a bend, and I spotted a tank. I stopped my driver immediately and shouted to him to back up. We got down from the carrier and crossed the road, taking my Piat [hand-held anti-tank weapon] gunner with me. Cutting carefully down the hedge we discovered it was a disabled British tank and returned to the carrier. Lo and behold another tank appeared over the brow of a hill. I got my Piat gunner down behind the hedge and said to him: "You've got one shot; get his track and he's disabled." But it was yet another British tank with a chap with his beret on sticking out of the turret. He was holding a bright fluorescent orange recognition panel. He said: "Who the hell are you?" I said: "Vanguard of the battalion." He replied: "Well get the hell out of it, I'm in the middle of a tank battle." Our Essex officer was sent for and agreed that we should turn around the carriers. We couldn't do this in the road as it was too narrow, so we smashed our way through a five-barred gate into an orchard and out the other end. The farmer was there doing his nut.[6]

---

4   Manuscript sent to the author by P. Cuerden (Hampshire, 1987).
5   Manuscript forwarded to author by H. Wernemann (Germany, 1989).
6   C. Benford, correspondence with author (Essex, 1993).

Private Ernest Partridge, 2nd Gloucesters, was about to go out on patrol when he was asked to take the lead by his officer:

> Our captain, who was a nice chap, said to me: "Would you be scout today?" I said: "Christ, why me?" He said: "Well somebody's got to do it." I said: "If I do it today, I won't get it tomorrow." So off I goes, and the section was some 50 feet behind me. I crept up to this shed and surprised a German and before I could shout out this Jerry bayoneted me through the leg. The men behind me shot him dead before he could have another go. I don't remember a lot after that.[7]

Sergeant Richard Philips, with the 2nd South Wales Borderers, commented on the ferocity of the fighting:

> The shelling was really hairy, we were crouched in this slit-trench and a mortar bomb landed a couple of yards in front of us, but we got away with it. The reaction of some people under fire was strange, chaps were laughing saying: "Bloody hell that was a close one." Despite the area being devastated by shelling there was no mark on a nearby crucifix [–] so many times I have seen this. I was glad to get out of that bloody place.[8]

Private Tony Mansi pressed on slowly with his 2nd Essex unit as casualties began to mount:

> Lads were being shot by snipers and we lost a lot to the heavy mortar fire as we moved forward, we passed three badly wounded Glosters huddling under a groundsheet. Then we went up this small lane and at the top of the track we saw Germans hanging from trees, having been blown there by our shellfire. I couldn't see a mark on them, they had been blasted up into the trees. Some of our chaps opened up on them thinking they were snipers.[9]

Mansi and his comrades found a dry ditch leading in the direction of the attack and began to dig in. There was a lot of noise and the other men in the ditch began to bunch up, but Mansi decided to move further down to get some space:

> In moving down the ditch that's where I found poor Major Petre, CO of D Coy, who was on the top of a bank. So, I pulled his body down into the ditch so he wouldn't get hit any more.[10] Suddenly small arms fire came from the bridge, [and] a bullet passed in front of me and went into the leg of a chap third along. At the same time bullets hit behind me and went into Sparrow's pack, he was sitting next to me.[11]

---

7   E. Partridge, correspondence with author (Gloucestershire, 1990).
8   Newspaper cutting forwarded to author by R. Jones (Essex, 1990).
9   Newspaper cutting forwarded to author by R. Jones (Essex, 1990).
10 Major Gerald Malcolm Mary Laurence Petre, 2nd Battalion Essex Regiment, was killed on 11 June 1944, aged 27. He is buried in Hottot-le-Bagues War Cemetery, France.
11 Newspaper cutting forwarded to author by R. Jones (Essex, 1990).

After two days of fighting, the 7th Armoured Division's advance was slow and costly. Eventually, their orders were changed by Montgomery, and they were told to make straight for Villers Bocage. This was part of Operation Perch, which was intended to make a wide sweeping right-hook movement south of Caen around the rear of the *Panzer-Lehr-Division* on 12 June.

More than one senior officer claimed this plan as their own after the war. For instance, Major General George ('Bobbie') Erskine, CO of 7th Armoured Division, wrote:

> After some unsuccessful stabs at Tilly, I suggested the use of the 7th Armoured Division's mobility to be used around the right flank of 50 Div. I was sure there was a soft spot here and had in fact reconnoitred routes and had a cut and dried plan for a swoop on Villers Bocage. The plan was eventually accepted after much delay. It could have been carried out 24 hours earlier and those 24 hours were vital.[12]

The tanks of the 4th County of London Yeomanry were dispersed over open fields on 12 June, north of Tilly-sur-Seulles, resting and refitting after their recent troubles. According to Major Ian Basil Aird, DSO, new orders were expected at any time:

> The Colonel, Lord Cranley, was away and there was a vague expectation among the squadron leaders as to what fresh orders he would bring back with him. They did not have long to wonder, for he was soon back and jumping out of his scout car with orders to move immediately. We were in for a long march along a complicated route and an attack the regiment was to lead, and in which surprise was to be the most important factor. The objective was the township of Villers Bocage. Maps were marked and orders given, and in a short time the tanks were marshalled[. T]he men were glad to leave the uncomfortable and unpromising area north of Tilly, though a little dubious of the advance along a centre line so tenuous and thin on the map and with so much at stake at its end.[13]

Disaster at Villers Bocage, 13–14 June

The *2. SS-Panzer-Division 'Das Reich'*, having been alerted to the possibilities of a British flanking movement at Villers Bocage, had moved from its position north of the Seine near Amiens to Normandy. It established new positions in the Villers Bocage sector to block any British advance. The division moved by night to avoid the Allied fighter-bombers that were causing such havoc with the German reserves. The British were totally unaware that two companies of the *I SS-Panzerkorps* had already arrived in the sector around Villers Bocage and were in position on 13 June. One of these units, *2. Kompanie, Schwere SS-Panzer-Abteilung 101*, was commanded by the famous tank ace *SS-Obersturmführer* Michael Wittmann, who would make history on this day. The 7th Armoured Division had no idea that this force of Tiger tanks lay in wait outside the town. German reinforcements had been hastily ordered forward to help plug the gap in the defences on the left flank of the *I SS-Panzerkorps*. Major Stuart Frederick

---

12 Hamilton, N., *Monty* (London: Hodder & Stoughton, 1981), p. 305.
13 Graham, A., *Sharpshooters at War* (London: Sharpshooters Regimental Association, 1964), p. 177.

Lever of the 7th Armoured Division had been given no indication that they now faced such a powerful force:

> Intelligence indicated enemy forces along the way, including armour, but with absolutely no suggestion that these included Tiger or Panther tanks.[14]

Major Aird commented on the move forward that the British made:

> The axis of the advance was a narrow road along the extreme western flank of the British army running parallel to the Americans. After 15 miles of jolting and dust the head of the column reached the main lateral road from Caumont to Caen, and away to the right could be seen the fires and smoke where the 1st American Infantry Division were fighting to hold the ground that they had taken in their rapid advance of the last few days. On our left the 8th Hussars had a tank bazooka'd and the leading Honey [nickname of the Stuart light tank] of the regiment had been fired on by an anti-tank gun from the east. As it was now dusk it was decided not to push on and the regiment leaguered for the night in a field north of the crossroads. Early next morning the advance continued, A Squadron leading, followed by some Honeys and A Company of the 1st Rifle Brigade. Then came B and C Squadrons, followed by Tac Brigade. The orders were to push on as fast as possible, there being no further opposition from the crossroads area. The country was very close, the road wandering over switchback hills, gradually swinging east towards Villers. Within a few hours, the leading elements, moving fast, were in sight of the small town. From brigade came the information that the place was clear of the enemy, and the cheering villagers on the side of the road seemed to confirm this. In consequence A Squadron galloped through the town, seeing no Germans, and reached their objective on the farther side, a hill which commanded the road to Caen.[15]

Sergeant Robert Bramall, MM, of B Squadron, 4th County of London Yeomanry, commented on the quality of the tanks his unit was using:

> Most of the lads were in Cromwell tanks, which I still think was a useless tank, fast enough but without adequate armour and under gunned. Fortunately, I had a [Sherman] Firefly, which had a 17-pounder gun, and we could take on anything. On June 13th, that fateful day, we leagured [sic] the night before at Livry, a bit east of Caumont, and were on the move at first light against no opposition to speak of. It was a beautiful day, at least it began that way, in contrast to the afternoon. Brigade said Villers was clear of the enemy and although the colonel wanted to do a recce first, looney [a friendly nickname for the 22 Armoured Brigade CO due to his courage and eccentricity] Brigadier Hinde came up and ordered us to push straight on down the road at maximum speed.[16]

---

14 D'Este, C., *Decision in Normandy* (London: Collins, 1983), p. 177.
15 Graham, *Sharpshooters at War*, pp. 177–78.
16 Neillands, R., *The Battle of Normandy 1944* (London: Cassell, 2002), p. 102.

A Squadron of 4th County of London Yeomanry and A Company, 1st Battalion the Rifle Brigade, entered Villers Bocage at 0800 hours on 13 June, with elements reaching Point 213 at 0905 hours. They received a rapturous reception from the local populace, *Gendarmes* having to hold the crowds back as they threw flowers onto the Cromwell tanks and offered cider to the troops. To take such a strategically important town so easily seemed too good to be true. The only sign of the enemy had been the sighting of a German half-track as they entered the town, which had turned tail as soon as it saw the British tanks. Lieutenant Charles Pearce, 4th County of London Yeomanry, spotted the half-track:

> I saw a German eight wheeled armoured car, half hidden in an orchard, on the facing slope 600 yards away. I could clearly see its commander watching our column. I was following behind the second in command's tank and shouted a target indication of the enemy vehicle over to him. Unfortunately, his turret was jam packed with kit and he could not traverse it, and nothing happened. I broke radio silence and spoke to RHQ troop leader but again nothing happened. A few minutes later the enemy armoured car disappeared into the trees of the orchard.[17]

Major Aird[18] had received a report from a troop leader of the 4th County of London Yeomanry that a German armoured car had been seen observing the British movements from a hill to the north of Villers Bocage. However, others disputed this report and the warning was disregarded.

To hold the town securely, Brigadier Robert Hinde, CO of 22 Armoured Brigade, knew that they must occupy and hold Hill 213, which was situated on the north-east side of the town.

The renowned war reporter, Alan Moorehead, was present and wrote of the swift entry into Villers Bocage:

> Here we were in the first week of the battle exploiting a possible breakthrough with very little opposition, an armoured brigade in front and the infantry coming along behind in lorries. It was exciting to be on the move at such a pace. We bypassed Tilly-Bocage where the Germans were still holding out and early the following morning, 13th June, the tanks ran through to Villers Bocage. It was a neat little crossroad town. The central square, the church, the restaurant called Vieux Puits, which was famous for its tripe and its *Escalope a la Normande*. Just over 1,000 inhabitants. The tanks roared through to the slopes beyond. The infantry followed in single file along the side of the road and presently we were all standing in the square together.[19]

Captain Patrick Dyas, MC, 4th County of London Yeomanry, marvelled at the lack of opposition after the bitter fighting of the past week:

> It seemed unbelievable that, after being contained for so long, the Sharpshooters were to drive unmolested through the villages of welcoming French people until, approaching from Tilly-sur-Seulles via Caumont, they reached their first objective, the road junction in the town of Villers Bocage, where little resistance was found. Some German billeting parties,

---

17   Saunders, *Battle for the Bocage*, p. 198.
18   Major Ian Basil Aird, DSO, was involved in an accident in late 1944 and was sent back to England. He died on 17 December 1944, aged 39, and is buried in Wooton Hill (St Thomas) Churchyard, Hampshire.
19   Moorehead, A., *Eclipse* (London: Hamish Hamilton, 1945), p. 97.

seen to be marking up French houses, were more surprised to see the British tanks than the Sharpshooters were to see them.[20]

Lieutenant Bruce Campbell, 1st Rifles, was astonished at the welcome the troops were given:

> Once in the main street of Villers Bocage we were amazed at the terrific reception which we received from the dense crowd of gaily dressed civilians who thronged the pavement. Everything seemed normal and even the *gendarmes* had turned out in their khaki and blue uniforms to guide us through the town.[21]

What the British did not know was that some of the massive and heavily armoured Tiger I tanks of the *Schwere SS-Panzer-Abteilung 101* had arrived on the outskirts of Villers Bocage. These lethal weapons of war lay hidden in a wood not far from the road up which the British Cromwell tanks had advanced. Their commander, *SS-Obersturmführer* Michael Wittman, was already famous as a *panzer* ace credited with 137 kills on the Eastern Front. Enraged by the Allied bombing of German cities, he had informed his men: "We have only one watchword and that is revenge!"

Major Aird remembered that all seemed quiet as the 4th County of London Yeomanry's Regimental Headquarters moved over the River Seulles and into the main square of the town:

> Recce sent a patrol to the south on the road to Aunay, perhaps the deepest penetration into France that had been made up to that time. The patrol shot up

Captain Patrick Dyas, MC, 4th County of London Yeomanry, Royal Armoured Corps. (Author's collection)

Major Ian Basil Aird, DSO, 4th County of London Yeomanry, Royal Armoured Corps. (Courtesy of P. Cuerdon)

---

20 D'Este, *Decision in Normandy*, p. 176.
21 Manuscript forwarded to author by P. Cuerdon (Hampshire, 1991).

a German car and captured the occupants, which included an officer who volunteered the information that he was billeting.[22]

The Battle of Villers Bocage took place on 13 and 14 June and involved significant elements of 7th Armoured Division, who were opposed by numerically inferior German forces. Supporting the 7th Armoured were the infantry and anti-tank guns of the 1/5th and 1/7th Queen's Regiment of 131 Brigade.

SS-Obersturmführer Wittmann[23] watched the seemingly endless British column, which consisted of A Squadron, 4th County of London Yeomanry, Stuart tanks of the recce group and A Company, 1st Rifles in carriers. The main tank and infantry column consisted of some 25 half-tracks, carriers and tanks. They halted under cover of a hedge-lined section of the road and awaited further instructions before they advanced to Point 213 to join their comrades who were already there.

SS-Standartenführer Kurt Meyer,[24] commander of the *12. SS-Panzer-Division 'Hitlerjugend'*, worried that if this attack succeeded the enemy would be able to outflank the German forces in the area and move into their rear. He watched events with interest and not a little concern:

> Wittmann had moved in front of his company to conduct a terrain reconnaissance, when he encountered a column of enemy tanks near Hill 213. The enemy was completely unprepared, Wittmann hesitated for a few moments and was undecided whether he should withdraw or attack the superior enemy forces. His unit had taken heavy losses through bombing attacks during the past few days. He knew every single tank was important and that he should not act carelessly. He had to attack as the advanced guard of the 7th Armoured Division would drive into the rear of *Panzer Lehr*. If a breakthrough of the German front succeeded, the defence of Caen would be lifted off its hinges.[25]

Major Aird watched Lieutenant Colonel Arthur Cranley, CO of the 4th County of London Yeomanry, move forward:

> Colonel Cranley now decided to go in his scout car to see how A Squadron and the infantry company were getting on and he left his headquarters with all its appendages covered by a troop of the Recce and some Green Jackets, instructing them to move into the main street towards the eastern exits. For a time, all seemed quiet.[26]

---

22 Graham, *Sharpshooters at War*, p. 178.
23 *Obersturmführer* Michael Wittmann was killed on 8 August 1944, aged 30, at St-Aigan-de-Cramesnil, France. His Tiger was hit by a Sherman Firefly tank of the Northamptonshire Yeomanry commanded by Captain Tom Boardman, the gunner was Joe Edkins. He was buried at the side of the road with his crew in an unmarked grave, which was lost. In 1983, the German War Graves Commission located the burial site and reinterred Wittman and his crew in La Cambre German War Cemetery, Normandy, France.
24 After the war, Kurt Meyer was sentenced to death for war crimes, but this was commuted to life. He died on 23 December 1961 and is buried in Hagen, Westphalia, Germany.
25 Meyer, K., *Grenadiers* (USA: Stackpole Books, 2005), p. 237.
26 Graham, *Sharpshooters at War*, p. 178.

The dreaded Tiger was more than a match for the British armour, with its massive 88mm high-velocity gun and heavy armour. (Author's collection)

Cranley had been informed that the area was safe to move through, but had asked for permission to make a proper reconnaissance before moving off. This was denied and he was ordered to press on regardless. The easy entry into Villers Bocage must have cancelled out any doubts about the wisdom of doing this, and the British armour moved off along the road in the direction of Point 213, unaware that every movement was being closely observed by hostile eyes.

Wittmann drove his Tiger, followed by two Panthers, into Villers Bocage and had to make a swift decision as to what he should do. He commented:

> I was in my command post and had given no thought to the idea that the enemy might suddenly appear. Then a man suddenly came into my command post and declared: "*Obersturmführer*, tanks are driving past outside. They are a peculiar round shape, and I don't think they are German." I immediately went outside and saw tanks rolling past about 150/200 meters distant. They were English and American types; at the same time I saw the tanks were accompanied by armoured troop carriers. It was an entire armoured regiment which had taken me by surprise. The decision was a very difficult one, never before had I been so impressed by the strength of the enemy as I was by those tanks rolling by. But I knew it absolutely had to be, and I decided to strike out at the enemy.[27]

27 Manuscript forwarded to author by Brian Cook (Carnegie Heritage Centre, Hull, 2016).

Kurt Meyer later wrote:

> Brigadier Hinde moved into Villers Bocage meeting no resistance. Because of this unexpected development, the lead armoured elements carelessly rolled further along the road to Caen to its objective, Hill 213. The motorised infantry company that followed took a break on the road.[28]

Wittmann watched as the squadron of Cromwells, Shermans and armoured carriers halted on a high-banked stretch of road and immediately saw his chance. Some of the British crews had already dismounted and started to brew up, upon seeing which Wittmann's tank driver said: "They are behaving as if they have already won the war." Wittmann replied: "We're going to have to prove them wrong."

Wittmann moved out of cover at 0905 hours and went onto the attack at once, bringing the British armour to a shuddering halt. His intention was to use his speed and superior firepower to block the road and prevent the British force from being reinforced or from withdrawing. Wittmann knew that the high-hedged banks were too thick for the lightly armoured British vehicles to get through to escape, while the road was too narrow for them to turn around. He commented: "They never left the road, they were so surprised that they took flight, but not in their vehicles, instead they jumped out and I shot up the battalion's vehicles as I drove by." His first victim was a carrier near the road on which he was travelling; as it was hit by the Tiger's high-velocity gun, it swung out across Wittmann's path from the force of the impact and started to blaze, clouds of black smoke billowing upwards. The Tiger continued on its way, smashing the stricken carrier out of its path.

Lieutenant John Leonard Cloudsley-Thompson, 4th County of London Yeomanry, was heading for Point 213 when Wittmann's devastating attack unfolded:

> We set off at dawn with A Squadron, the countryside was lovely and there was no resistance, and so we hoped to take the hill beyond Villers Bocage before we were noticed. Villers Bocage is a fair-sized county town, there was no sign of the enemy, so we drove straight along the main street. Brigadier Hinde and the colonel went forward in their scout cars to join the leading troops. A Squadron had got right through and RHQ, which I was commanding, were just leaving the town when the rear tanks of A Squadron burst into flames and the crews bailed out. Every RHQ tank began to reverse at speed.[29]

Rifleman Harold Hopkins, of the 1st Rifles, arrived at the crossroads as his officers went forward to be briefed on the situation. It was ominously quiet as his carrier stopped:

> We relaxed in the sun beside our half-tracks. Suddenly there was a loud bang, and the front vehicle went up in smoke. The next vehicle to brew-up was one near the rear, thus blocking any chance to escape for us. Casualties were mounting as other vehicles were destroyed. Three of my section, along with myself, crept along a ditch and managed to escape the fire

---

28 Meyer, *Grenadiers*, p. 237.
29 Cloudsley-Thompson, J.L., *Sharpshooter* (London: Arcturus Press, 2006), p. 89.

that was sweeping the column. Later we hid in a chicken coop and eventually made our way back to a very depleted battalion.[30]

Wittmann, realising he had to act quickly and assuming that his enemy had already spotted him, passed orders to his other tank commanders that they were to stand their ground if attacked. Meanwhile, he moved out to the give battle with his lone Tiger:

> I drove up the column and surprised the English as much as they had surprised me. I first knocked out two tanks from the right of the column, then one from the left, then turned about to the left and attacked the armoured troop carrier battalion in the middle of the armoured regiment. I drove toward the rear half of the column on the same road, knocking out every tank that came towards me as I went.[31]

Two Panther tanks of the *Panzer-Lehr-Division* then swung towards the column and opened fire, and as they did so Wittmann charged forward. He knocked out the rear tank of the column, after which he advanced up the column line, machine gunning vehicles and men as he went by them from as close as 50 yards. A horrified British despatch rider saw the looming threat: "I called out to Mr De Pass and told him, and he said something like: 'it was one of ours'. At this point I decided to tell Major Wright. He calmly informed me that he knew and that they were all around us." As 6-pdr anti-tank crews tried to engage the Tiger, they were mown down in a hail of fire. Others fled across country as machine-gun fire raked the open fields. With wrecked half-tracks and tanks burning furiously, British dead littered the scene as Wittmann's 60-ton monster thundered on its course.

The inhabitants of Villers Bocage ran for cover, the narrow streets of the town and surrounding areas echoing to the sound of gunfire as the British armour and the troops and tanks of the *Panzer-Lehr-Division* and the Tigers of *Schwere SS-Panzer-Abteilung 101* fought it out.

Kurt Meyer described the scene as the battle rolled on:

> The thunder of a main gun cut through morning silence. The lead vehicle stood there burning and, at a distance of 100 metres, a Tiger came roaring out of the woods. It turned onto the road, rolled along the line of the half-tracks and fired them all up, one after the other in quick succession. That was followed by a dozen armoured vehicles of the regimental headquarters and the artillery observers and a reconnaissance platoon, that happened to be behind a row of vehicles. A 75mm round from a Cromwell tank, fired at point blank range, bounced off the Tiger without effect. Within minutes the road was like an inferno, [and] 25 tanks and vehicles were in flames.[32]

Major Aird of the 4th County of London Yeomanry commented on the events of that fateful day:

---

30 H. Hopkins, correspondence with author (Catford, 1991.
31 Agte, P., *Michael Wittmann and the Waffen SS Tiger Commanders of the Leibstandarte in WW2* (USA: Stackpole Books, 2006), pp. 19–20.
32 Meyer, *Grenadiers*, p. 237.

The most indescribable confusion broke out. Up the street in front Lt Ingram's Honeys and a dozen half-tracks of the Rifle Brigade were burning. The RHQ tanks started to move backwards down the narrow street. As they did so, Spandaus opened up from the windows above and the street began to fill with smoke and the noise of falling slates, punctuated by the sharp crack of an 88. Out of the smoke trundled slowly a German Tiger tank. Major Carr, the second in command, fired at it with his 75mm, but, heart-breaking and frightening, the shots failed to penetrate the side armour. Almost immediately his tank was on fire, he himself seriously wounded and other members of the crew killed or wounded. The Tiger went on to shoot up the Shermans of the OPs [Observation Posts] with their poor [dummy] wooden guns, the IO's scout car and the MO's halftrack.[33]

Sergeant Robert Bramall, 4th County of London Yeomanry, also watched events unfold:

It was about 10:00 a.m. that we first heard firing from the town, machine guns and the vicious crack of an 88, which is something you don't forget, believe me. That was the first hint anything was wrong. A Tiger came into the village, I think from up the road from Longvillers, and first it wiped out the artillery observer tanks, these were Sherman tanks with the gun removed to make space for the radio but equipped on the outside with a dummy wooden gun barrel, poor devils. Then it got most of the recce troop. This Tiger smashed its way through Villers to the western outskirts on our front where my colleague, Sgt Lockwood, also in a Firefly, engaged it with his 17pounder; he didn't knock it out, but he certainly scared it off. However, that was only the start of it, [and] by now other German tanks were at work attacking A Squadron beyond the town. Villers Bocage was a bloody shambles.[34]

Having reduced the standing column to a blazing inferno, Wittmann then drove into Villers Bocage, to the Rue Georges Clemenceau, where he knocked out three Cromwell tanks that were taken by surprise, plus three Stuart light tanks of the HQ Group. One Honey tank, commanded by Lieutenant Rex Ingram, steered into the road in a futile attempt to block Wittmann, but his tank was no match for the heavy Tiger; the last thing he and his crew heard was the resounding crack of the Tiger's 88mm gun. The Tiger then smashed into Ingram's burning tank, with the crew still inside, knocking it off the road as it continued on its journey.[35] With the British formations in a state of total panic and with no obvious resistance in sight, Wittmann's panzers advanced through Villers Bocage.

When Wittmann journeyed into the centre of Villers Bocage, his luck finally ran out:

I then drove straight into the town, where I was hit by an anti-tank gun and my tank was disabled. Without further ado I fired at and destroyed everything around me that I could reach. I had lost radio contact and was unable to summon my company, [as] my tanks

---

33 Graham, *Sharpshooters at War*, p. 178.
34 R. Bramwell, correspondence with author (London, 1994).
35 Lieutenant Rex Sidney Anthony Ingram, 4th Battalion County of London Yeomanry, Royal Armoured Corps, was killed in action on 13 June 1944, aged 19. He is buried in Bayeux War Cemetery, France.

were out of sight. Then I decided to abandon the tank, taking all the weapons we could carry. I didn't destroy the tank as I believed that we could regain possession of it. Made my way to division, about 15 kilometres and had to dodge enemy tanks several times. Could have taken them out but had no close-range anti-tank weapons, so with a heavy heart had to leave them be. I reached the division and immediately reported to it and to corps. Subsequent counterattack destroyed the enemy. The bulk of the armoured regiment and its rifle battalion were destroyed.[36]

A Sherman Firefly had fired at and hit Wittmann's Tiger no less than four times, at which point the Tiger had returned fire and brought half the building above the Sherman down onto its hull.

Sergeant Bramall outlined other events he was in the thick of in and around Villers Bocage that day:

SS-*Obersturmführer* Michael Wittmann, *Schwere SS-Panzer-Abteilung 101*.
(Courtesy of H. Wernemann)

> Other German tanks were attacking. They blew up the leading tank and then the one at the back, which pinned the rest of the squadron down. He then rolled down the line knocking out all the rest, killing and capturing a lot of our lads. It was a shambles. Villers was a large village really with lots of firing going on, mainly concentrated on a square near the high street. Soon afterwards three German tanks came down the high street. I am sure the one in the lead was a Mark IV. I fired at it and missed. Fortunately, a 6-pounder anti-tank gun of the Queen's was brought up and they knocked it out. The next tank along was a Tiger. I had to reverse back a bit, but I could see it through the windows of the house on the corner. We traversed our gun and began to engage it through the windows, firstly with high explosive, which made a terrible mess of the house, and then with armour piercing. I don't know how many shots we fired but we knocked it out.[37]

The Mark IV panzers belonged to the *Panzer-Lehr-Division* and the Tiger that Sergeant Bramwell's tank knocked out was commanded by *Oberscharführer* Ernst.

Lieutenant John Cloudsley-Thompson was sitting in his 4th County of London Yeomanry Cromwell tank when he saw the tank ahead of him burst into flames and explode. Seconds later, a solid shot hit his own tank:

---

36 Agte, *Michael Wittmann and the Waffen SS Tiger Commanders*, p. 20.
37 R. Bramwell, correspondence with author (London, 1994).

It was so vicious, a supersonic shell passing so close, and this was the first time I think I'd ever been frightened. After that I tended to feel that nothing could ever miss me again. I was partially deaf until the next day, even though I had my headset on. I instructed my driver to drive on the left side and we pushed through a hedge between two houses. Pat Dyas, the Adjutant, turned his tank beside mine, his forehead was bleeding. At this point all the tanks to our front were burning. Suddenly the gigantic shape of a Tiger loomed out of the smoke and gloom, [and] even though we fired at point blank range our 75mm shells just bounced off the massive armour of the Tiger. It traversed its big 88mm gun very slightly when wham! We were hit. The shell passed between my legs because I could feel a kind of tingling from it, then it sped into the engine compartment and engulfed the tank in flames as we bailed out. A lance of fire swept over the turret and my mouth was full of sand and burnt paint. I shouted: "Get out!" and jumped out of the tank. I saw my crew get out. The Tiger rumbled by us and left a trail of carnage and black smoke that marked its progress. As I lay in the grass I heard my name softly called, I looked around, [and] it was my crew who had hidden themselves in a currant bush. Luckily all were unhurt. My troop sergeant had been leaning sideways when our tank was hit, the shell passed over his shoulder and between my legs and struck the motor, [and] a piece of metal had struck him behind the ear. Joe, the driver, was pale and trembling. Once again shells and machine-gun fire whizzed over our heads, [so] I quickly threw myself to the ground.[38]

Major Wilfred Herbert James Sale, MC, 4th County of London Yeomanry, watched the progress of the Tiger as it smashed its way forward:

A Tiger immediately knocked out Arthur's tank, Lord Cranleigh [sic], and that of the second in command, Major Carr, who was seriously wounded. Followed by the regimental sergeant major's tank. Captain Dyas in the fourth tank reversed and backed into the front garden of a nearby house.[39]

In the artillery line outside of Villers Bocage, Gunner John Coombs, of the 5th Regiment, Royal Horse Artillery, followed events with interest as he listened to the battery radio and saw ominous black plumes of smoke rising from the village:

When the leading tanks reached a point just beyond Villers Bocage they were ambushed by a single Tiger and the CLY lost their leading squadron and regimental HQ. Andy Merrifield, who drove the G Battery OP tank, managed to escape with his tank. K Battery CO's Sherman was in the main street of the town when the driver, Jock Rae, saw the Tiger and alerted the major who escaped through the turret, while Jock went through the escape hatch on the floor as the first 88 round blew the track off. The second shot set the tank ablaze. Like all command tanks in the regiment this one had a dummy wooden gun [–] I often wonder what the Germans made of that. We with the guns back at Tac HQ were following this unfolding drama thanks to the adjutant's radio[;] the ominous sounds of continuous gunfire and the sight of black smoke rising from the town was very disturbing.[40]

---

38 Cloudsley-Thompson, *Sharpshooter*, p. 93.
39 Addington, S., *Invasion* (London: Unicorn Publishing, 2019), p. 201.
40 *WW2: People's War* <www.bbc.co.uk/ww2peopleswar> (accessed 14 July 2017).

In the early afternoon, German tanks and infantry renewed the attack on Point 213 against Cranley's outgunned and outnumbered tank and infantry force. Those British tanks that had survived now came under the command of B Squadron, whose commander concentrated on the defence of his unit. A Mark IV Special and three Tigers were knocked out by the anti-tank guns of the 1/7th Queen's, but the German crews got away on foot as there was not enough British infantry present to stop them.

Private Albert Kingston recalled his 1/7th Queen's anti-tank platoon receiving the order "Take post":

> When we were ordered into action the ammunition trucks were driven into side streets and all the rifle sections were told to take up positions in the windows of houses on the enemy side of the town. There were several loud bangs which came from our 6-pounder anti-tank guns going off and then one very loud explosion when a Bren Ammo carrier went up. The firing seemed to spread, and we could see Jerry infantry working their way into the town. There was more tank and machine-gun fire, then dead silence. We waited. The street was a mess with bricks and rubble all over the place. A couple of hundred yards up the road the biggest tank I have ever seen came into view and it looked undamaged. Opposite our house one of our 6-pounders had been hit and was lying on its side.[41]

Just before noon, the *4. Kompanie, Schwere SS-Panzer-Abteilung 101*, commanded by *Hauptsturmführer* Rabe, reached Villers Bocage and immediately engaged in combat, attacking isolated British units on Hill 213. The 1/7th Queen's fought on from house to house, trying to push the Germans out of the town. The encircled and isolated units of the 4th County of London Yeomanry on Hill 213 found it impossible to pull back, being under constant German bombardment. The tanks and infantry of the *Panzer-Lehr-Division* pushed on into Villers Bocage and launch a violent assault from the south. The troops of A Company, 1/7th Queen's, were hit hard, and some sections were overrun in the first shock.

Lance Corporal James Kay, 1/7th Queen's, wrote of the fright he received as he saw his first Tiger tank come into view:

> We were shelled and fired at by Spandaus, which caused absolute havoc among our troops. The frightening sight of Tiger and Panther tanks was somewhat removed from the days of playing a trumpet in a dance band. Spandaus were firing from house windows and there was the sound of clattering roof slates and breaking glass falling everywhere. The Tigers seemed to be unstoppable and the guns of our Cromwells had no effect on these giants. This was a gruelling battle and many of our lads were lost.[42]

Colonel Desmond Spencer Gordon, CO of the 1/7th Queen's, looked on as a Tiger rumbled down the main street, shelling the tanks of the County of London Yeomanry and knocking down buildings in the process:

---

41   A. Kingston, correspondence with author (St Albans, 1994).
42   J. Kay, correspondence with author (Stevenage, 1996).

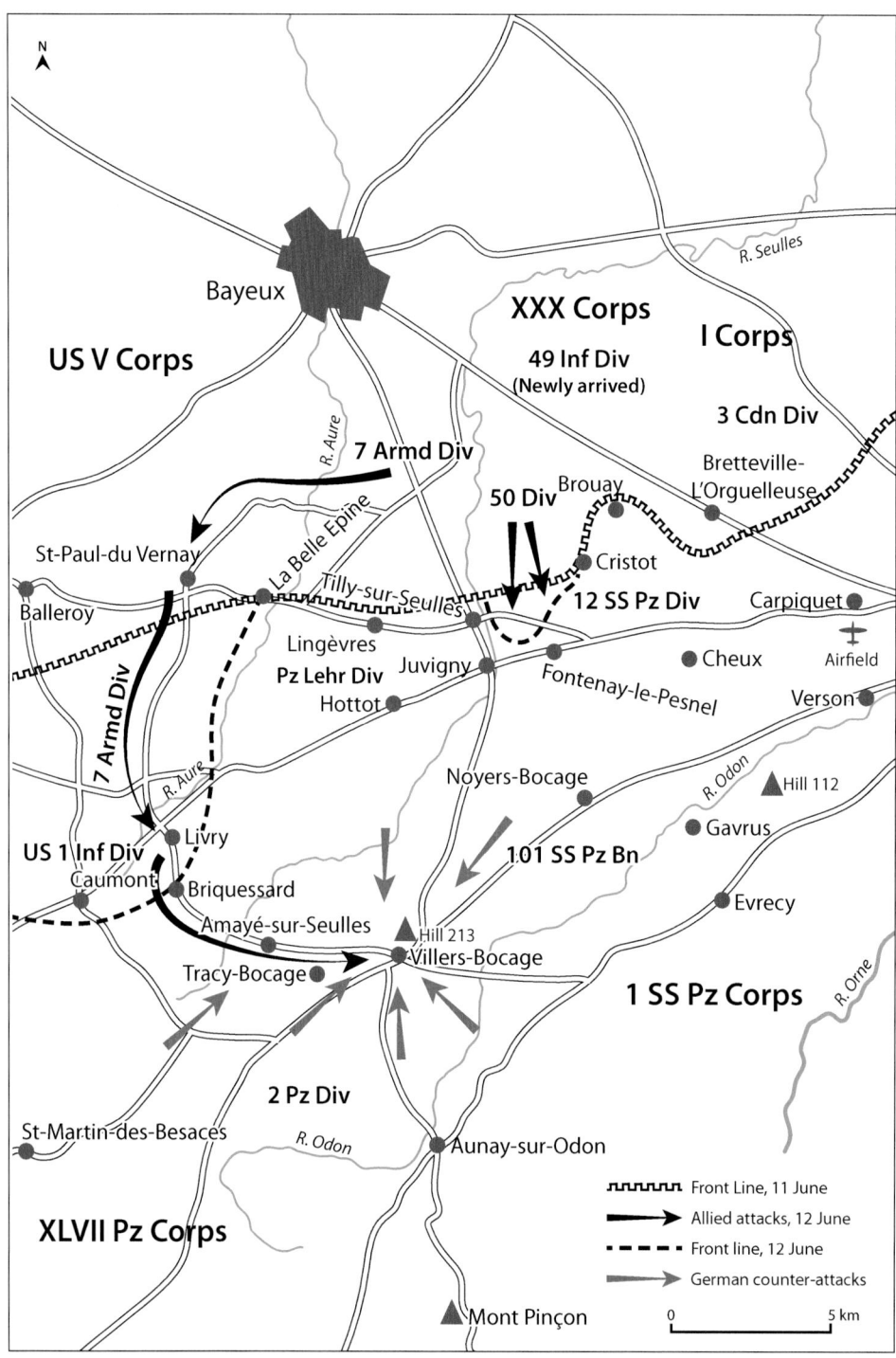

Disaster at Villers Bocage.

Panzergrenadiere of the *Panzer-Lehr-Division* being addressed by their officer before going into action. (Author's collection)

This caused confusion and the troops were ordered to get into the ruins and use their Piats, whilst the Cromwells and our 6-pounders covered all approaches to the high street. Further tanks, Tigers and Mk IVs, appeared in the main street. A Coy meanwhile encountered infantry opposition on the south-east face of the village and were pinned to the ground while an armoured battle raged for some time. Battalion 6-pounders in the area of the station had acquitted themselves well and claimed four tanks, Tigers were knocked out and two were hit without apparent damage.[43]

A forlorn hope

The road out of Villers Bocage to Point 213 was now crowded with German armour moving forward to reinforce the units in and around the town. The worsening situation for the British became hopeless, and all troops were ordered to withdraw and regroup. Luck ran out for Trooper

---

43 Saunders, *Battle for the Bocage*, p. 216.

T.D. Hawken, who was with the 4th County of London Yeomanry that day, as the enemy moved in for the kill:

> Early in the morning while we were cooking breakfast came the order to move at once. As we approached the town of Villers we came under heavy shellfire. On reaching the town Lord Cranley left our tank and went ahead to A Squadron by scout car. Major Carr took over command. We were able to see the Honey tanks ahead being knocked out and the crews being machine-gunned as they bailed out. This sight I will never forget. Major Carr, on seeing what was happening, ordered me to turn right into a field. I drove into the field straight through the gate and turned around facing the road. We saw a Tiger tank rumbling down the road. Sgt Jack Pumphrey called for Harry Ramsbottom who was sat next to me, a wireless operator to brigade, to come and load the gun. Harry was able to do this, and Jack fired two shots both hitting the enemy tank at close range but not powerful enough to do any damage. The Tiger traversed its gun, fired, and we received a direct hit and immediately caught fire.[44]

Trooper T.D. Hawken, 4th County of London Yeomanry, Royal Armoured Corps. (Courtesy of T.D. Hawken)

Hawken struggled out of his stricken tank through the co-driver's door, then heard Sergeant Pumphrey shouting to him: "Help me with Harry." A Sergeant Francis then appeared and helped Hawken to get the two men out. They dragged the men behind a hedge with a big tree in it to give extra cover. Hawken said that Pumphrey and Ramsbottom were both badly burned. He continued:

> I have no recollection of Major Carr however, as having received a direct hit at such close range had left me rather dazed. By this time the German infantry had arrived, and we were taken prisoner. One of them pinched my cap badge and I wish he would return it. As we prisoners moved off in column a German officer came up to us in a staff car, a Volkswagen, shouting and raving, and then he stopped and fired his pistol. Of course, we all scattered and then the guards got hold of him and put him back in the car. It turned out all his family had been killed the day before in Berlin during the bombing. He had already killed six of our soldiers at the back of the column; I was lucky I was at the front.[45]

---

44 T.D. Hawken, correspondence with author (Surrey, 1991).
45 T.D. Hawken, correspondence with author (Surrey, 1991).

For the 1/7th Queen's, the situation in the afternoon was now critical and they were ordered to move back to their original positions to cover the approaches to Villers Bocage. As they did so, reports came through of approaching German armour from all directions. Colonel Gordon described events:

> This was found to be a most difficult task as personnel of Coys had got very scattered throughout the houses of the village. By late afternoon the most serious problem now was some pockets of German infantry attempting to work their way through the village. A Coy had been driven back from their original positions near the station and there was a large gap between the south and north-western edge which was not covered by any of our Coys and there was no Coy available to do it.[46]

Gunner John Coombs was in position with his 5th Regiment, Royal Horse Artillery, battery of Priest self-propelled guns on the outskirts of Villers Bocage in the lull before the German counter-attack came in:

> About 3pm Captain Hill, our Adjutant, said that as it was now quiet he would have a sleep and walked up the slope of the field to lie in the lee of the sun. Almost at once three shells landed just where we could see his feet and we thought it was a shovel job for sure until he came running down the hill. Then all hell broke loose with a barrage of shells landing on our positions and heavy mortar bombs landing on the infantry in front. This went on for some time and then we were horrified to see groups of the Queens running between G [Battery's] guns. They looked like young boys to us in our mid-twenties and they were whimpering with terror. There was no sign of an officer, only a youthful sergeant major doing his best to stem their headlong flight. Major Holman drew his revolver but that only increased the panic. Eventually we managed to persuade them to dig-in next to us.[47]

As this was happening, the eight guns of G Battery were blasting away, making speech impossible. All the gunners knew that they were the only thing between them and the advancing enemy. Gunner Coombs recalled:

> It was not a situation we were used to; our little trench was ten yards behind the left-hand gun which completely obscured my view. I was calm and determined to fight it out with anything in grey or black that came round the corner of the self-propelled gun in front. This has always surprised me since faced with danger I am usually frozen in terrified immobility. I picked up a Sten-gun and carefully cocked it, making sure that the safety catch was off.[48]

The *Panzergrenadiers* and tanks of the recently arrived 2. SS-Panzer-Division 'Das Reich' advanced upon the British positions, and it looked as though they would not be stopped. Just in the nick of time, rocket-firing Typhoons appeared overhead and poured their rockets

---

46 Saunders, *Battle for the Bocage*, p. 219.
47 *WW2: People's War* <www.bbc.co.uk/ww2peopleswar> (accessed 12 October 2015)
48 *WW2: People's War* <www.bbc.co.uk/ww2peopleswar> (accessed 12 September 2016)

and cannon-fire into the German ranks, sending men and machinery flying into the air. The counter-attack was halted.

Major Charles Gregson, 7th Armoured Division, also remembered the timely intervention of the American artillery stationed around Caumont:

> I had with me a US liaison officer, Captain Chuck Babcock, and he called for a "Serenade".[49] The target was only some 300 metres in front of us, [and] I remember Babcock said: "If we get out of this I'll be court-martialled, only commanding generals can order a 'Serenade'." The Serenade duly arrived in minimum time and was very accurate. I don't ever again wish to be so close to such a volume of fire. The effect was devastating, and we knocked out some 11 tanks and completely broke up the attack [–] all was now quiet except for snipers in the trees outside our positions.[50]

All 7th Armoured Division units that were able to were sending back deeply disturbing reports from the battle area of the pressure they were under and of the casualties being taken. The infantry of the Queen's Regiment pleaded for reinforcements to enable them to stem the tide of German troops infiltrating the area, but none came.

The infantry and tank crews had taken hundreds of casualties in and around Villers Bocage, with many more taken prisoner. Gunner John Coombs, with the 5th Royal Horse Artillery, had been giving supporting fire to the attack. There were so many wounded still lying on the battlefield that the infantry stretcher-bearers couldn't cope, so the artillerymen were asked to volunteer to go and help. No volunteers came forward, so men were given a stretcher and ordered to bring in the casualties. Coombs was one of these men:

> We were given a stretcher and detailed, [and] we wasted no time in getting forward and finding a customer, one who seemed to hate our guts. A mortar fragment had taken him across both shins leaving his lower legs dangling. We manoeuvred him onto the stretcher as carefully as we could, [and] he is cursing us the whole time. Then we ran and walked with him for several hundred yards, bullets singing around our heads. As we reached the barn where the MO had set up the Regimental Aid Post, I sought to reassure him that Jerry was letting ambulances through to the rear and that he would be in Blighty in no time. "You said that well" he said sarcastically, then went right on hating me.[51]

The success of the action being fought by the 7th Armoured Division depended on the capture of Villers Bocage, to enable the British to threaten the supply lines of the German forces opposing the 50th Northumbrian Division to the north. The attempt on the town failed, the enemy getting the better of the first clash there, which represented the loss of the last opportunity to develop the Battle of Normandy into the mobile one which the Allied planners had hoped for. The battle was not handled well by the British XXX Corps commander, Lieutenant General Gerard C. Bucknall. The lack of any hands-on, flexible approach resulted in a sluggish response when the lead brigade of 7th Armoured Division should have been reinforced. This

---

49 A term used to describe a concentration of all available artillery fire on a specific target.
50 D'Este, *Decision in Normandy*, p. 189.
51 *WW2: People's War* <www.bbc.co.uk/ww2peopleswar> (accessed 14 July 2019).

Tiger 121 was caught out in the open and struck by British artillery fire in Villers Bocage. (Courtesy of T.D. Hawken)

led to confusion, the loss of many tanks and the death of many good men. The 7th Armoured Division was forced to withdraw to the high ground east of Caumont after having suffered severe casualties in both tank crews and infantry. They then made contact with the Americans and took their place in the line to the right of the 50th Northumbrian Division.

The history of the 4th County of London Yeomanry described the withdrawal:

> The enemy, after a failed counterattack, started to shell all they could see and the German infantry in the houses and hedges became more active. A few hours before dark the order came to withdraw from the town to the village of Amaye-sur-Seulles, some 4,000 yards to the west where Tac Brigade had been all day. This was not easy as part of the road was exposed to anti-tank and machine-gun fire, while the sunken portions of the road were too narrow to allow a Cromwell tank to turn. Eventually, under a heavy barrage of smoke and high explosive by the American 155mm and British 25 pounders, the Queens infantry and the two surviving squadrons were extricated to leaguer in the village of Amaye. Tanks of the 8th Hussars were there, and the lines of communications were being protected by 1st Royal Tanks.[52]

---

52 Graham, *Sharpshooters at War*, p. 180.

Sergeant Robert Bramwell looked back on a trying day for the 4th County of London Yeomanry:

> We pulled out at nightfall and went back to Amaye-sur-Seulles, near Tracy Bocage, west of Villers Bocage, and counted the cost. The regiment had been badly mauled, we lost our CO, Colonel Onslow was taken prisoner, all of A Squadron, most of the Recce Troop and RHQ, a lot of good people. Villers Bocage was a hard battle, believe me.[53]

Colonel Gordon found his widely dispersed 1/7th Queen's under intense pressure from the German infantry and recognised that something had to be done to retrieve the situation:

> A decision had to be made as to whether we could hold the village that night or not; without further infantry Coys it did not appear possible, and Brigade Command issued orders for the Battalion and 4th CLY to withdraw onto the high ground west of the village, from where we had started that morning, and there join up in a firm base position with the remainder of 22 Armoured Brigade.[54]

The retreat of the 7th Armoured Division was greatly assisted by a ferocious artillery barrage from British and American units. That night, RAF bombers also rained down high explosive bombs onto Villers Bocage and practically flattened the whole area. The people of the town, who had welcomed the British armoured units so joyfully, were now dead, injured or homeless. Most of the survivors sought shelter in the cellars of a nearby chateau. The War Diary of 22 Armoured Brigade recorded that well over 100 tanks were available to enter the fight at Villers Bocage after the withdrawal, but they never fired a shot all day.

Major Ian Aird, now commanding the 4th County of London Yeomanry, commented on the withdrawal:

> A few hours before dark the order came to withdraw from the town to the village of Amaye-sur-Seulles, some 4,000 yards to the west along the main axis, where Tac Brigade had been for most of the day. This was not easy, as part of the road was exposed to anti-tank and machine-gun fire, while the sunken portions of the road were too narrow to allow a Cromwell to turn. Eventually, under a heavy barrage of smoke and HE by the American 155mms and British 25-pounders laid just before dark, the Queen's infantry and the two surviving squadrons were extricated to leaguer in the village of Amaye. Tanks of the 8th Hussars were there, helping to remove an uncomfortable feeling of loneliness.[55]

Wittmann's victory had great significance for the *I SS-Panzerkorps*, as without his sacrificial attack on the British armoured column the 7th Armoured Division would have been able to drive unopposed down the straight national highway towards Caen, pushing deep into the rear of the German corps involved in heavy fighting further to the north. This potential catastrophe was averted only by Wittmann's attack. The advance by the 7th Armoured Division completely collapsed as Wittmann and the *Schwere SS-Panzer-Abteilung 101* went into action. After the

---

53   Neillands, *The Battle of Normandy 1944*, pp. 103–04.
54   Saunders, *Battle for the Bocage*, p. 220.
55   Graham, *Sharpshooters at War*, p. 181.

A knocked-out Tiger and a Panzer IV hit by shelling and air attacks in the ruins of Villers Bocage after the 7th Armoured Division had withdrawn. (Author's collection)

initial attack, serious losses were inflicted on the British force in the town and on Point 213, with more than 30 tanks and numerous Universal Carriers, anti-tank guns and trucks being destroyed. Many men were killed, wounded or taken into captivity. For his bravery and determination, *Oberstgruppenführer* Sepp Dietrich, commander of the *I SS-Panzerkorps*, recommended that Wittmann be awarded the Knight's Cross with Oak Leaves and Swords. His recommendation was granted.

Many historians have tried to depict the events at Villers Bocage as a draw, but to any dispassionate observer it is impossible to view them as anything other than a crushing defeat for the 7th Armoured Division. The first British attempt to capture Villers Bocage and Tilly-sur-Seulles to help them achieve a breakout had ended in humiliating failure. It was XXX Corps commander Lieutenant General Bucknall who had determined the outcome of the fight at Villers Bocage. Rather than acting quickly to requests for support by sending an infantry force to oppose the *Panzer-Lehr-Division*, hopefully advancing to Villers Bocage and relieving the situation, his response was sluggish. *Panzer-Lehr* was fully engaged around Tillysur-Seulles and Villers Bocage, and the *2. SS-Panzer-Division 'Das Reich'* was only just arriving in the area in strength. This left a gap along the Aure River that was still unplugged by the Germans. However, Bucknall did not read the signs that made it obvious that the 7th Armoured Division was desperate for reinforcements while time still allowed. The losses of men and machines on Point 213 and the need to withdraw from Villers Bocage were severe setbacks, but they were by no means decisive. The division still posed a serious threat to the German flank, but only if urgent steps were taken to press home what remained of their advantage before the *'Das Reich'* could arrive in any great numbers, so preventing any further movement towards Caen. Major General Erskine, commander of 7th Armoured, sent the following message to XXX Corps: "I consider that 2nd Panzer Division were taken by surprise, but they can be expected to react fairly violently. Can you give me an indication of what the corps commander intends if their reaction is violent?"

Bucknall had planned that the 50th Northumbrian Division should attack towards Hottot on the Caumont–Tilly road, and with artillery and air support should fully occupy the *Panzer-Lehr-Division*. This misplaced optimism bore little relation to reality, as *Panzer-Lehr* had been strengthened considerably in this sector and had proved immoveable in previous attacks. The end result was a bloody slogging match in which the 50th Division failed to make any significant headway, leaving Hottot in enemy hands. In a post-war interview, Lieutenant General Miles Dempsey, GOC British Second Army, commented on the Villers Bocage operation:

> This attack by 7th Armoured Division should have succeeded. My feeling that Bucknall and Erskine would have to go started with that failure.[56] Early on the morning of 12th June I went down to see Erskine, gave him his orders and told him to get moving and that I would tell corps commander what he was doing. If he had carried out my orders he would never have been kicked out of Villers Bocage, but by this time 7th Armoured Division was living on its reputation and the whole handling of that battle was a disgrace. Their decision to withdraw from Villers Bocage on 13th June was made without consulting me: it was done by the Corps Commander Bucknall, and Erskine.[57]

These failed attempts to outflank Caen were an early demonstration of the flaws in British tactics in Normandy. The debilitating effects of the confined Normandy terrain and the staunch fighting abilities of the German forces made the 7th Armoured Division's previous experience of mobile warfare in North Africa ineffective in a congested European battlefield. With its infantry support left far behind, the division had been stopped in its tracks in a landscape unsuitable for the large-scale deployment of tanks. It was becoming obvious that attacks led by tanks were doomed to fail without sufficient infantry and artillery support. Armoured units slowly began to adapt to the new way of warfare by mixing tank and infantry brigades, but the successful coordination of the two arms was never entirely achieved in the Normandy campaign. As the front lines congealed, it became clear that the fixation on Caen was pulling in all the best German formations, but in doing so it meant that all the British troops in the Bocage were committed to a bloody slogging match with the most elite German formations in Normandy, including nearly all the panzer divisions available. With finite resources in manpower, such a war of attrition could not be sustained indefinitely by the Germans.

---

56 In August 1944, both Erskine and Bucknall were relieved of their commands. Lieutenant General Brian Horrocks took over command of XXX Corps.
57 D'Este, *Decision in Normandy*, p. 196.

Men of the 4th County of London Yeomanry, who were captured on Hill 213, being marched into captivity. (Courtesy of T.D. Hawken)

Meanwhile, despite storms in the English Channel, Allied strength was building up in the Normandy bridgehead. But although troops and materiel poured into the bridgehead from the sea, it was not expanding as quickly as hoped. Endless streams of jeeps, lorries, tanks and armoured cars now clogged up the narrow roads of Normandy. This was a volume of traffic these lanes were not constructed to cope with, and they were soon pounded to dust. Among all of this bustle and confusion, a great force was being concentrated in the bridgehead, getting ready for the day it would burst forth across France and Belgium, and eventually into the Reich itself. But this was in the future, and XXX Corps had been fighting for nearly two weeks while the main force was still landing. For the troops in the front line, all they could do now was to continue to press forward, probing and grinding the enemy down, backed up by a never-ending stream of artillery, naval and air firepower. For XXX Corps' battalions and tank support, there was no immediate relief from the deadly Bocage.

Life in the line, 13 June

XXX Corps was about to enter upon one of the most unpleasant periods in its history. It was here in the Bocage that its men would fight a deadly war of attrition in the coming weeks, centred around the area of Tilly-sur-Seulles, Hottot and La-Belle-Epine. The German units facing them were the troops and tanks of the *Panzer-Lehr-Division*, tough, brave and committed fighters who would not easily give up the ground they held. In the recent fighting,

British and Canadian forces had suffered heavy casualties, but they were achieving exactly what Montgomery intended: the destruction of the German armoured formations being sent to Normandy. Montgomery's policy was to pull as many German divisions as possible onto the British Second Army in the Bocage so that the US First Army to the west could carry out its tasks against lighter opposition. The progress of XXX Corps was thus to be slow and painful.

The life of an infantryman, on both sides, in this bloody slogging match was often short. Two armies, each possessing enormous firepower, were locked in furious close-quarter combat in the maze-like Bocage, and mere men stood little chance of survival in this technologically driven warfare. Tanks and anti-tank projectiles blasted the infantry at close range, shells would come down without warning and deadly accurate mortar bombs took a steady toll in lives. At times it was impossible to see a man or a machine in the closely hedged Norman Bocage, but on the soft summer breezes there could be seen the black clouds of flies, and the smell of cordite and charred flesh filled the nostrils. All around were to be found sad little mounds of earth topped with wooden crosses or boltless rifles with a steel helmet hanging on them, marking the spot where some young man had met his end in this verdant but deadly countryside. Hundreds of dead farm animals also lay about in the fields, each one grotesquely bloated, stinking and crawling with maggots. Bulldozers buried those in the safe areas, but others in or near the killing zone were a constant torment to troops who lived with the thought that an erupting shell might throw one of these stinking apparitions near them, or worse, into their trench. The rancid stench of putrefaction was at times overpowering on these hot summer days in the Bocage.

The attritional battles of June 1944 ground on without pause. Rommel was during this time unable to mount any serious counter-attacks on the British sector, having been forced to squander his precious panzers to plug holes in the line to hold the Allies back. At this point the American forces were running low on ammunition and had to postpone their planned breakout for three days. This meant that the British and Canadian forces had to go on fighting the bulk of the German divisions for longer than anticipated, and because of gales in the Channel three British divisions had to delay their landings, leaving the men already fighting in the bridgehead to soldier on with fewer numbers than expected. Against this background, the battalions of XXX Corps prepared for the next bloody round amid the sunshine and deep meadows of the French countryside.

Major John Stirling, 4/7th Royal Dragoon Guards, remembered the nature of the fighting:

> If ever a piece of country was ideal for defence by tanks and a nightmare for them to attack in, it was Normandy in summer. The countryside is so like England, luxuriant green grass, tall thick hedges bounding small pasture fields, little sunken lanes with grassy banks and clumps of grey stone buildings forming a farm or a village. A delightful spot for a picnic, but a death-trap for an invading army. In this cover a tank or a gun could hide completely and bide its time. You only became aware of its existence when your leading tank went up in flames and often several more went up before you had any exact idea of its position. It was difficult to see or shoot more than a few hundred yards. Instead of tanks picking a position on a flank and sitting there shooting while the infantry went forward, now they had to go forward side by side with the infantry and were duly picked off.[58]

---

58 Stirling, J.D.P., *The First and the Last, The Story of the 4/7th Royal Dragoon Guards 1939–1945* (London: Art and Educational Publishers, 1946), p. 137.

During a lull in the fighting, Private Thomas Tateson watched a friend in the 7th Green Howards, 69 Brigade, try to milk a cow, much to the amusement of everyone:

> One morning everything was peaceful and calm for a change and a cow was grazing quite close to us. All the civilian farm workers having disappeared the cow's udders were very distended, and we decided we could do both the cow, and ourselves, a good turn by milking it. One of our number took the task upon himself and a hilarious half-hour ensued as he stealthily approached the animal mess tin in hand. The cow would docilely suffer him to take up position before gently strolling away. Each time this happened the lad was successively cheered on and then greeted with howls of derision as the cow negligently defeated his efforts. During this brief period in the cow pasture, we made ourselves very comfortable in our hole in the ground. We lined it with our capes and installed one of our radios which we illegally re-tuned to the home service. The contrast between our recent experiences and the sound of Vera Lynn singing 'We'll meet again' was profound and very moving, however corny and sentimental that may sound now.[59]

Trooper Don Aitken, 61st Reconnaissance Regiment, recalled a pause for a couple of hours, when as they smoked and rested, he and his comrades explored the area:

> Upon investigating the familiar smell of death nearby we found a German soldier lying in a covered slit trench. His face was a ball of maggots. We managed to get hold of some chloride of lime and scattered this all over him. I still recall with horror the disgusting sight of maggots flowing from his face like a living stream.[60]

The German infantry in the line suffered the same deprivations and horrors as their British opponents. *Sturman* Decker, of the *Hitlerjugend's 25. SS-Panzergrenadiere*, told of being in the line for over nine days and being unable to perform the normal operations of washing, as a result of which the curse of lice plagued them:

> Disruption on the railways caused by Allied bombing, and increased partisan activity, meant supplies were no longer reaching the

Trooper Don Aitken, 61st Reconnaissance Regiment. (Author's collection)

---

59 T. Tateson, interview with author (Sheffield, 1989).
60 *WW2: People's War* <www.bbc.co.uk/ww2peopleswar> (accessed 19 July 2016).

fighting troops at the front. As a result, we were given permission to enter French houses and to take whatever was necessary for personal use, such as clean underwear and so on, but nothing more. We were not allowed to take any more than was absolutely essential. I can remember cutting up a bed sheet and wrapping the strips around my feet because I didn't have any socks. Conditions in the field meant we were unable to wash or clean our uniforms regularly and this led to many of us catching lice. The lice used to gather in the crotch of our trousers and drive us mad. When we had time, we would remove our trousers, turn them inside out and hold the crotch over a lighted candle. This was a horrendous job, but it killed most of the little blighters. When we were finally taken prisoner, one of the first things they did was to delouse us with DDT. They sprayed every nook and cranny; they had to.[61]

49th West Riding Division joins XXX Corps, 13–14 June

On 13 June, the 49th West Riding Division came into the line on the left of the 50th Northumbrian Division, relieving 69 Brigade who had been involved in some hard fighting east of the River Seulles. Lieutenant H. Taylor, 6th Green Howards, recorded in his diary the arrival of these untested troops straight from England:

On Tuesday 13th June there was plenty of buckshee compo and enormous numbers of eggs produced by Robertson – we are feeding very well indeed. 49 Div arrived to relieve us this afternoon, fresh from England and it was to be their first time in action. They were all wearing steel helmets and had their faces blackened, which rather amused us, and were treated with superior grins from us. Moved out in the evening, slept in a room, ate at a table for a change and sat on a chair. Talked to a pretty French girl who, however, chewed gum and much preferred to sleep with the SS. Everyone feeling happy about being out of the line, not having to stand-to and lay lines. Unfortunately, a medium [artillery] regiment had set up shop in a neighbouring field and fired regularly during the night. Slept well though. Had a bath which cost 10 cigarettes. These people are very polite and hospitable, but obviously not glad to see us.[62]

The whole brigade marched off to a rest area in the rear and Private Thomas Tateson remembered the pleasure of having a bath in Bayeux:

On the afternoon of June 13th the 7th Green Howards handed our positions over to the King's Own Yorkshire Light Infantry of the 49th Division and we moved off to a rest area near Condé-sur-Seulles. Here we bivouacked in some orchards adjoining the Manoir-de-Ghene. The following day we were taken to Bayeux and visited the baths there for the luxury of a shower. We also had an hour to ourselves and a few of us indulged in the exotic pleasure of visiting a wine bar. Our approach to this period of freedom was not that of tourists admiring the ancient churches and buildings.[63]

---

61 Manuscript forwarded to author by H. Wernemann (Germany, 1989).
62 H. Taylor, correspondence with author (Richmond, 1988).
63 T. Tateson, interview with author (Sheffield, 1989).

Sherman tanks of the 7th Armoured Division move down a narrow lane in the close countryside of the Bocage. (Author's collection)

Private Reg Pope was feeling weary after going through so much in recent days with the 2nd Machine-gun Battalion the Cheshire Regiment, and felt great relief when he was told 69 Brigade was being pulled out of the line for a rest in Bayeux:

> What a difference from the horrors we had been through in the line. We got to Bayeux and although it was packed with troops and vehicles it was peaceful, the civilians were very friendly and treated us so well. They could not know what this meant to us. Eventually we went to the local baths where we took all our clothes off and jumped into the clear cool water. It was so refreshing and for a short while all our cares disappeared.[64]

The 49th West Riding Division was committed north-east of Tilly-sur-Seulles on the night of 13 June and would shortly be moving to the Fontenay front. With little battle experience, this green division would be in action before much longer, fighting the battle-hardened German SS units. However, they quickly settled in and it was not long before patrols from the 1/4th Battalion King's Own Yorkshire Light Infantry (1/4th KOYLIs) were probing forward in no-man's land. Private Rex Flower recalled:

> We took over the mortar pits of the outgoing Green Howards and got our mortars set up and settled down. The countryside was beautiful, the sniping was not. Next day we fired

---

64   R. Pope, interview with author (Durham, 1991).

our mortars for the first time in anger at an enemy spotted digging in. We soon dispersed them and caused some casualties. We had got our first blood. It was here the battalion took its first prisoners, [when] a patrol led by Lt N.L. Wilson captured two Germans and killed and wounded others. The two sergeants concerned were awarded the MM. They also won the two prizes promised from the Div GOC General Barker for the first German to be killed and for the first prisoners. Sadly, Captain Wilson[65] was mortally wounded later at Tessel Wood.[66]

Captain Richard Newsum, 4th Battalion Lincolnshire Regiment, was dug-in around Coulombs and was the commander of a carrier platoon. His men settled down and made themselves as comfortable as possible in their slit trenches:

Apart from the fairly regular shelling and mortaring life was a bit tedious. The worst thing was the dusk and dawn stand-to. With very short nights dusk stand-down was about 23:00 hours and dawn stand-to at about 02:00 hours which meant very little sleep. Our CO liked to keep his officers on the go and shortage of sleep was my worst enemy. Fortunately, the MO had a large supply of wakey-wakey pills. Later when I was wounded my first reaction was "Thank heaven, now I can get a decent kip".[67]

On 14 June, Lieutenant Colonel Trevor Hart-Dyke, DSO, commanding the Hallamshire Battalion, York and Lancaster Regiment, received news of the first offensive role to be given to the 49th West Riding Division. The village of Audrieu, its chateau and the woods to the east of the village were to be cleared of the enemy. Two companies, accompanied by a carrier platoon, advanced over the Bayeux–Caen railway line and occupied Audrieu without a shot being fired. The woods to the east and south, however, were not to be so simple as the enemy were established there in company strength. Major Ivor Slater led the attack on the chateau and its surrounding woods. The artillery and the mortars of the Hallamshire Battalion plastered the eastern woods before Major Peter Newton led his men into the attack. Under this assault, the weak German units retreated, though snipers took a steady toll of the attackers.

Lieutenant Colonel Hart-Dyke was pleased with the performance of his as yet untried troops, but darker things came to light as they moved into the grounds of the chateau:

The following day I came across the bodies of 14 soldiers of the Regina Rifles lying in a row in front of a hedge. They had obviously been stood up against the hedge of the chateau orchard and murdered. All had shots to the forehead. They had been dead for some days, and I arranged for our Padre Thomas to bury them. I felt very bitter about this callous act.[68]

---

65 Captain Norman Lee Wilson, 1/4th Battalion King's Own Yorkshire Light Infantry, was killed in action on 6 July 1944. He is buried in Fontenay-le-Pesnil War Cemetery, Tessel, France.
66 Delaforce, P., *The Polar Bears* (Gloucestershire: Sutton Publishing, 1995), pp. 35–36.
67 Manuscript forwarded to author by D. Eshelby (Leeds, 1991).
68 On 8 June, 64 Canadian troops were taken prisoner at the village of Putot-en-Bessin. They were marched to the Chateau Audrieu, where the HQ of the *12. SS-Panzer-Division 'Hitlerjugend'* was situated. Forty-five Canadians were murdered in batches in the grounds of the chateau by the troops of the *'Hitlerjugend'*.

The chateau itself had been the scene of a desperate fight earlier on as dead bodies littered the stairs.[69]

The troops of the 49th Division settled down in their new positions and looked to an uncertain future, it would not be long before they would be called forward to play their part in the most vicious and costly fighting for the Norman Bocage.

Attack by 231 and 151 Brigades, 14 June

On 14 June, the 50th Northumbrian Division was to launch an attack headed by 231 and 151 Brigades. On the left, the 9th Durhams would advance on the village of Lingèvres on the main road 3 miles west of Tilly, with the 6th Durhams having as its objective the neighbouring village of Verrières, with the intention of pushing on south to Hottot if possible. The 1st Bttalion Hampshires and 1st Dorsets on the right were to advance to the crossroads and surrounding areas of the village of La Senaudiere.

On 13 June, Lieutenant Colonel HumphreyReginald Woods, DSO, MC and Bar, CO 9th Durhams, and Lieutenant Colonel A.C. Green, CO 6th Durhams, were ordered to attend a meeting at brigade headquarters by Brigadier B.B. Walton to receive their orders for the coming battle. The commanders of the 1st Hampshires and 1st Dorsets did the same. When both brigades had been given their orders, it became obvious that an attack of this nature would involve each brigade having to take horrendous casualties. Little reconnaissance had been carried out and the assault was to be launched in daylight. The high command knew that it was imperative that the breakout should continue to move forward as German resistance was stiffening all the time as new units moved into the area. The official attitude was that if it meant heavy casualties, then so be it. To 50th Northumbrian Division's front were flat open cornfields, with woods screening the villages; church towers could be seen above the trees and a few red house roofs were also visible. Country roads ran alongside the fields with walled enclosures, and the exact positions being held by the enemy were unknown. It was obvious that the enemy held the woods and ditches and that they had good fields of fire across the open land. Corn in front of the woods had been cut by the Germans, but this was unknown to the attackers as it could not be seen from the British line. All of this had been carefully prepared by the enemy to make an effective killing ground.

Patrols of up to company strength went out into no man's land from both brigades on the evening of 13 June, the Germans allowing them to advance into the middle of the standing corn, where they were subjected to a withering fire. The Germans were obviously seasoned troops, holding their fire until it would be most effective. The British, having also spotted German tanks camouflaged in the woods, were forced to withdraw after suffering considerable casualties. The patrols proved without doubt that the enemy was there in considerable strength and was full of fight. The Germans holding these positions were *Panzergrenadiere* and tanks of the *Panzer-Lehr-Division*.

---

69   Manuscript forwarded to author by P. Graham (Barnsley, 1994).

The assault on Verrières and Lingèvres by 151 Brigade on the morning of 14 June was set to begin at 1015 hours, with 231 Brigade to start its attack at 1130 hours. Tension was running high among the troops as they prepared for the move forward. Support for this enterprise was considerable, coming in the form of the self-propelled guns of the 86th, 90th and 147th Field Regiments, Royal Artillery, plus the whole of 5th Army Group's artillery, which consisted of three medium regiments, a heavy regiment and an American artillery battalion. Their guns were to target the edges of the woods held by the Germans, then the barrage would creep forward as the infantry advanced behind it. Fifteen minutes before the attack, Typhoon fighter-bombers would drop 120 tons of bombs and rockets into the woods. In addition to all this firepower would be the Sherman tanks of the 4/7th Royal Dragoon Guards, commanded by Major Jack d'Avigdor-Goldsmid, actively supporting the infantry in their assault. Cooperation with the infantry had already been practised: the attackers would carry yellow reflecting panels to mark their position to friendly aircraft and to communicate enemy positions to the tank commanders of the three troops involved.

151 Brigade at Verrières and Lingèvres, 14 June

As the barrage opened up on the woods, the attacking infantry watched the display of immense firepower with a sense of great satisfaction. Lieutenant Jack Williams of the 9th Durhams observed:

> We were treated to a front row seat of a very accurate and sustained 25 pounder barrage and the woods literally jumped and danced in front of our eyes and not 300 yards away. Each of the Typhoons dived on the woods and released two bombs and 10 rockets that straddled and plastered the wood. Surely nothing could live in that now.[70]

Private James Radcliffe, serving in a mortar section with the 9th Durhams, watched the violence of the barrage as it thundered down:

> The German front line ran along the leading edge of a wood; the scene looked like something from World War One. I saw a mass of bursting shells and big trees were being thrown into the air. The place was blazing as planes dive bombed it, a real hell upon earth. It was hard to imagine anything could survive such an onslaught, but when the rifle companies started to advance through the cornfields the Spandaus started to chop them to ribbons.[71]

The 6th Durhams lined up on the main Tilly–Bayeux road on the left of the 9th Battalion. Unknown to them, there was an undetected major strongpoint in farm buildings on the route of their advance. They immediately came under heavy fire from mortars and Spandaus.

Captain Stephen Perry, a Forward Observation Officer (FOO) with the 86th Field Regiment, Royal Artillery, was with the 6th Durhams as the barrage came down:

---

70 Manuscript forwarded to author from W. Ridley (Durham, 1991).
71 J. Radcliffe, correspondence with author (Durham, 1987).

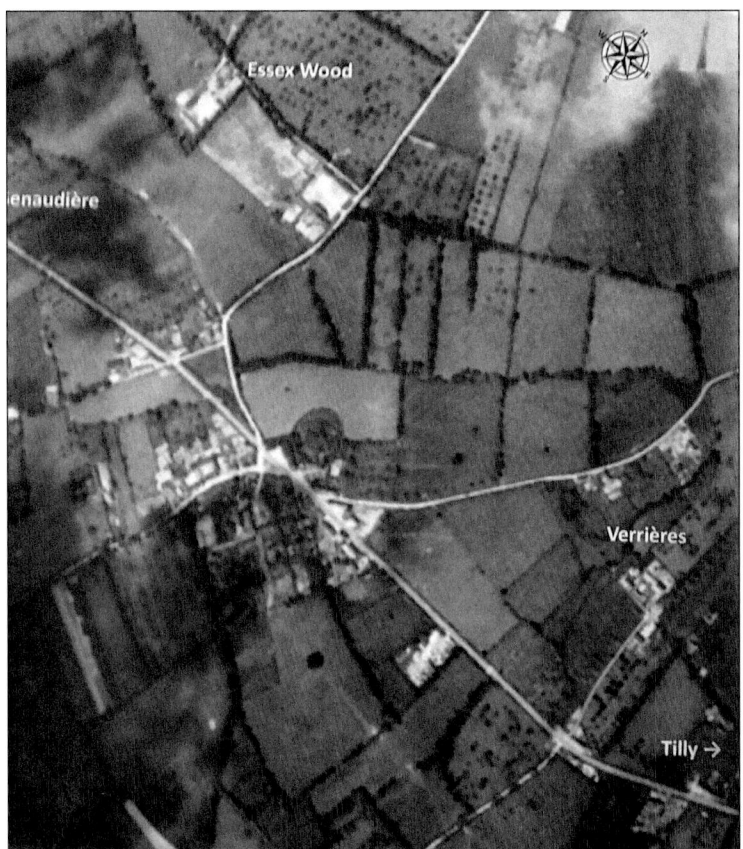

Aerial view showing Lingèvres, bottom left, and Verrières, bottom right. (Courtesy of M. Denney)

Men of the Durham Light Infantry entering the cornfield through which they must attack. (Courtesy of R. Pope)

> We were at the start line with the 6th DLI. The company commander, the enormously tough Spike Galloway, was wearing the MC and Bar. The barrage starts and 120 guns pound the country in front of us unceasingly for half an hour, but the infantry can't keep up and the barrage rolls away. Now the fun starts, [as] mortars, anti-tank guns, SP guns, Spandaus and rifles all open up on the infantry who are advancing now over flat wheat fields. Galloway orders a halt. We bury our heads in the ground when the moaning minnies whine over. This really is a rough battle. Everything on earth seems to be landing in our field. If we poke our noses above this corn the Spandaus in those farm buildings will knock us down like ninepins. We lie in the open for about half an hour while the battalion CO sums up the situation. Then we get orders to advance. It seems like suicide to stand up in the corn with a dozen Spandaus in front ready to knock us down. But Spike Galloway is a grand chap, and with a cheerful "Come on chaps" we all get onto our feet and start walking forward. The Spandaus open up, a dozen of our chaps go down, and after 100 yards down we go down again in the corn and get ready for the assault. As we go down there is a shout from Spike, he is shot through the shoulder. We help him back to the stretcher bearers. I walk back to the carriers expecting every moment to be my last, but for some reason nothing opens up.[72]

Private Ken Lodge, 6th Durhams, dived for cover from this hail of fire:

> All of a sudden, the Spandaus opened up, what a mess. That was probably the fastest I have ever hit the deck and we were just lying there taking it. We had no cover on either side of the road. Up on the right there was a bit of a building. We were the forward section, and we were getting it. All I could hear was bullets thudding into the ground and the muck flying into my face. I could hear the bullets going into the ground buzzing and buzzing and I said: "Good God, what am I going to do now?" The lads behind me could get back behind the road and they were setting up the Bren-guns and someone was shouting: "Fire into the barn." Anyway, they got everyone in my section but me and I was the only one that wasn't hit. The first four were killed and I lost my mate Eddie Fenwick.[73] They got poor Lt Bell,[74] the corporal, Eddie, Bennet,[75] and then they got this other lad in both his legs. The lad lying beside me got hit in the wrist. I was just lying there, and I thought I'll never get out of this. I honestly thought I was gone.[76]

Private Ernest Harvey recalled the slaughter amid the corn for the men of the 6th Durhams:

> We were all going into the attack across this cornfield and got about 20/25 yards out when Gerry opened up with Spandaus. Well, there was a small groove in the ground where, fortunately, I got down into it. The men were getting mown down left, right and centre. In

---

72   S. Perry, correspondence with author (Durham, 1990).
73   Private Edward Albert Fenwick, 6th Battalion Durham Light Infantry, was killed in action on 13 June 1944, aged 18. He is buried in Tilly-sur-Seulles War Cemetery, France.
74   Lieutenant F.W. Bell, 6th Battalion Durham Light Infantry, survived the war.
75   Private Cyril Frederick Bennet, 6th Battalion Durham Light Infantry, was killed in action on 13 June 1944, aged 30. He is buried in Tilly-sur-Seulles War Cemetery, France.
76   Moses, *The Faithful Sixth*, p. 288.

fact, the company was being slaughtered, it's as simple as that. As those were going down more men were moving up and they were getting knocked down. They cried: "Mother, Mother". Eventually two tanks came up behind us after a long while [–] the corn had been completely mown down as if it had been done with shears. The Spandaus had us pinned down and we couldn't move.[77]

The 6th Battalion pressed forward toward their tormentors in the farm buildings, many men falling in the process while the others went to ground to escape the deadly fire. Major K.M. Wood, MC, ordered an attack to be put in on the right flank in order to take the enemy from the rear. Major Reginald Atkinson, MC and Bar, led B Company down the line of a small stream, but as the leading sections advanced they were caught in a volley of *Nebelwerfer* bombs that fell among them. Major Atkinson recalled:

> Busson was among the wounded in the *Nebelwerfer* attack on the leading platoon of B Company as it commenced its right flanking movement from Le-Pont-de-la-Guillette when A Company was held up. The salvo of bombs landed in the middle of the leading platoon as it made its way along a small stream. It was a horrific sight as you can imagine. I saw Lt Bell[78] being carried back on the front of a tank of the 4/7th Dragoon Guards.[79]

The 9th Durhams formed up along a dusty track before the woods, then its companies moved to the attack at 1015 hours, their axis being a road that led in the direction of Lingèvres. The troops advanced at a steady pace with rifles at the port and bayonets fixed. On the flanks, the tanks of the 4/7th Royal Dragoon Guards moved forward as the barrage thudded and rumbled before them. Major Darcy Irvine, 9th Durhams, was in command of A Company:

> Initially all went fairly smoothly, and we kept very close up behind the barrage. There was a little smoke to begin with, but this cleared very rapidly. We had some tanks with us in the early stages. However, when we got to within 50 yards of the woods all hell was let loose, and we could see the Spandaus in enfilade cutting through the corn all around us. My left forward platoon reached the woods and quite a considerable number of Germans climbed out of their weapons pits with their hands above their heads. I cannot to this day understand why some of them were not shot, but the Geordies paid no attention to them, despite the havoc they had wrought among us and the fact that their compatriots were still keeping up a continuous hail of fire. It was at this stage, just short of the edge of the woods, that I was hit.[80]

Lieutenant Jack Williams of the 9th Durhams was given the task of accompanying Lieutenant Colonel Woods' carrier in his own carrier to protect him as he moved forward:

---

77 Moses, *The Faithful Sixth*, p. 290.
78 Lieutenant John Lawrence Bell, Somerset Light Infantry, attached to the 6th Battalion Durham Light Infantry, was wounded on 14 June and sent back to England, where he died of his wounds on 19 June 1944, aged 25. He now lies in Mill Hill (St Paul) Churchyard, Middlesex.
79 Moses, *The Gateshead Gurkhas*, p. 281.
80 Moses, *The Gateshead Gurkhas*, p. 283.

> For seven or eight minutes nothing happened and then an enemy tank in the left-hand corner of the wood fired and set one of the Shermans on fire. The fire was returned with good effect by the remaining two. Another Hun tank opened up from the right-hand side of the wood and then the woods came to life. Our leading troops were now in the middle of the stubble and were caught there by a withering fire from Spandaus and snipers, but still they kept going.[81]

In the meantime, the enemy positions were being heavily engaged by artillery and mortars, and a troop of Sherman tanks also came forward in support. But behind the hedgerows that criss-crossed the entire area, the Germans were well concealed and dug in.

Sergeant Charles Eagles, 9th Durhams, went forward in the carrier of Lieutenant Jack Williams to guard Lieutenant Colonel Woods and his party during the action:

> We passed over the road and entered a large cornfield, the men were well spread out with rifles at the port position as they waded waist high through the corn. We would be about 500 yards up the field, which was triangular in shape, and were advancing towards the apex when all hell was let loose. A withering fire from Spandaus and snipers caught us in a cross-fire. Men were falling all around, and I jumped from the carrier followed by Jack Williams. We ran over to the other carrier which had been hit and pulled Corporal Sowerby clear, he was screaming in agony as his leg and arm had been blown off. The driver, a young ginger haired lad, was in a terrible state but he was dead having been killed immediately. There was dead and dying all around us and gruesome screams filled the air, mingled with the sound of machine-gunfire, which was so intense it was cutting the corn like a scythe.[82]

As the survivors of the Durhams closed in on the woods, the attackers could at last dish out the kind of punishment they had been receiving. Corporal R. Cork, 9th Durhams, left his fallen comrades lying in the corn and at last came to grips with his enemy:

> As we came out of the high corn Spandau machine-guns opened up all along our front and many men fell. I was so close to the one Spandau nearest to me I saw the dust blown up in little spurts as the bullets left his gun. He was firing straight ahead as I ran forward with Sten-gun firing towards him, and as I got close the firing stopped and I pulled the gun away. He lay dead in the trench, and I hauled his very terrified comrade out. He had to stand on his dead mate, I called: "Hands on head and walk" which I think he was glad to do back across the cornfield while I went to the next trench. On the parapet lay a pair of binoculars, something must have told me to keep back, and I knocked them into the trench with a couple of shots. I went to the next trench but that also was empty, but to be certain I fired four shots into each one. I stood back to see what was happening but saw no one else left standing. Just then a burst of Spandau from deeper in the woods hit me and I fell.[83]

---

81 Moses, *The Gateshead Gurkhas*, p. 282.
82 Moses, *The Gateshead Gurkhas*, p. 282.
83 Moses, *The Gateshead Gurkhas*, p. 283.

Panzergrenadiere and tanks concealed on the edge of a cornfield wait for the Durhams to attack. (Author's collection)

Private James Radcliffe, 9th Durhams, was supporting B Company with his mortar section when his carrier came under intense small-arms fire:

> We moved into position just outside of Lingèvres and as we advanced heavy fire was coming from the direction of a hedge just to our left, [so] we jumped out of the carrier. I was carrying a Sten-gun at the time and Sergeant Joe Farage ordered me to rake the hedge with it. I gave it a couple of bursts and the firing stopped.[84]

Sergeant Eagles heard Lieutenant Williams scream over the noise of battle "This way" as he ran towards Lieutenant Colonel Woods' carrier:

> The colonel was standing with another officer and shouted some order to Jack who then turned and ran towards me. Then he staggered and fell at my feet, blood pouring from his thighs. He gasped: "Take a look Eagles, if they've shot my balls off shoot me."[85] I pretended to look and said: "You're ok" then somehow managed to get him across my shoulders, how

---

84 Arthur, *Forgotten Voices of the Second World War*, p. 285.
85 Lieutenant Jack Williams survived the war.

I'll never understand, and carried him back 50 or 100 yards. I spotted a medic and dropped Jack at his feet, and he passed out.[86]

Lieutenant Colonel Woods, the 9th Durhams' commander, reached the outer perimeter of the woods and realised that A and B Companies had been decimated in the attack. He issued orders to Major John H. Mogg that the remaining companies were to continue the advance and reinforce C and D Companies. This was the last message Woods would ever issue, as his carrier received a direct hit from a mortar bomb and he was killed.

Sergeant Eagles returned to his comrades in the apex of the cornfield after taking his officer to a First Aid Post, and saw Lieutenant Colonel Woods at the head of his troops:

> We scrambled through a hedgerow into a chaotic scene and as we tried to gather our composure and wits together the colonel shouted: "This way lads." We were bunched together when we noticed the turret of a Tiger tank behind a copse of trees and we scattered in all directions, flinging ourselves down for cover. All except for Colonel Woods who stood there watching and ordered: "Get that tank!" I couldn't believe I was hearing him correctly as it was a totally impossible task, sheer suicide. There was a hell of a lot of noise as mortar shells were landing between us and I dived for cover. By this time, I was six or eight feet away from Colonel Woods and crawled over to him, his eyes were wide open as he uttered his last words and then he died.[87] He had terrible wounds, about the worst I had seen, he was virtually cut in half.[88]

One of the main difficulties in the morning was the loss of the FOOs of the Royal Artillery. This meant that information on troop positions and movements was desperately lacking for the supporting guns. It was the Durhams' good fortune that the tanks of 4/7th Royal Dragoon Guards accompanied the attack throughout. The support of this armoured unit was essential, for as the Durhams entered the village just before noon German tanks appeared in the streets. Infantry, artillery and tank cooperation was working well for the British.

FOO Captain Stephen Perry, 86th Field Regiment, Royal Artillery, watched in awe as the 6th Durhams fought their way into Verrières:

> We are going into the assault and the Durhams go like mad with fixed bayonets into the farm buildings. No wonder we had such a tough time getting here, there are two 75s, three self-propelled guns, a half track and seven Spandau positions dug into the bank of a sunken lane. As we were going in a bullet whistles through my battledress but does no more damage than a graze to my shoulder blade. Casualties are so heavy after the battle that two composite companies had to be formed from the whole battalion. But what magnificent troops these Durhams are. It was just sheer guts that got them into Verrières.[89]

---

86 *WW2: People's War* <www.bbc.co.uk/ww2peopleswar> (accessed 3 September 2019).
87 Lieutenant Colonel Humphrey Reginald Woods, DSO, MC and Bar, King's Royal Rifle Corps, attached to the 9th Battalion Durham Light Infantry, was killed on 14 June 1944, aged 28. He is buried in Bayeux War Cemetery, France.
88 *WW2: People's War* <www.bbc.co.uk/ww2peopleswar> (accessed 3 September 2019).
89 Delaforce, P., *Monty's Northern Legions* (Gloucestershire: Sutton Publishing, 2004), p. 75.

Anti-tank gunners of the 9th Battalion Durham Light Infantry guarding an approach road to Lingèvres. (Author's collection)

After five hours of vicious fighting, the Durhams took many of the enemy positions. They found that they had been deeply dug-in, with large quantities of weapons and ammunition littered about the defensive ditches. These were gathered up by the 6th Durhams and turned upon their previous owners. The surviving attackers remained in the enemy defences while other companies entered the village of Verrières, trying to press on along the main road to Tilly. As the 6th Durhams reorganised in Verrières they found they had suffered 108 casualties during the attack. Prisoners were taken to the rear, and Private Ernest Harvey was ordered by his sergeant to collect ammunition and weapons from the wounded and the dead:

> We eventually took the position, but the point was that nearly all the men had gone. I thought that only went on in WW1 and I never thought it could happen in 1944. The stretcher bearers had come up and were tending to the few wounded that were left. Suddenly this voice said to me: "Leave that alone, don't touch them" [–] it was the Padre and tears were streaming from his eyes. So I went back to the hedge and saw this German running across a field and someone started firing at him and the Padre knocked the gun out of his hands and said: "There's been enough killing for one day." The sergeant and he had words.[90]

Just before midday, the badly mauled companies of the 9th Durhams entered the village of Lingèvres. Major John Mogg heard of the death of Lieutenant Colonel Woods and had to step

---

90 Moses, *The Gateshead Gurkhas*, p. 290.

into his shoes in overall command of the battalion. He immediately set about organising the defence of Lingèvres:

> By 12 noon I found myself in command of what was left of 9th DLI in the village of Lingèvres, [and] I ordered D Company to occupy the east and SE edge of the village facing towards Tilly. C Company of one platoon, all that was left of them, covered the approaches from the south. I made a defence fire plan with Major Ken Swann, 86th Field Rgt, and ordered support weapons to move forward. Carriers guarded the western approaches and Bn HQ was set up in the area over the stream north of the village. I sited the remaining anti-tank guns singly down the road approaches.[91]

Counter-attack at Lingèvres

The long and confused battle for the village of Lingèvres continued in earnest, and it was not long before the Germans began to mount a series of determined counter-attacks. The Durhams had winkled out the Germans one house at a time in vicious close-quarter fighting as the rapid fire of Spandaus and Bren guns echoed around the streets. A German 88 had got the range of the village and sent over airbursts in quick succession to explode above the village war memorial, sending shrapnel flying into the buildings and among the troops. The centre of Lingèvres was a decidedly unhealthy place to be. Shortly after noon, the counter-attacks began, a Panther tank entering the village down the Verrières road. A Sherman of the 4/7th Royal Dragoon Guards, commanded by a Sergeant Roberts, opened fire and the Panther exploded in a ball of flame.

Captain Alastair Morrison, 4/7th Royal Dragoon Guards, witnessed the gallant actions of an anonymous Bren-gun carrier driver:

> The wounded and the dead were propped up against the hedge and the church wall on the home side of the building to gain what shelter they could from the constant shelling and small arms fire. A Bren-gun carrier was in use as a makeshift ambulance driven by a soldier of the Durhams. He brought the carrier up from the rear, skid-turned it and reversed it under the trees by the church porch. Single handed he loaded it up with wounded men and then drove off slowly, so as not to jolt the passengers, to a first aid post in the large farmhouse by the bend in the road. He was to make the same solitary, dangerous journey many times during the afternoon, until towards evening the inevitable end came and his carrier remained stationary in the village centre, its devoted driver and his last cargo still and silent where a chance shell burst had killed them all.[92]

Major Mogg was busy organising the defence as the last Germans were driven out of the village. D Company was down to two platoons because of the heavy casualties they had taken in the initial attack and they were stationed astride the Tilly-sur-Seulles road. C Company's

---

91 Moses, *The Gateshead Gurkhas*, p. 285.
92 Johnson, G. and Dunphie, C., *Brightly Shone the Dawn* (London: Frederick Warne, 1980), p. 113.

survivors were ordered to position themselves astride the road running from Longraye. A and B Companies had suffered the most in the attack and were ordered to hold positions at the rear of the village.

Two German tanks appeared and were immediately engaged by the anti-tank gunners blocking the road. As Sergeant Harry Burton directed fire at the German armour, the first tank was knocked out by a 6-pdr shell. The tanks returned fire and scored a direct hit on the anti-tank gun, destroying it and causing the ammunition to explode. Burton and his crew were all wounded. The attack continued and the other anti-tank gun teams were in turn attacked by the German armour. The tanks of the 4/7th Royal Dragoon Guards gave much-needed support to the infantry, Major Mogg walking into the village to contact and direct them, finding them at the war memorial. Major Ken Swann,[93] artillery battery commander, jumped from his tank and the pair worked out the best defensive fire programme needed to support the Durhams and the Dragoon Guards. All the while there was a ferocious din from exploding German shellfire and British tanks banging away nearby, the sound of falling roof slates and masonry adding to the general cacophony.

Trooper M. Bullen, of the 4/7th Royal Dragoon Guards, was told to wait, engine running, while Swann talked to Major Mogg:

> The commander called a greeting and waved, [and] in answer to a request from our skipper he pointed to the Firefly. Our commander ran across the road, climbed on the Firefly and pointed to something out of my vision. I didn't have a chance to wonder what he was pointing at. Our wireless operator shouted into the intercom: "Driver reverse, right hand down and go like fuck." By the last word I was already going. The tank lurched, a building to our right collapsed, followed by a loud explosion and pieces of flaked enamel came flying around inside the driving compartment of the tank. For a minute I couldn't gather my thoughts. I remember saying: "Christ". We learned from Major Swann that he had seen a self-propelled gun that required the attention of the Firefly's 17-pounder. While he was directing the fire, he spotted a Panther up the Tilly road bringing its gun to bear in our direction. He shouted to our operator to move as the HE shell took us on the right-hand side while we were in reverse. It ricocheted off and exploded in the shop we were trying to get behind for cover. The side of the tank was slightly concave for about two feet. Inwardly, the front set was out of commission, as was the forward Browning.[94]

A second anti-tank gun received a direct hit, killing all of the crew, then another was hit, sending it and its crew flying through the air. An urgent report was received from Sergeant Wilfred Harris, 4/7th Royal Dragoon Guards, claiming that a tank was coming down the Tilly-sur-Seulles road towards Lingèvres, but to his great surprise he saw it was a Sherman. It was assumed it was a lost soul from B Squadron, which was supporting the attack at Verrières by the 6th Durhams. As the Sherman approached the village, it turned off the road to reveal it was being chased by German Panthers.

---

93 Major Kenneth Geoffrey Swann, MC, 342 Battery, 86th Field Regiment Hertfordshire Yeomanry, Royal Artillery, was killed in action on 20 June 1944 and is buried in Tilly-sur-Seulles War Cemetery, France.
94 M. Bullen, correspondence with author (Essex, 1992).

A knocked-out Tiger in the town centre near the Lingèvres Great War memorial. (Author's collection)

Sergeant Harris, in a Firefly covering the road east out of Villers Bocage that led to Tilly-sur-Seulles, dismounted from his tank to talk to his troop leader:

> He gave me the direction of two Panthers, plus other information, and asked me to take up a position not far from him, [so] I found a very nice defensive position and put the tank there. Keeping my eyes open I picked up the two Panthers about 1,200 yards away creeping down a hedge. I was confident they couldn't see me, so I held my fire and let them get closer. By this time my gunner, Ian Mackillop, had the leading tank well in his sights and when it was about 400 yards away I opened up. To my amazement the first shot sent it into a mass of flames and with the second

Sergeant Wilfred Harris, DCM, 4/7th Royal Dragoon Guards, Royal Armoured Corps. (Author's collection)

shot we did the same to the second Panther.[95] I immediately trained onto a third tank and brewed that one up as well.[96]

Lieutenant Michael Trasenster, in the thick of the action with the 4/7th Royal Dragoon Guards, was called forward in his Firefly by his commander to engage a Tiger that had been spotted:

> A 75mm gun is a doubtful starter against a Tiger. The crew were feverish with excitement. I got the gunner on to the target, and we let fly, Bang! And the tank rocked slightly. I saw a spurt of dust in front of the Tiger but by then another shot was on the way and another. As the third shot flew to the target, I saw a tongue of flame lick around the cupola. For a moment I could not believe my eyes. Then more wildly excited than I think I have ever been I grabbed the mike: "Hello X-Ray, I've knocked out a Tiger and it's brewing up," I babbled: "Well done," came the reply. We rejoined Jackie in the village, Stirling had bagged a Panther. Moreover, Sgt Harris of 4th Troop with his Scots gunner, Mackillop, had knocked out an amazing five Panthers in the village. It was a sight for sore eyes, and everyone was in terrific heart. The infantry was swarming round the tanks, it was a great victory.[97]

Lieutenant Michael Trasenster, 4/7th Royal Dragoon Guards, Royal Armoured Corps. (Courtesy of T.D. Hawken)

The armament of one of the Panthers, however, was still very active, and it was situated out of sight of the Shermans of 4/7th Dragoon Guards. Major Mogg, deciding it was too dangerous to be left, organised three tank-hunting patrols. His own patrol, consisting of himself, Captain Roy Griffiths, Sergeant Jordon and two private soldiers, stealthily moved from cover to cover until within range of the disabled Panther. Mogg recalled:

> Having crept under Bocage banks, across four fields and sited the Piat anti-tank weapon on top of a bank to fire at the Panther, I ordered the gunner to fire. The Geordie said: "I don't know how this bloody thing works." He had carried it across the Channel and for seven days in Normandy, a lesson perhaps. In fact, the enemy Panther was made a non-runner by this Piat, Major Mogg had to fire it himself, and the crew bailed out.[98]

---

95 Sergeant Wilfred Harris, 4/7th Royal Dragoon Guards, was awarded the Distinguished Conduct Medal for the action at Lingèvres.
96 Forty, G., *Villers Bocage* (Gloucestershire: Sutton Publishing, 2004), p. 172.
97 M. Trasenster, correspondence with author (Essex, 1991).
98 Moses, *The Gateshead Gurkhas*, pp. 287–88.

A knocked-out Sherman of the 4/7th Royal Dragoon Guards in the ruins of Lingèvres. (Courtesy of T.D. Hawken)

Mogg fired at the retreating tank crew with his revolver but missed, and the small party sprinted back to their own positions as fast as they could. At the same time as this action was being fought, Lieutenant Ken Whittaker, Anti-tank Platoon Commander, was siting one of his guns when he spotted a Panther tank in a barn on the Longraye road; plans were made to deal with it. Whittaker took his small band of tank hunters round the left flank, while a Sherman tank stationed itself along a narrow track to the rear of the barn. On a given signal, the Durhams would fire their Piat at close range into the tank and the Sherman would fire at a point on the barn wall where it was judged that the Panther was parked. Upon the signal to fire, the Piat didn't go off, and although the Sherman fired three rounds as agreed one after the other, the Panther was unscathed, backed out of the barn and escaped.

Another Panther was spotted on the Longraye road. Corporal Clifford Johnson's[99] Sherman tank was ordered forward to have better observation of the road, but as he did so he was hit by an armour-piercing round that struck his vehicle in the transmission, sending up a great shower of sparks. Luckily, the Sherman did not burst into flames and the crew scrambled out. As Corporal Draper escaped, he realised that he had left the gun off centre, knowing that unless it was pointing straight ahead it prevented the driver from opening his hatch. The driver, Trooper

---

99 Corporal Clifford Johnson, 4/7th Royal Dragoon Guards, died of his wounds on 15 June 1944, aged 26. He is buried in Bayeux War Cemetery, France.

Dagley, and co-driver, Trooper McDermott, were thus trapped in the tank. Draper braved the enemy fire to rescue his comrades, climbing into the tank and traversing the turret until it was straight, enabling him to open the driver's hatch. McDermott scrambled out, but Dagley was not moving so Draper pulled him out by his webbing and carried him to the shelter of the church wall, where he died.[100]

Private R. Mawson, a despatch rider with the 86th Field Regiment, Royal Artillery, had to stop for a call of nature but found himself in the middle of a battle among the Durhams:

> It was like hell let loose and everybody was on edge. I had to relieve myself and I went into a hedgerow and came across an infantryman who said: "Keep down there's a sniper in that tree, hold on I'll get him", and he did, the sniper dropped like a stone. I looked over a hedge and there were dozens of Boches, some sitting and some lying but all dead. I asked the infantryman about them, and he said: "We have to make good our losses", and he never batted an eye lid. I left soon after this, but the chain came off my motorcycle and I got busy putting it back on as it was not a healthy place to be caught in. Someone tapped me on the shoulder, and I nearly jumped six feet in the air. It was a German giving himself up; he even helped me with my chain. When it was fixed, I told him to get on the back and took him several miles to a prisoner of war cage. I made sure he didn't get shot.[101]

The German counter-attacks continued all afternoon in the dust and heat, but each one became less co-ordinated than the one before. Artillery fire and rocket-firing Typhoons rained fire and death as the German troops formed up, stopping them before they could get started. The combined fire of the Durhams and their tank support did the rest, and suddenly the firing died down The Durhams then scrambled out of the remains of the town's buildings and weary tank crews came out of their tanks to get some fresh air. The tension of the last few hours evaporated, but the price of victory had been high: the 9th Durhams had suffered 246 casualties at Lingèvres.

Sergeant Charles Eagles of the 9th Durhams took a moment to look at the scene of desolation around him as things became quieter, and suddenly realised that he seemed to be alone. However, his war was about to come to an end:

> I remember standing up and looking around me, nothing but bodies scattered everywhere, a dreadful, ghastly and gruesome sight. I don't really have the words to describe the horror of what I saw. The tank had gone, and everything was quiet again. I seemed to be on my own but then I saw Cpl Wood sitting at the side of the road looking a bit worse for wear, I sat down beside him, and three or four other lads joined us. We were covered in mud and dust, filthy in fact. We picked ourselves up and went towards a farmhouse, we crossed a ditch and saw six of our lads lying as though observing ahead. Woody crept over to them, and we lay down to give him some cover. He ran back to me panting and said: "They're all dead sarge and there's not a bloody mark on them." We were wondering what to do next when I heard a little cough and standing over me was a German officer with a number of German soldiers:

---

100 Trooper Reginald Dagley, A Squadron, 4/7th Royal Dragoon Guards, died on 14 June 1944, aged 33. He is buried in Jerusalem War Cemetery, France.
101 R. Mawson, interview with author (Hull, 1991).

Major John H. Mogg, 9th Battalion Durham Light Infantry, being presented with the ribbon to the DSO by General Montgomery for the action at Lingèvres. (Author's collection)

"Throw down your weapons you are surrounded," he said in perfect English. Much to our surprise we weren't searched for any hidden weapons, but merely ambled side by side down a minor road. We were treated very well.[102]

After their disastrous attack through the open fields that morning, one company of the 6th Durhams advanced through the village of Verrières without opposition, with a tank of the 4/7th Royal Dragoon Guards, commanded by Lieutenant S. Jenkins, up in support. Unbeknown to the advancing infantry, a German tank was stationed at Les-le-Gallois crossroads, covering the track the troops were moving down. The Durhams went to ground as they came under intense fire from the tank's machine gun and accompanying German infantry in well-concealed positions. Several men were killed and Major Wood withdrew the company to the north of Verrières, where they dug in. In their bid to outflank the enemy, the 6th Durhams had suffered 100 casualties.

Sergeant Bert Davies, of the 6th Durhams, recalled large numbers of hidden snipers in the trees:

> There were so many snipers there. I'd been across the cornfield and back again, but we didn't see the snipers in the treetops, they had proper wooden hideouts. I was behind a hedge and Sgt Ingram says to me: "Hey Bert, watch out there's a lot of snipers about in this area." Just as he said that a shot scalped him across the head. He spun round and dropped on the deck; he was whipped off to the first aid post. As long as you're a moving target you're difficult to hit, but as soon as you stand still you're an easy target.[103]

After some five hours of heavy fighting, the assault by the 6th Durhams got no further that night and Verrières remained in enemy hands.

---

102 *WW2: People's War* <www.bbc.co.uk/ww2peopleswar> (accessed 3 September 2019).
103 Manuscript forwarded to author by W. Ridley (Durham, 1994).

231 Brigade at La Senaudiere, 14 June

An attack by the men of 231 Brigade was to be led by the 1st Hampshires on the left and 1st Dorsets on the right. The 2nd Devons would remain in reserve at La Belle Epine. The troops before them were the *Aufklärung Abteilung* (Reconnaissance Battalion) of *Panzer-Lehr*. The fire plan that had been agreed to support the attacking infantry consisted of the guns of six British field regiments, an American 155mm battalion, naval gunfire and close air support. This deluge of fire was timed to land just before 1130 hours. Rocket-firing RAF Typhoons of 83 and 84 Squadrons would strafe and bomb the enemy defensive line and local villages.

The Hampshires advanced from Le Belle Epine to the area surrounding the village of La Senaudiere and its crossroads. They were held back 500 yards from the start line to allow the Typhoons to soften up the enemy positions. The Dorsets moved to their forming-up place through difficult terrain, with A and B Company leading. The British barrage, however, came down on the 1st Dorsets as they advanced, inflicting many casualties on B Company. The Dorsets' war diary recorded:

Troops of the *Panzer-Lehr Aufklärung Bataillon*. (Reconnaissance Battalion). (Courtesy of M. Denney)

> Misfortune overtook us from the outset when our own barrage came down on our start line and inflicted severe casualties on B Coy, and to a lesser extent on A Coy. The former coy being considerably shaken and disorganised, and Major Chilton wounded. The unfortunate mistake had occurred owing to our start line being taken by the gunners as the 'opening line' of their barrage.[104]

The war diary of the Hampshire Regiment described the start of the attack and the results of having been withdrawn before the barrage:

---

104 National Archive WO 171/336.

Artillery barrage covering 1,000 yards in three minutes was laid on. Supporting arms consisted of a troop of Crocodiles [flamethrower tanks] and a troop of M10s of the Northumberland Hussars. The battalion moved off already deployed and opposition was met north of La Senaudiere, showing the enemy had occupied the same ground which we had given up when the air attack began.[105]

The Hampshires met opposition from the start, which hampered their advance; they made several attacks on the enemy positions but failed to break through. Lieutenant Geoffrey Picot, of the 1st Hampshires' 3-inch mortar platoon, said they were moved 500 yards to the rear as the barrage on the enemy lines began:

> For this first attack we would have RAF support. Light and medium bombers were going to be used on enemy forward positions and heavy bombers on targets some way back. In order to prevent casualties to our own troops we had to withdraw about 500 yards and dig ourselves well in. This would allow a fairly large safety area in case there was any mistake. As it turned out the air support looked puny to me. I saw a few fighters in the distance that was all, the heavier machines must have gone farther on.[106]

The flame-throwing Crocodile tanks went ahead of the infantry and created havoc with their great spouts of fire, incinerating buildings and men in the village. However, the Germans soon recovered, their anti-tank gunners and tank crews entering the action and knocking out all but one of the Crocodiles, which, faced with the fire from Panthers, Panzer IIIs and anti-tank guns, withdrew.

Private Timothy Dudley-Ward came under heavy fire as his 1st Hampshires unit neared the village and was unable to progress very far:

> We caught it hot and strong, [and] a crowd of fellows and me got pinned down between the two lines with both sides slinging everything they had at each other. I decided to get out so another fellow and myself made a dash for it and much to our surprise we made it. Then Topper, our platoon commander, asked me to go along with him as I was the only one of his platoon he could find, [and] we picked up three others on the way. We lined a bank to help give covering fire, but this was as far as any of us got. Over came a mortar bomb and I felt the shrapnel bang into my leg, [and] when the dust cleared I saw the others were dead. A padre and a stretcher-bearer helped me back to the ADS [Advanced Dressing Station] and that was the end of my fighting career for a while.[107]

Lieutenant Picot's orders were to carry out a fire programme with his mortars against selected targets, after which his platoon was to move forward with the advancing troops and establish an observation post in the attic of a house, from which he could see the woods and buildings the enemy were thought to be occupying:

---

105 National Archives WO 171/336.
106 Picot, G., *Accidental Warrior* (London: Penguin, 1994), pp. 66–67.
107 *WW2: People's War* <www.bbc.co.uk/ww2peopleswar> (accessed 19 July 2016).

> The mortars were positioned in a farmyard not more than 30 yards from the observation post. In order to get a decent view, I had to peep through a small window which I could only reach by standing on a small ladder which threatened to collapse at any moment. Jimmy, my company commander, was in the attic with me to help. Our system of fire control was this, I observed through the window and gave the order to him. He leaned out of the lower window and bellowed the order down to a man standing outside the back door, who shouted the order to Sergeant Wetherick standing near the mortars, who gave the order to the mortar crews. We ranged and got onto our targets and bombed them severely.[108]

Picot was spotted by the Germans as he leaned out of the window, and it was not long before bullets began to fly uncomfortably around his little observation window:

> So, I stood away from the window and gave my orders: "Six rounds fire." I listened to the bombs being fired, counted to 25 to estimate the time they were in the air, then I popped my head up just in time to see them land and explode. Then I ducked down again and worked out the necessary correction, gave the new order and did not look out of the window until the next bombs were about to land.[109]

Lieutenant Colonel Charles Howie, commanding the 1st Hampshires, was in the thick of the action with the forward troops, encouraging them to keep up the momentum of the attack before La Senaudiere. "Nobody is to fall back," he told his junior officers. Men took cover behind the ruined buildings of the village while mortar crews dropped bombs on the enemy locations, the Hampshires' light machine guns and riflemen keeping up a steady fire on the German positions as enemy mortars bombs and shellfire in turn fell around them.

Having reorganised themselves by 1215 hours, the Dorsets resumed their advance, but as they approached to the west of the La Senaudiere crossroads they met increasingly heavy opposition from the entrenched Germans. The advance was now very slow through heavily wooded countryside, as they winkled out the Germans from their positions with bayonet and bomb. By 1600 hours, one company had reached the Balleroy road, and the advance continued from here for 600 yards until, by 1700 hours, they had reached a deserted chateau. The battalion concentrated to the north of the main road, an anti-tank gun being manhandled forward by Captain Hebden and his crew from D Company, knocking out two Panthers. In the melee, Company Sergeant Major Nicholas O'Connell[110] was hit and killed as he rallied the 1st Dorsets. The enemy remained in close contact during the hours of darkness before withdrawing at dawn.

The men having been without proper sleep for more than a week, the strain was beginning to tell on them all. As the battle died down, it was obvious that the attack had been halted. Men who had been kept going by the excitement and rush of the assault now found themselves feeling indescribably tired. Geoffrey Picot recalled the compulsion to sleep as he took stock of the situation:

---

108 Picot, *Accidental Warrior*, p. 67.
109 Picot, *Accidental Warrior*, p. 67.
110 Company Sergeant Major Nicholas O'Connell, MiD, 1st Battalion Dorsetshire Regiment, was killed in action on 14 June 1944, aged 33. He is buried in Hottot-le-Bagues War Cemetery, France.

> I smoked cigarettes just to stay awake, [though] I did not smoke normally. I splashed water into my eyes. I dare not sit down on the roadside or in the hedge, much as I wanted to, because I knew that if I did I would fall asleep, and if I fell asleep the whole platoon would follow suit. Some were already dozing on the road, [while] others kept awake with difficulty. The riflemen were not capable of going forward anymore but we had won the crossroads. We stayed at the La Senaudiere defensive positions for four days.[111]

That night, Allied artillery put down a very heavy barrage on the Germans just in case they should think of making a counter-attack while the Hampshires were feeling so run down. German heavy-calibre guns kept up a steady fire on the British in return, but most men were so exhausted that they slept through it all.

As casualties began to mount in the Normandy bridgehead, fresh troops were being sent from England to make up the numbers of the most depleted units. The majority of these were very young and had been given only the most basic training. Private Norman Cornwall of the 1st Hampshires was one such young man:

> After six months of intensive training, at the age of 18, I was part of a large contingent of men deposited by troop ship on the beach at Arromanches in France. We walked to Bayeux to a tented transit camp and stayed for one night, and on the following day we all left for front line duty. Before being posted to our relevant regiments a short church service was held and several of us took Holy Communion kneeling on a tarpaulin in the heather. Then I joined the 1st Battalion Hampshire Regiment of the 50th Division which had landed on Gold Beach on D-Day.[112]

Major Alexander Edward Craven Bredin, 1st Dorsets, saw men from other regiments drafted into his unit but thought that the quality of the replacement troops was not as good as the men they replaced:

> The number of reinforcements which arrived to rebuild our strength meant that very few Devon shoulder flashes could be seen for a while, there being so many men from other regiments attached to our unit to renew our effectiveness. The name Green Howards stands out in my mind, but I can't remember any of the other regiments involved. There were insufficient reserves of men immediately available to bring our brigade back to full strength, so we had to rely on a number of our own wounded who were considered to be fit for further action after having been patched up for return to the fighting lines by the field hospital. Some of the men were well below fighting standard, but because they could walk and were able to use their trigger finger, they were passed as fit enough to carry on. Many of them who were definitely not fit to continue were passed and somehow kept going.[113]

---

111 Picot, *Accidental Warrior*, p. 70.
112 *WW2: People's War* <www.bbc.co.uk/ww2peopleswar> (accessed 19 July 2017).
113 A. Bredin, correspondence with author (Hampshire, 1992).

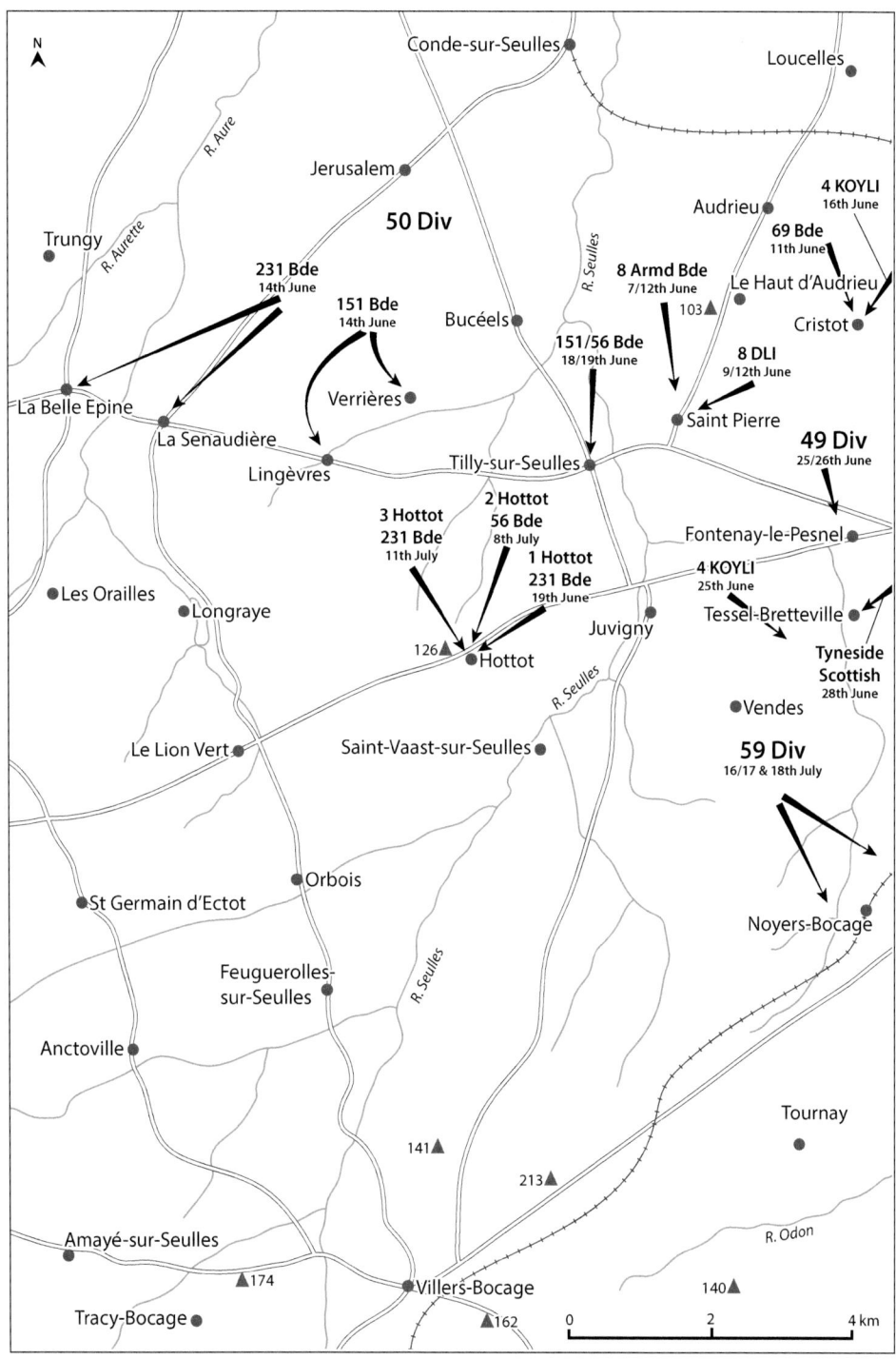

The deadly Bocage: June/July 1944.

The bloody road to Hottot, 15–19 June

On 15 June, 69 Brigade advanced 4,000 yards from the Seulles sector, encamping north of Verrières as a prelude to a full brigade attack the following day. Their main objective was to be the road south of Lingèvres and Tilly-sur-Seulles that lead to the village of Hottot. The 6th Green Howards were to advance from Bernieres-Bocage, through the positions being held by the 2nd Devons to the south of La-Belle-Epine and to secure L'Oraille as a base by 0900 hours. The 5th East Yorks were tasked with turning the enemy out of the woods to the west of Longraye, then advancing up the road supported by a troop of AVREs. The 7th Green Howards and a squadron of the 24th Lancers were to advance in a southerly direction towards the wooded area at Longraye.

Trooper Don Aitken, with the 61st Reconnaissance Regiment, moved in front of the main body, always trying to find the enemy positions so he could report back:

> We continued to probe along the byways, making contact with the enemy and reporting to base what we had seen. On the morning of 15th June, when my vehicle had been leading the patrol along a particularly nasty stretch of road, it was decided to pass the job over to our Bren-carrier troop. We pulled into the side of the road to let them pass, [but] when the lead carrier had gone less than 100 yards it blew up on a land-mine, killing all the crew and one German prisoner.[114]

Sixty years after the war, Aitken would find out that the explosion had been caused by mines that were carried in the Bren-carrier; a German prisoner had lost his balance and fell on them. The same incident was seen by Trooper Eric Postles, also of the 61st Reconnaissance Regiment, who identified the men who were killed:

> Sgt Griffiths' carrier reached the first building, where there was debris on the road, when there was a huge explosion, and the carrier was blown several feet into the air and came crashing down. We found one body, Trooper Webb, who was badly injured, we gave him morphine, but he died.[115] The others killed were Sgt William Griffiths,[116] Walter Collier[117] and Ronald McHugh.[118][119]

Private Thomas Tateson, 7th Green Howards, who had been in practically constant action since D-Day, mentioned the deadening effect of constantly moving from one attack to another:

---

114 *Chotie Darling* <www.chotiedarling.co.uk> (accessed 12 May 2020)
115 Trooper John Webb, 61st Reconnaissance Regiment, Royal Armoured Corps, was killed on 15 June 1944, aged 26. He is buried in Hottot-le-Bagues War Cemetery, France.
116 Sergeant William Arthur Griffiths, 61st Reconnaissance Regiment, Royal Armoured Corps, was killed on 15 June 1944, aged 26. He is buried in Hottot-le-Bagues War Cemetery, France.
117 Trooper Walter Collier, 61st Reconnaissance Regiment, Royal Armoured Corps, was killed on 15 June 1944, aged 22 years. He is buried in Hottot-le-Bagues War Cemetery, France.
118 Trooper Ronald McHugh, 61st Reconnaissance Regiment, Royal Armoured Corps, was killed on 15 June 1944, aged 22. He is buried in Hottot-le-Bagues War Cemetery France.
119 *Chotie Darling* <www.chotiedarling.co.uk> (accessed 12 May 2020).

Morale was pretty low all-round, and the heavy casualties of previous days had a depressing effect on everyone. While fear is forgotten when everything is happening, the dread moment comes when, after a few hours' rest, the word is given, and we are to make another attack. The stomach sinks and a leaden feeling spreads through the body. By this time the battalion had lost 15 officers and over 200 NCOs and soldiers.[120]

The men of 69 Brigade were roused at 0300 hours on 16 June and began the move forward. Their attack was to be supported by the guns of the 90th and 147th Field Regiments, Royal Artillery, and the mortars and machine guns of the 2nd Cheshires.

Lieutenant H. Taylor, 6th Green Howards, wrote of the move to the start line in his diary:

We set off early and met no trouble at La-Belle-Epine. Resistance on the way to L'Oraille held us up for a while. Went through L'Oraille and had to stop. Nonetheless, the battalion had secured the start lines for the remainder of the brigade by 09:00 a.m.[121]

On the morning of 16 June, despite their feelings of gloom and doom, Private Tateson and his comrades picked up their weapons, buckled on their equipment and prepared to move forward again at 0930 hours as they were ordered:

Almost immediately as we crossed the start line the battalion encountered strong opposition. An 88 was firing directly down the road and the two leading companies came under heavy mortar and machine-gun fire. Their commanders, Major Bowley[122] and Major Boyle,[123] were killed. On our wireless I heard the signaller who was with Major Bowley desperately pleading for the medical officer to come to the major's aid as he was dying. Major Bowley was a gentle-mannered, civilised man and it affected me to hear so poignantly of his actual dying. Major Boyle was also a popular officer but of an entirely opposite personality, extrovert, dashing and courageous to the point of foolhardiness, a bit of a showman. The sudden loss of these two officers had a depressing effect on all of us. I was constantly hearing the message that one or another platoon was pinned down. The tanks, which were endeavouring to give us support, lost contact since they had no clear field of vision. On one occasion our section was crawling along the side of the hedge when the chap in front of me disturbed a wasps' nest. The wasps came up in a swarm around our heads, but round his in particular; he immediately came up on his knees and started beating around with his hands in spite of urgent demands of: "For Christ's sake get down." Whether he was seen or not I don't know, but soon afterwards a burst of machine-gun fire rattled through the hedge and twigs dropped on us as we lay motionless.[124]

---

120 Thompson, *Victory in Europe*, p. 93.
121 Saunders, *Battle for the Bocage*, p. 303.
122 Major Horace Edward Bowley, 7th Battalion Green Howards, was killed on 16 June 1944, aged 31. He is buried in Bayeux War Cemetery, France.
123 Major Samuel Malcolm Boyle, 7th Battalion Green Howards, was killed on 16 June 1944, aged 34. He is buried in Bayeux War Cemetery, France.
124 Manuscript forwarded to author by T. Tateson (Sheffield, 1991).

Sergeant D.E. Gray, MM, advanced with his comrades of the 7th Green Howards in the direction of Longraye Woods:

> Started to advance but didn't get far before the boys ran into hellish Spandau fire and dug in tanks. Casualties were rising and we were kept busy getting them out. Christ but it was hell and old Jerry knows his ground [–] the tanks were unable to move because of the closeness of the country.[125]

As Private A. Mountford advanced with the 7th Green Howards, he found the German defenders ready for them:

> They were well concealed and were waiting for us, dug-in *Hitler Jugend* troops and armour. We became hopelessly pinned down in a shallow ditch alongside a hedge which we had just scrambled through with what little was left of two rifle companies.[126]

Sergeant Gray looked on as *Panzergrenadiere* worked their way round and infiltrated the flanks of the advancing British, while others, who had been missed in the advance, attacked them from the rear:

> The boys reached their first objective but had to pull back because of fire from the rear [–] you can't see the bastards, which makes things so nerve wracking. Strengthened A Company in front with our Brens, nearly copped it that time. Was in a cottage with Captain Murray and the Brigadier when Jerry brought up a tank and let fly at close range. Brigadier was wounded with two killed, but my luck held out again, wish I could stop a cushy one. It's about time they brought a fresh division in, our lads have had it. Knocked the hell out of us all night. [There are] very few of the old lads left now.[127]

Although they were outnumbered and pinned down, Private Mountford and his comrades did not surrender until the situation became hopeless; eventually, their colonel ordered them to do so. They were then marched to the rear past German tanks and heavy guns:

> After being disarmed we were marched off the battlefield past a line of heavy tanks; it was no wonder that the stuff that was fired at us was on the heavy side. Then we went across a field and there was a main road to our front which we had been ordered to take. Marching back from the front we found to be a bit hazardous as some of the German truck drivers tried to skittle us, knock us over, as they drove past. Overnight was spent in a farmyard with their artillery blasting away in the next field.[128]

---

125 Saunders, *Battle for the Bocage*, p. 305.
126 A. Mountford, interview with author (Beverley, 1989).
127 Saunders, *Battle for the Bocage*, p. 306.
128 A. Mountford, interview with author (Beverley, 1989).

The Deadly Bocage: June–July 1944   325

A very young and weary-looking but well-armed soldier of the *12. SS-Panzer-Division 'Hitlerjugend'*. (Author's collection)

As darkness fell, men in advanced positions realised that the enemy was closing in all around them. In the confusion, many were taken prisoner. Private Thomas Tateson was among their number:

> As night fell there were four of us in an advanced position near wooded country into which the enemy had withdrawn that day. Sgt Potterton told us that he didn't know where the hell Major Spark had got to. He had told us to stay put under cover of a ditch while he went off to arrange for more ammunition. He did not return, and it soon became obvious that under cover of darkness the Germans had put in a heavy counter-attack and that in fact we had walked into a carefully planned trap. They were all around us, tanks were on the road to our rear, and we could hear German voices shouting in the woods close by. There was heavy and constant firing all around, but mostly from the rear, and we realised we were completely cut off. Ted Russel, now being the senior NCO, told us to ditch our equipment, including our wireless sets, and this we did.[129]

It was hoped by Tateson and his comrades that if they travelled light there might be a chance of slipping through the German forces and returning to their own lines. But the Germans were around them in great numbers and no way through could be found:

---

129 T. Tateson, correspondence with author (Sheffield, 1990).

However, matters were decided for us when, hearing Germans approaching our scanty cover, Ted leapt up and surrendered. The psychological effect of being taken prisoner is an almost complete numbing of the senses. We were line up with our hands on our heads by men with Schmeisser automatics [MP 40 submachine guns] and it went through my head that they might shoot us out of hand. The dulling effects of anti-climax however meant simply that this thought left me with a detached feeling, almost curiosity, rather than fear. From prolonged intense excitement, leading to near exhaustion, we now experienced a complete lowering of the senses, even that of self-preservation. When dumping my kit, I had recovered a leather writing wallet containing a photograph of Olive in it and her letters to me. I slipped this inside my battledress. Now with my hands on my head the wallet slipped down and fell to the floor. I stooped and picked it up, in so doing risking an instant burst of fire and a quick death. We received demands for clocks, so I slipped my watch off and wrapped it around my ankle under my sock. I was re-tying my bootlace when a guard hit me across the face demanding: "Clock". I responded: "*Nix* clock" and he passed on to gather his harvest elsewhere.[130]

On 18 June, the 7th Green Howards were to relieve the 5th East Yorks in the woods at Longraye, the 5th East Yorks in turn relieving the 6th Green Howards at L'Oraille, who would be used for the planned attack. Sergeant Gray, 7th Green Howards, duly relieved the 5th East Yorks with his unit, which then attempted to push forward:

Took over from East Yorks and once more we tried to push on, but it was sheer suicide. The land was absolutely rotten with snipers and Spandaus. The lads have had it and they will have to pull them out. My section of carriers takes over A Company's positions while they try to advance, and did we get hammered, but we had to stay there. Poor old Sergeant Topliffe runs into a Spandau and gets five bullets in him. Marvellous piece of work by an officer in getting him out. The Doc thinks he might pull through; hope so, as he is the best sergeant in the battalion and hates Jerries more than anyone, on account of him seeing his brother killed next to him at Akarit.[131]

The 5th East Yorks and 7th Green Howards were counter-attacked by armour and infantry of the *Panzer-Lehr-Division*, forcing them to withdraw to the west. Sergeant Max Hearst of the 5th East Yorks remembered:

We took over from the Hampshires and as we moved in they moved out and everybody was in the open when mortar bombs began to drop amongst us. Blokes were hit by the dozen, mainly Hampshires. Sergeant Major Bert Greener was hit. We had served together in the Territorials since the '30s and had served together in France 1940, the Western Desert 1942 and in Tunisia and Sicily 1943. We'd started to dig in and Bert and I were sat facing each other with our tin hats touching when a mortar bomb landed behind me; it missed

---

130 T. Tateson, correspondence with author (Sheffield, 1989).
131 D.E. Gray, correspondence with author (Yorkshire, 1991). Sergeant Topliffe survived the war; his brother, Lance Sergeant John Edward Topliffe, was killed on 6 April 1943 at the Battle of Wadi Akarit, aged 23, and is buried in Sfax War Cemetery, Tunisia.

me but got him. I said: "Are you hit Bert?" He held his hand up and you could see through the hole in it. I said: "It's nowt Bert, you'll be alright", applied pressure to stop the bleeding and put a couple of field dressings on it. I set off with Bert to the Casualty Clearing Station and there were casualties laid everywhere. Blokes were pinned under trees, others had been impaled and were screaming, it was bloody chaos.[132]

Bombardier Jack Styan was caught in a barrage with Battle Axe Company, Royal Artillery, that night. He later recalled with vivid clarity the sight of his first casualty:

That night the tanks moved into the field beside us. The Germans must have had the range and started shelling us like hell. I heard one of our lads cry out and I went over to him. He was sat against a wall with his legs stretched out before him. I went to pick him up and his body just parted in the middle; I put him back and that was the first real casualty I had seen.[133]

Sergeant D.E. Gray found his unit held up short of their objective, as was the 6th Green Howards. Enemy mortar and machine-gun fire swept the area and the advanced companies pulled back to find some protection:

At 16:00 p.m. A Company starts to pull back and Jerry spots them. He sent over everything he had, and I just missed it again. I saw three chaps killed by the same shell that knocked me daft, not three yards from me and Ike. Dick Staveley and Allen [were] wounded and that left three of us to go and get them out. God knows why we weren't hit; much more and I would have had it, I was shaking like a leaf, so we got a brew on as darkness fell.[134]

The badly battered and exhausted men of the 7th Green Howards fell back to the positions being held by the 5th East Yorks as the light failed, and dug in for the night. The weather grew worse, and it began to rain as a cold northerly wind made the situation even more miserable for the depleted companies. Brigadier Fergus Y. Carson Knox saw how his 69 Brigade had suffered and declared them "Unfit for further offensive action". In driving rain, the men regrouped as best they could, reinforcements beginning to arrive during the night and the following morning. CSM Jack Verity reflected on the survivors' situation: "We were soaked to the skin and in a sorry state as we sorted ourselves out and couldn't even begin thinking about going back into action. It took a while, but we eventually bounced back."[135]

The 1/4th Battalion King's Own Yorkshire Light Infantry at Cristot, 16 June

The men of 69 Brigade having attacked Cristot on 11 June and being badly mauled in a failed attempted to take the village, it now fell to the 1/4th KOYLIs of 146 Brigade, 49th West Riding Division, to take this position by storm.

Unlike on 11 June, this assault would be preceded by a full-scale fire-plan involving seven artillery regiments from the 49th and 50th Divisions, along with naval gunfire from warships off the coast and the rockets and bombs of RAF fighter-bombers.

---

132 M. Hearst, interview with author (Hull, 1992).
133 Manuscript sent to the author by J. Styan (Hull, 1991).
134 D.E. Gray, correspondence with author (Yorkshire, 1991).
135 J. Verity, interview with author (Beverley, 1991).

The 1/4th KOYLIs were stationed at Bronay on 11 June and were relieved by the Royal Scots Fusiliers, thereafter moving on to La Motte in preparation for the coming assault. HQ Company commander Major Godfrey Harland met up with his commanding officer, Colonel Johnny Walker, who was looking very run down from the pressures of command:

> After Bronay my CO, Johnny Walker, asked me to accompany him to meet Brigadier Andrew Dunlop at a grid reference in a little wood. This brilliant young commander, who had won the DSO in the desert, now looked pale and anxious. He said: "The divisional commander wants me to attack Cristot tomorrow, it's over there." [H]e pointed to it: "I want your battalion to do it." A few days later Brigadier Dunlop was invalided home sick and never returned, a sad loss.[136]

For two days before the attack, the tiny hamlet of Cristot was pummelled by a storm of heavy shells and rockets. The troops in the front line watched in awe as the ruins of the village jumped and shattered even further with every explosion.

On 16 June, the assault troops moved to their start line, marked with white tapes, with A Company on the right led by Major A.R. Keeping and B Company on the left under Major A.B. Little. The Sherman tanks of C Squadron, 24th Lancers, and the guns of the 55th Anti-tank Regiment moved up in support.

Sergeant Rex Flower, serving with the Mortar Platoon of the 1/4th KOYLIs, was detailed with his section to advance behind the creeping barrage with A Company during the attack. As the men prepared themselves, the battalion padre turned up and, in the sunshine, led them in a short prayer, the men quiet and thoughtful as they contemplated their immediate prospects. Sergeant Flower had been briefed by his commanding officer: "We were told that 400 enemy infantry of 12th SS Panzer Division *Hitler Jugend*, supported by self-propelled guns, mortars and tanks, were defending Cristot."

As the men left the start line and the creeping barrage began to roar overhead, Sergeant Flower was taken aback by the violence of the shellfire:

> It was about noon when suddenly, with a terrific crash and roar, our guns opened up. I had never seen or heard anything like it. In front, where the shells were bursting, nothing could be seen but a huge wall of fire and smoke where the world seemed to end. 'A' Company and the tanks moved off and a few seconds later it was our turn to go into what looked like bloody hell. Talk about Dante's Inferno.[137]

Pte John Longfield of the 1/4th KOYLIs recalled:

> At about mid-day the attack commenced through a waist high cornfield. I well remember passing an enormous unexploded naval gun shell. We were very happy to get through the cornfield and into the village.[138]

---

136 Delaforce, *The Polar Bears*, p. 47.
137 Manuscript forwarded to author by Brian Cook (Carnegie Heritage Centre, Hull, 2016).
138 *WW2: People's War* <www.bbc.co.uk/ww2peopleswar> (accessed 3 April 2019).

The Sherman tanks of the 24th Lancers fired their heavy Besa machine guns into the hedges on the flanks and to the front. Sniper fire was not too heavy, and no opposition was met by the 1/4th until they were about 500 yards short of the ruins of the village. Heavy concentrations of mortar bombs then fell among the advancing troops, coming from the direction of Cristot, observation becoming very poor owing to the smoke and dust thrown up by the British barrage.

The advance was recalled by Lieutenant Robert Stanley Chadwick of the 1/4th KOYLIs:

> Colonel Walker, our battalion commander, was viewing the enemy area, [having] positioned himself in the centre of the forward line. My carrier was on his left. The company was under heavy fire from the Germans when our supporting artillery started firing and the colonel gave the order to move off. German artillery fired at us and all hell was let loose. I was moving on foot to direct my carrier to the routes that provided most cover, [and] it was a miracle we got through. I passed several men who had been hit by shrapnel, but we couldn't stop to help them.[139]

Sergeant Flower followed the lead troops through the cornfield with his mortar section:

> There had been casualties already, [and] I could see rifles stuck in the ground among the waist high corn to indicate the position of a wounded man. Suddenly, with a stupefying crash, enemy mortar bombs began exploding all over the field. One dropped nearby and the air hummed with splinters[;] this stonk went on for about 15 minutes solid.[140]

The Sherman tanks fired high explosive shells into the village and at its church, which was thought to be used as an observation post by the Germans. As the troops moved into the western edge of Cristot, the enemy mortar fire ceased, Sherman tanks then moving around the left flank.

Among those moving into the village was Lance Corporal Geoffrey Steer, B Company, 1/4th KOYLIs:

> The village of Cristot had been bombed and shelled for two days prior to our attack. The sunken road from the start line to the village was littered with rotting horses and cows killed by our shelling. The church was used by the Germans as an OP and snipers were using it as well. Our officer told me to go in at the front while he went in at the back. As I

Lance Corporal Geoffrey Steer, 1/4th Battalion King's Own Yorkshire Light Infantry. (Courtesy of M. Denney)

---

139 *Scholars Common Wilfrid Laurier University* <www.scholars.wlu.ca/cmh/vol13> (accessed 15 December 2020).
140 *Scholars Common Wilfrid Laurier University* <www.scholars.wlu.ca/cmh/vol13> (accessed 3 April 2019).

went in firing rang out in the vestry – he had shot the sniper. Cristot was an unhealthy place as the German gunners had got the range. The support we got from the 24th Lancers was first class; their tanks were always at the forefront of the attack.[141]

Major Godfrey Harland entered Cristot with his men of the 1/4th KOYLIs:

> The village was a shambles after the barrage. The crossroads was a nightmare and the Germans shelled it so accurately and repeatedly. The artillery bombardment was shattering in sound and spectacle as the soldiers of the first two companies moved through the standing corn behind the creeping barrage, supported by the tanks of the matchless 24th Lancers. In the village itself the consolidation phase was carried out successfully, despite the inevitable shelling and mortaring by the Germans.[142]

After the ruined village of Cristot was finally taken, the Germans, in their usual fashion, attempted to launch a counter-attack, but this was broken up by the mortar platoons of the 1/4th. Patrols were sent out as far as Le Hamel to the south as the rest of the battalion consolidated their positions. Some 30 casualties had been taken in taking the position. At dusk on 17 June, the 1/4th KOYLIs were relieved by the 1/7th Duke of Wellingtons.

151 Brigade and 56 Brigade at Tilly-sur-Seulles, 18–19 June

On the morning of 18 June, *Oberleutnant* Schone, officer commanding the *2. Bataillon* of *Panzergrenadier-Regiment Lehr*, was rallying his men to resist the expected British attacks. His troops had been holding Tilly-sur-Seulles for over a week and had suffered horrendous casualties; companies had been reduced to platoon strength in the fighting, and the survivors were very weary. He sent the following briefing to his junior officers:

> You have finally unified your entire force in the village, but the two companies who held the village against the first British attacks have suffered horribly. Since the Tommies have made no more direct attempts to take Tilly since the 11th your positions have been shelled sporadically and the crossroads have been bombed on a number of occasions. The village has been reduced to rubble yet still the French civilians remain, living where they can. The British have not been idle; on [the] 13th they drove a whole division around *I Panzerkorps* and briefly succeeded in taking Villers Bocage, however this assault was blunted by the newly arrived SS Tigers before *2. Panzer-Division* stabilised the situation. The British succeeded in taking Lingèvres on [the] 14th and have been making repeated attempts to retake St Pierre on your right.[143]

Oberleutnant Schone asked his troops for one more valiant effort to stand firm in the face of the expected assault:

---

141 G. Steer, correspondence with author (Wetherby, 1990).
142 Manuscript forwarded to author by P. Rose (Surrey, 1994).
143 Manuscript forwarded to author by Brian Cook (Carnegie Heritage Centre, Hull, 2018).

Panzergrenadiere of the *Panzer-Lehr-Division* await the next British assault. (Courtesy of M. Denney)

You are to hold the line at Tilly-sur-Seulles with the intention of keeping the vital crossroads and Seulles bridges open. The retention of Tilly-sur-Seulles is essential to the divisional plan and the loss of the crossroads and bridges would effectively cut the division in half. General Bayerlein has once again ordered you directly to hold firm; should the Allies break into the town he has promised to mount a counter-attack, but he has precious little left to send.[144]

The German forces in the town braced themselves for the coming attack; trenches were deepened and positions strengthened, ammunition and supplies were distributed to the defenders and, as the rain began, they sat and waited. Tanks with *Panzergrenadiere* clinging on to them had moved into the countryside around Tilly, taking up carefully selected positions and camouflaging themselves so as not to be seen from the air or from the ground. This game of hide and seek was a deadly serious business, as once a tank was spotted by the marauding fighter-bombers it was done for. The Allies' numerical superiority on the ground and complete supremacy in the air could only be countered by cunning. The German tank, mortar and machine-gun crews surveyed their whole field of fire and made themselves familiar with the distances of any feature, no matter how small.

Gefreiter Westphal, a panzer commander with the *Panzer-Lehr-Division*, looked to his front and saw 10 Tommies manhandling an anti-tank gun into position across a field. He sent out a warning over the radio: "Alarm! 10 Tommies with an anti-tank gun, they're crossing the field now and taking up position!" This galvanised his men into action, and the young tank

---

144 Manuscript forwarded to author by Brian Cook (Carnegie Heritage Centre, Hull, 2018).

commander barked out his orders: "Shrapnel 400 metres – fire!" The first 75mm shell burst in front of the anti-tank gun, killing several of the British soldiers. The surviving three ran off and took cover behind an apple tree, after which Westphal ordered: "Turret eleven-o-clock, shrapnel 420 metres – fire!" The upper part of the tree was torn to shreds, then his tank fired again. This time there was nothing left of the tree or the men behind it, other than a tangle of smashed branches. An hour later, a British spotter aircraft was seen circling above the German positions looking for the tell-tale signs of hidden tanks and guns. Westphal knew he had been spotted and his tank crew waited for the inevitable response:

> And then it came, at first only a few roving guns did the ranging. But presently we were under concentrated fire. The field of oats was ploughed over, and the hedges were torn to shreds. There was a continuous thumping against the outside of the tank, death was knocking at the door. The shelling increased until it was a veritable hurricane. The outer plates and additional armour along the sides were riddled like sieves. The blankets draped around the turret with their twigs and greenery had been swept away: "Smoke shells!" shouted Hammerle. The smoke outside was thickening and visibility was less than ten yards. Any moment now they would come.[145]

Private Gordon Duffin, of the 2nd Gloucesters, was part of a fighting patrol that was probing on the flanks of the main attack. They advanced through difficult terrain and ended up in sunken lane:

> We got so far then there was a forward slope, [and] I thought I don't like the look of this, because at the bottom is another thick hedge, hiding no doubt another sunken lane with a thick hedge on the other side. So, we get halfway down this forward slope and a Spandau opens up from the middle of the hedgerow. So down we all dive into the grass which is about a foot and a half high. The Spandau kept spraying the field we were in. A tank arrived, the lid is up and a head is sticking out. Then our officer, Wakefield, has stood up and is throwing a salute to the Herbert in the tank. I thought: "I don't believe this." He says: "Hello, what seems to be the trouble?" Wakefield says: "See the hedgerow in front? Well we are in a bit of bother, there is a Spandau in the hedgerow, can you help us?" He says: "Just a minute, ah, I've got the bugger." Well, I can't believe what I'm seeing or hearing. How they both were not shot to pieces is beyond me, but they are not.[146]

The 6th Durhams of 151 Brigade and the 2nd Essex of 56 Brigade launched an attack on Tilly-sur-Seulles in the pouring rain that was to last all day. Lieutenant Colonel Geoffrey Grahame Elliot, 2nd Essex, described the ground over which the attack would have to take place:

> We were asked to advance more than 2,000 yards through the thickest Bocage imaginable. Some of the fields were no longer than tennis courts and all were banked and ditched with thick hedges interspersed with large trees.[147]

---

145 Carell, *Invasion – They're Coming!*, pp. 157–58.
146 (accessed 13 December 2020).
147 Manuscript forwarded to author by N. Doherty (Essex, 1994).

The attacking troops were preceded by a creeping barrage fired by three regiments of artillery that would move forward at a rate of 100 yards every five minutes. Tanks would advance in line with the infantry, raking the hedgerows with their main armaments and heavy machine guns. Machine guns mounted on Bren-carriers took on the function of light tanks. Both battalions began their attack at 1430 hours, when a storm of fire and steel was laid down by the gunners of the Royal Artillery, the infantrymen plodding forward as the deafening barrage rumbled and danced before them.

Major Ewart W. Clay later described the essential support that was given by the artillery and tanks to the hard-pressed infantrymen:

> Tanks crashed through the hedges, shooting into hedge junctions and giving magnificent support. The fire brought down on the enemy was simply terrific and he was well and truly blasted out of his positions.[148]

Sergeant Charles Benford, with the 2nd Essex, watched as a four-man section of sappers was sent out onto a bridge to clear it of mines:

> On the other side of the bridge there was a German sniper; he killed two of the pioneers and pinned the other two down. Another section went out to try and bring them back, [but] they got pinned down and dare not approach the bridge. Finally, Captain Harrison decided he could get the men out and went onto the bridge. The sniper killed him;[149], he was a bit of a daredevil.[150]

Crocodile tank commander Lieutenant Andrew Wilson advanced with the knowledge that there might be a Tiger lurking in the ruins of Tilly-sur-Seulles that would make short work of his Churchill:

> You wondered if they had done the reconnaissance properly and if you would again recognise those small landmarks, the isolated bush, the dip in the ground, which showed you where to cross the start-line. I wondered if in the smoke and murk of the half-light, with your forehead pressed up to the periscope pad, you would ever pick out the target. All the while you saw in your imagination the muzzle of an 88 behind each leaf. Then the bombardment grew louder, and the order came to advance. There was the run-in with the blurred shapes, and Spandaus were firing but you couldn't see them. A Sherman officer was telling his troop to close up. The distance to our objective shortened and the Crocodiles began to speed up, firing their Besas all the time. Individual shapes stood out now, when something slammed through the air; it was an anti-tank gun. We poured in the fire when suddenly it was all over, and the infantry came up and ran in through the smoke. As I drove back to refuel, I saw the field we advanced through was littered with dead infantry and one Sherman tank blazing that had been hit through the turret.[151]

---

148 Clay, *The Path of the 50th*, p. 263.
149 Captain Norman Frank Harrison, 2nd Battalion Essex Regiment, died on 18 June 1944, aged 24. He is buried in Bayeux War Cemetery, France.
150 C. Benford, correspondence with author (Essex, 1991).
151 A. Wilson, correspondence with author (Leeds, 1991).

Corporal Anthony Mansi took part in a flanking attack with the 2nd Essex on a large house on the outskirts of Tilly-sur-Seulles. An AVRE Petard tank was called up, pumped three shells into the house, and the infantry moved in:

> There were slit trenches in the front garden, and I remember firing down them. I went to fire again and all I remember is an explosion, a terrific blast and that was it. I think we had been left for dead. When I came to, I was face down. The sleeve of my jacket and the legs of my trousers had gone where the blast had taken away the material. As I lay there, I could see my arm was covered in blood, [and] leaves and grass had stuck to it. I had lost my helmet and as I tried to look around, I could see a pair of boots and a voice calling out for help. It was the chap following me as I moved into the trench.[152]

Mansi and his section had walked into a booby-trapped section of trench. An S-mine had been triggered and jumped into the air, exploding at waist height for maximum effect. Mansi described his injuries: "It caught me up each leg, on one arm and on the buttocks. The chap behind me got it full face; he was calling for help and I joined him." It seemed like an eternity before a medic arrived, but Mansi could see trip wires all over the place and told the medics not to enter the trench. The medics, to their credit, made their way around the trip wires and dragged both men clear of the trench. Mansi recalled: "He cut my kit off me and shook white powder over my wounds and bandaged me up, [and] they then did the chap next to me who had a very bad face wound, it was terrible." The medic told Mansi the house had been taken and a jeep appeared. Mansi gave the medic the rations in his pack as thanks, and both men were taken to the rear.

Private Patrick Corden recalled events as his section of the 6th Durhams entered the village:

> We were working our way through the wreckage of people's houses. After days of shelling most had lost their roofs and bits of stone were constantly falling around us, dislodged by bullets and shells splinters. Our tanks would shoot up a building with HE and MG and in we would go. We quickly learned to avoid doorways, which could be booby-trapped with jumping mines, and went through windows which were all smashed, or holes blasted in the buildings by the tanks. We were getting on when their artillery and mortars seriously started up and we heard the sound of German tanks coming our way; by now we knew what Shermans sounded like.[153]

Sapper Sidney Blaskett, of No. 1 Troop, 81st Assault Squadron, Royal Engineers, advanced in his Petard tank and at once came under fire:

> As we came near the cross-roads there was an explosion near the front of our AVRE. I immediately sprayed MG rounds at some bushes where we thought they had fired at us. At the same time a German tank, possibly a Panther, came out of the road across our front. Captain Davies told us to fire a dustbin, a 290mm Petard round, at it, only 50 yards away.

---

152 Manuscript forwarded to author by A. Mansi (Manchester, 1992).
153 P. Corden, correspondence with author (Durham, 1993).

The Deadly Bocage: June–July 1944 335

Troops of the 2nd Battalion Essex Regiment clearing houses in Tilly. (Courtesy of A. Mansi)

A dead *Panzergrenadier* lies among the ruins of Tilly-sur-Seulles. (Author's collection)

> I traversed our turret slightly to our right, took aim and fired at its turret ring. The round hit a telegraph pole about three feet from the enemy tank. When the smoke and dust had cleared the tank had stopped and did not move again. The blast had put it out of action.[154]

Trooper S. Dewar supported the infantry in his Sherman tank of the Sherwood Rangers:

> A small French girl in a village we liberated gave us a tame live rabbit which I called Abdul. He was our lucky mascot and lived in the turret on my great coat. Captain Fern said he saw what he said were Germans with horses through his binoculars and he ordered us to fire high explosive shells at some buildings. I loaded and fired about 20 shells and Abdul scampered into the side sponson as hot empty shell cases fell upon the turret floor. Nitro cellulose fumes from the gun are inevitably inhaled, filling the lungs unpleasantly. We proceeded, firing our sponson at various German targets seen running.[155]

Once the momentum of the attack got under way there was no stopping it, the troops keeping pace with the barrage. Many of the German soldiers had had enough and ran to the rear. The 6th Durhams reached their objective by 1700 hours and dug-in, the supporting tanks staying with them and accounted for two Panzer Mk IV Specials.

Corporal S. Root, with the 6th Durhams, found the German positions well dug-in and the infantry still full of fight:

> It helped that we knew a bit about the ground from the last time we were there. Rather than going across the fields as a platoon, we sections worked our way up the hedges and ditches with another section ready to give covering fire. As we did the time before we used smoke, but when Jerry got wise, we fired it to his rear to worry him and draw his fire. It wasn't quick but it worked, and I remember when we got round him, we used up a lot of grenades.[156]

Private Corden sat amid the melee with his 6th Durhams comrades as the tanks fought it out in the streets:

> The sound of the tanks firing their main guns at each other, machine-guns going and exploding shells was terrible, and the building I was in was collapsing around me. All we could do was to keep our heads down until our corporal shouted "Enemy infantry" and kicked those who were too slow getting to their feet. Across this open area we could see through the smoke and flames figures moving through the houses, heading towards our boys. We shot at them, taking care to fire from well inside the rooms; if a tank saw the flash of a rifle or a Bren, the next thing would be boom! and you would be gone.[157]

---

154 *WW2: People's War* <www.bbc.co.uk/ww2peopleswar> (accessed 23 September 2016).
155 S. Dewar, interview with author (Richmond, 1992).
156 S. Root, correspondence with author (Durham, 1993).
157 R. Corden, correspondence with author (Durham, 1993).

Terrified French women and children abandon their homes as they flee the battle zone. (Author's collection)

The British troops had been involved in heavy fighting for days now and this victory over their tormentors raised their spirits. Indeed, the co-operation between infantry, artillery and tanks had shown the way forward for the future.

On 19 June, the 2nd Essex of 56 Brigade completed the capture of Tilly-sur-Seulles, meeting minimal opposition. The sight that greeted them was heartbreaking; the whole village had been destroyed and was unrecognizable to the inhabitants when they eventually returned. Private A. Vince of the 2nd Essex recalled entering the village:

> As we wound our way through the battle-scarred lanes, we saw plenty of evidence of the fighting in the form of knocked-out Cromwell and Sherman tanks, fewer German tanks and numbers of hastily dug graves. Not a building was untouched by war, and as we came nearer to the centre of the village every house was wrecked and broken. The Boche had hastily withdrawn ahead of us and on the western side we saw only a handful of horribly wounded civilians. In the centre of what once had been a village, all kinds of mines and booby traps had been left to slow down our advance and several casualties had been caused by the unwary who had tried to enter a house without first making sure it was safe. The rest of the day was spent trying to waterproof our slit trenches and taking evasive action against

exceedingly heavy stonking in which 88mm airbursts figured prominently. Casualties were not light.[158]

Trooper Eric Postles of the 61st Reconnaissance Regiment also remembered his time at Tilly-sur-Seulles:

> We were patrolling in the Tilly area, but the tactics had changed by providing a tank or a self-propelled gun to trundle along behind us, adding to our fire power. We had to admire the military police controlling the road junctions, often under shellfire. A number were killed, especially at the busy Jerusalem Crossroads, where they lie in a small cemetery cared for by the locals. We did long stops as the infantry attacked, [and] it was bad to see the wounded coming back in jeep ambulances. On advanced patrols we sometimes came across snipers operating in no-man's land[;] they were a menace and got short shrift from us when they were caught.[159]

Trooper Eric Postles, 61st Reconnaissance Regiment, Royal Armoured Corps. (Author's collection)

Another shocked by what he saw as he entered Tilly was Sergeant Charles Benford of the 2nd Essex:

> When we eventually got into Tilly, it was devastated, a complete ruin. The civilians were living in trenches dug in their front gardens, the poor devils.[160]

Corporal Philip Mailou moved with his gun crew of the 2nd Essex's Anti-tank Platoon across the Bayeux road and dug-in for the night:

> It was pouring with rain, and we needed a bulldozer to get through the bank and off the Bayeux road. Here we dug-in the guns in case of any counter-attack. We were really keeping our heads down and what a miserable time we had; it was so bad we even got an issue of rum. We did a guard or two, one [hour] off, two on. I recall my turn was at four in the morning. When I got up there was no-one on guard. If an officer had come along, we would all have been shot at dawn.[161]

---

158 A. Vince, correspondence with author (Essex, 1989).
159 *Chotie Darling* <www.chotiedarling.co.uk> (accessed 12 May 2020).
160 C. Benford, correspondence with author (Essex, 1992).
161 P. Mailou, correspondence with author (Essex, 1989).

Sappers sweep the streets of Tilly-sur-Seulles looking for mines after the Germans had left. (Author's collection)

The Germans eventually pulled back to Juvigny after thoroughly mining the village roads and leaving a profusion of booby traps for the unwary. All through the pouring rain of 19 June, the 2nd Essex was subjected to very heavy artillery fire, with German 88s sending over frighteningly accurate air bursts that exploded directly above the ruined hamlet

When Tilly-sur-Seulles finally fell to the 50th Northumbrian Division, it presented a view of utter desolation. Artillery and naval shells and bombs had battered it beyond recognition, leaving a pitiful sight for the victors and the surviving people who had lived there. This was to be the first of many such Normandy towns and villages liberated by XXX Corps that would be well and truly obliterated in the process. Heavy casualties had been taken in the storming of Tilly-sur-Seulles: the whole division had suffered 1,404 killed, 3,072 maimed and wounded and 505 missing. Yet this vicious killing match in the Bocage was by no means over yet, as the Germans dug-in and waited for them in the next village.

231 Brigade at '1st Hottot', 19 June

The vice-like grip of the German forces on Tilly-sur-Seulles had been prised loose at great cost, but the enemy was still holding nearby Hottot. On the afternoon of 19 June, two battalions of 231 Brigade moved to their start line in pouring rain opposite the village of Hottot, the 1st

Hampshires on the right and 2nd Devons on the left. During the morning, the 1st Dorsets took over the defences around Point 103 that were being held by the 6th Green Howards. Brigade CO Brigadier Alexander Stanier's plan was for the attack to be supported by the Sherman tanks of the Sherwood Rangers, flail and flame-throwing Crocodile tanks, massed artillery fire and the machine gunners of the 2nd Cheshires. They were to make a frontal attack on the village and advance to a ridge between Hottot and Villers Bocage, the final objective. The forming-up place was on the Tilly–Balleroy road. The actual start line, which had been marked with white tape by the intelligence sections, was some 600 yards to the south. The heavy rain had made it impossible for any close air support for the attack. Visibility for the infantry was limited to the next field, and in the tradition of the Bocage – and Hottot in particular – the fighting for this much-disputed village was to be bitter in the extreme.

It rained all day on 19 June, and the night before the battle for Hottot, Private Peter Cuerdon, 1st Hampshires, was in his slit trench when he had a close, but thankfully peaceful, encounter with a Tiger tank and its crew:

> Hottot? My God, that was a terrible place to be, dreadful country to fight in, all Bocage and perfect for Jerry, who was on the defensive. We went from field to field, and this was the place where we spent the longest time, about three weeks; we couldn't shift them out of Hottot. They started to bring up armour and we saw some Tigers. We had dug-in in a big field and a Tiger moved up to our front. There is nothing more eerie than the sound of a tank grinding and clanking its way towards you, [so] we put our heads down pretty sharp. He stopped quite close, and these two chappies got out to have sandwiches or something and then they suddenly pulled out much to our relief. There were times when even an infantryman thought the better of things; if you fired a shot in the evening, you would find it triggered off the other side to do the same and you ended up in the middle of a major confrontation for nothing. There were a lot of occasions when you kept quiet: gallantry wasn't always the best thing.[162]

Lieutenant David Holdsworth, who trudged forward with the 2nd Devons in the pouring rain, wrote:

> Someone, we were told, had laid out white tapes to mark the place from which our attack was to start. In bright sunshine these white tapes might have been easy to find, in teeming rain they were very nearly invisible. However, we found them, took up our positions, and prepared to advance on Hottot behind a creeping barrage.[163]

Tanks blasted away at each other and the cruel flame-throwing Crocodiles spewed out their venom in great arcs of blazing fire. Among all of this, the infantry of both sides fought it out in the ditches and hedgerows as the artillery barrage crashed and rumbled before them. The German troops holding the Hottot sector were experienced and dedicated fighters:

---

162 Manuscript forwarded to author by P. Cuerdon (Hampshire, 1992).
163 Holdsworth, D., *One Day I'll Tell You* (Yorkshire: Westfield Publications, 1994), p. 34.

Panzergrenadier-Regiment 25 of the *12. SS-Panzer-Division 'Hitlerjugend'* and a reconnaissance detachment and pioneer battalion of the *Panzer-Lehr-Division*.

Lieutenant A.E. Blackmore led forward his soaking wet men of the 1st Hampshires:

> No sign of the rain stopping after ten hours. The start line was neatly marked with white tapes and the enemy gave it and us a terrific plastering with his mortars. Everyone was tired and wet. We had moved nearly a mile from La Senaudiere with Hottot another thousand yards ahead. We pushed forward under a heavy barrage with our Bren guns fighting a staccato duel against the faster 'Burrup' of the Jerries' Spandaus. In the din it was difficult at first to know which was his artillery and which was ours. But one soon realised where the receiving end was when we reached a sunken lane, evidently well pinpointed by the enemy mortars. Several men in D Company, the leading formation, were also held up in this lane, but the place was decidedly too hot for comfort, so we climbed up a bank and dashed across the next field through a hail of mortar bombs and bullets.[164]

Lieutenant Geoffrey Picot, 1st Hampshires, advanced with his mortar teams behind the forward troops:

> The first firing position for the mortars was behind a garden wall about 100 yards off the road, [and] the medical officer asked me if we could move as his first aid post was nearby and the sound of our firing would not help his wounded patients. He accepted that the interests of the battle had to come first but if we could perform our tasks equally well somewhere else would we please do so. We did.[165]

During the morning, the battle increased in intensity, the noise level terrific and unceasing as each side pounded the other. The Hampshires were suffering particularly heavy casualties as they pressed forward against a determined foe. However, the tenacity of the attackers paid off and just after noon the lead platoons entered the outskirts of Hottot.

Lieutenant Picot was moving up slowly behind the main advance when he came under heavy artillery and mortar fire:

> Shells were bursting everywhere, some hitting the tops of trees and exploding there to create a wide fall out. A signaller sheltering beside me in a ditch was killed by an air burst, a large piece of shrapnel entering his back. I felt helpless and for a moment did not know what to do. But it did not matter, for nothing anybody could have done would have saved him. In a few minutes he was dead. Other shells bursting near my mortars wounded two men, one of whom died later that day. As we pressed on I found it very unnerving to see the bodies of those who had died leading the first wave of the attack, bodies that remained in strange postures, presumably where the blast had left them.[166]

---

164 S. Blackmore, interview with author (Hampshire, 1993).
165 Picot, *Accidental Warrior*, p. 73.
166 Picot, *Accidental Warrior*, p. 74.

The attacking companies advanced over difficult ground that was being swept by mortar bombs, artillery and Spandau fire. The village was held in strength by the Germans, but the British troops pressed on until they reached the outer perimeter. That achievement brought a most violent reaction from the enemy, who counter-attacked in force with Panther tanks and drove the Hampshires back. Lieutenant Blackmore later spoke of the experience of being in very close contact with the enemy:

> We got to close quarters with him at a farm when one of his Panther tanks came rumbling forward right up to our position, firing everything it had. With great presence of mind, one of our anti-tank gunners caught the Panther amidships, but not before it had managed to get one of our Shermans belonging to the Sherwood Rangers who were in support. Both tanks caught fire, but the Sherman crew managed to get out alright. The brewed-up tanks were now well ablaze and began to attract heavy mortar fire.[167]

Lieutenant David Holdsworth of the 2nd Devons led his men forward, and it was not long before the ruins of Hottot came into view:

> With my platoon I scrambled over a hedge and into a field on the far side. Shells burst only 100 yards ahead of us. But the artillery was as good as their word. As we advanced, so they increased their range. We were halfway across the field when enemy bullets began to zip around our legs and bodies. We didn't need much training to decide what to do next. We threw ourselves down into the soggy dripping grass, and then we remembered we too had firearms. I doubt whether we hit the enemy, but it did us the world of good to fire back. We got up and continued our advance and through the trees on the hill in front of us, we could just make out the vague outlines of some battered buildings [–] this then was Hottot.[168]

When Lieutenant Holdsworth reached the main road that ran through Hottot, to his right there was a Tiger tank with infantry on the turret and along its sides. Three Tommies walked down the road towards the Tiger, not showing any signs that they recognised it as German. The Germans seemed equally relaxed and had not noticed they were British. The crew casually clambered into their tank, and as the last one disappeared a rifle shot rang out, the lid of the turret clanged shut and the Germans machine-gunned the road for a number of seconds. As Holdsworth and his men dashed across the road, the tank came to life and rumbled past the hidden Tommies. Holdsworth wrote:

> A few minutes later shells crashed into the streets of Hottot, ripping up trees and gardens all around us. We dug ourselves deeper into whatever cover was available. We had great confidence in the Royal Artillery but wondered why it was necessary to be firing on us.[169]

Lieutenant Picot, 1st Hampshires, remembered that there were large numbers of snipers who were very active in the area:

---

167 S. Blackmore, interview with author (Hampshire, 1993).
168 Holdsworth, *One Day I'll Tell You*, p. 41.
169 Holdsworth, *One Day I'll Tell You*, p. 42.

A camouflaged German Panther tank fires into the ranks of the attacking Devons from a ruined farm at Hottot. (Courtesy of H. Wernemann)

Snipers were firing across the roadway from the woods. We answered by spraying the treetops with automatic fire, but the sniping continued. Bill Hand, who was commanding the anti-tank platoon, went off on his own with a Bren gun to stalk the snipers. Half an hour later he was carried back with a bullet through both legs. Our leading company got into Hottot only to be forced to withdraw when counter-attacked by tanks. On our left the 2nd Devons also got into the village, but they were ordered to make a similar withdrawal for the same reason.[170]

The Devons had achieved only a tenuous grip on the outskirts of Hottot, and to their left the Hampshires had been halted short of the village. Low cloud and rain meant that the troops and tanks of the *Panzer-Lehr-Division* could manoeuvre at will without fear of the dreaded *Jabos* that could create such havoc in clear weather. As the battle swayed to and fro, the newly reinforced Panther battalion enjoyed some success. Lieutenant Holdsworth received orders to withdraw at dawn:

At last, a message arrived by runner from the company commander telling us to hold our position and to withdraw at first light. It was the longest night I can remember. Even a cold tin of mixed vegetables was welcome. As we withdrew at dawn in single file, we had to negotiate a barbed wire fence. One of my soldiers bent down to get under the wire and

---

170 Picot, *Accidental Warrior*, pp. 74–75.

his finger touched the trigger of his rifle. The soldier in front of him was shot dead. A wet, tired and depressed platoon dug itself into a defensive position not very far from the point at which it had been launched into the attack.[171]

That same morning, the Germans reoccupied Hottot. Major John Leytham, 82nd Assault Squadron, Royal Engineers, wrote of the fighting around the village and the gruesome aftermath:

> As we moved towards the ruined village of Hottot on 19th June one of my leading AVREs was hit in the turret and exploded[;] the Germans put up a fierce resistance to our attack and then counter attacked us. It was only on the following day that we were able to advance and recover the disabled AVRE. Now once an armour[-]piercing shell enters the turret of a tank it acts in a manner similar to a domestic incinerator. The occupants of the turret are quickly smeared around the walls. I had given orders after the recovery that none of my men should look inside. A number were foolish enough to disobey my orders and it did not improve their morale. Vehicles like this should be taken back to the rear workshops where experts spray the inside with creosote. After a suitable interval they scrape off the remains from the wall of the turret.[172]

Geoffrey Picot commented on the failure to take Hottot on 19 June:

> We had been held up not only by tanks but by dogged and fierce infantry, by heavy defensive artillery fire brought down where we least liked it and by mines and booby traps left in the gaps in hedges and in all manner of places where a soldier would unsuspectingly go. Wet and tired I slept that night in a ditch.[173]

After the failure of the first attack upon Hottot, the 50th Northumbrian Division settled down to an unpleasant period of close-quarter combat with the enemy. The snipers' paradise that was the Normandy Bocage took a steady toll of men, even when no major action was being fought. The pressure was kept up on the Germans, mortar fire from both sides coming down without warning and both sides suffering casualties daily. Many good men lost their lives in this static form of warfare. Private Ronald Malabar was part of a draft of replacements which had joined the 9th Durhams near Hottot:

> When I got there, they looked pretty shattered[;] they had some terrible experiences, and I got the impression that they were rather weary. At the same time, they seemed to me very professional and knew exactly what they were doing. The battalion had seen a lot of action and suffered very heavy casualties. It was probably the reason for me being there. They were just out of the line when I joined them. The thing I remember about them was that they

---

171 Holdsworth, *One Day I'll Tell You*, p. 48.
172 Delaforce, P., *Marching to the Sound of Gunfire, Northwest Europe 1944–45* (Gloucestershire: Sutton Publishing, 1996), p. 38.
173 Picot, *Accidental Warrior*, p. 75.

had a pet goat at battalion HQ and every time a shell started to come over the goat used to beat everyone into the trenches.[174]

When time allowed, batches of men were sent back to Bayeux to enjoy the luxury of the baths, but for most men fighting patrols and the occasional limited advance was the order of the day. For nearly three weeks, the exhausted Northumbrians and the equally worn out *Panzer-Lehr-Division* had to accept a stalemate. Everybody lived in slit trenches, making sure to keep clear of any buildings, which were frequently booby-trapped or had been registered by the enemy artillery and mortar teams. The disposition of the 50th Northumbrian Division was now 231 Brigade north of Hottot, 151 Brigade in the Tilly-sur-Seulles sector and 69 Brigade south of Le Belle Epine and La Senaudiere. On their right was 56 Brigade.

Geoffrey Picot remembered the pause in the fighting as July approached and the 50th Northumbrian Division took on a posture of aggressive defence. This grim static warfare reminded the troops of how their fathers must have fought in the Great War. Lieutenant Picot commented on his commander of the 1st Hampshires:

> Colonel Howie was superb at aggression; this took on the form of sending out frequent fighting patrols to harry the enemy wherever they could be found and the ordering of many mortar and artillery barrages at suspected enemy positions.[175]

All troops in the forward areas were ordered to take out fighting patrols every day and night, and casualties mounted accordingly. Artillery and mortar shells would fall without warning, and meanwhile the snipers of both sides carried on their grim work. This was an unpleasant period of close contact with the enemy. All of these battles had a purpose, though it was not always known what they were by the men fighting and dying at the front. By the end of June, the 50th Northumbrian Division had suffered casualties of 300 officers and 3,000 other ranks. Major Peter Martin, 2nd Machine-gun Battalion the Cheshire Regiment, observed what was going on around him:

> Reinforcements came up every day to plug the gaps before the next day's attack. The individual soldiers were as super as they had always been, the courage was still there but the skills were going, and it showed. If our own artillery or mortar fire failed to dislodge the enemy our infantry seemed to become at a loss about what to do. Instead of using fire and movement to get forward they stopped. Untrained or semi-skilled 3-inch mortar men would fire their mortars from underneath trees, killing themselves with their own bombs exploding in the branches above. I began to see worrying signs in my own company, because there were four brigades in the division and only three machine-gun companies, we never got a rest. My soldiers had been with me right through the Western Desert, the invasion of Sicily and now Normandy. Battle fatigue was beginning to show. A superb corporal suddenly burst into tears and had to be sent back. We had this problem with new people too. One new officer who'd never seen a shot fired in the whole war broke down

---

174 Moses, *The Gateshead Gurkhas*, p. 294.
175 Picot, *Accidental Warrior*, p. 77.

completely under enemy artillery fire. In the First World War I suppose he would have been taken out and shot, but we felt sorry for him. He probably went and did a good, if less demanding job, elsewhere for the rest of the war.[176]

Lieutenant Picot also noticed how the effects of constant combat affected the troops and began to ponder his own mortality:

> Many veterans were running out of courage. Most men have a finite amount of this commodity, and it can get used up. The Germans had no such problem as all deserters were shot, thus everybody stayed in the firing line. The average infantryman who has fought six major actions without being hit, knows he won't last another six. There is a feeling that sooner or later death catches up with you, but casualties and death are synonymous. Three, four or five people are wounded and survive without permanent injury for every one that is killed. Not nice to think that the best that can happen is to be wounded or get a Blighty.[177]

The 49th West Riding Division in Operation Martlet/Epsom, the Battle for the Rauray Spur, 25 June – 1 July

As Caen had not yet fallen, Montgomery decided to set in motion Operation Epsom, which began on 26 June. After the fiasco at Villers Bocage, Montgomery intended to take no chances on another failure. Epsom was to be a return to his preferred tactic of building up a strong and powerful force to penetrate the German positions. He intended to use the full combat power of the Second Army to launch the strongest assault yet by the British in Normandy. Three British corps would be involved: I Corps, VIII Corps and XXX Corps. XXX Corps was on the right flank, and the codename for their attack would be Martlet, though it was also known as Dauntless. During the main advance on the 26th, the right flank of VIII Corps would be threatened in the Rauray area and so it became imperative that key points should be seized and held – the villages of Rauray, Fontenay-le-Pesnel, Tessel-Brettevillette and Juvigny. The 49th West Riding Division, supported by 8 Armoured Brigade, was allotted these tasks, to be executed on 25 June. German forces in this area consisted of the three battalions of *SS-Panzergrenadier Regiment 26*, as well as elements of the *12. Bataillon* of the *12. SS-Panzer-Division 'Hitlerjugend'*. Once the attack began, elements of the *21. Panzer-Division* would be sent to the area to reinforce the defending German units.

By midnight on 17 June, the 49th West Riding Division was holding a front some 2,500 yards long, from St Pierre in the west, through Le Haut d'Audrieu and Les Hautes Vents which overlooked Fontenay in the centre, to Hill 102 and Le Parke-de-Boislande on the eastern flank. Reinforcements intended for the division had not got through because of the storms in the Channel, and supplies and ammunition were also seriously delayed.

---

176 Arthur, *Forgotten Voices of the Second World War*, p. 335.
177 Picot, *Accidental Warrior*, p. 88.

Private P. Lawton, serving with the 1st Battalion Tyneside Scottish, commented that his comrades were only 18–20 years old, with no combat experience. All they had to fall back upon was their short basic military training:

> We debussed and as we moved round the end of a row of terraced cottages, I was struck by a feeling of apprehension which was not helped by the smell of burning cordite combined with that of putrefying flesh. We had some time to wait until we went into action, and it was a bit of a shock when an ME 109 flew quite low over our heads. It was the first time we had seen an enemy aircraft since our arrival in Normandy.[178]

Lieutenant Colonel Trevor Hart-Dyke, CO of the Hallamshire Battalion, Yorks and Lancs, recalled:

Lieutenant Colonel Trevor Hart-Dyke, DSO, Hallamshire Battalion, York and Lancaster Regiment. (Author's collection)

> Our battalion HQ was shelled, and we lost most of our signal equipment and both medical 15 cwt trucks were knocked out by shells landing on the medical post. This taught us never to leave our unarmoured vehicles in the forward area and to dump and dig our stores in. Rough seas had delayed the arrival of ammunition but the strength of the enemy defences at Fontenay and Tessel Wood was confirmed. The next few days were spent in conferences and reconnaissances for the big attack.[179]

Lance Corporal Geoffrey Steer, 1/4th KOYLIs, found his section had been singled out for a standing patrol led by a Lieutenant Trumper. They were to take a wireless with them and observe any enemy formations, calling down artillery fire on any significant targets or asking for support:

> We made our way through the wood and stopped at the edge[;] to our right was a copse about 30 yards wide and in front of it were fields as far as Vendes. Our patrol was about 15 strong and after about an hour of observation we heard the rumble of a tank. Across this field came a Tiger and it stopped 400 yards in front of our position. The crew got out and proceeded to camouflage the tank with a net, they then stood around the tank

---

178 Manuscript forwarded to author by P. Cuerdon (Hampshire, 1994).
179 *WW2: People's War* <www.bbc.co.uk/ww2peopleswar> (accessed 23 November 2014).

smoking. Lt Trumper crawled up to us and we discussed the situation with the other NCO. Three men were detailed to take the Piat and knock out the tank if they could and off they went while we waited. 10 minutes went by, and all hell broke loose, first rifle fire from our left, then the tank crew pulled the net off and jumped into the tank, just as our three lads returned at the gallop. Lt Trumper ordered the 25-pounders to open up while we started back through the wood. The first salvo of shells dropped in the wood amongst us but luckily no-one was injured. Then he lifted the range, and we could hear the shells going over us to the target. Later I asked the three lads: "What went wrong?" Thompson and Taylor smiled and told us that when they made their way through the copse they had spotted two German soldiers wearing camouflage capes up in the trees observing D Company's lines through binoculars. They then shot the soldiers out of the trees and came back to the patrol.[180]

Patrols of both sides were out constantly in no man's land as information was sought on their opponents' dispositions and strength. The enemy took a steady toll in men and carriers by shelling patrols with artillery and mortar fire when they were detected. On 20 June, the 1/6th Battalion Duke of Wellington's Regiment were resting at Brouay and counting the cost after their heavy casualties at Le-Parc-de-Boislande when tragedy struck. It was a sunny and peaceful afternoon, and no distant rumble of gunfire could be heard as the men went about their tasks, with a meal being cooked for the new arrivals. A German fighter then suddenly appeared in the sky and, spotting the assembled troops, immediately launched an attack, machine-gunning the gathering, although thankfully no casualties were suffered. Nevertheless, the pilot reported back what he had seen and shortly afterwards a screaming howl was heard as the first shell landed with a terrific explosion on the Dukes. Shells continued to arrive non-stop for 30 minutes. A fully loaded ammunition carrier was hit and exploded; the men had no slit trenches and no tools to dig any, and 20 of them were hit. The troops of the 1/6th Duke of Wellington's were due to be inspected by Brigadier Mahoney at 1445 hours that afternoon, and instead of postponing the inspection in view of what he occurred, it was decided to go ahead with it in a clearing in the wood. As the troops entered the wood at 1440 hours, shells began raining down on them. Headquarters Company received a direct hit, causing 20 casualties, with another 12 being hit in the wood. This had a demoralising effect on the young men of the Duke of Wellington's.

The divisional attack during Operation Martlet was to be made up of three distinct phases. The first objective was the taking of what was termed the Barracuda Line between Juvigny-sur-Seulles and Fontenay-le-Pesnel. The second objective was the securing of the Walrus Line: Tessel Wood and the farm at St Nicholas. The final objective was the capture of the Albacore Line at Rauray and the nearby high ground. On 24 June, air attacks were launched by rocket-firing Typhoons on Tessel Wood, Juvigny and Fontenay, and an artillery counter-battery programme against identified anti-aircraft positions took place the same day.

---

180 *WW2: People's War* <www.bbc.co.uk/ww2peopleswar> (accessed 23 December 2020).

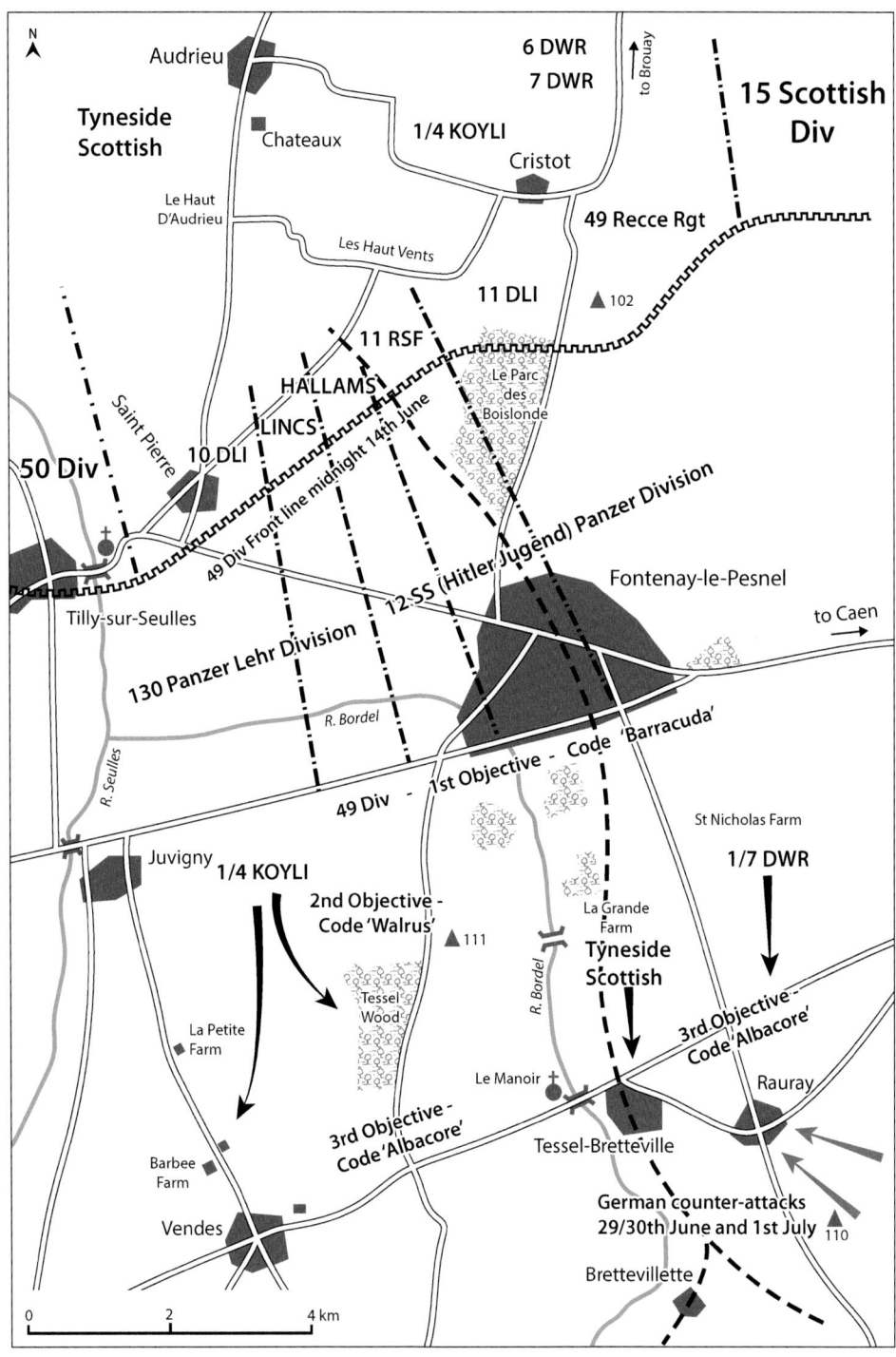

The 49th West Riding Division at Fontenay-le-Pesnel, 25 June –1 July 1944.

Fontenay: Into battle, 25 June (Barracuda Line)

This first attack would be led by three infantry battalions: the 4th Lincolns to the west near St Pierre, the Hallamshires in the centre and the 11th Royal Scots Fusiliers near Parc-de-Boislande. In reserve a mile to the rear would be the 1st Tyneside Scottish. The land over which they were to advance was a gentle slope through lush fields of ripe corn that led on to the close Bocage countryside.

The evening before the attack, the troops who would have to take the lead in the advance prepared themselves for the ordeal to come. Lieutenant David Render of the Sherwood Rangers recalled:

> It was dark by the time we had finished and the petrol-tin cookers that had heated our last proper meal before the off had long been extinguished by the time I crawled into the tank and brooded on the morrow, wondering what we had learned in the last few days and how my own performance would stack up. It was dark when we were woken from a few fitful hours of sleep. I looked at my watch, [but] the grey light of dawn was still over an hour away as we drove under radio silence to the assembly area near Point 102.[181]

Artillery observation officers accompanied the leading infantry companies, so that they could call down a barrage when needed. The artillery field regiments had worked out in great detail a timed firing programme for the advance, and a further defensive fire plan was made to cover 70 Brigade's final position. The 89th Light Anti-aircraft Regiment was tasked with providing a troop at Les-Hauts-Vents to fire on Tessel Wood and to protect the eastern flank, and another troop was attached to 49th Reconnaissance Regiment. Units from the 55th Anti-tank Regiment, Royal Artillery, were allocated as follows: 217th Battery went to 70 Brigade, 218th Battery to 146 Brigade and 219th Battery to 147 Brigade; 220th Battery was kept in regimental reserve in case of a German breakthrough. The 234th Battery and anti-tank regiments were to support 146 Brigade, with one troop going to support 147 Brigade.

The men of 70, 146 and 147 Brigades were roused by their officers at 0300 hours, and after a quick breakfast they set off to the start line. At 0400 hours, the Allied artillery opened up with a terrific roar and the rolling barrage came crashing down on the line of advance. At 0415 hours, 146 Brigade headed for their objective of Rauray, with 147 Brigade making for Fontenay-le-Pesnel; 70 Brigade was in reserve. The coolness of the morning had created a thick fog which, added to the smoke and fumes from the barrage, made for extremely reduced visibility.

As the barrage began, a young soldier of the 1st Tyneside Scottish, in reserve with 70 Brigade, turned and looked to his rear to see an amazing sight:

> Looking back behind me the sky was lit with flash after flash, increasing rapidly in tempo until the skyline was outlined almost in one continuous glow, as mediums, field guns and heavies joined in. All I could hear was the continuous whistle of shells passing low overhead, the stubborn rumble of the guns behind and the roar of bursting shells ahead.[182]

---

181 Render, *Tank Action*, p. 109.
182 Townend, W. and Baldwin, F., *Gunners in Normandy* (Gloucestershire: The History Press, 2020), p. 243.

Gunner John Mercer, 185th Field Regiment, Royal Artillery, remembered the start of the attack from the gunners' viewpoint:

> Two hours before dawn the guns began a barrage behind which the infantry, with supporting tanks, moved forward. Round after round was fired with the night sky illuminated by constant flashes of gunfire and the countryside filled with the heavy roll of the bombardment. Sustained enemy mortar fire could be heard like the thumping of a table by a hundred hands, and the rattle of machine-guns, audible in the distance, first the rat-a-tat of Bren guns and then the pop-pop-br-br-br of the German Spandaus in reply.[183]

David Render watched the barrage begin with his comrades from the Sherwood Rangers and wondered how anyone could survive such a maelstrom:

> It was 03:30 a.m. and the enemy were about to be pulverised by 60 minutes of intensive indirect fire. The horizon behind us was suddenly lit up by the muzzle flashes of 250 guns stabbing fire from their barrels into the retreating darkness. The 5.5-inch guns of the medium corps artillery, which fired projectiles weighing 100 pounds, supplemented the 25-pounders of the divisional gunner regiments and provided four times the destructive power of the lighter field pieces. The noise was terrific, and the shells screamed through the clouds overhead as a solid wall of sound. We could hear the crash of their explosions as the rounds landed unseen in the misty darkness less than a thousand yards ahead of us.[184]

SS-Standartenführer Kurt Meyer, commanding the *12. SS-Panzer-Division 'Hitlerjugend'*, was in Fontenay at the time and struggled forward to find his troops:

> Climbing over dead English bodies I reached the positions of the *SS-Panzergrenadier Regiment 26*. *Panzergrenadiere* with emaciated faces were crouching in foxholes and shell craters. There were no officers left, they were all killed or wounded. They talked about the enemy without hatred, repeatedly emphasising their outstanding morale.[185]

The young *Panzergrenadiere* expressed their bitterness to Meyer about the overwhelming amount of

SS-Standartenführer Kurt Meyer, Commanding Officer of the *12. SS-Panzer-Division 'Hitlerjugend'*. (Courtesy of H. Wernemann)

183 Delaforce, *The Polar Bears*, p. 63.
184 Render, *Tank Action*, p. 109.
185 Meyer, *Grenadiers*, p. 241.

enemy equipment compared to theirs, and where they would be if they had such an advantage. They all complained about the lack of their own aircraft in the skies, which enabling the British *Jabos* to roam unopposed. Meyer left the front line just as the British barrage was getting heavier:

> We were caught by a heavy barrage in the centre of the village, [so] I leapt behind some stone stairs and waited for this unpleasant morning greeting to pass. One of my companions lay on the street with smashed limbs; a direct hit had torn him to pieces. We dashed through the village pursued by heavy artillery fire falling on Fontenay and were glad to leave the ruins. Was this an overture to the expected offensive? The battalion command post was only 100 metres away, but the distance seemed endless.[186]

From his vantage point on Point 102, David Render had a grandstand view as the assaulting infantry and the tanks of B and C Squadrons of the Sherwood Rangers moved forward into the swirling mist, down the forward slope leading into Fontenay:

> The infantry moved in column beside the tanks, with their rifles at the port. Within minutes they were completely obscured as they advanced together into the thickening ground fog that had condensed in the lower reaches of the valley floor. Our artillery fire continued to land out of view ahead of them. Then we heard the unmistakeable battle-field signature of the German MG-42s, Spandaus, barking unseen through the mist. Soon it was joined by the sharp reports of German anti-tank guns and the crump of enemy mortar fire.[187]

Lieutenant Colonel Alexander William Henry James Montgomery-Cuninghame, DSO, CO of the 11th Royal Scots Fusiliers, assembled his troops at Le-Parc-de-Boislande and advanced with the Lincolns and Hallamshires into thick mist. They were supported by two mortar and machine-gun platoons of the 2nd Kensingtons, B Squadron of the Sherwood Rangers and various anti-tank units. They advanced down the western side of the thick woods at Le-Parc-de-Boislande, into the valley and across a road junction, named 'Hell's Lane' by the troops. With B and D Companies leading, they headed for Fontenay. Commanding B Company, 11th Royal Scots Fusiliers, was Major H. Macpherson, who recalled the orderly start as they crossed the start line on the day of the attack and the confusion which followed:

> We were the right forward coy and formed up for the attack at 03:45 hours and crossed the start line at 04:15 hours in a fairly compact bunch of units. The barrage was tremendous and our distance behind it was kept very well, as was direction. The men stood up to and kept behind the barrage like veterans. Just after the platoons had opened out a cloud of combined mist, smoke and dust started to rise. The fog rose so quickly that runners and platoons were lost. Enemy MGs on either flank then opened up. Visibility was down to five yards. 18 Set [portable man-pack radio transceiver] communication had gone and 12 Platoon on the left was completely adrift.[188]

---

186 Meyer, *Grenadiers*, p. 241.
187 Render, *Tank Action*, p. 113.
188 *WW2: People's War* <www.bbc.co.uk/ww2peopleswar> (accessed 21 May 2012).

Major W.F. Mackay, Officer Commanding D Company, 11th Royal Scots Fusiliers, led his men into the mist:

> We left the forward coy and proceeded when the first ground mist came down. After 100 yards visibility was down to about three yards. I lost touch with 17 Platoon and visibility became worse, [and] the rate of the advance slowed down resulting in the loss of the barrage. Luckily all platoon commanders had a compass bearing to the first objective. 17 Platoon was subjected to intense mortar fire, obviously an enemy defensive task. I was by this time completely out of touch with everyone, even by 38 Set, except for Lt Irvine and fifteen other ranks, when we reached Hell's Lane.[189]

Lieutenant Stuart Hills moved to the attack in his Sherwood Rangers Sherman tank:

> We moved down the hill behind the barrage. Halfway down into the valley we encountered a heavy ground mist which thickened the further we went, and eventually reduced visibility to a few feet. Tanks and infantry lost contact, and everything became confused. The enemy opened up with machine-guns, mortars, the lot, [and] the infantry had a particularly hard time.[190]

Trooper Austin Baker was with C Squadron of the 4/7th Royal Dragoon Guards, supporting the 1st Tyneside Scottish, and as usual in the Bocage visibility was limited to one field:

> The field sloped down-hill away from us, [and] the leading troop bowled off merrily down the field. None of the tanks fired, but the infantry charged blazing away from the hip. Nobody fired back and I was beginning to think that this was going to be a quiet affair, [but] I was very much mistaken. Second Lieutenant Thompson, on our right, came over the air with a message that made my stomach turn over. His tank had pushed through a hedge and had been knocked out by a Jerry tank just across the field. None of the crew had been hurt and amazingly had stayed in the tank and knocked out Jerry before bailing out. I guessed there would be other Jerry tanks about, and there was.[191]

Lieutenant Stuart Hills, MC, Sherwood Rangers, Nottinghamshire Yeomanry, Royal Armoured Corps. (Author's collection)

189 Delaforce, *The Polar Bears*, p. 73.
190 Hills, *By Tank into Normandy*, p. 103.
191 Thompson, *Victory in Europe*, p. 97.

Major W.N. Richardson, 189th Battery Commander, 69th Field Regiment, Royal Artillery, advanced with the Lincolns when they dug in. As FOO, he called down defensive fire to deter any enemy counter-attack:

> We went forward in the fog. There was a good deal of small arms fire, some Boche but mainly friendly, all unaimed but to some extent dangerous and certainly frightening. As the fog lifted Dick started to shoot regimental and then battery targets at some tanks which he had seen poking their 88mm guns out of the wood at Juvigny. As we shot at them, our 24th Lancers Shermans were lying off in a good position, popping off their 75s at them. The KOYLI went through about lunchtime and with them was Boy Carter and Ken Johnson, BC [Battery Commander] and FOO from 448th Battery. There were a lot of dead Germans, knocked out half-tracks and motorcycles about.[192]

Lieutenant Robert Woolcombe, 11th Royal Scots Fusiliers, moved off to the start line, his men in extended line. When they advanced, he saw dark shapes emerging out of the mist:

> The stray figures in battledress materialised before us, coming back from the battle. Each with levelled bayonets prodding two or three helmetless and sullen, bewildered looking youths in grimy camouflage smocks and trousers. They held up their hands in a resigned way. We stared after them and morale soared. The sight did the world of good to the younger ones among us who had been feeling the strain. Rifle at the hip, safety catches off, we shouted. Two motionless figures were sprawled nearby, we had a glimpse of twisted legs in SS canvas, a crooked arm, a swollen belly, and you looked away. We were past the start line now and moving forward through the corn.[193]

Lieutenant Leslie Skinner, Sherwood Rangers, moved downhill in his Sherman tank into the mist, which thickened the further he went, until visibility was down to a few feet:

> Our only contacts were by radio, and we were at a stand-still, [but] infantry sections near us moved a little further forward and dug-in fast.[194]

Skinner could see that the infantry in the slit trenches lower down the slope were having a rough time of it, so he decided to relieve their suffering by taking down to them water bottles full of rum that he had scrounged from the medical officer. He passed the precious containers to any officers and infantrymen he encountered, who were only too happy to be given some Dutch courage, until the bottles were empty. As he was about to return to his tank, the Germans opened up with heavy concentrations of Spandau fire:

> I had dived into a slit trench and landed on top [of] a young soldier who was somewhat scared by my arrival. Others were dug-in nearby, but in the mist were quite invisible. I assured him the MG fire was way up in the air, [but] he swore at me and to prove his point

---

192 Townend and Baldwin, *Gunners in Normandy*, p. 244.
193 *WW2 Today* <www.ww2today.com> (accessed 18 December 2020).
194 Thompson, *Victory in Europe*, p. 99.

picked up a ration box lid and held it above ground. A burst of MG fire cut it in two. It shook me and I didn't know which of us was the more frightened. When the firing stopped, I moved out, [though] he, poor devil, had to stay. As the mist slowly lifted the attack started moving forward again and casualty collecting began. A mortar shell landed nearby, and a piece of shrapnel got me across the forehead and knocked me out.[195]

Trooper Austin Baker watched from the turret of his Sherman tank as the infantry became pinned down by heavy machine-gun fire, while mortar bombs dropped all around the battlefield with a frighteningly regular precision:

Knocker Bell, the squadron leader, was prowling around on foot, under heavy fire, with a pair of field-glasses around his neck[;] I admired his nerve. A tank on the other side of the field was brewed-up, it was Sergeant Andy Rogers' tank from 1st Troop. We watched as the ammunition inside began to explode, [and] flames and black smoke poured out of the turret. Eric Santer and Cowper bailed out, but Sid Francis was killed[196] and Andy, having been carried away delirious with one leg sliced off, died shortly after.[197] We sprayed the hedge from end to end with Browning fire.[198]

By 0900 hours, visibility improved somewhat and the advance began to speed up. The Hallamshires had reached the western parts of Fontenay when German tanks arrived and began to shell them. Sergeant Williams fired his anti-tank gun at the first tank and it burst into flames. Although wounded, Williams took on the second tank and knocked that out as well.[199] Lieutenant Colonel Trevor Hart-Dyke, commander of the Hallamshires, received orders to contact the Royal Scots Fusiliers on the left flank, and he found them at Fontenay digging in with only 40 men left. Their commander, Lieutenant Colonel Alexander Montgomery-Cuninghame,[200] spoke with Hart-Dyke and informed him of the desperate situation they were in. The Hallamshires at this time were being shelled by the *Hitlerjugend*; mortar bombs fell one after the other on their positions, knocking out the majority of the mortar platoon's carriers before they could dig-in. The ammunition in the carriers exploded, adding to the chaos, and Company Sergeant Major S. Morton was killed. Lieutenant Colonel Hart-Dyke commented:

It was sad to see and hear as the carrier's ammunition and mortar bombs went up. A bomb killed CSM Morton[201] and wounded Lt Brinton, a South African officer. All day

---

195 Thompson, *Victory in Europe*, p. 99.
196 Trooper Sydney Francis, 4/7th Royal Dragoons Guard, was killed in action on 26 June 1944, aged 31. He is buried in Manvieu War Cemetery, France.
197 Sergeant Andrew Rogers, 4/7th Royal Dragoon Guards, died on 26 June 1944, aged 21. He is buried in Tilly-sur-Seulles War Cemetery, France.
198 Thompson, *Victory in Europe*, p. 98.
199 Sergeant Williams was awarded the Military Medal for the action at Tessel Wood.
200 Lieutenant Colonel Alexander William Henry James Montgomery-Cuninghame, 11th Battalion Royal Scots Fusiliers, was killed in action on 3 July 1944, aged 35. He is buried in Manvieu War Cemetery, France.
201 Company Sergeant Major Stanley Morton, Hallamshire Battalion, York and Lancaster Regiment, was killed in action on 26 June 1944, aged 33. He is buried in Bayeux War Cemetery, France.

our doctor, Major Alfred Alexander Gregory-Dean, MD, worked like a trojan under fire. Many ambulances were knocked out working between Les-Haut-Vents and Fontenay, [and] evacuation was no longer possible. Sergeant Goodliffe and his stretcher bearers were heroic, L/Cpl Penn[202] rescued 32 men, 11 of whom he saved under close small arms fire.[203]

Lieutenant Stuart Hills, with the Sherwood Rangers, found the fighting very confused. He was confronted by tanks of the *12. SS-Panzer-Division 'Hitlerjugend'*, many of whom were dug-in to the east of the town. The numbers of British infantry were now decreasing markedly, and the attack eventually ran out of steam by 1600 hours Hills' squadron withdrew to the high ground on Point 102 above Fontenay, where they expected to rest after they had refuelled and replenished their stocks of ammunition. However, an Orders Group was called at 1900 hours and they were informed that the attack would be renewed two hours later. The tank crews who had been fighting all day were not at all happy to hear this unwelcome news. They dragged themselves back to their tanks and began to prepare for the ordeal ahead. Hills remembered:

> Doug Footy and Arthur Reddish put extra tracer rounds into the MG belts[;] we had to be careful of our own infantry straying into our line of fire. Arthur got some grenades in case we were attacked. I was by no means certain that we would be coming back. About 9pm we climbed into our Sherman, warming the engines and marshalling into line. After 15 minutes we moved off into the night, over the crest of Pt 102 and down towards Fontenay.[204]

As the tanks moved forward, the infantry of 147 Brigade were on the right and were advancing with great caution, alert to any strange noises and trying to get their bearings in the darkness. Stuart Hills remembered:

> We passed all the ground we had passed earlier in the day and still there was no response from the enemy [–] perhaps we had taken him by surprise. Then suddenly an MG opened up and the infantry scattered. Bullets hit the tank like the rat-tat-tat of a hammer. I ordered the tank to slew right and Doug Footy opened up with his MG on the enemy positions, and then fired two HE shells which set a two-story [sic] building alight. Gradually we worked our way into the town, [where] the infantry was running in and out of the houses. I then received orders to accompany a Churchill tank to blast a German HQ in a chateau which we duly destroyed. We moved off with Arthur outside of his hatch and holding a Sten-gun to deal with any *Panzerfausts*.[205]

Major John Stirling, 4/7th Royal Dragoon Guards, recalled: "Tanks were being hit all the time by the defensive anti-tank fire coming from the area of Fontenay."[206]

---

202 Lieutenant Colonel Hart-Dyke recommended Lance Corporal Penn for the Victoria Cross, but he was awarded the Distinguished Conduct Medal instead. He was so badly injured in the action that he had to have a leg amputated.
203 Delaforce, *The Polar Bears*, p. 71.
204 Hills, *By Tank to Normandy*, p.104.
205 *WW2: People's War* <www.bbc.co.uk/ww2peopleswar> (accessed 16 December 2020).
206 Stirling, *The First and the Last*, p. 98.

As night fell on 25 June, 146 Brigade, attacking with two battalions, captured Bas-de-Fontenay against stiff opposition, advancing in the afternoon to the edge of the woods that crowned the spur to the north of Vendes. Meanwhile, on the left, 147 Brigade, attacking with a single battalion, found the fortified village of Fontenay a hard nut to crack. They fought hard and suffered many casualties in the battle, but could not get past the northern outskirts of the village. For some reason a second battalion was not ordered forward to bolster the attack until 2100 hours, when most of the village was occupied, but the enemy was still not driven out completely and house-to-house fighting and sniping continued throughout the night.

The German *Heeresgruppe B* reported recent events in this part of the Normandy front as follows:

> After heavy fighting on the severely weakened left of 12th SS Panzer Division, and on the right of Panzer Lehr Division, attacks by successive waves of enemy troops, supported in the air by continuous enemy sorties. Succeeded in tearing open a gap 5km wide and 2km deep.[207]

Lieutenant Colonel Stanley Christopherson, CO of the Sherwood Rangers, remembered the hard fighting at Rauray:

> Days of the most unpleasant fighting followed by misty and wet weather, which at times reduced visibility to nil. The fighting was confused and after the first day the Germans still held the southern edge of the village.[208]

The fight for Tessel Wood and Barbee Farm, 25 June, 1/4th Battalion King's Own Yorkshire Light Infantry

Sergeant Robert Sheldrake, serving with the mortar platoon of the 1/4th KOYLIs sat in his new positions at Le-Parc-de-Boislande as the German artillery began to get their range. The inexperienced troops of the 49th Division looked on, not knowing what to do as the ranging shells slowly crept towards them:

> Our attention was naturally attracted to the first enemy ranging shot which landed 400 yards to the front of the wood. The next came down 100 yards closer in a direct line between the first and our wood. I could see the others wondering what to do as slit trenches had always been a nuisance inflicted on tired troops by officers. Fascinated we watched them, like giant footsteps marching diagonally, marching towards us. I heard cries and the crashing down of undergrowth in the trees as tank men rushed for shelter. I shall never forget the moment I went to earth, I found myself on my hands and knees at the bottom of a tiny slit trench, ramming my head into the ground in an effort to get down a few more inches. Then, as the German gunners found our range, they slammed away at our poor little wood, [and] the

---

207 Ellis, L.F., *Victory in the West, Volume 1, the Battle for Normandy* (London: HMSO, 1962), p. 277.
208 Holland (ed.), *An Englishman at War*, p. 402.

clang of bursting shells and the shrapnel that rained off the trees passed over me as I lay there. When it was over, we were shaken but much wiser, [and] we made for the green fields and dug out new living quarters much further underground.[209]

To the south-west of the attack stood Barbee Farm, which had been turned into a formidable strongpoint by the Germans. Information on the German units stationed there was required by the planners of the attack, so a patrol of picked men – nine other ranks, one corporal and two officers, one of them Canadian – was sent to bring back a prisoner for interrogation. Private Patrick Stafford, 1/4th KOYLIs, was chosen to be part of the patrol. The night before the main attack, they set off in the darkness along a road that ran up the side of Tessel Wood. The Hallamshires held the line only 400 yards from Barbee Farm, so an officer from that unit guided the patrol forward for 100 yards until they reached white tapes that marked the route through a minefield that led to the farm. Stafford stated:

> We started to crawl through no-man's land, crossed a cart track and into a field of standing corn which was opposite our objective. We re-grouped under the closest tree to the farm, speaking in whispers as we were only 50 yards from the German positions. The corporal and a firing section moved off in the direction of the farm.[210]

The firing section disappeared into the darkness and with no word coming back, the officer told Stafford to creep forward, locate the section and return with some information on their progress. Stafford crawled into the gloom:

> With great caution I parted the corn and there stood a German sentry, he was standing side on to me and was easily identifiable by his steel helmet and was no more than 12 feet away. I was certain he had heard me but didn't know where I was. I decided not to fire at him but to return to the officer and report what I had seen.[211]

Private Stafford turned and, keeping as low as possible, quickly crawled back through the corn the way he had come. The Germans, having been alerted that something was happening, opened up with machine-gun fire through the cornfield, tracer rounds flying just above the head of the retreating soldier. More machine guns joined in the cacophony of fire in the hope of deterring the expected attack. Stafford got back to his officer and saw the fire section had returned, explained what he had seen and said it was now impossible to get a prisoner because the Germans were on full alert. As the fire increased, the men were ordered to retire as tracer rounds scythed through the corn: Stafford continued:

> Next the enemy started illuminating the area with flares that lit everything up like day. Now we were being plastered with mortar bombs and a shell exploded near me and blew me over, [and] in my daze I could see all kinds of different colours, how I remained unscathed

---

209 Delaforce, *Marching to the Sound of Gunfire*, pp. 38–39.
210 *WW2: People's War* <www.bbc.co.uk/ww2peopleswar> (accessed 12 December 2017).
211 *WW2: People's War* <www.bbc.co.uk/ww2peopleswar> (accessed 12 December 2017).

was beyond belief. The exploding mortar bombs urged us on ever faster back to our own lines.[212]

Sergeant Robert Sheldrake, with the mortar platoon of the 1/4th KOYLIs, prepared for the move forward with his officer:

> As daylight dawned over the cornfield, we watched our first 25-pounder shells come down on a line of trees across the field to our front. The Guv pointed to a hedge on a bank some 25 yards away, behind which crouched dark shapes and small groups of men: "That's the front-line Shelley, we are the point of the arrow at last, tell everyone to dig like hell because at first light we'll get a hell of a pasting here."[213]

The 1/4th advanced through the 4th Lincolns, with the tanks of the 24th Lancers in support, from the hamlet of Bas-de-Fontenay, west of Fontenay village, and along the Juvigny road on their way to their objective, Walrus, at Tessel Wood on the spur to the north of Vendes. The troops followed a thundering creeping barrage uphill for 100 yards, at which point the Germans launched a heavy *Nebelwerfer* attack on the British infantry and tanks, causing the advance to falter and inflicting many casualties. Eventually, the KOYLIs arrived at the edge of the wood and dug in.

Lieutenant Thomas Canning of D Company, 1/4th KOYIs, had been given the task of taking the enemy-held strongpoint at Barbee Farm, to the south-west of Tessel Wood near Vendes:

> An attack was something to be dreaded by any sane infantryman. [Particularly a] frontal attack in the open, on a heavily defended strongpoint, in daylight. I remember making our way forward in the gloom of early dawn, up to the western side of Tessel Wood to our start line. We turned right and we were facing Barbee Farm, which was 300 yards south-west of us. Between us and the farm were several small fields with thick hedgerows, [and] we advanced with caution to the first hedgerow, [which] was our start line. We lay down glad of the cover the hedgerow gave us, when the enemy opened up and began to plaster the ground behind us. The very ground we had traversed minutes before. We did not escape this stonking without casualties. Just to the right of me was our bugler and three officers synchronizing their watches. Our Company Commander for the attack was Major Derreck Dunnil, MC,[214] [who] had taken over from Major Roberts[215] who had been killed [earlier that day]. I was looking back to the edge of the wood where we had just walked and the shells were falling like rain, they were hitting the ground like machine-gun fire. At this point my stomach felt like lead, [...] akin to a solid weight holding me down.[216]

---

212 *WW2: People's War* <www.bbc.co.uk/ww2peopleswar> (accessed 12 December 2017).
213 *WW2: People's War* <www.bbc.co.uk/ww2peopleswar> (accessed 27 December 2020).
214 Major Derreck Hoyle Dunnil, MC, 1/4th Battalion King's Own Yorkshire Light Infantry, was killed on 4 November 1944. He is buried in Roosendal-en-Nispen Roman Catholic Cemetery, Nord-Brabant, Netherlands.
215 Major Gerald Philip Roberts, 1/4th Battalion King's Own Yorkshire Light Infantry, was killed on 25 June 1944, aged 25. He is buried in Tilly-sur-Seulles War Cemetery, France. His two brothers also died on war service.
216 *WW2: People's War* <www.bbc.co.uk/ww2peopleswar> (accessed 27 December 2020).

German anti-tank gunners of the *12. SS-Panzer-Division 'Hitlerjugend'* wait amongst the ripe corn. (Courtesy of H. Wernemann)

Lance Corporal Geoffrey Steer, 1/4th KOYLIs, recounted the start of the action:

> The Battalion Padre conducted a short service and said "God be with us" just before the barrage started. We gazed up the hill and it was all open fields, no cover at all. Some of our shells dropped short. On the way up we saw dead Germans in the cornfields, but we were also getting a pasting from the German mortars, especially the Moaning Minnies, their six-barrel mortars. It was about 3pm when we finally reached the wood along with the 24th Lancers. A good job too as we were being counter-attacked by enemy tanks, but the Lancers brewed-up two of them and the rest withdrew.[217]

Sergeant Robert Sheldrake took his 1/4th KOYLIs mortar platoon team into action as the Germans responded in kind:

> Our artillery threw over everything they had at Jerry and shells whizzed overhead to come crashing down on the enemy. Our mortars were pumping bombs over and the Brens were puttering away mingled with rapid rifle fire. The rasping quick action rattle of German Spandaus cut into the corn around us, backed up by a heavy stonk on our position. They threw mortar bombs at us and now and again a Moaning Minnie joined in [–] at the moment of release these gave off a weird loud wailing sound calculated to strike terror into us. They shelled us with 88s which reached us almost as soon as we heard the guns fired, [and] the corn wavered and shuddered among the smoke that enveloped all. The whole area quickly became a ragged shell torn corner, dotted here and there with slit-trenches

---

217 Manuscript forwarded to author by H. Chester (Durham, 1991).

in which we cowered and waited. Now and again a Sherman tank would come along, fire a few rounds and then withdraw. It was always our fear that they would run us over. The smiling eyes of the driver, as we desperately waved him aside, was very reassuring. It was no picnic for the tank men as two or three of them were brewing up in the vicinity, adding billowing black oily smoke to a cloudy scene.[218]

Lieutenant Lewis Keeble moved up to Tessel Wood with his young soldiers of the 1/4th KOYLIs, who had not experienced battle before and were having a hard time coping:

> It was bloody murder and people were dropping dead all around. We were there so I sent up the success signal and we start to take *Hitler Jugend* prisoners. There is an ominous looking bunker ahead, but it held no enemy. During the attack one of my platoons ran away and had to be brought back at pistol point by Tug Wilson, my 2 i/c. As we dug-in we heard that [Major] Gerald Roberts had been killed. D Coy had ground to a halt and Tony Little passed through them to the objective.[219]

Lieutenant Robert Stanley Chadwick, 1/4th KOYLIs, advanced and positioned his men on the corner of Tessel Wood facing the north-eastern side:

> Two light tanks were on our left supporting us, then I spotted a Tiger tank under cover. A machine-gun opened up on us and the Tiger opened fire on the supporting tanks. Two shells each put them out of action, [and] one man got out of one of our tanks badly shaken. I ran over to him, but he was shell-shocked, so we passed him on to the medics. The Germans didn't give us any rest, they were continually firing airbursts and machine-gun fire at us.[220]

Lance Corporal Geoffrey Steer moved forward alongside the armoured support:

> Men were falling on all sides. One man of D Company was walking by the side of a tank when a mortar bomb dropped nearby. We hit the deck and heard a scream, and on getting to our feet saw a terrible sight. The lad had been hit by shrapnel that had gone through his ammo pouch where he kept his phosphorous grenades, they all began to burn, and he died terribly within minutes. Times like that were very hard to take.[221]

Lewis Keeble led his reticent raw recruits to the start line:

> It was a hell of a day and was the most exciting day of my life. When we got word, we went down the hill to the village and lay up north of the main road. I tried to march the men to our forming up place on a compass bearing, [but] an RE [Royal Engineers] officer diverted us as a minefield was in our path. We got to the forming up place on time, but H Hour had been postponed. Two members of the company couldn't stand it anymore and had shot

---

218 *WW2: People's War* <www.bbc.co.uk/ww2peopleswar> (accessed 12 June 2016).
219 *WW2: People's War* <www.bbc.co.uk/ww2peopleswar> (accessed 12 September 2016).
220 *WW2: People's War* <www.bbc.co.uk/ww2peopleswar> (accessed 18 December 2020).
221 *War Experience.org* <www.war-experience.org> (accessed 5 January 2021).

themselves in the foot. Off we went when a blast from a shell knocked me over, only a little flesh wound though. Up the hill and through the first hedge, binoculars torn away, and trousers ripped. Where are the boys? Not here. I go back and shout: "Come on!" through the hedge again but still no boys. I go back again: "Come on!" and eventually they came.[222]

Sergeant Rex Flower was given orders by Captain Dixon to go with C Company, 1/4th KOYLIs, on the left to the start line:

We went down that bloody slope like bats out of hell to get to C Coy on time. Down we went into the smoke and dust, death and destruction, bodies and the noise of battle. We reached the cross-roads in Fontenay and there was a very dead German in the middle of the road, flat as a pancake. He was a patch of blood six feet across, and everything had gone over him. We went over him as well, turned right and joined the Juvigny road at a fair clip. I shall never forget the military policeman; he was calmly directing traffic in that frigging lot.[223]

Corporal William Gould, 1/4th KOYLIs, came to the same crossroads and also saw the crushed body in the road:

It was too much for me to bear and I rasped out: "Stop!" The driver obeyed but said in some bewilderment: "Why? It's only a dead German and he's past feeling." I stepped down on the roadway and dragged the mangled body into a ditch. I thought of his mother or wife, and I felt easier in my conscience for this small mark of respect for a fallen enemy. We had become so brutalized in the heat of battle.[224]

Lieutenant Thomas Canning stood up with his men of the 1/4th KOYLIs and in open order made for Barbee Farm on the right flank:

Corporal William Gould, 1/4th Battalion King's Own Yorkshire Light Infantry. (Author's collection)

In all of this mayhem our bugler stood to attention and sounded the attack. I thought that this was a throw-back to a past age, but it was also very inspiring, and we were immediately off to take Barbee Farm. The shells were not falling close to us now but there was small arms fire that built up as we progressed. The noise of heavy gunfire filled the air as we went over this small protective rise and the pace of the advance increased, [while] the men were all firing

222 *WW2: People's War* <www.bbc.co.uk/ww2peopleswar> (accessed 12 September 2016).
223 Newspaper cutting sent to the author by H. Thompson (Cottingham, 1992).
224 W. Gould, correspondence with author (Goole, 1989).

from the hip. The enemy machine-guns had us in their arc of fire and bullets buzzed past me. We were almost there when the enemy fire tightened up on us and the bullets were very close and seemed much faster.[225]

Private John Longfield of the 1/4th KOYLIs was in the advance as shells were falling all around him and his comrades:

> A small splinter hit the man next to me, it went through his foot and came out at the knee, and he was screaming in agony, [so] I called for a stretcher-bearer and carried on up the hill. The tanks of the 24th Lancers were behind me and when they fired the sound was unbelievably loud. I felt as though I was being torn in two. In Tessel Wood, moving through the thick undergrowth, I came across an enormous crater. I was about to shoot a German sitting there on the edge of the crater, his arms resting on his knees. When he raised his arms, I was so horrified at his predicament when I saw he had no hands, that I considered killing him to put him out of his misery. Stretcher-bearers took him away and he survived. We finished the day at the top of the hill pinned down by Spandau fire and I was told to take my Bren-gun and sort it out. Two tanks of the 24th Lancers were then hit. The first tank was by now burning merrily and it was not long before it was red-hot, remaining that way for the rest of the night. The smaller tank also brewed-up and the pair then made a very unpleasant fireworks display.[226]

As the final assault went in to take Barbee Farm, Thomas Canning was hit, but he realised that if he stayed where he was he would still be vulnerable to being hit again by the machine-gun fire that was sweeping the area. He thus ran 20 yards to find cover on the northern side of Barbee Farm, where he slumped to the ground to gather his thoughts and to inspect his wound:

> The bullet had hit me on the back of my hand and had shattered the bones, [and] my index finger was hanging by a piece of skin. At this time another section was passing me, and I took out my field dressing to staunch the flow of blood, [but] I realised that I could not even unfasten it with only one hand. The blood was pouring from me when a corporal from the following section saw my predicament. He stopped for a few seconds to help me and quickly unwrapped [the dressing] and placed it on my hand, telling me to hold it there. While I was doing this, I saw my battledress was ripped at the elbow and that blood was pouring from the rip. I had received another wound I knew nothing about, and the bullet had entered the arm at the elbow and come out six inches down the forearm. I was losing a lot of blood and realised I had to seek medical help.[227]

Private John Longford was in Tessel Wood with the 1/4th KOYLIs when he saw a figure lying in the undergrowth:

---

225 *WW2: People's War* <www.bbc.co.uk/ww2peopleswar> (accessed 27 December 2020).
226 Delaforce, *The Polar Bears*, p. 75.
227 *WW2: People's War* <www.bbc.co.uk/ww2peopleswar> (accessed 27 December 2020).

> I found the youngest lad in the company lying on his back in front of a hedge, with his tin hat over his face. When I lifted it up, I saw that the front of his head was missing and there was a grey mash of brains mixed with blood. The poor lad was only 17 years old, and he had got into the army by falsifying his age, what a dreadful waste.[228]

The mortar platoon of the 1/4th was now positioned in the line just short of the wood. Sergeant Flower and his men found the work of digging-in hard on this hot sunny day: "It was the hottest day up to now, in more ways than one as it was to prove. We got the ammo off the carriers and into the pit and we were all ready for action."

Sergeant J. Bell, serving with the anti-tank platoon of the 1/4th KOYLIs, saw the German counter-attack come in with a number of tanks:

> The Gun-layer identified the tanks as Panthers, I got sighted onto the first tank, the range was about 600 yards, but I got a hit with the first shot. Flames began to pour out of the stricken Panther. I then lay the gun onto the next tank and this also I got with the first shot, [and] it went up in smoke. I gave it another round just for luck. That was three rounds fired so far. The third tank was just about to disappear into the wood, but I had time to fire my fourth round and again scored a hit. This tank also burst into flames. The fourth tank fell to a corporal with a Piat.[229]

Lieutenant Lewis Keeble had just reported back to advanced Headquarters when the counter-attack came in:

> I had only been there for a few minutes when there was a great blast of artillery and machine-gun fire[;] we were being counter-attacked by infantry and two tanks. The same platoon ran away again. Tug got the spare Bren off the carrier, and I got the spare two-inch mortar and the CSM fed us with ammunition. This somewhat unconventionally composed battlegroup put down some pretty rapid fire. I thought our remaining forward platoon was likely to be overwhelmed and got the rear platoon organised to counter-attack if this happened. The enemy eventually retired leaving two knocked out tanks and quite a lot of dead. I was sure they would return and kept the company 'stood to' all night. It was during our time at Tessel Wood that exhaustion began to bite [–] the oldest and youngest were the worst affected.[230]

On the opposite side, *Hauptsturmführer* Seigel of the *'Hitlerjugend'* watched the performance of his young *Panzergrenadiere* with pride during the battle:

> During the enemy artillery strikes they sheltered in their trenches, often for half an hour at a time. They endured a hail of shell splinters, which were joined by branches from the explosions in treetops and chunks of brick from the ruined buildings. At the moment when the enemy's infantry fire heralded their attack, the grenadiers rose up out of their trenches

---

228 *WW2: People's War* <www.bbc.co.uk/ww2peopleswar> (accessed 27 December 2020).
229 Delaforce, *Marching to the Sound of Gunfire*, p. 50.
230 *Scholars Page Wilfrid Laurier University* <www.scholars.wlu.ca> (accessed 12 December 2020).

Gunners of the 55th Anti-tank Regiment, Royal Artillery. (Courtesy of *The War Illustrated*, December 1944)

and machine-guns and steel helmets faced the enemy. There was no shooting until the enemy, with flat helmets, were moving about in the chaos of the houses and streets, as ammunition was limited. But when they were almost within touching distance, bursts of machine-gun fire came from the German trenches they thought to be destroyed.[231]

All day the tanks of the 24th Lancers continued to sufferer heavy casualties as mortar fire was directed upon them. Enemy tanks added to their problems, but the Lancers and the anti-tank gunners engaged many of them successfully. The Lancers held their nerve and remained in their positions protecting the Yorkshiremen. The anti-tank guns of the 218th Battery, 55th Anti-tank Regiment, came forward to strengthen the front line just in time as the *12. SS-Panzer-Division 'Hitlerjugend'* launched a counter-attack on C Company's sector. Sergeant Flower recalled: "At 1700 hours the vicious crash of artillery fire spoilt my reverie; shells were dropping all over the field and they were enemy ones. The long-awaited counterattack was upon us. We kept firing and firing." This determined counter-attack was eventually beaten off, and Flower and his men spent the night in the positions they had defended: "In the baleful flickering light of burning tanks, amid the smoke and smell of battle, we spent the night there just in case Jerry came again, [but] he didn't."

Lance Corporal Geoffrey Steer, 1/4th KOYLIs, settled into his new position for the night but could not relax as the Germans were still sending over harassing fire into the British line:

> Making my way through a hedge I saw the grub wagon approaching, [then] suddenly Jerry opened up with 88s. There was a terrific bang and clouds of smoke and dust as part of the

---

231 Manuscript forwarded to author by H. Werncmann (Germany, 1987).

hedge fell on top of me. I dived into a trench, [where] there was already a lad at the bottom asleep. I lay still and heard the next two salvoes coming in, but they went over to the road. The lad under me was going berserk and when I got out, he ran down the hill. I never saw him again, [and] later reports said he was bomb happy.[232]

An observation post a little further along the line from Steer had been hit, and a wounded man came staggering by:

> His boot toecap was missing, shot off by shrapnel, and his toes were bleeding. He said: "Never mind me, see to the others." They had dug-in before a hedgerow and when the shells exploded into the trees the blast came down into the trench. The toll was 4 dead and two wounded. Major Little came across and was very upset, [and] he asked if we would do the honours for the dead. We dug a new trench for them[;] now you could say we were in a graveyard, with crosses on each side of us.[233]

Private Vernon Church of the 68th Anti-tank Regiment recalls the terrifying effect of the German barrage at night:

> The wood was frightening at night times in the Bren-carrier, because the road sloped away very steeply to the side. We were mortared and shelled, and I remember laying on the ground and hearing the sound of shrapnel whizzing through the trees. I was laid down holding my tin hat on, not knowing where the next one was going to land. The loud whizzing sound was the most frightening part.[234]

Rex Flower helped bury the dead at Barbee Farm:

> The bodies had been left in the hot sun and the stench was awful, indescribable. It was a terrible thing to see them now, [as] they had once been young men in the prime of life. There was a number of Germans, grotesque in their tight-fitting helmets, their heads swollen. It was a charnel house. We started burying them from the right. The enemy had a nasty habit of putting grenades under corpses, even their own, and when somebody went to bury them, instead of burying him, they joined him. They were lousy swine.[235]

The fighting around and in Tessel Wood was brutal in the extreme. A report sent by the *Panzer-Lehr-Division* that was intercepted by British intelligence stated that the division had suffered heavy losses on the first day of fighting. One soldier of the 1/4th KOYLIs remembered: "The order came to us while we were at Tessel Wood – No prisoners!" After this action, the men of the 49th Division were referred to as the "Polar Bear Butchers" by Lord Haw-Haw.[236]

---

232 *War Experience.org* <www.war-experience.org> (accessed 5 January 2021).
233 *War Experience.org* <www.war-experience.org> (accessed 5 January 2021).
234 V. Church, correspondence with author (Leeds, 1994).
235 Delaforce, *Marching to the Sound of Gunfire*, p. 85.
236 William Brooke Joyce was an American-born British Fascist and traitor who broadcast Nazi propaganda from Germany to Britain throughout the war. Each broadcast would begin with

The German command believed that the attack on 25 June by the 49th West Riding Division was the main assault, not a preliminary to Operation Epsom. They ordered the immediate movement of reserves to the area to bolster the badly battered ranks of the *Panzer-Lehr-Division*. The commander of the *12. SS-Panzer-Division 'Hitlerjugend'*, *SS-Standartenführer* Kurt Meyer, questioned the movement of his precious panzer units as he had received information that the main attack would come elsewhere:

> That evening the Corps ordered the deployment of our last tank battalion to restore the situation in that sector the next morning. The *Panzer Lehr Division* was to be assisted at all costs. I asked that the order be rescinded. The Chief of Staff's graphic situation report that friendly reconnaissance had identified the staging of strong enemy forces, especially armour, in the sector of *SS Panzer Grenadier Regiment 26* did not influence the Corps to change their order. My remark that an enemy tank attack was expected at any moment and the *2nd SS Panzer Regiment 12* was in a very favourable defensive position was also dismissed. And so it was, that on 26th June there was not a single tank in the divisional sector.[237]

By the evening of 25 June, the men of the badly mauled 49th West Riding Division had fought their way forward against a determined defence, but were still short of their main objective, the village of Rauray and the high ground beyond. The hot, sunny summer weather was about to change and dark heavy clouds began to envelop the area.

The Battle of Fontenay, 26 June (Walrus Line), 1/7th Battalion Duke of Wellington's Regiment

The 11th Royal Scots Fusiliers of 147 Brigade arrived at Fontenay-le-Pesnel, where there had been fierce fighting on the 25th. The village was being defended by *III/SS-Panzergrenadier Regiment 26* of the *12. SS-Panzer-Division 'Hitlerjugend'*. During the day, the German units had been reinforced by two companies of the *21. Panzer-Division* and by elements of the *Panzer-Lehr*. They had repulsed the British attacks on the northern suburbs of the village, and artillery duels from both sides were taking place, creating even more chaos and destruction. The German line had been pushed back but remained unbroken.

SS-Standartenführer Meyer, CO of the *'Hitlerjugend'*, had been at his divisional headquarters the night before:

> The burning front presented a ghostly picture. The remnants of some trucks were smouldering on the Caen/Villers Bocage road, they were supposed to be bringing ammunition to the front. Fighter bombers had relieved them of their responsibility. The ammunition exploded some meters behind the front.[238]

"Germany Calling". He was given the name Lord Haw-Haw by the British. He was hanged in Wandsworth Prison on 3 January 1946 and buried in Ireland.
237 Meyer, *Grenadiers*, p. 234.
238 Meyer, *Grenadiers*, p. 242.

His meeting with other panzer commanders was not a happy one, as they all knew that a catastrophe was in the making. This static form of warfare north of the River Orne could only result in the destruction of the panzer divisions that were deployed there. Meyer commented:

> The tactical fixing along the battlefield had cost us the irreplaceable blood of our best soldiers and was destroying precious equipment. Up to that point we had not received a single replacement for our wounded or killed soldiers, or a single tank or artillery piece. After a few hours' sleep we were dragged back to reality by the noise of the front.[239]

With a sense of foreboding, Meyer returned to his beloved division at Fontenay, where the battle had already begun:

> I returned to the *III/SS-Panzergrenadier Regiment 26*, [and found] the left flank of the division was in danger and heavy fire was falling on the whole battalion sector. You could hardly recognise Fontenay, [as] screaming rounds were tearing the last buildings to pieces. Each attack on the village had been repulsed up to that point. Communications with the companies was broken and the smoke from exploding projectiles obscured the view. It was impossible to determine the main defensive line.[240]

The main task of Private Cecil Heald, a Bren-gunner with the 11th Royal Scots Fusiliers, was to give covering fire to an anti-tank crew while they were stalking German tanks:

> We had reached a road junction to the east of Fontenay Church, and we were to cover the road. A short distance away was a small bridge over a stream, we heard the noise of tank engines revving up and saw three tanks approaching. The detachment commander, a L/Sgt, called his gun crew to action stations, then we waited until the first tank was on the bridge. The order to fire was given and L/Cpl Taffy Williams fired, destroying the first tank which blocked the bridge. The second tank turned to the left, exposing its tracks to the gunners. Taffy fired again, blowing off the track, and his second shot destroyed it completely. By now we were under heavy fire from the third tank which was reversing to the rear. Taffy was wounded and we carried him to a farmhouse where we dug in for the night in an orchard.[241]

Lieutenant David Render of the Sherwood Rangers had dismounted from his tank to talk to Captain Neville Fearn, and as he scrambled onto Fearn's tank a movement to his right caught his attention:

> Travelling proud above the top of a high banked hedge that flanked the road that I had just left was the head and shoulders of a tank commander motoring back towards the village. For a moment I thought it must have been one of C Squadron's tanks, as they were securing the higher ground ahead of us. Then I caught sight of the distinctive headgear the man was

---

239 Meyer, *Grenadiers*, p. 242.
240 Meyer, *Grenadiers*, p. 242.
241 Manuscript forwarded to author by A. Chester (Hull, 1991).

wearing and the field grey flash of the tank's paint. The hat was the black, silver edged, side cap, favoured by panzer commanders and the man wearing it was commanding a Tiger tank. "Shit," I said to Fearn, "it's a bloody Jerry and he is heading straight for the crossroads and A Squadron!" I was already yelling at the crew to turn and aim as I took the side of the tank at a sprint and hauled myself into the turret. I screamed at the driver to get into Fontenay as I scrambled for the headset and microphone to send a warning to Semken over the radio. We broke back onto the road and headed, at full tilt, into the village when I heard the first rounds of tank fire ring out and saw billowing smoke less than 200 yards ahead of me on the other side of the crossroads.[242]

The 1/7th Duke of Wellington's was now given the task of clearing the village of Fontenay, the first objective being St Nicholas Farm just beyond Fontenay on the road to Rauray. At 2100 hours, the Duke of Wellington's left their start line, supported by the tanks of the Sherwood Rangers and the mortars and machine guns of five platoons of the 2nd Kensingtons. The wrecked village had been under attack for 16 hours, and the troops fought their way into the ruins in the first hour of the assault.

Kurt Meyer, commanding *'Hitlerjugend'*, was in Fontenay and has left a vivid account of the hell that had been created there:

> The village was like a simmering cauldron, [as] heavy rounds drilled deep into the earth and left smoking craters behind. Based on an old soldiers' saying: "A round does not hit the same crater twice" I jumped into a crater and watched the enemy tanks attack Fontenay. Firing continuously and feeling secure, the steel colossi were moving slowly towards the rubble of Fontenay. Our anti-tank guns were destroyed by the insane artillery fire. The Panzer grenadiers held their *Panzerfauste* tightly, man against machine, what contrast and what a heroic spirit this contrast revealed. The first tank was smoking by that point, and I could see how the soldiers were leaping onto the vehicles. The enemy artillery was firing over our heads and tank rounds were spitting above us.[243]

The German armour gathered for a counter-attack as the British armour fought the *panzergrenadiere* in the rubble of Fontenay. The German armoured force crossed the Fontenay–Cheux road amid the thunder of battle and a tank-versus-tank combat ensued. As both sides took casualties, thick, black oily smoke from stricken tanks rolled over the battlefield. The ferocious action ebbed back and forth among the rubble for the whole day, neither side wishing to concede defeat. Kurt Meyer, always one to take risks by being at the front, advanced behind the tank of one of his company commanders, *Obersturmführer* Ruckdeschel, as battle-weary soldiers shouted greetings to him amid a storm of steel. The company commander's tank received a direct hit, the top hatch flew open and smoke gushed out of the turret, followed shortly by the tank commander. Meyer recalled:

---

242 Render, *Tank Action*, pp. 115–16.
243 Meyer, *Grenadiers*, p. 242.

Troops of the 1/7th Battalion Duke of Wellington's Regiment enter Fontenay. (Courtesy of *The War Illustrated*, December 1944)

> He staggered towards us, stumbled and collapsed; a panzer grenadier pulled him behind the remains of a wall. We then realised that *SS-Obersturmführer* Ruckdeschel had lost an arm, [and] the bleeding stump was bound up and a medic summoned.[244]

The German grenadiers and well-camouflaged panzers repulsed the British attacks and held on until the evening. After a heavy artillery barrage, the British infantry then attacked again and took the village and the ground beyond. The tanks of the Sherwood Rangers advanced to the crossroads north of Rauray, and the position was consolidated when the 11th Durhams arrived late that night.

Lieutenant David Render described the sights encountered in the village of Fontenay by the Sherwood Rangers:

> The scattered houses of Fontenay had been badly knocked about by our own artillery and I noticed how the stout Norman farm buildings had been incorporated into the German defences as strong points. A number of dead Germans lay, wax like and stiff, around their former positions. There was no sign of their armour that had been dug in among the houses and outbuildings. Files of our own weary infantry marched by the side of our tanks or were digging into the side of the road for safety.[245]

---

244 Meyer, *Grenadiers*, p. 243.
245 Render, *Tank Action*, p. 115.

Lieutenant Colonel Stanley Christopherson of the Sherwood Rangers remembered the poor weather conditions at Fontenay at the time:

> It was the most unpleasant fighting, in the most appalling misty wet weather, which at times reduced visibility to nil. B Squadron started off supporting the Royal Scots Fusiliers on the right, and C Squadron the Duke of Wellingtons on the left; A Squadron remained in reserve. The fighting in Fontenay was most confused, and after the first day the Germans still held the southern end of the village, which was finally cleared on the following morning.[246]

Lieutenant Stuart Hills of the Sherwood Rangers also commented on the fighting around Fontenay:

> The fighting had been heavy and unpleasant, something to which the steadily mounting casualty toll bore witness. The quality of the German resistance had been predictably good; these were troops from crack panzer divisions who had already gained much experience in Russia. We had also been handicapped by low cloud, which prevented our usual close air support from flying.[247]

A patrol moved cautiously forward towards Tessel-Brettevillette, and although the village had been attacked by rocket-firing aircraft during the day, it was found to be crawling with German infantry, the woods nearby being held by a number of tanks.

Rauray, 26 June

A new attack was now planned in a south-easterly direction, the starting point being the Juvigny–Fontenay road towards the heavily fortified village of Rauray. However, before Rauray could be taken there were three strongpoints that would have to be eliminated: St Nicholas Farm, Le Grande Ferme and Le Manoir. The main attack would then advance on Rauray. The 1st Tyneside Scottish was to lead the advance from the north of Tessel Wood, 1,000 yards south-east of La Grande Ferme, supported by the Sherman tanks of the 4/7th Royal Dragoon Guards. The 12th Battalion King's Royal Rifle Corps (KRRC) would secure the open right flank, aided by the tanks of the 24th Lancers.

Lance Corporal Anthony Hughes, a wireless operator in A Squadron, 24th Lancers, moved off with the KRRC:

> We were to exploit towards the villages of Le Manoir and Tessel-Brettevillette in support of the Motor Battalion, 12th King's Royal Rifle Corps, 5 Troop leading. At first light snipers were discovered in the hedges around our position and the first hour was spent

---

246 Holland (ed.), *An Englishman at War*, p. 402.
247 Hills, *By Tank to Normandy*, p. 109.

flushing them out. At about 9am we advanced along the road which ran down the east side of Tessel Wood. As was our practice the troop leader's tank was leading.[248]

At 0650 hours, the men of the 1st Tyneside Scottish stood up and began their advance, A Company marching off as the regimental piper played. Before them, enemy tanks were cleverly concealed in dug-in positions. Snipers were also waiting for the attack: the Scots had fallen into a German trap. A major disadvantage for the operation was the absence of a heavy bombardment in support of the infantry attack; most of 49th West Riding Division's firepower had been transferred to the main Epsom attack in support of VIII Corps. The consequences of this were soon felt as the first waves came under heavy fire from German tanks, mortars and machine guns. Concentrated Spandau fire forced the attacking infantry to go to ground, but the area they took cover in had been registered by the German artillery, and mortar and *Nebelwerfer* fire was poured upon them. Rockets and mortar bombs exploded in the trees, showering the British with shrapnel and splinters, which caused more casualties.

Private P. Lawton of the 1st Tyneside Scottish was just 18 years old and had not experienced combat, but his baptism of fire was about to commence:

> We moved forward in open order across a field and took up positions along a hedgerow and ditch. The field in front of us was littered with debris, dead cattle and a knocked-out Sherman. Shells and mortar bombs were bursting all around us. I think we found the airburst shells particularly disturbing. I know that I was worried in case a piece of shrapnel drove part of my helmet into my skull. I am sure that many other soldiers must have been troubled by such irrational thoughts in these traumatic times.[249]

Several Sherman tanks of the 4/7th Royal Dragoon Guards fell victim to the German anti-tank gunners. Try as they might, the British armour could not break through the tall hedgerows. The attack had lost its impetus by 1120 hours at a cost of 48 casualties and six tanks. Under cover of smoke, the Dragoon Guards withdrew back to Point 102.

Major John Stirling, 4/7th Royal Dragoon Guards, had moved forward with the Tyneside Scottish in the direction of Tessel-Brettevillette when he saw a German self-propelled gun manoeuvring in the grounds of a farm. His tank fired six high-explosive rounds at it and he thought that was enough to silence it. Sergeant Harris then reported over the air that he was being fired on from the farm and Stirling made the long-since famous last words "It's alright it's only a mortar":

> I saw a flash from above the village and the next moment a shell hit our turret with a terrific bang. After that everything was vague and ponderous like a dream. I heard Murphy shout: "Bale out, bale out." It seemed cowardly to leave the tank when we could still fight. Then I saw the gun mantle spinning slowly down the gun with a great hole in it. I realised the tank was useless and that we must bale out. I struggled upward and I was halfway out when I saw the flash again and again that terrible crash as we were hit. Something hit me in the

---

248 Doherty, R., *Normandy 1944 – the Road to Victory* (Kent: Spellmount, 2004), p. 178.
249 Manuscript forwarded to author by P. Cuerden (Hampshire, 1994).

back, and I was flung to the ground. I got up and hobbled about, [and] I was alone. The tank was on fire now and from inside the turret came the screams like a trapped animal. I got up on the front, both drivers' hatches were open and empty. Murphy's hands were grasping upwards, I caught them in mine and pulled: "Come on Murphy" I almost whispered, his eyes were closed and sightless and where his legs used to be hung two little black charred stumps. His hands were limp and clammy in the last nervous convulsions of death that was spreading a yellow stain across his face.[250] The operator was lying peacefully dead on the floor.[251]

Captain John Sinclair Highmore, 1st Tyneside Scottish, saw a group of German soldiers working their way towards an anti-tank gun position, under cover of a hedgerow:

They were engaged with small arms fire which would have been pretty ineffective because of the valley between the high banks topped with trees and thick hedging. I remember climbing onto a Sherman tank of the 24th Lancers parked in the Company HQ area, another one had been knocked out by this time. I asked the commander if he could fire a few rounds of HE to explode in the branches of the trees above the ditch and stop the enemy filtration. He obliged effectively because nothing further developed from that hedge.[252]

Corporal J.W.H. Tipler, 1st Tyneside Scottish, witnessed a tank being struck:

A squadron of tanks joined us at Tessel Wood, and during one stonk I saw one of them suddenly blazing from the open cupola[;] one man got out of the driver's compartment, and another came out of the turret. Both dropped to the ground and their mates went to help them.[253]

Private Robert Nixon was in reserve with the 1st Tyneside Scottish near Fontenay and watched the Sherman tanks advance. He was very frightened as this was his first action, but the sight of the armour pressing forward so confidently raised his spirits. Nixon's unit was mortared heavily, and he and several of his comrades were wounded by shrapnel and machine-gun fire. They were taken back to the RAP. Nixon commented: "Of about 12 Dundee blokes in my company only two of us came out alive."[254]

On the right flank, the 12th KRRC reached Le Manoir Farm and the 24th Lancers engaged Panther tanks that were in the area. Lieutenant Anthony Hughes of the 24th Lancers remembered when his Sherman was hit in the melee:

---

250 Trooper Edward Murphy, 4/7th Royal Dragoon Guards, Royal Armoured Corps, died on 28 June 1944, aged 35. He is buried in St Manvieu War Cemetery, France.
251 Stirling, J.D.P., *The First and the Last, The Story of the 4/7th Royal Dragoon Guards 1939–1945* (London: Art and Educational Publishers, 1946), p. 106.
252 Kite, B., *Stout Hearts, The British and Canadians in Normandy, 1944* (Solihull: Helion & Co, 2016), p. 74.
253 Baverstock, K., *Breaking the Panzers* (Gloucestershire: Sutton Publishing, 2002), p. 36.
254 R. Nixon, correspondence with author (Hartlepool, 1996).

> A tank behind us radioed that there was a tank in the hedge on our right. I looked through my periscope and saw a puff of smoke from the hedge about 40 or 50 yards away. The gunner yelled that we had been hit. Next thing I knew the whole turret was ablaze, [and] there was a blinding white flash. I remember struggling through the hatch and I think I succeeded in getting the whole of my body out when the tank blew up and I found myself on the other side of the hedge with a shower of flaming objects all around and I crawled as fast as I could away from the tank and into a slit-trench.[255]

Lieutenant Hughes was burned badly about the face but survived. Others were not so lucky and perished in that struggle. Because of the lack of success on their left and the precarious situation they were in, the KRRC was ordered to withdraw.

Corporal John Cropper, 24th Lancers, remembered the constant pressure to get forward and the encouragement he received from his superiors to do so:

> The basic tactic seemed to be to press on. We constantly seemed to be pushing forward and then pulling back to refuel and rearm. The most common type of message picked up on the net at that time was: "Press on, there's nothing in front of you, intelligence says there's nothing there", followed by: "Fuck intelligence, who the hell's shooting at me if there's nothing there?"[256]

Lieutenant Anthony Richardson, an artillery FOO, was with the Rifle Corps forward units:

> The first thing was to range on the church, [and] using close target procedure I got onto the church and ordered 90 rounds of gunfire at 5 second intervals to support the advance across the field. The battalion attack was stopped in a fold in the ground not far from the church. I asked if I could have the support of the whole regiment to get them onto the objective. This I was granted provided I range each battery separately as there were other troops nearby. This I did and was ready to fire when the CO said he wanted to withdraw the battalion, so I ordered the regiment to fire smoke instead of HE. Two rounds gunfire followed by six rounds gunfire at 60 seconds intervals produced the most wonderful smokescreen and the whole battalion was successfully withdrawn without any further casualties.[257]

At 1600 hours, the day's action was brought to a close and the Tyneside Scottish pulled back 3 miles to Haut d'Audrieu. The men were marched to the rear in single file, with a lone piper playing a lament. The casualties had been heavy for the attacking companies.

Trooper Austin Baker, a wireless operator with the 4/7th Royal Dragoon Guards, felt disheartened at the lack of progress:

> The whole squadron was now in the field with the tanks scattered around by the hedges. We soon discovered from the wireless that we were in a trap. There appeared to be Tigers and Panthers all around us, there were about six on the high ground ahead, four in the edge

---

255 Doherty, *Normandy 1944*, p. 178.
256 J. Cropper, correspondence with author (Nottingham, 1993).
257 Townend and Baldwin, *Gunners in Normandy*, pp. 245–46.

of the wood just across the field to our left. Between them they covered all the gaps. The hours dragged by, and in our tank we sat without saying much, listening intently to what was going on over the wireless. I was eating boiled sweets by the dozen and the others were smoking furiously. I don't know how long we had been sitting there when the tank behind us was hit, it was Joe Davis's tank, [and] I saw a spout of earth shoot up near it as a shot ricocheted through it. Some smoke curled up from the turret, but it didn't actually brew up. The whole of the turret crew had been killed. Brian Sutton and his co-driver bailed out. Six of the squadron were killed that day. In Lilly's crew Fairman[258] had been killed inside the tank and Digger James had been blown apart by a mortar bomb as he jumped off the turret.[259] Charison was badly burned, and George Varley was rumoured to be dead. One of Thompson's crew, Jackie Birch,[260] had been shot through the head by a King's Royal Rifle Corps man who mistook him for a Jerry after he had bailed out. The Tyneside Scottish came back across the field in single file, led by a piper who was playing what sounded like a lament. I just felt lucky to be alive that day.[261]

Sergeant Robert Sheldrake of the mortar platoon of the 1/4th KOYLIs, looked on at the scene around him and commented on the experience of war:

Hell-fire Corner had been the scene of many clashes with the enemy and many of their dead were strewn across the road. Who was fool enough to stay there long enough to move them? As tanks and carriers passed to-and-fro they charged over these bodies, churning them to a pulp of flesh and rag. I saw one carrier make a skid turn on the corner and strip the skin backwards over a ghastly trunk until the flesh lay exposed, vividly pink and shining. For a brief moment it arched as if in living torment before it slumped back into the ignominy and desecration of the mud. So, this is war, here was no glory, no proudness, but a bloody mashing and pulping of human beings. The ordinary man's war cannot be glorified; necessary it may be, but it is vile in the extreme.[262]

At 0930 hours the same day, on the divisional left flank, a second assault was being launched by 1/7th Duke of Wellington's, supported by the tanks of C Squadron of the Sherwood Rangers and the guns of the divisional artillery. As the barrage thundered down on the enemy lines, the Duke of Wellingtons sat in their trenches on the outskirts of Fontenay. They then stood up on the start line and moved across the open ground in the direction of St Nicholas Farm, their objective. The farm was held by the *VI/SS-Panzergrenadier Regiment 26, 12. SS-Panzer-Division 'Hitlerjugend'*. It had been turned into a formidable strongpoint by the Germans, its walls concealing tanks and anti-tank crews who waited patiently until the barrage had passed.

---

258 Lance Corporal Frederick Ernest Fairman, 4/7th Royal Dragoon Guards, Royal Armoured Corps, was killed in action on 26 June 1944, aged 25. He is buried in St Manvieu War Cemetery, France.
259 Trooper Edward Ernest James, 4/7th Royal Dragoon Guards, Royal Armoured Corps, was killed in action on 26 June 1944, aged 24. He is buried in St Manvieu War Cemetery, France.
260 Trooper John William Birch, 4/7th Royal Dragoon Guards, Royal Armoured Corps, was killed in action on 26 June 1944, aged 20. He is buried in St Manvieu War Cemetery, France.
261 Delaforce, *The Polar Bears*, p. 81.
262 R. Sheldrake, correspondence with author (Preston, 1991).

In the area around the farm, the *'Hitlerjugend'* waited for the attackers. The most terrific German fire came down on the advancing infantry and tanks, who fought back as much as was possible while mortar bombs and shells rained down upon them. Having advanced only 300 yards under such intense fire, it became impossible for them to go any further. What was left of both companies retired to their starting point at Fontenay.

The battlefield was a blazing charnel house of burnt-out tanks and torn bodies, a scene of great desolation. By midday on the 26th, all of the morning attacks had failed.

At 1550 hours, a new assault was ordered, to be launched by A and B Companies of the 1/7th Duke of Wellington's and the tanks of the Sherwood Rangers. The CO of the Sherwood Rangers, Lieutenant Colonel Stanley Christopherson, called a conference to enable the infantry and gunners to synchronise their timetable for the battle. Before the attack began, Major John Semken of the Sherwood Rangers drove his Sherman down the main street of Fontenay and was immediately confronted by a German Tiger tank. Luckily, they had been alerted that enemy tanks had been seen in the vicinity and the tank gunner had a round in the breech just in case as they rounded a corner and the monster came into sight. Fellow Sherwood Ranger Lieutenant Stuart Hills recalled the incident:

> As they cleared Fontenay they were suddenly confronted by an enormous tank coming round the bend in front. It was hard to know who was most surprised, but John shrieked: "Fire it's a Hun!" and they fired off several rounds into the smoke. As this smoke cleared away it was observed that the crew was baling out of the Tiger as small flames appeared to come from the inside of the tank. It was a Tiger of the 12th SS Panzer Division Hitler Jugend and the first Tiger to be captured in Normandy. It made an impressive sight at close quarters as both size and thickness of armour became apparent. 'A' Squadron squeezed past the Tiger and into a field on the right where they deployed.[263]

As Lieutenant David Render, Sherwood Rangers, waited for the off in his Sherman, he could see clearly before him the debris of the earlier attack:

> The infantry of the DWR [Duke of Wellington's Regiment] formed up next to us, crouching on one knee with their spiked pig-sticker bayonets fixed to the ends of their rifles. The patchy fog that had plagued C Squadron throughout the day finally began to lift and the early evening sun reflected off the ripening corn ahead of us. C Squadron had already secured the start-line for us, but they had lost two tanks in the process and their knocked-out hulls continued to burn. One smudged the sky with an ominous thick oily smokestack. I wondered whether the crews had got out and had they been badly burned. My own crew was apprehensive and tense as we waited for the artillery to commence firing.[264]

At 1530 hours, the British barrage began as the 1/7th Duke of Wellington's and their support tank crews looked on. The main attack went in at 1550 hours, the tanks and infantry pressing on to their objective, St Nicholas Farm, which was soon captured.

---

263 Hills, *By Tank into Normandy*, pp. 107–08.
264 Render, *Tank Action*, p. 119.

Stuart Hills was accompanying the infantry in his Sherman:

> During the next two hours we systematically shot up every hedgerow as we advanced. Some of John Sempkin's[265] tanks were Fireflies and they started knocking out one German tank after another. Sergeant George Dring, MM,[266] claimed no less than four himself. A Panther was shot up by the whole squadron as it drove across our front, its crew baling out as it was still moving. The German infantry started to surrender, leaping out of the ground under the noses of the tanks, while our own infantry came up to finish things off. 13 Panzer IVs had been knocked out along with a Tiger and a Panther. In spite of the casualties, we had won a tank battle against significant opposition, and this gave our confidence an important boost.[267]

Sergeant George Dring, MM and Bar, Sherwood Rangers, Nottinghamshire Yeomanry, Royal Armoured Corps. (Author's collection)

Stanley Christopherson advanced in his Sherman tank to the village:

> The squadron had a most successful shoot and knocked out approximately 13 Enemy tanks, of which Sergeant Dring bagged four. A Squadron completed the last part of the attack without infantry support over very open ground, finally finding itself on the outskirts of the village among a platoon of German infantry, well dug-in and refusing to surrender.[268]

Lieutenant Colonel Stanley Christopherson, DSO, MC, Sherwood Rangers, Nottinghamshire Yeomanry, Royal Armoured Corps. (Author's collection)

265 Major John Semken was awarded the Military Cross for the action at Rauray and the American Silver Star in late 1944. He was awarded the CB in 1980 and the Legion D'Honneur in 2015. He died at the age of 95 on 8 March 2016 and his obituary appeared in the *Telegraph* on 14 April 2016.
266 Sergeant George Dring, MM and Bar, was given the nickname of 'Killer' by his comrades because of his uncanny knack of hunting down German tanks and knocking them out. For the Rauray action he was recommended for the DCM, but was instead awarded a bar to his Military Medal. His war service affected him badly and for years he would not speak of it. He died at the age of 85 and his obituary appeared in *The Telegraph* on 14 March 2003.
267 Hills, *By Tank to Normandy*, p. 108.
268 Holland (ed.), *An Englishman at War*, p. 402.

Captain R.P. Grellis, with the lead troop of the Sherwood Rangers, hurled grenades at the German troops in an effort to dislodge them, but to no avail. Frustrated that his best efforts were producing no results, he dismounted his tank, pistol in hand, and forced them to surrender. Lieutenant Colonel Christopherson commented:

> In his excitement he forgot, as so often happened, to switch his wireless from the regimental external frequency to his tank internal communication, both of which work off the same set. As a result, the whole regiment heard the most thrilling and enthralling conversation between him and his crew and appreciated the shouts of encouragement from his crew as he dealt with the Germans.[269]

Lieutenant David Render received the order "All stations advance!" and the tanks lurched forward, with the infantry on either side tramping through the waist-high corn:

> As we fanned out, we crushed the crops flat with our tracks. We stopped to plaster every hedge in front of us with 15 minutes of HE and machine-gun fire before moving forward another bound. Despite our speculative fire and the artillery fire that preceded it, a German Spandau opened up from the bottom of the hedge. The infantry went to ground and stayed down, [which] was our cue to get forward and deal with it. The MG42 fire rattled off the side of the tank like a jackhammer. I ordered Martin to fire three rounds of HE to airburst in the foliage above the machine-gun nest. The explosive force of the fragmenting rounds and a few belts of 30-calibre fire were enough to silence them. We moved forward cautiously when suddenly there was a blur of movement to our front, as field-grey clad figures broke from the corner of the hedge line in a desperate bid to get away from our troop of tanks. Our tank machine-guns burst into life, cutting them down in a hail of bullets. I watched in fascinated admiration as the crew worked like a well-oiled automatic machine, as practised drill and killer instinct combined to deadly effect. The inside of the tank was a thick haze, but the job was done, and the riddled remains of several Germans lay sprawled face down along the line of the hedges.[270]

The attacking troops of the Duke of Wellington's were now in among the enemy dugouts, stabbing, firing and hurling grenades in order to kill or eject any Germans who were still hiding. Those who survived staggered out into the light in a dazed state with their hands raised, fully expecting to be shot; many were spared but others were not as the momentum of the assault swept through the enemy positions. The adrenaline-fuelled frenzy of an infantry attack was a wild affair and many men took revenge for their dead comrades who had fallen in the rush forward.

David Render watched from his tank turret as a young SS trooper was dragged out roughly from a bunker by furious infantrymen, his face swollen and bloody from the beating of rifle butts and boots he had received as he was captured. Lieutenant Render commented:

---

269 Holland (ed.), *An Englishman at War*, pp. 402–03.
270 Render, *Tank Action*, p. 120.

He was probably no more than 18 years old and was clearly angry that he had been captured. A Teutonic arrogance shone out from his clear blue eyes. He refused to put his hands up as he was searched for his pay-book and looked up at me as if I was something off the bottom of his boots. Suddenly, enemy mortar fire crumped all around us. The infantry threw themselves prone into the dirt and some scuttled behind the tank to shelter from the blasting shrapnel. But the young SS man stood his ground and didn't move a muscle. He laughed at those who had taken cover and I can still remember the startled look of momentary surprise on his face as a shell splinter struck him square on the forehead and he crumpled to the ground dead.[271]

The advance continued for another 300 yards beyond the farm. The reserve companies and their supporting tanks were then launched to the next objective 1,000 yards short of Rauray. The tanks of the Sherwood Rangers reached the crossroads north of Rauray, and by 1800 hours all objectives had been captured at the cost of 120 casualties. At 2230 hours, the 11th Durhams, commanded by Lieutenant Colonel Hamer, passed through for the final assault on Rauray. The town itself had been pummelled by rocket-firing Typhoons and its buildings and orchards were smashed into ruins. A patrol was sent out to obtain information on the situation in Rauray and came back with bad news: the village was full of alert SS troops, and in the surrounding woods the sound of revving tank engines could clearly be heard. It was apparent that more hard fighting would be needed to take this position, and Operation Martlet was now running way behind schedule.

To the east of the 49th West Riding Division, in the early hours of 26 June, VIII Corps had begun its advance. The going was hard and because of the bad weather, with rain and low cloud, air support had to be grounded. Detailed air attack plans had been prepared to support the advance of VIII Corps, and the lack of it was a great handicap. The 15th Scottish Division, supported by flail tanks, had at first made steady progress and reached the village of Cheux to the south of St Nicholas. But here they were confronted by the dedicated fighters of the *12. SS-Panzer-Division 'Hitlerjugend'*, who resisted their attacks with great ferocity and skill, stopping the British from advancing to the River Odon. As had been feared, heavy shelling from the Rauray Spur, which was still in German hands, was directed onto the 15th Division, causing many casualties and knocking out many tanks of the 11th Armoured Division.

Rauray, 27 June

Montgomery, not wanting to give Rommel more time to regroup his battered forces, decided that, even without the planned air support, Operation Epsom would continue.

Lance Corporal Kenneth Tout moved to the front with the Sherman tanks of the Sherwood Rangers and was to rendezvous at the Jerusalem Crossroads before going into action:

> We trundle through the narrow Normandy lanes between the high fortress hedges. From time to time the sun bursts through the leaves and branches to make our badges glint and

271 Render, *Tank Action*, p. 121.

sparkle. We sing contented little songs in low key, not the brash strains of 'Roll out the barrel' or the poignant wistfulness of 'We'll meet again' or the martial pace of 'Tipperary' but the softer songs like 'Nelly Dean' and 'Danny Boy'. For we are rolling though the quaint, shell-battered villages with exotic saints' names on the way to our pre-ordained destiny. What makes this place different are the huge, turreted, Sherman tanks standing between the trees and the crowd of tired, ashen faced men. Nobody takes any notice of us.[272]

At 0700 hours on 27 June, the 11th Tyneside Scottish advanced to Fontenay-le-Pesnel as a reserve battalion and dug in. *SS-Standartenführer* Kurt Meyer, commander of the *12. SS-Panzer-Division 'Hitlerjugend'*, recalled the situation at that time at Rauray:

I was in Rauray when morning dawned, watching the last tank roll into its jumping off position. It got lighter and lighter; it would not be much longer before the dance of death was to continue. The German batteries then fired their barrages, [and] low flying British planes roared overhead and fired their rockets into Rauray. The hell of attritional warfare had begun. The first tanks rattled forward, tracks clanking. Our attack initially gained ground but was stopped by an English counterattack and a bitterly contested tank versus tank engagement ensued. The tell-tale columns of oily smoke hung in the sky again, each column indicating the grave of a tank. But what happened then? The earth seemed to open and gobble us all up, all hell had been let loose, [and] we all stared spellbound at the murderous spectacle as fiery steel hurtled over us as it drilled into the ground. All that remained of Rauray were fragments of smashed trees and buildings.[273]

During the morning, the 11th Durhams, supported by the tanks of the Sherwood Rangers, tried hard to infiltrate Rauray. The *'Hitlerjugend'* fought ferociously among the ruins, and German tanks and 88mm guns poured their fire into the flanks of the attacking British armour and infantry.

Lieutenant Stuart Hills of the Sherwood Rangers recalled:

We sent out two troops to Rauray but ran into several Panthers which must have been brought up during the night. Three Shermans were destroyed and troop leader Ray Scott[274] and the experienced sergeants Biddell[275] and Green[276] were killed.[277]

---

272 Tout, K., *Tanks, Advance!* (London: Robert Hale Ltd, 1987), p. 45.
273 Meyer, *Grenadiers*, pp. 244–45.
274 Lieutenant Desmond Raymond Scott, Nottinghamshire Yeomanry, Sherwood Rangers, Royal Armoured Corps, died of wounds on 28 June 1944. He is buried in Bayeux War Cemetery, France.
275 Sergeant Lionel William Biddell, Nottinghamshire Yeomanry, Sherwood Rangers, Royal Armoured Corps, was killed in action on 26 June 1944, aged 37. He has no known grave and is commemorated on the Bayeux Memorial to the Missing.
276 Sergeant George Green, Nottinghamshire Yeomanry, Sherwood Rangers, Royal Armoured Corps, was killed in action on 27 June 1944, aged 29. He is buried in Fontenay-le-Pesnel War Cemetery, France.
277 Hills, *By Tank into Normandy*, p. 108.

Men of the 11th Battalion Durham Light Infantry moving into Rauray. (Courtesy of W. Ridley)

The Sherwood Rangers CO, Lieutenant Colonel Christopherson, remembered B Squadron sending two troops to reconnoitre the position at Rauray:

> Unfortunately, the Germans had brought up some tanks during the night, which were cleverly concealed in the trees at the edge of the village. All the tanks of Ray Scott's troop were knocked out. Sergeants Biddell and Green were both killed during the morning.[278]

Sergeant Monty Satchell, 49th Reconnaissance Regiment, was ordered to clear the corner of a cornfield as he approached Rauray, his first action, when he came under fire:

> I called out "Bloody Hell what was that!" as a ricochet whipped over our turret. Driver Dave said: "I could do with a Jimmie riddle." Everybody was tensed up and sweating. Then Spandaus and snipers opened up on us. This was it, our first taste of action. I had put my bloody head out of the turret to see properly, [and] two more Shermans had been hit up front. From Sunray over the radio came: "Squadron advance, turn right, good hunting." "What do you see Ron?" I said, as MG bullets hit the turret. Suddenly a German soldier stood up in the cornfield aiming a *Panzerfaust* at the carrier in front: "Gunner traverse left 100, co-axial fire, give him a long burst." Nearly up to the woods now, Dave had done well weaving his way across the cornfield: "Second target traverse right 200" and so it went on. We all agreed after that we had been frightened in this our first action.[279]

---

278 Holland (ed.), *An Englishman at War*, p. 403.
279 Manuscript forwarded to author by J. Styan (Hull, 1991).

Kurt Meyer, the *12. SS-Panzer-Division 'Hitlerjugend'* commander, watched as the action thundered on:

> Tanks and halftracks were advancing into the positions held by *SS-Panzergrenadier Regiment 26*. The barrage rolled over the earth like an enormous steel roller, crushing everything that lived. Only rarely did I see movement from the brave *Panzergrenadiere*. They held their ground stubbornly, fighting with the courage of despair. Flashes of dazzling destruction from Rauray hit the oncoming tanks, [and] British tanks were burning north of Rauray.[280]

So many tanks were lost that the survivors of the Sherwood Rangers had to withdraw, leaving the infantry to fight on alone. Corporal R.C. Baxter of the 11th Durhams described the attack:

> The attack on Rauray was timed for 11:00 hours, [and] D Company moved across a very flat field and was soon under fire from Spandaus. There was no cover at all, and we could see the enemy very clearly. After an attempt to advance further with help from our mortar platoons, a number of us were hit including myself.[281]

Eventually a platoon did fight its way to the centre of the village, led by Lieutenant K. Hoggard, who was badly wounded in the process. Other companies of the 11th Battalion took many casualties too from the accurate mortar fire being directed upon them by a German observer equipped with a radio on a well-camouflaged tree platform. Tank support could not now be expected, and it was obvious that if they were going to make any progress drastic measures were called for.

It was decided by the officer commanding that a full-scale infantry assault was called for, and later that morning the troops were ordered to stand-to and fix bayonets ready for the advance. The Durhams advanced with B Company on the right and D Company on the left, C Company waiting to follow up. An artillery barrage was put down in support but had little effect on the outcome. As the men moved forward in line abreast, machine-gun fire cut down many, while hidden snipers also took a steady toll. Both lead companies suffered heavy casualties, and NCOs and privates had to take over command of sections and companies as officers and senior NCOs were hit. When B Company reached its objective, it had only five men left. D Company suffered equally, and as C Company followed through they too lost many men, including their company commander, Major John Low,[282] who was killed.

By midday, the slaughter was so great that a ceasefire was agreed by both sides so that the dead could be moved and the wounded rescued from the killing zone. At 1400 hours, the attack was resumed and the Durhams managed to evict the young soldiers of the *'Hitlerjugend'* from Rauray. The snipers who had been tied into the branches of trees now hung lifeless from them, and the tanks of the Sherwood Rangers moved forward to support the infantry in case of an armoured German counter-attack. Major Martin Lindsay of the Sherwood Rangers advanced into the fields around Rauray and found it still a lethal place to be in:

---

280 Meyer, *Grenadiers*, p. 243.
281 Baverstock, *Breaking the Panzers*, p. 39.
282 Major John Low, 11th Battalion Durham Light Infantry, was killed in action at Rauray on 27 June 1944, aged 26. He is buried in Fontenay-le-Pesnel War Cemetery, France.

In Rauray we found nine knocked out enemy tanks, including a Tiger and a Panther, which had been abandoned intact and which we towed back to our lines. Major Hanson-Lawson went to have a look in Rauray for another abandoned Panther. A live enemy tank, hidden in trees, shot him up from behind. He was wounded and Sgt Crookes[283] who was with him died later of his wounds.[284]

As the battle drew to a close, the German infantry fought for their lives while artillery shells tore up the earth around them, hurling great lumps of clay and masonry skyward. Slowly, the German anti-tank guns were destroyed and the first German trenches were overrun by the British infantry. In desperation, the German commanders asked for artillery support, but it never came, and the British tanks ground their way through the chaos. Meyer watched helpless as his division was shredded by the enemy fire:

> I felt a burning emptiness in my heart for the first time and cursed the endless slaughter. What was happening at that point had nothing to do with war, it was outright murder. I knew every one of these young soldiers, the oldest was barely 18. The boys had not learned how to live but, by God, they knew how to die. Grating tank tracks ended their lives, tears ran down my face and I started hating the war.[285]

Stanley Christopherson looked on as the commander of B Squadron, Sherwood Rangers, Captain John Hanson Lawson, stalked a German tank that appeared to be knocked out:

> However, a Mk IV, shooting from the flank brewed him up, [and] John and his signal sergeant were both wounded, but all the crew managed to bail out from the burning tank, and thanks to Bill Wharton, who dashed out on foot to help, the whole crew, including the wounded, were brought back to safety in an old farmhouse, at which I established Regimental Headquarters. Sergeant Crookes was in a bad condition, but when I spoke to him, he smiled and told me he suffered no pain. He died shortly afterwards from shock and loss of blood. John Hanson Lawson had to be evacuated, suffering from a nasty wound and shock.[286]

Lieutenant Stuart Hills recalled the hard fighting for the Sherwood Rangers on the 27th:

> Later that afternoon B Squadron ran into more trouble around Rauray and by the end of the day only had seven tanks still serviceable out of their usual sixteen. John Hanson Lawson, squadron leader, was badly burnt when his tank was hit, and Sgt Crookes, his signal sergeant, later died of his wounds. He had been with the regiment since before the war.[287]

---

283 Sergeant William Percival Crookes, Nottinghamshire Yeomanry, Sherwood Rangers, Royal Armoured Corps, died of wounds on 27 June 1944, aged 23. He is buried in Bayeux War Cemetery, France.
284 Manuscript forwarded to author by A. Green (Sussex, 1993).
285 Meyer, *Grenadiers*, p. 257.
286 Holland (ed.), *An Englishman at War*, p. 404.
287 Hills, *By Tank to Normandy*, p. 109.

A carrier of the 2nd Kensingtons near a knocked-out panzer in the ruins of Rauray. (Author's collection)

From Tessel-Brettevillette, up the side of Tessel Wood, the Hallamshires advanced towards Vendes, and at 2100 hours the 1st Tyneside Scottish advanced to their starting point to the south of Fontenay-le Pesnel, where they dug in and prepared for an assault on Bretteville on 28 June. It was pouring with rain on the night of 27 June and the troops were given a rum ration to raise their spirits.

Lance Corporal Kenneth Tout arrived at the front to find the rest of the Sherwood Rangers had been in action, locating them in the rear licking their wounds. The reinforcements gathered round their freshly blooded comrades and wanted to know what the battle had been like:

> "Bloody awful!" says Mike. I am disappointed as I wanted to hear heroic words and to shake hands with the victors: "We got clobbered as the fields are so small, you go through one great hedge into a field and within 50 yards you have to crash through another hedge even thicker. And the orchards and farm buildings are ideal places for the Jerry tanks to hide waiting for us. We lost some tanks but got some of theirs as well. Harry Graham knocked out a Panther at 50 yards with his first shot." Great, good old Harry, they're bigger than Shermans aren't they? "Who cares," replied Mike: "What's more important is Frank Hickson's dead."[288] Oh no, not Frank, that big hearty, smiling fellow whom everyone liked[;] he was a corporal

---

288 Corporal Frank Edward Hickson, Sherwood Rangers, Northamptonshire Yeomanry, Royal Armoured Corps, was killed in action on 27 June 1944, aged 25. He is buried in Hottot-le-Bagues War Cemetery, France.

commander of a Sherman tank who never raised his voice to give an order, always so friendly and happy, [but] he's gone. "And Tommy Madelaine's had it."[289] No, not Tommy, tell us it's not true. Tommy as well as Frank and George Valentine.[290] The Gods have been unkind to the squadron. I noticed my two reinforcement companions have wandered away, the medicine is too strong for them. Mike continues to tell his story, almost oblivious of me, letting out the horrors of yesterday, exorcising the ghosts of the German guns behind the hedges.[291]

1st Battalion Tyneside Scottish at Rauray and Brettevillette, 28 June

At 0700 hours on the morning of 28 June, the weary troops of the 1st Tyneside Scottish formed up for yet another attack, supported by the machine guns of the 2nd Kensingtons. The men crouched low as the barrage from four field regiments thundered down quite close in front them, pummelling the countryside ahead. The troops moved slowly through the Bocage countryside, keeping behind the creeping barrage. Opposition appeared on the left, but in nothing like the strength that they had already experienced. Within 40 minutes, the forward companies had penetrated as far as Tessel-Brettevillette.[292]

Corporal S. Hebdige, 2nd Kensingtons, went with his platoon officer, Lieutenant J.T. Griffiths, on a reconnaissance patrol, and found the road to Bretteville blocked by German forces. They looked for another route forward and made contact with the nearby 1st Tyneside Scottish. Hebdige said they found a man in a slit trench who told them that the Headquarters was on the other side of an open field, which they duly went across:

> A Spandau opened up and the Tyneside Scottish in the slit-trench shouted to us to get down, but we were already down with bullets whipping through the hedge like a swarm of wasps.[293]

They finally made it to the Tyneside Scottish HQ, only to be told by the officers there that the road was now open, so they had to return the way they had come to deliver this news to their comrades. Hebdige continued:

> Head down I ran as fast as I could and caught my foot in a molehill, twisting my knee so badly I could not put any weight on it. The officer and sergeant came back thinking I had been hit and when I told them what had happened, they told me to crawl towards the Tyneside Scottish as they were nearer. This I started to do but had not got very far before a Moaning Minnie opened up and I heard mortar bombs dropping in the field. I then found

---

289 Lance Corporal Reginald Henry Madelaine, Sherwood Rangers, Northamptonshire Yeomanry, Royal Armoured Corps, was killed in action on 27 June 1944, aged 23. He is buried in Hottot-le-Bagues War Cemetery, France.
290 Lance Sergeant George Albert Valentine, Sherwood Rangers, Nottinghamshire Yeomanry, Royal Armoured Corps, was killed in action on 27 June 1944, aged 32. He is buried in Hottot-le-Bagues War Cemetery, France.
291 Tout, *Tanks, Advance!*, p. 46.
292 Tessel-Brettevillette was codenamed 'Jock'.
293 Baverstock, *Breaking the Panzers*, p. 40.

myself up and running and it was not until I reached the infantry that my knee gave way and I fell to the ground.[294]

C and D Companies consolidated their newly won positions, and about midday on 28 June A and B Companies passed through them to head for the village of Brettevillette,[295] once again an artillery barrage preceding the attack. It was not long before intense Spandau fire harassed the advancing infantry, while mortar bombs and shellfire fell on the rear of the attack. Doggedly, the men pressed forward through the explosions and machine-gun fire, and by 1430 hours fighting was going on in the village itself. Private P. Lawton of the 1st Tyneside Scottish carried a Piat anti-tank gun along with his rifle, ammunition and grenades, while a comrade carried the shaped charges for the Piat:

> We advanced along a hedgerow and the first thing we saw was the mutilated and dying Pte Ross,[296] who had been hit by shrapnel just a few moments earlier. Although still alive it was patently obvious that he was not going to last long. Pte Ross survived for 2 more days before he died. On reaching the road leading to the village, I was instructed to set up the Piat to ensure that no nasty surprises, in the form of enemy armour, was able to come up in the rear of 18 Platoon. We had come under shellfire during the attack, and now, as we lay half expecting an enemy tank to appear round the bend, we could hear rifle and machine-gun fire coming from the village behind us.[297]

Corporal J.W.H. Tipler of the 1st Tyneside Scottish also saw the unfortunate Private Ross being treated by medics:

> We had some food and sleep before moving to Rauray and as we marched in, we saw Pte Ross sitting on a box and being attended to, [and] one of his arms was missing. He looked deathly pale, but he managed a smile. I heard he died later.[298]

The Tyneside Scottish holding the village were counter-attacked by the tanks and infantry of *Kampfgruppe Weidinger*[299] at 1500 hours, and their hold on the position was looking precarious. As the 'Das Reich' SS troops and armour fought to dislodge the British from Brettevillette, Lieutenant Griffiths, 2nd Kensingtons, recalled the moment a German tank broke through and killed three of his men:

> By the time we got to the village the infantry was under attack from German troops and tanks and some of the wounded were returning out of the battle area. By standing on the

---

294 Baverstock, *Breaking the Panzers*, p. 40.
295 Brettevillette was codenamed 'Jones'.
296 Private John Johnson Ross, 1st Battalion Tyneside Scottish, Black Watch, died of wounds on 30 June 1944, aged 19. He is buried in Tilly-sur-Seulles War Cemetery, France.
297 P. Lawton, correspondence with author (Newcastle, 1991).
298 Baverstock, *Breaking the Panzers*, p. 48.
299 *Kampfgruppe Weidinger* was under the command of *SS-Major* Otto Weidinger and was composed of elite troops of the *2. SS-Panzer-Division 'Das Reich'*.

engine compartment of my carrier I was able to see beyond the edge of the village where enemy reinforcements were arriving. I manually signalled to one of the sections to fire its two machine-guns over the village at the enemy and this successfully disrupted them until a German tank emerged from the village, fired twice and destroyed and set on fire two of my carriers; three of the section were killed, Cpl F.S. Bushnell,[300] L/Cpl J.P. Wallace[301] and Pte Perry,[302] and one wounded, Sgt Bone. Both gun teams had gallantly fired at the tank, but .303 bullets are no match for armour. Luckily for me in my exposed position, the tank withdrew without firing at the carrier I was standing on.[303]

The Tyneside Scottish were driven back time after time, but on each occasion Company Sergeant Major Shanks rallied their dwindling numbers and led them back into the village. After so many losses, Lieutenant Griffiths[304] took his surviving troops back to another sector to form a defensive position in order that the men of the Tyneside Scottish would have a rallying point should they need it. Other men arrived and a strong defensive position was formed. By now all the Tyneside Scottish reserves had been flung into the battle, but the situation became so bad for the beleaguered troops that they had to be withdrawn to Tessel-Brettevillette. Corporal Tipler reached the village when the fighting was at its height and at once received orders to pull back as the British gunners were about to stonk the area. As he left in confusion, he came across his Company Commander, Major Harry Boyne, who had been badly wounded in both legs. They dressed his wounds as well as they could and put him on a stretcher on a jeep to be taken to the rear. CSM Shanks had now taken command of the company and he organised the retreat out of the ruins of Brettevillette. Private P. Lawton was ordered to stay in position and cover the withdrawal of his comrades, and when the last had left he was told to get out quickly:

> Pte Roper and I withdrew back along a hedgerow where we had advanced earlier in the day. About halfway down the field there was a Bren-carrier of the Kensingtons carrying a Vickers heavy machine-gun and as we approached the officer in charge called me over and pointed out an enemy tank with troops riding on the outside. It was driving along the road which, only a few minutes earlier, we had been guarding.[305]

The Tyneside Scottish had regrouped by 1800 hours to a position 400 yards from Brettevillette. Both sides had taken heavy casualties in the fighting and the village was shelled all evening and throughout the night.

---

300 Corporal Sidney Bushnell, 2nd Battalion Princess Louisa's Kensington Regiment, was killed in action on 28 June 1944, aged 18. He is buried in St Manvieu War Cemetery, France.
301 Lance Corporal John Penman Wallace, 2nd Battalion Princess Louisa's Kensington Regiment, was killed in action on 28 June 1944, aged 30. He is buried in St Manvieu War Cemetery, France.
302 Private Ronald Francis Perry, 2nd Battalion Princess Louisa's Kensington Regiment, was killed in action on 28 June 1944, aged 21. He is buried in St Manvieu War Cemetery, France.
303 Manuscript forwarded to author by H. Black (Exeter, 1989).
304 Lieutenant J.T. Griffiths was awarded the Military Cross for his actions at Rauray.
305 P. Lawton, correspondence with author (Newcastle, 1991).

Counter-attack at Rauray, 29 June

By first light on 29 June, it became obvious that *Kampfgruppe Weidinger* was firmly established in the area, with any attempt to move by the Tyneside Scottish bringing down a storm of fire from machine guns, mortars and tanks. All day they were harassed by the Germans' aggressive defence. Major John Stirling, 4/7th Royal Dragoon Guards, stationed on the high ground south of Bretteville, described the situation:

> The place was stiff with dug in tanks and anti-tank guns, and we lost several of our tanks while reconnoitring the feature. For days and days nothing anyone did could shift them. The tanks tried, the infantry tried, and the gunners had a go with everything they had. It was still suicide to poke your nose out onto that forward slope.[306]

The weather on the morning of 29 June was bright and clear, allowing Allied aircraft to make numerous sorties against German reinforcements that were travelling to the Odon area.

An attack by the 11th Durhams on Bretteville was planned, the forward positions held by the 1st Tyneside Scottish ordered to pull back so as not to fall foul of the coming barrage that would herald the assault. The enemy observers saw the rearward movement by the Tynesiders and sent the information back to their *Nebelwerfer* batteries, and it was not long before their missiles came screaming through the air to fall upon the hapless British troops, causing numerous casualties. The Tyneside Scottish were relieved by the 4th Lincolns at 0600 hours on 30 June, while to the south the 10th Durhams and 4/7th Royal Dragoon Guards were having a rough time because of accurate *Nebelwerfer* and artillery fire. As the Shermans attempted to reconnoitre forward, they lost several tanks to enemy anti-tank guns.

German armoured units of the *II SS-Panzerkorps* were at this point threatening to counter-attack at the junction of the 15th Scottish and 49th West Riding Divisions; the inter-corps boundary was between Rauray and Le-Haut-de-Bosq and was important as the Germans viewed it as the weakest point in the Allied line. The attack by the tanks of *9. SS-Panzer-Division* was about to cross the front held by XXX Corps to the south of Brettevillette. As the German forces assembled, no air strike was possible because of the cloudy weather, but they were severely delayed as artillery fire and shells from the ships in the Channel tore into their ranks as they manoeuvred into attack formation. This bombardment continued all day, the German being pounded so hard that communications were destroyed and all cohesion vanished. Without air or artillery support, their attempt to drive a wedge between XXX Corps and VIII Corps was doomed to fail, and by late evening, amid torrential rain, they were driven back with tremendous losses.

SS-Obergruppenführer Paul Hausser, commander of the *II SS-Panzerkorps*, commented in his report:

> Hardly had the tanks assembled when they were attacked. This disrupted the troops so much that the attack did not start until 2.30 in the afternoon. But even then, it could not get going, [as] the murderous fire from naval guns in the Channel and the terrible British

---

306 Stirling, *The First and the Last*, p. 108.

A *Nebelwerfer* battery firing numerous rockets onto the British positions. (Author's collection)

artillery fire destroyed the bulk of our attacking force in its assembly areas. The few tanks that did manage to go forward were easily stopped by the British anti-tank guns.[307]

The British commanders viewed this counter-attack as being only a rehearsal for a bigger attack the following day. The men of the 49th West Riding Division used their time to consolidate, reorganise their positions and bury their dead, as the guns fired throughout the day on selected targets.

On the night of 29 June, the forward troops of the 49th West Riding Division steeled themselves for the expected counter-attack the following morning. Sappers passed through the infantry loaded with anti-tank mines to be planted in no man's land ready for the panzers. Lance Corporal Geoffrey Steer was finding the weather quite mild, and instead of sleeping in his slit trench he and his comrades of the 1/4th KOYLIs were sleeping under a blanket on the top of the trench when tragedy struck:

> An explosion, different to shelling, tore through our section, the blankets went with the blast, and we all hit the trench floor together. I looked up and the trees were on fire along with our blankets. More explosions came one after the other and we were praying it would stop. When it did, we at once put the fires out and waited for daylight which was about an

---

307 Townend and Baldwin, *Gunners in Normandy*, p. 259.

hour away. Sgt Bell and the platoon commander, Lt Trumper, were both bleeding from their ears and were taken back to HQ for treatment. Nobody knew what had caused the explosions, so someone went to find out. Down the field somebody shouted: "Look out for unexploded mines!" The field behind our trenches was absolute carnage, I found pay-books, identification discs and other personal belongings. It turned out the pioneers were carrying primed boxes of mines through our lines, [and] they detonated in the open ground in front of us. One man tripped up and the blast blew the others following him off their feet. 14 men died and I collected their remains, [and] they were buried in one grave [–] that was another episode to try the nerves.[308]

On the night of 29/30 June, *Kampfgruppe Weidinger*'s shattered remnant regrouped in preparation for the day ahead. In the bitter fighting of the previous days, their casualties had been great, but yet more sacrifices would be required of them.

Counter-attack at Rauray, 30 June, hold the line!

At 1500 hours, an attack was made on the 15th Scottish Division, and on the left flank of the 49th West Riding Division, by the *2. SS-Panzer-Division 'Das Reich'*. The fighting was hard and bitter, but eventually the Germans were beaten back. Another attack began to form on the 1st Tyneside Scottish front west of Tessel Wood, but the 49th Divisional artillery broke it up with concentrated shellfire, knocking out three enemy tanks. Shelling from both sides was constant, and machine-gun and mortar fire ploughed up the terrain. Meanwhile, the poor infantry sat amid this hell on earth waiting for the next move, which would not be long in coming.

Lieutenant J.T. Griffiths of the 2nd Kensingtons became alarmed early that morning when shells burst all around his machine-gun positions. Platoon Headquarters was situated in a ditch at the edge of a large field, to his front was a section dug-in at the corner of a badly knocked-about copse, and another section was several hundred yards forward in shallow slit trenches beside a knocked-out Sherman tank. Griffiths recalled: "The infantry was well dug-in to our front and now, beyond them, emerging from the smoke, German tanks with infantry in support appeared."[309]

The 11th Royal Scots Fusiliers held the right flank near Juvigny and were in touch with the 50th Northumbrian Division to the west. In the east, the 1/4th KOYLIs were dug-in at the western edge of Tessel Wood, while the Hallamshires held the south-west corner of the wood, north of Vendes. The 4th Lincolns held the line at Tessel-Brettevillette and were linked up to the Hallamshires. The 11th Durhams were dug-in near Rauray, linked to the 1st Tyneside Scottish on the high ground. To the left of the 49th West Riding Division, the 6th King's Own Scottish Borderers (KOSBs) from the 15th Scottish Division were dug-in. The three 49th Division field artillery regiments, tanks of the 24th Lancers, guns of 217th Anti-tank Regiment and Vickers machine guns of the 2nd Kensingtons were made ready to support the infantry.

308 *WW2: People's War* <www.bbc.co.uk/ww2peopleswar> (accessed 28 December 2020).
309 J.T. Griffiths, correspondence with author (London, 1995).

At 1800 hours on 30 June, the attack by the 11th Durhams was cancelled and the two Durham battalions were relieved at Rauray by the 1st Tyneside Scottish. The Tynesiders of A and B Companies sited their 6-pdr anti-tank guns to the front, giving them a good field of fire and observation over the flat terrain, a perfect killing ground should the Germans tanks appear.

Private J.L.R. Sampson, of the Anti-tank Platoon of the 1st Tyneside Scottish, found his gun placed very close to the infantry. Pits were dug as tracer from intermittent fixed-line Spandau fire flew over their heads, while flares lit up the night with an eerie light that gave the whole place an air of unreality. Sampson recalled: "We finished our spade work and the five of us got into our slit-trenches very tired. Even with all the firing I soon fell asleep."[310]

Private T.J. Renouf moved with his 1st Tyneside Scottish platoon through the countryside along a track near the front line to relieve the Durhams. As he approached the front, the terrain changed to typical Bocage, with narrow lanes below field level topped with trees and hedges that looked impenetrable. He and his comrades were given an excellent slit trench that would provide them with some safety for the night and hopefully in the battle to come: "There was a streaky mist floating in the air and signs of a heavy dew." Renouf asked the Durhams what was going on to their front: "The DLI boys told us things were quiet and that the Germans were in the wood about 200 yards across an open field to our front. They also mentioned hearing the sound of armoured vehicles being moved around."[311]

Captain John Sinclair Highmore of the 1st Tyneside Scottish was ordered to take command of D Company and to moved forward to relieve a company of the 10th Durhams. Once his men were in position at dusk, Captain Highmore visited his platoons to make sure all was well: "When I was trying to find my left platoon's position, I blundered into a small copse in the dark and found myself surrounded by *Achtung Minen* signs, erected by the previous owners. However, luck was with me."[312]

During the night of 30 June, the anti-tank gun teams of the 1st Tyneside Scottish prepared their defensive positions. Lieutenant B.T.W. Stewart felt the urgency of the moment:

> The night before the battle we were ordered to move to defensive positions in the Rauray area. The guns were positioned by map references, although to some extent we were committed to the DLI's dispositions and ordered to dig in in readiness for a possible attack by German armour at first light next morning. I have a clear recollection of a sense of urgency and in view of the shortness of time available, I told the detachment commanders to blow themselves in with their anti-tank mines to ensure they were thoroughly dug-in in the minimum amount of time. They accomplished this task successfully and the whole platoon was poised for action before dawn.[313]

All through the night of 30 June and early morning of 1 July, the ominous revving sound of tank engines on the move could be heard in the darkness, patrols reporting back constantly of the movement of men and machines behind the German lines.

---

310 Beaverstock, K., *Breaking the Panzers* (Gloucestershire: Sutton Publishing, 2002), p. 127.
311 T.J. Renouf, correspondence with author (Newcastle, 1991).
312 Manuscript forwarded to author by P. Liversidge (Exeter, 1999).
313 Manuscript forwarded to author B. Stewart (Durham, 1990).

Captain A. MacLagan, 1st Tyneside Scottish, made sure his anti-tank crews were all settled in and ready: "I was very much aware of enemy activity, tank engines revving and moving about, warning us that an attack was imminent. I recall being near Major Mirrielees[314] as he gave orders for his company to 'Stand to'."[315]

Counter-attacks at Rauray, 1 July, the "Polar Bear Butchers"

To the south-east of Rauray was a five-sided field, roughly the size of two football pitches, the south-facing side forming the boundary between VIII Corps and XXX Corps. It was in this field that A Company of the 1st Tyneside Scottish were situated in slit trenches to the front of a tree-lined bank. To their left were the 6th KOSBs of the 15th Scottish Division. To the right of A Company, anti-tank guns had been positioned as the terrain was perfect for an attempted breakthrough by German armour. To their right, the battalion's central forward position, B Company of the 1st Tyneside Scottish, sat dangerously exposed in slit trenches. C Company defended the battalion's right flank on the other side of the lane to Rauray. To the left of Rauray, D Company was held in reserve. The 4th Lincolns and 11th Durhams were in prepared positions in the fields and orchards at Rauray. The anti-tank gunners had set up their 6-pds so as to have interlocking arcs of fire across each other's front. To draw the enemy's fire, three knocked-out Sherman tanks and a captured German anti-tank gun were positioned prominently so as to attract the attention of German observers.

A considerable amount of firepower was now available to support the nervous British infantry units, with the 69th, 143rd and 185th artillery regiments stood ready for the next day, as were the tanks of the 24th Lancers plus the 217th Battery of the 55th Anti-tank Regiment. The heavy machine guns of the 2nd Kensingtons waited in their positions for the moment of action. Meanwhile, the RAF dropped 1,300 tons of bombs on Villers Bocage in the space of 20 minutes, obliterating the town.

Private T.J. Renouf of A Company, 1st Tyneside Scottish, looked to his front and heard disconcerting noises in the darkness:

> During the night, the noise of moving tanks and vehicles continued. I remember Very lights being fired from time to time so as to illuminate the field ahead of us and expose any attempts at infiltration by the enemy.[316]

Sergeant A.R. Esplin, dug-in with the Mortar Platoon of the 1st Tyneside Scottish in the grey light just before dawn, had an observation post set up to their front and ranging shots were fired on prearranged targets. Esplin organised his men: "As the daylight broke through, we knew we were in for a fight and that we would be staying for a while, [as] the ammunition trucks were by this time unloading more mortar bombs than I ever thought we would need."[317]

---

314 Major John Currie Mirrielees, MC, was killed in action commanding a company of the 5th Battalion Black Watch on 29 August 1944, aged 29. He is buried in St Desir War Cemetery, France.
315 A. MacLagan, correspondence with author (Devon, 1994).
316 T.J. Renouf, correspondence with author (Newcastle, 1991).
317 Beaverstock, *Breaking the Panzers*, p. 139.

Armoured units of *SS-Panzer Regiment 9* move forward for the counter-attack at Rauray. (Author's collection)

Private A. Norris, with A Company of the 1st Tyneside Scottish, could see very little through the mist, so he and his friend got out of their slit trench to stretch their legs. But what he thought was mist turned out to be smoke laid down by the enemy, and slowly it began to disperse. The pair then looked over a nearby hedge: "In the field to our front were rows of enemy tanks, silent and motionless. Presumably they had crept up in the night." His comrade commented: "That's going to piss on the chips."[318]

At first light, the Tynesiders looked on as the Germans sent over intermittent salvoes of mortar bombs, each one getting nearer to their positions. It became obvious that these volleys were ranging shots, aimed at pinpointing the British positions. Eventually, a heavy bombardment by artillery and mortars fell upon 70 Brigade's front, and with tanks reported south of Brettevillette, the 1st Tyneside Scottish were ordered to 'Stand to'.

Private Renouf recalled this ranging fire: "After a lull it started up again but this time it was nearer. The process was repeated and soon the bombs were dropping around our positions. For the first half-hour or so the enemy was ranging more and more accurately onto our trenches."[319]

---

318 Beaverstock, *Breaking the Panzers*, p. 141.
319 T.J. Renouf, correspondence with author (Newcastle, 1991).

Captain Highmore, 1st Tyneside Scottish, sat in his slit trench when things began to happen: "A cascade of Very lights went up over the German held area and the ominous sound of tanks on the move grew louder by the minute. Heavy fire came down on the battalion front and the fog of war rolled over the battlefield."[320]

The air reverberated to the sound of gunfire as the Germans softened up the British line. The first assault launched by *Kampfgruppe Weidinger* and armoured vehicles from *SS-Panzer Regiment 9* was on 70 Brigade's right flank and the junction of the 15th Scottish and 49th West Riding Divisions. At 0640 hours, the battle began in earnest, the German armour standing at a distance and bombarding the Tyneside Scottish as the *panzergrenadiere* advanced under cover of smoke and the barrage. The Germans set up their machine guns and fired upon C Company trenches at very close quarters, while the tanks rolled forward through the smoke and passed C Company's positions. They were heading for B Company, where the battalion anti-tank crews lay in wait and were fully prepared to meet them.

Messages got through to Headquarters at 0640 hours that C and B Companies were being attacked by a strong enemy force of infantry supported by tanks, advancing under the cover of a smokescreen. The attackers were an infantry battalion of the *2. SS-Panzer-Division 'Das Reich'* and a tank battalion of the *9. SS-Panzer-Division*. The German thrust also came in on the right of the 1st Tyneside Scottish, on the boundary between the 4th Lincolns and the 11th Durhams.

Major W.K. Angus, commanding C Company of the 1st Tyneside Scottish, was in a desperate situation with his men as the German assault moved in. Lieutenant Donald Charles Wallace[321] and his sergeant were killed, and it was not long before his position was overrun.

Private A Henderson and his mate, Private John Laing, of C Company, 1st Tyneside Scottish, were in a well-camouflaged slit trench in the middle of a hedgerow when the barrage came down, which seemed to them to last for a long while. Henderson remembered: "I spotted German soldiers across the other side of the field, they were trying to work their way past us, [but] we fired our rifles at them, and their heads soon went down."[322] The enemy continued to infiltrate in a bid to reach Rauray. The defenders of the Tyneside Scottish were doing their best to hang on, but German machine-gun fire was inflicting enormous numbers of casualties and some sections start to give ground. Carriers carrying the wounded were braving the intense fire, but the situation soon began to look hopeless.

Once informed of the situation, the tanks of the 24th Lancers, from their positions in Rauray, started shelling the Germans with their 75mm guns. The mortar crews of the 1st Tyneside Scottish were also in action, firing their 3-inch mortar bombs at prearranged targets, and from the small villages around Audrieu the guns of the 143rd and 185th Field Regiments opened up with defensive fire. Sergeant H. Cooke, who was with the 185th Field Regiment, Royal Artillery, remembered the heavy casualties taken by the FOOs as they bravely accompanied the forward troops to observe the fall of shot and to call back any adjustments to the gun positions. Cooke recalled: "When I look back at the infantry doing their dangerous job, I think we were very lucky. They were in direct contact with the enemy and bore the brunt of everything. Thank

---

320 Manuscript forwarded to author by P. Liversidge (Exeter, 1999).
321 Lieutenant Donald Charles Wallace, 1st Battalion Tyneside Scottish, Black Watch, was killed in action on 1 July 1944, aged 20. He is buried in Bayeux War Cemetery, France.
322 Beaverstock, *Breaking the Panzers*, p. 150.

God for the Infantry was a well-used expression by us."³²³

Corporal G. Cowie, 1st Tyneside Scottish, had just joined D Company in reserve when the whole battalion was put on alert. Tank support moved forward, and prearranged defensive targets were bombarded by artillery and mortar fire. Cowie recalled:

> In the dawn light enemy troops managed to get in close, coming from Bretteville and Queudeville, [and] the 6-pounder anti-tank guns were soon in action. Sgt O'Brien's gun was operated with the greatest coolness and courage by its crew, [and] they knocked out five tanks with the first six shots, two of them at point blank range.³²⁴

Private John Murray of D Company, 1st Tyneside Scottish, fell victim to the violent momentum of the assault as his forward position was overrun:

Corporal George Cowie, 1st Battalion Tyneside Scottish, Black Watch. (Courtesy of M. Denney)

> We were attacked in full force when a mortar shell landed in front of me and my chest was pierced by shrapnel, the force of which lifted me up and dropped me onto my back in a ditch. At the same time my uniform was ripped to shreds. I was unable to see what was going on around me, but I could hear the German troops passing by. I was then left with only the sounds of the injured and dying filling my ears, then it became very quiet. Sometime later I heard gunfire approaching from the rear and eventually directly overhead. I then received gun-shot wounds to both legs.³²⁵ Shortly after this I heard the voices of our own troops around me. Luckily I was found and placed on a Bren-carrier and taken away for treatment.³²⁶

Lieutenant W.S. Vaughn, serving with the 55th Anti-tank Regiment, was north-east of Rauray and looked on as fierce fighting was going on in the forward positions. Troops of the 1st Tyneside Scottish pulled back in the face of the counter-attack and German tanks crept towards Vaughn's position:

> At about 06:00 a.m. information was obtained that an attack was imminent from the south. This was preceded by a very heavy mortar barrage, closely followed by infantry supported by tanks, [and] the forward companies of the TS withdrew past our positions.³²⁷

---

323 Townend and Baldwin, *Gunners in Normandy*, p. 238.
324 Delaforce, *The Polar Bears*, p. 107.
325 Private John Murray survived the war but had to have his right leg amputated below the knee.
326 *WW2: People's War* <www.bbc.co.uk/ww2peopleswar> (accessed 12 December 2020).
327 Townend and Baldwin, *Gunners in Normandy*, p. 267.

It soon became clear that the attack was in considerable strength and that the whole corps artillery and naval gunfire from the Channel would have to be called upon to start bombarding all along the 49th West Riding Division's front.

Lieutenant Vaughn[328] was informed that enemy tanks were infiltrating his positions on the right and a ferocious battle ensued between them and the anti-tank crews. Teams moved their guns to better positions in order to get a clearer arc of fire, and as a Tiger came creeping up, using a knocked-out Panther as cover, it received numerous hits from the anti-tank gunners and burst into flames. Another Tiger came up behind the cover that the two blazing tanks provided. The anti-tank gunners were working feverishly, and it was not long before this tank was also hit and burning. Vaughn looked on as the battle developed:

> Then a Mk IV moved across the front from some trees on the right and fired, killing one infantryman and wounding several others, [but] after a few rounds the tank withdrew and was observed by me to be in flames. Later there was a concentrated effort by four tanks in our gun area, but we had been warned and were ready. The remaining infantry, seeing the tanks, then retired leaving only myself and the gun team in the field. Sgt Hall engaged the targets as they appeared and was fired on in return. Two other tanks were in our area, one was blazing furiously, and the other was smoking.[329]

Sergeant Swaddle, 1st Tyneside Scottish, commanded a 6-pdr anti-tank section in this action:

> We stood by our guns as the battle started [–] most of the trouble seemed to be coming in on Sgt Watson's number three section, I was listening to the gun shots. Everyone was on the alert as riflemen, until tanks appeared on our front. Five tanks came along the road, three carried straight on and the other two came through the fence of the field in front towards my gun. I let the two tanks come to within 100 yards of us. We attacked the second tank first, [but] our first shot went into the embankment five feet in front of us, so we pushed the gun forward placing the barrel over the embankment. Our second and third shots killed the second tank. We then turned to the first tank and hit the target with two shots, [and] it stopped dead [–] we had fired five rounds of Sabot.[330] I then began to wonder about the other three tanks, so I left my team to find out what had happened to our number two gun. I found it had taken a direct hit on the barrel, [and] Pte Allen was wounded in the legs. I told him to make his way back, but he could not walk of crawl. With the help of L/Cpl Barclay, we took him to safety, running under small arms fire with Hughie on our shoulders.[331]

In the first 20 minutes of the attack, the 1st Tyneside Scottish suffered terribly but refused to give ground. The artillery fire from both sides was tremendous, but the Germans still could not

---

328 Lieutenant W.S. Vaughn was awarded the Military Cross for this action, and Sergeant Hall was awarded the Distinguished Conduct Medal.
329 Townend and Baldwin, *Gunners in Normandy*, p. 267.
330 The armour-piercing discarding Sabot round was used effectively in the Second World War by anti-tank crews to smash through the heavy armour of German tanks.
331 Manuscript forwarded to author by W. Gilson (Hull, 1990).

break through. German tank shells and British anti-tank shells screamed across the battlefield, and amid this inferno the Tynesiders gave all they had. Sergeant David Watson, serving with the Anti-tank Platoon, recounted that day of frantic action:

> My Bren-gunner, Pte J. Walker, was severely wounded in the hand and I sent him back to the Regimental Aid Post. We kept on firing at the tanks, but then my aimer, Pte C.D. Tierney, got hit in the face and I got him away too. I took on the job of aimer, the loader kept pushing shells in and we managed to take a few of the tanks out.[332]

Sergeant David Watson, MM, 1st Battalion Tyneside Scottish, Black Watch. (Courtesy of M. Denney)

Sergeant Watson, seeing that they were running out of ammunition, sent Sergeant O'Brien to the nearest company so that they could call back for more shells. However, O'Brien found it impossible to get through:

> Then I was hit in the knee by a piece of shrapnel and my loader, Pte W. Cook, was hit on the back of his hand which kept on bleeding. We just carried on until we had no more ammunition and as my loader and I were both wounded we had nothing left to do but to leave the gun.[333]

Watson's team had successfully knocked out five tanks in front of B Company's position and had helped blunt the German attack. Black oily smoke rolled over the battlefield from these burning wrecks. Faced with a head-on attack by SS tanks, Watson had handled his gallant team with cool determination and bravery. Many such acts were played out that morning. Lieutenant B.T.W. Stewart later found Sergeant Watson's gun position abandoned in no man's land, surrounded by a number of wrecked German tanks which he and his two guns had destroyed.

Ammunition was being called for all the time as the battle raged, the carriers of HQ Company travelling backwards and forwards to the leading companies as shells rained down. The returning carriers brought the wounded back with them while under heavy shellfire.

At 0725 hours, the 11th Durhams counter-attacked the Germans from their positions at Rauray, supported by tanks of the 24th Lancers. *Kampfgruppe Weidinger* was attempting to infiltrate between the Durhams and the 4th Lincolns but was driven off by the counterattack. British tanks moved forward to help the hard-pressed infantry and began bombarding the enemy. However, in spite of all the hard work and sacrifice made halting *Kampfgruppe Weidinger*, by 0800 hours German armour had succeeded in piercing the outer perimeter of

---

332 Baverstock, *Breaking the Panzers*, pp. 79–80.
333 Baverstock, *Breaking the Panzers*, p. 80. Sergeant David Watson was awarded the Military Medal for this action.

70 Brigade. Some units entered the outskirts of Rauray and were immediately taken on by the tanks of the 24th Lancers.

By 0900 hours, the light of day revealed a confused situation, with the 1st Tyneside Scottish being pressed hard as the SS units tried to force their way through between VIII Corps and XXX Corps. However, the terrain, with its thick impenetrable hedgerows, large trees and orchards, prevented the British commanders from judging what was developing left and right of their units. The German armour had been stopped by the anti-tank screen set up in the forward areas, but small groups of *panzergrenadiere* had infiltrated between the companies and snipers were active in the orchards between the 11th Durhams and the 4th Lincolns. The defending troops were feeling very exposed, and if the enemy saw any movement he promptly sent over a shower of mortar bombs or *Nebelwerfer* rockets. Private J. Sampson was taking a carrier loaded with ammunition to the front when a mortar bomb landed in the engine compartment: "The carrier burst into flames, the driver jumped out and it was only a matter of seconds before the fire would reach the petrol tank. Mortar bombs, 6-pounder shells and small arms ammunition in the carrier were all exploding. Jerry must have spotted the blaze because mortar bombs came over far too fast for my liking."[334] All the men in the area dived into their slit trenches, but some were hit and became casualties.

The forward companies of the 1st Tyneside Scottish were continually pressed by the *panzergrenadiere* and the situation began to look bad. At one point, British prisoners of war were driven before the German troops as they advanced. Numbers 13 and 14 Platoon were overrun and the Tynesiders were eventually forced to give ground, falling back to form a link with the 11th Durhams to their rear at Rauray.

Lieutenant J.F. McLaren, B Company, 1st Tyneside Scottish, looked to his front as his men kept up a steady fusillade on the enemy, but visibility was poor and he could only see a part of one platoon on his left flank. Enemy tanks were already around his position, all communication was gone and the anti-tank guns were now silent: "I could see no sign of life other than some of my own platoon and at this point I took the decision to order the few troops I was in contact with to fall back to the hedge in our rear, then to the reserve company at the bottom of the field."[335]

The 11th Durhams, to the west of Rauray, began to take the infiltrating Germans to task. It was a day of bitter fighting as the Germans attacked again and again. The chaplain of the 1st Tynesiders, C.W. Chesworth, risked his life tending to the wounded whenever he could, but the shellfire was continuous and to show your head above ground was fatal. Although the initial morning attack had been stopped, the *panzergrenadiere* of *Kampfgruppe Weidinger* had penetrated deep into the positions being held by the 1st Tyneside Scottish. The support fire from the artillery regiments, tank fire and the naval guns of ships in the Channel prevented any serious breakthrough by tanks and armoured fighting vehicles. By 1100 hours, the first phase of the battle was over and the Durhams and Lincolns were busy mopping up west of Rauray.

The situation was now critical for the Tynesiders, and it was imperative that reinforcements got to them as soon as possible. A party from D Company, 1st Tyneside Scottish, was fighting

---

334 J. Sampson, correspondence with author (Beverley, 1992).
335 Beaverstock, *Breaking the Panzers*, p. 158.

Infantry of the 1st Battalion Tyneside Scottish move up the side of a hedged sunken lane towards the enemy. (Courtesy of R. Protheroe)

its way forward along the hedgerows to relieve B Company. Corporal George Cowie was in that group:

> We formed up with me leading and emerged into the field at a semi-crouch, moving up the left-hand side of it towards B Company's position. About 30 or 40 men were following me in single file. A few yards behind me was our own Bren-gunner Taffy Jones, followed by his number 2, then the new company commander, Captain J.R. Alexander, with the remainder of D Company. There was no cover on the right, just an open field with an amazing number of brewed-up tanks, [and] I felt somewhat exposed. Everyone, including the company commander, looked white and tense. Local support was much in evidence, [and] I could hear behind me Pipey McKay's Bren-guns and the tanks of the 24th Lancers firing their Besa machine-guns.[336]

Before noon, the second German attack came in from Bretteville and Queudeville, again on the hard-pressed B Company front, as mortar fire rained onto the battlefield. The Shermans of the 24th Lancers lay in wait for the panzers as the German artillery stonked the whole area. The assault smashed through the 6th KOSBs of 15th Scottish Division on 70 Brigade's left flank, and there was now a real danger of total envelopment. The attack was eventually stopped but the German units were gathering their strength yet again for another effort from the hamlets of

---

336 *WW2: People's War* <www.bbc.co.uk/ww2peopleswar> (accessed 22 December 2020).

Queudeville and Bretteville. Every artillery piece in VIII Corps and XXX Corps was brought to bear on the German formations gathering for the attack, hundreds of shells pouring into the concentration areas. Numerous tanks were hit and many men were killed, the disruption so serious that the *9. SS-Panzer-Division* was thrown into confusion and desperate messages were relayed to the rear command echelons. As this deafening barrage fell, the fighting still raged on the front of the 1st Tyneside Scottish, where stretcher-bearers worked with a will to get the wounded away from the battle area; many of them were regimental pipers, these brave men saving many a life and great numbers of them becoming casualties as the SS showed no respect for a man wearing the Red Cross. Private J. Munro recalled: "I knew many of the pipe band as I played chanter with Piper Forrest back in the UK. One of my good friends, Piper Jock Simpson[337] from Aberdeen was shot by a sniper while he was tending the wounded; he did wear the red cross insignia."

The men from D Company, 1st Tyneside Scottish, were still trying to get to B Company, and after being forced back by German fire eventually came across the unit's rear. Corporal George Cowie of D Company moved forward into B Company's position amid shot and shell:

> The big stuff from the enemy was still flying about and it was anything but quiet. Orders could not be heard even if you bawled them out. As we approached bullets started slashing the grass at my feet, I could have been hit standing up or lying down, so I just carried on at the same pace, except that I was now crossing my fingers and muttering a silent prayer. The small arms fire continued with bullets whining and pinging all around me. With only a few yards to go I ran up a small slope until my head was level with the ground of the field beyond. A few yards ahead of me were several slit-trenches and a group of German infantrymen were scrambling out of these towards a screen of trees about 400 yards to their rear. Taffy joined me at the top of the slope, I grabbed his Bren and fired several bursts after the fleeing Germans, who were zigzagging towards the trees and were running fast.[338]

D Company's Lieutenant I.W. Murray tried numerous different ways to get to B Company's line; when he did finally succeed, he walked around the corner of a hedge to find three fully armed Germans who had not seen him. Lieutenant Murray grabbed a Bren gun and at very close range opened up on the Germans, who took to their heels, with none of them being hit. By this time the area had come under artillery fire again, so all the men leapt into slit trenches. Murray raised himself up to see what was going on: "The sight was hardly encouraging; to the left of centre there were four tanks which, apart from all else, were spoiling our day. My companion, a corpse, concentrated my mind wonderfully. I was convinced that my fighting days were done, at worst I would be dead or wounded, at best I would be a prisoner." The day before, Lieutenant Murray had received from his parents a gold ring and watch for his 21st birthday, inscribed with the crest of the Black Watch. Not wanting the Germans to have these as trophies, he placed them in a small envelope, burying them at the bottom of the trench he was in: "And so on we sat in a hail of shells, bombs and bullets. At intervals, we watched the four German tank crews coming up and out for air. They smoked cigarettes and chatted, no one dared fire at them. The

---

337 Corporal John George Simpson, 1st Battalion Tyneside Scottish, Black Watch, was killed in action on 1 July 1944, aged 29. He is buried in Fontenay-le-Pesnel War Cemetery, France.
338 *WW2: People's War* <www.bbc.co.uk/ww2peopleswar> (accessed 22 December 2020).

tanks were so close that if they did open fire on the exposed slit trenches it would have been at point-blank range, and no one would have survived that."[339]

At 1245 hours, smoke was laid down by the Germans and their third attack came in under its cover. The British anti-tank teams fired into the advancing panzers, B Company requested a concentrated artillery stonk to their front and the guns of the 24th Lancers added to the barrage. The reinforcements from D Company were now making their presence felt with their extra firepower.

Private P. Lawton of D Company was in his trench with Private Hamer, when Private Holt arrived and brought him a full Bren-gun magazine. It was now Lawton's job to take it to the next trench:

> I climbed out of the trench and carried it to the next one. Within minutes a shell came over and hit the trench I had just left. I went over to see what I could do and found that poor old Hamer[340] had been cut in half by the shell. Pte Holt didn't appear to have suffered any physical damage at all, he was taken off to hospital suffering from shock and I never saw him again. I have no doubt that he has felt the effects of that moment ever since.[341]

Yet again, panzers and armoured vehicles began concentrating for a third attack on what was left of the 1st Tyneside Scottish positions. The British artillery observation officers had noted that there was a point on the German advance where the tanks were forced to bunch together; this area was given a code name and every time it was sent back to the artillery positions, a concentrated barrage would descend on the German armour, causing death and confusion. At 1400 hours, a machine-gun platoon of the 2nd Kensingtons arrived at D Company's positions and gave a great boost to their dwindling firepower.

So far, the German *Kampfgruppe*, after three attacks, had only succeeded in placing snipers in the hedges and orchards outside the village of Rauray. The Germans had suffered too many losses in their struggle to penetrate the British salient. Nevertheless, yet again the Germans rallied their depleted forces in the afternoon for a fourth attempt, this time on B Company's front. The manpower situation was now critical for the Tynesiders, and behind the British lines any man who could stand and hold a rifle was sent to the front to bolster the surviving troops that were holding on. Private George Cowie had been sent to a field hospital by his officer, suffering from enteritis. While he was having a mug of tea, a panicky officer came blundering in and ordered men to get into his truck as the situation was desperate. Cooks and other soldiers who worked behind the lines were also given a rifle and put in the truck. Cowie recalled: "We were definitely scraping the bottom of the barrel for reinforcements, even the battalion tailor went."[342] Cowie got into the truck with his comrades and they hurtled off for the front line. As he approached the forward area, the sound of battle was deafening.

---

339 Beaverstock, *Breaking the Panzers*, p. 124.
340 Private Cyril Hamer, 1st Battalion Tyneside Scottish, Black Watch, was killed in action on 1 July 1944, aged 19. He has no known grave and is commemorated on the Bayeux Memorial to the Missing, France.
341 Baverstock, *Breaking the Panzers*, p. 125.
342 *WW2: People's War* <www.bbc.co.uk/ww2peopleswar> (accessed 21 December 2020).

At 1605 hours, the fourth German counter-attack was in preparation and they were rushing more SS panzers and troops to the front to take part. At Queudeville, German infantry were spotted debussing from armoured vehicles and tanks were also seen in the area. A massive artillery and mortar barrage soon fell on the area and did great execution; the attack had failed before it could begin. C Squadron of the Buffs was now allocated to 70 Brigade and sent six flame-throwing Churchill Crocodile tanks to aid the 1st Tyneside Scottish and the front held by the 11th Durhams. They advanced towards the German positions, closely followed by infantry, slowly creeping forward along the lines of hedgerows seeking out their prey. German snipers hidden in the undergrowth must have looked on in terror as the Crocodiles approached, blasting the hedges with their powerful Besa machine guns. When they reach an area where snipers had been active, they belched out a tongue of fire some 60–80 yards long, which consumed great swathes of the countryside and covered the area in acrid stinking smoke, burning to death any Germans concealed there. German troops who had survived this terrible onslaught fled before this vision of hell. Despite curing the problem of snipers, on the Tynesiders' front the lead Churchill flamethrower was hit and exploded in a ball of fire that incinerated the crew. It is believed it was hit by friendly fire.

All the German infantry in the Rauray area were put to flight, and on the right of B Company, 1st Tyneside Scottish, it was reported that enemy tanks were withdrawing at 1730 hours. Slowly, 70 Brigade began to advance, still under heavy fire.

During the evening of 1 July, Lord Haw-Haw broadcast a message from Germany in which he referred to the men of the 49th West Riding Division as "You Polar Bear Butchers", threatening them with immediate execution if they were captured and claiming that they had massacred surrendering SS troops. Indeed, one officer, a Lieutenant Green, and two other ranks of the 1st Tyneside Scottish were captured on 9 July and 10 days later their bodies were found in the cellars of the Chateau Juvigny. They had been executed.

Enemy shelling continued all night and all forward troops 'stood-to' in the darkness. Flares climbed high into the night sky and tank engines could be heard revving up behind the German lines. The exhausted young British infantry stared into the gloom as each man listened for the sounds of German infantry moving through the fields and hedges. Engineers went out into no man's land to lay anti-tank mines, taking a risk that they may be killed by the Germans or by jumpy troops of their own side. Corporal George Cowie heard noises to his front and was about to fire when a subdued voice said: "Are you the Tyneside Scots?" The frightened engineers identified themselves, but no one had a password, without which troops usually opened fire without warning. But the engineers were lucky and were allowed to pass. As morning dawned on 2 July, the Tynesiders were relieved by the Durhams, and as the weary advanced companies moved to the rear they were able to see the full devastation in their sector. The dead of both sides were scattered around the fields and hedgerows in various grotesque positions. Blackened and burnt-out shells of Shermans, panzers, Bren carriers and half-tracks were everywhere, and the ground was so pitted by shellfire it looked like the surface of the moon. Every building in the area lay in ruins. Corporal Cowie said: "We came across one of our divisional MPs directing traffic at the cross-roads. He shouted out congratulating us, then came over and said we were the talk of the bridgehead and I thought that was nice. We were shattered."[343]

---

343 *WW2: People's War* <www.bbc.co.uk/ww2peopleswar> (accessed 21 December 2020).

German infantry, creeping along a hedge-lined ditch, infiltrate the British positions near Rauray. (Courtesy of H. Wernemann)

Other troops were left behind to bury the dead – a massive task. Limbs and other bits of bodies were collected, many of these having no identity and being thrown into a mass grave. C.W. Chesworth, the 1st Tyneside Scottish chaplain, described the situation as "one very long nightmare". The men who had fought in the bridgehead all talked of Rauray as the worst action they took part in during the war. Acting Corporal J.W. Barnes, 1st Tyneside Scottish, looked around him and saw "a mass of debris, bodies and burning tanks and at the risk of sounding melodramatic, it was a kind of Armageddon".[344] As the dead were lowered into their temporary graves, a lone piper played 'The Flowers of the Forest'. The survivors paraded in the rear areas, and when the Regimental Sergeant Major called the roll it was found that more than half the battalion was missing.

The German counter-attacks at Rauray had been the first and last chance of the panzer divisions to make a deep penetration into the Allied line. Their failure was a turning point for the Allies and heralded the start of the German collapse in the west of the front. For the Germans, the counter-attacks against the 15th Scottish and 49th Divisions had been a costly failure, leaving the remaining enemy forces on the Rauray Spur to adopt a position of passive defence. In the attritional battles at Rauray, Operation Martlet had achieved its objective in distracting the German forces from the area of Operation Epsom and inflicting heavy casualties on the panzer divisions involved. However, XXX Corps had failed to reach its objective of the high ground beyond Rauray, and even though the village had been captured, the Germans were still

---

344 *WW2: People's War* <www.bbc.co.uk/ww2peopleswar> (accessed 21 December 2020).

in a commanding position on the Rauray Spur. The 49th West Riding Division held the line around Rauray for nearly a month before leaving XXX Corps on 30 July.

The 1/6th Battalion Duke of Wellington's Regiment: disbandment

At the beginning of July, Montgomery received a report that made disturbing reading. It was from the commanding officer of the 1/6th Battalion Duke of Wellington's Regiment, Lieutenant Colonel A.J.D. Turner, MC, and made the claim that the unit was not fit to be in the front line. Turner had taken command of the battalion at the start of the Epsom offensive, and by the end of it he had concluded they should be disbanded. He stated:

> Being a regular officer, I realise the seriousness of this request and its effect on my career. On the other hand, I have the lives of the new officer personnel to consider. Three days running a Major has been killed or seriously wounded because I have ordered him to help me in effect to stop the men from running during a mortar concentration. Twice I had to draw my revolver on retreating men. NCO leadership is weak in most cases and the newly drafted officers are in consequence having to expose themselves unduly to try to get anything done.[345]

The breakdown of discipline was in part because of the lack of effective leadership. In 14 days of action, the battalion had lost all of its company commanders and 23 other officers. Some companies had lost more than their fair share of officer and NCO casualties. In its first engagement on 17 June, the 1/6th had received a terrible mauling. The Yorkshiremen had been looking forward to going into their first action in Normandy; having been preparing for it for nearly four years, they felt it was now their turn to join in the fighting that others had been doing. On 17 June, the battalion attacked Le-Parc-de-Boislande, a chateau in thickly wooded parkland not far from Tilly-sur-Seulles. They were given very little intelligence regarding their objective and were told they would not be facing first-grade German units. A creeping barrage thundered up the slopes of the ridge as the 1/6th advanced, accompanied by the tanks of the 24th Lancers. They were met by heavy mortar and Spandau fire, but within two hours the chateau and the surrounding woodland had been cleared. One officer recorded: "We were absolutely over the moon; it was our first success, and it was a very good feeling." However, casualties had been high, with 150 other ranks and nine officers having fallen in the fighting.

Lieutenant Leonard Willis of the 24th Lancers wrote of his unit's part in the action:

> The Parc-de-Boislande harboured tanks and infantry and caused us much trouble. The attack went well, little opposition was met until we reached the objective, [but] here stiff pockets of enemy resistance were encountered. Our tanks shot up well over 50 infantry in a hedgerow. The troops on our left worked round the forward edge of the objective and took up fire positions. On the right resistance was stiffer and the Duke of Wellington's had a

---

345 Report on the state of 6th Battalion Duke of Wellington's Regiment. Public Records Office WO205/5G.

heavy task in clearing the enemy out. We were in position by 4pm near the chateau facing east, when two of our tanks were shot up by 88mm guns.[346]

The 1/6th Duke of Wellington's dug-in around the chateau but their flanks were seriously exposed, and no support arrived. They were 2,000 yards in front of any other troops and their salient could be attacked from three sides. The whole area was under constant artillery and mortar fire, making it difficult to evacuate casualties, and as dusk fell the supporting anti-tank guns and tanks withdrew to the rear, leaving the infantry alone and exposed.

The following day, 18 June, a tremendous enemy barrage came down on the positions of the 1/6th between 1000 and 1400 hours and the expected counter-attack was launched on their positions by a large force of German infantry and tanks, supported by mortar and artillery fire. Captain John Allan was behind the front in support and watched as the lead companies were overrun: "We saw our troops running through the woods in some disarray, which was a terrible shock. We tried to stop them, but they were not ready to listen, they were on their way and were being shelled at the same time."[347] The whole battalion then rushed to the rear, retreating over the ground that they had won at such a heavy cost the day before, taking even more casualties. Lieutenant Colonel F.K. Hughes later wrote of the situation:

> The Dukes had dug in insufficiently during the night and were without adequate overhead cover. Many casualties were thus suffered from shells bursting in the treetops, and then the enemy followed up with a quick raid on the foremost positions.[348]

The machine guns of the 2nd Kensingtons were supporting the Duke of Wellington's, and Corporal J. Calland, MM, saw the German infantry advancing towards his platoon:

> We could hear shouts and see movement in the field and then they came on, some yelling and some weaving like Indians though the corn. I fired through the battle sights and saw them fall, it was a queer feeling because this was the first time I had seen the Germans and it all seemed unreal. We pulled them up in front of us, but they got by on either side and our infantry was running back. Grenades were bursting all around us and bullets were whistling through the branches of the trees. Our section commander told us to fall back, and we made our way through the woods. We had nine casualties and lots of equipment lost or destroyed. Later a burial party found 40 dead Germans in the field opposite our position.[349]

The 1/6th were withdrawn to Le-Haut-d'Audrieu to reorganise and refit from 19–24 June. Morale seemed to have been broken, and although over the next few days new arrivals came into their ranks, there were no NCOs or officers, and the men were in a depressed state. Captain

---

346 L. Willis, correspondence with author (Godalming, 1992).
347 Barclay, C.N., *History of the Duke of Wellington's Regiment 1919–1952* (London: William Clowes, 1953), p. 98.
348 Hughes, F.K., *A Short History of the 49th West Riding and Midlands Division* (Hertfordshire: Stella Press, 1957), p. 57.
349 J. Calland, correspondence with author (Brentwood, 1994). Corporal Calland was awarded the Military Medal for his actions on 17 June 1944.

Allan commented: "It was a very unhappy and distressing time. We were ashamed, so we dug holes and went into a defensive position until it was decided what to do with us; in three days there were five cases of self-inflicted wounds, and the men were jumpy under shellfire."[350]

Lieutenant Michael Trasenster, 4/7th Royal Dragoon Guards, was sympathetic to the 'poor bloody infantry', who he knew had an unglamorous role and always suffered the heaviest casualties. He commented:

> One of the most moving sights I have ever seen was an infantry regiment, 1/6th Duke of Wellington's, decimated by terror. Soldiers were retreating with most of their officers alive and still with them, [though] a few, Canute like, tried to halt the unstoppable tide. Weapons were abandoned, [and] people were clinging to the backs of Bren-gun carriers, anything to get away from the German dawn attack. The regiment concerned had an horrific night, with a flame throwing Panther tank driving around their slit trenches burying many men alive and using the roaring flames to light their way around.[351]

On 26 June, the 1/6th would fight its last battle as a unit, led by Lieutenant Colonel Turner. Their task was to plug the gap between Juvigny and the western outskirts of Fontenay-le-Pesnel. Brigadier C.N. Barclay described the terrain over which the troops would have to pass:

> The ground made it difficult to approach unseen, [as] the first half mile was a forward slope, a great cornfield, criss-crossed by the tracks of armoured vehicles, but with not a vestige of cover. After this came a stretch of fields, with their hedges running forward to drop sharply in a wooded bluff, down to the River Bordel Valley. Beyond it the orchards and fields rose gradually to the Juvigny/Fontenay Road, along which the country was more open.[352]

As the troops left their start line, they were in full view of the Germans, who rained down mortar fire upon them, but they pressed on. The mortar fire continued and the casualties began to mount as they moved towards their final objective. From that point on everything went wrong: the mortar and shellfire became more concentrated, and direct hits were being made on the British mortar teams and the Headquarters of the 1/6th. Carrying parties and stretcher-bearers worked feverishly amid this storm of high explosive, and were in turn bombarded with mortar bombs. Major George Henry Foster,[353] the new second-in-command, was killed when he advanced in a carrier that ran over a mine. His successor, Major K.E.F. Miller, was seriously wounded when his jeep also triggered a mine. The *Aufklärung Abteilung* of the *12. SS-Panzer-Division 'Hitlerjugend'* scored hit after hit with their mortar bombs as they pounded the 1/6th with frightening ferocity and accuracy. The badly mauled 1/6th were in some disarray and got no further, and on 30 June they were withdrawn into brigade reserve, where they dug in. By stages, the 1/6th was moved back slowly to the beachhead.

---

350 Barclay, *History of the Duke of Wellington's Regiment*, p. 98.
351 Kershaw, R., *Tank Men* (London: Hodder & Stoughton, 2008), p. 346.
352 Barclay, *History of the Duke of Wellington's Regiment*, p. 209.
353 Major George Henry Forster, MiD, King's (Liverpool) Regiment, attached to 1/6th Battalion Duke of Wellington's Regiment, was killed in action on 27 June 1944, aged 43. He is buried in Tilly-sur-Seulles War Cemetery, France.

The 1/6th Duke of Wellington's had generally been a well-trained and useful battalion when it came to Normandy. However, they had lost so many key personnel that the battalion was unable to assimilate the new men coming in. Many men were suffering from shellshock; when they went to the rear, it was up to the medical officer to sort out the malingerers from the genuine cases, and a number of men were returned to action. Montgomery was not happy with the situation and sent Turner's report on the battalion to the Secretary of State for War, James Grigg, with the comment: "I consider the CO displays a defeatist mentality and is not a proper chap."[354] Nevertheless, Montgomery followed Turner's advice and sent the 1/6th back to Colchester in August, where they provided reinforcements for the 1/7th Duke of Wellington's. This had been a brave, young and untried battalion which had met the full ferocity of the '*Hitlerjugend*' and other SS troops in the Bocage, but it was now the end of the line. Many men and officers were sent to other units and fought with distinction until the war ended. Many were killed or wounded.

56 Brigade at '2nd Hottot', 8–9 July

On 8 July, the battle for Hottot was taken up again as 56 Brigade pressed forward with the intention of getting across the main road west of the village. The two leading battalions would be the 2nd Essex on the left and on their right the 2nd South Wales Borderers. Private A. Vince recalled the preparations as the 2nd Essex got ready to make their attack:

> Reveille was at 03:00a.m. on the 8th and at first light we were forming up in orchards occupied by the advanced companies. A bulldozer was smashing through hedgerows for our vehicles to follow up behind the lead troops. As our barrage opened up the enemy were also preparing for an attack and our shells tore into one of their battalions as it formed up on one of our objectives.[355]

Lieutenant Hugh Barrett-Lennard of the 2nd Essex marshalled his men and led them to their start line:

> Reveille was at 03:00 and at first light we were forming up in orchards. A bulldozer was smashing a path through the hedgerows for our vehicles to pass through as they followed the leading troops. At this point the British artillery barrage tore into a German battalion, co-incidentally forming up to attack us at mid-day, causing them to suffer high casualties. Despite this the reason for the tough resistance encountered by 2nd Essex and 2nd South Wales Borderers was likely to be because the German infantry, and their supporting armour and artillery were well positioned to receive an attack. The SWB and 2nd Essex forged ahead but tanks were unable to follow due to the presence of mines. They harboured in a field and gave supporting fire while attempts were made to clear the road of mines.[356]

---

354 Hamilton, *Monty*, p. 278.
355 Manuscript forwarded to author by A. Vince (Essex, 1989).
356 P. Cuerdon, correspondence with author (Hampshire, 1991).

A Tiger II in a hull-down position firing at the attacking British troops and armour at Hottot. (Courtesy of M. Hearst)

Concentrations of enemy tanks and troops were situated in this area, and the attacking troops of 56 Brigade were met with heavy machine-gun and mortar fire. During the afternoon, they had managed to reach their objectives and as they dug-in and prepared defensive positions, German heavy tanks were rumbling forward to take part in a counter-attack.

Private Vince and his comrades sat tight in their hastily dug slit trenches: "We were stuck there all day under incessant shell and mortar-fire and casualties mounted."[357] By evening, the two attacking battalions had been forced to withdraw north of the road. Although 56 Brigade had brought the divisional front closer to the main road, the Germans were determined to take back the lost ground. During the night and in the early hours of 9 July, the 2nd Essex waited for the inevitable counter-attack, the air filled with ominous sounds coming from the German lines of heavy tanks on the move.

Private Vince sat in his slit trench as these frightening noises came to him through the gloom:

> Early in the morning of the 9th we could hear that for which we had been waiting, the preparations for a counterattack. The shouting of German officers and NCOs, as they sorted out their men, and the rumble of enemy tanks, as they took up their positions, came to us through the damp hazy first light. Artillery was quickly and accurately laid down on the

---

357 Manuscript forwarded to author by A. Vince (Essex, 1989).

Germans forming up places, but the attack came in at 06:00 a.m. Mark IV tanks bore down upon 7 Platoon and simultaneously hordes of infantry assailed B, D and A Companies.[358]

Corporal Philip Mailou of the 2nd Essex was manning a Bren gun and could see no more than 50 yards through the trees and hedges. In the gloom, figures could be made out as they moved about. Artillery and tanks in support fired over the heads of the Tommies:

> We were knocking these infantrymen over and afterwards we counted about 60 German dead to our front. We suddenly realised we had got a lot of empty magazines and two or three of us started loading the mags. We were behind a bank and a lot of stuff was going over. Suddenly there is a loud bang and I'm hit. "Get a stretcher-bearer," I shout. Someone shouts back: "Bugger off get one yourself." A ricochet had taken a lump out of my leg, and no-one was going back to the first aid post under that fire. Eventually I did get back to the first aid post where they put a bandage on it and had done with it, [and] I returned to duty.[359]

The battle went on without pause for two hours as both sides threw their full weight at each other, all the time being at very close range. The 2nd Essex held on with a grim determination; despite heavy casualties, each company re-formed and adjusted their positions. German tanks and *panzergrenadiere* pressed forward, and some platoons were forced to give ground. A Mark IV tank attacked HQ Platoon and destroyed it completely. The Piat gunners took on the tanks and knocked out three of them, after which the remainder, along with their infantry, began to pull back. As the battle subsided, the Essex men were subjected to terrific shellfire for the rest of the day; casualties and prisoners were sent to the rear. But their trials were not yet over, and later on 9 July the Germans launched yet another attempt to crush the 2nd Essex. Private Vince and his comrades counted 80 German dead only yards from B Company's front before the counter-attack was launched:

> At 18:00 p.m. the enemy put in his final attack. The whole of the balance of the German brigade was thrown in and, yelling and firing, they came across the fields right onto our automatics and rifles. Many were mown down but still they pressed the attack home until our Crocodiles, flame-throwing tanks, came up and wrought havoc in their decimated ranks. Gradually they broke and fled, chased by long tongues of flame 150 yards long from the Crocodiles and by our small-arms fire.[360]

The Crocodile crews used their weapons with lethal effect, but even so, when they saw the results of their work up close, it was distressing to see men burning to death before their eyes. Sergeant Reginald Webb was the commander of one Crocodile tank:

> The commander would give the order: "Flame-gun fire!" and a jet of flame would leap from the front of the tank with a roar. Everything in its path would be carpeted in burning fuel until the fire rose in one fierce red wall. The gun would splutter and hiss like an empty

---

358 Manuscript forwarded to author by A. Vince (Essex, 1989).
359 P. Mailou, correspondence with author (Essex, 1990).
360 Manuscript forwarded to author by A. Vince (Essex, 1989).

soda-water siphon. It was a formidable weapon, but it was horrible to use, and the result was terrible. You got the horrifying picture of somebody alight and running away. But do as you would be done by, if we didn't hit him, he might have a *Panzerfaust* and that was you finished.[361]

Lieutenant Andrew Wilson saw the effects of his flamethrower tank, and though it was shocking, men carried on as they knew the enemy would not shrink from doing the same to them:

> There were numerous bodies which seemed to have been blown back by the force of the flame and lay in naked blackened heaps. Others were caught in twisted poses as if the flame had frozen them. Their clothes had been burned away, only their helmets and boots remained, ridiculous and horrible. The stench of death was everywhere.[362]

The men of 56 Brigade had brought the British line nearer to the main road into Hottot. As they dug-in and consolidated their positions, it now fell again to 231 Brigade to launch another attack to take the heap of ruins that was the village of Hottot.

231 Brigade at '3rd Hottot', 11 July, "Protect me this day Lord"

The 1st Hampshires and 2nd Devons of 231 Brigade, supported by the tanks of the Sherwood Rangers, would make the assault. Lieutenant Geoffrey Picot of the 1st Hampshires received a detailed description of the coming attack from his CO, Lieutenant Colonel Howie, as did an unusually large group of officers:

> It was the largest orders group I had ever attended. Besides our own company and support platoon commanders there were tank commanders, flame throwing tank commanders, artillery representatives, heavy mortar and machine-gun commanders, one or two liaison officers, the medical officer and the padre. The size of the group was an indication of the amount of help we were going to get. As we sat on the grass, Lt Colonel Howie strode up and down in front of us: "This battalion will capture Hottot" he shouted with great emphasis. "We will capture Hottot, and we will hold it at all costs, this is how we will attack." He went on to give specific orders to everyone. Howie was fierce, storming and confident. But there were some of us who couldn't feel so confident. Since our first attack we had sat outside the village and given it the name of Hot spot. We were now banging our heads against a brick wall.[363]

Lieutenant David Render moved to the front with his Sherwood Rangers squadron in support of 231 Brigade:

---

361 R. Webb, correspondence with author (Huntingdon, 1986).
362 A. Wilson, correspondence with author (Melton Mowbray, 1990).
363 Picot, *Accidental Warrior*, p. 91.

It took all night to move into our positions on the start line for the attack, which would be the standard 'two up' infantry brigade affair. Two of the brigade's battalions, each supported by a squadron of tanks from the Sherwood Rangers, would form the initial assault force, while C Squadron would remain in reserve with the brigade's third infantry battalion. That first night snipers crept forward to infiltrate our positions and there was always the risk that a German with a *Panzerfauste* might work his way through the infantry protecting us. I strained my eyes into the blackness around me, closing one eye to protect my night vision when flares bathed the ground ahead of me in brilliant light before dying out to cast eerie flickering shadows all around. The occasional stream of tracer cut through the darkness which was alive with strange shapes that played tricks on the mind and stretched my imagination as I struggled to stay awake and focused.[364]

The night before the battle, men slept fitfully where they could under their ground sheets and tarpaulins. Some were lucky and found a damaged barn or the ruins of a house to bed down in. Just before first light, breakfast and tea was prepared; many feared that this may be their last meal. At 0630 hours on 11 July, the attacking brigades moved to their forming-up positions. Officers and NCOs looked at their wristwatches as the hands crept slowly to 0700 hours. Lieutenant Picot said to himself: "I wonder how many people are praying from the bottom of their hearts: Protect me this day Lord."[365] As the second hands of watches ticked inexorably to zero-hour, tense and stressed men stood to their arms waiting. At 0700 hours, from the rear came a deafening roar as artillery, mortars and machine guns opened up. The soldiers stood up in the half-light and walked towards the thundering barrage as it blasted trees, earth, machines and bodies high into the air. Picot had to shout orders in order to be heard among this deluge of fire:

On the start line Major Littlejohns will be saying: "Ok away we go." For a long time the roar of the artillery does not stop as terrific salvoes swish overhead and we wish our riflemen luck. The bark of machine-guns is so continuous that it gets on one's nerves. For a time, the attack goes well, and I move one of my sections of mortars 1,000 yards forward. The engineers have blown gaps in hedges immediately behind the assault troops and vehicles are passing through the gaps moving across countryside. Many salvoes from the enemy are landing near a hedge 300 yards behind us and I am thankful they didn't land there when we were moving up. All the same the shelling is uncomfortably close. The loud crack of explosions, the sight of disintegrating hedges, the thick black smoke that hangs around and the reeking smell of burning cordite gives me a sinking feeling.[366]

David Render moved forward with the infantry in his Sherman:

The artillery barrage began to creep forward as dawn broke over the eastern horizon and there was little time to marry up with the infantry before we began to move forward. The first light revealed the nature of the ground over which we would have to advance, sloping

364 Render, *Tank Action*, p. 131.
365 Picot, *Accidental Warrior*, p. 106.
366 Picot, *Accidental Warrior*, p. 94.

upwards to the northern side of the village. It was typical Bocage, studded with orchards and clumps of trees among a patchwork of small hedge bound fields little bigger than a football pitch. Due to the noise of our engines, we couldn't hear the scream of the incoming shells, but the infantry could, and they sank to the ground like moles just before the first of the rounds began to land. Those infantrymen that made it to cover, or avoided a direct hit, survived, others caught out in the open became casualties.[367]

Lieutenant A.E. Blackmore, 1st Hampshires, remembered the fierce defence he faced:

The attack began with a hand-to-hand party in an orchard. I got the leading section of 7 Platoon near to the southern end under covering fire without too much trouble and then Jerry gave us everything he had at point-blank range. At this stage Horace Wright, who was in the adjoining field, crawled up through the hedge to give me further orders and while he was talking, I had the uncomfortable sensation that my backside was being made a target for Spandau fire. From his position in the ditch on the side of the hedge he couldn't see the ground being churned up behind me, whereas I was uncomfortably aware of the fact.[368]

Lieutenant Render remembered the heavy German counter-barrage and the snipers up in the trees which ensured he kept his head well down while placing a decoy helmet near his hatch:

We hosed down every likely tree and piece of cover with machine-gun fire. The German snipers often tied themselves into the trees to stop them falling out when wounded. We only knew if we hit one when a German soldier toppled from the branches to have his fall smartly arrested by a piece of rope. The first hedge line was sanitised with 15 minutes of 30 calibre and 75mm HE, [then] we positioned ourselves to deal with the next hedgerow. Rapid fire of HE shells could smash an enemy tank's optics or damage its tracks, however we never remained static for too long as constant fire and movement was the way to stay alive. Having fired three or four rounds at a target in rapid succession, each Sherman would jockey backwards and then drive back into a new attack position. We put these tactics into operation at Hottot.[369]

The situation became confused as the smoke from exploding shells and burning tanks and carriers obscured the view of the battlefield. The Germans showed no signs of weakening, keeping up a stout defence in the face of the onslaught. Throughout a very hot day, the British fought their way forward against fierce and determined opposition. They were at the point of gaining their first objective when shells from their own artillery came down among them, inflicting more casualties on the surviving troops. Lieutenant Blackmore struggled through the chaos and took his first prisoners:

---

367 Render, *Tank Action*, p. 132.
368 A.E. Blackmore, correspondence with author (Hampshire, 1992).
369 Render, *Tank Action*, p. 134.

The enemy now began to surrender and 14 of them came out, two or three of who were boys of about 18 years or so, but fierce fighters for all that. I counted seven enemy dead in the orchard and there were also several badly wounded Huns who seemed glad enough to be put into the bag after their ordeal. After a brief pause to regroup A Company advanced to its first objective known as 'Orange'. After we consolidated all hell was let loose on us for two hours, causing further casualties among the company. In the afternoon we moved forward again and reached the outskirts of Hottot at about 15:30 p.m. after getting some really heavy mortar fire. Here we dug in; there were woods to our left and right and the houses, or what was left of them, of Hottot itself could be seen about 500 yards to our immediate front. Tanks of the Sherwood Rangers, complete with flails and flame-throwing Crocodiles, were now in close support.[370]

At this moment one of those tragedies of war occurred. The drone of rocket-firing Typhoons was heard overhead, and the British troops looked up in the expectation of them blasting the German positions. The fighter-bombers' engines roared as they went into a steep dive, and Lieutenant Geoffrey Picot of the 1st Hampshires recalled Lieutenant Colonel Howie going forward to see why his men were held up:

The issue of the battle was hanging in the balance when we hear RAF rocket firing Typhoons coming to support us and we are thrilled. With eager anticipation we see the Typhoons fly in and dive to the attack. Surely, they are diving early, yes, they are, what on earth are they up to? And then, slap in the middle of the battalion area, they loosed off their rockets, there is a swish and then a shuddering explosion. As I crouch in a slit trench the earth trembled beneath me, but I trembled more. I did not know whether to stay there or get out of my trench and wave our identification flags. There is only one thing I really wanted at that moment and that was for the earth to open and swallow me up for safety. The planes circled around again, and I notice one lad wildly waving identification flags at them. Finally, the Typhoons got the message and flew home.[371]

David Render also told of the friendly-fire his fellow Sherwood Rangers suffered at Hottot:

I heard the high-pitched roar of an aero engine. I looked up behind me and saw the first black shape of a Typhoon diving towards us. The leading edge of its wings seemed to be on fire, and I initially thought that it might have been hit by German flak. Then it began to bank and climb upwards and that's when I saw the smoke trails betraying the presence of rockets streaking towards us. I had just enough time to shout a frantic warning to the rest of the troop to batten down and managed to get one half of my own hatch closed, when the screaming projectiles exploded on either side of us and showered the tank with steel splinters.[372]

---

370 A.E. Blackmore, correspondence with author (Hampshire, 1992).
371 Picot, *Accidental Warrior*, p. 95.
372 Render, *Tank Action*, p. 137.

Render looked through the half-open hatch of the tank turret and watched as three more Typhoons circled in the sky. As they went into a steep dive, they swooped down one after the other, 60mm rockets speeding off their wings accompanied by bursts of 20mm cannon fire that tore up the ground around the stationary tanks:

> Some of the rounds hit us but none of the rockets did, which would have opened us up like a tin of beans. While it was over in a matter of seconds, being under air attack is a frightening experience. It was made worse by the fact that we were suffering at the hands of our own air force, [and] the language in the tank was foul. Dickie Holman in 4 Troop was particularly upset as the RAF shot up all the presents he had just received for his 21st birthday, which were strapped under the tarpaulin on the back of his tank.[373]

Lieutenant Blackmore of the 1st Hampshires also left a detailed account of this friendly-fire incident:

> At 16:00 p.m. I heard the drone of approaching aircraft; our Typhoons were coming over. The engines of the nearest aircraft roared as the plane began to dive, and with a feeling that quickly changed from one of relief to one of horror, I realised that our RAF friends were attacking our positions. Not altogether surprising as the picture was very confused, our tanks being in close combat with the enemy tanks. The rocket fire came down with a mighty roar and I felt a somewhat queasy sensation in the pit of my stomach as the rockets exploded in the wood about 70 yards away. The Typhoon in question banked for a second attack when one of our tanks managed to fire a yellow identification signal just in time to warn the pilot. He rose steeply and flew on without firing. Then a Panther tank opened up on our right flank and moved towards us, but another Typhoon spotted it and attacked immediately. There was an ear-splitting explosion and the Panther rocked sideways and then halted while red and orange flames rapidly engulfed it and set fire to its ammunition. Another tank was also hit judging by the smoke and flames that rose from a nearby copse. It was now becoming impossible to see anything clearly through the thickening smoke.[374]

Lieutenant Render wrote of the subsequent hard fight to get into the village:

> It took another day of difficult fighting to grind our way slowly up the hill towards Hottot and to break into the village. The enemy continued to shell us heavily as we eventually fought our way down the long narrow high street. The tanks dealt with any machine-gun positions and any elevated structures that might conceal a sniper or an artillery spotter, by pumping 75mm rounds into the church spire and the upper windows of any prominent building. Then the infantry would enter and clear the houses on either side of the street with grenades and bursts of automatic fire. We progressed through the village in this manner until we were engaged by anti-tank fire and forced off the road to seek cover. The

---

373 Render, *Tank Action*, p. 137.
374 A.E. Blackmore, correspondence with author (Hampshire, 1992).

Troops of the Hampshires and tanks of the Sherwood Rangers enter the ruins of Hottot. (Author's collection)

first round hit one of our tanks and caused it to brew-up. I hoped the crew got out as within seconds the Sherman was a raging inferno. For once I was thankful for the constant loud noise of our own engine and the battle around me, as it would drown out the animal like screams if any of the men were still trapped inside.[375]

The Sherwood Rangers had knocked out several German tanks, but their own losses had been considerable. Lieutenant Render looked back on the men he knew who had become casualties:

Captain Ronnie Gellis was cruelly maimed when he had his jaw shot away by a sniper. Mike Howden received shrapnel wounds to his face when in the lead up the road to Hottot.

375 Render, *Tank Action*, p. 136.

Geoffrey Malkins[376] was seriously wounded by artillery fire when out of his tank, [and] tragically he was to die of his wounds sometime later.[377]

Lieutenant Stuart Hills was acting as a liaison officer with the Sherwood Rangers and gleaned information about the progress of the battle as he moved around:

> My own tank was very much involved, and all its periscopes were smashed by mortar fire. Again, the infantry was taking very heavy casualties. The CO of the 1st Hampshires was killed and his counterpart in the 2nd Devons wounded. Sadly, the Sherwood Rangers also had losses, and one of them was my old tank gunner Doug Footitt, who was killed in action the first time he commanded his own tank.[378] Arthur remembers shaking hands with him just before the action, as they wished each other good luck: "I'm not looking forward to this lot," Doug had said. Five other tank commanders were killed or wounded in this action.[379]

Shortly after 1600 hours, a barrage of artillery and mortar fire was laid down on the German positions, but the attackers were now in a poor condition after what they had been through; morale was in a fragile state, the Typhoon attack having made it worse in the forward companies. A second attack was launched with Lieutenant Colonel Howie directing the two leading companies, but it did not get very far as the enemy returned the barrage with interest. Howie was killed in this last abortive assault.[380]

For the 2nd Devons, on the left of the Hampshires, it was the same story. They advanced and fought bravely all day on 11 July, initially making good progress. They knocked out six enemy tanks but were eventually stopped and finally driven back by troops of the *Panzer-Lehr-Division*. The first and second attacks were stopped in their tracks, causing many casualties, including several officers, as the deadly accurate German artillery fire came down on the advancing troops. Dozens of German prisoners were taken, but the attack had lost all cohesion as the depleted companies struggled to get forward. At the end of the day, 231 Brigade had reached a line just north of Hottot, but the Germans still held on to the pile of rubble that was the village.

Lieutenant Blackmore sat with his men in the forward positions of the 1st Hampshires as the Germans laid down a prolonged and accurate bombardment:

> We hung on to our forward positions with our right flank dangerously exposed. During much of the time there was a lot of confused firing in our rear, and it seemed as if the enemy

---

376 Major Geoffrey Ernest Malkins, 1st Battalion Royal Dragoons, Royal Armoured Corps, was wounded and sent home to England; he died of his wounds on 4 September 1944, aged 28. He is buried in Rotherfield Greys Churchyard, Oxfordshire.
377 Render, *Tank Action*, p. 136.
378 Corporal Douglas Haig Footitt, Sherwood Rangers, Nottinghamshire Yeomanry, Royal Armoured Corps, was killed in action at Hottot on 11 July 1944, aged 27. He is buried in Bayeux War Cemetery, France.
379 Hills, *By Tank to Normandy*, p. 114.
380 Lieutenant Colonel Charles Henry Roger Howie, King's Liverpool Regiment, commanding the 1st Battalion Hampshire Regiment, was killed on 11 July 1944 at Hottot. He was awarded the Distinguished Service Order posthumously for the Hottot action and is buried in Bayeux War Cemetery, France.

were launching some kind of counter-attack from the woods south of the Chateau-de-Cordillon. We heard later that they had done so twice with limited success against the 1st Dorsets, who were able to prevent them from making any serious penetration.[381]

That night, the assaulting brigades sat tight in their positions and licked their wounds. It had been a day of trauma and stress in the extreme, and many familiar faces were now missing. Lieutenant Blackmore received the order to pull back:

> After nightfall on 11 July, 'A' Company was given orders to withdraw, which we managed to do in orderly fashion and without further incident, passing silently within less than 200 yards of the enemy, who made a great deal of noise digging in. However, they didn't hear us, and we got back to a position some 250 yards north-east of the Ferme-de-la-Briajere. Although most of us could cheerfully have fallen asleep standing up, we were pretty tired to put it mildly. It was irritating to yield ground that we had won at the cost of such losses.[382]

On the night of 18/19 July, the enemy finally withdrew from Hottot, leaving behind them a scene of death and devastation. This beautiful little Norman village had been ground to dust as the Germans resisted the British advance with everything at their disposal. Before they left Hottot, the Germans had spent a lot of time laying mines and booby traps in profusion, and as the British entered the village many a curious soldier looking for souvenirs paid the price.

During the early hours of 19 July, Lieutenant Geoffrey Picot led a patrol of the 1st Hampshires towards Hottot as they had received intelligence that the enemy had withdrawn:

> The advance began and went on into the early hours[;] the night was very black and there was inevitably plenty of confusion. The men leading the patrols never knew when they might encounter booby traps or enemy soldiers. Vehicles got bogged down and a lot of noise was made freeing them. But the patrols did their job well, their companies were able to build on them and at daylight the rest of the battalion followed. Our advance was smoothly accomplished, and the intelligence assessment was right, the enemy had gone. The village of Hottot, through which we passed, was very unimposing, just a row of deserted and damaged ruined houses on either side of the road which was covered with rubble. This, for which we had fought so hard, had now fallen into our hands like a ripe plum. There was no sign of the enemy anywhere and we rode joyously over a crest into the valley below. I think we could be seen on this crest from some hills in the distance as the Germans sent over a certain amount of artillery fire. So, we quickly cut and blasted routes through hedges and woods so that supplies could be taken to the front line without any movement being observed.[383]

This ended a bitter and bloody phase in the story of XXX Corps, with no successful set-piece battles and no swift *Blitzkrieg* assaults in which the enemy was routed. It was instead a bloody slogging match to take one ruined village after another, slowly grinding down the German divisions that opposed them. In the process, the divisions of XXX Corps were being bled white in

---

381 A.E. Blackmore, correspondence with author (Hampshire, 1992).
382 A.E. Blackmore, correspondence with author (Hampshire, 1992).
383 Picot, *Accidental Warrior*, p. 104.

A wounded soldier of the *Panzer-Lehr-Division* being taken into captivity.
(Courtesy of H. Wernemann)

the Norman Bocage, and the manpower situation was now becoming critical. In the Normandy battles, the 50th Northumbrian Division alone had suffered 4,476 casualties; companies were below strength and the green recruits that were taking the place of veteran soldiers were not arriving in sufficient numbers to compensate for the troops lost in this bloodletting.

Private Albert Carman had been called up in 1943 at the age of 18, and after completing his training was among a draft of new troops that were posted to the 50th Division in July 1944. As a young boy, he had read with relish newspaper and magazine reports about the exploits of the division as they fought their way through North Africa, Tunisia and Sicily. He was delighted to find he was to join his boyhood heroes, having never dared to dream that he would one day become a part of such a prestigious and respected formation:

> We landed at Arromanches and from there marched to Bayeux; the action had moved inland, and we could hear the ominous rumble of gunfire in the distance. The best way I can describe our feelings is to say we were very apprehensive. At Bayeux we went into a reinforcement holding unit and waited there while units needed reinforcing. In my case it happened to be the 6th Battalion Durham Light Infantry who were part of the 50th Northumbrian Division. I'd read about them when they were fighting in North Africa when I was only 15 or 16, [and] I never thought I'd become part of them. They were great lads and a lot of them were veterans. I felt quite honoured to be with such experienced people. A lot of these chaps were older than me; when you're 18 someone who is 25 is old.

Us rookies would be talking together, and the older chaps would be talking knowing that we would be listening. They would be saying: "Remember old so and so, aye, lost his leg he did didn't he." They were only saying this to frighten us to death and of course they succeeded. But they were very good to us and took you under their wing. They were good lads.[384]

As the struggle for Hottot was raging in July, the other brigades of XXX Corps held the line and inched forward where they could. Reinforcements came into their ranks, enabling them to maintain an aggressive posture towards the enemy. Extensive patrolling was undertaken by all units not involved directly in the fight for Hottot. This was tiring and dangerous work as the enemy had planted mines and booby traps in and around hedges and any other places where the Tommies could advance through. Private Ratcliffe of the 9th Durhams recalled one reconnaissance patrol he took part in:

After we had gone further down the road the officer who was leading decided to turn into a field. This led to some high ground where he thought he could possibly catch sight of the enemy. There was a gap in the hedge, and we were going through it[.] I had an uneasy feeling about this, and I said to Sergeant Farage: "did we need to be with the leading section." I explained how I felt, and he said: "OK, we'll hang on a minute." The leading section went through the gap and one of the lads stood on an S mine, these are anti-personnel devices that, when activated, fire a canister up into the air which explodes firing shrapnel in all directions. Very nasty and much feared by the infantry. Quite a few men in the platoon were hit, including Corporal Cowell[385] who got it in the back.[386]

Enemy shelling and mortar fire was experienced on most days when in the line, while machine guns fired on fixed lines across the landscape in the hope of catching a patrol unawares in no man's land. All German positions at the front had been turned into strongpoints, with armour lurking nearby, and the snipers of both sides were kept busy every day lying in wait for the unwary.

Major Reginald Atkinson of the 6th Durhams remembered the dangers they faced even in relatively static positions:

The grounds of the Chateau-de-Cordillon were littered with S mines when the Germans had withdrawn. A nice young platoon commander, Norman, was permanently blinded here. I lost a platoon commander called Gardner[387] on patrol in this section, he had only joined the company the day before. One young NCO and a private soldier couldn't take it

---

384 Manuscript forwarded to author by A. Carman (Durham, 1991).
385 Corporal Cowell survived the war.
386 Moses, *The Gateshead Gurkhas*, p. 293.
387 Lieutenant Thomas James Gardner, King's Own Lancaster Regiment, attached to 6th Battalion Durham Light Infantry, was killed on 11 July 1944. He is buried in Hottot-le-Bagues War Cemetery, France.

Men of the Dorsetshire Regiment and Durham Light Infantry serving meals to homeless French civilians. (Courtesy of W. Gilson)

anymore and had to be sent back out of the line. At the time of the German withdrawal from Hottot the strain on the rifle companies was beginning to tell.[388]

The 50th Northumbrian Division had taken 3,000 prisoners, mainly from the *Panzer-Lehr*. As the enemy pulled back, all civilians in the area were collected in holding camps where they could be sheltered, cared for and fed; their homes were destroyed, so tents were erected to provide temporary cover for families. The troops set up large field kitchens to feed these poor people and medical assistance was provided where necessary.

The dead were buried without ceremony. The brigades of the 50th Division came out of the line in late July, when they were given time to replenish their stocks of equipment and have a well-earned respite from the horrors of the front. In the rest camps, the luxury of large tents and hot meals were provided for troops who had been living in the open for nearly a month. Parades and battle training took place, which was intended to assimilate the new recruits into the ranks of the veteran formation.

By the end of July, more than a million men were living, fighting and dying in the orchards and fields of the Bocage. The battle meandered through crushed cornfields and shattered villages, where gains were measured in metres as the battle swayed to and fro. All of this took its toll on men as they struggled to come to terms with this new dark and violent world in which

---

388 Moses, *The Faithful Sixth*, p. 297.

they existed. It was XXX Corps' great misfortune to have some of the most formidable German SS divisions confronting them. The men in these German formations were tough and merciless fighters who considered themselves superior to the Allies and to their comrades in the regular German army. *SS-Hauptsturmführer* Hans Bernhard commented: "The soldiers of the division were to demonstrate a toughness to do one's duty no matter what the cost and to go on to the limits of physical and mental endurance. What was at stake for them? We were fighting for our Fatherland."[389] Recruitment into their ranks was based along rigid physical and racial lines, and as such there was a hard ideological edge to their soldiering, with an unquestioning devotion to the *Führer* and the Fatherland.

Major Peter Martin of the 2nd Machine-gun Battalion the Cheshire Regiment looked back on his experiences over these days with a critical eye:

> We, of course, the wretched people on the ground, had no idea of the great Monty plan and we went through a phase when it all seemed totally pointless. Every day a battalion from each brigade would launch an attack to capture another couple of hedgerows. They would probably lose something like two to three hundred men in the process. Up with the rations the next day would come another two hundred men to fill the gaps, then another battalion the following day would do a similar attack and the casualties were enormous. It all seemed to us on the ground totally pointless. Why did we have to expend all those lives capturing the hedgerow in front? Wasn't there some better way of doing it? That's the only time during the whole war when I was ever critical of higher command.[390]

Sergeant James Bellows of the 1st Hampshires recalled one day in Normandy when he passed through an area that had been fought over by the Durhams:

> We got new reinforcements, and one job they were given was to collect the dead for burial. One lad found his twin brother and it shattered him. As we went into the attack in Normandy we passed through a place where the Durhams had gone in, [and] the place was covered with their graves; CO, Adjutant, 2ic, the lot in one field. You can never forget that; little things trigger it off when you wake in the night. Even after all this time it's still so clear.[391]

Normandy was primarily an infantryman's battle, with little quarter given on either side. The tone of the fighting was established early on during the push inland when SS troops began executing prisoners. Several miles north-east of Tilly-sur-Seulles, in the villages of Le-Mesnil-Patry and Audrieu, atrocities were committed against Canadian troops by the *12. SS-Panzer-Division 'Hitlerjugend'*. In mid-June, the same division committed an even worse atrocity at the Chateau Audrieu, where a number of Canadian and British prisoners of war were stood up against a stone wall and summarily executed. Thereafter, the fighting in Normandy took on a level of savagery that was to characterise the whole campaign. After the initial landing and move inland, the enduring memory of the men of XXX Corps in Normandy was one of grim

---

389 Manuscript forwarded to author by H. Wernemann (Germany, 1991).
390 Williams, *D-Day to Berlin*, pp. 133–34.
391 J. Bellows, correspondence with author (Hampshire, 1994).

struggles for survival. Those who fought in the Bocage remembered the fear of unseen mortar and sniper fire, the constant artillery fire day and night, the mud and filth and the loss of many friends to an invisible enemy. Rommel summed up the thoughts of many when he said: "It was one terrible blood-letting."[392]

Rommel leaves the field, 17 July

On the high ground south of the city of Caen, the German forces strengthened their defences as Montgomery pulled back his battered armoured divisions. Back in Blighty, the press muttered angrily at the lack of progress as the British lion licked its wounds. On afternoon of 17 July, however, the British scored one victory which may well have outweighed all the German defensive successes. *Generalfeldmarschall* Rommel had been making a visit to the front and had called in at the Headquarters of the *I SS-Panzerkorps* to discuss the situation with *Oberstgruppenführer* Sepp Dietrich. As Rommel was about to leave for his own HQ at La Roche-Guyon just before 1600 hours, Dietrich advised him to change his large Horch staff car for a less visible and more manoeuvrable Volkswagen because of the Allied fighter-bombers marauding about the skies. Rommel thanked him but declined the offer as he looked up into a now-clear sky. He told his driver, *Oberfeldwebel* Daniel, to get a move on and at Livarot he turned down a side road. Three miles from Vimoutiers, he was forced to rejoin the main road and one of Rommel's party cried out "Low-flying aircraft!" Allied fighter-bombers came from behind as they swept up the Livarot road less than 100ft above the ground. Rommel called to his driver: "Try to make the village." Daniel put his foot down as they roared into the bend, but they could not hope to match the speed of the fighter-bombers; 20mm shells passed through the car, tearing up the upholstery and ripping open the left side of the vehicle.

Daniel was hit in the arm and shoulder, slumping forward over the wheel, and the car swerved to the right and crashed into a tree. It then spun to the left, blocking the road. Rommel, who had been thrown out of the car and had hit his head against the windscreen, was bleeding heavily. He hit the road with a crash and fractured his skull. Daniel died later of his wounds. Other men in the car – *Major* Niehaus, *Hauptmann* Lang and *Feldwebel* Holke – escaped with only cuts and bruises. They ran back along the road and dragged Rommel behind a hedge, and as soon as the fighter-bombers had disappeared they took him to the nearest village, ironically named St-Foy-de-Montgomery. Germany's great hope for the Normandy campaign and the hero of Africa had fallen victim to a fighter-bomber attack, like numerous other men on the invasion front. He would never command again.

---

392 Liddell Hart, *The Rommel Papers*, p. 341.

8

The Road to Mont Pinçon: July–August 1944

In Normandy, by late July 1944 the Allied armies that had fought so hard and sacrificed so much were ready to break out in a movement that would take them to the borders of the Reich.

On the evening of 7 July, Allied bombers dropped 1,800 tons of bombs on Caen. They were careful not to bomb on or near their own troops, and as a result the bombs landed more on the city than on the German defences. The infantry assault opened at 0400 hours on 8 July, and by the evening I Corps had reached the outskirts of the city. The Germans withdrew their heavy weapons and troops to the south of Caen, while the *12. SS-Panzer-Division 'Hitlerjugend'* fought a rearguard action, after which they in turn pulled back.

Major William Renison, 2 i/c of the 2nd East Yorks, watched the aerial assault:

> The final assault on Caen opened with the heaviest bomber attack I have ever seen. We were only about four miles from the target and plumb in the line of their fly in, we had a grandstand view. It was magnificent to see the majestic approach of wave after wave of big bombers flying quite low and in perfect formation at an almost pin-point target. As far as the eye could see they stretched out towards the sea and the sinking sun. As the raid progressed a cloud of dust rose high into the air and blotted out almost everything, drifting slowly towards us and up the valley of the Orne. By the end of the raid the troops were standing on the end of their slit-trenches clapping and cheering[;] the effect on morale was electric.[1]

Lance Corporal Kenneth Tout of the Sherwood Rangers sat in his Sherman tank as he heard an unusual distant rumble:

> At first there was just a distant drone, then a louder booming, a noise which should indicate great numbers of bombers above our heads. But no planes were yet visible. The noise increases until the sound of the planes reverberates inside our skulls, the very bones in our heads setting up fresh echoes to torment us, until we become scared, we are hearing ghost planes, the ghosts of all the dead planes since the war began, for the sky above our heads

---

1 Thompson, *Victory in Europe*, p. 105.

was clear of both planes and clouds. At first in the distance, we see a few specks above the horizon that hardly justifies the ferocity of the noise. The specks accumulate, spread and advance and accelerate. The noise becomes unbelievable and even greater. The planes are near enough to quantify as flights and squadrons and groups of higher massed formations. They are now near enough to [be] identified, the wide wings, the smooth lines, the gun turrets, the RAF roundels, as Lancasters. They are now overhead, high but linked to us by the noise which laps about us as an invisible ocean.[2]

Lance Corporal Tout looked on as the waves of closely packed bombers thundered overhead, extending to the farthest horizon. He watched in awe as the flak and tracer rose to meet the Allied fleet of aircraft, looking like latticework reaching up into the sky. The formations of Lancasters droned inevitably on into this storm, maintaining height and speed. Incendiary bombs and flares fell from the leading aircraft, giving a grim warning to the people in the city of what was about to descend upon them. The endless succession of heavy bombers rolled on, the tank crews and infantry beginning to cheer as they sat on the outskirts of Caen. Tout remembered:

We saw clusters of tiny black bombs detaching and winging diagonally towards the target area and hear the concussion. The anger of their bomb-flashes surges above the trees like a swelling fiery sea. The impregnable curtain of anti-aircraft fire begins to waver, droop in places, thin, splutter and disappear. The planes continue to come and one or two swing away smoking suspiciously. The distant concussions continue to pummel our faces like punches. Finally, the inevitable smell, compounded of cordite, burning buildings, disembowelled streets and singeing flesh.[3]

SS-Standartenführer Kurt Meyer, CO of *12. SS-Panzer-Division 'Hitlerjugend'*, was on the receiving end of the British bombardment:

Fighter bombers continually attacked the approach roads to Caen, any movement into Caen had become impossible, [and] we could not evacuate our wounded or receive supplies. The roads had become death runs and bombers roared through the sky once more from the north. We could hardly believe that this tormented town was to suffer yet again. The gods only know why this unoccupied town was being razed to the ground. The waves of bombers made for the bridges, causing fires south of the Orne. The town centre was again blanketed with bombs, [and] Caen was enveloped in flames, smoke and ashes.[4]

Meyer looked on in awe as the waves of British bombers released their loads upon the ruined town, and it was not long before it was his unit's turn to be given a taste of what the citizens of Caen were receiving:

---

2   Tout, *Tanks, Advance!*, pp. 55–56.
3   Tout, *Tanks, Advance!*, p. 56.
4   Meyer, *Grenadiers*, p. 261.

A British soldier picking his way through the ruins of Caen. (Author's collection)

The last wave of bombers released their bombs, [and] I jumped through the cellar entrance of our command post and threw myself into the furthest corner of the cellar. A tremendous noise shook the vault, and the candles went out, I couldn't breathe. I could barely see my hand in front of my face through the dense dust cloud. Hubert Meyer called out to me, and more voices could be heard. Suddenly a soldier called out: "We've been buried alive!" The young soldier could only be calmed down with some effort. The outside concussion had hurled him through the open door into the cellar.[5]

All around Caen, the ground heaved and trembled as each new load of high explosive detonated on the undefended city, the stink of cordite filling the nostrils and the air thick with brick dust as each building was razed to the ground. Even with this sledgehammer blow from the air, all did not go well with the ground attack. It was left to the US First Army to set the ball in motion on 25 July; supported by another vast air armada, they struck south along the west coast of the Cherbourg peninsula and in gloriously sunny weather swept through Le Mans and on in a great arc to Argentan. Pressing south to meet them came the British Second Army, advancing to the general line Vire–Condé-sur-Noireau–Falaise. Here was formed the infamous Falaise Pocket,

---

5   Meyer, *Grenadiers*, p. 261.

in which a whole German army would be slaughtered by the bombs, rockets, artillery and tanks of the Allied forces.

The 59th Staffordshire Division joins XXX Corps: Noyers Bocage, 13–24 July, '2nd Battle of the Odon'

The 59th Staffordshire Division joined XXX Corps on 13 July and moved to the Loucelles, Cristot and Fontenay-le-Pesnel area to prepare for the '2nd Battle of the Odon'. Their objectives were the capture of Haut-de-Forges, Landelle, Noyers, Missy and its surrounding orchards. The main objective was Noyers, which was to the north of the Odon valley, astride the main road from Caen to Villers Bocage. Noyers was the key to controlling the valley and essential to any subsequent operations to cross the river. The area was held by German troops of the *276.* and *277. Infanterie-Division*. In support of the 59th Staffordshire Division would be elements of 33 Armoured Brigade and the 79th Armoured Division.

Kenneth Tout was in his Sherwood Rangers Sherman as daylight broke on the 16th:

> Our troop was lined up in a lonely stretch of French lane, totally anonymous, no houses, no signposts, no animals, no people and no outlook. Both sides of the lane are obscured by hedges taller than our tank. Hedges, for all we can see, wider and deeper that our tank. All about us the fury of an artillery barrage crashes and whistles and flashes. We can see nothing of it except the brightening of the early light with each hidden flash, but none of it touches us. We are in a tiny leafy asylum for psychotic youths who leave their ploughing, baking and clerking to go hunting men as though beasts of the jungle. The engine is switched off as the troop leader mounts his tank turret behind us: "Five minutes to go," he says. "Just turn your tank like a damn hunter and take that fence on your right, God knows what you will find, probably a tiny field. If you can't see me report in at every hedge and wait for the rest of the troop to move into line, you know the form, good hunting."[6]

The first phase of the attack started at 0530 hours on 16 July. On the right was the 5th Battalion East Lancashire Regiment (5th East Lancs) from 197 Brigade, while on the left was the 1/6th and 5th Battalions of the South Staffordshire Regiment (South Staffs) from 177 Brigade. They cleared several villages and farms which lay on the approaches to Noyers. The 5th East Lancs were held up by severe opposition, their commanding officer being wounded, and it was not until 0800 hours that they were able to reach their first objective east of Vendes. Here they stayed, unable to complete the capture of the whole of Vendes.

Lance Corporal Tout continued to crash through hedge after hedge as he approached Vendes, all the time being watchful for enemy tanks and anti-tank gunners. Suddenly, the cry went up:

> Germans by the next hedge! But all dead. Lying in a group face downwards as though having been blown there by some almighty blast. I pointed my guns at them, then traverse away towards more ominous areas. As we begin to cross this further field Rex calls out:

---

6   Tout, *Tanks, Advance!*, p. 75.

"Those Jerries aren't dead." I swing the guns and see the Germans leaping to their feet, hands held high and empty mouths expressing the words "*Kamerad! Kamerad!*" and trembling into incontinence as my gun almost grazes their faces in its onward swing. Corporal Snowdon, up above, and Rex, opening up his lower hatch cover, by dint of much waving and *kamerad*ly grinning, manage to persuade our petrified enemies to work their nether limbs back towards our Staffordshire cousins in the hedgerow behind us. To the front another German hops across a gate space like a scared rabbit, [but] I am too astonished to react. Another German runs across the same space, and I douse the right-hand hedge with machine-gun bullets. A third German makes the leap and I press the floor button, [and] tracer spits into the hedge on the right of the gate. I am waiting for the fourth German, with his basin shaped helmet, his wide neat tunic, his sloppy baggy trousers and his carbine in hand. As he sprints across the gate I fire into the hedge, his destination, [but] he keeps on running and I am perplexed.[7]

At 1430 hours, German infantry and armour counter-attacked and overran the right-hand British company in the first rush. The Germans pressed on aggressively and forced the remainder of the 5th East Lancs back to their start line.

Regimental Sergeant Major Brookes of the 7th Battalion Royal Norfolk Regiment (7th Royal Norfolks), who had been a soldier since he was 15 years old, recalled:

We were somewhere near Vendes with all the panzers before us and as they opened fire I didn't duck quick enough. I was outside my slit-trench when Jerry started to shell our positions very heavily and as I jumped for my trench a shell hit it on the edge. The trench caved in with me underneath it. When they dug me out, they found I'd been cut badly about the face and head and the blast had made me practically stone-deaf. The MO evacuated me to the rear.[8]

Lance Corporal Tout became convinced that the hedge in front of him was shielding a trench, so his tank sent high-explosive rounds into the hedge at very close range. The concussion of the explosions hit the tank turret as more rounds were slammed into the breach, the tank rocking like a ship in a storm. Flame, sods of grass, smoke, and burning leaves and branches fell on and around the tank, what is left of the hedge began to burn and no more Germans tried to leap to safety. A German self-propelled gun, hidden behind a hedge in the distance, then started to shell the British positions, the location of the first shots going undetected. Tout, ordered to advance and engage the hidden threat, passed through a gate and spotted the most likely location for the self-propelled gun. He opened fire, tracer rounds ripping through the hedge at various points but with no reaction. The troop commander then ordered Tout to fire high-explosive rounds into the supposed enemy position:

These explode in or behind the hedges, causing eruptions of smoke, earth and branches, which only intensify the impression of indecipherable mess in the distance. Then men

7   Tout, *Tanks, Advance!*, p. 77.
8   bbc.co.uk/ww2peopleswar (accessed 19 January 2021).

German troops of the *277. Infanterie-Division* watch as British tanks approach Noyers. (Author's collection)

appear in khaki, the South Staffs are moving forward slowly, well dispersed, into the gateway and through the gaps which we have caused in our hedge. Beyond the gateway, among the apple trees, is a small black and white timbered farmhouse. The windows are shattered and smoke drifts lazily from an outbuilding with a galvanised iron roof, [but] otherwise, stillness. Another Sherman rolls up to the farm, [and] infantrymen run into the farm and outbuildings. Near us a South Staffs captain stands with two or three soldiers and nonchalantly lights up a cigarette. He notices us watching and gives us a thumbs-up signal.[9]

Meanwhile, the two South Staffs battalions on the left fared better, and by 0645 hours the 1/6th South Staffs had captured Bretteville and taken very heavy casualties in the process. Two-thirds of the supporting tanks had been lost to mines and many of the infantry had lost direction in the thick morning mist. The 5th South Staffs captured the orchards to the west of Grainville-sur-Odon and then took Nouillons by noon. All of 177 Brigade's objectives had thus been taken, and at 1330 hours the flail tanks of the 79th Armoured Division came forward to breach the large German minefield at Queudeville.

9 Tout, *Tanks, Advance!*, p. 79.

Lieutenant Arthur Buller, a flail tank commander, pushed his tank forward and began clearing the mines:

> At Queudeville an infantry officer waved us on, we had our orders and got busy straight away. We smashed through fences to get into the fields and a path was soon cleared. Smoke concealed the battlefield, but we knew that a number of tanks had been hit that morning and their burning hulks added to the confusion. We expected to be attacked at any time by anti-tank gunners as we knew Jerry was not too far in front of us.[10]

In view of the lack of progress on the right flank and the heavy losses in tanks and men during the first phase of the operation, the second phase was delayed as the enemy was present in great strength at Noyers. At 1730 hours, the 2/6th South Staffs launched an attack against Noyers, and 45 minutes later the 6th North Staffs attacked Haut-des-Forges. The 2/6th South Staffs forced their way forced their way into Noyers, but were pushed back out by fierce German resistance. The 6th North Staffs attacked at 1815 hours and met with less opposition, capturing Haut-des-Forges and holding on to it. During the day, 177 Brigade captured 369 prisoners, all from *277. Infanterie-Division*. After dark, the 2/5th Lancs Fusiliers attacked at 2230 hours and were met by a storm of Spandau and mortar fire, failing to make any material progress.

On 17 July, a series of attacks on Noyers was launched by 177 Brigade. At first light, the 2/6th South Staffs and one company of 5th South Staffs fought their way forward to Noyers railway station, supported by the tanks of the 1st Battalion Northamptonshire Yeomanry (1st Northants). However, they got no further and were halted there until 1330 hours, when they were withdrawn.

Lance Corporal Tout of the Sherwood Rangers was feeling very exposed after the previous day's activity of milling around in very small French fields, recalling the start of the early-morning advance as they moved into what he described as "The biggest field on earth". The other tanks of his squadron then entered the field and arrayed in line in front of a hedge:

> At dawn we advanced along yet another French lane and then turned right into an endless field, whose far side is bounded by a hedge and the main Caen–Villers road. That road is now effectively cut, [and] nobody can use it without being blasted away by our guns.[11]

Beyond the road lay an area of the French countryside intersected with narrow lanes which gradually fell away to the River Odon, one of the arterial ways for the retreating German forces. Tout said the tank crews began to feel naked in this exposed position:

> Tommy grumbles: "What a marvellous target for any Tiger out hunting, he could pop us off one by one, just like that." We've got a few of our own to bring to bear I respond: "And what odds will you give me on a Sherman against a Tiger at this range?" argues Tommy with considerable justification: "Give some Jerry tank commander a bloody good birthday present, 20 Shermans in the bag and the Iron Cross with Oak Leaves on his chest": "Go

---

10 A. Buller, interview with author (Richmond, 1991).
11 Tout, *Tanks, Advance!*, p. 80.

and stick your Iron Cross up your arse Tommy," answers Hickey: "You're getting us all scared."[12]

In the afternoon, the 5th South Staffs attacked Noyers from the north-east, but only managed to enter the outskirts. At the same time, the 1/6th South Staffs advanced from Brettevillette towards Bordel, but were met with the most violent resistance. The Germans brought forward anti-tanks guns to support their infantry, and the sound of tracked vehicles could be heard as their enormous self-propelled guns crept forward. Lance Corporal Tout sat in his Sherman on that hot afternoon when he got his first inkling that self-propelled guns were in the vicinity:

> All afternoon, hot and drowsy, in a world of droning bees and shimmering squadrons of gnats in the still air. A black object, like the head of a seal in a harbour, scythes through the heads of the corn across our front. A puff of smoke arises from beyond a distant hedge. One rending howl, like a dog in pain, rushes past the left shoulder of our tank, and a noise like a huge door slamming comes from across the main road: "SP" shouts the commander. "Gunner traverse left and fire."[13]

The driver of Tout's Sherman tried to start the engine, but it failed to respond as the tank's batteries were flat. No power was getting through to the electrical system, meaning the turret could not be traversed to enable the crew to fire at the imminent threat. Tout tried to ratchet the turret around manually, a hard and lengthy job. The tank engine jumped into life, but still no power came through as a third shot from the German self-propelled gun scythed through the corn and passed the tank with a screaming howl. Slowly, Tout brought the turret around until he had the target in the crosshairs, but as he did so a flame shot up from the hedge as another Sherman nearby let fly with a high-explosive round:

> I tread the button and tracer shoots for the hedge and other tracers arrow in as other gunners along our line of tanks sight and fire. The hedge becomes a blazing beacon and whatever was lodged there, crewed by suicidal idiots or inveterate heroes, has retreated or been blasted to Valhalla. Above the hedge, on the gentle breeze, there writhes a grotesque shape of smoke like a human being suffering pain in extremis: "He missed us twice," I babble: "He missed us three times, I saw the third," says Rex. The gruff voice of Bill Fox came over the net: "Let that be a lesson to you, keep your eyes open as well as your bowels and keep your batteries charged. This happens to be a war not a bloody Sunday School picknick [sic]."[14]

After dark, all units drew back from Noyers so that the artillery and mortars could pummel the village.

On the front held by 177 Brigade, the 1/7th Royal Warwickshires, with the support of the 1st Northants and flame-throwing Crocodile tanks, attacked and regained the first-phase

---

12   Tout, *Tanks, Advance!*, p. 80.
13   Tout, *Tanks, Advance!*, p. 81.
14   Tout, *Tanks, Advance!*, pp. 81–82.

objectives at 1230 hours. During the night, the headquarters of the 1/7th Royal Warwickshires was hit by two large shells, which caused serious casualties.

At 1000 hours on 18 July, 177 Brigade launched a full-scale attack on Noyers, with the 1/6th and 5th South Staffs supported by tanks, Crocodiles and armoured engineers. This attack pressed vigorously into the teeth of the enemy defences, but the Germans stood their ground and refused to give way; casualties were heavy on both sides. Five Sherman tanks were lost by the already depleted squadrons to the German anti-tank gunners. The British withdrew, reorganised and launched another attack in the afternoon, but this also failed. The attackers then pulled back for the night so that Noyers could be subjected to another overnight bombardment.

Kenneth Tout looked on as rocket-firing Typhoons attacked the German positions:

> I ducked abruptly as something screams overhead, like the scream of a shell, but this scream goes on and on, over the hedge held by the enemy, beyond the road and above the trees, [as] a slim winged shape comes hurtling earthwards. I have just got time to identify it as a Typhoon with what appears to be fizzing flame shooting from its wings. The plane swoops upwards out of the dive and is chased by an immense cauldron of flame and smoke bubbling up from its target area. Tommy screams: "Rockets! Bloody hooray, Typhoons with rockets," The second Typhoon dives and scatters fire beneath it, a third, a fourth and a fifth. The boiling concussions sweep across the field like a veritable China Seas typhoon and rock our tank back on its suspension: "Pity the poor sods under that lot, Jerries or not," gulps someone: "Make the bastards squirm," cries a voice over the wireless. Tommy Walsh adds: "That little twit Montgomery will be pissing himself with delight having brought all those Tigers over this way[;] wish the bugger was sitting in my seat and I was sitting in his just now." The patch in front was now sprouting a sky-high crop of black vegetation as unexplained infernos of fire rage where the rockets had hit [–] are they Tigers on fire?[15]

In the early hours of 19 July, it was reported that the 49th West Riding Division had advanced to Vendes. However, Noyers was still held by the German *276.* and *277. Infanterie-Division*, who had been reinforced by the *Aufklärung Abteilung* of the *9. SS-Panzer-Division* and elements of the *2. SS-Panzer-Division 'Das Reich'*. A new assault was being prepared, but the XXX Corps commander, Lieutenant General Gerard Bucknall, called it off; the 59th Staffordshire Division was to remain in the line and be on full alert.

Although the battle for Noyers had yielded no prize, casualties had been very severe. In three days of fighting, the 59th Division had suffered 1,250 casualties, killed, wounded and missing. The division then left XXX Corps and was returned to XII Corps on 24 July.

On 30 July, the British Second Army launched its offensive, Operation Bluecoat. On the right flank, directed towards Vire, was VIII Corps, newly refitted and rested after its costly attack south-east from Caen. In the centre was XXX Corps, consisting of the 50th Northumbrian Division, 43rd Wessex Division and 7th Armoured Division. In line eastwards stretched the units of XII Corps, I Corps and the Canadian II Corps.

---

15 Tout, *Tanks, Advance!*, p. 83.

56 and 231 Brigades, 50th Northumbrian Division, at Launay Ridge, 31 July

Against slackening opposition, the troops of 56 and 231 Brigades pressed forward to the high ground in the vicinity of Anctoville and Feuguerolles-sur-Seulles. The morning of 30 July was fine and the troops about to go into action had a grandstand view of the heavy bombers attacking Villers Bocage. On 31 July, the 2nd Gloucesters made limited attacks on their front and on the same day orders were issued for a full-scale attack on enemy positions, which would commence at 2000 hours. The troops of 56 Brigade approached their start line, which was marked with white tapes on a reverse slope of a ridge; over the top of the ridge, the ground dropped away across the main road to a wooded valley before rising steeply again to Launay. Whoever was in possession of the Launay Ridge could control the country for miles around. This objective was to be taken by 2145 hours. A creeping barrage was thundering in front of the lead troops as they set off on time to cover the 1½ miles approach march. Directly in front of the start line was a minefield that had to be crossed, and when this was achieved the men opened up in perfect formation, with the company commanders leading as they followed 25 yards behind the barrage. The firepower of 5.5-inch howitzers, machine guns of the 2nd Cheshires, mortars and tanks added to the deluge of fire, while Typhoons dived out of the sky to release their rockets on the enemy positions. The advance was made at the rate of 100 yards every two minutes, and all seemed to be going well.

Private A. Vince of the 2nd Essex recalled the events of that day:

> I shall always remember it, as not once did the staggered line of infantry pause as they climbed the last slope firing from the hip as they went. Casualties were incredibly light and in front of us the Boche could stand it no longer. They broke and fled, and it was a long time before they stopped running. Only a few remained behind their guns, and these were soon killed or captured and at the same time all companies reported their objectives secured. Over 100 prisoners, 43 Spandaus, brand new *Panzerfausts*, masses of small arms, indeed the entire equipment of two whole battalions was the spoil we collected that evening. Their food was still in the pots and their mess tins; surely no-one will say the enemy left all this willingly.[16]

By 1 August, the British troops were firmly entrenched here. Trooper Sandy Handley recalled one incident in which he was involved with the 61st Reconnaissance Regiment:

> With four Bren-carriers we had to charge across to the corner of a field, I was firing away, no question of taking aim, as with the motion over the bumpy field the bullets went everywhere but to the corner of the field. We got closer and a white flag came up. One German officer and six troopers were taken prisoner. Captain Truman ordered all the Bren gunners and NCOs with Tommy-guns to get out of their vehicles, spread out and walk forward while firing. When we did this the bullets started bouncing off the trees and branches, it was pretty frightening. Any minute we expected a burst of Spandau fire to come at us.

---

16 Manuscript forwarded to author by A. Vince (Essex, 1989).

Troops of 231 Brigade get a lift forward in preparation for the attack. (Courtesy of P. Cuerdon)

When we were well into the wood another dirty white rag went up and we took six more frightened Germans with hands raised.[17]

The men of 231 Brigade were in the line on 30 July and began to prepare for their move to the start line the next day. Lieutenant Geoffrey Picot, with thee Mortar Section of the 1st Hampshires, watched as aircraft appeared on their way to bomb Villers Bocage:

> Little black dots appeared in the sky behind us, they came nearer and we recognised them as aircraft, flight after flight of aircraft. They were Lancaster and Halifax heavy bombers flying in formation with a magnificent and impressive disregard of the anti-aircraft defences. Scores of bombers came overhead, and their targets were not very far away, [so] we felt the earth tremble as their bombs exploded. For half an hour the attack continued, and I did not see one bomber come to grief.[18]

---

17 *Chotie Darling* <www.chotiedarling.co.uk> (accessed 17 September 2019).
18 Picot, *Accidental Warrior*, p. 122.

Once 231 Brigade launched their attack, it was up to the mortar platoons to support them by bombarding targets as they were recognised. Lieutenant Picot viewed events as the lead troops pressed on and tried to keep close to the attack with his mortar crews:

> The attack progressed and I moved up two of my sections into shell holes. We were preparing to fire from here when I heard a tremendous explosion behind us. I turned and near the shell hole I saw a cloud of black dust where a few seconds ago Sergeant Johnson had been standing. Agonizingly slowly the dust disappeared, and I saw Johnson again, evidently unhurt, perfectly calm and walking in the open towards the slit-trenches where his section was sheltering and signalling to them to remain steady and start firing. As more shells landed nearby he continued to spread calm where others would have magnified their fear and spread terror. Bravery wears many faces and I decided that includes remaining cool and calm under fearsome shelling. Accordingly, I wrote a recommendation that Sergeant Johnson[19] should be awarded the Military Medal.[20]

Panzergrenadiere Fritz Jeltsch of *Infanterie-Regiment 736, 716. Infanterie-Division*, was holding the line opposite 231 Brigade and came under fire from artillery and from the air, his unit being destroyed in the terrible rain of death that fell on their positions:

> Our position came under the most terrible fire, and we were surrounded. They were shooting from every direction and almost everyone in my unit was killed, it was awful. I remember one of my friends running just in front of me when we were attacked again. He was hit and fell on me, so I got hold of him and dragged him to one side. An ambulance came along, and I was crying out to this first aid man: "Can I put him in?" and he said to me: "It's too late, you can't do anything for him anymore, save yourself." So I left him and ran into a field to join the other survivors. I couldn't do anything about it, but it's laid on my conscience for many years.[21]

With 56 and 231 Brigades having secured their positions, 69 Brigade attacked and captured an important hill to the west of Villers Bocage known as the Amaye feature on 2 August, encountering only small-arms fire. This was followed by the capture of Tracy Bocage, which stands on the high ground just outside of Villers Bocage. These new positions were shelled frequently by the enemy, the CO of the 5th East Yorks, Lieutenant Colonel Robert Brian James, DSO and two Bars, being killed by shellfire.[22]

The advance to Tracy Bocage and the southward pressure being applied on the left flank by the 49th West Riding Division tightened the Allied grip on Villers Bocage. On 4 August, the final enemy Hate (a term used by the infantry for incoming fire) came down on the 1st Dorsets, a parting shot from a departing enemy. C and D Companies of the 1st Dorsets sent out patrols

---

19 The recommendation for the Military Medal for Sergeant Johnson was granted.
20 Picot, *Accidental Warrior*, p. 124.
21 Arthur, *Forgotten Voices of the Second World War*, p. 339.
22 Lieutenant Colonel Robert Brian James, DSO and two Bars, Essex Regiment, commanding 5th Battalion East Yorkshire Regiment, was killed on 3 August 1944, aged 31. He is buried in Hottot-le-Bagues War Cemetery, France.

which took many prisoners, and on the afternoon of the 4th a patrol from C Company, headed by Corporal Boydell, reached the outskirts of Villers Bocage. Permission was given for them to press on, and a patrol under Sergeant Moss entered the town. The scene that greeted them was one of utter desolation: burnt-out British and German tanks littered the streets, bearing witness to the savage struggle that had taken place there between 7th Armoured Division and the *2. SS-Panzer-Division 'Das Reich'* and *Panzer-Lehr-Division*.

Private James Ratcliffe of the 9th Durhams wrote of his time at Villers Bocage:

> Another vivid memory about this time was watching the RAF bombers destroy Villers Bocage. They came over in a huge bunch, no real formation, and all the bombs seemed to be released at the same time. You could actually see them falling from the planes. Then there was a noise like a rolling clap of thunder, a huge column of smoke and that was it, a town wiped out. We went through it after and what a job to get through; there was rubble everywhere. There was supposed to have been panzers in the place but apart from smashed ones we never saw any.[23]

Lieutenant David Render of the Sherwood Rangers watched the destruction of the town from the turret of his Sherman tank:

> We had a grandstand view of the bombing of Villers Bocage as RAF Lancasters pulverised the place. The large lumbering aircraft came in low over our heads with their bomb bay doors open, and we could clearly see the bombs slung inside their fuselages. We watched in fascination as thousands of pounds of steel cased high explosive ordnance fell away from their bellies and rained down hell on that wretched town. The bombers then altered their course to the north and left the prevailing wind to cover us in brick dust from the devastation they had wreaked, as they headed for home.[24]

The journalist and writer Alan Moorehead witnessed the devastation at Villers Bocage:

> When we got to Villers Bocage there was nothing you could really recognise anymore. The bulldozers arrived and drove new roads through the 20-foot-deep rubble. It was like an archaeological excavation into a lost world. It was generally agreed that this was just useless destruction, for it did not prevent the movement of German vehicles, they simply went round instead of through the town.[25]

Major Peter Martin, 2nd Machine-gun Battalion the Cheshire Regiment, was called to a meeting to meet his new corps commander, Major General Brian Horrocks, DSO, MC, who had replaced Lieutenant General Bucknall:

> I learned that Villers Bocage had been captured, two months after we were supposed to have captured the place on D-plus 1. For the first time since D-Day the whole company was

---

23 J. Ratcliffe, correspondence with author (Durham, 1990).
24 Render, *Tank Action*, p. 126.
25 Moorehead, A., *Eclipse* (London: Hamish Hamilton, 1946), p. 247.

relieved, and we went into a rest area where we stayed for a couple of days. The following day I was ordered to attend a briefing by XXX Corps commander. He congratulated us all on what 50 Div had done and there was a feeling of great exhilaration.[26]

Each street of Villers Bocage had had its buildings smashed and broken after incessant poundings by the RAF and Allied artillery. Quietly, the dazed troops of XXX Corps picked their way through the rubble, always mindful of booby traps on this bright and sunny August day. The name of Villers Bocage had become a household name in England as the vicious battle for its possession had rumbled on, and at long last it was in the hands of XXX Corps, just under two months behind schedule.

On 5 August, the 50th Northumbrian Division was relieved and moved out of the line, their first complete break from the front line since they landed on D-Day, and what a welcome experience it was. The companies of the division were badly depleted, and during the next three days new recruits swelled their ranks. Elsewhere, the attack continued in full swing as American troops forced a passage through the Avranches bottleneck, virtually cutting off Brittany from the rest of France, then pushing on to form the Falaise Pocket by sending their armoured formations eastwards. To the east of the pocket, a route remained wide open, through which a German withdrawal to the line of the Seine was still possible. Hitler, however, had other ideas, being determined not to yield a yard of ground; he foolishly ordered a counter-attack to the west from the Mortain area.

The 43rd Wessex Division, Operation Bluecoat, 30 July – 9 August

A certain amount of regrouping took place on Second Army's front, and for the first time the 43rd Wessex Division came under the command of XXX Corps. On 27 July, Montgomery ordered the Second Army to attack from Caumont in a southerly direction, hopefully capturing Mount Pinçon by the 30th. For this operation, XIII Corps was on the right flank and XXX Corps on the left. This would be the first venture into the genuine Bocage for the 43rd Wessex Division; ahead of them were heavily wooded hills, rivers, winding tracks and lanes and the usual fields surrounded by tall hedgerows with high banks. The German forces had been given plenty of time to sow assorted mines in profusion throughout the area. Fifteen miles to the front of the 43rd Wessex sat the commanding slopes of Mont Pinçon; all of this was good ambush country, as the Wessex men were about to find out the hard way.

The 43rd Division's plan was for 130 Brigade to penetrate the enemy positions at Briquessard and Cahagnes. The troops of 214 Brigade would then advance to the crossroads at St Pierre-du-Fresne, after which 129 Brigade would take Point 361 on the heights above Bois-des-Hommes. They would have the tanks of 8 Armoured Brigade supporting them. The 50th Northumbrian Division would be positioned on the right, supported by the tanks of the 13/18th Hussars of 8 Armoured Brigade. It was their task to capture the Amaye-sur-Seulles feature and then to advance towards Villers Bocage, finally pressing forward to Condé-sur-Noireau. The 7th Armoured Division would follow the advance in reserve.

---

26 Thompson, *Victory in Europe*, p. 120.

The people of Villers Bocage saw their homes destroyed in the fighting; many were killed, some fled the battle zone and others hid in cellars and were buried alive, in the hope they would be rescued later. (Author's collection)

The Bocage countryside around Caumont, July 1944. (Courtesy of J. Betts)

Trooper William Hewson of the 1st Battalion Royal Tank Regiment (1st Royal Tanks), 7th Armoured Division, passed through the shattered city of Caen to reach XXX Corps and take part in Operation Bluecoat:

> I've never seen such devastation in my existence. Practically the whole city was a mass of rubble, slivers of walls, lone chimneys and standing parts of buildings. Jerry's retreat was orderly, with their pivot on Caumont. 43rd Div and 50 Div progressing slowly, we are waiting until there is some sort of breakthrough.[27]

General Ivor Thomas, DSO, MC and Bar, CO of the 43rd Wessex Division. (Courtesy of I.R. English)

The commander of the 43rd Wessex Division was the fiercely aggressive Major General Ivor Thomas, DSO, MC and Bar, known to his troops as Von Thoma because of his unbending character, always exerting maximum pressure on his subordinates. An officer of the 13/18th Hussars commented: "Brigade and battalion commanders were somewhat fearful of Von Thoma, who at the same time infuriated them, [as] he insisted on fighting their battles and would not leave them alone even after the final operational orders had been issued."[28]

The attack began as daylight broke on the morning of 30 July. Along with the 50th Northumbrian Division on the right, the 43rd Wessex Division was in the centre and the 15th Scottish Division on the left. The 43rd Division was to force a passage through the enemy forces at Briquessard and then to proceed to the important St Pierre-du-Fresne crossroads and take the heights south of Jurques, while at the same time protecting the flank of the XXX Corps attack. The Wessex Division would be supported by 8 Armoured Brigade, commanded by Brigadier George Erroll Prior-Palmer, DSO. The brigade consisted of the Sherman tanks of the 4/7th Royal Dragoon Guards, 13/18th Hussars and Sherwood Rangers.

Briquessard, 30 July

At 0800 hours on 30 July, 130 Brigade set off from the village of Livry, north-east of Caumont, and made for their first objective, the village of Cahagnes a mile to the south. The brigade was reinforced by the 4th Battalion Somerset Light Infantry (4th Somersets) from 129 Brigade

---

27 Thompson, *Victory in Europe*, p. 121.
28 Delaforce, P., *The Fighting Wessex Wyverns* (Gloucestershire: Sutton Publishing, 1994), p. 71.

and the Sherman tanks of the Sherwood Rangers. The 5th Dorsets were on the right, with the 4th Somersets on the left and the 7th Hampshires in reserve. The men of 214 Brigade would follow the advance, with 129 Brigade following behind them. As the attack went in, the troops watched as a massed formation of Lancaster bombers passed overhead to drop their bombs on the enemy positions. Lieutenant Stuart Hills of the Sherwood Rangers was supporting the 7th Hampshires when he heard a roaring noise and looked up:

> Then came the growing roar of aero engines as hundreds of Lancasters came over searching for their targets. We could see the bomb doors open and seconds later we felt the earth shake with the percussion of the bombs exploding. Huge clouds of dust and smoke rose lazily from the target area, and we could only imagine what it was like to be underneath it all.[29]

The troops had to advance through closely wooded countryside, astride the narrow country lanes leading to Briquessard. From the start, casualties were being taken from mines and heavy Spandau fire, and on the first day the troops covered only 1,000 yards. Providentially, a British bomber flying at low altitude dropped several bombs on the German positions at the northern edge of the village.

Lance Corporal Richard Henry William Brew, fighting with the 4th Somersets, recalled the difficulties they had when moving forward:

> Briquessard loomed up ahead of us, but all was chaos, at least to me. We were on our way again, but we were held up at the bottom of a slope by heavy small-arms fire and we took shelter in a long hedgerow. We were all lined up along this hedgerow, looking at this big farmhouse, and the hiss and crack of bullets passing through it told us that this was not a healthy place to be. Then I heard the hiss of a bullet very close by. I don't know where it had come from, but it passed so close it cut the straps of my equipment and as my pack went backwards, I went forwards. It was a lucky break as I only got a crease. We achieved our objective at Briquessard which was a bridge to the south of the village and were relieved by 43rd Reconnaissance Regiment.[30]

Corporal Douglas Procter of the 4th Somersets remembered the problems they faced as they tried to move forward: "We were one of the forward platoons on the left flank; it was impossible to observe anything beyond the nearest hedgerow and it seemed a hopeless situation."[31]

Lieutenant David Render drove through a wooded area with the Sherwood Rangers. As his Sherman neared the village of Briquessard, the morning mist began to clear, but pockets of patchy fog clung to the ground between the trees. The wall of a large house loomed out of the mist at the side of the track he was on, indicating he had reached the outskirts of the village. His tank slowly crawled down the track until it joined a road that ran down the centre of the village. He stopped to get his bearings and could see a triangular village green with cottages on either side. Lieutenant Render viewed the windows of the cottages suspiciously but could see no sign

---

29 Hills, *By Tank to Normandy*, p. 119.
30 R.H.W. Brew, correspondence with author (Suffolk, 1989).
31 D. Procter, correspondence with author (Dorset, 1992).

of the enemy. The only noise was from the idling tank engine and the radio static; the village was ominously silent. Other tanks arrived on the scene and Render's tank lurched forward:

> Lane's Sherman moved forward when a bloody great explosion ripped into the grass bank a few feet to the left. The enemy bazooka team was located less than 30 yards away in the garden of one of the cottages, [and] they must have panicked as their second shot was also a miss and went high over my head, shattering the roof of the cottage next to us and showering the tank with shards of slate. I was already shouting fire-control orders into the mike as the Germans managed to get their third shot in. Martin traversed the turret fast to the left, firing the coaxial 30 calibre as he went. Stamping on the main armament fire button as soon as the turret slewed to a stop, he was spot on with the first high explosive shell. He then swivelled the turret a few inches from left to right as he continued to hose the front of the houses down with machine-gun fire. Mayo had already slammed another 75mm round into the breach by the time I slapped Martin hard on the shoulder again. I watched the second round impact among a score of scurrying figures. They were trying desperately to get out of the gardens and escape the heavy weight of fire we were pouring back at them by running between the houses. But at that range we couldn't miss, and machine-gun bullets and shell fragments cut them down to a man.[32]

Lieutenant Render grabbed the Schmeisser he carried and jumped down from his tank, being covered by other tanks that had arrived as he did so. The once-smart cottage gardens were now strewn with German dead: "The bodies lay across the well-cut lawns and flower beds, they were *Fallschirmjaeger*, with their cut down helmets and baggy jump smocks[;] we had not come across German paras in Normandy before."[33]

The infantry of the 43rd Wessex Division pressed on and walked into dense unmarked minefields, where they suffered many casualties. Corporal Douglas Procter of the 4th Somersets remembered the struggle to get forward:

> The barrage started and all hell was let loose. We began to advance and immediately ran into a hail of small-arms fire that flew around us. Flinging ourselves to the ground, we tried to locate the Spandaus. The field was strewn with anti-personnel mines, and it was a lottery where one trod.[34]

According to Private Victor Caldwell of the 4th Somersets: "Schu mines could blow your feet off or you could lose your manhood, they were deadly."[35] On the evening of 30 July, the 7th Hampshires moved around the right flank of the Dorsets towards Cahagnes, and by midnight all the companies of the Hampshires were advancing towards the slope that led to the village. Cahagnes had been bombed by the RAF and was still burning brightly as night fell, and the Germans had well-concealed defences before and in the ruins of the village.

---

32   Render, *Tank Action*, pp. 153–54.
33   Render, *Tank Action*, p. 146.
34   D. Procter, correspondence with author (Dorset, 1992).
35   Delaforce, *The Fighting Wessex Wyverns*, p. 211.

Panzergrenadiere, armed with a *Panzerschreck* anti-tank rocket launcher, await the arrival of the British armour in Briquessard. (Author's collection)

At 1730 hours, the brigade broke through and the 1st Battalion Worcestershire Regiment, riding on tanks, had advanced around and beyond the burning ruins of Cahagnes by nightfall. In the darkness, the 7th Somersets cleared houses and fought off a counter-attack, aided by the Shermans of the 4/7th Royal Dragoon Guards. Private Leonard Stokes took part in this action with the 7th Somersets:

> In the dark two enemy half-tracks drove right into our midst firing their machine-guns like mad. This was nothing like 43rd Division battle-school. Most of us were scurrying around looking for non-existent cover in the dark. Major Whitehead took immediate action, he snatched the loaded Piat gun out of my hands and thrust his rifle at me. He then fired one shot at the first half-track which exploded and burst into flames. He then took back his rifle and fired at a German and the man fell back into the flames with his arms outspread. Number 10 Platoon had not got their Piat ready, [and] because of this the second half-track escaped.[36]

Cahagnes, 31 July

It was not until the following morning of 31 July that a path through the minefield was cleared, and the advance was restarted towards Cahagnes by 214 Brigade and the tanks of 4/7th Royal

---

36   Delaforce, *The Fighting Wessex Wyverns*, p. 118.

Dragoon Guards. Lieutenant David Render, Sherwood Rangers, watched as a raid by the RAF preceded the next assault:

> We watched them come in low over our heads in the early morning light as dawn was breaking on 31st July. The sky was suddenly full of the throbbing foreboding roar of engines as hundreds of Lancasters and Halifaxes streamed black against the sky. The doors of their bomb bays were already open, and they lumbered on in the direction of Cahagnes. We watched as the bombs started to fall and the ground beneath our feet shook as they began saturating the German positions with thousands of tons of high explosives. Great gouts of flame and clouds of dust and debris plumed ahead of us and we were glad we were not on the receiving end. But any sympathy we may have felt for the Germans was short lived as anti-aircraft tracer rose up to meet the bombers. We watched in horrified fascination as the wing of a Lancaster folded up and it began to spiral to the ground. We saw the white billowing canopy of a parachute and then a second one pop below the doomed aircraft. We knew Lancasters had a crew of seven and we willed more to follow, but none did, as the crumpled black shape plummeted out of sight behind a ridgeline, where a thick ball of flame plumed momentarily against the horizon. Suddenly the bombing stopped, and an uncanny silence settled across the landscape, until it was broken by the sound of tank engines starting up.[37]

Fellow Sherwood Ranger Lieutenant Stuart Hills wrote of the depressing sight Cahagnes presented as he entered on the main road:

> Cahagnes was a terrible mess, like every other Norman village we fought our way through, it had been bombed and then smashed up by the guns and tanks. If any civilians were still there, they would have been hiding in deep cellars.[38]

SS-Untersturmführer Walter Hahn of *Schwere SS-Panzer-Abteilung 101* wrote of his unit's action in the Cahagnes sector:

> We carried out an attack east of Cahagnes which got bogged down because of the concentrated artillery fire of the enemy. Hannes Philipson's tank suffered engine damage and the crew had to abandon their vehicle in the midst of all this terrible artillery fire. Hannes returned to the tank during the night, repaired the damage in spite of the ongoing heavy artillery fire, and brought the vehicle back to the company.[39]

By the late afternoon, the smoking ruins of Cahagnes was firmly in the hands of the 43rd Wessex Division. Some 180 prisoners were taken, but the enemy had put up a determined resistance; in the village streets and in the well-concealed strongpoints, over a hundred German soldiers lay dead.

---

37 Render, *Tank Action*, pp. 156–57.
38 Hills, *By Tank to Normandy*, p. 121.
39 Agte, *Michael Wittmann and the Waffen SS Tiger Commanders*, p. 51.

St Pierre-du-Fresne, 1 August

At 0200 hours on 1 August, the 7th Somersets were in position in an orchard on the outskirts of St Pierre-du-Fresne, where they dug-in during the hours of darkness. Patrols were sent out to locate the enemy positions and a Tiger tank was reported to have been seen only 300 yards away. As the morning mist lifted, a strong enemy force was seen to be forming up for a counter-attack, and Major K.J. Whitehead contacted the divisional artillery to call down a stonk on the German position.

Brigadier Hubert Essame, DSO, MC, commanding 214 Brigade, described the scene in the area on 1 August:

> The prolonged bombardment and dense traffic had raised a cloud of fine dust which, mingling with the smoke put down by the divisional artillery on the left flank, enveloped the battlefield in a thick fog through which the sun shone deep a red.[40]

Private Leonard Stokes of the 7th Somersets was out on patrol when he came face to face with a Tiger: "I cautiously looked to my left and found myself looking down the barrel of the biggest gun I had ever seen, on the biggest tank I had ever seen, which was encased in a layer of concrete and slowly moving towards me."[41]

Two enormous German self-propelled guns, Ferdinands, came forward up a sunken lane with infantry support and fired into the British positions at close range. The Ferdinands were in turn stalked by Piat teams, with one being knocked out and the second withdrawing. When the morning mist lifted completely, a large force of German infantry launched a counter-attack on the Somersets, the brunt of which was taken by B Company. The Somersets' outposts were overrun, and as the Germans broke into the British position, fighting began at very close quarters.

Brigadier Essame commented on the strength of this German attack:

> Close quarter fighting with the enemy's infantry, who were bravely and resolutely led, now ensued in which the whole company, including headquarters, joined in. The first tank, covered by the second, was now in the middle of the company, firing viciously. Suddenly the crew abandoned it, leaving it still grinding forward in gear. The other tank, blinded by phosphorus grenades bouncing on its roof, withdrew.[42]

The British mortar teams fired continuously during the attack. Private Eric Codling of the 8th Middlesex Machine-gun Battalion remembered:

> The mortar barrels became hot enough to cook toast on and after a while the battering on our ear drums caused us to reel about like drunks, such was the deafening noise. Mortar

---

40   Essame, H., *The 43rd Wessex Division at War 1944–45* (London: William Clowes, 1952), p. 56.
41   L. Stokes, correspondence with author (Devon, 1994). The Tiger tanks had a rough exterior finish known as *Zimmerit* that resembled rough-cast concrete; it prevented magnetic anti-tank mines from being attached to them.
42   Essame, *The 43rd Wessex Division at War*, p. 57.

barrels had to be taken down and rolled in the lush grass to cool them because licks of flame were coming from the barrel mouths after a bomb had been fired, threatening to explode the next bomb about to be dropped in.[43]

Private Stokes commented on the German counter-attack at St Pierre-du-Fresne:

> The mist in front of our position now suddenly cleared. Several hundred German soldiers were seen to be coming down the hill towards us. Major Whitehead managed to call down heavy artillery fire on the enemy who were caught out in the open. The barrage was also called down on our own positions to clear the enemy who were infiltrating. The attack was smashed to smithereens and eventually the enemy scarpered leaving 20 bodies behind and 40 prisoners. Incredibly, B Company only had four killed and seven wounded. Major Whitehead[44] was a first-class officer.[45]

Lieutenant Sydney Jary, MC, a platoon commander with the 4th Somersets, was briefing his runner in a house at about 0900 hours when a Private Thomas cried out:

> "Sir they are charging us." Sure enough, from about 150 yards ahead, a well spread-out line of about 20 Germans were putting in a bayonet charge. They were brave lads, but they didn't stand a chance. I gave no orders except: "Cease fire." Not one got to within 70 yards of us.[46]

As the attack came in, the tanks supporting the Somersets opened up a barrage with their heavy Besa machine guns and scattered the German troops. Three-inch mortars and artillery fire added to the mayhem, the field before the advanced troops being covered with German dead and wounded. Patrols were sent out after the attack had been broken to collect prisoners. To the south of Cahagnes, the 5th Battalion Duke of Cornwall's Light Infantry was busy clearing out any pockets of resistance that had been bypassed in the advance. The 1st Worcesters got a surprise when a German commander, *Oberst* Taistler of the *21. Panzer-Division*, and his adjutant marched 58 German soldiers into captivity; they had simply had enough.

Lieutenant David Render of the Sherwood Rangers advanced steadily in his Sherman on the right flank, fighting actions as his troop moved forward. On the evening of 1 August, he took stock of the situation:

> The distance the regiment had covered in 48 hours was greater than any previous operational advance and was an indication that the German line was beginning to fold in on itself. The regiment's axis would now swing to the south-east towards Mont Pinçon. The Sherwood Rangers would continue to support 130 Brigade and ahead of us lay the villages of Jurques and Ondefontaine, which would soon be our objectives. Beyond them lay the dominating feature of the massif and 43rd Wessex Division's ultimate objective. The total

---

43 Manuscript forwarded to author by M. Hirst (Hull, 1993).
44 Major Whitehead was awarded the Military Cross for his actions on 1 August 1944.
45 L. Stokes, correspondence with author (Devon, 1994).
46 Jary, S., *18 Platoon* (Somerset: Light Infantry Office, 1998), p. 34.

Troops of the 5th Battalion Duke of Cornwall's Light Infantry clearing houses in St Pierre-du-Fresne. (Courtesy of M. Denney)

distance was less than five miles but advancing on a frontage of a single road would take a week of relentless bloody fighting to get there. The further we advanced towards Mont Pinçon, the more difficult the terrain became. The Germans sought to make the most of the advantage that the ground gave them.[47]

At 2000 hours on 1 August, the 5th Battalion Wiltshire Regiment moved forward to the base of the slopes of the Bois-du-Homme in preparation for the next day's operations. They were tasked with taking the steep approaches of the Bois-du-Homme leading to the highest peak, Point 361. This was located on a thickly wooded ridge that ran 2 miles long from west to east and was situated 3 miles to the south of St Pierre-du-Fresne. That night the heavens opened and torrential rain poured down, filling slit trenches and making the tracks on the slopes before them thick and slimy with mud.

The Bois-du-Homme and Hill 361, 2 August

At 0200 hours, 129 Brigade began its march to Ondefontaine. From the commanding German positions on the Bois-du-Homme, rifle and machine-gun fire fell upon the advancing columns. It was to be a day of slow but steady progress as 214 Brigade worked its way forward in the

---

47 Render, *Tank Action*, pp. 157–58.

Men of 129 Brigade, 43rd Wessex Division, on their approach march to the Bois-du-Homme. (Author's collection)

direction of Mont Pinçon. The 5th DCLI, supported by the tanks of the 4/7th Royal Dragoon Guards and divisional artillery and mortars, reached the top of the ridge and engaged the enemy armour and infantry. At the same time, the 1st Worcesters moved around the flank and took the crest. During the afternoon of 2 August, the outskirts of La Bigne village were reached by patrols of the 43rd Reconnaissance Regiment, who were in advance of the main body. They reported that the dense woodland that stretched to Ondefontaine, a distance of 5 miles, was strongly held by German infantry and armour.

Driver Arthur Eade, with 504 Company, Royal Army Service Corps, was called upon to transport troops to the forward area:

> I was detailed to pick up a load of soldiers and drive them up into the woods, where we stopped and unloaded while fire was going on all around us. In the wagon we carried picks and shovels with which we dug a shallow trench, just deep enough to get below ground. I put my tin hat on, and I listened to the exploding mortar bombs and the Moaning Minnies as they came screaming down exploding all around us. I was glad to get out of that place, but the poor bloody infantry had to stay.[48]

---

48 A. Eade, correspondence with author (Bradford, 1991).

Jurques-du-Fresne, 2 August

Major Desmond Scarr of the 43rd Reconnaissance Regiment advanced to the village of Jurques, on the lower slopes of the Bois-du-Homme:

> The division carried out a night approach march in order to advance on Mont Pinçon. We took up positions in the village of Jurques. There was a great deal of noise and smoke, much of it coming from a Sherman tank that was burning with its ammunition exploding, on the outskirts of the village. The ground we stood on was high and overlooked a road that ran down into a valley and then rose up to a wooded ridge.[49]

Sergeant Walter Caines of the 4th Dorsets remembered the hot summer weather in which they fought. Men had been going without sleep for a while and would often drop off while on the march, being lifted onto a tank to help them along:

> On the way to Jurques it was a terrible night. A signals scout car went off course and was blown up in a minefield, killing the Adjutant Captain Goddard[50] and the control operator Cpl Penny.[51] The battalion passed through Jurques fairly easily; it was a battered town. We then faced a hell of a lot of resistance, [as] Jerry opened up with everything he had. Self-propelled guns fired like hell let loose. Spandaus rattled away and several of our tanks were knocked out by carefully concealed anti-tank guns. La Bigne, south of Jurques, was captured but the battalion suffered numerous casualties again and we were now feeling the worse for wear.[52]

Lieutenant Whittle came within half a mile of Jurques with his 4th Dorsets comrades when they were delayed by mines:

> The road was heavily cratered and while we were searching for mines a machine-gun opened up on us. Patrols pushed forward and met opposition for the first time, a few fanatics holding out in the village itself, [but] these fools were quickly dealt with and then they were no more. At this point the Adjutant, Captain Goddard, in trying to catch up with the column, took a different route and entered Jurques in front of us. We heard an explosion and pushed forward and halfway between Jurques and La Bigne we found the Adjutant's scout car blown up on a mine. Captain Goddard had been killed instantly, and Lt Brogan, the signals officer, was badly burned.[53]

---

49 *WW2: People's War* <www.bbc.co.uk/ww2peopleswar> (accessed 24 January 2021).
50 Captain William David Goddard, Adjutant 4th Battalion Dorsetshire Regiment, was killed on 2 August 1944, aged 25. He is buried in Hottot-le-Bagues War Cemetery, France.
51 Corporal Hubert Richard Penny, 4th Battalion Dorsetshire Regiment, was killed on 2 August 1944, aged 28. He is buried in Tilly-sur-Seulles War Cemetery, France.
52 Manuscript forwarded to author by W. Caines (Dorset, 1989).
53 Watkins, G.B., *From Normandy to the Weser, the War History of the 4th Battalion Dorsetshire Regiment, June 1944 to May 1945* (East Sussex: Naval and Military Press, 2015), p. 20.

Lieutenant Stuart Hills of the Sherwood Rangers sat in the dark interior of his Sherman tank as it rumbled forward:

> Through the night we continued our advance with the infantrymen riding at times on the back of our tanks. There was the odd skirmish and as dawn was breaking, we reached Jurques. Dropping the infantry off just outside the village, we entered at speed with our tank leading. The place had earlier been bombed and there was a lot of dust and smoke still hanging about on the damp morning air. Some buildings were on fire, but we roared on without being fired upon. Then we found the road to La Bigne.[54]

Fellow Sherwood Ranger Major T.M. Lindsay felt that the high command was almost hysterical in its efforts to press on and force a breakout:

> We were ordered to carry on towards Jurques. There was heavy shelling on the approach road. The attack went in at night, C Squadron was peacefully waiting for zero hour, sleeping or brewing tea on small stoves in the bottom of our tanks. Suddenly German planes swooped over flying very fast and very low, dropping flares right on our positions. It was as bright as a sunny day, there was the crump of bombs falling, but two of the enemy planes go down in flames. But now all surprise had gone from our attack. The carriers, tanks, guns and lorries of the 7th Hampshires were all clearly silhouetted in the glaring light.[55]

A Private Pickford found he and his comrades in the 5th Wiltshires attracted the attention of a German sniper:

> We passed a gap in a hedge which was being watched by a sniper tied to a tree. He killed two of our lads and our officer and put a bullet through my helmet, which I have kept. When the tanks were informed of what was happening one moved forward and ripped the tree to pieces with its machine-gun. The sniper fell out of the tree and hit the ground with a thud.[56]

Private Eric Codling of the 8th Middlesex Machine-gun Battalion entered the village of Jurques and found bicycles left by the Germans; the tyres had been let down, but the pumps had been left. After pumping up the tyres, the men had some fun careering around the streets. Outside a deserted café, Codling saw a stationary Sherman tank: "The flies were clustered around the open turret and inside the tank was the commander and gunner slumped forward in their seats, very dead. A small hole in the turret, by an AP shell, caused their deaths."[57]

Later in the morning of 2 August, the 7th Hampshires occupied Jurques and were shelled for the remainder of the day by 88mm guns to their front. Tiger tanks could be seen rumbling about on the higher ground which dominated the road running uphill to the south. Rocket-firing

---

54 Hills, *By Tank to Normandy*, p. 123.
55 Lindsay, T.M., *Sherwood Rangers* (London: Burrup & Mathieson, 1952), p. 95.
56 Letter to author from Mr Pickford (Chippenham, 1991).
57 E. Codling, correspondence with author (Hampshire, 1991).

Typhoons attacked the German position, but to no avail, and the German forces sat tight while their artillery bombarded the British line.

Stuart Hills was impressed by the power of the Typhoons:

> The air officer accompanying us called up four Typhoon fighter bombers off the cab-rank to fire their rockets at the Tigers. We fired some red smoke to identify the target and then the planes came in very low with a tremendous roar. It was an awesome display of firepower. We came under heavy enemy shellfire, and it became too dangerous to leave the tank. The high ground dominated the whole area and until we could capture these positions enemy artillery observers could bring down accurate fire on us.[58]

Lieutenant Colonel Stanley Christopherson, CO of the Sherwood Rangers, remembered coming across the biggest tank he had ever seen during the advance:

> A Squadron was involved with 214 Brigade in capturing some high ground south of the Bois-du-Homme. They advanced steadily during the day, meeting moderate opposition and reached their objective that evening. During the advance they met a Jaguar[59] for the first time, the heaviest of all German tanks. It was immobilised at 30 yards range[;] three shots were fired, none of which penetrated it, but the track was damaged, and the crew bailed out.[60]

The British unit commanders then decided that a night attack stood a chance of success, but as darkness fell a thick mist descended as the attackers tried to work their way around the right flank. Two such attempts were made, only to be repulsed by the fire from dug-in tanks and continuous Spandau fire from the well-prepared infantry positions. No artillery fire could be brought to bear on the Germans because the mist only allowed limited observation. Lieutenant Sydney Jary of the 4th Somersets remembered the effects such heavy Spandau fire had on the attackers:

> My first reaction to the angry crushing fire power of the Spandau came in July 1944. They were very rapid firing guns. The Germans fired in long sustained bursts, the object of which seemed to me to be to keep us pinned to the ground regardless of the expenditure of ammunition. The German infantryman rarely fired his rifle[;] he was the carrier of light machine-gun ammunition, of which they seemed to have an endless supply.[61]

La Bigne, 3 August

Lieutenant Jeremy Taylor, 43 Reconnaissance Regiment, was with his unit on 3 August and had orders to pass through the infantry and to reconnoitre a route towards Jurques and Ondefontaine. He could see clearly the sights of the fierce struggle that had taken place there:

---

58 Hills, *By Tank to Normandy*, p. 121.
59 The Jaguar referred to by Lieutenant Colonel Christopherson was a *Jagdtiger*, or Hunting Tiger, a huge tank destroyer of 72 tons.
60 Holland (ed.), *An Englishman at War*, p. 406.
61 Manuscript forwarded to author by G. Hilton (Hull, 1992).

A violent battle had been fought over the fields in which we harboured, and the ground was littered with dead, British and German. Arriving in darkness, with a German air-raid in progress near-by, several of the men settled down for the night by their vehicles to discover in the morning that they had been lying near corpses. One corporal mistook a body for a sleeping comrade who he needed for a job and made some attempt to rouse him, needless to say he failed.[62]

Before dawn on 3 August, the 43rd Wessex Division advanced towards the village of La Bigne and came under heavy shellfire which inflicted many casualties. The padre of the 5th Dorsets, the Reverend Francis William Musgrave,[63] was killed and Major Newton, 2 i/c 5th Dorsets, was wounded.

As 214 Brigade moved forward on 3 August, the 5th DCLI was ordered to help the Hampshires to clear the opposition confronting them around Jurques, to enable the advance to continue. At 0815 hours, the attack went in. According to Lieutenant F.W. Durden: "We were advancing close to our own barrage when we saw the enemy in their slit trenches. We charged forward firing from the hip and killed several of them. The rest got up and ran away but we hit a number of them as they did so." As they pressed forward they came across dug-in and well concealed tanks, but could not get close to them; 88mm shells and mortar bombs burst in the trees and casualties began to mount, two Shermans being knocked out and left blazing. Durden was particularly disturbed as the concentrated mortar fire got closer and closer: "It was a frightening sight as it crept its sinister way forward towards our command post until the bombs were exploding around us."[64] The Duke of Cornwall's sent out snipers to harass the German mortar teams, but eventually the battalion had to withdraw so that the artillery could be called upon for help.

Facing the DCLI were 10 enemy tanks, Tigers and Panthers of the *10. SS-Panzer-Division*, that were firmly dug-in on what the troops christened Tiger Hill. Typhoon fighter-bombers swooped out of the sky, but instead of hitting the German positions they hit the 43rd Reconnaissance Regiment and the gun positions of the 94th Field Regiment.

Lieutenant Stuart Hills of the Sherwood Rangers looked on as the enemy mortar and artillery fire passed over him to land in the rear areas:

> The rear troops were not so lucky. There was a pair of enemy 88mm guns covering the La Bigne Road, where there was little cover. Two of our tanks were knocked out. The La Bigne Road was heavy with our traffic and infantry carriers virtually head to tail for about half a mile. Suddenly two German self-propelled guns were spotted on the high ground and Lt Alan Birkett and his troop were sent off to engage them. They hit and damaged one SP but Alan's tank was then hit by the other and set on fire. The tank was on a slope at the time, and it began to run back down towards a bunch of infantry carriers and vehicles at the

---

62 Taylor, J., *A History of the 43rd Reconnaissance Regiment 1939–45* (Bristol: White Swan Press, 1950), p. 70.
63 Chaplain 4th Class the Reverend Francis William Musgrave, Royal Army Chaplain's Department, 5th Battalion Dorsetshire Regiment, was killed on 2 August 1944, aged 39. He is buried in Hottot-le-Bagues War Cemetery, France.
64 Manuscript forwarded to author by A. Hills (Durham, 1994).

bottom, its ammunition exploding all the time inside the burning tank. Then Sergeant Guy Sanders, MM, leapt aboard and steered the tank into a ditch, thus avoiding a major catastrophe. Alan Birkett[65] was killed and what remained of him and his crew inside the burnt-out tank was buried by the infantrymen of the Dorsets. The brewed-up Shermans in the defile on the way to La Bigne were a macabre marker of the dangers we faced in advancing on a narrow front consisting of a single road. The burning hulks made a dreadful sight.[66]

Fellow Sherwood Ranger Lieutenant David Render passed through Jurques with his troop. As they left the village they moved into a fold in the ground, and he said it was here the trouble started:

> A pair of 88s, firing from an elevated position, engaged and knocked out two Shermans, from one of C Company's troop, as they crested the steep road running out of the defile. Lt Jock Campbell[67] was the leading troop commander and he and a number of his men were killed. When a second troop from C Squadron was sent forward up the road, two German self-propelled guns engaged them. The advancing Shermans managed to return fire, damaging one enemy SP, but the second SP hit and brewed up the lead tank commanded by Lt Alan Birkett.[68]

Render's troop took up a position on a ridge which overlooked a small wooded dale, with the village of La Bigne just visible. It was an exposed forward slope where they would be vulnerable to any concealed 88s on the far side of the valley. The tanks spread out as the commanders scanned the ground to their front with their binoculars, with the sun behind them, looking for any sign of the presence of an enemy tank crew or self-propelled gun. To Render's front, a target unexpectedly came into view:

> I saw a company of German infantry moving in column of route along the front of a pine forestry block to our front. There must have been about 150 of them and they were marching four abreast as if on their way to a military parade, clearly unaware of our presence. I ordered the troop to engage, and we opened up on them with machine-gun fire and began to shoot them down. Those who survived the initial burst scattered towards the shelter of the forest. In response we switched to High Explosive from the 75mm, deliberately aiming into the pines to create an airburst effect to cause more casualties. By the time we had finished firing, what remained of the slaughtered company lay in crumpled heaps of field grey at the foot of the pine trees.[69]

---

65 Lieutenant Alan Martin Birkett, Sherwood Rangers, Nottinghamshire Yeomanry, Royal Armoured Corps, was killed in action on 2 August 1944, aged 24. He has no known grave and is commemorated on the Bayeux Memorial to the Missing, France.
66 Hills, *By Tank to Normandy*, p. 124.
67 Lieutenant Donald Edward Campbell, Sherwood Rangers, Nottinghamshire Yeomanry, Royal Armoured Corps, was killed on 2 August 1944, aged 20. He is buried in Bayeux War Cemetery, France.
68 Render, *Tank Action*, p. 158.
69 Render, *Tank Action*, p. 161.

A German Ferdinand self-propelled gun. (Courtesy of H. Wernemann)

La Bigne was still in German hands as daylight faded, but the British commanders knew that to leave it occupied by the enemy for another day would mean that they would be able to reinforce during the night. Consequently, the Sherwood Rangers and the infantry of the 7th Hampshires put in a night attack. The German machine-gun positions were blasted at close range by HE from the tanks, then the Hampshires moved in to systematically clear each house with grenades and bayonets. La Bigne was taken that night. Stuart Hills remembered the night action well:

> We moved from our orchard and into La Bigne, hosing down the houses as we went, systematically working our way through with the infantry. Once or twice the infantry was pinned down by machine-gun fire and we moved in to support them, all the time apprehensive that we might meet a *Panzerfaust* in a doorway or an upstairs window. It was again a bottleneck with no room for manoeuvre. The weather was dull with low circling clouds overhead and we anticipated meeting both enemy tanks and anti-tank guns. But resistance was not unduly strong, and after the village was cleared, the infantry dug-in about a mile beyond it and we passed through on our way to Ondefontaine.[70]

Stanley Christopherson, the Sherwood Rangers' CO, recalled his time at La Bigne:

> On 3rd August the attack went in with C Squadron supporting the 5th Dorsets and the village of La Bigne was captured after some sticky fighting[;] the squadron lost Lt

---

70 Hills, *By Tank to Normandy*, p. 126.

Campbell and two of his crew. Progress was slow owing to the numerous mines that had been recently laid and the REs attached to C Squadron did some magnificent work in clearing them. After the fall of the village C Squadron advance 300 yards south, and having consolidated, A Squadron passed through it with the 5th Dorsets to capture Ondefontaine, which the enemy intended to hold, as soon became evident. A Squadron had to proceed along the one and only road, which was narrow and bordered by a high hedge on either side. Along the whole length of [this road] the high ground to the right flank, containing Le-Bois-de-Buron, commanded an ideal view. In the wood the Germans had placed their OPs and tanks.[71]

Ondefontaine, 4 August

The next objective for the 43rd Wessex Division, as it slogged its way up to Mont Pinçon, was the village of Ondefontaine, which was only 10 miles from their ultimate objective. The ground over which the division had to advance became more difficult, progress being further slowed by constant artillery and mortar fire. Yet again, the advance was funnelled down a single narrow road, flanked by high-banked hedges. There was a thickly wooded ridge called the Bois-de-Buron which would have to be cleared of the enemy when the village fell.

The attack on Ondefontaine began at dawn on 4 August. The 4th Dorsets were called forward and given the task of taking the village. D Company advanced into heavy Spandau and mortar fire that inflicted heavy casualties.

Signals Sergeant (later Lieutenant) Walter Caines of the 4th Dorsets remembered how the men were shaken by the German defensive fire:

> Casualties were heavy and many wounded still lay out in the cornfield. Some managed to crawl back, others lay out until dark or died silently of their wounds where they fell. Those that were left were tired and badly shaken up. I was feeling in no stout-hearted mood as we moved up a sunken road when suddenly shells whistled over us. All was quiet for a moment, followed be a hell of a stonk and we dashed for cover behind a bank. One shell burst on the bank above Harris and dented his helmet. Another crashed down knocking us silly.[72]

Private Ernest Hodge, MM, had good reason to remember that terrible day fighting with the 4th Dorsets:

> We ran into a village which was supposed to be clear of Germans, [and] once in Jerry began to shell us. I remember this lad who was next to me, he got his head blown off and I was shell-shocked. I did not want to go on anymore, I was bomb happy as they called it at the time. I was crying and couldn't go on. A tank crew got hold of me and said: "Come on boy, drink this nice, sweet tea and you'll be alright." The tank crews always had a cup of tea on the go. They were the making of me from that day on.[73]

---

71 Holland (ed.), *An Englishman at War*, p. 414.
72 Thompson, *Victory in Europe*, p. 124.
73 E. Hodge, correspondence with author (Exeter, 1993).

The German artillery fire was to continue all day. Two signallers, Corporal Harris and Sergeant Caines, worked hard at the dangerous job of laying wires to enable the companies to keep in touch by radio. While carrying out this task, Caines was shot by a sniper: "I really did feel scared, probably because I had been without sleep for so long. As I lay on the ground I quietly prayed."[74]

Lieutenant Stuart Hills was in the lead troop of the Sherwood Rangers when his unit entered the village:

> As the light improved, we could see the small village perched on top of a ridge. The access road ran up its right-hand side and was heavily wooded and narrow. Enemy fire was much lighter than expected as we came out of the wood and into open ground. We moved cautiously to the churchyard at the edge of the village, then past the church to a T-junction. Tension rose as a platoon of infantry slipped past us and hid behind a stone house. Geoff Storey edged the nose of the tank past a protecting church wall, when Swish, swish! two anti-tank tracer shells whistled past: "Reverse," I shouted, and Geoff promptly complied[;] they had tried to lure us into a trap.[75]

Lieutenant David Render was near Lieutenant Hills during the attack and came under fire from the wooded area on the high ground on the flank:

> Being the lead tank of the leading troop, advancing down a single road was quite frankly bloody dangerous. My heart would sink when the squadron commander told me that 5 Troop would be in the lead. Covering 1,000 yards of exposed road, dominated by wooded high ground requires cautious movement. We had only covered 400 yards when the first high-velocity armour piercing round screamed past us at over 3,000 feet per second, from somewhere in the trees above us on the right flank. I had just enough time to say: "What the fuck was that?" before my brain engaged and I yelled: "Anti-tank, reverse!" into the microphone.[76]

Render's driver changed gear and pulled back while at the same time trying to pinpoint the position of the offending gun. As the tank moved into a hull-down position, a second shot screamed over the turret, but their luck held. Another tank had seen where the shot came from and started pumping high-explosive shells into the position. A battery of Sexton self-propelled guns of the Essex Yeomanry was in close support, and their fire was directed onto the suspected location. A volley of shells smashed into the German position and knocked out whatever it was that was giving them so much trouble. Nevertheless, there were other guns and tanks to be dealt with, which made for slow progress.

The officers of the Dorsets urged the tank crews to advance and give protection to the exposed infantry, but Stuart Hills believed such a mission was akin to committing suicide. At this point the Dorsets identified strong German tank and infantry units at the far end of the main street. Both the Sherwood Rangers and the men of the Dorsetshire Regiment pulled back as an

---

74 Thompson, *Victory in Europe*, p. 124.
75 Hills, *By Tank to Normandy*, p. 127.
76 Render, *Tank Action*, p. 165.

artillery stonk was called for on the enemy gathering on the other side of the village. A young infantry officer of the Hampshires had seen some movement in the village church tower and thought that a German observer up there had been directing the accurate mortar fire that had been tormenting the British troops throughout the morning. A tank gunner of the Sherwood Rangers, Trooper Dick Dexter, fired two shots, the second of which went straight through the steeple.[77]

Major Loosley, commanding 217 Battery, Royal Artillery, engaged the Germans with the corps artillery, and it was not long before the crushing power of the British barrage descended on the far side of the village. Whole houses disappeared in the deluge as the village was destroyed, the Germans caught in a death trap. However, accurate German mortar fire fell upon the artillery batteries and Major Ronald Tomlinson[78] was killed. The 5th Dorsets' war diary commented: "This officer had been with us since the beginning of our operations and with his battery had given us great support. Bn HQ felt his loss keenly."

The tanks of the Sherwood Rangers prepared to follow on the heels of the barrage and force a way through to the far end of the village, accompanied by the infantry of the 7th Hampshires. Stuart Hills moved through the village unopposed in his Sherman tank:

> We passed the church and sprayed the houses with machine-gun fire. There was no opposition as we moved right through to the far end.[79]

Any Germans who were able to had withdrawn, leaving behind their dead and wrecked weapons among the ruins. Lieutenant Hills identified one dead German officer as being a member of the *10. SS-Panzer-Division*. The British tanks rumbled past the village and onto the high ground beyond. Ondefontaine had fallen.

After days of constant pressure to keep on the move, the fighting and stress, along with the effects of sleep deprivation, were now being felt by all the troops at the front. Men were at the limits of their physical and mental endurance. David Render found it difficult just to stay awake:

> Our eyes were red raw with the grit that comes from lack of sleep, and it became an increasing effort to stay awake and keep focused. I had to chide and cajole the crew to remain alert, but I could feel my own attention span slipping. Our own commanding officer was becoming concerned at our condition and the regimental medical officer had warned him that we would struggle to remain effective as a unit if we were not rested.[80]

Private Sandy Handley of the 43rd Reconnaissance Regiment was placed on night vehicle guard and recalled the effort it took to stay awake. As he attempted to reach the guard post, the other men in his unit got under his feet in the dark:

---

77 After the attack, a dead German observer was found in the ruins of the church steeple.
78 Major Ronald Rendell Tomlinson, 112th West Somerset Yeomanry Field Regiment, Royal Artillery, was killed in action on 5 August 1944, aged 26. He is buried in Tilly-sur-Seulles War Cemetery, France.
79 Hills, *By Tank to Normandy*, p. 109.
80 Render, *Tank Action*, p. 167.

> It was pitch black, [and] me and another trooper kept stumbling over our sleeping mates, they were so tired that they had just dropped down where they were and gone to sleep. At the end of our two-hour stint, we found the next two men to go on vehicle guard and woke them up. We wandered off and dropped down anywhere and were soon asleep.[81]

His troop was ordered to be up at 0500 hours and on the move an hour later, but the men were so tired that nobody woke the guard commander. The troop sergeant eventually woke the men and there was a terrific row, all the guards being put on a charge pending court martial, for being asleep on duty. Private Handley remembered: "What a shambles we all looked as it got light."[82] Luckily for the men, their officer was sympathetic as he knew how tired his men were and the charges were quietly dropped.

Sergeant Walter Caines of the 4th Dorsets watched the hard-pressed stretcher-bearers at work:

> Shells fell in the area and the unit suffered several casualties, some really badly wounded. The medics were excellent[;] one could see the wounded being brought in by stretcher-bearers who would be sweating in streams after their arduous slogging to and from the RAP, a hundred yards away from Tactical HQ. One could hear the wounded moaning, sometimes crying with pain as they passed. The boys would walk alongside saying: "Cheer up mate, have a fag" and stuff a lighted cigarette in their mouths. A cig always helped soothe the pain, this was well known to all.[83]

As the 43rd Wessex Division pressed on in the direction of Mont Pinçon, Major A.D. Parsons of the 4th Wiltshires sat on the back of a tank with his men:

> [I had] an uncomfortable feeling as we rode along, packed tight on the top of the Sherman tanks of the 13/18th Hussars and our already overloaded wheeled and tracked vehicles. The countryside on the way to Mont Pinçon resembled Devon, steep and wooded hills, lanes with high banks and large undulating cornfields. The weather was very hot, [and] the roads lay thick with white dust and dead horses. There was a new danger of roadside mines.[84]

Late on 4 August, the weary column reached Mont Chauvet. The 43rd Reconnaissance Regiment, which had been well forward scouting the land ahead of the main advance, had been in action with the enemy all day, and skirmishes continued throughout the night.

Mont Pinçon: a daunting prospect, 4th Battalion Wiltshire Regiment, 5 August

Mont Pinçon stands some 1,200ft above the Bocage and is the highest hill in Normandy, totally dominating the landscape for miles around. From this high ground, German observers could see any movement on the surrounding areas and call down accurate mortar and artillery

---

81 *Chotie Darling* <www.chotiedarling.co.uk> (accessed 14 January 2021).
82 *Chotie Darling* <www.chotiedarling.co.uk> (accessed 14 January 2021).
83 Newspaper cutting forwarded to author by A. Hunt (Leeds, 1993).
84 *WW2: People's War* <www.bbc.co.uk/ww2peopleswar> (accessed 23 January 2021).

The Road to Mont Pinçon: July–August 1944   457

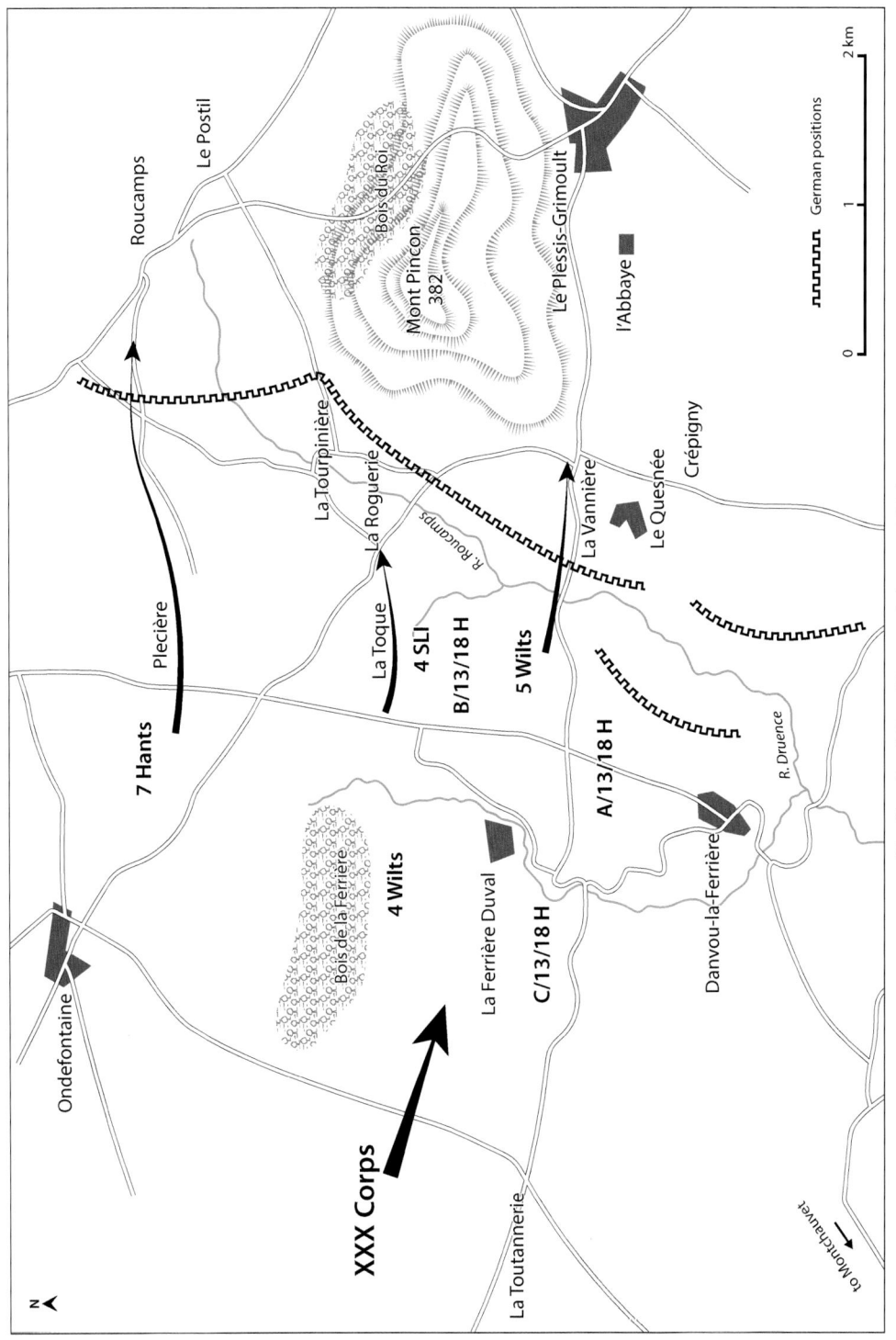

The Road to Mont Pinçon, 6 August 1944.

fire at will. The upper slopes were very steep, and well wooded on the southern and southwestern sides. Thick hedges divided small fields on the lower slopes, enabling the Germans to put up a strong defence. The British plan for 5 August was for 129 Brigade to assault the hill from the west and south-west, advancing through the villages of La Variniere and St Jean-le-Blanc. These were typical of villages in the Bocage, with hardy solid buildings and thick walls made of stone. The whole area was covered by a maze of sunken lanes that were surrounded by numerous thick orchards. The Germans quickly reorganised their battered surviving units into ad hoc battle groups. Information on these groups is scant, but among the units known to be in the area were elements of the *267.* and *326. Infanterie-Division, 21 Panzer-Division* and *9. SS-Panzer-Division.*

The German defenders were in a desperate situation, their front between Vire and Mont Pinçon being under great pressure from the advancing British units. Later in the day on 4 August, the Americans broke through the German lines at Avranches and Patton's armour began streaming into Brittany.

At 0800 hours on 5 August, the tanks of B Squadron, 13/18th Hussars, and the infantry of the 4th Wiltshires moved to the attack. To the north, the tanks of A Squadron, 13/18th Hussars, moved on a parallel route, carrying the men of the 5th Wiltshires. In those narrow lanes, speed was out of the question, the troops also having to deal with the possibility that some of them had been mined. Nevertheless, the men of the 4th and 5th Wiltshires clung to the outside of the tanks as they headed towards Mont Pinçon.

St Jean-le-Blanc

Where the 4th Wiltshires approached St Jean-le-Blanc, the road sloped down to a stream, the bridge over which had been blown, with its banks mined. C Company, 4th Wiltshires, waded across the stream and moved up the steep, wooded slope beyond. The enemy was close by and waiting in well-concealed trenches, and a battle started that was to last all day. Major Parsons of the 4th Wiltshires remembered the difficulty they had attempting to come to grips with the German positions:

> A large chateau was burning, the bridge had been blown and both banks were mined. Getting up the steep slopes was slow, costly and bitter work for C Company, they had eight hours of desperate fighting under a burning sun.[85]

The commander of the battalion's C Company, Major David Ivor Mathie Robbins – known to his friends as Dim Robbins – was ordered to press on over the stream. Major Parsons continued:

> The bridge, which we had expected to cross, was blown. My commanding officer said: "The orders are to get on, let the tanks stay here for now, continue on foot to that river and get across to the village, which is only a mile or two." Once we got into the rougher ground, getting higher and higher, it was very steep, very hot and sporadic fire broke out.

---

85 *WW2: People's War* <www.bbc.co.uk/ww2peopleswar> (accessed 23 January 2021).

The battle lasted for several hours because of the close nature of it. Every time we tried to advance it drew very heavy fire.[86]

The Wiltshires battled their way forward against determined opposition as they fought from house to house, neither side giving any quarter in close combat. Platoon commanders and NCOs were killed or wounded, but still the men fought on. Major Robbins looked on as a lance corporal took over command of one section and led it forward:

> He was a battalion boxer called Jenkins, he had given me a lot of trouble, but he was an excellent fellow. I saw him leading a small counterattack and meeting head on, with Germans doing the same thing, with about ten men. It was fascinating to watch as Jenkins won. This kind of thing was going on all the time. Jenkins's platoon was practically knocked out, but it stayed. On the left there was similar fighting, and this went on all day.[87]

Captain Thomas Powell led the battalion's mortar platoon forward to give added firepower to C Company's attack: "C Company was having a really rough time of it and drew enemy fire whenever they moved. I think we fired a couple of thousand bombs at their positions as we had unlimited ammunition."[88]

Captain Thomas Powell, 4th Battalion Wiltshire Regiment. (Courtesy of M. Denney)

As the battle was being fought, British engineers built a makeshift bridge over the stream while under fire from *Nebelwerfers* and mortars, and at 1600 hours the tanks of B Squadron, 13/18th Hussars, rumbled across the stream and up the slope to support the infantry in the battle zone. Another company advanced to St Jean-le-Blanc and found there German infantry and tanks that were well dug-in among the orchards and cornfields.

Major Robbins recalled that the casualties on both sides were heavy: "No Germans surrendered, they fought to the end and clearly must have been a rear-guard company set with that task. By 18:00 p.m. they had all been shot or withdrawn."[89]

Major Robins and a Forward Observation Officer, Captain John Fletcher from the 94th Field Regiment, Royal Artillery, left the men digging-in and moved forward to get a good observation position for the artillery. As they advanced, another ridge loomed before them and they

---

86 A.D. Parsons, correspondence with author (Hampshire, 1990).
87 Manuscript forwarded to author by L. Procter (Bedford, 1996).
88 T. Powell, correspondence with author (Wycombe, 1991).
89 D.I.M. Robbins, correspondence with author (Hampshire, 1990).

surprised two Germans, each armed with a Schmeisser. Captain Fletcher shot one and the other one ran off. Looking down a slope, they spotted German infantry and tanks forming up for a counterattack. Fletcher immediately radioed back the coordinates, and shortly after a barrage fell on the unlucky Germans and dispersed them before they could get moving. Major Robbins then returned to his company:

> Night was falling and the troop of tanks withdrew to do whatever it is they do at night. So, we were left in this rather eerie position digging in with the Germans quite close, no grub, and waited. We did not quite know what to do next except to defend this place.[90]

Major Parsons remembered the night after the battle for St Jean-le-Blanc:

> That night C Company dug-in, hungry and exhausted with the sad task of burying the dead. As night fell the tanks withdrew, [and] our only friends were the gunners. Enemy tanks and self-propelled guns were defending St Jean-le-Blanc. [There had been] a bitter and largely fruitless day's fighting in difficult country under a hot sun and [with] little or no food. We lost 22 killed, 39 wounded, a bitter day for the battalion.[91]

The whole battalion was across the stream by nightfall, but the opposition they faced was too strong to enable them to take the village, and when darkness fell they were withdrawn.

5th Battalion Wiltshire Regiment, La Variniere-Duval, 5 August

As the 4th Wiltshires battled for St Jean-le-Blanc on 5 August, the 5th Wiltshires were also in action. The tanks of A Squadron, 13/18th Hussars, carried the 5th Wiltshires – 25 men to a tank – to the crossroads near La Variniere-Duval. The plan was for the Wiltshires to advance to Mont Pinçon, supported by tanks, by way of Chante-Pie and La Variniere, but between them and their objective were two wooded depressions which acted as good tank obstacles. Towering above all of this were the formidable heights of Mont Pinçon.

The advance began at 1300 hours on 6 August. Corporal Ronald Garner of the 5th Wiltshires remembered: "There was a lot of mortar fire coming down on us as we moved forward."[92] The platoons also came under fire from Spandaus in the wooded areas and some were pinned down. The Sherman tanks moved up to the infantry to shell and machine-gun the woods, and the opposition was quickly dealt with.

Major Desmond Scarr of the 43rd Reconnaissance Regiment scouted the positions on the slopes of Mont Pinçon:

> It was late in the day when we finally launched ourselves down the hill. It appeared at first that the Germans had pulled back, and we were able to advance. When we made contact, it was we who caught the Germans unawares at a place called Duval and we were able to

---

90 D.I.M. Robbins, correspondence with author (Hampshire, 1990).
91 *WW2: People's War* <www.bbc.co.uk/ww2peopleswar> (accessed 23 January 2021).
92 Hunt, E., *Mont Pinçon* (London: Leo Cooper, 2003), p. 96.

Men of the 5th Battalion Wiltshire Regiment await the order to move forward. (Courtesy of M. Denney)

inflict casualties and take prisoners. We were far from battle-hardened and as yet unaccustomed to the eerie contrast between the glorious Normandy countryside and the strong presence of death which pervaded the scene and accompanied our every action. The waiting moments were the worst and once or twice over the coming days I found myself hating it.[93]

As darkness fell, it was realised that further attacks were impracticable so the remaining companies formed an all-round defensive position. Battalion headquarters move into a farmhouse and came under mortar fire, as Adjutant Captain Harry Peace recalled:

A mortar shell dropped on us and sadly our much-loved padre, Jimmy Douglas,[94] the cook, Double Davies and several others were killed. Not exactly a good start to a battle. Dusk was falling and there we were; the Germans and ourselves seemed to be mixed up. We had one company across the river and that was the situation.[95]

Private Victor Coombes of the 5th Wiltshires recalled that German patrols were infiltrating the battalion area in the moonlight. He was ordered to take part in a counter-patrol and moved out into the darkness:

---

93 *Chotie Darling* <www.chotiedarling.co.uk> (accessed 1 February 2021).
94 The Reverend James Douglas, MiD, Chaplain 4th Class, Royal Army Church Department, 5th Battalion Wiltshire Regiment, was killed on 5 August 1944, aged 34. He is buried in Tilly-sur-Seulles War Cemetery, France.
95 Manuscript forwarded to author by P. Cuerdon (Hampshire, 1993).

The enemy must have had this road under observation as they opened up with a machine-gun and literally sprayed the area with bullets. Lt Chittenden[96] was killed instantly. Vic led the rest of the patrol back. Lt Colonel Thomas arrived, Commanding officer 5th Wiltshires, having run the gauntlet from C Coy's bridgehead to report that they were surrounded, and their position was untenable. "He was given permission to withdraw," said Cpt, Adjutant Harry Peace, MC and Bar. D Company was extricated with great difficulty, with only 38 survivors. Battalion casualties were now so high that A and B Companies were merged under the command of Major Milne and C and D Companies were merged under the command of Major Field. Lt Colonel Thomas[97] had been riddled with MG bullets during D Company's withdrawal from the bridgehead.[98]

Captain Henry Gifford Wells, MC, of the 8th Machine-gun Battalion Middlesex Regiment, arrived at the positions held by the Wiltshires as night fell:

Lieutenant Colonel Richard Michael Collette Thomas, CO of the 5th Battalion Wiltshire Regiment, who was killed in action on 5 August 1944. (Courtesy of P. Cuerdon)

We followed a Wiltshire company into an orchard at a little place called Danvou, overlooked by Mont Pinçon. We spread out and concealed our vehicles in the dark as best we could and dug slit-trenches, but the ground was like rock.[99]

The tanks of the Sherwood Rangers had been in action almost every day and had sustained terrible casualties. The Reverend Leslie Skinner had the unpleasant task of recovering the bodies of men whose tanks had been hit:

---

96 Lieutenant Alan Reginald Chittenden, MC, Royal Sussex Regiment, attached to the 5th Battalion Wiltshire Regiment, was killed in action on 5 August 1944, ages 21. He is buried in St Manvieu Cemetery, France.
97 Lieutenant Colonel Richard Michael Collete Thomas, Commanding Officer 5th Battalion Wiltshire Regiment, was killed in action on 5 August 1944. He is buried in St Manvieu War Cemetery, France.
98 Manuscript forwarded to author by P. Cuerdon (Hampshire, 1993).
99 *WW2: People's War* <www.bbc.co.uk/ww2peopleswar> (accessed 25 August 2021).

Located previously brewed-up tanks on foot, Watson[100] and Heselwood[101] died of wounds at Dorsets RAP. Only ash and burnt metal in Birkett's tank. Dorsets MO says other members of crew consumed by fire having been KIA. Searched ash and found remains of pelvic bones. At other tank three bodies still inside, partly burned and welded together. Managed with difficulty to identify Lt Campbell. After a long struggle, unable to remove bodies, nasty business, sick. C Squadron still wanting me for two burials, but after three unsuccessful attempts to reach them had to give up. Heavy fire each time I tried.[102]

Reverend Leslie Skinner, Sherwood Rangers, Royal Armoured Corps. (Author's collection)

The taking of Mont Pinçon, 6 August

Rather optimistically, the planners expected the 43rd Wessex Division to capture the summit of Mont Pinçon by 1000 hours on 6 August, and then to advance 9 miles to the south. The attack was to be launched by the 4th Somersets on the left and the 5th Wiltshires on the right. In reserve would be the 4th Wiltshires.

Captain Thomas Powell of the 4th Wiltshires sat in reserve as the morning light appeared on 6 August:

> Our concentration area as dawn broke was in full view of the enemy. They were in Danvou, or had OPs in Danvou, and while we were at last having an early breakfast, they shattered us with very heavy mortar and artillery fire. During this ten-minute shelling D Company lost one officer and nine men killed, and two officers and 27 men wounded.[103]

Captain Wells sat with his 8th Machine-gun Battalion Middlesex Regiment in an orchard as daylight broke on the 6th:

> Down came the enemy shells hitting the apple trees and showering the troops below with splinters of shell. There was no let-up and nothing we could do. We had several killed and more wounded. We had no idea where the shells came from. I did what I could to patch

---

100 Trooper Leslie William Watson, Sherwood Rangers, Nottinghamshire Yeomanry, RAC, was killed on 2 August 1944, aged 26. He is buried in St Charles de Percy War Cemetery, France.
101 Trooper Frederic Heselwood, Sherwood Rangers, Nottinghamshire Yeomanry, RAC, was killed on 2 August 1944, aged 22. He is buried in St Charles de Percy War Cemetery, France.
102 Thompson, *Victory in Europe*, p. 127.
103 Hunt, *Mont Pinçon*, p. 105.

up the wounded and got them sent back. But then came another salvo and Harewell[104] was killed while attending the wounded. I was hit slightly in the shoulder.[105]

The men of 130 Brigade launched a diversionary attack from the north, as 129 Brigade struck out from the west. These attacks would be launched up the steepest slopes; to the north there were less steep-sided approaches, but shortness of time prevented any movement of troops to that area. Leading 130 Brigade into the attack at 1100 hours were the 7th Hampshires. As they moved forward, mortar and machine-gun fire cut many men down and A Company had to withdraw. An attempt was made to outflank the enemy as the guns of 112th Field Regiment bombarded the German positions. At 1400 hours, the advance was taken up again, but once again heavy defensive fire held them up and inflicted numerous casualties. It soon became apparent that no further progress was possible, and the companies were withdrawn. Plans were made for a further attack later that day with artillery support.

The move forward was recalled by Lieutenant Sydney Jary of the 4th Somersets:

> The approach march to our forming-up place had been a nightmare of swirling abrasive dust, shelling and the stench of exhaust fumes from the tanks that transported us forward. We were due to attack at 15:00 p.m. The ground before us descended to a small stream at the foot of Mont Pinçon, then rose steeply through typical Bocage fields with thick hedgerows, to a thickly wooded area. Mont Pinçon loomed above us menacingly. The top of the hill was open and crowned with gorse.[106]

As the Somerset Light Infantry advanced along a narrow sunken lane in shirtsleeve order because of the hot weather, Lieutenant Jary looked through his binoculars but could see no sign of the enemy. The 4th Wiltshires were following behind:

> The forward platoon had barely crossed the stream when concentrated Spandau fire came from the front and both flanks. This devastating firepower stopped the battalion dead in its tracks. There was no way forward or round it and no way to retire, [and] Private Morris was killed.[107] Powerless and crouching in a hedgerow I tried to identify the Spandau positions, but this proved impossible.[108]

The German defenders used the contours of the landscape to maximum effect, it being easy for them to move freely and unseen under cover of the high banks that surrounded them. Corporal Douglas Procter of the 4th Somersets looked up the slopes of Mont Pinçon as Spandau fire flew over his position:

---

104 Private William Frederick George Harewell, 8th Machine-gun Battalion Middlesex Regiment, was killed on 6 August 1944, aged 36. He is buried in Tilly-sur-Seulles War Cemetery, France.
105 *Chotie Darling* <www.chotiedarling.co.uk> (accessed 23 January 2021).
106 Jary, *18 Platoon*, p. 41.
107 Private Reginald Morris, 4th Battalion Somerset Light Infantry, was killed in action on 6 August 1944, aged 37. He is buried in Banneville-la-Campagne War Cemetery, France.
108 Jary, *18 Platoon*, p. 41.

3-o-clock was zero hour when the barrage started, and the first two companies started advancing. The enemy waited until all the battalion was exposed, every man jack of us. Then they opened up with about a dozen Spandaus strategically placed all over the hillside and we couldn't spot them at all. All we could do was hug the ground for five or six hours, attempt any movement and a hail of bullets came over.[109]

The 5th Wiltshires and Shermans of the 13/18th Hussars continued to resume the attack on the bridge over the stream. The Wiltshires had to reorganise into two companies because of their heavy casualties, sappers accompanying them for mine clearance and tanks leading the way. The troops had just got over their start line when the German barrage came thundering down on them, and at the same time machine-gunners and snipers opened up. As the tanks proceeded across the open ground, they laid down a suppressing fire on the German positions. Under tremendous fire, the surviving Wiltshires made their way through an orchard and down to the stream, taking cover behind its high banks. Corporal Patrick Hennessey moved forward in his 13/18th Hussars Sherman to the foot of the hill:

Corporal Douglas Procter, 4th Battalion Somerset Light Infantry. (Author's collection)

> We had fought our way forward against very heavy mortar and machine-gun fire, which was taking a steady toll of the infantry. The day was hot and sultry, and the air was laden with dust and the stench of dead cattle. Every movement of a vehicle stirred up more dust, which drew more fire from the enemy and curses from the infantry, who lay in shallow slit trenches waiting for the word to move across the river and up the steep scarp. The pioneers were working to clear the mines on the bridge under cover of a smoke screen and in the face of considerable enemy fire. As soon as the bridge was clear our artillery put down a barrage on the far bank and we went across the bridge in tanks with the infantry following. They had got about halfway across when the enemy came to life with machine-guns and mortars, catching them in the open. Within minutes the two leading companies were practically wiped out.[110]

Major Derrick Wormald, DSO, MC, of A Squadron, 13/18th Hussars, took up a position to the north of La Variniere and came under heavy artillery fire, so decided to move his tank:

---

109 Manuscript forwarded to author by G. Sale (York, 1995).
110 Hunt, *Mont Pinçon*, p. 114.

> There was a huge explosion, and we came to a shuddering halt, I thought we had been hit by a medium shell. After the stonking ended, I dismounted to inspect the damage. As I jumped from the hull, I noticed that I was descending with my feet about to land on a German Teller mine. I separated my feet and landed astride it. I then radioed for the squadron recovery vehicle which came to our assistance.[111]

Lieutenant Colonel John Harold Child Pearson, CO of the 5th Wiltshires, realising his troops were pinned down, left his carrier and went ahead on foot to see the situation for himself and to try to rally the men. As he approached the bridge, he was shot by a sniper, Captain Harry Peace thereafter assuming command of the battalion.[112] The heavy machine-gun fire all around them was relentless.

Corporal Ronald Garner, with HQ Coy, 5th Wiltshires, dug furiously to get below ground and gain some protection from the German fire:

Major Derrick Wormald, DSO, MC, 13/18th Hussars, Royal Armoured Corps. (Author's collection)

> Every few minutes a German MG would fire into the area making us duck. After we got two feet down we struck water. Once, when a salvo of mortar bombs landed, I dived into a sewer to find three other men already in occupation, one was reading his pocket bible. After Harry Peace took command, our IO, Lt Keeling, became Adjutant. We had well over 100 prisoners and had only 66 men left from all four rifle companies put together.[113]

Captain Peace recalled:

> I got to brigade and said that we would attempt a limited objective of the crossroads at La Variniere, and we did at least have a better idea of where some of the enemy opposition was coming from. We were able to lay on a revised fire plan, which, instead of a general barrage, was more likely to hit where we wanted it to hit.[114]

The only original surviving company commander was Major Field, who together with Peace rallied the men and encouraged them to keep moving under cover of fire from the tanks and the

---

111 Miller, C.H., *History of 13/18th Royal Hussars 1922–47* (London: Blackwood, 1949), p. 87.
112 Lieutenant Colonel John Harold Child Pearson, DSO, South Lancashire Regiment, commanding the 5th Battalion Wiltshire Regiment, died on 7 August 1944. He is buried in Tilly-sur-Seulles War Cemetery, France.
113 R. Garner, correspondence with author (Wiltshire, 1992).
114 Hunt, *Mont Pinçon*, p. 115.

fresh barrage that roared before them. Once over the bridge, the men approached the houses on the outskirts of La Variniere and the enemy started to come out with their hands raised; over 100 prisoners were taken. Captain Peace then gave orders that all the nearby hedgerows were to be cleared. The troops advanced down the main road of the village and the whole place was occupied in less than 30 minutes. The 5th Wiltshires now had more prisoners than men, so Captain Peace said to his sergeant major: "Look, we can't afford two men to take these prisoners back. If there is anybody who is a bit shaky send him back with the prisoners." The sergeant major replied: "To tell you the truth sir, they are all a bit shaky."[115] Several German prisoners were taken to the side of the road and told to dig graves. They were very frightened, fearing the graves were for themselves, and were thus digging very slowly. They were in fact for the British dead, and the prisoners were eventually marched off into captivity after completing their task.

Captain Noel Denny of the 13/18th Hussars moved to a relatively safe location with other tanks from his regiment and took up position there:

> The remainder of the squadron were now over the river and at this point in the proceedings, five Boche infantry, all armed with bazookas, who had been sitting beside my tank on the road, came out of the hedge and gave themselves up, to my intense relief.[116]

German 150mm shells falling on the crossroads kept the infantry pinned down, and the battalion strength was now at just 70 men and five officers. Reports were sent to Brigade HQ that La Variniere had fallen, and a message came back for them to press on past the village. Captain Peace had set up his HQ in a sunken lane that was littered with dead Germans, when Major Milne – who had been commanding the combined A and B Companies – arrived at the run. He had been captured by the Germans, but when the barrage came down on them he had played dead as they all withdrew in terror. A German barrage then landed on Captain Peace's HQ in the sunken lane and wounded many who were sheltering there, including Peace: "I felt as though someone had hit me with a bloody sledgehammer. I was quite vocal, or so I'm told. They picked me up and that was the end of my military career."[117]

New orders were now received: the 5th Wiltshires were to stay put and hold the crossroads as the 4th Wiltshires would be passing through them to attack the hill itself. This order was received at 1800 hours, but the 4th Wiltshires were at the time on the left flank some 2 miles away. Lieutenant Colonel Vincent Dunkerly, officer commanding the 13/18th Hussars, was impatient and ordered the tanks of his A Squadron to advance to the high ground. The 13/18th Hussars Sherman of Corporal Patrick Hennessey had crossed the stream and was dealing with pockets of Germans still hiding in the scrub. At about 1800 hours he spotted a track that went up the hill, and when he reported this find he was told to press on up it as fast as possible.

Major Derrick Wormald of the 13/18th Hussars had been warned that infantry and 88mm anti-tank guns were in position on the summit: "I viewed the future with the gravest possible concern and gloom."[118] On the way up one tank slid off the road and dropped into a quarry, and

---

115 Hunt, *Mont Pinçon*, p. 89.
116 Newsaper cutting forwarded to author by J. Sadler (Malton, 1996).
117 Hunt, *Mont Pinçon*, p. 91.
118 Miller, *History of the 13/18th Royal Hussars*, p. 94.

another had its track blown off by an armour-piercing shell. Captain Noel Denny spoke of the action on that warm summer evening:

> Second Troop and I laid a smoke screen. Lt Jennison's tank then raced to the top of the hill, followed shortly afterwards by Lt Elliot's. During this movement we were not once shot at, the Boche being caught on the top looking east instead of west. By half-past six we had seven tanks in an all-round defensive position on the summit.[119]

Patrick Hennessey was just about to ascend the track up the slope when he came across another Sherman:

> From my left another Sherman appeared and came racing across my bows with a friend of mine, Cpl Hammond, leaning out of the turret, roaring with laughter and waving at me, and away he went up the track and I had to follow him. We both started racing up this track as if it was something of a game. I was furious with Hammond for going in front in piratical fashion, but away we went crashing up to the top. There was a bank on the right and a steep drop on the left. Sgt Rattle's tank, he was the troop sergeant, slithered into a quarry and very nearly overturned, but it didn't.[120]

When Trooper George Treloar of the 13/18th Hussars reached the peak he found the enemy to be close by:

> I recall firing our machine-guns and the enemy putting up flares to find us. We got to the top and one man from each tank had to get out and act as infantry in the hedgerows, while lying there I remember hearing the Germans talking. Finally, the infantry came up, the Wiltshires, having lost a company of men that day by the river.[121]

That evening, Lieutenant Colonel Dunkerley led the remains of A Squadron to the crest, followed by the 4th Somersets who dug-in there. Major A.D. Parsons led B Company of the 4th Wiltshires up the slopes and found only minimal resistance, the main difficulty being the actual physical effort of climbing the steep slopes that were covered in scrub:

> It was a strange feeling as we toiled upward, heavily laden with weapons, ammunition, picks and shovels, expecting to find ourselves surrounded at any moment. As we neared the top a thick mist came down. We could see no landmarks, but we found the tanks and they were relieved to see us. Germans could be heard shouting and digging close by. We were as tired as any troops could be and many of us fell asleep as we were digging positions in the rocky soil, falling headlong, pick in hand, into the half-dug trenches, dead to the world. For us the Mont Pinçon operation was bitter and fruitless, not a battle against the Germans so much, as against the burning sun and the choking dust, our parched throats and empty

---

119 Delaforce, P., *Monty's Marauders* (Gloucestershire: Sutton Publishing, 1993), p. 167.
120 Hennessey, P., *Young Man in a Tank* (London: privately published, 1988), p. 56.
121 Neillands, *The Battle of Normandy 1944*, p. 311.

bellies, the craggy slopes and tangled thickets, the rocky earth and above all against our utterly weary bodies.[122]

Major Henry Gifford Wells of the 8th Machine-gun Battalion Middlesex Regiment followed the infantry up the hill:

> We ascended up the road to Mont Pinçon, which had by then been taken by our tanks. As we went up we passed a knocked out German self-propelled gun at the side of the road, with the gunners still sat in their firing positions, they were both dead.[123]

Trooper Henry William Brew of the 43rd Reconnaissance Regiment moved up to the top of Mont Pinçon before dusk:

> We fought our way to the top, it was a very hard battle as the Germans had a complete view of the battlefield and could move about easily, covered as he was by thick hedgerows and high banks of earth. It was only when one tank fought its way through various minefields that we headed for the summit.[124]

As night fell, a thick fog enveloped the peak as the infantry dropped into their slit trenches. Trooper Brew and his comrades were tired and hungry, and because they were dressed in shirt-sleeve order, they now began to feel the cold of the night:

> We were still in our shirtsleeves that were so comfortable on that dry sunny afternoon, but now it was dark and cold. We knew there was no chance of a hot drink or food reaching us in our exposed positions, so I decided to go over and ask a tank commander nearest to us if he could let us have some water for a brew, [and] he kindly let us have some from the Jerry cans strapped to the side of the tank. As we drank it became obvious that the cans had also been used for fuel and we were nearly all sick. So, there we were cold, thirsty and now sick; me and my big ideas.[125]

Corporal Douglas Procter of the 4th Somersets commented on the difficulties of digging-in that night:

> Mr Jary gave us orders to dig-in. It's easy giving an order but complying with the order is a different matter. We dug about six inches deep and then we hit solid rock. We had only small entrenching tools so we put the spoil to the side of the trenches to give ourselves as much protection as we could. Meanwhile we were in shirtsleeves, cold and shivering. All we wanted was something to eat and drink.[126]

---

122 Manuscript forwarded to author by D. Eshelby (Wiltshire, 1997).
123 *WW2: People's War* <www.bbc.co.uk/ww2peopleswar> (accessed 14 July 2020).
124 *Chotie Darling* <www.chotiedarling.co.uk> (accessed 12 August 2020).
125 www.chotiedarling.co.uk (accessed 12 August 2020).
126 Manuscript forwarded to author by P. Macksey (Beverley, 1998).

Lieutenant Sydney Jary also recalled the discomfort of that night:

> A cold damp mist descended which, with the fading light, gave us welcome cover but also wretched discomfort. We were still in our shirtsleeves, which became damp from the sweat of our exertions climbing the steep lower slopes. Alert, with pistol in hand, I anticipated a sudden brush with an enemy post. Not a shot was fired. By some miracle we had passed right through their positions without being detected. Our luck had changed. Through the mist German voices could be heard calling to each other, unaware that, by stealth, we were now king of the castle.[127]

Lieutenant Sydney Jary, MC, 4th Battalion Somerset Light Infantry. (Courtesy of M. Denney)

The news of this successful operation was relayed to headquarters and on to XXX Corps' new commander, Major General Brian Horrocks, who later reflected:

> As I returned to my headquarters that evening Pyman came running towards me. Now senior staff officers are not in the habit of running round their headquarters, so I wondered what had happened: "We've got it sir!" he called out while still some distance away. "Got what?" I said. "Mont Pinçon," he replied. I couldn't believe it. He told me a message had come through that two troops of tanks belonging to the 13/18th Hussars were now on the top of the hill. They reported, however, that they were feeling very lonely as there was a thick mist all around them and they could hear the Germans moving about everywhere. This was wonderful news.[128]

The weary troops of the 4th Wiltshires, who were practically at the end of their tether after some 48 hours of continuous fighting, were roused by their commander, Lieutenant Colonel Edward Lancelot Luce, to relieve the troops on the crest. Luce personally led the transport column in single file, in the dark, to the top of the hill. Lieutenant Hugh Franks, 13/18th Hussars, supported the infantry as they advanced and was soon in action:

Lieutenant Hugh Franks, 13/18th Hussars, Royal Armoured Corps. (Author's collection)

---

127 Jary, *18 Platoon*, p. 52.
128 Horrocks, B., *A Full Life* (London: Collins, 1960), p. 189.

I was beginning to hear quite a bit of machine-gun fire ahead of me, so I went forward and saw a group of infantrymen lying flat on the ground or crouching behind trees, taking cover wherever they could. I remember seeing fire coming from one of the Spandaus which was holding up the infantry. I was able to send over a few high explosive shells that way and also to fire our Browning machine-gun from the turret and that silenced them.[129]

Private Albert Kings, 1st Battalion Worcestershire Regiment. (Courtesy of M. Chalk)

It had been the task of 130 Brigade to make a diversionary attack on the northern flank of Mont Pinçon, and at 2300 hours on 6 August the 7th Hampshires duly made a frontal assault on the villages of Pleciere and Pasty. The leading companies took heavy casualties in the process as the Germans had well-prepared defences. The Hampshires battled their way forward in the thick fog and relieved the hard-pressed 4th Somersets on the crest of Mont Pinçon by 2330 hours, the 1st Worcesters meanwhile relieving the 4th Wiltshires. Private Albert Kings wrote of that gruelling climb to get to the top with the 1st Worcesters:

> In the climb up Mont Pinçon I thought I had reached the limits of human endurance. We were heavily loaded, and the sweat ran into my eyes so I could hardly see. I felt absolutely shattered. At the top, digging-in was impossible in the chalky soil. We lost Lt Booth[130] that day, killed by an 88mm shell.[131]

The troops who had just arrived on the peak in the early hours of 7 August dug-in frantically as 88mm shells burst on their positions, but luckily for them the Germans were firing blind through the fog and could not see their targets. Major K.J. Whitehead of the 7th Somersets made it to the peak, but enemy 88 fire was taking a steady toll of his men:

> Shells were still raining down and three brewed up Sherman tanks exploded violently on the main road. An exploding tank is a strange sight as its ammunition is detonated by fire. As each shell explodes it leaves a smokers-ring of quivering smoke about it. It is frightening too.[132]

---

129 Hunt, *Mont Pinçon*, p. 124.
130 Lieutenant Arthur Jack Booth, 1st Battalion Worcestershire Regiment, was killed in action on 7 August 1944, aged 28. He is buried in Tilly-sur-Seulles War Cemetery, France.
131 A. Kings, correspondence with author (Devon, 1992).
132 www.bbc.co.uk/ww2peopleswar (accessed 12 October 2016).

Major Whitehead was hit in the chest by shrapnel as one 88mm shell exploded nearby, wounding many other men, while Lance Corporal Arthur Reilly[133] and Private Ronald Oldfield[134] were killed on the spot. Major Whitehead remembered:

> I thought I was going to die; the shock stuns the senses. Stretcher bearers arrived and bound me up and at once and I felt better. The RAP was a haven of rest, the MO was cool but obviously very upset by the casualties.[135]

On the morning of 7 August, mortar bombs and bullets, with the occasional shell, still fell upon Mont Pinçon, but as the mist evaporated the men on the top had a magnificent view of Normandy and the parts of it they would soon have to fight for. The loss of the Pinçon feature was a serious blow for the Germans, and a large-scale counter-attack was expected but failed to materialise.

Trooper George Trelour of the 13/18th Hussars sat in his Sherman tank on the morning of 7 August:

> In the morning Lt Adam tried his hand at shooting at a church spire which he said was a German OP, bringing fire on us and killing our infantry, but after 12 shots he had not hit it. I asked if I could have a go. I set the crosswires in the corner of the tower of the church, put a HE round in the breach and fired, the spire came crashing down and a great cheer went up from the boys.[136]

Early on 7 August, an officer of the 4th Somersets was standing on Mont Pinçon when a voice behind him asked: "Have you seen the Corps Commander?" He never even turned round but replied: "Good heavens, you don't expect to find him this far-forward do you?" He then turned round and found himself face to face with Major General Horrocks.[137]

Brian Horrocks was indeed on Mont Pinçon that morning, walking among the men. When asked if there was any news by a Private Pursey of a mortar platoon, who had no idea to whom he was talking, he stopped to show him a map

Major General Brian Horrocks, DSO, MC, XXX Corps' Commanding Officer. (Author's collection)

---

133 Lance Corporal Arthur Robert Moyes Reilly, 7th Battalion Somerset Light Infantry, was killed in action on 7 August 1944, aged 30. He is buried in Tilly-sur-Seulles War Cemetery, France.
134 Private Ronald Oldfield, 7th Battalion Somerset Light Infantry, was killed in action on 7 August 1944, aged 29. He is buried in Tilly-sur-Seulles War Cemetery, France.
135 www.bbc.co.uk/ww2peopleswar (accessed 12 October 2016).
136 Neillands, *The Battle of Normandy 1944*, pp. 311–12.
137 Gill, R. and Graves, J., *Club Route, 30 Corps in Europe* (Hanover: Werner Degener, 1945), p. 39.

and told of the dramatic change in the general situation. Horrocks would become a familiar and much-loved figure to the men of XXX Corps as he drove around in his jeep, and was often found at or near the front. Major General Gerald Lloyd Verney, part of Horrocks' staff, drove up Mont Pinçon with the corps commander to set up a forward observation post. Verney later wrote:

> A more unpleasant drive it would be hard to imagine. The road up was frequently shelled, and it was considered wise to park the cars on the reverse slope and then to run to reach the pit. General Horrocks was one of those rare people who was stimulated by being shelled, rather as some are stimulated by a good gallop. It was nice for him being made like that but no fun for his companions.[138]

Brigadier Hubert Essame, CO of 214 Brigade, commented:

> The capture of Mont Pinçon will go down in history as a very great feat of arms achieved at maximum possible speed, over an enemy into the minds of whose forward troops the thought of defeat had not yet entered and fighting under conditions which gave every advantage to the defence. Above all shines the great sacrifice, endurance, courage and fighting skill of the infantry and the pitifully few survivors of the 5th Wiltshires, who at the crisis of the battle, finally carried the cross-roads at La Variniere and turned the tide.[139]

Beyond Mont Pinçon, the 43rd Wessex Division at Le-Plessis-Grimoult, 7–8 August

During 7 August, the DCLI reconnoitred in the direction of Le-Plessis-Grimoult and found the area to be strongly held by the enemy. Brigadier Essame, 214 Brigade's CO, moved to the front in the late afternoon to get a good view of the village from a hill:

> After a dramatic passage through La-Variniere, we arrived on a hill and crawled forward to a large hole in front of the Worcestershires' positions. The view ahead was excellent, but only the roofs of the houses of the objective, Le-Plessis-Grimoult, could be seen. The plan decided on was a noisy feint attack down the road which approached Le-Plessis-Grimoult from the west, while the bulk of the 5th Duke of Cornwall's was to move silently along the lower slopes of Mont Pinçon, then execute a right wheel and attack the village from the north.[140]

The 1st Worcesters moved down the slopes of Mont Pinçon to occupy the crossroads at La Variniere. B Squadron, 4/7th Royal Dragoon Guards, and C Company of the DCLI advanced eastwards from La Variniere. Finally, the rest of the Duke of Cornwall's silently crept southwards into the northern area of Le-Plessis-Grimoult. A barrage from the divisional artillery,

---

138 Verney, G.L., *The Desert Rats, A History of the 7th Armoured Division 1938–45* (London: Hutchinson, 1954), p. 86.
139 Essame, *The 43rd Wessex Division at War*, p. 72.
140 Essame, *The 43rd Wessex Division at War*, p. 70.

Panzergrenadier Heinz Degenhardt of *SS-Panzergrenadier Regiment 26* of the *12. SS-Panzer-Division 'Hitlerjugend'* being awarded the Iron Cross 1st Class by his commanding officer, *Brigadeführer* Wilhelm Mohnke. Degenhardt was killed on 8 October 1944. (Author's collection)

mortars and machine guns covered the right flank, and as the light was fading the barrage thundered down on the village. The Shermans of the 4/7th Royal Dragoon Guards advanced on the village, firing with all guns.

Company Sergeant Major Reginald Philp of the 5th DCLI descended Mont Pinçon with D Company to the northern end of the village, where they quickly disposed of two German positions:

> We moved down to Le-Plessis-Grimoult. It was evening by then, [and] we linked up with the road which runs down the east side of Mont Pinçon. The company had 8 Platoon on the left-hand side of the road, and I was with company HQ, another platoon was on the right-hand side of the road with a third platoon in reserve. There was a bit of cover, no problems, and we did not come up against any Germans until it was getting dark, and we came down the road junction.[141]

Private George Taylor moved forward silently with the 5th DCLI at 2200 hours as the barrage began in the fading light:

> There was a deafening explosion as an enemy ammo store exploded in a fury of gold and red flame. This magnificent bonfire acted as a beacon for the attack. The night was lit up with

---

141 Manuscript forwarded to author by L. White (Aberdeen, 1992).

tracer bullets, but heavy mortar fire was coming down on all our tanks. A mortar bomb landed on an ammunition lorry that had come up to replenish the tanks and was enveloped in flames.[142]

When the barrage stopped, the troops moved into the ruined village and began working from house to house, raking each one with small-arms fire before hurling grenades through the windows. The buildings were set ablaze by phosphorus grenades and the flames spread quickly. At the far end of the village, German vehicles could be seen moving about and the unmistakeable outlines of Tiger tanks were spotted, one of which was being loaded with fuel and ammunition. With the only Piat having been destroyed, a Major Parker of the DCLI ordered that rapid fire be brought down on the crossroads with everything at the men's disposal. CSM Philp realised that his party had not yet been seen by the Germans:

> To our surprise, across the other side of the road against some houses there was a large German tank being loaded with ammunition from a lorry which was parked right against it. We stopped under cover and watched the Germans carrying ammunition, smoking cigarettes, talking casually, and they weren't aware that we were there. Then a message came to me from the company commander telling me to mortar them. The first HE landed right in the truck, it blew up, caught fire and killed the crew, it must have killed them all. The tank also caught fire and exploded from inside.[143]

As the tank burst into flames, a second tank moved off and a half-track was left behind. Other British troops arrived and began clearing more of the houses. Most of the Germans gave themselves up, having been quite shaken by the explosions. The Duke of Cornwall's had cleared the village by 2300 hours after an hour of fighting, the German defence collapsing and prisoners being taken. Private Taylor remembered:

> I will never forget the sight of enemy prisoners being marched down the village street by the glow of burning houses. German dead and wounded lay scattered about.[144]

Private William Edwards, a stretcher-bearer with the 1st Worcesters, had to deal with the numerous casualties on the battlefield, often running backwards and forwards through shell and small-arms fire to collect the wounded. Many of the old hands had been wounded or killed by now, and the new men coming in to take their place were often not around long enough to become more than a number:

> Someone would come into the battalion one morning and disappear the same evening. Nobody knew him and after a while nobody could ever recall him being there. And for relatives it can be quite upsetting. They would say: "Well we know he was in your battalion, why doesn't anybody know him?" It was because they came up and were gone so soon, that was not unusual. The casualties in the infantry battalions were the highest, some rifle

---

142 Delaforce, *The Fighting Wessex Wyverns*, pp. 139–40.
143 Hunt, *Mont Pinçon*, p. 151.
144 www.bbc.co.uk/ww2peopleswar (accessed 3 July 2010).

companies turning over nearly 100% of their total strength. Night-time was the worst, you would hear the call "Stretcher-bearer!" in the dark while under bombardment and you would look at your mate and it was obvious the same thought was passing between you – do we go? We are safer here than we would be out there. And then you go because you have to, and you find the casualty, he's in a hole so you don't know how badly he's wounded. Getting him out of the slit-trench is difficult and you don't know what extra damage you might be doing. There was a lot of noise crashing around us, and you were doing something that was physically and emotionally difficult, but you got on with it. Then you go back to your hole in the ground and thank God Almighty you are safe; I don't want to do that again.[145]

On the morning of 8 August, two German counter-attacks were beaten off and a Royal Tiger tank was captured, the first of its kind to be seized in Normandy.[146] Daylight revealed the extent of the victory: 31 Germans lay dead in the streets and houses, and 125 prisoners had been taken into captivity. The equipment left behind by the fleeing Germans included a complete half-track, two *Nebelwerfers* and a staff car. During the morning counter-attack, an 88mm gun opened fire and Major Parker was hit in the jaw and shoulder, with CSM Philp buried alive: "Fortunately, I was not wounded and was only suffering from shock when they pulled me out."[147] It was only a matter of days before they were both returned to their battalion.

Shortly after midday on 9 August, the 50th Northumbrian Division advanced through the 43rd Wessex Division and took up the attack on XXX Corps' front, while the 7th Armoured Division was ordered to press forward at once with the 50th Division following to mop up any remaining opposition. However, the armour found it difficult to make any great progress in the enclosed countryside and the 50th Division found itself in the van once more.

The advance on Condé-sur-Noireau, 9 August, 50th Northumbrian Division

XXX Corps' battle plan was for 151 Brigade to attack to the south from Le-Plessis-Grimoult, astride the road to Condé-sur-Noireau. From there they were to advance over the southern slopes of Mount Pinçon and then move down the road from Plessis Grimoult as it falls away for nearly 4 miles until it reaches St Pierre-la-Vieille on the road to Condé. On either side of St Pierre-la-Vieille stand two hills; on the western side is Point 229 and on the eastern side is Point 266. From here the road runs over higher ground to the north of Proussy and down into the valley at Condé.

Condé-sur-Noireau is a small town at the junction of two rivers and a road bottleneck. The Americans, sweeping around from the Cherbourg peninsula, and the Canadians and British, attacking south of Villers Bocage and Caen, were gradually enveloping the German forces who had been ordered by Hitler not to retreat. Condé-sur-Noireau was the town through which many German troops caught in the trap would have to pass if they wished to extricate themselves. The capture of this town was essential, one more step to snapping the trap shut.

---

145 W. Edwards, correspondence with author (Worcestershire, 1993).
146 The Royal (or King) Tiger was a great monster of a tank, with thick armour and heavy armaments. Its weight was some 68 tons.
147 Hunt, *Mont Pinçon*, p. 132.

The 9th Durhams would be left in reserve to hold Le-Plessis-Grimoult as a secure base, with the assaulting battalions being the 6th Durhams on the left and the 8th Durhams on the right. Each battalion would have a squadron of the 13/18th Hussars in support, and five field regiments of artillery would lay down a creeping barrage for the infantry to follow. The La Riviere feature was to be the objective of the 8th Durhams and La Cannardiere for the 6th Durhams, which meant an advance of nearly 5 miles. Once the objectives were taken, 69 Brigade was to pass through, followed by 231 Brigade the following day. The track to Le-Plessis-Grimoult moved directly over Mont Pinçon, which had been taken by the 43rd Wessex Division on 6 August at great cost, opening the way southward to Condé-sur-Noireau. Once on the crest of Mont Pinçon, it was possible to look down on the bridgehead and over the Loire valley. However, not many people stopped to admire the view as the German artillery had registered the road over Mont Pinçon, which was shelled constantly and with great accuracy.

Lieutenant Geoffrey Picot of the 1st Hampshires crossed Mont Pinçon in the early hours of 9 August:

> Late at night we received orders to move forward, and we left our harbour at 03:00 a.m. In the dark we drove over the steep Mont Pinçon, passed through a village and reached our assembly area where we waited for several hours. We had been warned that the village, Le-Plessis-Grimoult, was often the target for the German artillery, but there was no shelling as we passed through it.[148]

Lieutenant R. Brewer moved over Mont Pinçon on the morning of 9 August with the 9th Durhams to relieve the 6th Queen's in Le-Plessis-Grimoult:

> The road to Plessis led almost over the top of the Mount and was straight and fairly open into the village at the bottom. The plan had been for us to take over the area before first light and the DCLI and the Queens to be away. That was the plan. The CO being relieved had different ideas and our own company had to be downright rude to get him to move at all. "Six-o-clock would be good enough for him," he grumbled. Nobody it appeared had any clear idea of the picture of where their own troops were, to say nothing of the Jerry positions. And so, dawn found us all lined up on the forward slope of the hill almost head to tail, like coconuts at a shy. And Jerry wasn't slow to start shying everything he could lay his hands on. It would not have been a surprise to us to see the kitchen sink being thrown at us as well. Shrapnel rained down in torrents, or so it seemed. Lt Nichols and I had the delightful job of wandering around choosing gun positions, [as] those that were already made were useless, going back and getting the guns, leading them in and checking on the progress of the work, when the only place any normal person wanted to be was underground. We had eleven casualties in the platoon that day and that was the only time I really hated being an officer. I had to order the men, all credit to them for the way they obeyed, from the comparative safety of the ditch in which they were waiting, onto their carriers and into the hailstorm of death.[149]

---

148 Picot, *Accidental Warrior*, p. 139.
149 Moses, *The Gateshead Gurkhas*, pp. 298–99.

Troops inspecting a knocked-out King Tiger in the ruins of Le-Plessis-Grimoult. (Author's collection)

The Germans, having spotted the movement of hundreds of troops and vehicles coming over Mont Pinçon, began to lay down a ferocious barrage on the approach road and on Le-Plessis-Grimoult itself. The Durhams ran through heavy concentrations of shellfire to get through the village, passing as they did so a knocked-out King Tiger tank at the crossroads. The Durhams arrived at their starting place just in time and so had little opportunity to liaise with the tank crews. At midday, the creeping barrage started and the advance got underway. The history of the 8th Durhams comments:

> The barrage started with the usual whine and crash of shells. There was no time for section and platoon commanders to pause and pick up their bearings. However, the men soon settled down and the advance got underway very quickly.[150]

As the Durhams started across the last 2,000 yards to their objectives, enemy resistance stiffened, but they rushed forward while firing their weapons from the hip and hurling grenades before them. This close-quarter fighting broke the German resolve, and the momentum of the attack was never checked. Major James Kailofer[151] led C Company, 8th Durhams, forward and was hit by shellfire. His men laid him by the side of the track to await the arrival of

---

150 Lewis and English, *The 8th Battalion Durham Light Infantry*, p. 266.
151 Major James Kailofer, 8th Battalion Durham Light Infantry, was killed on 9 August 1944, aged 27. He is buried in St Manvieu War Cemetery, France.

stretcher-bearers, but as he lay there he was hit again and killed. They reached their objective of La Riviere by mid-afternoon. The headquarters of the 8th Durhams was positioned in an orchard on the southern outskirts of the village and came under heavy artillery fire. The HQ men had not had time to dig slit trenches when the barrage came down and were caught in the open by the terrible bombardment, with many casualties being taken. Major E. Wakelin of the 74th Field Regiment, Royal Artillery, commented: "This is quite the worst shelling I have had since Mareth."[152]

The 6th Durhams advanced in orderly fashion behind the creeping barrage, with tanks in close support, reaching their objective of La Cannardiere at 1430 hours. As they dug-in, the German artillery laid down a heavy bombardment on the whole area, resulting in numerous casualties. The tank support by the 13/18th Hussars had been most effective, raking each hedgerow with their heavy Besa machine guns and main armaments, which was good for morale and encouraged the troops. Many prisoners were taken, mainly from the *276. Infanterie-Division*.

The Durhams of 151 Brigade had reached a point some 2½ miles north of St Pierre-la-Vieille, and at 1400 hours on 9 August 69 Brigade passed through them, with the 6th and 7th Green Howards leading. They made slow progress in the face of fierce resistance from 88s and heavy-calibre artillery, moving forward for only a mile before being checked. By 2200 hours the advance came to a halt, and the men dug-in for the night with the enemy in close proximity.

Private Patrick Hearn of the 6th Green Howards recalled the advance and the terrible fire that held them up:

> We were advancing in single file through the Durhams' positions. The signs of battle were all around us and were not pleasant to see. Shells and mortar rounds thudded before us and all of a sudden there was an almighty noise; yes, it was the moaning Minnies. I have never been so scared in all my life. I dived into a pile of stinging nettles near a wall for some protection, and when the explosions had stopped I got up to find I was covered in cow shit and stinking to high heaven. My pals had been hit and when I got to them, I could see the first one I got to was already dead with a big lump of shrapnel sticking out of his back. Others had damaged legs and other wounds. The stretcher-bearers earned their money that night.[153]

The attack would be renewed on the morning of 10 August by the 5th East Yorks, with the intension of capturing St Pierre-la-Vieille and Point 229. During the night of 9/10 August, the Yorkshiremen were shelled heavily, the only suitable forming-up place for the assault being under direct observation by the German gunners. It seemed that the men of the 5th East Yorks would suffer heavy casualties before they even began the advance. As daylight broke on 10 August, Lady Luck smiled on the Yorkshiremen; a thick early-morning fog had descended over the whole area in a dense blanket, concealing both infantrymen and tanks as they gathered to prepare for the move forward. The Yorkshiremen set of with their supporting tanks into the mist, the German outpost line being taken unawares and overrun in the first rush, many of the Germans being killed or taken prisoner. Two companies tried to storm Point 229 but were met

---

152 Townend and Baldwin, *Gunners in Normandy*, p. 276. The British Eighth Army toiled for two weeks before breaking through the Mareth Line in southern Tunisia in March 1943.
153 P. Hearn, interview with author (Scarborough, 1989).

by a storm of high-explosive shells from tanks and self-propelled guns on the crest. The companies re-formed and attacked again, but the result was the same and they were hurled back with heavy casualties before their objectives could be reached.

Sergeant Max Hearst of the 5th East Yorks remembered the terrible fire that kept them pinned down:

> God, I didn't like that place. We started receiving all this shit and all of a sudden there was a hell of an explosion near us, covering us with muck. One of the most nightmarish things was hearing the cries of those who had been badly hit; we couldn't get to them as to stand up meant certain death. One lad, who I couldn't see, was sobbing in his pain and calling out for his mother. I asked Sgt Turnbull what was happening now. "I haven't a clue," he replied. At this time, I had a Tommy-gun and I started firing in the direction of the enemy, and the lads joined in as stuff screamed over us.[154]

The men of the 5th East Yorks took heavy casualties. The dire straits they were in is illustrated by the fact that in one platoon the only section commander left standing was a Corporal J. Grace. This brave young man took charge and organised the survivors to best effect, all the time under heavy fire, running from one man to another directing their fire. One man was hit moving across open ground that was being swept by Spandau, snipers and mortar fire. Without regard for his own safety, Corporal Grace ran across the fire-swept battlefield and brought him back to safety.[155]

With the whole of 69 Brigade held up short of St Pierre-la-Vieille, 231 Brigade now prepared to take up the lead towards Condé-sur-Noire. At 0830 hours on 11 August, a brigade attack was launched with the 1st Hampshires leading and the 2nd Devons on their left.

Fortunately, an early-morning mist hid the battlefield as the troops and tanks passed the start line. Lt Geoffrey Picot of the 1st Hampshires sited his Mortar Platoon teams in a farmyard, moved to the cover of a hedgerow to give supporting fire and then watched the infantry move off:

> Soon shells were falling all around us, [and] after firing for some time I was called to the command post where I found a collection of unhappy officers sheltering behind a Sherman tank. Lt Colonel Turner, smoking his pipe as ever, muttered an annoyed oath every now and then when a shell landed near.[156]

The Germans resisted tenaciously in and around the village of St Pierre-la-Vieille and the high ground of Point 249, and only slight progress was made by the Hampshires. Lieutenant Picot made some interesting comments about the failure of the attack to take its objectives:

> He, Lt Colonel Turner, attacked initially with one company of about 100 men because there was supposed to be only 30 enemy soldiers in the village, but there were many more

---

154 Max Hearst, interview with author (Hull, 1991).
155 Corporal J. Grace was awarded the Military Medal for his leadership and bravery in the face of the enemy.
156 Picot, *Accidental Warrior*, p.139.

and the company was held up. So, Turner sent in a second company to help them, and more progress was eventually made.[157]

Lieutenant Colonel Turner then needed to reinforce the attackers with carrier-borne anti-tank guns and mortars. An officer was sent to reconnoitre a route forward for them but he was held up by the heavy artillery fire that saturated the area. When he reported back to Turner, he brought news of a stream that would bar the way for the carriers and that the area was being heavily shelled, preventing any movement over it. At 1845 hours on this hot summer's day, the 1st Dorsets moved to the attack in support of the Hampshires who were fighting in the south of the town.

At 0600 hours on 12 August, the 1st Dorsets and 2nd Devons were ordered to push home the attack. By 1000 hours they had advanced nearly 2 miles south of St Pierre-la-Vieille. This had pushed a salient deep into the German gun positions, and both flanks were now vulnerable to counter-attack. In addition to their problems, the enemy was still in good positions behind the town. German self-propelled guns, tanks and artillery were now shelling the forward British troops from three sides.

To the east of St Pierre-la-Vieille, early on 12 August, the men of the 9th Durhams were ordered to take Points 249 and 262, but as they assembled they were shelled by the enemy, taking numerous casualties. Their attack was eventually postponed until 1330 hours that day; by 1500 hours Point 249 had been reached by the supporting tanks, but communication with the infantry was poor. Lieutenant Colonel John Mogg (now promoted from major, and having received the DSO for the action at Lingèvres) and Lieutenant D.W.R. Bowden had to go forward to ascertain the positions of the infantry companies. Captain Roy Griffiths, 9th Durhams, described events:

> Shortly after crossing the start-line, Denis Hurst,[158] a New Zealander who commanded the carrier platoon with Jimmy Casey, was killed. We proceeded to our objectives, which were two points on the map 249 and 262. It was a strange attack, [as] we moved straight forward from the start-line and after a short distance moved out at an angle of 90 degrees to the objective. We came under Spandau and small-arms fire but again our casualties were light. Roy Hill's platoon was allocated Point 262, with myself and the rest of the company occupying Point 249. On reaching our objective it was reported to me that someone had noticed that the corn sheaves below us were moving. I found this hard to believe. I watched through glasses and indeed there was movement in the corn that had been cut and sheaved. I arranged for a shoot with Brens and amongst the corn several of the enemy appeared, showing on their left arms red-cross arm bands, but around their shoulders were two belts of ammunition. I signalled for some artillery support onto their position and the enemy withdrew.[159]

---

157 Picot, *Accidental Warrior*, p. 139.
158 Captain Denis James Sutherland Hurst, The Queen's Royal Regiment (West Surrey), attached to 9th Battalion Durham Light Infantry, was killed in action on 12 August 1944, aged 22. He is buried in St Manvieu War Cemetery, France.
159 Moses, *The Gateshead Gurkhas*, p. 300.

Counter-attack, 12 August

As the light faded on the evening of 12 August, the Germans marshalled their forces for a counter-attack on the 1st Dorsets. The enemy assault came in from the west and south, and one party broke into the Dorsets' headquarters. For over two hours they fought a spirited action on a reverse slope, the situation so desperate for the Dorsets that cooks, batmen and orderly room staff were called upon to defend the sector. Lieutenant Geoffrey Picot of the 1st Hampshires was in the rear of the Dorsets and watched the struggle developing:

> Just in front of us the Dorsets were having a frightening time. In the area of their battalion headquarters shots were being fired. The alarm was raised and the Dorsets began to shoot back. My opposite number, Jackie, a Canadian, jumped into his battle trench and found a German there who had surrendered. For some moments there was confused and frantic firing, until someone realised that no more bullets were coming from the enemy. All the surviving raiders were captured, and they quickly told their story, the Germans were pulling out and to cover their withdrawal they had sent this party in to counterattack us.[160]

Eventually the enemy disengaged after taking numerous casualties, many inflicted by the guns of 90th Field Regiment. On the night of 12/13 August, Captain Sherratt, MC, of the 7th Green Howards took a patrol out in the direction of St Pierre-la-Vieille and, after finding no opposition, entered the village. After Captain Sherratt had reported his findings back to headquarters, the whole battalion entered the ruins soon after midnight in a dense fog and intense darkness. As daylight dawned on 13 August, the devastation became apparent. Company Sergeant Major Jack Verity of the 7th Green Howards described the scene:

> It always seemed like an anti-climax when we finally took places as there was so little left of them. The poor bloody French people had lost all they had, and I wondered where they were now. The village was pummelled to brick dust and scattered among all of this lay the Jerry dead, always a sad and pathetic sight. A small number of Jerries were found alive and taken prisoner; they were totally shell shocked, poor sods. German equipment was everywhere but most of it was ruined and the whole place was one fucking great mess.[161]

Company Sergeant Major Jack Verity, 7th Battalion Green Howards. (Courtesy of J. Verity)

160 Picot, *Accidental Warrior*, p. 148.
161 J. Verity, interview with author (Beverley, 1992).

The backbone of enemy resistance north of Condé-sur-Noire had been broken, and by 16 August the armoured cars of the 61st Reconnaissance Regiment entered the town of Condé, a week after the advance had started from Le-Plessis-Grimoult. XXX Corps had fought numerous bitter actions to reach this point, but for the troops still in the lead there would be no immediate respite as the Germans continued to shell the British, causing yet more casualties. Private Kenneth Lodge, with the 6th Durhams, remembered the intermittent shelling that continued even though the fighting had stopped:

Major Renton Galloway, MC and Bar, 6th Battalion Durham Light Infantry, after being wounded at Verrières. He was killed in action on 12 August 1944. (Courtesy of W. Ridley)

> I was standing beside a hedge, and he came walking up, Major Spike Galloway, he always took an interest in the youngish chaps, like myself, and he said: "How are you going on?" I said: "Oh fine sir" and he said a few words: "Thank you all for your good work" and that sort of thing. My mate was across there in a slit-trench, and he shouted: "Get here!" and as I ran over and jumped in there was a great almighty, ear-splitting bang and it went quiet, then the screaming started, and this lad came past me and he had a huge scar across the calf of his leg which was like a burn. There wasn't any blood, just a burn and he was screaming. Major Galloway was dead,[162] he was lying there, and they picked him up. There was another four of them lying dead; a shell had hit a tree, otherwise it would have gone past. There were ever so many wounded. The dead lads didn't have a mark on them. We had lost a good leader in Major Galloway, a very good officer, anyone would follow him.[163]

With death and destruction all around them, individuals coped in various ways to get through these dark times. Men relied on their comrades in the most trying of circumstances and the bonds formed would last a lifetime for those who survived. Private Ronald Mallabar of the 9th Durhams pondered his own mortality as he viewed the desolation all around him:

> Burnt out farmhouses, dead animals, batches of graves, little mounds of earth with a cross on the top, a wooden cross, a rifle with a helmet stuck on top of it. It was quite worrying seeing them at battalion HQ making these crosses in case we had to push anyone under the ground. If anybody was killed, we just had to wrap them in a blanket and bury them

---

162 Major Renton (known as Spike) Galloway, MC and Bar, 6th Battalion Durham Light Infantry, was wounded at Verrières and killed in action on 12 August 1944, aged 32. He is buried in St Manvieu War Cemetery, France.
163 Moses, *The Faithful Sixth*, pp. 299–300.

and that was that. They would be fished out later by proper war graves people. It wasn't going to happen to me, people around me were falling down dead and lying about badly wounded, but it wasn't me. When I was eventually wounded, I realised just how mortal I was. I decided that the war would go on for ever until I was killed. Life consisted of the battalion and when you're away from it you feel lost and want to be back, even though you know you may be going back to be killed. It dominated your life, there was nothing else. You had such a deep bond with the fellows you worked with, you had to rely on them many a time to save your life and [it was] the same for them. You loved each other with a deep brotherly love, and you just wanted to be with them.[164]

The 50th Northumbrian Division was withdrawn on 13 August, when the 43rd Wessex Division once again took up the lead for XXX Corps. Condé-sur-Noire was now within reach and the Normandy campaign was reaching a climax. The Allied forces had almost surrounded the whole German *7. Armee* and nearly half of the *5. Panzerarmee* in the ever-shrinking pocket to the west of the Falaise–Argentan road. The only way of escape eastwards for the Germans was through the 15-mile gap between those two places, which was being kept open by the *5. Panzerarmee* and by the divisions of *General der Panzertruppe* Heinrich Eberbach's armoured group holding the Argentan area to the south. On 16 August, *Generalfeldmarschall* Gunther von Kluge, *Oberbefehlshaber West* (high commander in the West), placed *7. Armee* commander *SS-Obergruppenführer* Paul Hausser in command of all troops fighting in the pocket and ordered their withdrawal eastwards, crossing the Orne that night. The net was closing and one of the greatest military catastrophes ever seen was about to unfold.

164 Moses, *The Gateshead Gurkhas*, pp.301–02.

9

Breakout and Pursuit

Operation Blackwater, 43rd Wessex Division

The signs of a slow but inevitable withdrawal by the enemy were obvious as the German line buckled under the enormous pounding it was receiving from the Allied air and land forces. XXX Corps was to keep up the pressure on the enemy, and on 13 August the 43rd Wessex Division took up the chase. The previous day, the Germans had continued to resist resolutely, supported by armour, and the Allied advance southwards had left the mountainous wooded country around Mont Gaultier and Culey-le-Patry still occupied by enemy forces. Later in the day on 12 August, the 7th Somersets and 5th DCLI advanced and were ordered to eject all enemy forces as far as the Orne. The task of clearing Mont Gaultier was given to the 7th Somersets, while the 5th DCLI was to occupy the village of La Trulandiere. The men of the 43rd Wessex Division clashed with enemy forces in the fields and hedgerows, mortar fire falling upon the attackers as each slit trench was cleared one at a time in hard close-quarter fighting. The commander of the 7th Somersets' Pioneer Platoon, Lieutenant Donald Francis Bean, cleared the roads of mines while under fire, and with this done he led his platoon against the enemy and drove them off. Once in position, German mortar teams caught Lieutenant Bean and his men in a heavy concentration, inflicting many casualties. Bean saw one of his men fall and at once threw himself over his comrade's body, only to be hit and mortally wounded himself.[1]

The 5th DCLI advanced on the left flank, attempting to clear the spur that ran down from the village of La Trulandiere near Culey-le-Patry to the Orne. H-Hour was at 2000 hours on 13 August, and as the troops advanced they came under heavy fire from mortars and Spandaus. However, the enemy were driven from their positions and forced back over the Orne.

Major Desmond Scarr of the 43rd Reconnaissance Regiment reconnoitred the high ground in the area and unexpectedly came in for some special treatment from the RAF:

> By way of a welcome, a group of Typhoons decided that 6 Troop was on the wrong side and singled us out for special attention. Diving down on us they fired salvoes of rockets. The

---

[1] Lieutenant Donald Francis Bean, 7th Battalion Somerset Light Infantry, was wounded on 12 August and sent home to England, where he died of his wounds on 30 October 1944, aged 28. He is buried in Sheviock St Mary Churchyard Extension, Cornwall.

noise was indescribable, and we flattened ourselves in our vehicles or in the nearest ditch. It was a miracle the troop suffered no serious injuries. We were shaken for a while and I never again trusted any nearby aircraft, German or otherwise.[2]

Private Ronald Garner, with the Intelligence Section of the 5th Wiltshires, was struck by the plight of the French people whom they helped liberate:

On the 14th the battalion moved to La Rue, in a valley near Condé, as hundreds of French refugees came to greet us and to beg for food. They were a pitiful sight, and we couldn't very well refuse them. Out came our tins of sardines and corned beef. What they wanted most of all was bread. They were given our army dog biscuits and seemed to enjoy them quite a lot. It was a very upsetting sight for us and I felt so sorry for them.[3]

Proussy, 14 August

Proussy was a village on the road south from Aunay, a mere 3 miles from Condé-sur-Noireau. It was strongly held by the enemy, and the 5th Dorsets were given the unenviable task of clearing it of the German forces entrenched there. In the early morning of 14 August, a British barrage fell upon Proussy, heralding the imminent attack. The Dorsets, supported by the tanks of the Sherwood Rangers, moved forward behind the thundering creeping deluge of artillery shells. The text-book operation was successful and 165 Germans surrendered.

Lieutenant David Render was in support of the 5th Dorsets at Proussy with the Sherwood Rangers:

Our assault on Proussy was a success. As we entered the village, we put HE rounds through every building that might contain a sniper or an artillery observation officer. The infantry then flushed out the German defenders from each of the houses and rounded up over a hundred prisoners. The rest of the day was spent in conducting mopping-up operations, but a route to the home bank of the Noireau, north of Condé, had been secured.[4]

Lieutenant Colonel Basil Aubrey Coad of 130 Brigade directed the 7th Hampshires, supported by the B Squadron tanks of the Sherwood Rangers, to capture the rambling village of St Denis-de-Mere, to the south of Proussy. Their assault began at 1400 hours on 14 August, when as usual a massive barrage preceded the infantry and tanks. German self-propelled guns immediately knocked out four Sherman tanks, but after a fierce struggle the village was eventually cleared by 1900 hours. Seventy-two soldiers of *Grenadier-Regiment 752* were taken prisoner, the Hampshires suffering 29 casualties in the fighting.

Lieutenant Colonel Stanley Christopherson recounted what happened next for his Sherwood Rangers and the Hampshires:

2 *Chotie Darling* <www.chotiedarling.co.uk> (accessed 24 November 2020).
3 R. Garner, correspondence with author (Wiltshire, 1994).
4 Render, *Tank Action*, p. 169.

German prisoners passing a group of Tommies. (Courtesy of M. Denney)

After the capture of Proussy and St Denis-de-Mere the Noireau river had to be crossed and the village of Berjou captured[;] it was situated on the high ground on the far side of the river and commanding a dominating view of the river and the whole countryside. As usual the enclosed country made tank fighting extremely difficult and unpleasant, and conditions were not improved by continuous rain, which lasted for two days.[5]

With the general situation improving for XXX Corps, its commander, Major General Brian Horrocks, issuing orders intended to finally drive the enemy beyond the Noireau and envelop his left flank. On 14 August, the 11th Armoured Division came under the command of XXX Corps and was given the task of pursuit, pushing forward as fast as possible to Vassy, Flers and on to Argentan. The 11th Armoured, with the 11th Hussars under its command, along with the 50th Northumbrian Division and 43rd Wessex Division, were to press forward on the right flank to the road which runs in a southerly direction from Condé to Flers, and then to advance on the whole corps front.

---

5   Holland (ed.), *An Englishman at War*, p. 419.

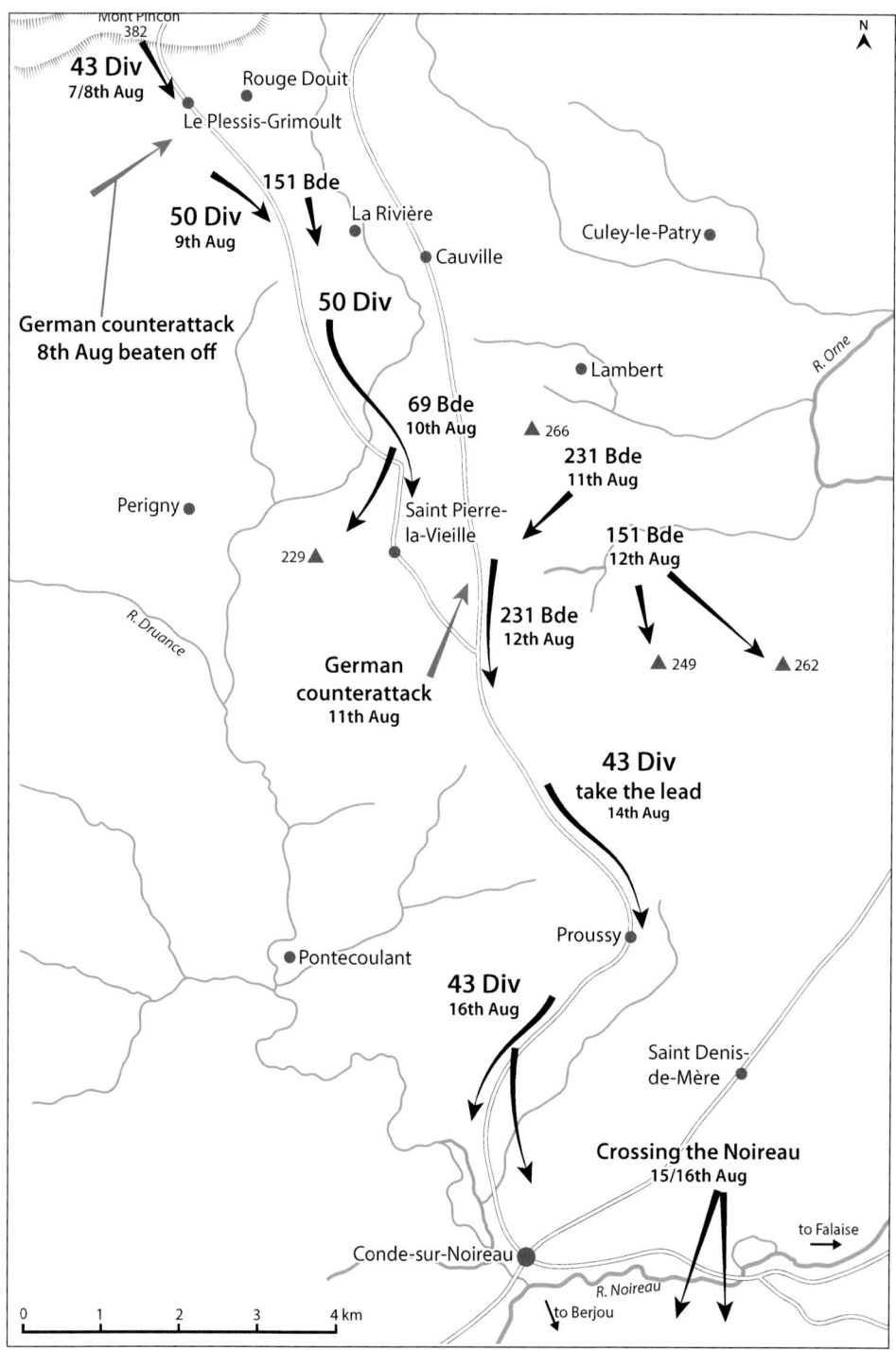

From Mont Pinçon to the Noireau River, 8–16 August 1944.

Crossing the Noireau, 15–16 August

The high ground on either bank of the Noireau was wooded and very steep on the southern side. Running due south from Thury was a railway line that entered a narrow ravine, crossed the Noireau and then joined the main line from Falaise to Condé to the south of the river. The narrow road that led to the river crossing point was winding and rough. Some 1,200 yards to the east stood a mill, not far from the village of Cahan, and it was between these two features that Major General Ivor Thomas of the 43rd Wessex Division intended to force a crossing. The river itself is only about 20 yards from bank to bank and is only 3ft deep, meaning troops on foot could easily cross but vehicles and tanks would sink into the soft sediment. Across the river, from the road running to Condé, thickly wooded hills rose abruptly to high ground containing the fortified villages of Berjou, La Canet and Le Hamel, this formidable feature running 2 miles to the south-east to Point 237. All bridges across the river had been destroyed by the retreating Germans (and possibly by the RAF).

Trooper S. Brownlie of the 2nd Fife and Forfar Yeomanry, 11th Armoured Division, advanced in his Sherman tank:

> In many small unspectacular actions we were delayed by mines and anti-tank guns, well sited by German officers who beat it and left a handful of men to hold us up. We went through St Germaine-des-Crioult, west of Condé, and the Fifes and 3rd Mons [3rd Monmouthshire Regiment] formed up in textbook formation, then advanced south-east. We got to the high ground overlooking the Noireau River. Here we sat all afternoon in the sun and had a wash and shave. A scissors bridge[6] was put over the river and we crossed about 6pm near a lemonade factory.[7]

The 7th Somersets were hot on the heels of the German forces as they crossed the Noireau, and at once set about reconnoitring crossing places for the 43rd Wessex Division. On the night of 14 August, patrols made their way to the riverbank without incident, and although a German sentry was spotted on the far bank he did not see them. The Somersets met a young Frenchman who lived nearby, and he gave them vital information about crossing points over the river. One patrol, led by Captain Baden and Pioneer Sergeant Martin, entered a mill, and from this vantage point could survey the Noireau and observe the Germans digging in their machine-gun positions. The whole area was liberally strewn with mines, which would cause numerous casualties, not only to the troops but to the unfortunate French civilians: on 15 August, a young boy was killed by a mine, and one poor woman lost her three children in the same way. During the night, members of the patrol crossed the river unmolested to complete their work, returning to report their findings to their superiors.

---

6   The scissors bridge was a converted Sherman tank manned by men of the Royal Engineers. It held a box girder bridge that unfolded like a pair of scissors to join the two riverbanks.
7   S. Brownlie, correspondence with author (Argyll, 1991).

Taking the high ground, Berjou, 16–17 August

Brigadier Hubert Essame, CO of the 43rd Wessex Division's 214 Brigade, recalled the plan of attack for his men:

> The plan included the most intense and elaborate fire support by the machine-guns of the 8th Middlesex, under Lt Colonel M. Crawford. Starting half an hour before the infantry were due to cross the start line of the river, the medium machine-guns of two companies drenched the attacking battalions' objectives with concentrated fire, continuing for one hour, whist the 4.2-inch mortar company blasted the ridge with HE and smoke. This, combined with concentrations by the divisional artillery, which set alight the wooded slope ahead and drove the enemy under cover, enabled the infantry to wade through the stream at 6pm with the certainty of success.[8]

At 1800 hours, near the demolished railway bridge, men of the 1st Worcesters stepped into the river with A Company leading. As they made for the high ground, several of them fell when mortar bombs crashed around them. The men pushed on to the main road, whereupon a number of Germans came out waving white flags. A little further along, they reached the junction with the track that led up the steep hill to Berjou. Teller mines in the ground were bypassed and left for the pioneer platoon to deal with. Lieutenant William Gould of the 1st Worcesters described the hard crossing of the Noireau:

> At the river crossing, Jerry brought down on us a most heavy bombardment of shells and mortars, and casualties started to mount. It was more than flesh and blood could take to go through this fire screen, and panic was much in evidence. Major Souper, CO A Coy, seeing the danger, walked calmly forward and urged us on. Up to this point I had been trembling in my shoes, but responding to such bravery I forced myself alongside him and my chaps backed me up. In a flash we had crossed the stream and we were on our way.[9]

A company of the 7th Somersets crossed the river at Le Rocray, heading for Le Hamel on the left. The remainder of the battalion followed the 1st Worcesters up the sheer track, swearing and cursing at the steepness of the gradient. On both sides of their ascent the woods were blazing, but up they went until they reached an open field in front of Berjou. Two white mortar flares, the signal for success, were fired, informing brigade headquarters that they were on the ridge. Other men then joined those on the crest and the position was quickly consolidated.

The 5th DCLI followed up behind the Worcesters in a cacophony of noise and exploding mortar bombs. Lieutenant Colonel George Taylor, the CO of the Duke of Cornwall's, recalled:

> With D Coy leading we went over the broken bridge, up the road and passed the railway station. The enemy mortar bombs exploded with deafening roars 200 yards to our right. We

---

8 Essame, *The 43rd Wessex Division at War*, p. 84.
9 Manuscript sent to author by W. Gilson (Hull, 1993).

waded across the shallow river and moved into the wood, which was still burning from the bombardment, [and] the acrid smoke caught in our lungs.[10]

As darkness fell, Spandau fire was raking the new positions, but it was too late to be effective. The Worcesters and DCLI, six companies in all, formed a tightly packed wedge on the edge of the plateau, dug-in only 80 yards away from the enemy. Casualties began to mount as the German mortar teams got to work. No artillery support was available as the heavy wireless sets needed to make contact could not be carried up the steep slopes, and there were also as yet no tanks, anti-tank guns or armoured vehicles of any sort.

The river crossing below was under constant German bombardment. The brave sappers worked feverishly under fire to make crossing points for the tanks and vehicles. The 553rd Field Company, Royal Engineers, erected a Bailey bridge on the site of the old demolished bridge, while the 204th Field Company built a tank ford and three trestle bridges. Bulldozers, lorries and carriers scuttled back and forth, all the time avoiding mines and booby traps. The commander of the Royal Engineers, Lieutenant Colonel Harold E. Pike, was seriously injured when his reconnaissance vehicle overturned in the darkness, and the sapper companies suffered numerous casualties from flying steel as they worked. Several tracked vehicles and trucks received direct hits and lit up the hellish scene as the men laboured to complete their tasks on a grim moonless night. At 0200 hours on 16 August, the heavens opened to complete their misery. The tanks of the Sherwood Rangers, along with the anti-tank guns and transports of the attacking battalions, had by now converged on the narrow track leading to the river; just before dawn, the congestion was serious, many vehicles hitting mines on their journey to the crossing point.

Counter-attack at Berjou

As dawn broke, it became possible to take stock of the situation. On the crest above, an uncanny lull reigned over the battlefield. The men had spent a cold and miserable night in their slit trenches, drenched by the thunderstorm. During the early hours, a Major Brewis of the DCLI had managed to get a big artillery wireless set up the hill and was now able to communicate with Brigade Headquarters. The quiet did not last long, mortar bombs crashing into the British positions with loud bangs and vivid flashes. A company of the DCLI attacked and knocked out two German machine-gun posts, but heavy Spandau fire drove them back with many casualties.

On the morning of the 16th, the Germans rallied their forces in front of Berjou for a counter-attack, troops of *Grenadier-Regiment 986* launching the initial assault on the left of the Worcesters. A further attack came in on the right flank of the DCLI. The Germans called heavy fire onto the track that ran down to the valley, where all the tanks and vehicles were waiting. Lieutenant Stuart Hills of the Sherwood Rangers described the scene from the valley below:

> It was dark and the battle for the ridge was still going on[;] one could hear the sharp bursts of machine-gun fire and see the shallow, curving trails of tracer bullets as they flicked

---

10   G. Taylor, correspondence with author (Exeter, 1991).

across the night sky towards the sterner gloom ahead. Just before first light the battle was renewed, and a steady stream of casualties came back down the hill.[11]

Tanks at last!

The column of Sherman tanks of the Sherwood Rangers, interspersed with armoured cars and carriers of the 43rd Reconnaissance Regiment, stood nose-to-nail at the river opposite the track leading up the hill to Berjou. Colonel Stanley Christopherson, CO of the Sherwood Rangers, rushed up the slope in his Sherman tank:

> Lt Stanley Perry's tank was the first to cross over the hastily constructed bridge over the Noireau and led the advance up the hill and through the small bridgehead which the infantry had made during the night. Frank Galvin was killed when an anti-tank gun brewed-up his tank,[12] Sergeant Sleep was killed by a sniper[13] and Sergeant Guy Sanders[14] was killed when trying to rescue his great friend Corporal Brooks, who had been wounded by shellfire while doing a recce on foot, he was killed by the same shell,[15] all of them first class tank commanders with great battle experience during their years with the regiment and, more important, greatly loved and respected by us all as fellow men.[16]

Stuart Hills was straight into action as he made his way up to the crest:

> We went for the top saturating the surrounding hedges and bushes with machine-gun fire. At the top we reached an open field on the right of the track. Here the mortaring was intense and to get out of the tank was certain death, but we waited there for further orders. The orders came that the objective was Berjou village, towards which we would move together with the DCLI [–] thank heavens it was not my turn to lead.[17]

Fellow Sherwood Ranger Lieutenant David Render watched as the tank squadrons crossed the river with infantry clinging on to their backs:

---

11 Hills, *By Tank to Normandy*, pp. 132–33.
12 Lieutenant James Francis Galvin, Sherwood Rangers, Nottinghamshire Yeomanry, Royal Armoured Corps, was killed in action on 16 August 1944. He is buried in Banneville-la-Campagne War Cemetery, France.
13 Sergeant William Arthur Ernest Sleep, Sherwood Rangers, Nottinghamshire Yeomanry, Royal Armoured Corps, was killed in action on 16 August 1944, aged 32. He is buried in Banneville-la-Campagne War Cemetery, France.
14 Sergeant Guy Sanders, MM, Sherwood Rangers, Nottinghamshire Yeomanry, Royal Armoured Corps, was killed in action on 16 August 1944, aged 35. He is buried in Banneville-la-Campagne War Cemetery, France.
15 Corporal Arthur Charles Brooks, Sherwood Rangers, Nottinghamshire Yeomanry, Royal Armoured Corps, was killed in action on 16 August 1944, aged 21. He is buried in Banneville-la-Campagne War Cemetery, France.
16 Holland (ed.), *An Englishman at War*, p. 420.
17 Hills, *By Tank to Normandy*, p. 134.

German *3. Fallschirmjäger-Division* machine-gun team. (Courtesy of H. Wernemann)

C Squadron attacked along the track that wound its way up the sharp incline of the ridge on the other side of the river. Co-operation with the infantry broke down as they pushed through the thickly wooded slopes that were thick with German snipers and paratroopers armed with anti-tank weapons. Six tanks were lost to *Panzerfausts* and six commanders were wounded or killed.[18]

Now that the infantry had reinforcements and the artillery FOOs were on the crest with them, plans were made to storm Berjou itself. The area to be advanced over by the Worcesters was flat and the village was held by a German company supported by tanks and self-propelled guns. Information on the enemy dispositions, and much more, had been provided by the French Resistance. The DCLIs were to clear the left side of the ridge.

Lieutenant Colonel George Taylor of the DCLI, who presented the battle plans to the brigade commander, remembered: "Brigadier Essame approved my plan and said increased firepower would be available to support the Worcesters attack."[19]

Lieutenant Colonel Robert Edward Osborne-Smith, DSO, CO of the 1st Worcesters, was given the task of destroying the enemy in Berjou. The attack would be led by D and B Companies on the right, while A Company would be following up with C Company behind

---

18 Render, *Tank Action*, p. 163.
19 Essame, *The 43rd Wessex Division at War*, p. 86.

them to mop up. The tanks of the Sherwood Rangers took up hull-down positions on the crest as a tremendous barrage of artillery and mortar fire fell upon the German positions. As the infantry swept up the slope, shells exploded before them, the full weight of the firepower of the Sherwood Rangers' guns adding to this support.

Lieutenant Hills watched the mayhem unfold from his Sherwood Rangers Sherman tank and felt very vulnerable in such a forward position:

> It was a glorious summer's day, but everything was dulled by the task in-hand and the extent of our casualties already. I had no idea what lay in front, the fatal shot might come from anywhere and I was constantly expecting it. We duly encountered Spandau fire on the crest and then renewed mortaring. I moved forward and opened up because I could see the enemy quite clearly dug-in under hedgerows. We must have done some damage because shortly afterwards a trickle of prisoners began to come in. The infantry began to round them up and some of my crew helped. They looked young, lean and tough and came from the 3rd German Parachute Division, elite troops. I directed Captain Arthur Warburton, Forward Observation Officer, and his Essex Yeomanry 25-pounders onto possible enemy positions, especially those of his mortars, which continued to give us hell. One of Warburton's stonks must have hit an ammunition dump because there was a big explosion.[20]

Lieutenant Colonel Taylor recounted the fierce action on the ridge and beyond:

> A Coy took the ridge, Les Monts, supported by tanks. A large number of the enemy were killed or captured in the process. In a farm on the plateau lay the bodies of five of our men, around them were 19 dead Germans. Covered by the great artillery barrage the Worcesters swept forward, taking Berjou and a considerable number of prisoners. The village was taken by 17:30 p.m.[21]

When Berjou fell, the roads around it were found to be strewn with mines, which continued to cause casualties for some days. As night fell on 16 August, the heavy enemy mortar and shellfire died down. Only a solitary 88mm and a long-range gun continued to bombard Berjou and its surrounding areas. One of the last casualties here was Regimental Sergeant Major John Hurd of the 1st Worcesters;[22] during the day's fighting, he had been seen bringing in 30 German prisoners at the double single-handed. Brigadier Essame of the 43rd Wessex Division commented on this veteran soldier:

> This redoubtable old Warrant Officer, he was over 50 [sic], had concealed his age so as to be able to accompany his battalion. Distaining cover and always among the first to seek out and kill the enemy, he embodied in his person the highest traditions of the regular infantry of the line. It is grimly appropriate that he should have fallen in the hour of victory on the Berjou Ridge.[23]

---

20 Hills, *By Tank to Normandy*, pp. 137–38.
21 Delaforce, *The Fighting Wessex Wyverns*, p. 151.
22 Warrant Officer 1st Class (RSM) John Hurd, 1st Battalion Worcestershire Regiment, was killed on Berjou Ridge on 16 August 1944, aged 45. He is buried in Banneville-la-Campagne War Cemetery, France.
23 Essame, *The 43rd Wessex Division at War*, p. 88.

Aftermath

Stuart Hills of the Sherwood Rangers was feeling melancholic after the battle on the morning of 17 August as he took stock of the situation:

> The whole of Berjou Ridge above the Noireau was now in our hands, [and] senior officers came forward to view where the fighting had taken place and expressed, with some astonishment, that we had stormed such a formidable position so quickly. Our own Brigadier, Prior-Palmer, wrote to Stanley Christopherson: "Your chaps really did do a superhuman job up that ruddy mountain and I am sure some decorations were well deserved." I, however, did not feel remotely euphoric. As dawn broke on 17th August, I stirred to the sound of birds singing and I looked around me at the silent forms of my troop who were still sleeping soundly. Only Arthur Reddish was up and about. Gradually the events of the previous day began to come back, and with them the realisation of what I had lost. Corporal Brooks, trying to summon help and then being wiped out as he bailed out. Sergeant Bill Sleep, seven years in the army, and Sergeant Guy Sanders, MM, 35 years old from Grimsby, whose loss was almost the hardest to take because he had been such a good soldier and seemingly indestructible. If he could be taken in an instant, gallantly trying to rescue his friend, what hope was there that the rest of us would survive? Then there was Frank Galvin, who I had just started to befriend, now he and all of his crew had perished almost as if they had never been. But there was the wounded too, and the knowledge that C Squadron had been decimated by the day's action. I was the only troop leader left and to get all of this into perspective was not easy[;] it was not surprising that the older heads noticed how low I was. I had come to rely on all these men, and we had shared much danger and discomfort since before D-Day. I sensed the unreal atmosphere around the survivors, one of heavy disillusionment and disbelief. It was too difficult and painful to grasp immediately, and I still expected that at any minute the casualties would suddenly reappear as though nothing had happened. But gradually this dream faded into grim reality.[24]

Lieutenant Colonel Christopherson, who knew Lieutenant Hills well, commented on the effect the fierce fighting at Berjou had on his friend:

> After the capture of Berjou no officer troop leader, except for Stuart Hills, remained in C Squadron. Stuart I'm afraid was terribly distressed about the loss of his fellow tank commanders. On the evening of the 17th after Berjou had been captured I walked to the end of the village and looked down onto the Noireau river. From there I had a wonderful view of the surrounding country and could fully appreciate why the mortar and shellfire had been so accurate. The Germans could see every movement that we made.[25]

The situation for the hard-pressed infantry on the ridge was the same, as they also counted the cost and buried their dead. Private Horace Trim of the 1st Worcesters never forgot that sad night:

---

24 Hills, *By Tank to Normandy*, pp. 139–40.
25 Holland J (ed.), *An Englishman at War*, pp. 420–21.

A German anti-tank gun team in a concealed position. (Courtesy of M. Denney)

"A pioneer brought along some crosses and asked Harry and me to bury the dead nearest to us as they were so busy. With tears in our eyes, we carried them to the chosen area and buried them a foot deep with an earth mound on top."[26] The exhausted men then slept a deep sleep in their shallow slit trenches, waiting for the dawn and the inevitable stand-to. The battle for crossing the Noireau and the capture of Berjou and the high ground was over. The 43rd Reconnaissance Regiment pressed forward seeking out the positions of the retreating Germans, which was always a dangerous task. Within three days they had reached St Honorine-la-Chardonne and Segrie-Fontaine on the River Orne. On 18 August they entered Athis and linked up with the 11th Armoured Division. The 5th Wiltshires occupied St Honorine-la-Chardonne to a joyous and enthusiastic welcome from the populace, while at La Fertie the 4th Somersets had a similar experience, the church bells ringing out to welcome the brave warriors.

Private Thomas Dutton of the 1st Worcesters was deeply touched by the joy of the French villagers:

---

26   Holland, J., *Normandy '44* (London: Bantam Press, 2019), p. 397.

Every town and village that we journeyed through, the inhabitants lined the streets waving flags, throwing flowers and issuing drinks. Mile after mile it was the same story. In return we offered cigarettes, sweets and chocolate. To see British soldiers so bedecked with flowers was unbelievable, such emotion was roused on both sides, the sheer flood of happiness was unreal.[27]

Private Ronald Garner entered the village of St Honorine-la-Chardonne with the 5th Wiltshires riding on the back of a Sherman and found a reception that warmed his heart:

Private Thomas Dutton, 1st Battalion Worcestershire Regiment. (Author's collection)

As the first troops and tanks entered the village the church bells began ringing and men, women and children ran into the streets to greet us laughing and smiling. The pavements were lined with the inhabitants offering us buckets and buckets of cider, calvados and abundant fruit. The scout cars of the Reconnaissance Regiment were decked with flowers. The German troops had left two hours before. A French liaison officer took charge of the administration, and the village was turned into a rest camp for us.[28]

Other XXX Corps units received the same joyous welcome as they pressed forward through villages and towns. As Lieutenant Geoffrey Picot advanced with his 1st Hampshires unit, they became very wary of the possibility that they could still become a casualty after going through so much. As they approached any village, they looked closely to see if any flags were flying, a sign that it had been liberated. If no flags were seen, his column would close with the objective very cautiously, observing all the while:

I shall never forget those tumultuous days in August, when France warmed to its liberation. Apples and pears were thrown at us as we passed through villages, bottles of local firewater were placed in our hands, little delicacies of food, that we knew people could ill spare, were showered upon us whenever we stopped for a moment, and it was all given with moving eagerness. The young and middle-aged waved flags, shook our hands, danced in the streets, kissed and behaved with enthusiasm and excitement. Old men wept for joy, who had fought their war and won it a quarter of a century previously and had lived through the shame and horror that had come to them when the next generation did not win over again what was

27 *WW2: People's War* <www.bbc.co.uk/ww2peopleswar> (accessed 25 April 2019).
28 R. Garner, correspondence with author (Surrey, 1993).

really the same war. A woman walking along a country road clapped her hands continuously saying: "*Merci, merci*" all the time as our column of 130 vehicles rumbled past her. On all faces were such expressions of thankfulness and joy as I had not seen anywhere before. For us also it was unforgettable, all the troops were deeply moved.[29]

Lieutenant R. Brewer of the 9th Durhams was amazed when he saw the flags of all the Allies flying in a village as his unit entered:

Not shabby ones but beautifully kept ones. The greatness of our reception grew and grew. Flags and bunting flew out of windows, across the streets and being waved, flags everywhere. To stop was to be besieged by thousands of people clamouring just to touch the men they had waited so long to see. Bottles of everything under the sun were produced for Tommy to drink. Flowers were strewn all over the roads, fixed to our jackets and all over our vehicles. Apples, tomatoes, pears and even hard-boiled eggs were given to us to eat. It was most gratifying to be liberators to such obviously pleased peoples and, of course, our morale was way up at the top.[30]

Lieutenant Tim Ellis and his men of the 4th Somersets were feeling tired, hungry and very fed-up, as they had not had a hot meal the night before. But things changed for them as they entered the town of Flers:

We had a hell of a good party; the civilians had not been evacuated and were out in strength to meet us. We were covered in flowers and offered all sorts of venomous drinks; I got an excellent Sauterne. Everyone was Boche Hunting, and it was priceless to see some of the 1914–18 French veterans suddenly appearing with a brace of miserable Boches in tow.[31]

Most of the fighting men of XXX Corps were now very tired. The brunt of the heaviest fighting in Normandy was borne now by the corps' 43rd Wessex Division and 50th Northumbrian Division, not forgetting the 15th Scottish Division of VIII Corps. Other unit commanders looked on incredulously; it was a mystery to them how the 43rd Wessex still retained the will to fight after all they had been through. Their commander, Major General Thomas, was ruthless in the demands he made of his men, and Montgomery was grateful to him for this. For his supposed insensitivity to losses, he had been given the nickname of 'Butcher'. Under pressure from their commanding officers, the infantry battalions of XXX Corps kept on pushing forward, taking their punishment and still coming on for more.

The riflemen trudged into battle with the knowledge that the odds were stacked against him, performing his tasks without promise of reward or relief. After every hill there was another hill, and after every river there was another river. After weeks in the line, only a 'Blighty' wound could provide him with the comfort of safety and a harbour from the storm. Those who remained evaded death as best they could, using the battlefield skills and instincts they had developed by experience. Each man knew that the longer he was at the front the less likely his

---

29   Picot, *Accidental Warrior*, p. 171.
30   Moses, *The Gateshead Gurkhas*, pp. 305–06.
31   Delaforce, P., *The Black Bull* (East Sussex: Tom Donovan Publishing, 1997), p. 106.

chances of survival became, and that sooner or later he would probably end up on a stretcher or in a grave. Even a very short break in the rear, from the din of the battlefield, was looked forward to by men, but the time spent resting could easily be disturbed by forebodings about the future and the inevitable return to action.

Courage is an expendable commodity and builds up in individuals over a period of time. Men who were in continuous contact with the enemy could find their stock of courage quickly exhausted; this was known as battle exhaustion. By August 1944, up to 20 percent of the men were suffering from this malady as they saw their friends, NCOs and officers killed or gravely wounded. The replacement officers did not at first command the respect and trust that had been earned by their lost comrades. When casualties among officers were extreme, others would be called upon to take over in a crisis and found it hard to cope with the demands made of them. By the end of July, 'exhaustion centres' had been established in Normandy and proved a great help in providing immediate help to psychiatric cases. By the end of August, infantry casualties had reached such proportions that a division had to be disbanded to provide reinforcements. Private Stanley Whitehouse of the 1st Battalion Oxfordshire and Buckinghamshire Light Infantry (1st Ox and Bucks), 53rd (Welsh) Division, part of XII Corps, began to feel that exposure to danger on a regular basis was blunting his combat effectiveness, and after an initial good start felt his spirits slowly begin to sink:

> About this time, I began to experience more acute symptoms of bomb happiness, or shell shock as it was called in the earlier Great War. I had been in the line now almost continuously for more than three months and as week succeeded week, I was having to dig deeper and deeper into those innermost resources of resolution, endurance and zeal to combat the knowing, nagging fearfulness that filled my waking, and often, sleeping hours. As the campaign progressed, I came to realise that for all the enemy's skill and doggedness he was more easily overcome than my troubled tortured mind. I had long since forsaken that spirit of adventure, that devil-may-care attitude that had sustained me in the early days, when mates around me were being killed and horribly maimed, and the whiplash of the murderous Spandau and the crunch of mortars had men quivering in the bottom of their slitters.[32]

Major Martin Lindsay of the 1st Battalion Gordon Highlanders, 51st Highland Division, part of the British I Corps, saw the effects on himself and other brave men as they were slowly being ground down by the constant pressure they were under:

> In the last hour I have been reading a *Sunday Times* review of Moran's 'Anatomy of Courage' [and] it quotes his theory that courage must be husbanded: "Courage is willpower, whereof no man has an unlimited stock, and when in war it is used up, he is finished. A man's courage is his capital, and he is always spending." How right he is! I can think of an officer with an MC and Bar and several NCOs with MMs who bear this out. They were all decorated for fine leadership in North Africa and Sicily and must have presumably been

---

32 Whitehouse, S., *Fear is the Foe: A Footslogger from Normandy to the Rhine* (London: Robert Hale, 1988), p. 125.

the pick of the battalion. The officer was finished before he was killed and the NCOs, the few that remain, are virtually useless today. They have all had to carry on for far too long. I can quote my own case too, until a month or two ago, though I hated being shelled, I used positively to look forward to the thrill of battle. Now, though I have not yet got to the stage of dreading an action, I get no pleasure out of it and look forward to the end of the war.[33]

The men of XXX Corps were, for the moment, out of contact with the enemy, but they knew it would not last as they followed up on a retreating foe. Their past experience had taught them never to underestimate the Germans' ability to make an improvised stand, and this force was still deadly and possessed a will to fight at any opportunity.

All units in the Bocage continued to take casualties on a daily basis. Lieutenant Richard Mosse, who fought with the 1st Welsh Guards, left a description of his time in the Bocage. It is a sobering read to anyone who supposes that by August the pressure was easing, as at the bitter end of that month the losses and suffering continued unabated:

> We turned off the main road to go down the side road to the top of a ridge. Dust means shells and notices were in great evidence, it was the worst place I have ever been in. Numerous bodies of our predecessors lay in the fields between the companies, with about 25 knocked out vehicles, mostly British. A thick dust covered everything, and over it all hung that sweet sickly smell of death. By day we could not move as we were under observed mortar fire, and going up to the forward companies, under machine-gun fire. Our guns had opened short again and Sergeant Lentle had been killed and several wounded. Sergeant Lentle I could ill afford to lose, he was a steady, sensible man.[34] He would not take risks as he had a wife and two boys he adored, but would obey any order however dangerous, I could always rely on him. Hugh, Fred and I were all that was left of the original company, so we helped hold a bit of the line. We had advanced some half a mile and our casualties amounted to 122. As long as I live that word Bocage will haunt me, with memories of a ruined countryside, dust, orchards, sunken lanes and the presence of death.[35]

---

33   Lindsay, M., *So Few Got Through* (London: Collins, 1946), p. 13.
34   Sergeant Clifford James Lentle, 1st Battalion Welsh Guards, was killed in action on 11 August 1944, aged 32. He is buried in Banneville-la-Campagne War Cemetery, France.
35   Hastings, *Overlord*, p. 385.

10

From Falaise to the Seine

As the men of XXX Corps battled their way forward, the situation for the German forces deteriorated quickly, the German high command becoming anxious that their troops would soon be enveloped by the wide American sweep that had begun. It was clear that should this eastward swing succeed, the German position in Normandy would soon become untenable, and unless sufficiently strong reinforcements were provided, they may have to evacuate the whole of northern France without a struggle. News that the left flank of *Heeresgruppe B* had collapsed reached its commander, *Generalfeldmarschall* von Kluge, who in turn sent an appreciation of the situation to Hitler:

> Whether the enemy can still be stopped at this point is questionable, losses in men and equipment are extraordinary. The morale of the troops has suffered very heavily under constant, murderous enemy fire, especially since all the infantry units consist of haphazard groups which do not form a strongly co-ordinated force.[1]

By stating such views, von Kluge was only repeating those of his predecessor, *Generalfeldmarschall* von Rundstedt, who had been sacked for coming to the same conclusion. The very best that the German Army could hope for now was to delay the American thrust, but they were powerless to prevent them from bursting out into the heartlands of France.

Montgomery realised that the German forces were faced with two bitter choices: they could compound defeat by concentrating their forces around Mortain or they could withdraw to the Seine and shorten their lines of supply. The British commander had already planned to destroy the German forces between the Loire and the Seine but realised that many might escape from the trap that was being set. To catch them, he was planning a second, wider encirclement where the pincers would snap shut at the Seine and issued orders for this on 11 August. Because Allied bombers had destroyed many of the Seine bridges, the two German armies – 7. *Armee* and 5. *Panzerarmee* – would be unable to extricate the bulk of their guns, armour and heavy equipment. Montgomery knew he could move his armoured forces faster than the Germans could

---

1 Lucas, J. and Barker, J., *The Killing Ground – The Battle of the Falaise Gap August 1944* (London: B.T. Batsford, 1978), p. 72.

withdraw and that the second pincer movement would trap and crush the great mass of the German troops in France.

During the first week of August, the Canadians, the British and the 1st Polish Armoured Division fought ferocious and bloody actions on the road to Falaise. Patton's Third Army had taken Rennes and stormed on into Brittany. On 6 August, Hitler ordered von Kluge to send his panzer divisions in an ultimately doomed counter-attack at Mortain in the hope of cutting off Patton's armoured thrust. This plan was militarily insane and only hastened the disintegration of the German armies in Normandy.

By 19 August the Allied trap had been sprung as Polish forces met up with the Americans in the area around Chambois. The final escape route for the Germans had been all but closed and the destruction of their units would now be undertaken by the Allied ground and air forces. The pocket into which thousands of German troops were now crammed was bounded by Falaise, Condé, Flers and Argentan. In the dust-covered lanes, roads and fields of this area, the greater part of the German 7. *Armee* was to die. The only options for the Germans were to break out eastwards or to hope that the armoured forces already extricated before the gap was closed could break back in. Inside the pocket, desperate German *kampfgruppen* fought to open the road to the east, while the units not involved in this effort moved slowly along crowded roads, desperately looking for any way out that might appear. In the fields and lanes, thousands of medical, supply and administrative units could do nothing but wait in their vehicles or on foot for their fate to be determined.

Slaughter in the Bocage, the *Westheer*'s Stalingrad

Outside of the Falaise Pocket, around the trapped German armies, the Allied forces massed their military might. The fields in the pocket occupied by the Germans were divided into killing grounds: one for the air forces, one for the artillery of XII Corps and one for the guns of an armoured brigade. Into these areas, an incessant storm of shells, bombs and rockets would be rained down upon the trapped and helpless Germans, day and night. The targets presented could not be missed, as long columns of up to 200 vehicles clogging the roads nose-to-tail were not uncommon. Horse-drawn transport columns also trudged along in the dust for mile after mile, looking for a way out as the slaughter began. *SS-Sturmmann* Egon Schulze recalled of that time:

> We were trapped and encircled in the vicinity of Falaise, and things became terribly confused. On 18th August we received orders to take our panzers and rescue some of our comrades who were encircled by the *Amis*. When we reached our destination about sixty percent of the place was already in enemy hands, and unfortunately all our ammo was located there. Undaunted we blew up the ammo to deprive the Allies of it, but by then the enemy had closed off the whole area. It was total chaos, with artillery duels going on, *Jabos* in the sky and panzer battles raging all over. The area we held got smaller and smaller. We tried to reach our own unit with our panzers, but it no longer existed, it was every man for himself.[2]

---

2   Williamson, G., *Loyalty is My Honour* (London: Motorbooks, 1997), p. 96.

Troops look on as the Falaise Pocket is bombarded continuously from land and air. (Author's collection)

Inside the pocket, under a torrent of high-explosive shells and bombs, chaos reigned as masses of desperate men and horses panicked in their confusion. Whole columns of tanks and vehicles were blown apart, while horse-drawn transports and columns of marching men stood no chance in this maelstrom. As the Allied pressure forced the pocket to contract, the congestion became worse and the slaughter more concentrated. The roads and tracks became clogged with blazing vehicles, dead horses and men, those who survived the first attacks being forced into the fields, where they were continuously and mercilessly strafed from the air and by artillery fire. Flight Sergeant Allen Billham of 609 Squadron, RAF, flew sorties over the doomed pocket in his rocket-firing Typhoon:

> British convoys would stretch over two miles and have the regulation fifty yards between each vehicle. The Germans had everything close together and had flak all the way round. When we saw these targets, it was too good to miss; well everything joined in the attack, Spitfires, Mustangs, Thunderbolts, you name it, roared down on the hapless Germans. But our Typhoons had the rockets and the 20mm cannon, so we did most of the damage, certainly against armoured vehicles.[3]

3 A. Billham, correspondence with author (Gloucestershire, 1993).

A Hawker Typhoon fighter-bomber being armed with rockets and 20mm cannon shells by ground crews. These aircraft attacked the Falaise Pocket with devastating effect. (Courtesy of M. Perkins)

Private Jim Betts, serving with the 5th East Yorks in 69 Brigade, moved up to the pocket with his unit as they headed for the Seine and looked on as the deadly Typhoons went about their grim business:

> There were dead horses and men everywhere, [and] smashed carts and burning tanks were scattered all over the place, it was a terrible thing to see. As Jerry tried to get away the rocket firing Typhoons caught up with them; it really made me cringe as the rockets hit the slow-moving columns. All sorts of stuff, people, horses and machines, were blown high into the air and as we moved up, we found what was left of the poor buggers, hundreds of dead Germans. It was a scene of hell upon earth.[4]

Hauptfeldwebel Eric Braun of the *2. SS-Panzer-Division 'Das-Reich'* was in the thick of the Allied assault. He recalled the horror he and his comrades had to endure:

> The never-ending detonations, soldiers waving at us, begging for help. The dead, their faces still screwed up in agony, were huddled everywhere in trenches and shelters. The officers

---

4 J. Betts, interview with author (Hull, 1992).

The wreckage of a German column caught out in the open by rocket-firing Typhoons. (Author's collection)

and men who had lost their nerve, burning vehicles from which piercing screams could be heard, and men driven crazy who were crying, shouting and laughing hysterically. The poor horses still harnessed in their shafts screaming terribly, trying to escape the slaughter on the stumps of their legs.[5]

Oberleutnant Hans Holler of *Panzergrenadier-Regiment 192, 21. Panzer-Division*, remembered desperately trying to get out of the pocket eastwards:

We received orders to abandon our positions during the night of 19/20 August, [and] the closer we got to the breakout point the ghastlier the scene that met our eyes. The roads were blocked by shot-up and burnt-out vehicles standing alongside each other. Ammunition was exploding, panzers were burning, and horses lay struggling on their backs until they were finally put out of their misery. In the fields far and wide was the same chaos. The enemy artillery fired into the turmoil from all sides as everything pressed eastwards.[6]

---

5   Hastings, M., *Das-Reich* (London: Pan Books, 1983), p. 237.
6   Trigg, *D-Day Through German Eyes*, p. 263.

British airmen flying over the Falaise gap were remote from the destruction that they wrought, but one anonymous pilot paid a visit on foot into the area of destruction after the firing had stopped and was shocked by what he saw:

> The roads were choked with wreckage and the swollen bodies of men and horses. Bits of uniforms were plastered to shattered tanks and trucks and human remains hung in grotesque shapes on the blackened hedgerows. Corpses lay in pools of dried blood, staring into space as if their eyes were being forced from their sockets. Two grey clad bodies, both minus their legs, leaned against a clay bank as if in prayer. I stumbled over a typewriter; paper was scattered around where several mailbags had exploded. I picked up a photograph of a smiling young German recruit standing between his parents who stared back at me in accusation. Suddenly I realised for the first time that each grey clad body was some mother's son. That area had to be passed with all speed.[7]

Major Peter Martin of the 2nd Machine-gun Battalion the Cheshire Regiment also passed through the pocket with the 50th Northumbrian Division:

> I can remember the scenes of absolute carnage. The German army, apart from the panzer divisions, relied on horse-drawn transport and so there were all these carts and dead horses in the shafts and the road was absolutely choked with the dead and dying. And the stench; it was a really horrific sight, and we were very glad to get past it and out onto the road to the Seine.[8]

Alan Moorehead, the famous war correspondent who was present at many of the most important events of the Second World War, left a blistering account of what he saw in the Falaise Pocket:

> When the first German columns came within the range of the British fire the horses stampeded, not half a dozen but hundreds. They lashed down the hedges and fences with their hooves and dragged their carriages through the farmyards. Many galloped for the banks of the river and plunged headlong, with all their trappings, down the twelve-foot banks into the stream below, which at once turned red with blood. Drivers of lorries panicked the same way and as more shells kept ripping through the apple trees, they collided their vehicles against one another with such force that some of the lighter cars were telescoped with their occupants still inside. For long stretches, vehicles, horses and men became jammed together in one struggling, shrieking mass. Engines and broken petrol tanks took fire and the wounded who were pinned in the wreckage were suffocated, burned and lost. Those who were lucky enough to get out scrambled up the ditches and ran for cover across open fields, [where] they were picked off as they ran. One belt of shellfire fell on the river bridge at the moment when two closely packed columns were converging upon it. Those vehicles, beasts and men on the centre of the bridge were all pitchforked into space at once. But so

---

7   Williams, *D-Day to Berlin*, p. 204.
8   P. Martin, correspondence with the author (Cheshire, 1993).

The crew members of this German tank had burned to death when their vehicle was hit from above by rockets. (Author's collection)

many fell that soon the wreckage piled up level with the bridge itself and made a dam across the river. It was exactly like one of those crowded battle paintings of Waterloo or Borodino, except of course the wreckage was different.[9]

In the area of destruction, the miasma of death was all-pervading and overpowering; so strong, in fact, that pilots of light artillery observation aircraft flying over the battlefield recorded in their reports how the stench reached them hundreds of feet in the air. Decay and putrefaction covered the land, with swarms of black flies and bluebottles carpeting everything. Cattle carcasses crawled with maggots in the hot summer sun and the grossly swollen unburied bodies of German soldiers lay with blackened faces in grotesque positions. There was no dignity for the dead, and in the most-bombarded areas parts of bodies festooned the trees. On the heights at Ormel, an entire convoy of ambulances had been hit and destroyed by the dreaded rocket-firing Typhoons, presenting a disgusting spectacle to the troops who had to pass by. The wounded, being immobile, had been trapped in the ambulances and burned to death in the blaze, their bodies shrivelled and shrunk.

9   Moorehead, *Eclipse*, p. 131.

General Dwight Eisenhower, Supreme Commander of the Allied Expeditionary Force, entered the pocket and commented on what he saw:

> 48 hours after the closing of the gap I was conducted through it on foot, to encounter scenes that could only be described by Dante. It was literally possible to walk for hundreds of yards at a time, stepping on nothing but dead and decaying flesh.[10]

When the firing finally subsided on 21 August, the survivors in the Falaise Pocket breathed a sigh of relief as they sat stunned among the burning carnage. The German field army in France had been destroyed, gradually ground down by a battle of attrition it could never hope to win. After Falaise, the German Army continued to occupy large tracts of France but was not in control of them. In a 10-week period, the German defenders of Normandy had lost 1,300 tanks, 50,000 dead and 200,000 men wounded or taken prisoner.

The Germans had lost so many vehicles and tanks in the Normandy campaign to Allied air attacks that the use of horses was the only feasible means of transport for the men and for hauling guns from position to position. A measure of the German situation in Normandy, in the age of *Blitzkrieg*, was the fact that one of the most modern armies in the world was now reduced to the use of horsepower to move troops and supplies.

XXX Corps in the van, Operation Loopy

On 22 August, XXX Corps advanced in the direction of the Seine, passing through the wreckage of a German army in the Falaise area. The men of XXX Corps could not believe their eyes when they witnessed such scenes of human and animal suffering. Private W.M. Hewitt of the 6th Durhams wrote:

> The Germans had a lot of horse transport, [and] dead men and horses were laid all over the place, just blasted to pieces. Behind the hedges there were rows of big guns that hadn't been used much. The rocket firing Typhoons were terrible, they roared out of the sky sending their rockets into this writhing mass of people and horses. It must have had a demoralising effect on the trapped Germans.[11]

Lieutenant William Jalland knew the rot had started for the enemy as his unit of the 8th Durhams chased over the northern side of the gap and witnessed a sinister sight:

> It was the first place I became aware of the fact that the Germans were hanging their own deserters. We came across a battered orchard, [and] there half a dozen to a dozen Germans had been hanged for running away. Their feet were just a few inches off the ground, swaying gently in the breeze, it was very moving and sad. We had never come across that sort of thing before.[12]

10 D'Este, *Eisenhower, Allied Supreme Commander*, p. 342.
11 M.W. Hewitt, correspondence with author (Durham, 1994).
12 Manuscript sent to author by W. Jalland (Durham, 1993).

As troops moved through the killing zone, many of the small lanes were impassable because of the numbers of dead men and horses and wrecked vehicles. (Courtesy of J. Betts)

Major Douglas Goddard was with his battery of the 112th Wessex Field Regiment, Royal Artillery, as they fired constantly into the mass of men, machines and horses:

> Two enemy armies were caught in the killing ground and were virtually obliterated by our artillery and air attacks. The carnage of tens of thousands of dead Germans, their horses, vehicles and weapons, went on for miles. It was a ghastly experience to witness that level of death, suffering and destruction, even over one's enemies.[13]

Private Harold Wood of the Royal Army Medical Corps and his comrades looked on at the carnage with incredulity as they passed by:

> The first thing that comes to mind is the number of dead horses on their backs, [as] their swollen bodies made their legs stick up in the air. The smell of death was all pervading and smashed vehicles littered the whole area. Plus, [there were] wrecked tanks and armoured cars still containing the bodies of dead soldiers. One horrible lasting memory for me is of one body still sitting in the driving position in his vehicle, with maggots falling out of his eye sockets. We felt sick as we drove through the wreckage in a long, slow, traffic jam and we were relieved to get past this nightmare.[14]

---

13 *WW2: People's War* <www.bbc.co.uk/ww2peopleswar> (accessed 27 March 2021).
14 *WW2: People's War* <www.bbc.co.uk/ww2peopleswar> (accessed 23 March 2021).

Lieutenant David Render of the Sherwood Rangers passed through the devastated area in silence in a column of Sherman tanks:

> Teams of horses sprawled dead in the traces of their gun limbers and carts, many with their bellies ripped open by shrapnel, which had spilled their entrails on the ground. Among them thousands of German dead lay thick where they had fallen, like wax figures contorted into grotesque attitudes that captured the last moments of their death. Some had arms twisted out as if in supplication, others were burned black, their shrivelled bodies fused into the twisted wreckage of vehicles. One Wehrmacht soldier had been crushed by a concrete lamp post felled by an exploding shell or rocket. Incongruous as it seems, amid all this death and destruction, his demise resulting from a piece of concrete, struck me the most. The entire area was pervaded by the stench of death and putrefaction. A blizzard of perhaps a million rapacious flies lifted as we passed. We couldn't avoid driving over the dead and our tracks ground their rotting bodies into the road that was now a sea of grisly mud. It was a relief to leave behind us the foul concentration of death that this area had become.[15]

Private Reginald Pope, serving with the 2nd Machine-gun Battalion the Cheshire Regiment, felt pity for the troops that had been trapped in the pocket as he viewed the carnage:

Private Reginald Pope, 2nd Machine-gun Battalion the Cheshire Regiment. (Courtesy of R. Pope)

> They had a terrible bashing there; I've never seen anything like it. It was just suicide for those poor devils as there was no way they were going to get out of there. Their artillery and transports were horse drawn and our planes just blasted them from the air. It was pure carnage, there's no doubt about it.[16]

Bombardier Jack Styan passed through the chaos with his battery of Battle-Axe Coy, Royal Artillery:

> You could see our bombers and fighters flying over, loads of them, to bomb and strafe way up front of us so we could push through. The roads were littered with burnt-out wagons, tanks and trucks. I remember looking into one of the burnt-out tanks and saw a foot, the sole of somebody's foot, and it was white, [while] the remainder of the body was charred black. It was one of those terrible sights you can never forget.[17]

Major Mathew Guymer of the 5th Royal Horse Artillery was scarred deeply by what he saw at Falaise, images that would stay with him for the rest of his life:

---

15 Render, *Tank Action*, pp. 173–74.
16 R. Pope, interview with author (Durham, 1991).
17 J. Styan, correspondence with author (Middlesbrough, 1994).

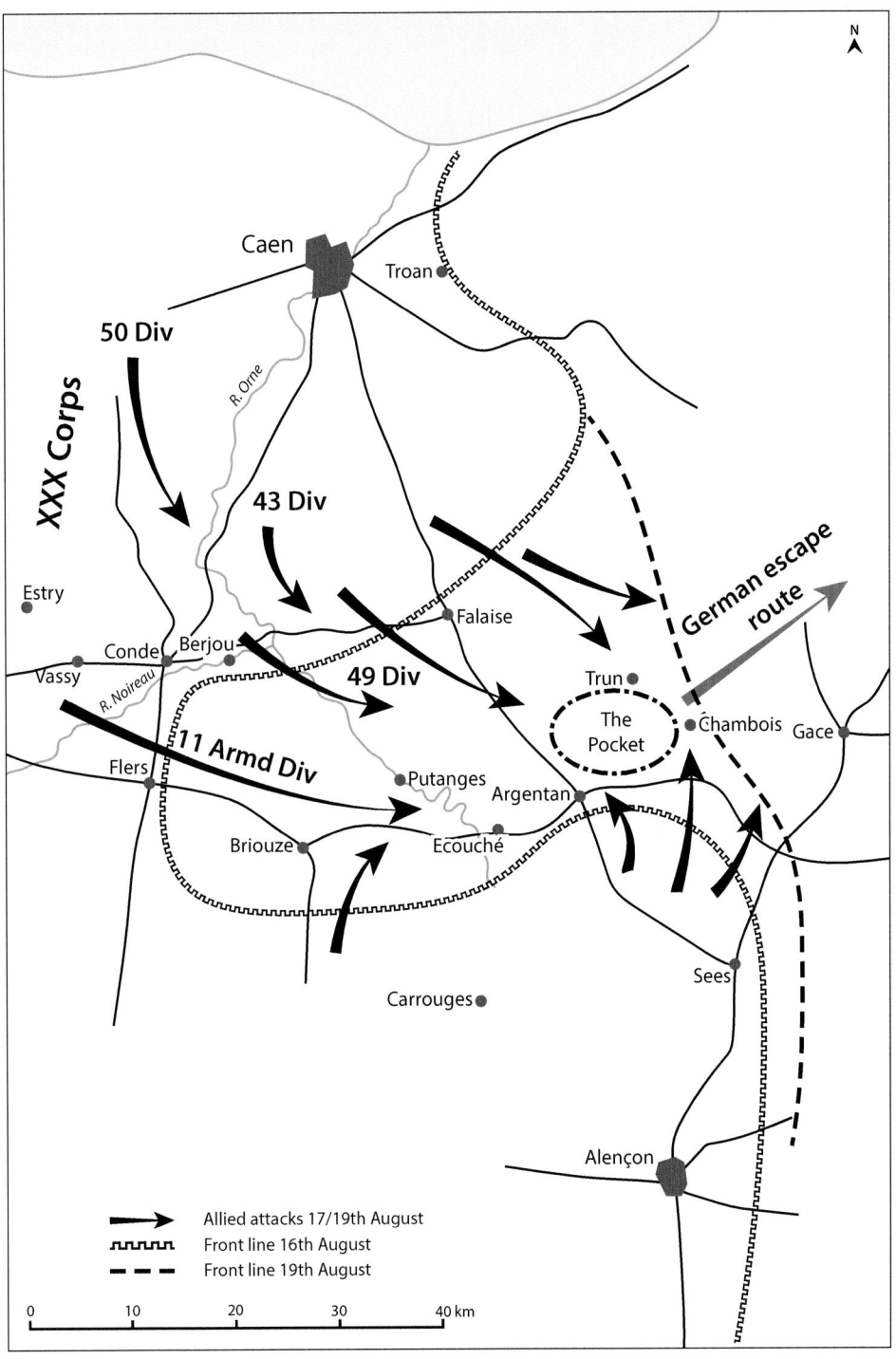

The Falaise Pocket, the *Westheer*'s Stalingrad.

Thousands of men and horses were killed and left on the roads and in the fields throughout the countryside. The abandoned ruined equipment and the bodies of men and horses that covered that beautiful part of Normandy was an appalling sight. We had to get our scarves and handkerchiefs to cover our mouths and noses to try and cut out that awful stench. Traffic jams clogged up the roads because of the numbers of vehicles on the move, as well as the abandoned equipment and the ruins of a retreating army. There were also hundreds of German prisoners who had to be dealt with. Those of us who were there and witnessed the carnage will never forget with revulsion the unspeakable dreadful horror of it all for the rest of their lives.[18]

Private Norman Hardy and his comrades from the 5th East Yorks entered a ruined farmyard and found civilians there. However, German troops outside the pocket were still sending over the odd shell to deter their pursuers, leading to events that left Hardy deeply scarred:

Private Norman Hardy, 5th Battalion East Yorkshire Regiment. (Courtesy of N. Hardy)

As we moved forward through the Falaise gap we saw all the dead horses and men laid about, [and] wrecked tanks and transports were everywhere. We stopped at a farmhouse, [and] this was the worst part of my experience during the whole of the war, I think. There was a young girl there, she was only about 12 and had a brand-new coat on. She looked really smart and was very excited to see us all. I hadn't left my carrier as we hadn't been there above ten minutes when Jerry sent over some 2-10s [shells] and she was killed in the explosions. I can always remember her happy smiling face after all this time and I often think that if we hadn't been there, she wouldn't have been killed. But I can always remember that girl coming to our carrier all fussy and pleased to see us. That did me in worse than anything else during the war.[19]

The German troops who managed to escape the slaughter at Falaise made for the Seine. *Unteroffizier* Otto Henning of the *Panzer-Lehr-Division* recalled the retreat:

---

18 WW2: *People's War* <www.bbc.co.uk/ww2peopleswar> (accessed 23 March 2021).
19 N. Hardy, interview with author (Hull, 1995).

We had to reconnoitre carefully before driving through a village to make sure the enemy had not yet been there and that we could get out if we entered it. The British and American advance was very fast and on a number of occasions we only just managed to escape. We drove through villages that had already been decorated with the Tricolour and French civilians thought we were Americans. Our vehicles were so carefully camouflaged that it was impossible to know if we were friend or foe.[20]

The campaign in Normandy was effectively over and the German forces were routed, suffering some 250,000 casualties in the process. But for XXX Corps, one more task remained before the Allied armies could break out of Normandy completely and sweep forward to the borders of the Third Reich. The River Seine was the last major obstacle to the Second Army, and XXX Corps was to make the first crossing of it by British troops.

Bounce the Seine, 43rd Wessex Division, Operation Neptune

Running from south-east to north-west, the River Seine forms a natural barrier for any army moving across northern France. Once the Germans had been forced back over the river, the Seine became a problem for the Allies, forming a formidable barrier to the further expansion of their advance. The route to Vernon via Argentan, Breteuil and Pacy cut right across the American lines of communication, but negotiations with the Americans regarding the passage of XXX Corps through them was undertaken successfully. Bridging equipment for the crossing of the Seine had been arriving since early August. Formations of engineers had been specially trained in assault and bridging operations and the specialist equipment needed, such as storm boats, close support rafts, Bailey and pontoon bridges, which had all been meticulously developed. A bridging column consisting of 366 vehicles was allocated to XXX Corps.

Major General Ivor Thomas, CO of the 43rd Wessex Division, was given the following instructions by Major General Horrocks at XXX Corps headquarters:

> Force a crossing of the Seine at Vernon on or about 25th August. Cover the construction of a Class 9 and a Class 40 bridge to form a bridgehead of sufficient depth to allow the passage through of the remainder of the Corps, i.e., two armoured divisions, one armoured brigade and one infantry division, to ensure the protection of the left flank of the Corps axis between the rivers Eure and Seine.[21]

Operations for XXX Corps were now developing with lightning speed as the British Second Army, with XXX Corps on the right and XII Corps on the left, advanced to the Seine. The 43rd Wessex Division was given the task of being the first British division to cross the Seine, and in the early hours of 25 August the leading troops reached Vernon. The Germans had left and the town itself had been liberated by the French Forces of the Interior (FFI), led by Georges André, who was confident that freedom was at hand. For the first time in four years, the French

---

20 Manuscript sent to author by H. Wernemann (Germany, 1989).
21 Essame, *The 43rd Wessex Division at War*, p. 91.

tricolour flew again from public buildings. American reconnaissance patrols arrived to explain that the town was to be liberated by British forces, who were on their way. André, deciding to hold on until they arrived, began the task of clearing all buildings of the last remaining Germans who were in hiding, having been left behind by their retreating comrades. Fourteen-year-old Guy Dugres joined in the manhunt with some of his friends:

> We found a terrified German hiding at the bottom of a well. I had my own machine-gun, although it did not have a breach mechanism and couldn't fire. Anyway, by threatening this soldier with it, we managed to get him out of the well and proudly marched him into Vernon along the Rue-de-Bizy. One frightened enemy soldier, with hands on head, followed by a group of small boys, it made a glorious sight. Then we handed him over to the FFI.[22]

A member of the FFI in Vernon. (Author's collection)

By 20 August, Vernon was in the hands of the FFI, which had taken over the old barracks and placed a guard on the road bridge to stop any Germans filtering back into the town. But with only light weapons, they were at the mercy of any significant armoured formation that wished to retake Vernon. Among the populace there was great rejoicing as they awaited the arrival of the British. Houses were bedecked with flags and a feeling of festivity was in the air when three German tanks rumbled into the town, retreating from the Americans. Nevertheless, the FFI had now tasted freedom and its members were not about to give it up. They clashed head-on with the German armour, with one of the tank commanders shot dead in front of the town hall. A young Frenchman, Pierre Zyslony, climbed onto the second tank and hurled grenades into the open turret, only to be killed by a burst of machine-gun fire. The third tank was set ablaze by a Molotov cocktail and its commander wounded. Thereafter, the Germans abandoned their tanks and took flight.

22 Ford, K., *Assault Crossing The River Seine, 1944* (Devon: David and Charles, 1987), p. 31.

Enemy reinforcements arrive, the *49. Infanterie-Division*

On 21 August, elements of the German *49. Infanterie-Division* arrived at Vernonnet, on the opposite side of the river from Vernon, having come from Boulogne to strengthen the line of the river in anticipation of a British crossing. This caused problems for the FFI, as there was now a substantial enemy force overlooking Vernon from across the river. The FFI snipers made any unfortunate German who came into view an excuse to partake in some target practise, and in the following days there were sporadic outbursts of small-arms fire from both sides. The Germans retaliated with shells and mortar fire on Vernon. Louis Le Maignon was positioned in an upper floor of a house at the Vernon end of the remains of the road bridge, guarding against any possible German attack:

> Our group was supposed to have a heavy machine-gun. I spent most of the day carrying ammunition to the basement, only to find out later that there was no machine-gun. I had an automatic rifle, but it seemed to me that I was only there to be shot at. The two men with me had a Tommy-gun and another rifle. We tried firing at the Germans a few times, but they never attempted a crossing. The next morning, we were relieved and went back home. My kids asked me if I had killed many Germans. I answered that happily they did not advance, so we did not have to do very much. It was just as well, for we had little ammunition that fitted our guns.[23]

The *49. Infanterie-Division* was commanded by *Generalleutnant* Siegfried Macholtz, an experienced and highly decorated officer who had been a regular soldier since 1909. The division was formed in February 1944, and at the start of June 1944 its order of battle was as follows:

Grenadier-Regiment 148, 149 and *150*
Artillerie-Regiment 149
49. Fusilier-Abteilung
149. Panzerzerstorer-Abteilung (Tank Destroyer Battalion)
149. Ingenieur-Abteilung (Engineer Battalion)
149. Nachrichten-Abteilung (Signal Battalion)
149. Division Versorgungsgruppe (Supply Group)

On paper, the *49. Infanterie-Division* was a normal *Wehrmacht* field division, but in reality it was more of a mobile reserve and was formed originally as the *191. Ausbildung-Division* (Training Division). It spent the early part of the war in Belgium, and after a stint in southern France in 1943 was moved to the Montreuil–Etaples–Boulogne area for coastal defence duties. In February 1944, it was converted into a field division and renamed the *49. Infanterie-Division*. For the next few months, it remained in the Boulogne vicinity as part of the German *15. Armee*, helping to strengthen Hitler's Atlantic Wall against attack. When Operation Overlord began, Hitler still believed that the main attack was coming in the Pas-de-Calais area and that the Normandy landings were a feint. Throughout June and most of July, while the battle raged in Normandy,

---

23   Ford, *Assault Crossing The River Seine*, p. 32.

Hitler left the *15. Armee* in place ready to meet the expected threat, and it took several weeks before Hitler realised that an Allied landing in the Pas-de-Calais was not going to happen.

As the German Army continued its struggle to drive the Allies back into the sea, so the strength of the *49. Infanterie-Division* declined, its commander, Macholtz, being compelled to provide the hard-pressed *7. Armee* fighting in Normandy with reinforcements. As the war of attrition rumbled on, Macholtz was told to part with mortars, heavy machine guns and vehicles. In return for the replacements sent to Normandy, he only received groups of foreign conscripts and very young *Hitlerjugend* (Hitler Youth). When the division finally got the call to move from the Pas-de-Calais to the front line on the Seine, it comprised a depleted collection of men from various countries, poorly motivated and poorly armed. Macholtz was ordered to hold the line of the River Seine between Giverny and Les-Andelys and to prevent any crossings. Vernon and its essential road network seemed to the Germans the likeliest place for the British to cross.

Kampfgruppe Meyer

Macholtz set up his divisional headquarters at Beauvais and quickly formed a battle group from the troops of *Grenadier-Regiment 150* who had arrived in the town. This group moved down to the Seine under the command of *Hauptmann* Meyer; they would be reinforced as soon as more troops arrived from the Pas-de-Calais. Unfortunately for Macholtz, American forces had crossed the Seine at Mantes and the need to stop this breakthrough meant that reinforcements meant for the *49. Infanterie-Division* were now diverted away to assist the German units who were trying to contain the American bridgehead. The remaining units of the *49. Division* began arriving in Beauvais in dribs and drabs in a variety of transports. Some were sent to the Seine, while others were held in reserve for the American threat.

Macholtz had correctly concluded that any Allied assault across the Seine must come in or near Vernon if it was to be effectively exploited. This made his defensive preparations easier to organise, which was just as well considering the limited number of troops he had available. The high ground beyond Vernonnet would prove to be the key to any successful action. Along the Seine, opposite Vernon, stand three high spurs; one directly to the rear of Vernonnet and another two to the left and right of the village. *Hauptmann* Meyer positioned his *kampfgruppe* on the high ground overlooking Vernonnet. These long escarpments, with their steep chalk faces, dominated the whole river front near Vernon. Meyer strategically established machine-gun positions all along the edge of the 300ft-high chalk-faced escarpments, and in between these were situated 20mm dual-purpose *flak* guns. As a whole, these deployments presented a strong and formidable defensive position covering the waterfront. Other positions covered the sites of the demolished road and rail bridges.

By 23 August, the German defensive line opposite the village of Vernon had been established. There were relatively few German troops in the area, but thanks to Meyer's organisational skills those who were present totally dominated the assault area. The German intelligence services knew that the Americans had arrived in Vernon but that they had only passed through the town as their forces headed towards Rouen. All the available signs suggested that an assault across the Seine at Vernon was very unlikely. The days passed by with little to do but to watch for the British troops. The occasional shell dropped in the area, and the French snipers continued to annoy the Germans. Macholtz knew that the main threat to his *49. Division* was the possibility

Troops of *Kampfgruppe Meyer* in cliff-top positions overlooking Vernon. (Author's collection)

of being outflanked by the American forces which had crossed the Seine upstream. It seemed to be increasingly unlikely that the division would have to fight its first action of the war on the banks of the Seine.

On 24 August, two American jeeps pulled into the main square of Vernon. The civilian population thought they had come to liberate the town, but were soon disappointed, as Jacques Cambuza, a member of the FFI, recalled:

> The American jeep contained soldiers who were specially trained for the job, interpreters who began lavishly to hand out cigarettes. They had a certain aloof look about them; they were not fighting soldiers. They imagined that they could buy us with their gifts, it wasn't very nice.[24]

The local population became anxious when the Americans left: was the town liberated or not? Would the Germans return, and where were the British?

As XXX Corps made the drive to the Seine, its units faced a sensitive problem, as blocking their way were the lines of communication of two American corps as they drove down the Seine valley. These lines of communication are guarded jealously by any army, as along such arteries pass all the essentials needed to supply the front line. XXX Corps was allocated periods when they could pass through: from 0800–1200 hours and 1400–1800 hours on 24 August, and between 0100 and 0500 hours on 25 August. It would mean that XXX Corps would need to be split up into three separate groups. The first group would be made up of the assault troops who

---

24   Ford, *Assault Crossing The River Seine*, p. 32.

would arrive at Vernon on the day of the assault, leaving no time for any last-minute adjustments to the battle plan. This assault group would need to have everything with it that it required, and consisted of 1,800 vehicles. The make-up of the other two groups was also of great importance and depended on the point at which the units they contained were to be introduced into the battle. All manner of possibilities had to be considered.

The bridge at Pacy

Early on 24 August, the long column of the British battle group passed through the ruins of Argentan and into the undamaged countryside beyond to Laigle and Breteuil. Cheering crowds of ecstatic civilians sped them on their way. Here and there they came across a wrecked 88mm gun and numerous abandoned enemy transports. During the afternoon, the column turned off the road in pouring rain west of Breteuil. An advanced guard of the divisional engineers was sent ahead to find out what the situation was at the River Eure at Pacy. St Acquilin-de-Pacy was situated about a mile from the river, its approaches pock-marked by bombing and burnt-out vehicles which blocked the way. They were to find worse news at Pacy, where the bridge over the river had been destroyed, along with the railway bridge to the eastern side of the town. The 260th Field Company, Royal Engineers, soon got to work filling in the potholes, but booby traps had been left and the first casualties were taken among the engineers. Meanwhile, 553rd Field Company's bridge reconnaissance party advanced on foot into Pacy, and all through the night of 24/25 August the 11th Field Company laboured to construct a Bailey bridge over the Eure. Thanks to their efforts, the road was opened at 1015 hours on the 25th and the race to get to Vernon began. All normal considerations of spacing and speed were abandoned, the drivers being told to go flat out. Heavily loaded tanks with infantry riding on them, jeeps, lorries, carriers and DUKW amphibious vehicles surged forward in a haze of dust and heat. In the time allotted, the entire assault battle group had made it through the Pacy defile. This gallop forward was only possible because of the complete superiority of the Allied air forces.

Captain Geoffrey Picot of the 1st Hampshires, 50th Northumbrian Division, was halted at Pacy with the rest of his battalion while they waited to hear what their next role in the advance would be:

> We remained at Pacy for a few days and [on the afternoon of] 24th August I took a jeep and drove into the town to see what it looked like. There was military traffic everywhere and it was all moving in different directions, so, not willing to be caught in the middle of a convoy I left Pacy and drove towards Vernon. There was a lot of transport on that road and I noticed General Horrocks pass me, driving his own car at high speed. Apart from a couple of ambulances going back with casualties there was little sign of fighting. As there was no shelling going on and people were walking about, I drove right on into Vernon. The town had suffered a lot of damage, so great that it could only have been done by heavy bombing. Possibly the bridge had been attacked several times before D-Day. A number of shops were open and in one I bought a bottle of perfume for my girlfriend in London. Before I returned, I had a drink in an *estaminet* that was being well patronised by British soldiers. The *mademoiselle* touched my pips asking: "What is that?" Someone told her I was a captain, so she said, apparently thrilled: "Oh *monsieur capitaine*" and beamed at me while standing

ready for me to order another drink. When I returned to our harbour area and spread the news that I had been to Vernon and found it quiet and that the hills on the other side of the river seemed deserted, the morale of the chaps went up as the farther the enemy was away, the higher was their morale.[25]

The town of Vernon was to provide a stable base from which the attack would take place, and one of the battalions earmarked for the assault, the 4th Wiltshires, was now given the job of occupying and controlling the town after their arrival. They would be supported in their task by a squadron of tanks from the 15/19th King's Royal Hussars, while to the north of Vernon more tanks from this regiment provided a defensive line in case the Germans tried to interfere with the crossing of the river once it started. The 43rd Reconnaissance Regiment was to carry out fighting patrols in the hope of picking up intelligence of the Germans' intentions. As the 4th Wiltshires were now committed to safeguarding the town in the initial stages, this left only three battalions to carry out the attack across the river. The shortage of infantry dictated that the initial bridgehead be concentrated around the proposed bridging sites. Speed and surprise were essential, and the new bridges would need to be erected in the vicinity of the damaged road bridge. The 43rd Wessex Division had three days to plan and execute Operation Neptune, which was no easy task. Major General Thomas had issued strict orders that no British troops should be seen by the enemy in Vernon or on the riverbank prior to the assault.

The village of Vernonnet, on the far bank, was concentrated around the exit of the old, now damaged, road bridge. This would be an ideal spot for the troops to land as they could quickly secure the bridging sites, and work on them by the engineers could begin at once. However, the assaulting troops would have the problem of clearing Vernonnet first, which could lead to delays and heavy casualties as they fought in the narrow streets, clearing the houses near the river one at a time. The final plan which was made dictated that the attack be launched on a two-battalion front, one on either side of Vernonnet. Along the Seine near Vernon there are a number of islands of various sizes, scattered about in the fast-flowing current. Reconnaissance photographs of these obstacles were in short supply; indeed, there was only one air reconnaissance picture available to the planners.

Some 400 yards below Vernonnet is a large island close to the eastern shore. Vernon and Vernonnet were linked by the now-demolished iron girder railway bridge that crossed this island, and the line then continued to the other bank. It was decided that the main cut here had only a trickle of water running over it, and that it would probably be dry. Passage for troops was thought to be possible, so this island was selected for the left-hand column, the 4th Somersets, to land upon. This decision was to have serious consequences for the attacking troops. Further upstream from the demolished road bridge was another island in mid-river, and directly above that was a shallow part of the river that ran over the island, an area considered to be perfect for a crossing. The approaches were good, and the far bank was a good landing place.

General Thomas decided that the right-hand assault by the 5th Wiltshires would take place in this area, where their boats could pass over the submerged island. The 1st Worcesters following behind would pass over the river at the same spot. The final make-up of the assault group to bounce the Seine was as follows:

---

25 Picot, *Accidental Warrior*, pp. 171–72.

>One squadron of the 43rd Reconnaissance Regiment
>One squadron of the 15/19th King's Royal Hussars
>The 4th Wiltshires, 129 Brigade, to occupy Vernon
>The 5th Wiltshires, 129 Brigade
>The 4th Somersets, 129 Brigade
>The 1st Worcesters, 214 Brigade
>94th Field Regiment, Royal Artillery
>129 Brigade Headquarters
>43rd Division Tactical Headquarters
>Royal Engineers Group

Before the XXX Corps assault group moved off on the last leg of its journey to Vernon, they were encamped at a staging area in Breteuil on 24 August. Tucked into every nook and cranny of every farmyard, orchard, field and meadow were the 1,600 vehicles that made up the assault group. Hedgerows were in full bloom and the cloudy sky had at last given way to a beautiful late summer's evening. In this pastoral setting the war seemed a distant memory and men enjoyed the luxury of doing very little. The prevailing feeling was generally that the German forces were close to collapse, and in quiet moments men looked back on past battles and thought of the friends they had lost. Some men were very sceptical of this view of the German Army, as they had thought them beaten before and every time they bounced back to give them a bloody nose.

The commanders of the brigades singled out to make the attack needed to assess the allocated areas where they would be expected to leave from on the near riverbank and where they would have to land on the opposite side. Lieutenant Colonel Christopher Godfrey Lipscomb, DSO and Bar, CO of the 4th Somersets, spoke to an American officer who reported to him that there was no sign of enemy occupation on the far bank and that a crossing place had been found:

> It was not a good one, but it was just possible to cross here. The whole of Vernon was under observation from the high ground on the other side of the river and the only covered approach to the bank was by a long straight avenue with a double row of trees in full leaf on either side. They would afford considerable concealment to men and vehicles. The houses on the waterfront ran parallel to the river and would give excellent cover for those waiting to embark. The river was 200 yards wide with steep banks on the home side and shallow muddy exits on the further bank.[26]

Signaller Frederick Greenwood, who was attached to the 5th Wiltshires, had served all through the Normandy campaign after landing with the 5th Berkshires on D-Day. One evening he overheard a group of young officers discussing the Seine operation that they were about to take part in and was deeply disturbed by what they said:

> They seemed to think that the crossing was going to be a piece of cake. The enemy was supposed to be very weak along the Seine, consisting of old men and those unfit for

---

26 Lipscomb, C.G., DSO and Bar, *History of the 4th Battalion the Somerset Light Infantry (Prince Albert's) in the Campaign in North-west Europe, June, 1944–May, 1945* (Taunton: Goodman, 1946), p. 41.

front-line duty. We were going to dash across the river with no trouble at all. It worried me to hear them talk about the coming battle as though it was just a game.[27]

Greenwood had a premonition that his luck was about to run out, and by lamplight he wrote a letter home to his fiancée in England, explaining that she was not to worry if she didn't hear from him for a while. The battle in which he was about to take part at Vernon would see him wounded and taken prisoner by the Germans, but he survived to return to his betrothed after the war. The officers whose conversation he had overheard were new to action and were soon to find out what it was really like to fight the Germans, even in their reduced state.

---

27   F. Greenwood, correspondence with author (Wiltshire, 1989).

11

A Calvary Called Vernon, 25–27 August 1944

This is the story of one of many crossings over the River Seine in late August 1944, and of how one British division of XXX Corps, free at last from the restrictions of the Normandy countryside, attacked the enemy-held far shore in daylight. After the halt at Pacy, XXX Corps approached Vernon and covered the last 8 miles at breakneck speed, moving quickly across a flat plateau towards the Seine. The early-morning sun was starting to bathe the land in brilliant sunshine as the advanced troops of XXX Corps flew along the dusty roads. Patrick Spencer-Moore, ADC to Major General Ivor Thomas of the 43rd Wessex Division, was in the van that day and recalled: "One of the most exciting trips I have ever had in my life. It was a marvellous summer's morning, and we were swanning through the countryside of France. The horrors of Normandy were all left far behind us, it was a wonderful thing."[1] When XXX Corps arrived at Vernon on 25 August, news came through that Paris had finally been liberated.

In between Pacy and the Seine, the advance by parts of XXX Corps was forced to slow down occasionally, the fields and roads having become pockmarked with numerous craters. The US 5th Armored Division had run into an ambush here just five days previously, resulting in three days of heavy fighting. Their air support had dropped 1,000lb bombs all around the area where the Germans were situated, making much of it impassable for vehicles. General Thomas was informed that the bulk of the American forces had been withdrawn from the area and that patrols had been left in Vernon until the British could get there to take over. Thomas was also told that there could be no guarantee that Germans were not in the area on XXX Corps' left flank. Luckily, Thomas had already allocated the 43rd Reconnaissance Regiment and tanks of the 15/19th Hussars to guard the area from the Eure to the Seine.

On the final approach to Vernon, the road descended at a sharp angle as it wound its way into the town. The columns passed through the Forest of Bizy, and from the cover of its great trees the leading vehicles emerged and were suddenly confronted with the town itself. They slipped quietly into the streets of Vernon unnoticed, the people living there having no idea they had been liberated until they looked out of their windows and doors to see these strange new vehicles. General Thomas was one of the first to arrive at Vernon and made his way to the river to inspect the crossing sites he had selected from an aerial photograph.

---

1 McKee, A., *The Race for the Rhine Bridges* (London: Pan Books, 1974), p. 135.

On a hot and dusty day, the troops that would lead the assault eyed the far bank of the Seine with suspicion. General Thomas was not happy as he viewed the situation by the river, with the white chalk cliffs across the wide river dominating the crossing places completely. He realised that a heavy smokescreen would be essential to give the assault boats any chance of survival. He eagerly sought intelligence from the local community and the FFI about the state of the river and the conditions on the far bank. The various units of the division that would be involved in the crossing sent reconnaissance parties towards the river; they crept over walls, around buildings and stealthily moved through gardens, always keeping out of sight of the German lookouts. Each team needed to gain a complete picture of their section of the riverbank. The officers of the assaulting companies were anxious to see their individual crossing places and the areas where they were to land on the far bank. All of this activity drew the attention of the local populace and crowds began to gather around the British troops, who were doing their best to be inconspicuous.

Major Michael Concannon of the 94th Field Regiment, Royal Artillery, entered the town and was seeking locations for his gun teams. He found the local FFI[2] to be in command and was approached by numerous people offering him the benefit of their local knowledge. They informed him of a group of Germans hiding in the town and were most put out when their liberators would not help in apprehending them. Concannon remembered: "We tried to explain that we had come to Vernon to do a specific operation and not to dash here and there after two or three Germans, we were after the whole lot. I think we may have annoyed some of them, but we had to be firm."[3]

Captain J.S. McMath of the 5th Wiltshires later wrote of the surreal atmosphere that pervaded everything:

> We found the atmosphere unreal enough, but it was harder for the new arrivals to realise that the whole position was overlooked by the enemy, and in our new capacity as traffic police we sweated blood in the afternoon sun, persuading men and vehicles to hide themselves away and not join the inhabitants in a liberation promenade. Now commanders of every rank and every arm crowded into our observation posts, and it took all our tact and persuasion to prevent their drawing an expected fierce enemy reaction.[4]

Sapper A.H. Harding, who had been a painter and decorator before the war, was given the job of making and erecting signs to inform the drivers of the hundreds of vehicles containing heavy bridging equipment, stores and ammunition where they should park:

> Sign writing under the noses of the enemy is not a practise to be recommended, [as] it is apt to lead to inaccuracies both in lettering and spelling. We were slapping it on fast, and it was the sloppiest bit of sign writing I've ever done. There was no time to make a good job of it.[5]

---

2   *Forces françaises de l'Intérieur* (French Forces of the Interior, or French Resistance).
3   Manuscript forwarded to author by M. Whiting (Gloucestershire, 1999).
4   McMath, J.S., *The 5th Battalion Wiltshire Regiment in North-west Europe* (London: Whitefriars Press, 1946), p. 163.
5   *WW2: People's War* <www.bbc.co.uk/ww2peopleswar> (accessed 21 March 2021).

This was the only aerial view of the battlefield at Vernon that the British commanders could consult as they planned for the crossing of the Seine. In midstream, the islands are clearly visible. (Author's collection)

General Thomas found the headquarters of the FFI in the Chateau-de-Bizy and was told that the landing site on the left, to be used by the 4th Somersets, was indeed an island, but that the cut that separated it from the far shore was dry and easily passed. He was also informed that the 5th Wiltshires' crossing place, on the right flank, would be easy to pass over as some weeds covered the shallows and the locals insisted that the submerged islands would not impede any boats. Thomas was assured that the water was deep enough. This was considered good news at the time and the attack could now go ahead as planned. However, the information he was given by the locals turned out to be incorrect, and that night the whole operation would be put in jeopardy because of it.

The die was now cast, but problems continued to emerge as the assault troops prepared for their task. Lieutenant Colonel T.H. Evill of the Royal Engineers reported that adequate launching sites for the DUKWs could not be found, and therefore storm boats were to be used by the assault troops. But when the ramps had eventually been completed by the engineers, the DUKWs could be put into operation. The infantry had no experience in the use of the rather awkward and heavy storm boats, but they would have to make the best of it as H-Hour had been set at 1900 hours that evening. Support for the attack was to be provided by the 94th Field Regiment and 121st Medium Regiment, Royal Artillery. Overlooking the river, the 8th Machine-gun Battalion Middlesex Regiment had placed three machine-gun platoons in the gardens and buildings of Vernon to give support. C Squadron of the 15/19th Hussars took up positions in gardens and streets near the river and would support the attack with observed fire. When the attack went in, there would be 15 minutes of preliminary bombardment, followed by a further 10 minutes when a smokescreen would be laid down and maintained during the remaining hours of daylight.

The commanding officers of the 5th Wiltshires and 4th Somersets rushed around in the short time left to them, issuing orders, seeing that their men had all they needed and that they had been fed before the off. The troops shouldered their heavy burdens and began their move through the backstreets leading to the river. The men of the 5th Wiltshires trudged silently past the Chateau-de-Bizy and entered the town by a boulevard now named Avenue Marechal Montgomery. The 4th Somersets passed down the Avenue des Capuchins, which was straight, tree-lined and led to the railway bridge, the mantle of the trees giving them all the cover they needed. Civilians, men, women and children crowded the streets, laughing and shouting at the men as they passed by. At 1845 hours there was a terrific roar as the barrage opened up on that fine summer's evening, and shells began to moan overhead on their way to the enemy positions. In an instant, the streets were empty of civilians. The chalk cliffs on the far bank became clouded in smoke and fire as the guns and mortars rained down high-explosive shells on the unsuspecting Germans. Tracer rounds flew upwards into this deluge of fire from the machine guns of the 8th Middlesex Regiment and the tanks of the 15/19th Hussars.

As the barrage roared overhead, Sapper Harding and his comrades were working furiously to erect the signs they had made indicating the parking areas for the convoys which continued to arrive in the town. At one point they had run out of boards and had to obtain more by ripping down anything they could find in the town that was suitable:

> What a noise when the artillery barrage came down, it was all hell let loose. The signs; Tippers here, Floating Bay units there, were made on the spot under machine-gun fire from the opposite bank. Once the signs were painted, they then had to be erected. The

Men of the 5th Wiltshires silently passing through the backstreets of Vernon on their way to the river. (Courtesy of M. Denney)

sappers, in between intervals of ducking and running, climbed lampposts, trees and walls to fix the signs in the most prominent positions.[6]

As the battle began, and the barrage thundered, the town was a hive of furious activity for the British. Assembly and forming-up areas on the riverside had been marked for the assault troops, and RASC lorries unloaded their storm boats and low-loaders carrying bulldozers as the infantry moved slowly through the narrow streets. The battle had begun.

The 5th Battalion Wiltshire Regiment crosses the Seine, 25 August

At 1900 hours, the artillery in the Forest of Bizy and the mortars in Vernon started sending over smoke shells, and clouds of white mist began billowing up the slopes between the trees, the opposite bank slowly disappearing under this protective mantle. The assault troops, who were crouching behind walls and buildings, then heard the familiar sound of Spandau fire coming out of the mist and knew then that the Germans were waiting for them.

Driver Clifford Roberts of the 553rd Field Company found great difficulty in moving his truckload of storm boats safely down to the river:

Men of the 5th Battalion Wiltshire Regiment climb into a storm boat on the banks of the Seine. (Author's collection)

The construction was still under shellfire. My truck had to be led through the town and down to the Seine. Sergeant Welland guided me along the main street, which was itself still under sniper fire. He walked about 60 yards in front of my lorry. If he crossed the road, I had to do the same at precisely that point. If he carried on along a pavement, I drove down the pavement behind him. When we got to the end of the road near the site, he directed me into an area at the back of a café surrounded by a high wall. When the sappers arrived to pick up the boats, they were not very happy, [as] there was still some distance to be covered before they reached the water's edge. They had to manhandle the cumbersome boats around the back gardens of some houses to get them down to the river. Once out in the open, they were forced to creep forward under the cover of an armoured bulldozer to escape the sniper fire. Whilst my truck was being unloaded, a house close by received a direct hit from a salvo of enemy shells which killed two medics and covered me with debris. Outside, just beyond the wall, other sappers suffered badly, one lost an arm and a leg. The atmosphere was electric and terrifying.[7]

The sappers of the 15th Kent GHQ Troops, Royal Engineers, manned the eight storm boats allocated to A Company for the crossing. The boats turned out to be very awkward and heavy to handle down to the river, and each needed a whole platoon to move it. At 1900 hours, the

---

7   C. Roberts, correspondence with author (1997).

first two boats, carrying 8 Platoon commanded by Lieutenant Leslie John Selby, slipped into the water and set off for the far bank. Recording this moment for posterity were two official war photographers, who took many pictures of the two boats moving out into the smoke-covered river until they were finally enveloped by the fog and disappeared. They did not know it at the time, but those images would turn out to the last time most of these men would be seen alive as they went to their deaths. All seemed to be going well until the last 30 yards from the far shore, when both boats grounded on a submerged island that the locals had assured General Thomas had enough water running over it to allow free passage. At the same time, the wind dispersed the smokescreen and the Germans on the far bank had a grandstand view of the luckless platoon.

The German machine-gun crews' response was immediate and savage. Spandau fire ripped through the small boats loaded with men. Lieutenant Selby's boat was hit by a hail of bullets and capsized, the men being thrown into the water. In the second boat, which was riddled with bullet holes from stem to stern, Sergeant Thomas Mackrell shouted to his men to swim for it and plunged into the water as machine-gun bullets churned up the water all around him:

> The smoke started to lift as we got under way, [and] we could see the opposite bank. Then the machine-gun fire opened on us, and as we neared the far bank, we got stuck on a sandbank. Several men in the boat were hit. I shouted to the men to jump off the boat and wade ashore; we were in four and a half feet of water. As the men got onto the bank, they spread out to gain cover and I lost touch with some. The boat was swinging about in the river with two Royal Engineers, the crew, hanging on. I managed to get one wounded man on board again and with the REs swam the boat back to the other bank. There were no survivors in Lt Selby's boat.[8] By the end of an hour only one of the eight boats had survived.[9]

Sergeant Mackrell looked along the river expecting to see other boats coming towards him, but there were none. The enemy Spandau fire passed just above his head and continued to rake the shoreline and river. Sheltering in the river at the stern of his boat was an engineer officer called Bellamy, but Mackrell saw no other sign of life as the rest of the platoon had been swept away downstream and were claimed by the river, their heavy packs dragging them under. With a wounded man in the boat, Mackrell and the engineers paddled it to the cover of the tree-covered island a little downstream, but when they tried to start the boat's engine this only drew the attention of the enemy gunners on the cliffs opposite. From there they made it back to the friendly shore.

As this tragic scene was unfolding, other boats had arrived at the water's edge, and once in the river they began to ferry the remainder of A Company across the Seine. Some had difficulty in starting up their engines, a task that could only be completed after the infantry had boarded as the Evinrude engines[10] had no clutch and could not be left running as the troops embarked. Without power, all the boats could do was drift with the current downstream and run aground in mid-river. What was left of the now patchy smokescreen was being carried

---

8 Lieutenant Leslie John Selby, MC, Queen's Royal Regiment West Surrey, died on 26 August 1944. He is buried in St Desir War Cemetery, France. Of the 35 men in Selby's storm boat, only 11 survived.
9 Manuscript forwarded to author by P. Cuerden (Hampshire, 1991).
10 Evinrude manufactured outboard motors for the military in the 1940s and is still in business today.

Troops of the 5th Battalion Wiltshire Regiment push off from the shore in a storm boat into the smokescreen that lay across the River Seine. Not long after this picture was taken, most of the men in this boat became casualties. (Author's collection)

away on the breeze and left many exposed to the view of the German machine gunners, who tore into them without mercy. The devastating enemy fire sank boats and picked off men struggling for their lives in the cold water; many of these men made it back to the friendly shore they had started from and sought cover from the German fire behind stone walls.

Lieutenant Colonel Lindley Robert Edmundson Fayle, DSO, CO of the 15th Kent GHQ Troops, Royal Engineers, watched the preliminary bombardment begin as after 10 minutes it changed to smoke. He was positioned lying behind a tree in a garden where he had a good view of the river:

> Owing to the smoke it was very difficult to see anything, but we heard the sound of the storm boat engines starting and the Boche replying with Spandau fire. I shot down to the river to see my own troops. I eventually met the officer in charge of the storm boats, Lt Bellamy, on the right battalion front. He was

Lieutenant Colonel Lindley Robert Edmundson Fayle, DSO, OBE, Commanding Officer of the 15th Kent GHQ Troops, Royal Engineers. (Author's collection)

slightly wounded and told me that the first wave consisted of two boats, but they had been heavily fired upon and most of the occupants killed or wounded. He had escaped without serious wounds and had got back to the bank to organise the remaining boats which had got about a platoon over the river, but the battalion commander had shut down the crossings until after dark, so the men were under cover.[11]

After an hour, only one boat was still afloat, manned by an officer of the Royal Engineers; disregarding the enemy machine-gun fire, he piloted his craft in a wide detour upstream of the submerged island, making several successful trips. In this way, this brave young officer ferried 60 percent of A Company to the far shore. Lieutenant Harry John Drake of the 5th Wiltshires and his party then headed for their objective, a large white house 200 yards from the landing spot.

Private Ronald Garner of the 5th Wiltshires recalled the moment he landed on the far bank:

> In the middle of the river the craft was hit in the rear and two men were wounded. We managed to scramble up the far bank and Lt Miald led the attack on some houses some 300 yards away. As we advanced our own smoke shells were dropping all around us.[12]

Corporal Victor Coombs, 5th Wiltshires, was in the furthest boat upstream, away from the worst of the firing and clear of the hidden shallow islands that had caused so much trouble for the first boats. He knew that the crossing was going to be a risky affair as the smoke had by now virtually disappeared. The pilot of the boat was of the same opinion as the hillside before them was in full view:

> We landed further upstream after a detour on the extreme right of the attack. Then it was heads down and run like stink for the road near a group of houses out of sight of the German machine-gunners. Lt Drake was to be killed there.[13]

Once on their objective, Lieutenant Drake organised an all-round defensive position, blocking the road from the right, but it was not long before things began to happen. Major John F. Milne, the company commander, now arrived after his second attempt to cross the river and saw to it that his men were well dug-in. Shortly after, an astonishing sight appeared from the right: oblivious to the presence of the British troops, a group of six whistling German soldiers cycled down the road in the direction of the British positions. They rode right up to the British lines before being taken prisoner, having no idea that the river had been crossed. A house was used as a prison for the new captives, and as darkness fell the 5th Wiltshires settled down to await developments.

The disaster with the storm boats had created a crisis for the British commanders in Vernon, who desperately needed to get more men over into the flimsy bridgehead. Lieutenant Colonel

---

11 Manuscript sent to the author by L. White (Hull, 1989).
12 R. Garner, correspondence with author (Exeter, 1993).
13 V. Coombs, correspondence with author (Tiverton, 1994). Lieutenant Harry John Drake, 5th Battalion Wiltshire Regiment, was killed on 26 August 1944. He is buried in St Desir War Cemetery, France.

A German Spandau team await the order to fire. (Author's collection)

William Roberts, CO of the 4th Somersets, decided that it was time to make use of the four DUKWs he had at his disposal, and they were duly launched into the dark waters of the Seine. Three grounded almost at once and became useless, but the fourth amphibious vehicle, carrying one platoon of C Company, made it to the far bank. When it had dropped off its cargo, it continued to make repeated trips back and forth until it had ferried across the rest of the 5th Wiltshires.

As the men in the bridgehead sat tight, shots could be heard coming from Vernonnet. All the action seemed to be taking place near the waterfront. The British guarding the road sat tight in their positions until a lone German cyclist appeared down the road. A soldier then foolishly took a shot at him with his Sten gun and missed, and the startled German retreated quickly the way he had come to report to his superiors that the British had arrived. The Germans now knew for sure that the enemy had crossed the river, and it would not be long before a counter-attack would be launched on this small outpost.

Major Milne and 15 men arrived at the white house, making it A Company's headquarters. The barn-like building and its outhouses had been abandoned for some time. Any counter-attack on the headquarters would first have to get by the section commanded by Corporal Coombs, who covered the road further up the valley from a group of houses. The Germans had gathered a force about 100 yards from Coombs' position and began to move stealthily along a ditch that ran by the roadside. The British opened up on the Germans, forcing them to retire. Later, a more determined attack was launched along the railway track and along the road, supported by heavy Spandau fire, and it was only after a furious exchange of fire that the

Germans retired again. Coombs and his men were by now feeling the pressure of these initial German probes. His small group had only the amount of ammunition that they could carry, and no other supplies had reached them so far. Ammunition was thus running low and it would not be long before they ran out completely, so Coombs decided to fall back down the road to a new position in a house near Major Milne's headquarters.

Sergeant Edward Gardner of the 5th Wiltshires remembered the strength of the German counter-attacks, which they found difficult to repel:

> The Germans put in a strong counter-attack as darkness fell. A Coy was virtually wiped out, [and] me and a L/Cpl lay at the bottom of a slit trench; we later scarpered back to the riverbank. Only 33 of us had got across the river, including Coy CO Major Milne, who was later taken prisoner.[14]

Private J.V. Webb of the 5th Wiltshires took part in the defence of the company headquarters:

> As we made for the white house across the water meadows, L/Cpl Coster, about two feet on my left, was hit by an empty smoke canister and killed.[15] During the defence of the house there were twenty of us, of whom 16 were wounded, at about 3am on August 26th. All night our signaller was calling for reinforcements and all night we were told they were on their way.[16]

Coombs' group finally got to the last group of houses and met Major Milne, who had come from his headquarters to see the situation for himself. Coombs and his men were down to their last bullets so Milne ordered them to fall back down the valley and join the rest of the company. The Germans were becoming bolder, having obviously assumed that the British had withdrawn. Coombs observed a German carrying a machine gun who was crawling along a ditch that ran by the side of the house he was in. The German proceeded to set up his weapon no more than 10 yards away. Coombs, now completely out of ammunition, scrounged a bullet from a comrade and shot the German dead. The Germans, realising that the British were still there and prepared to fight, reacted ferociously. Heavy machine guns raked the houses all along the road as the trapped British troops fired their last shots; a white towel, tied to a rifle, was held out of the house window, and Coombs and five men marched out of the house and into captivity.

At A Company headquarters, Major Milne was desperately trying to contact battalion headquarters. In the house with him was a Royal Artillery observer whose radio could send but not receive; eventually the radio operators managed to get through to battalion.

The Germans were now becoming more aggressive and had worked their way down the valley, clashing with A Company's outer perimeter. In resisting their attacks, A Company took numerous casualties. The enemy came on yet again, this time supported by a mortar barrage. A request was sent back to battalion for artillery support, but when it arrived it fell on the positions held by the Wiltshires as the two opposing forces were so close together. The British opened fire on the enemy with every available weapon as the Germans reached the house they were in, and

---

14   E. Gardner, correspondence with author (Wiltshire, 1994).
15   Lance Corporal Frederick Coster, 5th Battalion Wiltshire Regiment, was killed in action on 25 August 1944, aged 24. He is buried in St Desir War Cemetery, France.
16   Manuscript forwarded to author by J.V. Webb (Birmingham, 1992).

the attackers fell back once again under a withering fire, leaving their dead and wounded behind them. The remnants of A Company were quickly running out of ammunition. The follow-up companies which had crossed the river were too busy fighting their way into Vernonnet, so A Company would have to deal with the counter-attacks on their own as best they could.

The 4th Battalion Somerset Light Infantry crosses the Seine, 25 August

The crossing on the left flank was to be carried out by A Company of the 4th Somersets at 1910 hours near to the demolished road bridge downstream, and upstream from the railway bridge. Eight storm boats had been allocated and would be piloted by the Royal Engineers. Getting the heavy boats down to the river was found to be very difficult for the carrying parties, but as luck would have it, they had been dropped off near the Seine by RASC trucks so by H-Hour all the boats were in the water and ready to cross.

Lieutenant Colonel Christopher Godfrey Lipscomb of the 4th Somersets remembered:

> The first two companies over were to cross in storm boats and the follow-up companies in Dukws. We had never seen storm boats before, and they proved considerably heavier than we had been led to believe. We experienced great difficulty in getting them down the steep bank and into the water.[17]

On the far bank was a railway embankment lined with a few trees that ran inland from the Seine, the trees giving some concealment to the attacking infantry. However, this landing area was also overlooked by a high chalk cliff face that was occupied by the enemy.

Captain Hancock, FOO for the guns of the 94th Field Regiment, Royal Artillery, in Bizy Forest, recorded:

> On the dot we heard the dull thud-thud of the guns in the rear and in a moment the opposite hillside was carpeted with mushroom like puffs of smoke intermingled with tracer and HE from our tanks along the riverbank. Two minutes before the assault 468 Battery began to lay a smokescreen.[18]

The storm boats' engines revved up as the troops made for their objective across the river in a haze of smoke. In one of the first boats was Corporal S. Hitchcock of A Company, 4th Somersets:

> I remember coming under fire from a small anti-aircraft gun firing small shells that was probing through the smoke. Near the shore one boat was hit and sunk but the rest made it across. We leapt ashore and ran for the cover of the railway embankment as small shells burst all around us. Those that burst in the treetops were the worst, sending showers of splinters and steel in all directions. We dug-in like fury to get away from the probing fire that was coming through the smoke. A lot of men were hit as we dug our holes.[19]

---

17 Lipscomb, *History of the 4th Battalion Somerset Light Infantry*, pp. 42–43.
18 Delaforce, *The Fighting Wessex Wyverns*, p. 162.
19 Manuscript forwarded to author by M. Hearst (Hull, 1990).

A storm boat, carrying men of the 4th Battalion Somerset Light Infantry, moves across the smoke-covered Seine making for the far shore. (Author's collection)

The Army Photographic Section had identified a cut on the far side of the landing place and had to find out if it was dry and passable. Reconnaissance parties were sent over with the first assault to decide if this cut could be passed over by vehicles. Under machine-gun fire, the reconnaissance crews made their way to the old railway bridge, ducking and diving, the increasing smoke cover enabling them to complete their task. To their disappointment, this supposedly small cut turned out to be a deep watercourse 18 metres wide with steep muddy banks; it was very unlikely that it could be used for the crossing.

Sergeant Rex C. Hunt, Royal Engineers, had been given the job of landing with the 4th Somersets to make a reconnaissance of the site across the cut for a Class 9 bridge (a pontoon bridge with a capacity of 9 tons):

> Our storm boat driver made his way to the far bank and as we were about to embark a concealed German machine-gun opened fire on us and a few unhappy moments ensued. The bullets were hitting the bank all around us, so we dashed for cover. We tried again to get forward when the smoke had thickened and this time we were successful. We headed for a clump of fir trees upstream of the railway bridge, [and] among the trees we found the gunner forward observation officer already operating. Contacting an officer of the Somerset Light Infantry, we went forward with him towards the obstacle ahead. Halfway across the open ground a sniper got busy and caused us to dodge, but we gained the cover of the trees

Troops of the 4th Battalion Somerset Light Infantry clearing houses in Vernonnet. (Courtesy of M. Denney)

lining the bank of the other river. This proved to be an obstacle of some magnitude, some sixty feet wide with steep muddy banks and deep mud at the bottom. Far from being passable, it was unlikely that anyone would ever get across to the mainland that way.[20]

Unknown to part of A Company, they had landed on what was virtually an island; here they dug-in and the storm boats that had brought them returned to the near shore and loaded up with the troops of C Company who were to pass through A Company's positions and head inland. The problems began as the men of C Company arrived on what they thought was the hostile shore. They did not get far when it was realised that the two companies were on an island and were holding an area consisting of no more than 137m by 98m. FOO Captain Hancock noted: "After some confused fighting we discovered that the troops had landed on a bloody island, [and] here we dug ourselves in for the night and sat tight in our bridgehead of about 150 by 100 yards."[21]

Lieutenant Colonel Lipscomb decided to land B Company of the 4th Somersets, under Captain J.M.F. Hutchinson, in DUKWs 300 yards upstream to the right of the island where A and C Companies were stranded. Of the two DUKWs that entered the water, one grounded on

20 *Royal Engineers Battlefield Tour Normandy to the Seine* (British Army of the Rhine, 1946, completed under the direction of the Chief Engineer), p. 122.
21 Delaforce, *The Fighting Wessex Wyverns*, p. 213.

a mudbank and the other sank as it went into the river. The rest of B Company then crossed in storm boats without incident and formed a bridgehead to the left of the road bridge, clearing the area between the Seine and Vernonnet against considerable opposition.

Lieutenant Leo Davis, serving with the Signals Platoon of the 4th Somersets, wrote:

> We did not normally consider ourselves fighting soldiers, [but] for once at Vernon this altered. We had to cross the river and each group had to clear certain houses that were in view on the other side. I was given eight men to carry out the assault: my own signallers, a couple of company runners and two regimental policemen. For advice on how to conduct the assault I consulted the company runners, both riflemen. They told me that the leader dashes up to the door, kicks it open, and sprays the inside with his machine-gun and the rest follow him in. The leader was me I was plainly told. On the way over the boat engine spluttered, stopped and refused to restart and we wallowed helplessly. I had a sudden brainwave and told the men to take out their entrenching tools and to paddle like hell, [and] it worked beautifully. We arrived on the far shore and as I jumped off the boat, I fell flat on my face in the mud which blocked the mechanism of my Sten-gun. At the first house I kicked in the door and pulled the trigger and heard a dull thud as the breach-block slammed forward. Just as well really as the house was crammed with 30 to 40 women and children, refugees.[22]

When night feall, the Germans sent out strong patrols to probe the positions held by the Somersets, who could hear them clearly as they approached. Each time they got too close for comfort, Captain Hancock would call down a barrage on them, forcing them to retire. The remainder of the night passed peacefully for A and C Companies on the island.

At first light on 26 August, D Company, commanded by Major Garner, crossed in storm boats without incident. They proceeded to clear the remainder of Vernonnet and established themselves up the valley before them, turning the spur from the rear. On the spur they destroyed four German 20mm anti-aircraft guns that were dug into the side of a sunken lane, guns which had been responsible for many of the British casualties and were trained on the crossing sites.

Brigadier George Herbert Leo Mole, DSO,[23] CO of 129 Brigade, was by now very disconcerted regarding the situation at the start of the attack. In the original plan, the 1st Worcesters were to follow the 5th Wiltshires over the river and pass through their positions to the high ground above Vernonnet. After it was realised that the first waves of the assault were not going to plan, no orders for the Worcesters to advance were issued. Reports coming back to Mole were disturbing, and he met with General Thomas, 43rd Wessex Division's CO, near the river front. Lieutenant Patrick Spencer-Moore, ADC to Thomas, could see that the senior officers were not at all happy:

> I could see that Thomas was a little agitated and caught snatches of his conversation with Brigadier Mole. He seemed to be trying to get Mole to move the 4th Somersets to a new

---

22 Lipscomb, *History of the 4th Battalion Somerset Light Infantry*, p. 87.
23 Brigadier George Herbert Leo Mole, DSO and Bar, MC, Commanding 129 Brigade, was mortally wounded on 14 November 1944 and died the same day, aged 47. He is buried in Brunssum War Cemetery, Netherlands.

site and prodded the map saying: "Have you tried to get in round there?" The plan was obviously going wrong.²⁴

The 1st Battalion Worcestershire Regiment tries to cross the Seine

Headquarters of 129 Brigade now ordered Lieutenant Colonel Robert Osborne-Smith, CO of the 1st Worcesters, to cross by the badly damaged road bridge that night, and with this in mind the 1st Worcesters moved into the streets of Vernon and up a ladder onto the foot of the broken bridge. As A Company moved forward over the bridge, a hail of mortar bombs fell among them. A Sergeant Jennings led the first platoon onto the bridge and began to plod wearily across it in the dark amid the chaos, but as they approached the enemy side Jennings set off a booby trap and was wounded along with several others. A hail of Spandau fire swept the approach and bullets ricocheted off the steel work, one man being killed. To the right, about 50 yards from the bridge exit, was a large concrete emplacement, from where German machine gunners had the Worcesters pinned down, preventing any forward movement. The noise seemed to draw more fire onto the bridge access and the rest of the platoon withdrew hastily into the houses on the near shore at Vernon.

Lieutenant Stanley Trimnell was waiting to go forward with his men of the 1st Worcesters:

> We were ordered to retreat and find cover from the heavy mortar and machine-gun fire coming from the far side of the river. Our assault crossing was now postponed until first light next day. I took my platoon into the cellar of a second-hand furniture shop. Much to our delight it was stocked with old mattresses and a stock of home-made bottled wine.²⁵

Private Peter Mann of the 1st Worcesters was a very young recruit and was fretting about his future:

> I became quite anxious as we were told it would be up to us to cross the bridge the following morning. I spent the night in the porch of Vernon church near the river. I got no sleep and my thoughts raced in my head; would we get across? Would I survive? How would I cope?²⁶

Other men of the 1st Worcesters also spoke of how they spent that night before anticipating going into action. Captain Bryan Elder said:

Private Peter Mann, 1st Battalion Worcestershire Regiment. (Courtesy of P. Mann)

24 Ford, *Assault Crossing The River Seine*, p. 79.
25 *Worcestershire Regiment.com* <www.worcestershireregiment.com> (accessed 6 March 2021).
26 *WW2: People's War* <www.bbc.co.uk/ww2peopleswar> (accessed 21 May 2021).

> I found a fairly comfortable resting place in the local cinema and managed to get a few hours. precious sleep.[27]

Lieutenant John Davies recorded:

> I spent the night huddled up on a staircase in the Rue Carnot near the church. Although the place was not very comfortable I succeeded in getting a few hours' sleep.[28]

Corporal William Gould of the Signals Platoon added:

> After we were driven back, we lay down in any sheltered spot during the hours of darkness and fed on our iron rations. It was while we waited that Major Watson, the company commander, stressed upon us the vital importance of our job in providing communications when we do cross.[29]

Attempts to silence the German machine-gun fire with mortar and artillery fire failed, and another attempt to cross the river had come to nothing. Lieutenant Colonel Osborne-Smith was all ready to order the men over the bridge again regardless of the cost when Brigadier Mole decided to task the 5th Wiltshires with clearing the opposition from the far bank at first light.

The 5th Wiltshires had met with fierce opposition, the attempt to cross the road bridge had met with failure and two companies of the 4th Somersets were marooned on an island on the left. General Thomas' problems were increasing by the hour, and in the darkness the battle plan was falling badly behind schedule and needed reviewing. At midnight, Mole and Thomas met again and decided upon changes for the next phase of the attack. Lieutenant Colonel Lipscomb was now to land his next two companies of the 4th Somersets near Vernonnet further upstream, and the two companies on the island were to re-embark and follow them over. The 1st Worcesters were to make another attempt to cross the damaged road bridge at first light, whatever the cost. To assist this attack, the 5th Wiltshires would land their remaining two companies downstream of the hard-pressed A Company, near the old bridge, and capture Vernonnet. The clearing of the village was essential for the operation to succeed, and in the meantime the survivors of A Company, who were short of ammunition and holding off determined German counter-attacks on the white house, would have to manage as best they could.

Sappers under fire, 25 August

Lieutenant Colonel T.H. Evill, Royal Engineers, instructed 553 and 204 Field Companies to begin constructing the Class 9 bridge codenamed 'David'. The officer overseeing this operation had put armoured bulldozers to work at 2000 hours on the 25th to level the approaches to the bridge, but each time an engine started up a shower of mortar bombs would descend on the sappers as they worked. The construction area for the rafts that would make up the bridge

---

27 *WW2: People's War* <www.bbc.co.uk/ww2peopleswar> (accessed 6 March 2021).
28 *Worcestershire Regiment.com* <www.worcestershireregiment.com> (accessed 6 March 2021).
29 Worcestershire Regiment.com <www.worcestershireregiment.com> (accessed 6 March 2021).

Sappers working hard under fire preparing a raft, shielded by the trees of an island. (Courtesy of M. Hearst)

was sheltered from the enemy fire by an island and the raft building carried on apace, in the hope that the enemy would be cleared from their positions by dawn. The sappers constructed numerous rafts while the area around them was under fire from machine guns, 20mm anti-aircraft guns and mortar fire. The proposed bridging area was also under constant machine-gun fire, so the sappers moored all the completed rafts under the lee of the island, ready to be moved into position as soon as the enemy had been cleared from the high ground. At one point, men who were manoeuvring two completed rafts were killed by mortar fire and the rafts were washed downstream and disappeared into the night. As dawn broke, the enemy fire was as heavy as ever and movement was impossible.

Sapper James Collins served in the 584th Field Company, Royal Engineers, and although very young his hard training on the Isle of Wight now came into use:

> While we were building the rafts, our divers recovered an assault boat from the middle of the river that was full of bodies. We buried its occupants from the Wiltshire Regiment nearby. We were now being blooded into a real war.[30]

Sergeant Patrick Tucker, Royal Engineers, recounted what happened when they were spotted by enemy gunners:

---

30 J. Collins, correspondence with author (Exeter, 1987).

Troops of the *I/Grenadier-Regiment 148*, *49.Infanterie-Division*, one carrying a *Panzerfaust*, enter the rear of Vernonnet to the sound of gunfire. (Author's collection)

We were fired on by an anti-aircraft gun set high up on the clifftop. What made this particularly frightening was the fact that the enemy gun was firing tracer shells and the men could see the projectiles snaking towards them; when they hit, they flew all over the place. The only cover available to us was the bulldozer itself and it was an eerie sensation for us to shelter behind its thick blade as it was being spattered by small enemy shells. It was impossible to move without drawing enemy fire.[31]

German reinforcements arrive, 25 August

Part of the German *49. Infanterie-Division*, the *I/Grenadier-Regiment 148* left Boulogne on 15 August to reinforce defences on the Seine. The troops had no transport and had to rely on bicycles. On the way to Vernonnet, their numbers had been depleted because of problems with bicycles and other mishaps; the men who were left behind would have to make their own way on foot later, was a reflection of the disorganised state of the German forces in northern France at that time. They had no heavy weapons, tanks or artillery support. As the British formulated their new plan of attack, the infantry of *I/Grenadier-Regiment 148* arrived in Vernonnet from the direction of Gisors. As they entered the rear of the town, they walked into a battle now in

---

31 P. Tucker, correspondence with author (Somerset, 1992).

full swing; their original purpose had been to relieve *Kampfgruppe Meyer* for 24 hours and then to pull back into regimental reserve.

They expected to find quiet static positions along the Seine, but instead found themselves in the middle of a full-scale fire-fight. They were immediately used to fill gaps in the line as the battle thundered on around them. The *49. Infanterie-Division* had lost half its strength by providing reinforcements for the *7. Armee* in Normandy, its fighting capacity being eroded without ever seeing action. This had a demoralising effect, and as the division faced its first battle the bulk of its troops consisted of non-Germans and *Hitlerjugend*. However, their arrival in Vernonnet was most opportune for the German troops already fighting there, as they stiffened the defences at the moment they were most needed. It was to prove a most uncomfortable coincidence for the 43rd Wessex Division that fresh enemy troops had arrived just as the British assault to capture Vernonnet had got underway.

A Coy, 5th Wiltshires' last stand, 25–26 August

To the right of the positions being tenuously held on the enemy shore by C Company, 5th Wiltshires, were what was left of A Company. The large white building they occupied was under constant attack by the Germans, who were advancing down the main road and railway line. The hard-pressed defenders had twice repelled counter-attacks with small-arms fire. A third attempt got into the Wiltshires' outer perimeter before being driven off, but it had been a close-run thing; the Wiltshires were fast running out of ammunition and desperately needed resupplying. Their headquarters consisted of no more than 20 men, each one with only a handful of bullets. The troops outside the house knew that they faced further attacks by the Germans which they would not be able to resist, and that the time had come to withdraw and link up with C Company on the banks of the Seine. In pairs, they left what cover they had and retreated quietly into the darkness in the direction of the river. The men remaining in the HQ house itself knew nothing of this but realised that the end would not be long in coming. Radio codes were destroyed as the Germans raked the house with heavy machine-gun fire, enemy Very lights flying into the night sky to illuminate the scene. For those men still in the house, escape was impossible.

Major Milne, the company commander, steeled himself to make a last stand and ordered his men to pile their packs and radios across a big hole that had been blown into the front wall of the house by the Germans. Tense men pointed their weapons down the road and awaited the enemy counter-attack using what cover they could find. When it came, they held their fire and waited until the last minute: every precious round of their dwindling store of ammunition had to count. The Germans halted, waiting to see if their fire was being returned, and when none came they continued their advance, assuming that the Wiltshires had fled. The crunch of hob-nailed boots on tarmac became louder as the Germans approached the house, the troops inside holding their breath and lying motionless. At nearly point-blank range, four rifles, a Sten gun and Major Milne's pistol tore into the surprised attackers. The officer leading them fell dead just feet away from the house, and those that survived turned and fled into the night. The furious Germans retaliated by firing everything they had at the house: Spandaus, small arms, mortars and grenades. Everyone in the house became a casualty and at last their desperate defence came to an end. Major Milne lay on the floor with a dead private soldier on top of him, covering him in blood. The helpless wounded, now out of ammunition, crouched low and awaited their fate. The German troops arrived, calling out "Tommy" and "*Kamerad*". For A Company, the war was over.

In the middle of the night, battalion headquarters landed among the positions held by C Company. Immediately they were established, the Wiltshires sent a party of men down the road in the direction of A Company's position. They arrived in the area near the white house as the last German attack was about to fall on Milne's group. In the darkness, it was difficult to tell with any accuracy what exactly was happening as tracer rounds and explosions tore through the night. The troops settled down among some trees with bullets flying all around until eventually it was realised that A Company was no more.

The 1st Battalion Worcestershire Regiment's second attempt to cross the Seine, first light, 26 August

The members of A Company, 1st Worcesters, were roused from their slumber and silently filed down to the river in the darkness, each man alone with his thoughts and bad memories of their first attempt to cross the bridge. At dawn on 26 August, a patrol from A Company climbed the ladder that took them onto the first broken span of the road bridge and cautiously crossed over. To their astonishment and delight, they found that the enemy machine gunners had gone; the Germans had been prepared to hold fast under cover of darkness, but when dawn came they would have had to face the concentrated firepower of the British artillery, tanks and mortars, and had sensibly decided that discretion was the better part of valour.

Lieutenant John McGrath of the 1st Worcesters crossed the river successfully during the hours of darkness in a DUKW with his commanding officer:

> Once on the other side we lay flat on our faces in the long grass. I was trying to make myself heard over the 18 [communications] set whilst being told to be quiet by the CO. We had made many attempts under fire to get a cable across the river but had to wait until the cold light of dawn before a cable party was able to take one over the remains of the demolished bridge and establish a direct telephone line link.[32]

Corporal William Gould and his Signals Platoon comrades of the 1st Worcesters moved forward with the lead company, carrying heavy coils of telephone wire and radio equipment:

> Dawn came and we advanced over the bridge almost without incident, but our cable took some getting over and when we eventually managed it, we were an isolated unit. When laying telephone communications, it is almost impossible to keep up with the advancing infantry. For you have of necessity to make the line safe from clumsy feet and following vehicles.[33]

---

32 Manuscript forwarded to author by J. McGrath (Corby, 1992).
33 *Worcestershire Regiment.com* <www.worcestershireregiment.com> (accessed 12 April 2021).

A Company, 1st Battalion Worcestershire Regiment, climb the ladder leading to the first expanse of the broken road bridge. First light, 26 August 1944. (Courtesy of M. Denney)

Under the cover of an artillery smokescreen, the remainder of A Company crossed the bridge and entered Vernonnet, and the rest of the battalion was not far behind them. Private Thomas Dutton entered the town and found it mostly in ruins:

> Moving off the bridge and into the town of Vernonnet, we found it was badly damaged and still on fire. Lots of buildings were in a state of collapse with bricks and debris under our feet as we moved on down the street.[34]

Sergeant Harold Harrison of the 1st Worcesters recalled:

> I was commanding 14 Platoon and after crossing the bridge we turned left and pressed down the street in front of the church. Rubble and roof tiles were everywhere underfoot, the whole place was wrecked.[35]

---

34 *Worcestershire Regiment.com* <www.worcestershireregiment.com> (accessed 12 April 2021).
35 *Worcestershire Regiment.com* <www.worcestershireregiment.com> (accessed 12 April 2021).

Despite the early morning's events, Vernonnet was not clear of the enemy; they still held the three tree-covered spurs that dominated the bridging site and other crossing points. Silently in the darkness, men of the 1st Worcesters moved from doorway to doorway looking for the enemy.

Sergeant Harrison remembered his first contact with the Germans in the town:

> We had not advanced far when 13 Platoon ahead of us, commanded by Sgt Peter Saunders, came under MG fire. Corporal D.W. Priest[36] was killed leading the first section. We were pinned down and lay flat on the ground. The MG was on the left side of the street just behind a bend. CSM Jim Lane passed down orders for us to move down the right-hand side of the street, behind the back of some houses, and to try to locate the MG position. It was difficult to get past the house and gardens, so we had to go back to our original positions.[37]

Sergeant Harold Harrison, 14 Platoon, 1st Battalion Worcestershire Regiment. (Author's collection)

Private D. Hodgkins was among the first of the 1st Worcesters into the town:

> As the leading section of my platoon, 13 Pln, we were the first to encounter the enemy. As we moved round a corner, we were greeted with a burst of MG fire from the enemy concealed in a garden behind a wall. With two of my mates, we dashed into the nearest house and ran up the stairs to a bedroom window. From this vantage point we had a clear view of the enemy MG crew below, [and] with a burst from our Bren-gun the enemy machine-gunners were killed.[38]

William Gould of the 1st Worcesters' Signals Platoon was busy with his mate, Private Denby, following the advancing troops and laying telephone cable as they went:

> Dozy Denby, my most loyal companion, worked heroically to ensure we got our cables to the far bank. Several bursts of MG fire greeted us when we arrived in Vernonnet. However, we maintained progress and reached A Coy, who had dug themselves in around the church.[39]

---

36 Corporal Douglas William Priest, 1st Battalion Worcestershire Regiment, died on 27 August 1944, aged 19. He is buried in Vernon/Vernonnet Communal Cemetery.
37 *Worcestershire Regiment.com* <www.worcestershireregiment.com> (accessed 12 April 2021).
38 *Worcestershire Regiment.com* <www.worcestershireregiment.com> (accessed 15 April 2021).
39 *Worcestershire Regiment.com* <www.worcestershireregiment.com> (accessed 16 April 2021).

Men of the 1st Battalion Worcestershire Regiment press forward through the ruins of Vernonnet. (Courtesy of N. Hardy)

Private Thomas Dutton moved through the wreckage that had once been the town with the 1st Worcesters:

> We moved to a small church on our left, passing up the side of the church and through the churchyard and up through the cemetery. Then over a fence and into a small field beyond, it was surrounded with hedges. Suddenly we could hear volleys of small arms fire up ahead, 16 Platoon had encountered the enemy.[40]

Major Alfred Albert Grubb, MC, known as Algy, who commanded B Company, 1st Worcesters,[41] passed through the recently secured village of Vernonnet and pushed on up the spur to the high ground beyond. He was ordered to advance up a track to the right of the church but was not confident of his map-reading capabilities:

> My trouble was this, I was perfectly capable of reading a map, but I rarely believed it. Somehow, I always went in the wrong direction. I did not believe that the track by the

---

40 *Worcestershire Regiment.com* <www.worcestershireregiment.com> (accessed 16 April 2021).
41 Major Alfred Albert Grubb, MC, attended a ceremony to unveil a plaque to the 1st Worcestershire Regiment at Vernon on 25 August 1992; after the ceremony he returned to his hotel in Vernon and passed away there two days later on 27 August.

church was the one that the colonel intended me to go up, [as] it did not seem to go anywhere. There was a nice little road going up the side of the hill and I thought: "That's it, he's got it wrong", for the object of the exercise was to get on top of the high ground. The road I took went round some houses and then led out of the village. It wasn't long before I realised that I was on the wrong route, but what was I to do then? It was no good turning back, [so] I decided to go on and hope for the best.[42]

To his left, Major Grubb could plainly see the spur where he should be and decided to carry on, then cross over to his original objective, but the further he went, the ground on his left fell away sharply. He was now stranded on the wrong spur and found himself advancing on the road that led to La Capelle St Ouen, in the sector being held by the 5th Wiltshires overlooking the bridging sites:

The 5th Wiltshires were somewhere on my right but were nowhere to be seen. I carried along the road, which bore round to the left at the edge of Vernonnet and then continued straight for a few hundred yards. We were advancing in two columns, one on either side of the road. As we approached the end of the straight road, an enemy machine-gun opened on the leading troops.[43]

Private Albert Kings was with the lead section when the Germans opened fire:

As we moved up the hill from Vernonnet I was a Bren-gunner in the middle of the lead section. Suddenly a Spandau opened up and I heard a cry behind me, someone had been hit. We went to ground on either side of the road and took cover, [but] my best friend Joe Cartwright[44] was killed here. I looked behind me and saw Bert Smith[45] lying wounded and calling for a stretcher-bearer. Two bearers ran forward waving a Red Cross flag and lifted Bert onto a stretcher. Then the German machine-gun opened fire again hitting the two stretcher-bearers and mortally wounding Bert Smith. The stretcher-bearers were called Ernest Jones and Walter Greathead.[46][47][48]

Private Peter Mann was with B Company that day:

We were pinned down by a German Spandau and several of the chaps were hit. Our stretcher-bearers, who were waving a Red Cross flag, bravely attended to the wounded in the open, only to become victims of this machine-gun. As I hugged the ground, with

---

42   Ford, *Assault Crossing the River Seine*, p. 103.
43   Ford, *Assault Crossing the River Seine*, p. 103.
44   Private Joseph James Cartwright, 1st Battalion Worcestershire Regiment, was killed in action on 26 August 1944, aged 20. He is buried in Bayeux War Cemetery, France.
45   Private Bert Smith, 1st Battalion Worcestershire Regiment, died of his wounds on 27 August 1944, aged 34. He is buried in Bayeux War Cemetery, France.
46   *WW2: People's War* <www.bbc.co.uk/ww2peopleswar> (accessed 12 April 2021).
47   Private Ernest Jones, 1st Battalion Worcestershire Regiment, was killed on 26 August 1944, aged 32. He is buried in Bayeux War Cemetery, France.
48   Private Walter Greathead, 1st Battalion Worcestershire Regiment, was wounded but survived the war.

bullets whistling past my ears, I was terrified, but by then the adrenalin was flowing and we had no choice but to continue.[49]

The sight of unarmed stretcher-bearers, carrying the flag of the Red Cross, being killed as they tended the wounded infuriated those who witnessed it, but the Spandau fire kept them pinned down, unable to get at their tormentors. The continuous fire swept up and down the road, a stream of bullets ripping up the verges and killing any man who was exposed. Corporal William Gould was among the 1st Worcesters lying in a ditch as the bullets flew around them:

We were pinned down for some considerable time and could see the enemy bullets leaving white marks on the tarmac road as they ricocheted off it.[50]

With his men slowly being picked off one by one, Major Grubb knew the situation was critical. Further back down the road was a track that led to a chalk quarry, and Grubb decided to send Lieutenant Rex Fellows and a few men up it in an attempt to outflank the Spandau crews. Grubb commented on Lieutenant Fellows: "He was a good chap, but being new to the company, he was red raw."[51] Grubb's concerns were unfounded, Fellows leading his men to the quarry and putting in an attack only to find that the enemy were withdrawing. Fellows recalled:

Lieutenant Rex Fellows, 1st Battalion Worcestershire Regiment. (Author's collection)

As we moved quickly through the woods it was very noisy. We reached a location behind the German machine-gun, now only 50 yards away. We were charging down the steep slope, firing from the hip as we did so, and saw the Germans fleeing up the road.[52]

The men who had been pinned down for so long wanted revenge for the atrocity they had observed with the stretcher-bearers. As they consolidated near the fork in the road, the Germans began sending over mortar bombs in great numbers, forcing them to take cover. The Germans had a strong force hidden in the undergrowth before the Worcesters. To the right of the Worcesters were high cliffs and to their left the ground fell away steeply, and visibility was down to only a few yards. Suddenly, silence then fell as both sides paused for breath. Major Grubb

49 *WW2: People's War* <www.bbc.co.uk/ww2peopleswar> (accessed 21 May 2021).
50 *WW2: People's War* <www.bbc.co.uk/ww2peopleswar> (accessed 3 May 2021).
51 *WW2: People's War* <www.bbc.co.uk/ww2peopleswar (accessed 3 May 2021).
52 *WW2: People's War* <www.bbc.co.uk/ww2peopleswar> (accessed 5 April 2021).

looked down the road in the direction of Vernonnet and to his amazement saw his friend, the commanding officer of the 4th Somersets, Lieutenant Colonel William Roberts, walking up the road in full view. Roberts looked down at Grubb, who was laid in a ditch, and asked: "Bloody hell, what are you doing here?" As he was being told of the situation in the area, he remained stood upright on the road. Enemy fire then hit all around his feet, tearing up the road surface, to which Roberts exclaimed, "That was bloody rude!"[53], before starting back down the road at a steady pace.

In the meantime, the Germans had infiltrated along the high ground to Grubb's right. Sergeant David Kerrigan had been caught by them as he was relieving himself in the chalk quarry, being shot through the head.[54] With the whole company now in danger of being outflanked, Grubb decided to lead a patrol up to the high ground on the right to expel the Germans who were overlooking his position, only to find that when he got there that they had withdrawn. He left his patrol in position on the thickly wooded plateau and returned to the main force. Major Grubb had established his company in a solid position astride the main road, blocking any German moves down it, and they would now wait until the 5th Wiltshires could consolidate positions on the high ground, where they could protect his right flank in preparation for a further forward move.

During the afternoon of the 26th, Major Grubb's B Company, 1st Worcesters, was hidden down a road that led to the village of Bois Jerome, with the enemy concealed in woods just beyond them. Six Germans riding bicycles in the direction of Vernonnet took the Worcesters completely by surprise and were in among the British position before anyone realised. Corporal Chambers coolly took aim with his Bren gun and killed them all, leaving bicycles and dead Germans strewn across the road. The surprised Tommies leapt out of their hiding places and dragged everything off the road and out of sight before returning to their well camouflaged posts. A few moments later, a German lorry drove into view. A Bren gunner in close proximity opened up and the lorry hurtled forward as the alarmed driver put his foot down. As the lorry sped through the British positions, numerous bullets tore through the canvas sides but the driver continued on his way, weaving his vehicle from one side of the road to the other. He plunged down the hill and disappeared out of sight. Grubb could not believe the lorry had got through his position:

> The lorry was immediately captured when it reached the village of Vernonnet further down the road. It was subsequently found to contain a complete field photographic unit. Inside were numerous Leica cameras and other valuable equipment, none of which ever made it across the Seine: it all disappeared into kitbags as spoils of war. It was worth a fortune, and we missed it all.[55]

The 4th and 5th Battalions Wiltshire Regiment, 26 August

In the early hours of 26 August, the main body of the 5th Wiltshires stumbled over the old bridge, and after an exhausting night climb in the dark they reached the top of the escarpment,

---

53 Ford, *Assault Crossing the River Seine*, p. 110.
54 Sergeant David Hugh Kerrigan, 1st Battalion Worcestershire Regiment, was killed on 26 August 1944, aged 31. Kerrigan is buried in Bayeux War Cemetery, France.
55 Ford, *Assault Crossing the River Seine*, p. 117.

Men of the 5th Battalion Wiltshire Regiment crossing the Seine. (Courtesy of M. Denney)

dug-in and rested. As dawn broke, they realised that their present position was vulnerable. Enemy machine-gun posts and snipers were still on the spur in great numbers, and the thick woods on this high ground were only a few yards from their trenches. They awaited the expected counter-attack to throw them off the spur. C Company alone, led by a Lieutenant Holly, was not of sufficient strength to clear the high ground without support; D Company was in Vernonnet and B Company was blocking the road along the river valley. They had to wait for the 4th Wiltshires to cross into the bridgehead before further progress could be made in clearing out the enemy, who were creating havoc with the bridge-building below.

During the hours of darkness, news was received in Vernon of the progress of the 1st Worcesters in Vernonnet. The 4th Wiltshires then formed up in the streets of Vernon and filed down to the Seine. One company at a time crossed the old bridge and moved into the bridgehead without incident; it would seem that the enemy was busy giving the engineers their full attention as they laboured to build the bridges. News began to filter back of the trouble being experienced by the 5th Wiltshires. The 4th Wiltshires were alarmed at the news, so when they reached the far side of the river they moved up the river valley and soon arrived at the blocking position held by B Company, 5th Wiltshires. They passed through their sister battalion, and it wasn't long before they reached the white house where A Company had made its last stand only a few hours before. The wreckage from the fight lay all around the area, and the dead, still lying in the open, were slowly decomposing in the warm August sunshine. B Company of the 5th Wiltshires was now free to join Grubb's company on top of the spur, and once they arrived the two companies entered the woods and started the task of clearing the Germans from the dense scrub that covered the plateau. The Wiltshires slowly winkled out the enemy from their hiding places. On top of the spur, the 4th Wiltshires beat a path through the thick wooded undergrowth with machetes, which meant their progress was at a snail's pace. However, they made such a racket that the enemy's attention was diverted away from the riverbank to meet the new threat. At one point, the men of the 4th Wiltshires stumbled upon a group of Germans playing cards. The startled Germans grabbed their weapons and jumped to their feet, and both sides began blazing away at each other. After a fierce fire-fight, the surviving Germans pulled back into the protection of the wood, leaving their dead behind them. A and B Companies on the high ground and C Company at the bottom of the slopes slowly flushed out the Germans from their well-established positions.

Many of the machine-gun posts that were located along the cliff face had poured their fire upon the sappers below with devastating effect. Some had been knocked out by tank fire from Vernon, and the machine gunners of the 8th Middlesex had also taken their toll. The British troops advanced and carefully inspected each dug-out with great care, as booby traps were often left to maim or kill the unwary. In silence, they worked their way through well-camouflaged positions. Sergeant James Quigley remembered some tense moments:

> Each slitter had to be inspected to make sure Jerry had really gone, and some of the positions were quite elaborate with gear all over the place. No wonder most of them couldn't be spotted by our observers. It was a nerve-wracking experience and took us quite some time to complete, but eventually we moved on into the undergrowth.[56]

Further into the woods, D Company encountered several German self-propelled guns which opened fire on them, forcing the men to retreat as shells began to explode in the trees all around. The troops could not stalk these guns as the undergrowth was so dense, limiting visibility to just a few yards. The Wiltshires tried to close with the enemy on numerous occasions, but any movement brought down a hail of shells that broke up any attack. Darkness was falling as the self-propelled guns finally pulled back to prepared positions, by which time the whole cliff face opposite the crossing sites was cleared.

The completion of the first bridge, codename 'David', 26 August

The engineers below enjoyed only a brief respite from their tormentors as the harassing fire aimed at them was resumed. During the break, work was restarted on the folding boat bridge as numerous rafts were ferried upstream and put into position. The pontoon bridge at last began to take shape. As the enemy fire resumed, the sappers suffered numerous casualties in their exposed positions, but pressed on with their work resolutely.

Sapper Roy Young of 533rd Field Company, Royal Engineers, worked on the river crossing:

> Each landing bay, with their access ramps, was built on the shore and shoved into the river, [while] floating pontoon bays, that were to connect the two landing bays across the Seine,

---

56 J. Quigley, correspondence with author (Taunton, 1992).

were assembled downstream of the bridging site. It was my job to supervise the assembly of these bays. Each bay of two pontoons with Bailey panel superstructure was towed into position by a motor tug. The long access ramps of the two landing bays were on rollers to allow for ease of construction and to accommodate changes in water level.[57]

Sapper Leslie Trimmer, also with the 533rd Field Company, described the attempt to build the bridge under fire as one of the worst days of the war for him:

My friend Ted Lawless[58] was hit in the back by a mortar bomb fragment[;] he was a fine musician and spoke German. Bill Burns[59] also died that night which was dark and raining. Owing to intermittent shellfire we were forced to build some of the rafts for the bridge upstream and float them down into position. The bridge was nearly completed by mid-day only to have a shell land right in the middle of it. Sgt Petre walked out onto the bridge and carried a wounded man back to safety.[60]

In the late afternoon of the 26th, General Thomas and Brigadier Mole arrived at the banks of the Seine while it was under heavy fire. Both were alarmed by the noise of the battle taking place across the river and the situation the sappers found themselves in. Mole watched in fascination the movements of his men he could see on the high ground beyond the river. During the late afternoon, the sappers were able to continue their work on the Class 9 bridge, and, without the enemy's harassing fire, showed their skill at bridge building. Crowds of French civilians looked on in awe as the sappers worked hard to complete their task. Before they could finish, however, the Germans gave the exhausted engineers one more problem to solve. A dam downstream was destroyed, causing the water level to fall and exposing stretches of slimy mud on each bank. Lieutenant Colonel Evill of the Royal Engineers found that the new water level stopped him reaching the far bank, but after some thought and consultation with his men he decided to end the bridge just short of the far bank and to build a trestle that would enable his men to span the gap to the shore. This took more time, but the bridge, called 'David', was finally finished by 1730 hours, when the first vehicles moved across it into the bridgehead.

Private Arthur Eade, Royal Army Service Corps, arrived in Vernon with a lorry full of equipment for the troops on the far bank:

I drove my 3-tonner down a hill into Vernon where they had built a pontoon bridge over the river. I crossed it and drove to Giverny, where the 4th Somersets were stationed. They had cleared the woods on the high ground, so it was safe for us to get to them. Buildings were in a state of ruin because of the hammer they had taken but the French people were wandering all around and seemed really pleased to see us. The poor Somersets had taken a

---

57 *WW2: People's War* <www.bbc.co.uk/ww2peopleswar> (accessed 1 May 2021).
58 Sapper Terence Lawless, 533rd Field Coy, Royal Engineers, was killed in action on 26 August 1944, aged 26. He is buried in Vernon Communal Cemetery, France.
59 Sapper William Mellen Burns, 533rd Field Coy, Royal Engineers, was killed in action on 26 August 1944. He is buried in Vernon Communal Cemetery, France.
60 *WW2: People's War* <www.bbc.co.uk/ww2peopleswar> (accessed 1 May 2021).

pasting. We brought to them picks, shovels, blankets, overcoats, mortar bombs, fixed line tripods for their Bren-guns and everything they needed at the front.[61]

214 Brigade, 26 August

Now the infantry was on the enemy shore and consolidating the bridgehead, General Thomas decided that it was time he introduced a second brigade into the battle. The men of 214 Brigade, minus the 1st Worcesters, which had moved forward as part of the assault group, arrived in the sector the previous night and were camped 6 miles from Vernon in a large wood near Pacy. Lieutenant Colonel George Taylor, CO of the 5th DCLI, had been ordered to prepare his battalion to move over the newly erected boat bridge and to act as the advanced guard for 214 Brigade. News came on 26 August of the setbacks that had been suffered during the first assault, that there was no new road bridge and that the clearing of Vernonnet and the cliffs opposite had not yet been completed. The move across the river by the Duke of Cornwall's had to be postponed, but by 1600 hours most of them had arrived in Vernon. A report was received from across the river by battalion headquarters that the forest was clear of the enemy. Lieutenant Colonel Taylor rushed to tell brigade commander Brigadier Essame, who was talking to General Thomas, the good news. Thomas was delighted to hear something positive at last, and at the same time was told how the 4th Somersets had mopped up the machine-gun nests and sniper positions on the cliffs to the left of Vernonnet. Thomas made the decision to put 214 Brigade across the river without delay. He was committing his infantry into this tight bridgehead and was constantly on the alert for the expected German counter-attack.

The 7th Somersets were instructed to lead the way over the old road bridge and to advance into the forest of Vernon, with the DCLI following. They were to advance down the river valley and take the village of Pressagny L'Orgueilleux, which was a short distance from the proposed tank ferry site. As they entered Vernonnet, they were met by crowds of excited civilians eager to meet their liberators and show their gratitude; they lined the roads and pressed into the hands of the marching soldiers small gifts of fruit, cider and wine. The 7th Somersets marched up to the high ground and passed through their sister battalion, the 4th Somersets, before disappearing into the dark interior of the Forest of Vernon. They had been used to fighting in the close fields and meadows of the Bocage and to digging-in at the first opportunity to get below ground as quickly as possible. But here, in the deep and dark forest, the closely packed trees provided an abundance of cover. The men prepared themselves for an unfamiliar type of warfare, with the knowledge that every tree could conceal an enemy position or sniper. As the light faded, Lieutenant Colonel W.J. Nichol, CO of the 7th Somersets, decided to position his troops in a formation that would be ready for the enemy if they attacked during the night.

The 5th DCLI, commanded by Lieutenant Colonel George Taylor, followed closely behind the 7th Somersets over the old road bridge. They received the same ecstatic welcome from the populace of Vernonnet, and in spite of the distractions moved steadily on through the village. The troops advanced to the village of Pressagny L'Orgueilleux without incident, arriving there

---

61   A. Eade, correspondence with author (Castleford, 1990).

in the early evening. The battalion, consisting of only three companies because of the casualties it had sustained in the heavy fighting earlier, covered the left flank of the division's bridgehead. Lieutenant Colonel Taylor placed two companies just short of the houses of the village, with a third company 500 yards back in the direction of Vernonnet in the forest to block an area where various tracks met. He established his battalion headquarters in the Chateau-de-la-Madeleine, which was situated on the road that ran into the village. The house was being used as a home for orphan boys and was run by a monk, Brother Andre, who made the men feel most welcome. Taylor remembered the feeling of euphoria among the troops at the absence of any enemy in the area; many believed that the German Army was finished, but they were soon to be disabused of this notion:

> Having advanced all the way since beating the Germans in Normandy, one felt that the war had not long left to run. Later that night, as we were having supper, my intelligence officer David Wilcox asked: "What about the blackout sir?" to which I replied: "To hell with the blackout, the war is almost over." Rather a stupid remark on my part I'm afraid, as later events were to prove.[62]

The start of the second bridge: codename 'Goliath', 26–27 August

At 1400 hours on 26 August, the CO of the 15th Kent GHQ Troops, Royal Engineers, Lieutenant Colonel Lindley Fayle, was waiting in the centre of Vernon for the reconnaissance officer, Lieutenant Tanner of the 584th Field Company, to arrive. Tanner informed his superior that the remainder of the bridge-building party was having great difficulty getting there because the Americans would not allow the engineers to pass through their lines of communication. General Thomas had ordered that the tank raft was to be completed by the following morning, but it now seemed very unlikely that the units required to do this would get through to the Seine on time. Fayle was given the 207th Field Park Company, part of 43rd Division's engineers, and although it would take longer for these troops to fulfil their task compared to his own specialist engineers, the preliminary work had to be started in preparation for their arrival if the raft was to be completed by dawn. Lieutenant Tanner left with orders to get the rest of the units through to Vernon as a matter of urgency.

In the late afternoon of 26 August, work commenced on the Bailey bridge. The line of the bridge was to be between the new Class 9 bridge and the old demolished road bridge. The engineers had been waiting patiently, but as they began to get to grips with the filling-in of a large bomb crater on the Vernon shore it was realised that the pair of bulldozers needed for the task had been borrowed to repair the road between Pacy and Vernon. They were brought back to Vernon by 1700 hours, by which time work on both sides of the river was well under way. The construction of the Bailey bridge could now proceed unhindered as both sides of the river were in friendly hands and the towering cliffs opposite had been cleared of the enemy. The two engineer companies began to build out from both banks, while a third assembled the pontoons and towed them into position in mid-river. The masonry on the Vernon side was blasted away so

---

62 Manuscript forwarded to author by K. Hamilton (Worcestershire, 1991).

From the Vernon bank, lorries can be seen moving across the Class 9 bridge named 'David', while the engineers work to finish the heavier Class 40 'Goliath' bridge. (Author's collection)

that the engineers could make a gentle slope down the bank to the entry site, but the exit site on the far bank was piled high with large logs which had to be moved to another location. As the work progressed, Lieutenant Colonel Thomas Lloyd, Royal Engineers, looked on while stray shells fell around the engineers as they worked, each company reporting a few casualties. Lloyd remembered: "There was no stonking in the accepted meaning of the word and on the whole, it was good to be in Vernon on that August day."[63]

Sappers moved telegraph poles to the bank to allow easy access for the pontoons to be lowered into the water by the bridging sappers. Three-ton lorries stationed in the railway goods yards brought the pontoons to the assembly areas; each pontoon weighed a ton and was 6ft wide and 3ft deep. Piers were constructed and towed away to the bridging site, while on each bank large piles of Bailey sections were deposited. Once the preparatory work on the approaches was completed, construction could begin on the bridge itself. Though unrecognisable as a bridge so far, the Class 40 Bailey bridge, codenamed 'Goliath', would soon take an unmistakable shape.

Lieutenant Colonel Lloyd watched from the shore as his men toiled to finish their task:

> The company had three cranes spaced along the riverbank. As soon as a lorry had backed up alongside a crane a sapper clambered up onto the pontoons and fastened the crane

63 T. Lloyd, correspondence with author (Devon, 1991).

sling to the upper one. The crane took the weight and the lorry then shunted forward from under the pontoon, leaving it suspended, with the sapper still on board making sure the bungs were in. The crane then swung the pontoons out and lowered it onto the telegraph pole launching ways, broadside on to the river. Other sappers fastened reins to it; the original one then disconnected the crane sling, and then, clinging on to the hook, had himself swung up again onto the lorry, which by this time had shunted back into position to repeat the process. Often, he was hardly clear before the men holding the reins paid out, and let the pontoon go rushing down the ways in a crescendo that ended in an almighty splash. All to the accompaniment of much the same backchat as would have been used by Shakespeare's soldiery on an evening such as this.[64]

The people of Vernon were fascinated by all of this bustle and activity. One French civilian watching the bridge-construction was Jacques Cambuza:

It was miraculous to witness the orderly manner in which the English soldiers worked to build the bridge. Firstly, they had to demolish one of the two very superior residences which were on the main street close to the Pont-de-Vernon. Then they pulled down a house that had been burned by the Germans a few days previously. They moved hundreds of cubic metres of earth in order to make a smooth descent towards the bank of the Seine. All the while perfect order reigned. Some heaved heavy materials around, others in lorries brought up steel plates from a depot back in the town. Everything seemed to have been worked out to an exact plan. As a bulldozer lifted up building materials, the soldiers one metre in front of the machine, would drop back in perfect discipline. Not a moment was wasted. Out on the river, pontoons were manoeuvred into position by small boats. With the light beginning to fade, girders were thrown from one pontoon to another, and the bridges were built before my very eyes.[65]

By 2100 hours on 26 August, a stiff breeze had blown up, and the night was cloudy and heavy with rain. Meanwhile, the trucks and half-tracks belonging to the delayed engineers finally arrived in Vernon; it had taken some delicate negotiations to get past the American checkpoint and vital hours of daylight had been squandered. A relieved Lieutenant Tanner wasted no time in directing them down to the river. The rafting experts of the 15th Kent GHQ Troops were at last ready to begin work on the mighty 'Goliath'. The bridge was already taking shape as daylight faded, and the situation in the bridgehead had improved considerably: within 24 hours, two brigades were on the far shore, and thanks to the completion of the Class 9 bridge, more troops and vehicles were moving into the lodgement area to support the infantry.

General Thomas hoped to have the Bailey bridge completed so he could move tanks and guns over the river to further strengthen his position. Throughout the morning of the 27th, the newly arrived engineers worked on the Class 40 'Goliath' bridge under fire from the south by a distant enemy gun that was firing constantly. Two boats and two floating buoys were hit and sunk. One shell landed on the bridge itself, wounding or killing 20 sappers.

64   Manuscript forwarded to author by H. Williams (Hartlepool, 1994).
65   Ford, *Assault Crossing the River Seine*, pp. 123–24.

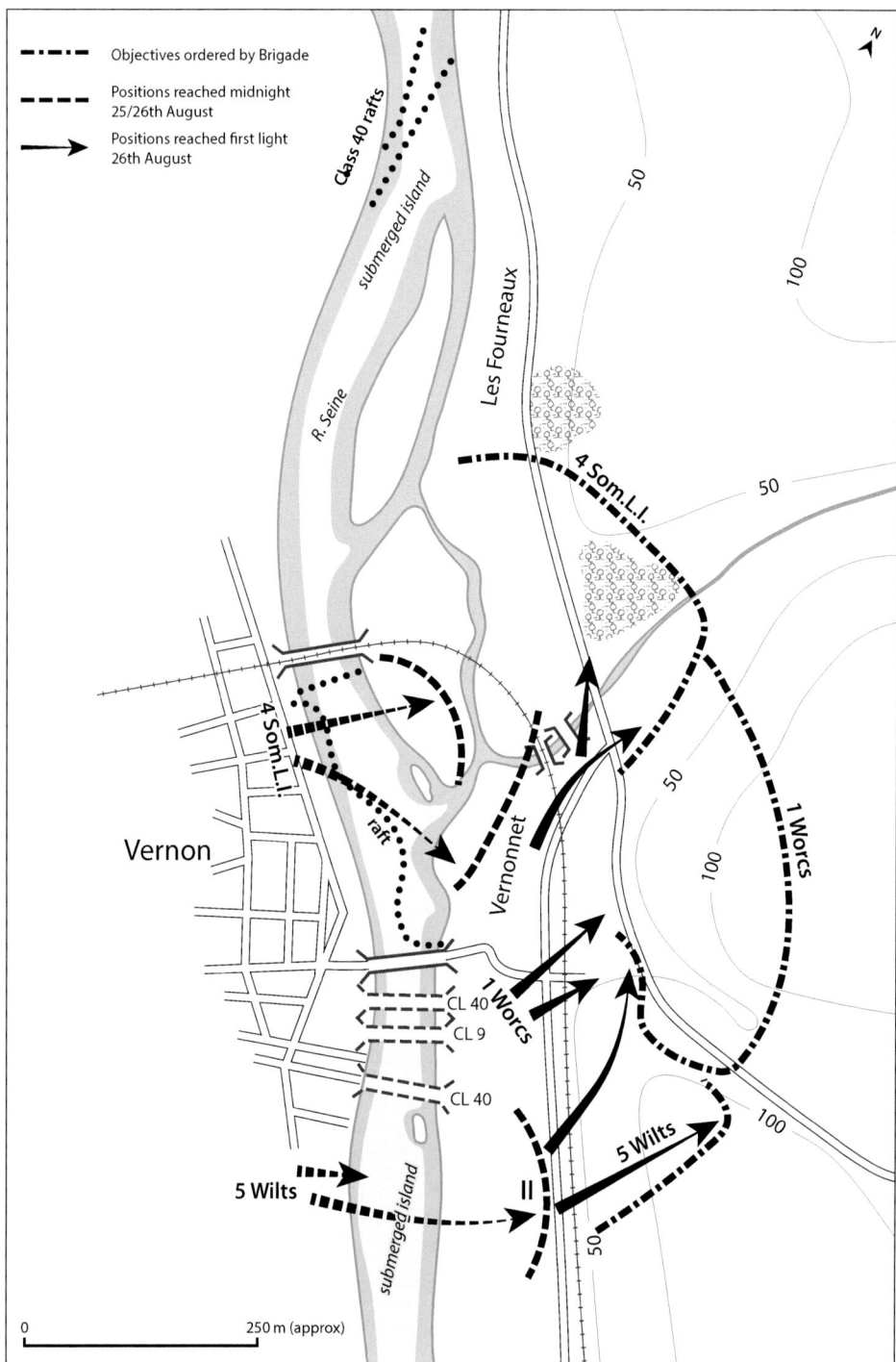

Assault Crossing at Vernon, 43rd Wessex Division, 25/26 August 1944.

The bridgehead was only 3 miles long and a mile deep, but the British controlled the area. The hard-pressed infantry dug-in for the night, ready to continue the advance at first light on 27 August. It was to be a quiet night for most troops, but unknown to them the Germans were silently gathering their strength ready for the dawn.

Kampfgruppen Meyer and *Schrader*, 27 August

During the late afternoon of 26 August, a reconnaissance flight by Messerschmitt 110s flew over the crossing area, revealing to the Germans the full scale of the assault taking place. *Generalleutnant* Macholtz, CO of the *49. Infanterie-Division*, had ordered a counter-attack on the night of the 26th, but in the chaos his orders went astray and an assault was not possible as German units had become inextricably mixed up. Macholtz had as his reserve the remainder of the *49. Infanterie-Division*, which was organised as *Kampfgruppe Schrader*, which was itself divided into two groups. The first group, consisting of four companies supported by three Tiger tanks, was given the task of advancing from Tilly to Vernonnet and taking the spur to the east which overlooked the site of the Class 40 bridge. The second group, comprising two companies, was to be the reserve and was to take Bois-Jerome-St-Ouen. Had these attacks been executed late on the 26th by *Kampfgruppen Meyer* and *Schrader*, the situation might have been very serious for the British, but when Macholtz and his staff finally got his formations organised and on the move the blow came far too late.

Counter-attack: *Kampfgruppe Meyer*, 27 August; the 5th Battalion Duke of Cornwall's Light Infantry

The 5th DCLI was sitting in an all-round defensive position south of Pressagny L'Orgueilleux. The Cornishmen were aware of the presence of German troops in or around Pressagny, and patrols went out during the night searching for intelligence on their dispositions. Eventually, the situation settled down during the hours of darkness. One patrol from B Company was returning through the village in the pouring rain when a German patrol spotted them. As the DCLI men reached their lines, shadowy figures could be observed moving behind the them. When they were challenged, the Germans replied with a burst of fire and within seconds were in among the British troops. In the confusion, both sides fired at anything that moved, it being impossible in the darkness to tell friend from foe. This brief but bloody struggle ended when the Germans withdrew back into the village.

When the main counter-attack came just before dawn on the 27th, by two companies of the German *Regiment 148*, the Cornishmen were taken completely by surprise as tracer rounds tore through their sector. After heavy overnight rain, the Germans had the benefit of the cover of a thick mist as they crept through the cornfields, rushing upon the exposed positions held by a platoon of B Company. Lieutenant Colonel Taylor received a garbled message that B Company had been overrun by a strong attack, but at dawn on 27 August B Company was still holding a defensive position to the south-east of the town. The first position fell quickly as the Germans were in superior numbers. Terrified survivors fell back on A Company as the enemy burst through the newly formed gap and surrounded A Company. The men of the 43rd Wessex were

Men of the 5th Battalion Duke of Cornwall's Light Infantry pass the bodies of German troops while stalking the enemy in a heavily wooded area. (Author's collection)

shocked to find just how quickly the Germans had encircled them, the enemy now being in the rear of both companies.

In the darkness and confusion, there now followed a deadly game of hide-and-seek as each side sought out their opposite number. From their slit trenches, the Tommies kept up a continuous fusillade with Bren-gun and rifle fire. Shadowy figures appeared and disappeared in the gloom, while stick grenades and Mills bombs burst to light up the area for a second or two. Company Sergeant Major Philip of A Company found a group of Germans very close by and killed them all with a burst from his Bren gun. Fighting at close quarters was continuous as tracer rounds cut through the darkness and explosions rent the air. As the enemy were all around the Cornwalls, Major Parker decided it was time for some drastic action to ease the situation. He issued orders for his men to cease fire, and in the silence contacted battalion headquarters by telephone. He explained his situation to Lieutenant Colonel Taylor and requested that an artillery stonk be put down on his own positions. Taylor agreed to this desperate measure in the hope that the slit trenches occupied by the DCLI men would give them at least some protection.

The first salvo of shells roared through the air to land on the positions held by A Company. Earth was torn apart and sent into the air in great fountains of debris as the Cornwalls cowered in their trenches and pressed their bodies into the soft ground, while at the same time praying that they would be spared. The startled Germans were thrown into a state of confusion, and as there was no cover for them they quickly took flight into the woods to get away from the explosions that were tearing through their ranks. A Company had taken only three casualties, but two men who had been taken prisoner by the Germans were later found, having been executed by their captors.

As the retreating Germans moved eastwards through the Forest of Vernon, it was now C Company's turn to be attacked, not as expected from the front, but from the area they assumed to be safe – their rear. C Company was positioned where tracks crossed in the forest, guarding the approach through the woods. The disorganised German troops who were now on the retreat ran headlong into their rear posts and a vicious fight ensued. The Cornishmen fought valiantly but were soon overrun by superior numbers and many men were killed. Confusion reigned in D Company as terrified stragglers fell back to battalion headquarters, but luckily for them the only thought the Germans had was to get away and they disappeared into the forest as quickly as they had appeared. The whole action lasted for just 20 minutes and the men of the 5th DCLI thought themselves fortunate to have got off so lightly. The Germans had passed through their positions in the darkness and had got to within a short distance of battalion headquarters. With more determination, the German attack could have been successfully pressed home, which would have been a disaster for the bridgehead at a crucial moment in the battle. However, nothing was lost but for a number of casualties and the Cornwalls were still in possession of the road to Vernonnet and the area that was covering the tank ferry site. As dawn broke, the finishing touches were being completed on the 'Goliath' bridge and tanks would soon be crossing into the bridgehead to assist the hard-pressed infantry.

The attack on the 5th DCLI positions during the early hours of 27 August had given 214 Brigade commander Brigadier Hubert Essame great cause for concern:

> The situation looked ugly, and I was anxious for the security of the rafting site that was being covered by the DCLI, on which the re-enforcement by the tanks of 4/7th Dragoon Guards depended, [so] I therefore diverted several armoured cars to the DCLI and would send the first troop of tanks when they had landed soon after 08:00 a.m. to this flank.[66]

Brigadier Essame ordered the 1st Worcesters to begin their advance on Tilly by the Gisors road, which wound up a steep re-entrant, trees and thick undergrowth coming down as far as the road and visibility being restricted to only 15 yards on either side. The 7th Somersets were to advance on the Worcesters' left through the thick forest as far as its northern edge south of Panilleuse. Both battalions started their advance at 0800 hours, and after an advance of some 400 yards the leading Worcester troops came under machine-gun fire. This was quickly dealt with and the advance continued to push forward, but the ominous sound of tank tracks grinding and clanking forward was then heard.

As the Worcesters fought on, the 7th Somersets pressed forward through the dark forest on the left flank, where they encountered opposition. A Company had been sent out to guard the south-eastern flank at 1000 hours and was too far forward from the remainder of the battalion to be supported. The isolated group of men were taken by surprise as the Germans surrounded them and took them prisoner. A Company was not at full strength, many of the men being new additions and the company commander also having no battle experience. Lieutenant Colonel

---

66 Essame, *The 43rd Wessex Division at War*, p. 107.

Nichol wanted to keep A Company in reserve so he could introduce them gradually to battle conditions, but instead they were thrown in at the deep end.

Lieutenant John Newmark of the 7th Somersets, who would be taken prisoner that day along with 60 other men, returned from patrol to find a shocking sight:

> I heard voices outside a house speaking in German. To my astonishment there was most of A Company lined up in two rows with the major at one end, all being searched by a German officer. Other enemy troops stood around in menacing positions. I was totally baffled: had they put up a fight? I felt sure they would not have surrendered meekly. After all they were fighting soldiers. What on earth could have happened?[67]

Lance Corporal William Baron of the 7th Somersets later recounted what had happened:

> The major was leading a patrol when they came across an open area of grassland. Suddenly they came under fire, and a sergeant and the company clerk were killed. Our company was overwhelmed by scores of Germans; we had our weapons removed and were escorted back to the farmhouse.[68]

The two advancing battalions had, like all the other battalions in the division, been sadly depleted after the savage battles they had fought earlier in Normandy. A large proportion of each company was now made up of reinforcements from other units and lacked the cohesion of more seasoned troops.

Two tanks enter the bridgehead

The men of the 5th DCLI were continually under fire, but things changed in their favour when two Sherman tanks of the 4/7th Royal Dragoon Guards turned up to stabilise the situation. The two tank commanders met with Brigadier Essame and Lieutenant Colonel Taylor at the Chateau-de-la-Madeleine before they crossed the river, and would be the first to get to the other side. Essame explained what he wanted from the tanks and gave both tank commanders a free hand as to how they would achieve it.

One of the 4/7th Dragoon Guards commanders, Lieutenant Michael Trasenster, recalled:

> There was nothing worse than being messed around by some indifferent infantry commander, trying to dictate tactics, as sometimes happened with quite fatal results for all concerned. It was harder for NCO tank commanders to resist these dictates, for they were often dealing with quite senior officers, sometimes, as in this case, as high as brigadiers. On this occasion, however, all was well; Essame and Taylor were true professionals.[69]

Lieutenant Trasenster was in the lead Sherman as the two tanks rumbled slowly up the rise leading to the road that ran up the valley, where they would be in a position to stop any further enemy attacks from the north. Once they had arrived, they took up a position covering the exit from the village. The 5th DCLI were still held up short of Pressagny, but with the arrival of

---

67 Manuscript forwarded to author by J. Newmark (Exeter, 1989).
68 W. Baron, correspondence with author (Worcestershire, 1990).
69 Manuscript forwarded to author by P. Cuerdon (Hampshire, 1995).

two tanks and several armoured cars, Lieutenant Colonel Taylor was confident enough to push a strong patrol, led by two of the armoured cars, into the village. There was no sign of the enemy as the patrol passed through the now-quiet village and pressed on into the open countryside in the direction of Notre Dame-de-l'Isle. In the eerie silence, the Tommies looked in vain for the enemy, while Taylor sent one company through the village with orders to establish an observation post on the far side. At this very opportune moment, the division's machine-gun battalion, the 8th Middlesex, turned up to accompany this advanced company, and they were soon joined by the two tanks of the 4/7th Dragoon Guards. In the early morning darkness of the 27th, there had been sharp clashes with the Germans by the 5th DCLI, but since then it had been quiet around Pressagny. The infantry, machine gunners and tank crews now felt safe enough to begin the morning ritual of the brewing of tea, and they sat around chatting.

However, this peace was not to last long as German troops were spotted 400 yards downstream at the water's edge, congregating near a barge. The two Shermans took aim and opened fire on the startled Germans, shells falling among them and onto the barge, which must have been carrying petrol or ammunition as it blew up in a terrific explosion of bright yellow flame and black smoke. Giving the enemy no respite, the tanks then opened up with their heavy machine guns and continued firing with spectacular results until their stock of ammunition had been used up.

Lieutenant Trasenster said that the Sherman gun crews could work very fast when the maximum number of shells were required on a target:

> At extreme range a good loader could sometimes get four or five shells in the air at the same time, before the first one landed. The gunner kept his foot on the firing pedal and the loader kept the rounds on his lap. As the round went in, the loader kept his arm moving up and over the breech block, which closed and fired. There were risks: you lost an arm if you hesitated as the gun recoiled.[70]

This fine piece of shooting had averted a possible strong attack against the Cornwalls' flank. Any surviving enemy troops fled inland through the thick forest.

Counter-attack: *Kampfgruppe Schrader*, 27 August; the 7th Battalion Somerset Light Infantry

The battalions of the 43rd Wessex Division that were in the bridgehead had all made contact with the German *49. Infanterie-Division,* but *Generalleutnant* Macholtz had by now managed to reorganise his troops, presenting a united front against any further expansion by the British. German resistance was stiffening and Macholtz was ready to launch his counter-attack proper. The British, however, felt that the Germans had missed their chance and were now in retreat to the borders of their homeland. Macholtz had other ideas and had assembled various units from the *49. Infanterie-Division*: *Grenadier-Regiment 149* and *150* and elements of the *149. Fusilier-Abteilung*, which were now placed under the command of *Colonel* Schrader. Orders for the

---

70 Ford, *Assault Crossing the River Seine*, p. 141.

Troops and armour of *Kampfgruppe Schrader* make their way forward to meet the units of the 43rd Wessex Division in the bridgehead. (Courtesy of H. Wernemann)

counter-attack were issued on the morning of 27 August; three Tiger tanks of *Schwere Panzer-Abteilung 205* would be in support. The *Kampfgruppe* was given its objectives, while at the same time the advancing British battalions were making for the same locations. On the British right flank, the *149. Fusilier-Abteilung* moved to secure the wood west of Bois Jerome, where the 4th Somersets were approaching as they moved in to attack the village. The centre of the German attack came down the Gisors–Vernonnet road, the 1st Worcesters advancing up this same road having no idea they were about to run headlong into a strong German force supported by tanks. On the British left flank, *Kampfgruppe Schrader* was to secure the track running through the Forest of Vernon from the direction of the Chateau-de-la-Madeleine. At the same time, A Company of the 7th Somersets were trying to establish themselves in this area.

By 1000 hours, the bridgehead was being expanded by the two British brigades facing the Germans. With the tank ferry now open for business, there was armour in the bridgehead too, although the British had no idea that a counter-attack was imminent. With 130 Brigade assembling in Vernon in readiness to enter the fight across the Seine, the sappers continued to work on the bridges in readiness for the crossing of the remainder of XXX Corps, who were fast closing in on Vernon.

At the headquarters of the 7th Somersets, tense staff officers, who did not yet know of the disaster which had befallen A Company, waited in vain for news of the unit. British tanks mistakenly sent back a message that they had reached the beleaguered British troops and were firing on the enemy. It seemed as though the situation was saved until, only a few minutes later, another message from C Company informed the headquarters that they had been joined by a troop of Sherman tanks that had joined in the fight against a large German force. The tanks had not made it to the men of A Company, who were now left to their fate. The tanks of the 4/7th Royal Dragoon Guards tried to push on to reach A Company, but they could not penetrate the dense undergrowth; one tank commander was killed and the relief party ground to a halt.

D Company of the 7th Somersets now moved up to support the tanks and became engulfed in a fierce fire-fight, taking numerous casualties. The British tanks and infantry were forced back in the face of this violent assault by *Kampfgruppe Schrader* and the 7th Somersets were hard pressed to hold the ground they had. A desperate battle for survival ensued as the two surviving companies tried to stem the German advance. Major David Drury of the 7th Somersets described the difficulties facing the British troops:

> In the thick woods you could never see the enemy, when suddenly the fire came at you from out of the trees, [then] everyone immediately went to ground and started to blaze away with Bren-guns in all directions. Then we began edging forward firing like mad, trying to identify where the enemy fire was coming from. It was slow process, made more difficult by the presence of enemy snipers. Nevertheless, we had one great asset in the shape of the forward artillery observation officer. Once we had identified an enemy location we would contact him to get the details passed back to the guns. It was very frightening to be in the forest when the shells arrived, the danger being not only from the shrapnel, but also from branches and whole trees crashing down around you. It was certainly discouraging for the enemy.[71]

The 7th Somersets found that they could advance no further forward than the first set of tracks, but the line held. *Kampfgruppe Schrader* had also been halted in the forest and, finding that no further advance could be made via this route, the counter-attack ran out of steam in the late afternoon. The men of the 7th Somersets scraped holes in the ground or sheltered behind trees and waited for further developments. To their right, the sounds of battle thundered and roared as the 1st Worcesters fought it out on the Gisors road with *Kampfgruppe Schrader*.

The 1st Battalion Worcestershire Regiment, tank alert!, 27 August

The 1st Worcesters' advance up the winding road out of Vernonnet, with its densely wooded slopes, had stopped when the forward platoon heard the ominous sound of a large tank grinding and clanking its way towards them. It was confirmed that it was a Tiger by a patrol, which had noted that it was accompanied by German infantry. Tanks were always feared by foot soldiers, but the Tiger was feared most of all because of its enormous size, thick armour and heavy

---

71 Ford, *Assault Crossing the River Seine*, p. 151.

weaponry. Private George Wyman of the 1st Worcesters recalled: "My heart sank as I listened to the dread sound of a German tank approaching making an unearthly noise; even though it was out of sight it still terrified us all."[72] Troops of the Worcesters moved up the wooded slopes on the right to protect the British flanks.

The Worcesters deployed their 6-pdr anti-tank guns on the road ready for action, one covering the bend and another 100 yards further back down the road. The anti-tank guns were loaded and ready, and the gun aimer waited to see his quarry at virtually point-blank range. Luckily for the anti-tank crews, they had been issued with sabot shells. These were made of a light steel sheath containing a solid tungsten centre, the shell being modified with a four-piece sabot jacket to build it up to the necessary 6-pound calibre. This produced a lightweight shell that was capable of penetrating thick armour, as the sabot jacket fell away as the shell left the muzzle of the gun and the tungsten shot then flew towards its target at a much higher velocity than a normal shell.

In the road verges, the infantry waited as the 60-ton monster noisily approached them. The Tiger slowly nosed forward around the bend, its great 88mm gun barrel leading the way. When the anti-tank gunners could see the off side of the hull and turret, they opened fire and hit the base of the tank's enormous gun with the first shot. Working feverishly, the anti-tank gunners reloaded and scored another hit with their second shot. The third and fourth shots hit the Tiger in the hull, after which it ground to a halt as the crew abandoned their burning machine. The gunners continued to fire as the tank exploded and burst into flames. The German crew were all killed, and as the firing stopped one man could be seen hanging lifeless out of the turret.

D Company's Sergeant Sidney Potter returned from a patrol and reported that another Tiger was on the move:

> Another tank appeared on the road with infantry in support. There was lots of shouting from the Germans up on the high ground and the verges were being fired on. This anti-tank gun of Sgt Guest was loaded and ready, the tank rumbled towards us round the bend and was just half visible when the order came to fire. The first shell was a hit and as the tank tried to wriggle back to safety more Sabot shells were fired into it, setting it on fire. As the crew bailed out, they were dealt with by the lads of the platoon. By this time, it was 11:00 a.m.[73]

For the German infantry accompanying the Tigers, their destruction proved too much and they quickly withdrew. Nevertheless, the Worcesters' advance was halted as it was evident that a counter-attack was taking place in some strength. Battalions on both flanks of the Worcesters were being held up by the same *Kampfgruppe*, and the advance up the Gisors road had to wait until tanks could get forward to support the infantry. C Company of the Worcesters moved to the high ground on the right flank to stop any enemy infiltration, while D Company consolidated its positions on both sides of the road, with A Company close by.

Further back down the road towards Vernonnet, B Company, under the command of the charismatic Major Alfred Grubb, was in reserve and waited in a lay-by with the mortar crews. In this clearing stands an obelisk that commemorates a local dignitary from the 18th century.

---

72 Ford, *Assault Crossing the River Seine*, p. 130.
73 S. Potter, correspondence with author (Bewdley, 1998).

British anti-tank gunners in action. (Courtesy of J. Styan)

It was here that Major Grubb had set up his headquarters, and as he was shaving he could hear the sounds of battle:

> I had my shirt off and was beside my company carrier in the process of having a shave in the Sunday morning sunshine. I could hear some commotion going on further up the road but felt that it was nothing for me to worry about, after all my company was number four in the queue. The first thing that attracted my attention, was men coming back down the road[;] there was a great panic and then a bullet ricocheted off the top of this monument alongside which I was standing, knocking down a great lump of stone. The bullet carried on and went through the head of a carrier driver killing him instantly. I thought to myself: "To hell with this!" Then things really started to boil up.[74]

The *panzergrenadiere* and fusiliers of *Kampfgruppe Schrader* had been successful in infiltrating both flanks and were raking D Company's positions with heavy and accurate machine-gun fire that came out of the undergrowth, making it virtually impossible to locate their position. The

---

74 *Worcestershire Regiment.com* <www.worcestershireregiment.com> (accessed 12 July 2021).

Germans pressed forward, inflicting numerous casualties on D Company while enfilading its positions from both flanks.

Corporal Alfred Banks of D Company cowered in his slit trench as the Germans moved in:

> We tried to engage Jerry but couldn't see a flaming thing and the Spandau fire just got worse. We had an armoured car with us and with his heavy-calibre machine gun he fired into the trees along with us. It was in this chaos that news came to us that another Tiger tank was on its way. I wondered if this was going to be the end for us. Eventually our own mortar and artillery shells began to arrive and the woods on each side of the road began to be torn apart by explosions and fire. Whole trees flew into the air as shells rained down on suspected German positions and we kept our heads down. What a sight! It frightened the hell out of me.[75]

The targets for the artillery were all the suspected forming-up places for the Germans, with the hope of breaking up any counter-attack before it began. All available guns kept up a constant barrage on the valley on the left flank. However, this side was not the main danger; it was the high ground on the right and the commanding view it gave that was of most concern, and this hillside was still wide open to any enemy outflanking movement. Major Grubb watched events unfold and saw the danger at once. He felt that to stay on the road was not the place to be as it was already congested with troops, so made the decision to take B Company up to the hill on the right. Grubb always had with him two men for his own personal protection: Joseph Cook, his batman, and George Bromwich, the company boot maker. Grubb never went anywhere without them.

Grubb had worked out a plan as to how he would stop any Germans who tried to move through the heavily wooded hilltop:

Major Alfred Albert Grubb, MC, 1st Battalion Worcestershire Regiment. (Author's collection)

> I intended to collect all my company's Bren-guns together and string them out so that anyone who came over the hill could bloody well have it. We had thirteen Bren-guns and four two-inch mortars in the company. We would line up the whole battalion along a ridge in front of some water and then get everyone to fire their weapons at the same time. I decided that if I grouped all my fire power together, then the enemy would have a bit of a job to get through. I took the company HQ's Bren-gun myself, while my two bodyguards carried my ammunition. The hill was very steep, thick with trees at the bottom near the road, then a grassy slope and finally another sprinkling of trees at the top. At the bottom of the

---

75 A. Banks, interview with author (Huddersfield, 1992).

hill the battalion's three-inch mortars were lined up under the control of Jock Bannister […] in the layby near the monument.[76]

Major Jock Bannister recalled:

> My mortars were pumping stuff over the top of the hill, they had been firing continuously and they had all overheated. What was happening was that as soon as a mortar bomb was put into the barrel its primary charge was igniting and the bombs were falling only twenty yards away. This in itself was safe enough, for there has to be a projection of X yards before the bomb is fused and could explode. But the mortars somehow had to be cooled down, [so] I lined up my men and got them to pee on the barrels by numbers.[77]

As Grubb got part of the way up the hill, he was surprised to find C Company dug-in, commanded by Major Gerry Glover. Further on, Grubb came across his friend Major Anthony Benn, who had joined the battalion only two weeks ago as second-in-command. Benn asked grub what was going on and was told of Grubb's plan, after which Benn headed down to the road. On the road, D Company was being threatened by another Tiger tank that was slowly making its way to their location. The Tommies took shelter in the trees and hedges as the tank kept up a steady stream of heavy machine-gun fire upon them. It was now the turn of the Germans to have the upper hand as the gunners of the first anti-tank gun, that had earlier been so successful, were forced to keep their heads down because of the fire coming from the enemy infantry on the right flank. The Tiger moved with great caution around the knocked-out Tigers, and once out in the open fired at the anti-tank gun before it could reply. The tank's high-velocity 88mm shell smashed into the anti-tank gun with devastating effect, reducing it to a pile of twisted metal and killing all the crew. The tank pressed on, its second shot hitting the anti-tank gun's carrier, which disintegrated into a ball of flame.[78] A heavy armoured car of the 43rd Reconnaissance Regiment was next in the Tiger's sights, and with a blinding flash and a roar it too exploded.

The war of Private Howard Francis of 16 Platoon, D Company, 1st Worcesters, ended that day:

> I saw the Tiger tank pull out onto the road just around a bend in front of us. Suddenly there was machine-gun fire all around us and I was hit in my left arm, breaking the bone. I passed my Bren-gun over to my colleague and then made my way back under the hedgerow cover to a heavily armoured scout car which was in the road and told them there was a tank just around the bend, their reply was: "Don't we know it mate". I then heard a man shout for the medics, [and] I must have passed out as I came to in a field hospital two days later on the 29th.[79]

The great lumbering form of the Tiger rumbled down the road unchecked as it made its way into the heart of D Company. Permission to withdraw was requested and granted immediately, D

---

76 Ford, *Assault Crossing the River Seine*, p. 156.
77 *Worcestershire Regiment.com* <www.worcestershireregiment.com> (accessed 12 June 2021).
78 This carrier was commanded by Sergeant G. Barraclough, and amazingly he and his crew survived the blast with only minor injuries.
79 *Worcestershire Regiment.com* <www.worcesterregiment.com> (accessed 12 July 2021).

Company being ordered to move to the rear through A Company's position, where they could form a new stable base.

Sergeant Sidney Potter of D Company recounted the retreat back towards A Company:

> We were ordered to withdraw back down the road to the next company's positions. No order was ever obeyed as quickly as this one, and with bullets at our heels we were jet propelled. Then we came upon one of our majors, Major Benn, on the side of the road shouting: "Stop! Stop!" We halted and he ordered us to go up the slope where we were to meet the attack. It was there I was struck by a German bullet and became one of the 65 casualties[80] from this action.[81]

A Company's Lieutenant Stanley Trimnell was caught by a burst of machine-gun fire as he watched parts of D Company passing through his positions:

> We had sections on either side of the road and as we stood up to move around the bend there was a burst of machine-gun fire that hit my batman, my runner and myself. Fortunately, the stretcher-bearers collected us with little delay.[82]

Private Thomas Dutton of D Company ran as fast as his feet would carry him:

> I was running like mad down this road with a comrade, Teddy Harris. A bullet hit the road behind him and flew up into his pack, but we still kept running. We then came level with one of our majors, Major Benn, [who was] shouting: "Stop!" so we halted. He first ordered us to dig-in where we were, then told us to go up the slope and meet the attack. On the way up Pte Les Lunnon, a Bromsgrove lad, was coming down carrying his Bren-gun by the carrying handle. Blood was oozing from a bullet wound in his wrist, [and] he asked someone to open his hand so that he could let go of the gun. We continued to clamber up the slope at the side of the road. It was thickly wooded and very close country. Halfway up I was struck by a German bullet, a scalp wound. The bullet penetrated the front rim of my steel helmet and came out through the back rim, running along the side of my head as it did so. I was covered in blood.[83]

D Company's Private Ronald Cherry was taken prisoner that day:

> I was part of a two-man Bren-gun team with Private Wilfred Edgington. We moved forward up the side of the road, and we could hear the noise of tank tracks heading towards us. A Tiger tank then appeared from around a bend in the road ahead with German infantry in support. Suddenly there was a burst of fire, and my mate Edgington[84] was

---

80 In this action there were 91 casualties: 26 killed and 65 wounded.
81 S.Potter, correspondence with author (Bewdley, 1989).
82 Manuscript forwarded to author by S. Trimnell (Bath, 1990).
83 T. Dutton, correspondence with author (Devon, 1993).
84 Private Wilfred John Edgington, 1st Battalion Worcestershire Regiment, was killed in action on 27 August 1944, aged 23. He is buried in Vernon/Vernonnet Communal Cemetery, France.

hit twice in the chest, killing him instantly. One of the bullets passed through him and hit me in the chest, knocking me down to the ground. The next thing I saw was a German soldier prodding me with his rifle and I thought I was about to be shot. Then a German sergeant came over and I was taken prisoner.[85]

As D Company retreated, the Tiger halted on the road to wait for its supporting infantry. Every British vehicle within sight of the Tiger was destroyed, which for the moment was master of this field of destruction. Even though it was halted, the monster tank kept up a steady stream of machine-gun fire on the fleeing men amid a scene of perfect chaos. Many fell back to the protection of the trees on the slopes; the men of A Company who saw the fleeing troops found it too much to bear, many of them jumping up and joining the flood of terrified men heading for the rear. For a while all control was lost as the men fell back. Major Benn tried to restore some semblance of order to the desperate situation: he stood in the open, revolver in hand, urging the men to stop and take cover off the exposed road, and as he did so the Tiger began to move forward once again, still spraying the road with machine-gun fire. Benn swore and cursed at the fleeing troops and eventually stemmed the flood, a selfless and heroic act that was needed to steady the troops' nerves. But just as order was starting to be restored, a hail of bullets from the tank tore through the ranks of the men still on the road, mowing them down, the brave major being among those killed.[86]

Private Ronald Cherry, 1st Battalion Worcestershire Regiment. (Courtesy of R. Cherry)

Sergeant Stanley Procter described the death of Major Benn in the chaos:

> That day will be etched into my memory forever, the trees in full leaf, the racket of the guns firing and the noise of tank tracks clanking and creaking. The infantry ahead was fighting on the right and suddenly they came back in a bit of a hurry towards our white scout car which was alone on the road. I saw Major Benn shouting: "Come on you buggers, follow me", waving his revolver and he started to lead the men back up the hill. He was killed almost at once.[87]

Once again, the Tiger halted on the road waiting for its infantry support to come up. Now the retreat by the had been Worcesters stopped, they began to keep up a hail of small-arms fire on

---

85 R. Cherry, correspondence with author (1991).
86 Major Anthony Alastair Benn, East Yorkshire Regiment, attached to the 1st Battalion Worcestershire Regiment, was killed on 27 August 1944. He is buried in Vernon/Vernonnet Communal Cemetery, France.
87 Delaforce, *The Fighting Wessex Wyverns*, p. 172.

the thick armour of the Tiger, but this had no effect on the tank as its crew were protected by up to 10cm of steel. However, the Tiger was now so far ahead of its supporting infantry that it was vulnerable; the tank commander realised this and backed his tank around the corner, after which a strange stillness descended over the battlefield. Both attackers and defenders sat in their positions and licked their wounds. It was unlikely that either side would advance any further that day.

At the Worcesters' headquarters, a troop of Sherman tanks of the 4/7th Royal Dragoon Guards arrived, fresh from the ferry across the Seine. One of them was a Sherman Firefly, armed with a large 17-pdr gun, and it was hoped that this would be a match for the Tiger. Commanding this group was Major Jack d'Avigdor-Goldsmid, MC, and after being briefed on the situation he sent the Firefly up the road in case the Tiger should appear at battalion headquarters.

To the right of this action, on the hilltop, *Kampfgruppe Schrader* still pressed forward. Major Grubb had by now positioned his Bren guns just below the crest, but he could observe no signs of life – all was eerily quiet. Grubb looked to his front but could see no one, when Captain Noel Watkins of the 1st Worcesters arrived to find out what was happening. Grubb asked where the riflemen were, and upon being told they were still at the foot of the hill he realised that his orders had been misunderstood. One of the basic rules for any infantryman is that you never put your head above the parapet in the same place twice. As Grubb looked up a second time, a burst of machine-gun fire cut across the bank and he was hit.

Private Peter Mann of B Company was nearby when Grubb received his first wound since landing in France:

> It was during the fierce fighting on the road to Tilly that we met a large-scale counter-attack. I was a Bren-gunner and we were up a thickly wooded hill and Major Grubb was lying near me in the wood. He was a colourful character and had taken his men up the hill to meet the counter-attack. As he looked up a bullet passed through his specially made helmet, but he was alright.[88]

Major Grubb recalled the good fortune behind his survival:

> I could never get on with a steel helmet as they cut into my head, so I arranged with the regimental hatter, Thomas Stone in Jermyn Street, to make me a custom helmet. I was measured and they made me a skull cap out of cork with pieces of rubber sewn on around the base to cushion the steel helmet which rested on top. It was this cork skull cap that saved my life. The first bullet hit the helmet at the front, went straight through and was deflected upwards by the cork skull cap and shot out the top of the helmet.[89]

The second bullet to hit Grubb passed through his jacket, setting fire to his clothing. The force of the impact knocked him over and he was left unconscious for a short time. Grubb and his company had no idea that the enemy were so close until stick grenades began to drop into their

---

88 P.Mann, correspondence with author (Exeter, 1989).
89 *Worcestershire Regiment.com* <www.worcestershireregiment.com> (accessed 13 July 2021).

positions, upon which the Tommies pressed themselves into the earth and waited for the explosions. Grubb shouted for all the grenades to be brought to him and he started throwing them at the enemy, but he couldn't quite make the range as he was lying down. He ordered Captain Watkins to take charge of the Bren guns and began to crawl back to where his 2-inch mortar teams were situated. He at once grabbed a mortar as others passed him the mortar bombs, and at a short range of just 20 yards he set the angle of the mortar in an almost vertical position. The first ranging shot nearly landed on top of him, but other bombs struck the German Spandau positions.

On the top of the hill, visibility was as little as 20 yards because of the trees and thick undergrowth. The terrain was ideal for small parties of Germans to infiltrate the crest armed with light machine guns, and *Kampfgruppe Schrader* now began to gather in strength for the final push over the summit of the hill. B Company came under heavy fire from their unseen opponents as Schrader's men edged ever closer to the British position. Major Grubb, still without his riflemen when he most needed them, ordered Captain Watkins to keep up a non-stop barrage of Bren-gun fire into the woods while he and his two bodyguards tried to outflank the enemy-held summit. As they crawled off into the undergrowth, the noise of battle rose to a crescendo as both sides fought it out at close quarters. The Worcesters put up such a curtain of fire that it was impossible for the Germans to get forward. On and on the struggle went without pause, leaving nothing for the beleaguered Germans to do but withdraw. Grubb's venture met with success as all the firing made the Germans keep their heads down, and tanks of the 4/7th Royal Dragoon Guards, newly arrived on the road below, were also sweeping the crest of the hill with their fire. The trio stayed where they were until night fell, when a search party rescued them.

The battalion commander called a meeting of his officers at his headquarters as dusk fell. Captain Bryan Elder, second-in-command of D Company, was given orders to take a night patrol up the road to the area they had previously held and to make contact with A Company, then to report back. Captain Elder recalled:

Captain Bryan Elder, 1st Battalion Worcestershire Regiment. (Courtesy of C. Milton)

> I selected my batman, Pte George Pound, and another private and we set off up the road to the position we had occupied before being relieved. My batman was on the left-hand side, I was in the middle and the other private was in the rear. As we neared the position we had held earlier in the day, a German machine-gun opened up hitting my batman in his right hand [–] later he had to have it amputated [–] he lay on the road, and I rushed to him and put him on my shoulder and took him back down the road to our stretcher point, where

the medical staff immediately took him to our RAP. I then reported to the CO and eventually crawled back to my company position feeling somewhat shattered.[90]

The 1st Worcesters spent the night dug-in astride the road in the same place they had started their advance on Tilly that morning. During the night there was a violent thunderstorm, the men sheltering under their gas capes to keep as dry as possible. Throughout the hours of darkness there would be the occasional stream of tracer bullets ripping through the trees, but most of it was high and did very little damage. The troops were so tired that they took little notice and soon fell asleep. The only ones to witness the gunfire were the sentries who tried hard to stay awake.

The 4th Battalion Somerset Light Infantry, 27 August

To the left of the 1st Worcester's positions, the 4th Somersets were advancing on the village of Bois Jerome on the morning of 27 August. As B Company moved forward, they came across a small chateau just short of the village which was occupied by the enemy. The Somersets, led by Captain J.M.F. Hutchinson, MC and Bar, put in a surprise attack and sent the Germans packing at the cost of four casualties. The Carrier Platoon was to take charge of the chateau while Hutchinson and his men pressed on to the village, so the troops who remained waited for the arrival of the carriers. D Company, which had become separated from the rest of the battalion, made a wide encircling advance through the woods searching for the bulk of the German forces. As they did this, enemy troops, who were withdrawing back to Bois Jerome, came across the chateau that was held by a platoon of B Company just as they were handing it over to the Carrier Platoon. The Germans took the Somersets completely unawares as they launched a surprise attack. Two Tommies were killed in the fire-fight, and it was not long before the Germans were in possession of the chateau once again. Lieutenant Colonel Lipscomb, commander of the 4th Somersets, later wrote:

> Whilst the hand-over was taking place, the chateau was counter-attacked. The enemy was supported by Armoured Fighting Vehicles firing solid shot and high explosive into the chateau and they succeeded in turning us out.[91]

In the rear, A and C Companies came under fire as the German *149. Fusilier-Abteilung* of *Kampfgruppe Schrader* attacked them from the cover of the woods. Lipscomb recounted:

> The tail, under the command of Major Brind, was ordered to form a base and to send out patrols to locate the enemy. At the same time B Company were to retake the chateau at all costs. The Regimental Aid Post retired to the bottom of the hill and made use of one of the numerous mushroom shaped caves to open shop. To support B Company three armoured

---

90 *Worcestershire Regiment.com* <www.worcestershireregiment.com> (accessed 13 July 2021).
91 Lipscomb, *History of the 4th Battalion Somerset Light Infantry*, p. 46.

cars, referred to as rubber tyred elephants on air, now arrived on the scene and turned the scales in our favour in the battle for the chateau.[92]

Captain Hutchinson recalled that a man from the chateau rushed up to tell him that the enemy was in their rear:

> That was the first I knew of our troubles and when the CO heard the news, he immediately ordered my company to retake the chateau at any cost. It was a sticky problem, for surrounding the house was a wire fence and wall. The only way through was the gate. At that time, we had three armoured cars with us and so I asked one of them if he could blow a hole in the wall of the chateau. The moment he had done that, I planned to rush through the gate with all my company; it seemed the only way. However, I do remember thinking to myself: "My God, what if the gate is covered by a machine-gun?" I was going to send the whole bunch of about forty men through that one gate. I told them that once they were through, to spread out quickly and get around the back. I must admit though, I was worried about the consequences of rushing the gate.[93]

B Company duly rushed through the gate, only to find that the Germans had pulled out in the direction of Bois Jerome, and they reoccupied the chateau unopposed. Lieutenant Colonel Lipscomb was now in a dilemma, for as the German defenders retreated before the 4th Somersets, *Kampfgruppe Schrader* was attacking the rear of the battalion. The possibility of the battalion being cut off from the rest of the division now became a real and present danger. With the rear companies strung out in the forest, Lipscomb ordered Captain Hutchinson to hold on to the chateau while he sent the three armoured cars of the 43rd Reconnaissance Regiment back to support A and C Companies. The infantry of the rear companies were hard-pressed to hold *Kampfgruppe Schrader* at bay as the Germans tested the line for weaknesses at every opportunity. Armoured cars, unlike tanks, can approach a position silently, and this is exactly what they now did to great effect. The Germans were taken totally by surprise as the armoured cars began to rake the trees and undergrowth with heavy and continuous fire.

Many German troops fled before the onslaught, and those that did not were slaughtered by the heavy machine-gun fire. Fortunately for the British, the enemy had no anti-tank guns to call upon, relying solely on 20mm cannons and machine guns, which did not worry the armoured cars as long as they had the support of friendly infantry around them. These three armoured cars effectively halted the advance of *Kampfgruppe Schrader*, but even so the Germans' 20mm cannons continued to keep up a steady fire and their small shells were exploding in the treetops above the heads of the Somersets, inflicting numerous casualties.

Once the enemy counter-attack locations were identified by the artillery FOOs on the ground, the information was quickly relayed back to the artillery positions of the 94th Field Regiment in the Forest of Bizy across the river, who harassed the enemy at every opportunity. Spotting the enemy in the dense woods was extremely difficult, and with the advance moving ahead the British gunners now needed to cross the river to be nearer to the infantry in the

---

92 Lipscomb, *History of the 4th Battalion Somerset Light Infantry*, p. 46.
93 Ford, *Assault Crossing the River Seine*, p. 133.

battle area. Major Michael Concannon, second-in-command of the 94th Field Regiment, was given the task of leading a survey party across the river to find a suitable site for the guns of his regiment. At this time the Germans were bombarding the bridging area on the Seine from several miles inland with captured 152mm Russian howitzers, and while most shells fell into the water, one lucky shot scored a direct hit on the folding boat bridge, killing an unfortunate despatch rider. When Major Concannon and his party arrived at the Seine, he discovered that he would have a long wait before he could cross. However, within 30 minutes a Class 9 raft was in operation, ferrying vehicles across the river. Once on the far bank, Concannon found his commanding officer, Lieutenant Colonel Thomas Irwin Bishell, in conversation with Brigadier Mole. Bishell ordered Concannon to press on into the forest towards the 4th Somersets, whom it was hoped would have taken Bois Jerome by the time he got there. Concannon's party located the Somersets' Regimental Aid Post, where they were informed of the fierce battle going on ahead. As Concannon and his men continued their move forward in two jeeps, the sounds of battle became ever louder. He decided to continue the search for the Somersets' headquarters on foot, and as soon as they had done so a German 20mm cannon started firing from what seemed like very close range down the track. Shells began to explode in the trees and undergrowth, trapping the survey party and pinning them down.

Lieutenant Peter Ost, Survey Officer with the 94th Field Regiment, was among those who came under fire:

> We then went through the glades of the forest leading to Bois Jerome until we reached the Somersets' RAP. The only sound of war was the occasional plop and crump of mortar fire and the sharp burst of Bren and Spandau in the distance. A Boche 20mm opened up with an unholy racket down the track by which we were parked, and its shells were bursting in the trees on either side. Bill Stockton, the signals officer, was wounded and the RSM's language was incredible. A Somerset carrier moved up in an attempt to knock the gun out, [but] it received a direct hit and burst into flames.[94]

Unknown to Concannon, another survey party from the 179th Field Regiment, Royal Artillery, led by Major John Edmund Backhouse, was also in the Forest of Vernon, searching for new sites for his artillery positions. Without any warning, the German 20mm gun opened fire on his scout car and Major Backhouse was struck in the head, and as he collapsed on the ground shells were bursting all around. Lieutenant Ost witnessed the attack:

> Unfortunately, at this very moment, Major Sir John Backhouse,[95] 2 i/c 179th Field Regiment, arrived and dismounted from his scout car when the Boche gun opened up. He fell at once, hit in the head. Gunner Stickley and his driver raced to his assistance oblivious of the fire.[96]

---

94 P. Ost, correspondence with author (Taunton, 1989).
95 Major John Edmund Backhouse, MC, second-in-command 179th Field Regiment, Royal Artillery, died of his wounds on 29 August 1944, aged 35. He is buried in St Desir War Cemetery, France.
96 Manuscript forwarded to author by P. Ost (Taunton, 1989).

German quad-mounted 20mm Flakvierling 38 gun. (Author's collection)

Major Concannon retreated to safety with his party, but after the troops of the Somersets had eliminated the danger he visited the site of the German 20mm gun position once the battle had moved on:

> Lying close by the gun was the four-man detachment; all had been killed at their posts. Around the site were great piles of empty shell cases, serving as testimony to the terrific fire they had put down and which caused us such trouble. They were very brave men sticking to their task as they did, even though they were hopelessly outnumbered and surrounded on all sides.[97]

As the 4th Somersets and 214 Brigade countered the attacks by *Kampfgruppe Schrader*, the other two battalions of 129 Brigade – 4th and 5th Wiltshires – continued to expand the bridgehead. On the south-eastern edge of the Forest of Vernon, the 5th Wiltshires advanced up the Gasny road but came up against opposition in the form of a well-sited 37mm gun that caused them to

---

97 Ford, *Assault Crossing the River Seine*, p. 166.

halt their move forward on two occasions. Patrols were sent out to locate the position of the gun, and each time an artillery barrage was put down on its location. Following on the heels of the barrage, the carrier platoon moved in, only to find that the Germans had withdrawn.

Private Ronald Garner of the 5th Wiltshires remembered the events of that morning:

> We came up against heavy opposition from light flak guns used in a ground role. The fire from these stopped everything dead as they tore through the trees, and we all dived for some kind of cover. An artillery stonk shifted the buggers out of it and the battalion dug-in for the remainder of the day. During the night we got flak fire constantly and it poured with rain; we were so cold that a rum ration was issued to keep us going.[98]

It took the 5th Wiltshires all morning to cover 2,000 yards to a point where they could dig in, where their slit-trenches had a clear view over the flat open countryside towards the village of La Chapelle-St-Ouen, about a mile-and-a-half distant. Major General Thomas was not sure where the next blow would fall and ordered the advance to halt until the German counter-attacks in other parts of the bridgehead had been contained.

The 4th Wiltshires at Giverny

The 4th Wiltshires had been given the job of clearing the high ground near the river, and during the early morning they moved forward up the Seine valley with the village of Giverny – famous for the home and gardens of French impresionist painter Claude Monet – as their objective. Two companies swept the lower ridge, while two other companies moved against the crest above them. At first the going was easy, with no enemy opposition before them, and the men ate ripe apples that were abundant in the orchards that peppered the hillside. As C Company, commanded by Major Derek Ivan Mathie Robbins, moved to the high ground, Giverny was spotted in the distance and the men were ordered to secure their position as a prelude to an attack that would be led by D Company along the road below.

Major Robbins ordered the troops of C Company to give supporting fire when D Company made their assault, but was taken aback by what he saw next:

> To my intense horror, I saw a long line of German soldiers marching along the road in good order, intent on reinforcing the village from the far end. I remember thinking to myself that with all those in the place it was going to be a hard fight. Then, I know I did wrong, I immediately ordered my men to open fire, even though the range was rather far. We hit a few, but most of them vanished into the houses. It was a bad move; we all knew how difficult a job it was to fight anyone out of a village.[99]

The Germans had been taken off guard when C Company opened fire, and D Company then rushed up the flat road, supported by armoured cars. The attack failed and an artillery barrage

---

98 R. Garner, correspondence with author (Bath, 1991).
99 Ford, *Assault Crossing the River Seine*, p. 167.

Tired sappers look on as XXX Corps armour crosses over the bridge 'Goliath'; the other bridge, 'David', can be seen on the right of the picture. (Author's collection)

was then called down on the enemy strongpoints in the area. During the afternoon, the 4th Wiltshires were joined by a troop of Cromwell tanks of the 15/19th Royal Hussars. A smokescreen was laid down to cover the tanks as they slowly worked their way forward in first gear up the steep hill to join C Company on the crest overlooking Giverny, giving badly needed firepower to the beleaguered infantry. The Squadron Commander of the 15/19th Royal Hussars then gave support to a second attack by D Company on Giverny. They attackers broke into the houses on the outskirts of the village as daylight was beginning to fade and, in the dark, began the onerous work of clearing the houses one by one. The commander of D Company then called a halt to the fighting and told his men to consolidate their gains until daybreak.

In Vernon earlier in the day, the folding boat bridge known as 'David' was damaged by shellfire and was out of action for over two hours. The brave engineers had suffered numerous casualties in the explosions and a pair of bulldozers, that had been busy ploughing a road through the back gardens of the houses that lined the approach to the old road bridge, were hit and destroyed. Their blazing hulks were left as a grim reminder that the Germans were still able to punish any movement on the far side of the Seine. However, it was of paramount importance that both bridges were completed as XXX Corps' armour and troops were moving at speed towards the river. As the sappers worked feverishly to complete the bridges, columns of tanks lined up ready to cross, giving the sappers renewed energy to finish their task.

The enemy stonk on the bridgehead turned out to be their last hurrah as the infantry on the far bank overran the final active German battery. The construction of the bridges thereafter continued in peace and the exhausted sappers looked on with pride as the first vehicles crossed into the bridgehead.

Company Sergeant Major Ernest Powdrill, MC, Royal Artillery, commanded four Sexton self-propelled guns and ordered them to the riverbank at 1800 hours just as the light was fading:

> Tank by tank negotiated the pontoon bridge, a procedure that did not increase my confidence. A pontoon bridge is no more than a series of flat sheets laid over a series of pontoons laid side by side. As it is a floating structure, secured to the banks at both ends, it is not, in my untutored opinion, a particularly stable arrangement. As the tanks went over, they appeared to wobble from side to side. If ever a jar of rum was needed, now was the time, but no such luck. On the banks, sappers and military police were in command, signalling each tank over at the appropriate moment. The richness and extent of their vocabulary was to be admired.[100]

CSM Powdrill saw the Seine stretching away on either side of the bridge he was about to cross; it was a forbidding sight in the half-light with its strong, fast running current in full flow:

> Then it was our turn and the driver's eyes were glued to the narrow line of the pontoon, his knuckles glowing white as his hands gripped the steering tillers. The first few yards were not too bad, but then as the pontoon sagged under the weight of the tanks, water began to slosh over the tracks, so that the roadway in front temporarily disappeared. It was a nightmare drive, and it was with huge relief that we found ourselves safely on dry land on the opposite bank.[101]

The mighty 'Goliath' bridge was open for business on the evening of 27 August, at a cost 20 men killed or wounded. It had taken 500 sappers 28 hours to build it under fire. The men of 130 Brigade now moved into the bridgehead, complete with vehicles, anti-tank guns and artillery. Following them came the tanks of 8 Armoured Brigade, in readiness for the 43rd Wessex Division's big push beyond the Seine. Reports were coming in from the lead battalions that there were no longer any enemy troops in front of them as the Germans were in the process of pulling back. However, the commanders at the front knew that to be complacent could be a dangerous thing. Lieutenant Colonel Lipscomb of the 4th Somersets was determined to press home his attack into the village of Bois Jerome now he had tank support. By the time the tanks had taken up their positions, the light was fading fast. The commanders complained that it was unsuitable to use tanks in the darkness, but their fears were dismissed by Lipscomb and A Company of the 4th Somersets was ordered to force a lodgement in the village and to attack it from due west. Lipscomb remembered:

> By now the light was almost gone and A Company commander, Major Acock, told the commanding officer that he considered it too dark to use tank support effectively. However, the tanks were already in position to shoot the company in and opened-up with a hail of

---

100 E. Powdrill, correspondence with author (Halifax, 1994).
101 E. Powdrill, correspondence with author (Halifax, 1994).

machine-gun fire as well as their main armament. The noise echoing and reverberating around the wood was almost deafening and A Company was ordered to press home the attack. This was entirely successful and a firm lodgement in the centre of the village was obtained. Lt Jary led a patrol into the north end of the village and reported that the enemy had withdrawn. D Company occupied that end of the village during the night. About midnight the most terrific thunderstorm broke over the battlefield turning the ground into a morass and filling every slit-trench with water. At the same time the enemy started lobbing heavy shells into and around the area of battalion HQ. As a point of interest 75 percent of these were duds and failed to explode. We silently blessed some underground worker in a German arms factory.[102]

The forest echoed to the sounds of battle as the tanks fired salvo after salvo with their main armaments and raked the area with Besa heavy machine guns. XXX Corps' artillery joined in the violent barrage that descended upon this usually quiet hamlet. Many of the poor civilians who had not abandoned their homes had to sit tight, pray and hope that they would be spared in what must have been a terrifying experience. When A Company followed up the barrage they found no opposition; the Germans had moved out. Burning houses lit the scene as the troops secured their position and the medics took care of the wounded civilians who had been on the receiving end of the barrage. Cpl S. Hitchcock of A Company, 4th Somersets, moved into the area to begin the task of clearing up:

> There was a complete row of houses on fire, and I think some people were trapped inside, I could hear some kiddies crying. Our job was to make sure there were no more Germans hiding in the ruins and we began to search every building. I remember one house had a chink of light showing in the darkness. It was to the left of a large manor with a walled garden, there were beautiful pears on the trees growing against the wall and we had our fill of them the next day. Two of us crept towards the door, listened and pushed it carefully open, grenades at the ready. Inside we were confronted by four women. One had suffered a bullet wound in her thigh from a stray shot fired in the bombardment. We were soon joined by others of my platoon, and you can imagine the ribald comments that were bandied about as we attended to the unfortunate woman's wound. Other men began to poke around, looking all over the house. Suddenly, a broad Somerset voice called out from upstairs that there was a Jerry under the bed. To which one wit replied that he also had one under his bed at home. In fact, there was a German hiding upstairs, but we soon had him out, tied his hands and sent him back to company HQ. I believe he was the only prisoner taken at Bois Jerome.[103]

The situation on the left of the Gisors road remained stable where the 1st Worcesters had fought off the counter-attack by *Kampfgruppe Schrader*. The Worcesters dug in and spent their time firing into the trees, as did the Germans, to dissuade any further movements. The men of the Worcesters had been in action all day on the 27th and were exhausted, but a small number of

---

102 Lipscomb, *History of the 4th Somerset Light Infantry*, p. 47.
103 Ford, *Assault Crossing the River Seine*, p. 173.

patrols were needed to be sent out in the darkness to find out if the Germans were still on the hill. Major Jack d'Avigdor-Goldsmid of the 4/7th Royal Dragoon Guards looked on as a very young and pale-faced officer was briefed to take a patrol up the hill to ascertain if the enemy were present:

> None of the preparation had been done before the patrol and this poor little bugger looked absolutely worn out. I remember thinking to myself that it would not be much good sending him out. As a spectator it was awful to see this poor chap go off up that hill towards the enemy in the pitch darkness. A while later the patrol came back. They had no information to offer, explaining they had got lost. The Lieutenant was rather shame faced about it, but nothing was said.[104]

During the night, a Tiger tank that had accompanied the German infantry withdrew, leaving them to prevent any forward movement by the British. It was still unknown if the Germans were on the high ground, but weaving tracer fire down the valley let the Worcesters know that the enemy were still holding their positions. The British troops were beyond caring and most of them slept throughout these bursts of fire. The Germans probably did the same. Major Grubb of the 1st Worcesters remembered the exhaustion that came over him as night fell:

> When it was all over, I collapsed into a very small slit trench and went completely out. In fact, I nearly drowned. A tremendous thunderstorm during the night had filled my trench with water and when I came to the next morning it was just below my nose. I had no idea it had been raining. I was carrying a picture of my girlfriend, now wife, in my blue Morocco wallet at the time. I still have it, all blue from the water.[105]

The bridgehead consolidated, 27–28 August

By 2100 hours on 27 August, the German counter-attacks had been beaten off and no ground had been ceded to the enemy. The bulk of the victorious 43rd Wessex Division was now across the Seine and the battle for the high ground beyond Vernon had been won. Monday, 28 August dawned dry and sunny, in stark contrast to the thunderstorm of the night before. Major General Ivor Thomas, CO of the 43rd Division, was confident of the security of his bridgehead as reports of a withdrawing enemy continued to come in. During the night, vehicles and tanks continued to enter the bridgehead in great numbers, travelling across the two bridges now in operation. Throughout the day of the 28th, the whole of the bridgehead continued their advance inland and a succession of villages were attacked, all falling without any serious casualties. Lieutenant Jary of the 4th Somersets looked back at his experience of battle and the lessons learned:

> Infantry had to fit in to the big picture, rarely operating without artillery and armoured support. The most successful actions fought by 18 Platoon were fought without the support

---

104 J. d'Avigdor-Goldsmid, correspondence with author (Warminster, 1991).
105 Manuscript forwarded to author S. Hamilton (Worcestershire, 1991).

of either. We had learned in a hard school how to skirmish, infiltrate and how to edge our way forward.¹⁰⁶

Following closely on the heels of the infantry came the artillery scouts in their carriers, looking for a place to site their guns. However, as one group passed through the area that had been fought over by the Worcesters they received a shock, according to Bombardier R. Barber of 220 Battery, 112th Field Regiment, Royal Artillery:

> I remember when our party had the living daylights frightened out of us. As we came round a bend in the road leading up from the river, there in front of us was an enormous Tiger tank. Fortunately, it had been knocked out and we motored on into the recently captured Tilly, where fires were still burning.¹⁰⁷

Bombardier Barber and his comrades pulled into the main square in Tilly and looked on with interest as the local fire brigade went into action:

> The firemen all seemed to be dressed in various braided uniforms and were manhandling an old hand-operated fire engine. It looked very amusing, like something out of a Chaplin film. But they were behaving very bravely, for there were still some Germans around, although most had been captured or fled. From the church tower I could see long lines of the enemy pulling out from the area. One thing I saw really upset me: female collaborators were being unceremoniously dragged out into the streets very roughly and having their heads shaved, poor girls.¹⁰⁸

Private Peter Mann of the 1st Worcesters entered a house in one village and found that his unit had appeared in a German newspaper:

> As members of the 43rd Wessex Division we wore a shoulder badge of a yellow dragon, a Wyvern. We were amused by a captured German newssheet which referred to us as the "Yellow Devils" who were to be feared. Looking around me at these exhausted young men it did not seem a very apt description.¹⁰⁹

Trooper Austin Baker entered the abandoned village of Gisors with the 47th Royal Dragoon Guards:

> One of the best days C Squadron ever had, [with] a spectacular charge from the high ground into Gisors. The brigadier in his scout car waved us on. An ammo dump went up in a terrific explosion. A peasant told Captain Gilbertson that three enemy tanks were just

---

106 Jary, S., *18 Platoon*, p. 87.
107 R. Barber, correspondence with author (Spalding, 1991).
108 R. Barber, correspondence with author (Spalding, 1991).
109 P. Mann, correspondence with author (Exeter, 1989).

ahead, two Mk IVs and a Panther, they had run out of fuel. The crews had set fire to them, and they were exploding all over the place.[110]

As the troops of the 43rd Wessex Division cleared the last of the villages, the Germans took flight, but as each village was taken the progress of the troops was impeded by the happy French population as they surged into the streets to welcome their liberators. Lieutenant Colonel Taylor, CO of the 5th DCLI, recalled:

> They welcomed our men with great enthusiasm, thrusting flowers on them, giving them wine to drink and kissing the somewhat embarrassed soldiers. One Frenchman, who was in a state of glorious intoxication, kept roaring the Marseillaise, and throwing his arms around the necks of the officers, had to be put under restraint. The French said that our attack had driven out about 80 of the enemy who fled up the road with more haste than dignity. By the lights of the burning buildings the position was consolidated.[111]

Down on the banks of the Seine, the sappers who had worked so hard and suffered so much looked on as XXX Corps' vehicles and tanks poured over the bridges. Sapper Roy Young of the Royal Engineers would never forget the sight:

> The bridge was completed by 18:30 p.m. on August 26th. Traffic then passed over continuously for three days and nights. Each vehicle was kept 80 feet apart. When we saw the tanks, lorries, armoured cars and vehicles of every description pass over the Goliath bridge to support the infantry and to prepare for the next phase of the advance, we were all gratified as it was a wonderful and rewarding sight.[112]

The battle for the Seine bridgehead was now over and the 43rd Wessex Division had completed its task of forcing a crossing of the river at Vernon. They had guarded the construction of the bridges across the river and formed a lodgement on the enemy side in sufficient depth to facilitate the passage of XXX Corps, which would act as the spearhead for the 21st Army Group as it headed into the French interior and on into Germany. The corps commander, Major General Brian Horrocks, commented on the move forward:

> On August 29th we burst out of the bridgehead on the Seine and set off on our chase northwards. This was the type of warfare I thoroughly enjoyed, who wouldn't? I had upwards of 600 tanks under my command, and we were advancing on a frontage of 50 miles. The 11th Guards Armoured Division and 8th Armoured Brigade were scything passages through the enemy rear areas, like a combined harvester going through a corn field, with my old friends 50th Northumbrian Division clearing up the mess behind them. Small battles to overcome hastily organised enemy defences at villages and crossroads were going on across this wide front. But there was no main enemy defensive position.[113]

110 Manuscript forwarded to author by P. Ford (Leeds, 2001).
111 Ford, *Assault Crossing the River Seine*, p. 182.
112 R. Young, correspondence with author (Bury, 1991).
113 Horrocks, *A Full Life*, p. 195.

12

Out of Normandy

The idea that the battle for Normandy was won in the first 24 hours of the invasion, and that once the troops were ashore the Germans had no opportunity to drive the Allies back into the sea, is very simplistic in its assertion. Montgomery was aware of the vulnerability of the situation in the early stages of the landings, and after the first 24 hours, although the beaches had been taken, the Allied lodgment was still somewhat tenuous. After XXX Corps had moved inland off the beaches, both sides became bogged down in a battle of attrition as the Allied forces slogged their way forward hedge by hedge, field by field and village by village, each one vital ground that had to be taken if a breakout was to be eventually achieved. The German armoured formations began to arrive slowly and haphazardly into the Normandy battle area, but thanks to the Allied air forces their efforts to move quickly forward were fought to a bloody standstill. Eventually, only travelling by night could enable them to evade the rocket-firing fighter-bombers, known to the Germans as *Jabos*, that ranged unopposed in the skies above them.

The Bocage proved to be a difficult battle ground tactically, and attacks by both sides were blunted in this close countryside which favoured the defending troops. During the first seven weeks of fighting in Normandy, the infantry battalions that made up XXX Corps had become badly depleted after suffering horrendous casualties during the landings and in the grinding Bocage battles. The incessant dangers and discomforts which the front-line soldier was called upon to endure for weeks and months without proper rest, inflicted stresses and strains on the individual that steadily accumulated over time. Some men broke under the strain, but the majority went on carrying their burden until wounded, killed or they suffered a nervous breakdown. As in past wars, the heaviest burden of battle casualties occurred among the infantry, few of whom went for a year without a wound of some kind. This steady drain on their numbers meant that the manpower of all infantry battalions in XXX Corps was always under strength. The green troops they received as replacements from England were quite often hurriedly trained and totally unprepared for the type of fighting that was taking place in the Norman Bocage. This placed the remaining survivors in the line under further pressure to carry on, as however rapidly the new men may have arrived it would be impossible for the past efficiency of a unit to be restored without a period of rest and training, when the new men could be assimilated into their new unit and be able to work with the men around them.

Periods of rest and refit during the Normandy campaign were uncommon, many units staying in the front line for long periods under constant fire. The new men were expected to learn very quickly the rules of the Bocage fighting. Many were killed or wounded not long after they arrived, while others soon learnt the lessons that would keep them alive. A distinct lack of enthusiasm when in action was displayed at times, especially by the old soldiers who had served in France in 1940, the Western Desert, Tunisia and Sicily. The outlook was bleak for the front-line soldiers, who knew that they had to carry on until they were either wounded, killed or taken prisoner. Those who did survive exercised greater caution in all they did. Many of the veteran troops had been wounded more than once in various theatres of war and knew that each time they were hit it lessened their future chances of survival when they returned to the front line again. They had seen too many of their comrades killed and maimed to take any more unnecessary risks, but the exhausted and depleted infantry battalions plodded remorselessly on through the Bocage against a determined and ruthless enemy. The Allied commanders were acutely aware of the situation and of the strains and stresses that the ordinary infantryman was under. General Omar Bradley, commander of the US First Army in Normandy, commented:

> The rifleman trudges into battle knowing that the statistics are stacked against his survival. He fights without promise of either reward or relief. Behind every river there's another hill and behind that hill another river. After weeks or months in the line only a wound can offer him the comfort of safety, shelter and a bed. Those who are left fight on, evading death, but knowing that with each day of evasion they have exhausted one more chance for survival. Sooner or later, unless victory comes, this chase must end on the litter or in the grave.[1]

Efforts were made to give the infantry units a rare visit to a rest camp, where they could bathe and have a change of clothes and underwear. Most men who were lucky enough to enjoy this treat talked of the pure relief of sitting quietly in the shade far from the continuous noise of the battlefield and the incessant traffic and all-pervading dust that covered everything in the bridgehead. However, during the time spent re-equipping and resting, each man had at the back of his mind deep forebodings that disturbed his sleep. Every infantryman knew that the small pleasures they were enjoying were only temporary; the official history of the rifle brigade summed it up nicely:

> When one's battalion has a period of rest in war, delight in washing and sleeping, in drinking perhaps Calvados, and buying eggs and butter, is tempered by the realization that this respite does not spring from the altruistic motives of the higher command, but that you are simply being fattened up, like pheasants in pre-war Septembers, for a particularly important occasion.[2]

The grinding battles of attrition fought by XXX Corps for each village they encountered was viewed by exhausted troops that had been in action for days with a detached, almost surreal vision of what they were going through. The enemy was mostly seen at a distance and the firing at long range; only occasionally did they close with their foe. For the Germans it was the same.

---

1   Belfield and Essame, *The Battle for Normandy*, p. 167.
2   Hasting, R., *The Rifle Brigade 1939–1945* (London: Gale and Polden, 1950), p. 236.

Herman Blocksdorf, who fought with the *Panzer-Lehr-Division*, commented on the British tactics in Normandy:

> If they received any infantry fire, they went to ground and would plaster our positions with bombs for hours on end. Following this they came at us with the terrible flame-throwing tanks that burnt down both men and buildings. Once a man was covered in flame oil nothing could save him, it was a terrible and painful death. Our hatred of the enemy continued to grow day by day. After these horrors had reduced us, they would advance and overrun us; we had left only a handful of men.[3]

Gradually, the attritional fighting increased in intensity. Once local attacks, by either side, had ground to a halt, frustrations developed into atrocities. The young, immature soldiers of the *12. SS-Panzer-Division Hitlerjugend* were told that defeat was not an option. Their whole philosophy encouraged them to be ruthless and to apply the use of violence in the most aggressive way in order to restore any given situation. There is much evidence of atrocities by both sides in the Bocage. Private N.L. Francis had joined the 4th Dorsets as a new replacement and was introduced to the realities of the current situation near Tilly in no uncertain terms:

> We were new recruits straight from Blighty, but the Dorsets had been in action since the landings. Being green, we expected a period of settling in, but we were soon to be disabused of this thought. Our Sergeant was called Anderson. He put us straight into the line and I'll never forget what he told us: "You are not to take any prisoners, shoot them on the spot." We looked at each other and realized that the time for playing soldiers was over.[4]

The difficulties facing XXX Corps in Normandy cannot be understood without credit being given to their relentless German opponents, who were fighting a defensive battle, in terrain that favoured the defenders, against increasingly superior numbers. As the Bocage battle developed, the Tommies got the measure of their opponents and fought them to a standstill. Time was on the Allied side and battle was a hard school of "kill or be killed", but caution was at times necessary. Without doubt there were tactical failures that should have been seen and ironed out earlier. Montgomery, once an attack had stalled, did not always push his men and tanks forward until he was sure of his logistical support. His long-time opponent Rommel wrote:

> The first essential condition for an army to be able to stand the strain of battle is an adequate stock of weapons, petrol and ammunition. In fact, the battle is fought and decided by the quartermasters before the shooting begins. The bravest soldier can do nothing without guns, the guns [are] nothing without plenty of ammunition, and neither guns or ammunition are of much use in mobile warfare unless there are vehicles available in sufficient quality to haul them around.[5]

---

3 Manuscript forwarded to author by H. Wernemann (Germany, 1989).
4 N.L. Francis, correspondence with author (Dorset, 1990).
5 Liddell Hart, *The Rommel Papers*, p. 212.

The dead being interred in Bayeux War Cemetery in August 1944. (Author's collection)

When we take into consideration the massive problems of supplying such a large army, the shortages of ammunition and the steady loss of men in this difficult battlefield, it is not surprising that Montgomery insisted on the organization of his logistical support before attacking again against a formidable foe. The complicated logistical problems facing the Allies were mind-boggling; by September, 39,000 vehicles, 220,231 personnel and 517,000 tons of supplies had been landed. Some 16,000 tons of supplies landed each day in the beachhead, with enough petrol to keep 100,000 tanks and vehicles on the road.

XXX Corps proved its worth from the storming of Gold Beach on the morning of D-Day to the bitter fighting for numerous villages and towns inland: Hottot, Tilly, Rauray, Tessel Wood, Noyers, Cahagnes, Plessis Grimoult and many more hamlets that took a steady toll of the attackers. Then it was on to the struggle for Mont Pinçon, which resulted in the advance to the Seine at Vernon and the struggle for the heights across the river as they drove the Germans back. The German panzer divisions were worn down by drawing them into battle before they were ready, thus ensuring that they could never manoeuvre freely in the manner to which they were designed. A picture is often painted of the British forces ramming their heads against a wall of panzer divisions in Normandy, when in fact the opposite was true.

By the last days of August, it was clear that the German armies in the West had lost France, XXX Corps' units pouring over the Seine in pursuit of a defeated enemy. The Germans had suffered immense losses and had been let down at every level by their own high command. Those who had survived the Bocage and the bloodbath around Falaise made their way eastwards in total chaos. After three months of bitter and bloody fighting, a turning point had been achieved in the war in Europe. Paris was in French hands once again and the Allied armies were streaming towards the borders of the Reich. XXX Corps had travelled a long, hard road to get to this moment. Major Peter Martin, serving with the 2nd Machine-gun Battalion Cheshire Regiment, recounted the move forward as he left the battleground of Vernon and crossed the Seine:

> It was hoped to capture Amiens within 48 hours, but when this was revealed to the men there were some cynical grunts from those who recalled the invasion plan for the D-Day capture of Villers Bocage. 50 Div was once again given the task of mopping up after the armour and was responsible also for the flank protection of XXX Corps. 231 Brigade was to move behind the Guards Armoured Division and 151 Brigade behind 11th Armoured Division. 69 Brigade was in reserve behind 8th Armoured Brigade in the centre. Our column, which included as it did a variety of captured vehicles, [and] had so far presented a picturesque and circus like appearance, was now reduced both in size and beauty by our having to hand in a number of German trucks and by an order issued at this time forbidding the carrying of flowers on the trucks and the long-established practice of painting the names of the owner's girlfriend on the front of each vehicle. During the evening of the 29th of August, in pouring rain, we left our comfortable chateau and, moving through Vernon in artificial moonlight,[6] crossed the river to leaguer in a muddy orchard at La-Chappelle-St-Ouen where, inevitably, half the trucks became bogged down. They were preceded by A Company who spent the night at a village somewhat distressingly called Tilly.[7]

Lieutenant Geoffrey Picot spent many a miserable night under his leaky tarpaulin with the 1st Hampshires and expected the order to move off at any moment:

> I shall never forget those tumultuous days at the end of August when France warmed to its liberation. After we passed over the Seine and began moving through numerous villages, some of the people brought out chairs and sat on these all day long at the roadside as the troops drove through. On all their faces there was [sic] such expressions of thankfulness and joy. I was confident that they would remember Britain with gratitude for the rest of their lives. For us also it was unforgettable, and all the troops were deeply moved by their reception. When that night I finally went to sleep there was no news of what might happen in the morning. At midnight a runner woke me up and told me the battalion had to move just before dawn. When I awoke drenching rain was falling and the night was as black as could be. We got onto the road on time and with the coming of the morning the rain stopped.[8]

---

6 'Artificial moonlight': lighting provided by large powerful searchlights reflecting their beams off the cloudbase.
7 Manuscript forwarded to author by P. Martin (Cheshire, 1989). Peter Lawrence de Carteret Martin reached the rank of major general after the war and was awarded the CBE for his service. He died at Lymington Spa, Hampshire, on 10 February 2013.
8 Picot, *Accidental Warrior*, p. 174.

Lieutenant David Render of the Sherwood Rangers took part in the final actions above Vernonnet, clearing the last of the Germans off the high ground:

> Once across the Seine, the ground east of Vernon opened up dramatically and allowed Horrocks to use the mobility of XXX Corps to fight a deep penetration battle in the relentless pursuit of a defeated enemy. To meet the pace and style of operations the corps commander envisaged, the Sherwood Rangers had reorganized into a regimental battlegroup. All three tank squadrons would now work together, combined with an integral company of infantry mounted in Bren-carriers from the 12th KRRC [King's Royal Rifle Corps], a battery of Sexton 25 pounders from the Essex Yeomanry and two squadrons of reconnaissance cars from the RAC's 61st Recce Regiment. For the first time since North Africa the regiment deployed in desert formation for the advance. Jerry was on the run and was being chased by four Allied armies of 37 divisions advancing on a front of 200 miles. Most Germans were only too willing to surrender at the first opportunity, while the occasional fanatical desperado, willing to die for his Fuhrer, was easily dealt with. As far as we were concerned, once across the Seine, the Great Swan of the pursuit battle, as it was called at the time, had begun.[9]

Fellow Sherwood Ranger Lieutenant Stuart Hills received orders to cross the Seine with his squadron, but his Sherman broke down and he had to take over a new one at Vernon. He was then ferried across the river to support the DCLI in the last of the fighting in the bridgehead:

> The tanks of the 8th Armoured Brigade found themselves in the vanguard of the advance in the general direction of Amiens. The country beyond the bridgehead is open and rolling with wide fields, no hedges and good roads; apart from a few woods, the only trees were those surrounding villages. How different we found it from the closeness of the Bocage, which had hindered us as much as it had helped the German defenders. Now all the advantage lay with the speedy Shermans, which could bypass potential sources of trouble and rely on their mechanical efficiency to cover ground very quickly. To travel at top speed across hard open country on a lovely morning, knowing that the Germans were on the run, was exhilarating to say the least. In every village we passed we received terrific welcomes.[10]

As XXX Corps flew through the French countryside, many men in its ranks enjoyed this new sensation, but they also knew that the fighting was still not over and looked to the future with trepidation. German forces were streaming back to the borders of the Reich, where they would fight hard in defence of the Fatherland. Sergeant Max Hearst of the 5th East Yorks, 69 Brigade, passed over the high ground above Vernonnet and saw bodies lined up at the side of the road. It was obvious to him that the 43rd Wessex Division had been given a tough time by the Germans:

> We passed through the bridgehead, and it was plain to see that a hard battle had been fought here. Knocked-out Tigers, carriers and anti-tank guns were smashed up all over the

---

9 Render, *Tank Action*, p. 175.
10 Hills, *By Tank to Normandy*, p. 148.

place and trees were torn out of the ground by the force of numerous explosions. The poor bastards who hadn't made it were lined up under their ground-sheets near the roadside, and the woods were still burning and smoking. The armour reassuringly moved before us, and we pressed on into open country that was, thankfully, not like the bleeding horrible Bocage we had just left. We didn't meet much opposition, but we cleared the odd pocket still in place and found the Germans more than happy to surrender; the poor buggers had been through hell and were worn out, just kids some of them. The advance went quickly, but us old lags knew how quickly the Germans could recover and expected to meet them at any time. It was a grim thought that never left us, and we would be proved right as future events would show.[11]

In the wake of the Allied invasion, the French civilians suffered grievously. Within the first 48 hours of D-Day, it is estimated that 3,000 men, women and children perished in the Allied coastal bombardment. By 25 August, the German Army had lost 400,000 men killed, wounded or taken prisoner; in material terms they had lost 20,000 vehicles, 1,300 tanks, 500 assault guns and 1,500 field guns. At every step during the Normandy campaign, after the battle had moved on, burial squads carried out their gruesome task of interring the remains of the dead. Theirs was the unenviable work of collecting the bodies – and parts of bodies – of soldiers for whom victory and defeat now meant the same thing. Most of these men rarely spoke of the grisly, if essential work they did, but one man, Private Thomas Bates of the 5th East Yorks, when interviewed was forthcoming when questioned about this:

> There were lots of unidentified men who had died, [and] some were in bits from a direct hit with a shell or a mortar bomb. Well you can imagine what would happen to them; sometimes all we found was an arm, a leg or a hunk of torso. Other men had been buried and it was our job to dig them up and move them, horrible work. Most were just rags and bones. The stench was terrible and it's something you never get used to as long as you live. Really bad visions appeared to me in dreams for years. I could never tell my family about these things, [as it's] best people don't know.[12]

Although there are many critics of the Normandy campaign, what cannot be denied is that it was the greatest military operation ever mounted, from the landings on 6 June 1944 to the battles that followed, leading to the destruction of *Heeresgruppe B*. As the battle passed on, Normandy took time for the scars of war to heal. It took many years to rebuild the shattered cities, towns and villages. Life slowly returned to normal as the detritus of war was cleared away. The numerous cemeteries that hold the remains of the fallen who were killed in battle in Normandy were eventually built, and stand today as silent witness to momentous events and the passage of XXX Corps. They are still visited continuously by the curious and those who have relatives who died or served there in those terrible times, making Normandy a place of pilgrimage. The place where so many died is now a beautiful part of the world, with holidaymakers enjoying all the pleasures it has to offer. Excellent museums have sprung up all along the

11 Max Hearst, interview with author (Hull, 1993).
12 T. Bates, interview with author (Beverley, 1995).

French civilians digging up the remains of British soldiers from their battlefield graves in the Bocage, August 1944. (Author's collection)

coast, where the great bunkers, in their grim splendour, resist the passage of time. The business of remembrance gives the people of Normandy a good living and the economy thrives; after all the people had suffered in 1944, who could deny them their economic success?

The story of the battle has been told and retold ever since 1944. Myths have grown up, changing the narrative as society itself changes. If you visit the peaceful Norman beaches and the Bocage, it is important to remember the carnage that took place there in 1944 and to recognize the enormous sacrifices that were made for us by that generation. Normandy was a terrible battle of attrition, but it did not end the war. Indeed, what followed before the final surrender in May 1945 was every bit as cruel and brutal. A better world eventually emerged after 1945 and long years of peace have ensued, a peace that Western Europe still enjoys to this day.

I visited Normandy recently with three friends and have always made time to visit the many cemeteries and memorials there. In the tranquil sad beauty of these sacred places, only the birds and the hum of passing traffic could be heard, and as we sat in the sunshine I thought of the many veterans I had interviewed and of the accounts I have read over the years. I heard once again their voices, which came to me as the ghosts of that terrible time flitted around my mind's eye, evocative in the now silent peaceful landscape. The Second World War generation who fought in the Normandy Bocage have now mostly passed away, taking with them the grief and pain that these cemeteries represent, scarring the countryside mile after mile. The events that took place here are now little known by the majority of the public, and with the passing of time the Second World War has become just another distant conflict in the mind of the nation. Nevertheless, the faithful still gather every year to remember these young men, who came from all walks of life and gave up so much that we might live in freedom.

Appendix I

Order of Battle, 50th Northumbrian Division, May/June 1944

GOC Major General D.A.H. Graham, CBE, DSO, MC
GSO 1 Lieutenant Colonel R.L.G. Charles

69 Brigade
Commander Brigadier F.Y.C. Knox, DSO
5th Battalion East Yorkshire Regiment
Commanding Officer Lieutenant Colonel G.W. White, MBE
6th Battalion Green Howards
Commanding Officer Lieutenant Colonel R.H.W.S. Hastings, MC
7th Battalion Green Howards
Commanding Officer Lieutenant Colonel P.H. Richardson
151 Brigade
Commander Brigadier R.H. Senior, DSO, TD
6th Battalion Durham Light Infantry
Commanding Officer Lieutenant Colonel A.E. Green
8th Battalion Durham Light Infantry
Commanding Officer Lieutenant Colonel R.P. Lidwell, DSO
9th Battalion Durham Light Infantry
Commanding Officer Lieutenant Colonel H.R. Woods, DSO
231 Brigade
Commander Brigadier Sir A.B.G. Stanier, DSO
1st Battalion Hampshire Regiment
Commanding Officer Lieutenant Colonel H.D.N. Smith, MC
1st Battalion Dorsetshire Regiment
Commanding Officer Lieutenant Colonel E.H.M. Norrie, OBE
2nd Battalion Devonshire Regiment
Commanding Officer Lieutenant Colonel C.A.R. Nevill, OBE
61st Reconnaissance Regiment
Commander Lieutenant Colonel Sir W.M. Mount, TD
2nd Machine-gun Battalion the Cheshire Regiment
Commander Lt Colonel S V Keeling, DSO.

56 Brigade
Commander Brigadier E.C. Pepper, OBE
2nd Battalion Essex Regiment
Commander Lieutenant Colonel J.F. Higson, MC
2nd Battalion Gloucestershire Regiment
Commander Lieutenant Colonel D.W. Biddle, DSO
2nd Battalion South Wales Borderers
Commander Lieutenant Colonel R.W. Craddock, MBE
Royal Artillery
Commander Brigadier C.H. Norton, DSO, OBE
74th Field Regiment
Commander Lieutenant Colonel H.W.W. Harris, DSO
86th Field Regiment
Commander Lieutenant Colonel G.D. Fanshawe, OBE
90th Field Regiment
Commander Lieutenant Colonel I.G.S. Hardie
124th Field Regiment
Commander Lieutenant Colonel P.H. Gough
147th Field Regiment
Commander Lieutenant Colonel R.A. Phayre
102nd Anti-tank Regiment
Commander Lieutenant Colonel A.K. Mathews
25th Light Anti-aircraft Regiment
Commander Lieutenant Colonel G.G.O. Lyons, MBE
Royal Engineers
Commander RE Lieutenant Colonel R.L. Willott, DSO
233rd Field Company
Commander Major J.R. Cave-Brown
295th Field Company
Commander Major C.W. Wood
505th Field Company
Commander Major C.A.O.B. Compton, MC
235th Field Park Company
Commander Major I.L. Smith
15th Bridging Platoon
Divisional troops
Commander Lieutenant G. Sumner
Royal Signals
Commander Lieutenant Colonel G.B. Stevenson
Royal Army Service Corps
Commander Lieutenant Colonel G.W. Fenton, MBE
346 Coy, 508 Coy, 522 Coy and 524 Coy RASC
Royal Army Medical Corps
149, 186 and 200 Field Ambulance
47, 48 Field Dressing Station and 22 Field Hygiene Section

Royal Army Ordnance Corps
Commander Major D.C.H. Merrill
69, 151 and 231 Workshop Sections
Royal Corps of Electrical and Mechanical Engineers
Commander Lieutenant Colonel E.H. Rundle

Appendix II

50th Northumbrian Division Honours and Awards, 6–14 June 1944

Abbreviations employed in text
VC: Victoria Cross
DSO: Distinguished Service Order
MC: Military Cross
DCM: Distinguished Service Medal
MM: Military Medal
BEM: British Empire Medal
MiD: Mentioned in Dispatches
Bar: If a bar was awarded it means an individual has been awarded the same gallantry medal for the second time. This bar was worn on the ribbon of the original award.
The following list has been taken from the original recommendations that were written 74 years ago. I apologise for any omissions or mistakes.
Each entry features name, initials, rank and any awards already given prior to D-Day; followed by the award, the date it was given for, the date it appeared in the *London Gazette* and the battalion and regiment the man served in.

69 Brigade
Addis, T., Pte: MM, 6 June 1944. Gazetted 31 August 1944. 6th Bn Green Howards
Backhouse, G., Pte: MM, 6 June 1944. Gazetted 31 August 1944. 6th Bn Green Howards
Baldwin, S., Pte: MM, 7 June 1944. Gazetted 31 August 1944. 7th Bn Green Howards
Bancombe, C.P., Lt: MC, 11 June 1944. Gazetted 31 August 1944. 6th Bn Green Howards
Clare, R., Pte: MM, 6 June 1944. Gazetted 31 August 1944. 5th Bn East Yorkshire Regiment
Calvert, G., CSM: DCM, 11 June 1944. Gazetted 31 August 1944. 6th Bn Green Howards
Clarke, A.E.V., Pte: MM, 11 June 1944. Gazetted 31 August 1944. 6th Bn Green Howards
Coles, C.J., Driver: MM, 11 June 1944. Gazetted 19 October 1944. 186 Field Ambulance
Davis, R., Sapper: MM, 6 June 1944. Gazetted 19 October 1944. 233 Field Coy, Royal Engineers
Goddard, G., Pte: MM, 11/12 June 1944. Gazetted 31 August 1944. 7th Bn Green Howards
Harrison, W.A., L/Sgt: MM, 6 June 1944. Gazetted 19 October 1944. 233 Field Coy, Royal Engineers

Hastings, R.H.W.S., Lt Col, MC: DSO, 6 June 1944. Gazetted 31 August 1944. 6th Bn Green Howards.
Henson, J.M., Pte: MM, 11 June 1944. Gazetted 31 August 1944. 6th Bn Green Howards
Hollis, S.E., CSM: VC, 6 June 1944. Gazetted 17 August 1944. 6th Bn Green Howards
Honeyman, F.H., Major: MC, 6 June 1944. Gazetted 31 August 1944. 6th Bn Green Howards
Joyce, A., L/Cpl: MM, 6 June 1944. Gazetted 31 August 1944. 6th Bn Green Howards
Kerr, G.S., Driver: MM, 11 June 1944. Gazetted 19 October 1944. RASC, attached to 69 Brigade
Knox, F.Y.C., Brig, DSO: Bar to DSO, 6 June 1944. Gazetted 31 August 1944. O/C 69 Brigade
Lamb, W.R., Capt: MC, 6 June 1944. Gazetted 31 August 1944. RAMC, attached to 5th Bn East Yorkshire Regiment
Leary, J., Pte: MM, 11 June 1944. Gazetted 31 August 1944. 6th Bn Green Howards
Livingstone, A., Sapper: MM, 6 June 1944. Gazetted 19 October 1944. 233 Field Coy, Royal Engineers
Lofthouse, R., Major: MC, 6 June 1944. Gazetted 31 August 1944. 6th Bn Green Howards
Marsden, W.M., Capt: MC, 6 June 1944. Gazetted 19 October 1944. 186 Field Ambulance
McDougal, W.E., CSM: MM, 6 June 1944. Gazetted 31 August 1944. 5th Bn East Yorkshire Regiment
Mills, T., L/Cpl: MM, 6 June 1944. Gazetted 31 August 1944. 5th Bn East Yorkshire Regiment
Philips, P.R., Lt: MC, 11 June 1944. Gazetted 19 October 1944. 2nd Machine-gun Bn Cheshire Regiment
Potterton, W., Sgt: MM, 7 June 1944. Gazetted 31 August 1944. 7th Bn Green Howards
Prenty, H., L/Sgt: MM, 6 June 1944. Gazetted 31 August 1944. 6th Bn Green Howards
Rice, A.N.M., Major: MC, 6 June 1944. 31 August 1944. 5th Bn East Yorkshire Regiment
Sandison, D.R., Major: MC, 11 June 1944. Gazetted 19 October 1944. 186 Field Ambulance
Showering, R.H., Cpl: MM, 6 June 1944. Gazetted 19 October 1944. 186 Field Ambulance
Thompson, J.T., Pte: MM, 6 June 1944. Gazetted 31 August 1944. 6th Bn Green Howards
Wallace, T.M., Sapper: MM, 6 June 1944. Gazetted 19 October 1944. 233 Field Coy, Royal Engineers
Watson, J., Sapper: MM, 6 June 1944. Gazetted 19 October 1944. 233 Field Coy, Royal Engineers
Webber, F., Sgt: MM, 6 June 1944. Gazetted 31 August 1944. 5th Bn East Yorkshire Regiment
White, J., L/Cpl: MM, 6 June 1944. Gazetted 19 October 1944. 186 Field Ambulance
Young, G.M., Major: MC, 11 June 1944. Gazetted 31 August 1944. 6th Bn Green Howards

151 Brigade
Atkinson, G.R., Major, MC: Bar to MC, 10 June 1944. Gazetted 31 August 1944. 6th Bn DLI
Botterman, W., Sgt: MM, 8 June 1944. Gazetted 31 August 1944. 6th Bn DLI
Bryges, S.L., Cpl: MM, 9/13 June 1944. Gazetted 31 August 1944. 8th Bn DLI
Cawley, J., Pte: MM, 11 June 1944. Gazetted 31 August 1944. 8th Bn DLI.
Chipchase, W.D., Pte: MM, 6/7 June 1944. Gazetted 19 October 1944. 149 Field Ambulance
Daw, I.A., Capt: MC, 7 June 1944. Gazetted 31 August 1944. 6th Bn DLI
Gallagher, T.W., Sgt: MM, 6 June 1944. Gazetted 19 October 1944. 149 Field Ambulance
Higginson, W., Cpl, MM: Bar to MM. 9 June 1944. Gazetted 31 August 1944. 8th Bn DLI.
Kirk, T.M., Lt: MC, 6 June 1944. Gazetted 31 August 1944. 6th Bn DLI

Laws, P.M., Lt: MC, 10 June 1944. Gazetted 31 August 1944. 8th Bn DLI
Michael, D., Cpl: MM, 11 June 1944. Gazetted 31 August 1944. 8th Bn DLI
Pickin, A., Sgt: MM, 9 June 1944. Gazetted 31 August 1944. 2nd Machine-gun Bn Cheshire Regiment
Protano, F., MM: 10 June 1944. Gazetted 31 August 1944. 8th Bn DLI
Richardson, W., Cpl: MiD, 8 June 1944. Gazetted 31 August 1944. 6th Bn DLI
Richmond, R., L/Sgt: MM, 9 June 1944. Gazetted 31 August 1944. 8th Bn DLI
Thomas, B., Cpl: MM, 12 June 1944. Gazetted 31 August 1944. 8th Bn DLI
Wallbanks, S.P., L/Sgt: MM, 10 June 1944. Gazetted 31 August 1944. 8th Bn DLI
Wear, J., L/Cpl: MM, 10 June 1944. Gazetted 31 August 1944. 6th Bn DLI
Wood, G., Major, MC and Bar: DSO, 10 June 1944. Gazetted 31 August 1944. 6th Bn DLI.

231 Brigade
Austin, J.N., Lt: MC, 6 June 1944. Gazetted 19 October 1944. 295 Field Coy, Royal Engineers
Bison, C., Sgt: MM, 6 June 1944. Gazetted 31 August 1944. 1st Bn Hampshire Regiment
Boys, J.N., Lt: MC, 6 June 1944. Gazetted 31 August 1944. 1st Bn Hampshire Regiment
Bradshaw, F.B., L/Sgt: MM, 6 June 1944. Gazetted 19 October 1944. 295 Field Coy, Royal Engineers
Burns, R.W., Cpl: MM, 6 June 1944. Gazetted 19 October 1944. 295 Field Coy, Royal Engineers
Burt, T., Sgt: MM, 8 June 1944. Gazetted 31 August 1944. 522 Coy, RASC, attached to 47 Royal Marine Commando
Butt, W.R., Pte: MM, 6 June 1944. Gazetted 31 August 1944. 1st Bn Hampshire Regiment.
Carter, V.E., Cpl: MM, 6 June 1944. Gazetted 31 August 1944. 1st Bn Dorset Regiment
Cooper, F.S., Lt: MC, 7 June 1944. Gazetted 19 October 1944. 200 Field Ambulance
Dyer, G.E., Cpl: MM, 7 June 1944. Gazetted 19 October 1944. 200 Field Ambulance
Farrow, C.W., L/Cpl: MM, 7 June 1944. Gazetted 19 October 1944. 200 Field Ambulance
Goddard, R., Pte: MM, 11 June 1944. Gazetted 31 August 1944. 1st Bn Dorset Regiment
Grimshaw, L., Pte: MM, 11 June 1944. Gazetted 31 August 1944. 231 Brigade Signals
Hawkins, W., Cpl: MM, 6 June 1944. Gazetted 31 August 1944. 1st Bn Dorset Regiment
Hayes, W.N., Major: MC, 6 June 1944. Gazetted 31 August 1944. 1st Bn Dorset Regiment
Holdsworth, M., Lt: MC, 11 June 1944. Gazetted 31 August 1944. 2nd Bn Devon Regiment
Huckley, G., Cpl: MM, 11 June 1944. Gazetted 31 August 1944. 1st Bn Dorset Regiment
Keenor, A., Pte: MM, 6 June 1944. Gazetted 31 August 1944. 2nd Bn Devon Regiment.
King, A.L., Lt: MC, 6 June 1944. Gazetted 31 August 1944. 1st Bn Hampshire Regiment
Kingswell, R., L/Cpl: MM, 6 June 1944. Gazetted 31 August 1944. 231 Brigade HQ Defence Platoon
Lindon, B.M.W., Capt: MC, 7 June 1944. Gazetted 31 August 1944. 522 Coy, RASC, attached to 47 Royal Marine Commando
Littlejohns, J.L.G., Major: MC, 6 June 1944. Gazetted 31 August 1944. 1st Bn Hampshire Regiment
McKenzie, D.S., Sgt: MM, 6 June 1944. Gazetted 31 August 1944. Royal Electrical and Mechanical Engineers, attached to 321 Brigade HQ
Miller, J., L/Cpl: MM, 6 June 1944. Gazetted 31 August 1944. 1st Bn Dorset Regiment
Nevill, C.A.R., Lt Col: DSO, 6 June 1944. Gazetted 31 August 1944. 2nd Bn Devon Regiment

Nichol, R.M., Major: MC, 6 June 1944. Gazetted 31 August 1944. 2nd Bn Devon Regiment
Norrie, E.A.M., Lt Col: DSO, 6 June 1944. Gazetted 31 August 1944. 2nd Bn Devon Regiment
Oldridge, C., Pte: MM, 6 June 1944. Gazetted 28 September 1944. 2nd Bn Devon Regiment
Perkins, A., L/Cpl: MM, 9 June 1944. Gazetted 31 August 1944. 2nd Bn Devon Regiment
Playford, R., Pte: MM, 12 June 1944. Gazetted 31 August 1944. 1st Bn Hampshire Regiment
Redpath, J., Cpl: MM, 9 June 1944. Gazetted 31 August 1944. 1st Bn Dorset Regiment
Richards, L.E., Cpl: MM, 12 June 1944. Gazetted 31 August 1944. 231 Brigade Signals
Rotherham, F., L/Sgt: MM, 8 June 1944. Gazetted 31 August 1944. 2nd Bn Devon Regiment
Sadler, F.D., Major, MBE: MC, 6 June 1944. Gazetted 31 August 1944. 2nd Bn Devon Regiment
Sear, J., Sgt: MM, 7 June 1944. Gazetted 31 August 1944. 2nd Bn Devon Regiment
Sippetts, A.E.C., L/Sgt: MM, 6 June 1944. Gazetted 31 August 1944. 1st Bn Hampshire Regiment
Slade, G., Cpl: MM, 6 June 1944. Gazetted 31 August 1944. 1st Bn Hampshire Regiment
Talbot, A.W., Sgt: MM, 6 June 1944. Gazetted 31 August 1944. 1st Bn Dorset Regiment
Tams, W.J., Sgt: MM, 11 June 1944. Gazetted 31 August 1944. 522 Coy, RASC, attached to 1st Bn Devon Regiment
Thompson, S., Cpl, MM: DCM, 6 June 1944. Gazetted 31 August 1944. 1st Bn Dorset Regiment
Waller, V., L/Cpl: MM, 6 June 1944. Gazetted 31 August 1944. 1st Bn Hampshire Regiment
Warren, D.J., Major, MC: DSO, 6 June 1944. Gazetted 31 August 1944. 1st Bn Hampshire Regiment
Webb, L., L/Cpl: MM, 6 June 1944. Gazetted 28 September 1944. 1st Bn Hampshire Regiment
Whittington, C.R., Capt: MC, 6 June 1944. Gazetted 31 August 1944. 1st Bn Dorset Regiment
Wicks, J.M.C., Capt: MC, 6 June 1944. Gazetted 28 September 1944. 1st Bn Hampshire Regiment
Williams, S., Sgt: MM, 11 June 1944. Gazetted 31 August 1944. 2nd Bn Devon Regiment
Wint, N., Sapper: MM, 6 June 1944. Gazetted 19 October 1944. 295 Field Coy, Royal Engineers

56 Brigade
Biddle, D.W., Lt Col: DSO, 11 June 1944. Gazetted 19 October 1944. 2nd Bn Gloucestershire Regiment
Boocock, A., Sgt: MM, 8 June 1944. Gazetted 31 August 1944. 2nd Battalion South Wales Borderers
Brain, G., Sgt: MM, 11 June 1944. Gazetted 19 October 1944. 2nd Bn Gloucestershire Regiment
Clark, G.R., Capt: MC, 8 June 1944. Gazetted 31 August 1944. RAMC, attached to 2nd Bn South Wales Borderers
Craddock, R., Lt Col: DSO, 8 June 1944. Gazetted 31 August 1944. 2nd Bn South Wales Borderers
Dauncey, G., Major: MC, 8 June 1944. Gazetted 31 August 1944. 2 Bn South Wales Borderers
Kenwood, R.C., L/Cpl: MM, 8 June 1944. Gazetted 31 August 1944. 2nd Bn South Wales Borderers
Lance, J.K., Major: MC, 6 June 1944. Gazetted 31 August 1944. 2nd Bn Gloucestershire Regiment.

Lockhart, J., Cpl: MM, 8 June 1944. Gazetted 31 August 1944. 2nd Bn South Wales Borderers
Murgatroyd, M., Pte: MM, 8 June 1944. Gazetted 31 August 1944. 2nd Bn South Wales Borderers
Over, D.G., Sgt: MM, 11 June 1944. Gazetted 19 October 1944. 2nd Bn Gloucestershire Regiment
Randell, D.M.E., Lt: MC, 8 June 1944. Gazetted 31 August 1944. 2nd Bn South Wales Borderers
Rhodes, F., Cpl: MM, 10 June 1944. Gazetted 31 August 1944. 2nd Bn Gloucestershire Regiment
Thomas, Leslie, Pte: MM, 8 June 1944. Gazetted 31 August 1944. 2nd Bn South Wales Borderers
Thomas, Leonard, Pte: MM, 8 June 1944. Gazetted 31 August 1944. 2nd Bn South Wales Borderers
Thomas, W.J., Cpl: MM, 7 June 1944. Gazetted 31 August 1944. 2nd Bn South Wales Borderers.
Thomas, W.R., Reverend: MC, 11/12 June 1944. Gazetted 31 August 1944. 2nd Bn Essex Regiment
Thompson, A.F., Capt: MC, 8 June 1944. Gazetted 31 August 1944. 2nd Bn South Wales Borderers

Royal Engineers Beach Clearance Party
Buckley, A.G.B., Lt: MC, 6 June 1944. Gazetted 19 October 1944. 73rd Field Coy, Royal Engineers
Close, A., Sapper: MM, 6 June 1944. Gazetted 19 October 1944. 73rd Field Coy, Royal Engineers
Fitzgerald, J.M., L/Cpl: MM, 6 June 1944. Gazetted 19 October 1944. 73rd Field Coy, Royal Engineers
Peard, Lt: MC, 6 June 1944. Gazetted 19 October 1944. 280th Field Coy, Royal Engineers
Wilson, I.T.C., Lt: MC, 6 June 1944. Gazetted 19 October 1944. 73rd Field Coy, Royal Engineers
Wyatt, L.E., Major: MC, 6 June 1944. Gazetted 19 October 1944. 73rd Field Coy, Royal Engineers

8 Armoured Brigade
Abbs, T.E., Lt: MC, 11 June 1944. Gazetted 31 August 1944. 4/7th Dragoon Guards
Bracegirdle, W., Sgt: MM, 6 June 1944. Gazetted 31 August 1944. Sherwood Rangers Yeomanry
Cracroft, H.J.B., Brigadier: DSO, 6 June 1944. Gazetted 31 August 1944. C/O 8 Armoured Brigade
D'Avigdor-Goldsmid, J.A., Major: MC, 13 June 1944. Gazetted 31 August 1944. 4/7th Dragoon Guards
French, E.M., Major: MC, 13 June 1944. Gazetted 31 August 1944. 1/7th Queen's Regiment.
Jenkins, R.M., Major: MC, 11 June 1944. Gazetted 31 August 1944. 4/7th Dragoon Guards
Wide, N.S., Lt: MC, 12 June 1944. Gazetted 31 August 1944. 4/7th Dragoon Guards

47 Royal Marine Commando

Donnell, P.M., Lt Col, MiD: Croix de Guerre with vermilion star (not gazetted). 47 Royal Marine Commando
Ellis, W.E., L/Sgt: MM, 8 June 1944. Gazetted 12 September 1944. 47 Royal Marine Commando
Emsley, R., Marine: MM, 7 June 1944. Gazetted 12 September 1944. 47 Royal Marine Commando
Gadsden, D.R., Marine: MM, 7 June 1944. Gazetted 12 September 1944. 47 Royal Marine Commando
Gardner, D.H.G., Sgt: MM, 7 June 1944. Gazetted 12 September 1944. 47 Royal Marine Commando
Griffin, J.A., Marine: MM, 7 June 1944. Gazetted 12 September 1944. 47 Royal Marine Commando
James, W.T.B., Lt: MC, 8 June 1944. Gazetted 31 August 1944. 47 Royal Marine Commando
Kendrick, P.G., L/Cpl: MM, 7 June 1944. Gazetted 19 October 1944. 47 Royal Marine Commando
Macdonald, W., Marine: MM, 7 June 1944. Gazetted 12 September 1944. 47 Royal Marine Commando

Provost Coy and signals
Bennet, R.W., L/Cpl, MM: Bar to MM, 6 June 1944. Gazetted 31 August 1944. XXX Corps, HQ Signals
Ford, J., Sgt: MM, 6 June 1944. Gazetted 31 August 1944. 50 Div Provost Coy, attached to 69 Brigade
Jacklin, R., Sgt: MM, 6 June 1944. Gazetted 31 August 1944. 50 Div Provost Coy

Royal Artillery
Barnett, R.A., Major: MC, 9 June 1944. Gazetted 31 August 1944. 102nd Anti-tank Regiment, Northumberland Hussars
Bayley, F., Sgt: MM, 9 June 1944. Gazetted 31 August 1944. 102nd Anti-tank Regiment, Northumberland Hussars
Bayliss, R.N., Lt: MC, 9 June 1944. Gazetted 31 August 1944. 102nd Anti-tank Regiment, Northumberland Hussars
Beresford, C.F., Gunner: MM, 9/10 June 1944. Gazetted 31 August 1944. 102nd Anti-tank Regiment, Northumberland Hussars
Bishop, N.J.D., Capt: MC, 7 June 1944. Gazetted 31 August 1944. 90th Field Regiment
Bowstead, D., L/Cpl: MM, 6 June 1944. Gazetted 31 August 1944. E Section, No2 Coy Signals, attached to 90th Field Regiment
Bramfeld, W.S., Lt: DSO, 6/9 June 1944. Gazetted 31 August 1944. 102nd Anti-tank Regiment, Northumberland Hussars
Down, A., Sgt: DCM, 6/9 June 1944. Gazetted 31 August 1944. 102nd Anti-tank Regiment, Northumberland Hussars
Edwards, E.C.B., Capt: MC, 6 June 1944. Gazetted 31 August 1944. 147th Field Regiment
Gilmour, G.H., Bdr: MM, 9 June 1944. Gazetted 31 August 1944. 102nd Anti-tank Regiment, Northumberland Hussars

Greig, G.D., Lt: MC, 6/14 June 1944. Gazetted 31 August 1944. 124th Field Regiment, attached to 86th Field Regiment, Herts Yeomanry

Hamilton, P.A., Capt: MC, 9 June 1944. Gazetted 31 August 1944. 74th Field Regiment, attached to 90th Field Regiment.

Hinder, E.C., Bdr: MM, 9/10 June 1944. Gazetted 31 August 1944. 102nd Anti-tank Regiment, Northumberland Hussars.

Mathews, A.K., Lt Col: DSO, 6/9 June 1944. Gazetted 31 August 1944. O/C 102nd Anti-tank Regiment, Northumberland Hussars

Mitchley, S.M., L/Bdr: MM, 6/14 June 1944. Gazetted 31 August 1944. 124th Field Regiment, attached to 86th Field Regiment, Herts Yeomanry

Munro, K., Lt: MC, 6/7 June 1944. Gazetted 31 August 1944. 147th Field Regiment

Palmer, R.E., Sgt: MM, 6 June 1944. Gazetted 31 August 1944. 147th Field Regiment

Phayre, R.A., Lt Col: DSO, 6/11 June 1944. Gazetted 31 August 1944. 147th Field Regiment

Seaton, G.H., Sgt: MM, 10 June 1944. Gazetted 31 August 1944. 102nd Anti-tank Regiment, Northumberland Hussars

Sidgwick, C.J., Major: MC, 6 June 1944. Gazetted 31 August 1944. 147th Field Regiment

Smith, J.B.M., Major: DSO, 6 June 1944. Gazetted 31 August 1944. 86th Field Regiment, Herts Yeomanry

Taylor, D.B., Capt: MC, 6 June 1944. Gazetted 31 August 1944. 147th Field Regiment

Thompson, W.D., Sgt: MM, 6/8 June 1944. Gazetted 31 August 1944. 102nd Anti-tank Regiment, Northumberland Hussars

Appendix III

Casualties to 50th Northumbrian Division, 6 June to 1 December 1944

Officers killed: 113
Other ranks killed: 1,045
Officers wounded: 339
Other ranks wounded: 4,967
Officers missing: 46
Other ranks missing: 1,752
Total casualties: 498 officers, 7,764 other ranks

Appendix IV

German Order of Battle, Gold Beach, 6 June 1944, 716th Static Infantry Division

---

Commanding Officer *Generalleutnant* **Wilhelm Richter**
726th Infantry Regiment
736th Infantry Regiment
716th Pioneer Battalion
716th Anti-tank Company
716th Signal Company
716th Artillery Regiment
1st Battalion 916th Grenadier Regiment, 352nd Infantry Division. Commanding Officer *Generalleutnant* Dietrich Kraiss. Stationed in fortified houses at La Riviere and Le Hamel.
The 716th Division was formed in April 1941 and consisted mainly of older personnel. At the start of June they were stationed near Caen, but then moved to the Normandy beach area.

Appendix V

Order of Battle, 7th Armoured Division, Villers Bocage, June 1944

Commanding Officer Major General G.W.E.J. Erskine

22 Armoured Brigade
Commander Brigadier W.R.N. Hinde
1st Royal Tank Regiment
Commander Lt Colonel R.M.P. Carver
5th Royal Tank Regiment
Commander Lt Colonel C.H. Holliman
4th County of London Yeomanry
Commander Lt Colonel Viscount A. Cranley
1st Battalion the Rifle Brigade
Commander Lt Colonel A.G.V. Paley
131 Queen's Infantry Brigade
Commander Brigadier M.S. Eskins
1/5th Battalion Queen's Royal Regiment (West Surrey)
Commander Lt Colonel H. Wood
1/6th Battalion Queen's Royal Regiment (West Surrey)
Commander Lt Colonel M. Forrester
1/7th Battalion Queen's Royal Regiment (West Surrey)
Commander Lt Colonel D.S. Gordon
Independent Machine-gun Company, 3rd Support Company, Royal Northumberland Fusiliers
Armoured Reconnaissance Regiment, 8th Royal Hussars
Commander Lt Colonel C. Goulburn
Royal Armoured Corps, 263rd Forward Delivery Squadron
Royal Artillery
Commander Brigadier R. Mews
3rd Royal Horse Artillery
Commander Lt Colonel J.A. Norman
5th Royal Horse Artillery
Commander Lt Colonel G.P. Gregson
15th Light Anti-aircraft Regiment

65th Anti-tank Regiment (Norfolk Yeomanry)
Commander Lt Colonel W.B. Stewart
Divisional troops
Royal Engineers
Commander Lt Colonel A.D. Hunter
4th and 621st Field Squadrons, 143rd Field Park Squadron
Royal Signals
7th Armoured Divisional Signals
Commander Lt Colonel G.S. Knox
Royal Army Service Corps
Commander Lt Colonel E.G. Hazelton
58th, 67th and 507th Companies
Royal Army Medical Corps
Commander Lt Colonel E.C. Eccles
2nd Light Field Ambulance, 131st Field Ambulance, 29th Field Dressing Station, 70th Field Hygiene Section, 134th Mobile Dental Unit
Royal Army Ordnance Corps
Commander Lt Colonel A.C. Lusty
Divisional Ordnance Field Park
Royal and Electrical and Mechanical Engineers
Commander Lt Colonel J.D. Berryman
7th Armoured Troops Workshop, 22 Armoured Brigade Workshop, 131 Brigade Workshop, 15th Light Anti-aircraft Workshop

Appendix VI

Order of Battle, 130th Panzer Lehr Division in the Bocage, June-July 1944

Commanding Officer *Generalleutnant* Fritz Bayerlein

Divisional Headquarters
130th Motorised Mapping Detachment
Divisional Escort Company
130th Motorised Military Police Troop
130th Panzer Regiment (*Oberst* Rudolph Gerhardt)
Regimental Staff Company
1st Panzer Battalion, 6th Panzer Regiment (*Major* Markowski)
2nd Panzer Battalion (*Oberleutnant* Prince Wilhelm von Schonberg-Waldenburg)
316th Radio-controlled Company
901st Panzer Grenadier Lehr Regiment (*Oberst* Georg Scholze)
Regimental Staff Company
1st Panzer Grenadier Battalion (*Major* Konrad Uthe)
2nd Panzer Grenadier Battalion (*Major* Schone)
Self-propelled Gun Infantry Company
Engineer Company
Light Flak Company
902nd Panzer Grenadier Lehr Regiment (*Oberstleutnant* Willie Welsch)
Regimental Staff
1st Panzer Grenadier Battalion (*Major* Zwierzynski)
2nd Panzer Grenadier Battalion (*Hauptmann* Muller)
Self-propelled Gun Infantry Company
Engineer Company
130th Panzer Artillery Regiment (*Major* Zeisler)
1st Panzer Artillery Battalion
2nd Panzer Artillery Battalion
3rd Panzer Artillery Battalion
992nd Medium Artillery Battalion

Divisional troops
130th Panzer Reconnaissance Lehr Battalion (*Major* Gerd von Fallois)
130th Anti-tank Lehr Battalion (*Major* Joachim Barth)
311th Army Anti-aircraft Battalion
130th Panzer Engineer Battalion (*Major* Herbert Eltrich)
130th Panzer Signals Battalion
130th Field Replacement Battalion
130th Supply Troop
130th Motorised Bakery Company
130th Motorised Butcher Company
130th Motorised Divisional Administration Company
130th Medical Battalion
130th Motorised Field Post Office

Appendix VII

Order of Battle, 101st SS-Panzer Battalion of the 1st SS-Panzer Division 'Leibstandarte SS Adolf Hitler' in the Bocage, June 1944

Commanding Officer *SS-Obersturmbannführer* Heinz von Westernhagen
1st Company (*SS-Hauptsturmführer* Rolf Mobious)
2nd Company (*SS-Obersturmführer* Michael Wittmann)
3rd Company (*SS-Obersturmführer* Hanno Raasch)
4th Light Escort Company (*SS-Obersturmführer* Wilhelm Spitz)
Tank Workshop Company (*SS-Obersturmführer* Gottfied Klein)

The following Tigers of 2nd Company fought in Villers Bocage on 13 June 1944:
Tiger 211 (*SS-Obersturmführer* Jurgen Wessel)
Tiger 221 (*SS-Obersturmführer* Georg Hantusch)
Tiger 222 (*SS-Obersturmführer* Kurt Sowa)
Tiger 223 (*SS-Obersturmführer* Jurgen Brendt)
Tiger 233 (*SS-Obersturmführer* Georg Lotzsch)
Tiger 234 (*SS-Unterscharführer* Herbert Stief)

Appendix VIII

Biographical details of Company Sergeant Major Stanley Elton Hollis, VC, 6th Battalion Green Howards

Stanley Elton Hollis was born on 21 September 1912 at 46 Archibald Street, Middlesbrough, Yorkshire, and was the second son of Alfred Edward Hollis, a labourer at the ironworks at the Rye Product Plant on Teesside, who later would be a fishmonger. His mother was Edith Jane Hollis, nee White. His parents had three sons; one died in infancy and Allan Hollis later emigrated to Florida. The family grew up in the difficult time of the First World War and its aftermath.

The cousin of Stanley Elton Hollis, Mrs Dorothy Bird, who emigrated to Quebec in Canada, recalls the early history of the Hollis family:

> We all went to Carlin How School at the beginning of the First World War. Stan's father was away serving in the army, he was gassed but survived and returned home safely at the end of the war. From there we went to Fylingthorpe, part of Robin Hood's Bay, near Whitby. It was a beautiful old house and my mother called it Newton House. Then my family moved to Robin Hood's Bay, quite close to the slipway near the sea. Aunt Eddie and Stan had a house next door. Stan and I first started school there and it were lovely being close to the beach. Stan had a whale of a time playing with toy boats, exploring the rugged coastline and scrambling up the cliff-top paths. I don't remember how long we lived there but Aunt Eddie decided to take a job in munitions and go back to Carlin How near Loftus. After the First World War we moved to Dundas Street, Loftus. Uncle Alf came home after five years away. Aunt Eddie had another baby to add to Stan and his younger brother Alan. This was Stan's brother Billy who only lived two weeks and is buried in a grave in Loftus Cemetery. Stan, Bill Horobin (Stan's cousin) and I went to school there, Liverton Mines Infant School, only Stan didn't go much. He would take off then meet us on the way home, just like us all coming back from school together. He got found out eventually and was in deep trouble. From there Aunt Eddie, Stan and family went to Dormanstown, Middlebrough, when Stan was 11 and then to Beaumont Road, North Ormesby. After school Stanley worked in his parents' wet fish shop.[1]

---

1   Morgan, M., *D-Day Hero, CSM Stanley Hollis VC* (Gloucestershire: Sutton Publishing, 2004), p. 12.

At the age of 14, Stanley met his future wife, Alice Clixby, as they both worked behind the counter of the fish and chip shop. Despite his poor attendance at school, Stanley was awarded a scholarship to go to Sir William Turner's School at Redcar. However, he was needed in the shop and his parents could not afford to let him go. Stanley ran away to sea several times before his father decided to apprentice him in the merchant navy with a Whitby firm, Rowland and Marwood Shipping Company, so he could be trained as a navigation officer. His first vessel was the *Dunsley* of Whitby, in which he made his first voyage, and later he would join the *Elder* of the Dempster Line, which made regular voyages to the West Indies. In 1930, as his ship docked in West Africa, he was taken seriously ill with blackwater fever (a complication of malaria), which ended his naval career. Upon arriving home, Stanley followed his doctor's advice and took a shore job as a lorry driver/mechanic for Tarmacadam and Crossley's Brick Company and continued his courtship of Alice Clixby. His earlier attempts at courtship had ended in failure as Alice had told him he was too short and that she didn't like his red hair. When he left the Merchant Navy he was over 6ft tall and tough looking, so Alice gave in and the couple fell in love. They married at Middlesbrough Registry Office in 1931 and resided at 19 Park Avenue, Ormesby.

In the recession-hit 1930s, Stanley took on any kind of work rather than be unemployed. With the declaration of war in 1939, Stanley was employed by the army driving munitions to the docks. Eventually he joined up with the 4th Battalion Green Howards with a promise by the recruiters that he would be moved to his first choice of the Royal Navy, an empty promise that was never honoured. His application to serve as an officer came to nothing because of his lack of education. At the outbreak of hostilities, he was posted to the 6th Battalion Green Howards, 69 Brigade, 50th Northumbrian Division, and went to France in April 1940 as part of the British Expeditionary Force. He at once stood out to his officers as someone who had potential and was promoted to corporal. After the Dunkirk evacuation, in which he was wounded, he was promoted to the rank of sergeant. The 50th Northumbrian Division was then sent to Iraq, Palestine and Cyprus before being posted to the Gazala Line in the Western Desert and serving with distinction at the Battle of El Alamein in late 1942, moving on to the Tunisian Campaign of 1943 as part of the victorious Eighth Army.

Stanley was promoted to the rank of company sergeant major just before his unit landed in Sicily on 10 July 1943. Here he was seriously wounded during the battle for Catania Airfield and was recommended for the Distinguished Conduct Medal by Lieutenant Colonel Robin Hastings of the 6th Green Howards, but the recommendation was never acted upon. Stanley was, however, Mentioned in Despatches for his bravery in taking out a machine-gun post. Major R. Lofthouse of the 6th Green Howards commented: "If it hadn't been for Hollis we would have been shot up pretty badly." Stanley's wounds took him out of the war for a while and he went to hospital in Algeria for several months until he recovered sufficiently to return to his unit in 1944.

The 6th Green Howards landed at La Riviere on Gold Beach, as part of the spearhead of 69 Brigade at 0730 hours. The details of the actions fought by the 6th Green Howards are covered in this book in detail. Hollis was always in the forefront of the action, and for his fearlessness and bravery was eventually awarded the only Victoria Cross to be given on 6 June for Normandy. During the summer of 1944, Hollis was wounded in the leg by splinters from a mortar bomb and sent home to recover. Many who knew him thought that it was this last wound that saved his life. Hollis commented:

> We were just waiting for the company commander to come back when a whine came through the air. A mortar bomb fell right into the headquarters. The signaller was killed stone dead where he sat, [and] I was sitting not a yard from him."[2]

This was the end of the fighting war for Hollis. He was advised by his doctors, who had to put a steel plate into his skull, that his body could not take any more punishment and he was sent home for good. At the age of 32, he arrived at the family home in Park Avenue North, Old Ormsby, where he slowly recovered from his wounds. When notification of the award of the Victoria Cross arrived, he was a mentally and physically damaged man. His wife Alice commented in 1983:

> When the King's telegram came saying he had won the VC he was still suffering from his war wounds. He just glanced at it, screwed it up into a ball and threw it at the fire. I dare not touch it or he'd have torn it up. When he wasn't looking I rescued it, ironed it out and it's a precious souvenir now.[3]

Once back in civvy street, Hollis went back to driving and labouring work, eventually taking over the management of a pub in the Market Square, North Ormsby, which he renamed The Green Howards. He was a very popular landlord and enforced a strict 'no swearing' policy. Hollis commented: "My customers know I won't stand for any nonsense. In 1970, The Green Howards pub was demolished and he moved on to the Hollywell View public house in Liverton Mines, North Yorkshire.

Later in life, the numerous pieces of metal inflicted by his war wounds came back to haunt Hollis with a vengeance. His leg wounds gave him a lot of serious trouble. During the 1950s he was admitted to hospital to have four deeply embedded bullets removed. They had slowly worked their way from his shoulder and down his arms, to eventually exit from his hands. Other bullets lodged in the bones of his feet would still be there on the day he died.

Stanley Hollis died in North Ormsby Hospital on 8 February 1972, aged 59. He was buried in Acklam Cemetery, Middlesbrough, on 12 February. His old regiment turned out in force to pay their respects to a brave man. Six pallbearers from the Green Howards carried the coffin and a bugler played 'The Last Post' as he was lowered into the ground. Two other VCs were present: Sergeant Bill McNally and Major Edward Cooper. Other officers in attendance were Colonel John Forbes and Brigadier Cooke-Collis, DSO and Bar. In 1982, Mrs Alice Hollis, at the age of 71, sent her husband's group of six medals for auction at Sotheby's, where they fetched a record £32,000. Alice received abusive letters when it became known that she was about to sell her husband's hard-won medals, but it was his dying wish that the money raised in this way should benefit the family. Alice commented:

> He was a wonderful man, so much fun to be with, but he wouldn't have approved of my holding on to his medal, he used to keep it in the button box with the milk tokens. It was not that he wasn't proud of it, that was just him. I wish I had sold the medals ten years

---

2   Morgan, *D-Day Hero, CSM Stanley Hollis VC*, p. 102.
3   Newspaper cutting sent to author by W.F. Vickers, ex-6th Green Howards (1994).

ago he always said it should be sold for the grandchildren, it was doing no good lying in a drawer getting scratched among the bottle tops and I couldn't afford to insure it. He had terrible nightmares after the war, reliving the battles and screaming out. When he first came home he said: "I'm a cripple, lamed for life" then he shut himself up in the bedroom for a week, pushing letters under the door telling me to "Push off" and leave him.[4]

The pain had been eased for Hollis when he was taken into hospital to receive treatment for his wounds and a metal plate was fitted into his skull, and he thereafter began to take an interest in his children, as Alice related:

Brian [their son] grew up to be a Scotland Yard detective, he didn't want me to sell the medal, but it was what his dad wanted. It's all for the grandchildren, all I've bought for myself is a car my daughter drives, I just use the interest on the money to pay the household bills. Everyone thought Stan was a hero except for the government, he died with bullets still in his feet, yet they said he wasn't entitled to a disability pension. I don't think we treat our heroes right. One man stopped me in the street and said it was thanks to Stan that his boy came back alive. Stan would be down sometimes and talk about sending his medal back, but he soon bounced back up again, he was that kind of man. Stan was a wonderful man, and when he died everything collapsed, but he never really left me.[5]

On 6 June 1944, CSM Hollis was to be found where the fighting was heaviest. During all of that day he displayed the utmost gallantry, courage and initiative, and his actions undoubtedly saved the lives of many of his men. In November 2015, his hometown of Middlesbrough paid homage to this brave man and unveiled a bronze statue of him in action carrying a Sten gun. It is situated near the Cenotaph on Linthorpe Road. Brian Bage, who was chairman of the Stanley E. Hollis VC Memorial Fund, said:

This seven-foot magnificent bronze statue was a fitting tribute to a true hero. It's taken a lot of hard work by a great many people, but it's been more than worthwhile. I hope people will come from far and wide to see it, and to remember the actions of a very brave man.

In 2021 I visited the Green Howards Museum in Richmond. The medals of CSM Stanley Hollis were on display, and it was my privilege to see them and to know that the memory of Stanley Hollis is alive and well and will be so for as long as we keep written records of these momentous times.

---

4   Newspaper cutting forwarded to author by W.F. Vickers, ex-6th Green Howards (1994).
5   Newspaper cutting forwarded to author by W.F. Vickers, ex-6th Green Howards (1994).

Appendix IX

German reinforcement divisions which moved into the Normandy battle area between 6 and 18 June 1944

21st SS-Panzer Division (6 June 1944)
12th SS-Panzer Division 'Hitlerjugend' (7 June 1944)
130th Panzer Lehr Division (8/9 June 1944)
346th Infantry Division (8/9 June 1944)
77th Infantry Division (11 June 1944)
2nd SS-Panzer Division 'Das Reich' (13 June 1944)
3rd Fallschirmjaeger Division (13 June 1944)
353rd Infantry Division (16 June 1944)
1st SS-Panzer Division 'Leibstandarte Adolf Hitler' (18 June 1944)

Appendix X

British operational codenames, 1944

Anvil (later rechristened Dragoon): Allied landing in the south of France (August).
Bluecoat: British Second Army offensive towards Mount Pinçon and Vire (begun 30 July).
Bodyguard: Cover and deception plan for the Allied strategy in Europe.
Cobra: American break-out at St Lo (begun 25 July).
Dauntless: XXX Corps operation in the Epsom battles (25 June).
Epsom: British Second Army offensive to cross the Odon and Orne Rivers south-west of Caen (26 June to 1 July).
Fortitude: Cover plan for Overlord.
Goodwood: British Second Army offensive south-east of Caen (18–21 July).
Gooseberry: Artificial breakwaters for offshore anchorages and Mulberry Harbour, largely composed of block-ships known as Corncobs.
Jupiter: VIII Corps attack towards the upper Orne (10 July).
Maple: Mine-laying programme during Neptune operations.
Mulberry: Artificial harbour off the Normandy coast.
Neptune: Naval assault phase of Overlord.
Overlord: Plan for the invasion of France.
Phoenix: Concrete caisson for Mulberry breakwaters.
Pluto: Acronym for 'Pipeline under the ocean', a scheme to supply petrol from England to the continent by underwater pipeline.
Totalize: Canadian First Army offensive towards Falaise (Phase 1, 8–11 August).
Tractable: Canadian First Army offensive towards Falaise (Phase 2, 14–16 August).

Appendix XI

Order of Battle, 49th West Riding Division, attached to XXX Corps from 13 June–30 July 1944

Commanding Officer Major General E.W. Barker

70 Brigade
CO Brigadier Edward Cooke-Collis
10th Battalion Durham Light Infantry
11th Battalion Durham Light Infantry
1st Battalion Tyneside Scottish
146 Brigade
CO Brigadier J. Walker
4th Battalion Lincolnshire Regiment
1/4th Battalion King's Own Yorkshire Light Infantry
The Hallamshire Battalion, the York and Lancaster Regiment
147 Brigade
CO Brigadier James Mahoney
6th Battalion Duke of Wellington's Regiment
7th Battalion Duke of Wellington's Regiment
11th Battalion Royal Scots Fusiliers
Divisional troops
228, 229, 230, 294, 756 and 757 Field Coys, Royal Engineers
231 and 289 Field Park Coys, Royal Engineers
23 Bridging Platoon, Royal Engineers
49th Divisional Signals
69th, 70th, 71st, 79th, 80th, 178th and 185th Field Regiments, Royal Artillery
55th, 58th and 88th Anti-tank Regiments, Royal Artillery
89th and 118th Light Anti-aircraft Regiments, Royal Artillery
2nd Machine-gun Battalion Princess Louisa's Kensington Regiment
49 Royal Army Service Corps

Appendix XII

Order of Battle, 79th Armoured Division, June 1944

Commanding Officer Major General G.G. Roberts, DSO and Two Bars, MC

30 Armoured Brigade
22nd Dragoons
2nd County of London Yeomanry, Westminster Dragoons
1st Lothian and Border Horse
Other divisional troops
1st Assault Squadron, Royal Engineers
149th Assault Park Squadron, Royal Engineers
5th Assault Regiment, Royal Engineers
26th, 77th, 79th and 80th Assault Squadrons, Royal Engineers
6th Assault Regiment, Royal Engineers
81st, 82nd, 87th and 284th Squadrons, Royal Engineers
42nd Assault Regiment, Royal Engineers
16th, 222nd, 557th and 617th Assault Squadrons, Royal Engineers

Appendix XIII

Order of Battle, 43rd Wessex Division, joined XXX Corps, 13 June 1944

Commanding Officer Major General Ivor Thomas, DSO, MC and Bar

129 Brigade
CO Brigadier G.H.L. Mole, DSO and Bar, MC (KIA 14 November 1944)
4th Battalion Somerset Light Infantry
4th Battalion Wiltshire Regiment
5th Battalion Wiltshire Regiment
130 Brigade
CO Brigadier N.D. Leslie
7th Battalion Royal Hampshire Regiment
4th Battalion Dorsetshire Regiment
5th Battalion Dorsetshire Regiment
214 Brigade
CO Brigadier H. Essame, DSO, MC
7th Battalion Somerset Light Infantry
1st Battalion Worcestershire Regiment
5th Battalion Duke of Cornwall's Light Infantry
Divisional troops
43rd Reconnaissance Regiment, the Gloucester Regiment
8th Battalion Middlesex Regiment (Machine guns and Mortars)
43rd Wessex Divisional Signals
Royal Artillery
94th, 112th and 179th Field Regiments, 59th Anti-tank Regiment, 110th Light Anti-aircraft Regiment
Royal Engineers
204, 260 and 553 Field Companies
207 Field Park Company
13th Bridging Platoon
Royal Army Service Corps
54, 504, 505 and 506 Companies

Royal Army Medical Corps
129, 130 and 213 Field Ambulance
14 and 15 Field Dressing Stations
38 Field Hygiene Section
43rd Ordnance Field Park
306 Mobile Laundry and Bath Unit

Appendix XIV

Order of Battle, 11th Armoured Division, August 1944

Commanding Officer Major General G.P.B. Roberts, DSO and Two Bars

29 Armoured Brigade
23rd Hussars
2nd Fife and Forfar Yeomanry
3rd Battalion Royal Tank Regiment
8th Battalion the Rifle Brigade
30 Armoured Brigade
22nd Dragoons
Westminster Dragoons
1st Lothian and Border Horse
2nd Queen's Westminsters
12th Battalion King's Royal Rifle Corps
159 Infantry Brigade
4th Battalion King's Shropshire Light Infantry
3rd Battalion Monmouthshire Regiment
1st Battalion Herefordshire Regiment
Divisional troops
2nd Independent Machine-gun Company
2nd Battalion Northamptonshire Yeomanry Reconnaissance Regiment (disbanded 17 August 1944)
15/19th King's Royal Hussars Reconnaissance Regiment (disbanded 17 August 1944)
13th Regiment, Royal Horse Artillery
151st Field Regiment, Royal Artillery
58th Light Anti-aircraft Regiment, Royal Artillery
13th and 612th Field Squadrons, Royal Engineers
147th Field Park Squadron, Royal Engineers
10th Bridging Platoon, Royal Engineers
11th Armoured Division Signals, Royal Corps of Signals

Appendix XV

Order of Battle, 59th Staffordshire Division, joined XXX Corps, 13 June–24 July 1944 (disbanded August 1944)

Commanding Officer Major General L.O. Lyne, DSO

176 Brigade
6th Battalion North Staffordshire Regiment
7th Battalion North Staffordshire Regiment
7th Battalion Royal Norfolk Regiment
177 Brigade
5th Battalion South Staffordshire Regiment
1/6th Battalion South Staffordshire Regiment
2/6th Battalion South Staffordshire Regiment
197 Brigade
5th Battalion East Lancashire Regiment
2/5th Battalion Lancashire Fusiliers
1/7th Battalion Royal Warwickshire Regiment
Divisional troops
7th Battalion Royal Northumberland Fusiliers
59th Reconnaissance Regiment, Royal Armoured Corps
Divisional Artillery
61st, 110th and 116th Regiments, Royal Artillery
Divisional Engineers
257, 509 and 510 Field Companies, Royal Engineers

Appendix XVI

Order of Battle, 12th SS-Panzer Division 'Hitlerjugend', Normandy, June 1944

Commanding Officer *SS-Brigadeführer* Fritz Witt (KIA 14 June 1944, replaced by *SS-Standartenführer* Kurt Meyer)

25th SS-Panzer Grenadier Regiment; 1st, 2nd and 3rd Battalions, each consisting of four Companies
13th Anti-tank Company
14th Flak Company
15th Reconnaissance Company
16th Pioneer Company
12th SS-Panzer Regiment
1st Battalion, consisting of four companies
2nd Battalion, consisting of six companies
12th SS-Artillery Regiment, consisting of three battalions
12th SS-Motorcycle Regiment
12th SS-Reconnaissance Battalion, consisting of five companies
12th SS-Panzerjager Battalion, consisting of two batteries
12th SS-Nebelwerfer Battalion, consisting of three batteries
12th SS-Flak Battalion, consisting of four batteries
12th SS-Pioneer Battalion, consisting of three companies and one bridging unit
12th SS-Panzer Signals Battalion
12th SS-Panzer Instandsetzungs-Recovery Unit
12th SS-Nachschub-Supply Troops
12th SS-Wirtschafts-Labour Company
12th SS-Fuhrerbewerber Lehrgange
12th SS-War Reporter Platoon
12th SS-Feldgendarmerie Company
12th SS-Field Post Office
12th SS-Medical Battalion

Appendix XVII

Biographical details of Lieutenant General Sir Brian Horrocks, KCB, KBE, DSO, MC, LL.D

Brian Horrocks, the only son of Colonel Sir William (RAMC) and Mina Horrocks, was born in Ranikhet, India, on 7 September 1895. He entered the Royal Military Academy, Sandhurst, in October 1912 and was in his own words "idle, careless about my turnout and scruffy". He was an unpromising student, who may never have received a commission at all if it was not for the outbreak of the Great War. He was commissioned as a 2nd lieutenant into the Middlesex Regiment on 8 August 1914 and joined the 1st Battalion, part of 19 Independent Brigade, with the British Expeditionary Force. On 21 October 1914, at Armentieres, he received a bullet through the abdomen and was taken prisoner. He was promoted to full lieutenant on 18 December 1914, despite being in captivity. Horrocks made numerous attempts to escape and was eventually placed in a Russian officers' compound, where he became fluent in the Russian language. His resistance to being in captivity earned him a Military Cross, awarded in 1920.

In 1919, Horrocks was posted to Russia as part of the Allied intervention in the Russian Civil War, returning home on 29 October 1919 and rejoining his regiment based in Germany as part of the British Army of the Rhine. From there he was posted to Ireland, which was then embroiled in the Anglo-Irish War. This was followed by a stint in Silesia to keep the peace between the German and Polish populations. When he returned to Britain, he took up the Modern Pentathlon and was picked for the British team for the 1924 Paris Olympics.

During the interwar years, he received a variety of postings that included: Adjutant 9th Middlesex; student at the Staff College, Camberley; Staff Captain at the War Office; Brigade Major, 5 Infantry Brigade; and instructor at the Staff College. In 1928, Horrocks married Nancy Kitchin and they had one daughter, Gillian, who drowned in the River Thames in 1979. At the outbreak of the Second World War, he was promoted to lieutenant colonel and went to France to command the 2nd Middlesex, taking over as they retreated to Dunkirk. He was then promoted to brigadier and commanded 11 Brigade. Upon their return home he took over 9 Brigade to defend the south coast against invasion. His next promotion was to acting major general in command of the 44th Home Counties Division.

In March 1942, he took over command of the newly formed 9th Armoured Division and gained the temporary rank of major general, and in spite of never having commanded a division in battle was given the command of XIII Corps under Montgomery. Once in North Africa, Horrocks' corps was given the task of defending Alam Halfa Ridge, which they did successfully, the Germans being repelled with heavy casualties. XIII Corps held the southern sector at Alamein in the autumn of 1942 while the main thrust was launched by Montgomery near the coast. In December 1942, Horrocks relinquished command of XIII Corps and took over command of X Corps, and on 31 December was appointed a Companion of the Distinguished Service Order.

At Mareth in Tunisia 1943, Horrocks carried out one of his most successful actions, a flanking manoeuvre that rendered the Mareth positions untenable, forcing the Axis forces to retreat. Horrocks then transferred to First Army to take over IX Corps and led them in the final offensive in Tunisia. He was Mentioned in Despatches in June 1943 and was appointed a Companion of the Order of the Bath on 5 August, being given the temporary rank of lieutenant general. In June 1943, he was commanding X Corps and was watching the 46th Division at Bizerte as they practised for the landings at Salerno, when he was hit by bullets from a German fighter plane. The bullets passed through his upper chest and carried on through his body, piercing his lungs, stomach and intestines. He spent 14 months recovering and underwent five operations. It was a year before he was ready to serve again, being restored to the rank of lieutenant general and given command of XXX Corps in August 1944, leading them through the Bocage to the Seine and beyond. In September 1944, XXX Corps received the task to lead the ground assault in Operation Market Garden, but the British advance never made it to the beleaguered paratroopers at Arnhem. After this failed operation, XXX Corps took its first German town, Geilenkirchen, during Operation Clipper. During the Battle of the Bulge, Horrocks, having become nervy and difficult to deal with, was relieved of his command by Montgomery so he could go home and rest, and was replaced temporarily by Major General Ivor Thomas of the 43rd Wessex Division.

Horrocks was back with XXX Corps in 1945, and the whole corps was transferred to the Canadian First Army to take part in Operation Veritable. He accepted the need for the massed bombing of the town of Cleves, a decision that haunted him long after the war, but the German Army was forced back over the Rhine. XXX Corps then broke through the Siegfried Line and advanced into the heart of Germany, crossing the Rhine on 23 March. XXX Corps had reached Cuxhaven by the time hostilities ceased in May 1945. Horrocks was Mentioned in Despatches twice in 1945 and was appointed Knight Commander of the Order of the British Empire on 5 July that year. He was also honoured with awards from Belgium, France, the Netherlands, Greece and the United States. On the day the Bergen-Belsen Concentration Camp was liberated on 5 April 1945, Horrocks was given the task of rescuing the thousands of inmates. He requisitioned all food stores in the area, water trucks and army medical services that were available. He continued to serve in the British Army until he fell ill in August 1948.

In 1949 he was appointed Gentleman Usher of the Black Rod in the Houses of Parliament and held this post until 1963. He later had many articled published on military matters and this led to a short but successful career as a television presenter, appearing in the landmark television series *The World at War*. His autobiography, *A Full Life*, was published in 1960, and he also co-authored *Corps Commander*, an account of the battles in North-West Europe, published in 1977. In the film *A Bridge Too Far*, based on Operation Market Garden, he acted as military advisor; he was portrayed in the film by Edward Fox.

Horrocks died on 4 January 1985, aged 89, at Fishbourne, West Sussex. A well-attended memorial ceremony for him was held in Westminster Abbey. His body was cremated and the ashes deposited at the crematorium near Chichester until 2022, when the Princess of Wales's Royal Regiment, a successor to his own Middlesex Regiment, organised a private burial at St Paul's Church in Mill Hill.

Bibliography

Addington, S., *Invasion* (London: Unicorn Publishing, 2019).
Agte, P., *Michael Wittmann and the Waffen SS Tiger Commanders of the Leibstandarte in WW2, Vol. I* (USA: Stackpole Books, 2006).
Agte, P., *Michael Wittmann and the Waffen SS Tiger Commanders of the Leibstandarte in WW2, Vol. II* (USA: Stackpole Books, 2006).
Arthur, M., *Forgotten Voices of the Second World War* (London: Ebury Press, 2004).
Badsey (ed.), S., *World War Two Battle Plans* (Oxford: Helicon Publishing, 2000).
Bailey, R., *Forgotten Voices of D-Day* (London: Ebury Press, 2009).
Barclay, C.N., *History of the Duke of Wellington's Regiment 1919–1952* (London: William Clowes, 1953).
Bastable, J., *Voices from D-Day, Eyewitness Accounts of 6th June 1944* (Newton Abbot: David and Charles, 2004).
Baverstock, K., *Breaking the Panzers* (Gloucestershire: Sutton Publishing, 2016).
Beckett (ed.), I.F.W., *Rommel, a Reappraisal* (Barnsley: Pen & Sword, 2013).
Beevor, A., *D-Day, The Battle for Normandy* (London: Penguin, 2010).
Belfield, E. and Essame, H., *Sir Brian Horrocks, Corps Commander* (London: Sidgwick & Jackson, 1977).
Belfield, E. and Essame, H., *The Battle for Normandy* (London: Purnell, 1965).
Bowman, M.W., *Air War D-Day. Gold, Juno and Sword* (Barnsley: Pen & Sword, 2013).
Bowman, M.W., *Remembering D-Day* (London: Harper Collins, 2004).
Carell, P. (trans. from the German by E. Osers), *Invasion – They're Coming!* (London: Harrap and Co, 1962).
Carruthers, B., *Voices of the Luftwaffe* (Berkshire: Archive Media Publishing Ltd, 2011).
Carruthers, B. and Trew, S., *The Normandy Battles* (London: Cassel, 2000).
Cawthorne, N., *Fighting them on the Beaches, The D-Day landings, 6th June 1944* (London: Arcturus Publishing, 2017).
Clay, E.W., *The Path of the 50th* (Aldershot: Gale and Polden, 1950).
Cloudsley-Thompson, J.L., *Sharpshooter* (London: Arcturus Press, 2006).
Collier, R., *D-Day, June 6th, 1944* (London: Cassel, 1992).
Crookenden, A., *History of the Cheshire Regiment* (London: Evans, 1949).
Cooper, M., *German Army 1939/45* (London: MacDonald and Jane's Publishers, 1978).
Cooper, M. and Lucas, J., *Panzer – The Armoured Force of the Third Reich* (London: MacDonald and Jane's Publishers, 1979).
Delaforce, P., *Churchill's Desert Rats* (Gloucestershire: Sutton Publishing, 1994).

Delaforce, P., *Marching to the Sound of Gunfire, Northwest Europe 1944–45* (Gloucestershire: Sutton Publishing, 1996).
Delaforce, P., *Monty's Marauders* (Gloucestershire: Sutton Publishing, 1993).
Delaforce, P., *Monty's Northern Legions* (Gloucestershire: Sutton Publishing, 2004).
Delafore, P., *The Fighting Wessex Wyverns* (Gloucestershire: Sutton Publishing, 1994).
Delaforce, P., *The Polar Bears – Monty's Left Flank: from Normandy to the Relief of Holland with the 49th Division* (Gloucestershire: Sutton Publishing, 1995).
D'Este, C., *Decision in Normandy* (London: Collins, 1983).
D'Este, C., *Eisenhower: Allied Supreme Commander* (London: Weidenfeld & Nicolson, 2002).
Doherty. R., *Normandy 1944 – the Road to Victory* (Kent: Spellmount, 2004).
Doherty, R., *Hobart's 79th Armoured Division at War* (Barnsley: Pen & Sword, 2011).
Dunphie, C. and Johnson, G., *Gold Beach* (Barnsley: Pen & Sword, 1999).
Ellis, J., *Brute Force* (London: Andre Deutsch, 1990).
Ellis, L.F., *Victory in the West, Volume 1, the Battle of Normandy* (London: HMSO, 1962).
Essame, H., *The 43rd Wessex Division at War 1944–45* (London: M. Clowes, 1952).
Ford, K., *Assault Crossing the River Seine, 1944* (Devon: David and Charles, 1987).
Forty, G., *Battle Zone Normandy – Villers Bocage* (Gloucestershire: Sutton Publishing, 2004).
Gill, R. and Groves, J., *Club Route, 30 Corps in Europe* (Hanover: Werner Degener, 1945).
Graham, A., *Sharpshooters at War* (London: Sharpshooters Regimental Association, 1964).
Greenwood, T. (ed., Partington, S.V), *D-Day to Victory, The Diaries of a British Tank Commander* (London: Simon & Schuster, 2012).
Gilchrist, R.T., *Malta Strikes Back, the Story of 231 Brigade* (London: Gale & Polden, 1954).
Hamilton, N., *Monty, the Battles of Field Marshal Bernard Law Montgomery* (London: Hodder & Stoughton, 1981).
Hart-Dyke, T., *Normandy to Arnhem: A Story of the Infantry* (Sheffield: Greenup & Thompson, 1966).
Hastings, M., *Overlord, D-Day and the Battle for Normandy* (London: Michael Joseph, 1984).
Hastings, M., *Das-Reich* (London: Pan Books, 1983).
Hasting, R., *The Rifle Brigade 1939–1945* (London: Gale and Polden, 1950).
Hennessey, P., *Young Man in a Tank* (privately published, 1988).
Hill, M., *D-Day to Victory* (London: Atlantic Publishing, 2002).
Hills, S., *By Tank to Normandy* (London: Orion Publishing, 2003).
Holdsworth, D., *One Day I'll Tell You* (Yorkshire: Westfield Publications, 1994).
Holland, J., *Normandy '44, D-Day and the Battle for France* (London: Bantam Press, 2019).
Holland (ed), J., *An Englishman at War, the Wartime Diaries of Stanley Christopherson, DSO, MC, TD 1939–45* (London: Corgi Books, 2014).
Holmes, R., *D-Day, from the Invasion to the Liberation of Paris* (London: Carlton Books, 2004).
Horrocks, B., *A Full Life* (London: Collins, 1960).
Howarth, D., *Dawn of D-Day* (London: Odhams Press, 1959).
Hughes, F.K., *A Short History of the 49th West Riding and Midland Division* (Hertfordshire: Stellar Press, 1957).
Hunt, E., *Mont Pinçon* (London: Leo Cooper, 2002).
Isby (ed.), D.C., *Fighting in Normandy, the German Army from D-Day to Villers Bocage* (London: Greenhill Books, 2001).
Jary, S., *18 Platoon* (Somerset: Light Infantry Office, 1998).

Johnson, G. and Dunphie, C., *Brightly Shone the Dawn* (London: Frederick Warne Ltd, 1980).
Jolsen, H.F., *Orders of Battle 1939–1945* (London: HMSO, 1960).
Keegan, J., *Six Armies in Normandy* (London: Jonathan Cape Ltd, 1982).
Kershaw, R.J., *D-Day, Piercing the Atlantic Wall* (Surrey: Ian Allan, Publishing, 1993).
Kershaw, R.J., *Tank Men* (London: Hodder & Stoughton, 2008).
Kite, B., *Stout Hearts, The British and Canadians in Normandy, 1944* (Solihull: Helion & Co, 2016).
Lee, D., *Beachhead Assault* (London: Greenhill Books, 2004).
Lewis, P.J. and English, I.R., *The 8th Battalion Durham Light Infantry 1939–1945* (Newcastle: J. & P. Bealls, 1949).
Liddell Hart, B., *A History of the Second World War* (London: Cassell, 1970).
Liddell Hart, B., *The Other Side of the Hill* (London: Pan Books, 1983).
Liddell Hart, B., *The Rommel Papers* (London: Da Capo Press, 1953).
Lindsay, M., *So Few Got Through* (London: Collins, 1946).
Lindsay, T.M., *Sherwood Rangers* (London: Burrup & Mathieson, 1952).
Lipscomb, C.G., DSO and Bar, *History of the 4th Battalion the Somerset Light Infantry in the Campaign in North-west Europe, June, 1944 – May, 1945* (Taunton: Goodman, 1946).
Lucas, J., *Das-Reich – The military role of the 2nd SS Division Das-Reich* (London: Cassel, 1991).
Lucas, J. and Barker, J., *The Killing Ground – The Battle of the Falaise Gap August 1944* (London: B.T. Batsford, 1978).
Macksey, K., *Anatomy of a Battle* (London: Stein and Day, 1974).
Mayo, J., *D-Day Minute by Minute* (London: Short Books, 2014).
McKee, A., *The Race for the Rhine Bridges* (London: Pan Books, 1974).
McMath, J.S., *The 5th Battalion Wiltshire Regiment in North-west Europe* (London: Whitefriars Press, 1946).
Miller, C.H., *History of the 13/18th Royal Hussars 1922–47* (London: Blackwood, 1949).
Miller, R., *Nothing Less than Victory, the Oral History of D-Day* (London: Michael Joseph Ltd, 1993).
Milton, G., *D-Day, the Soldier's Story* (London: John Murray, 2019).
Mitcham, S.W., *Hitler's Legions* (London: Leo Cooper, 1985).
Mollo, B., *Sharpshooters* (Kent: Historical Research Unit, 1970).
Montgomery, B.L., *Memoirs* (London: Collins, 1958).
Moorehead, A., *Eclipse* (London: Hamish Hamilton, 1946).
Morgan, M., *D-Day Hero, CSM Stanley Hollis VC* (Gloucestershire: Sutton Publishing, 2004).
Moses, H., *The Faithful Sixth* (Durham: County Durham Books, 1995).
Moses, H., *The Gateshead Gurkhas* (Durham: County Durham Books, 2001).
Neave, J.A.S., *The War Diaries of Julius Neave, 13/18th Hussars* (Essex: privately published, 1995).
Neillands, R., *The Battle of Normandy 1944* (London: Cassell, 2002).
Neillands, R. and Norman, R., *D-Day 1944, Voices from Normandy* (London: Cassel, 1993).
Neville, R.F., *The First Northamptonshire Yeomanry in North-west Europe* (Brunswick: J.H. Meyer, 1946).
Nightingale, P.R., *The East Yorkshire Regiment in the War, 1939–45* (Howden: Mr Pye Books, 1952).
Picot, G., *Accidental Warrior* (London: Penguin Books, 1994).
Poppel, M., *Heaven and Hell, the War Diary of a German Paratrooper* (Kent: Spellmount, 1988).

Powdrill, E., *In the Face of the Enemy, A Battery Sergeant Major in Action in World War Two* (Barnsley: Pen & Sword, 2009).
Reddish, A., *Normandy 1944: From the Hull of a Sherman* (New Zealand: Battlefield Associates, 1995).
Render, D., *Tank Action, An Armoured Troop Commander's War 1944/45* (London: Weidenfeld & Nicolson, 2016).
Rissik, D., *The DLI at War* (Durham: DLI, Brancepeth Castle, 1953).
Royal Engineers Battlefield Tour. Normandy to the Seine (British Army of the Rhine, 1946. Completed under the direction of the Chief Engineer).
Saunders, T., *Commandos and Rangers: D-Day Operations* (Barnsley: Pen & Sword, 2012).
Saunders, T., *Gold Beach – Jig* (Barnsley, Pen & Sword, 2002).
Saunders, T., *The Battle for the Bocage, Normandy 1944* (Barnsley: Pen & Sword, 2021).
Saunders, T. and Hone, R., *12th Hitler Jugend SS Panzer Division in Normandy* (Barnsley: Pen & Sword, 2021).
Schneider, W., *Tigers in Normandy* (Barnsley: Pen & Sword, 2011).
Stafford, D., *Ten Days to D-Day, Countdown to the liberation of Europe* (London: Little, Brown, 2003).
Stirling, J.D.P., *The First and the Last, The Story of the 4/7th Royal Dragoon Guards 1939–1945* (London: Art and Educational Publishers, 1946).
Synge, W.A.T., *The Story of the Green Howards, 1939–1945* (Richmond: The Green Howards, 1952).
Taylor, J., *A History of the 43rd Reconnaissance Regiment 1939–45* (Bristol: White Swan Press, 1950).
Tout, K., *Tanks, Advance! Normandy to the Netherlands 1944* (London: Robert Hale Ltd, 1987).
Townend, W. and Baldwin, F., *Gunners in Normandy, The History of the Royal Artillery in North-West Europe January 1942 to August 1944* (Gloucestershire: The History Press, 2020).
Trigg, J., *D-Day Through German Eyes, How the Wehrmacht lost France* (Gloucestershire: Amberley Publishing, 2019).
Urban, M., *The Tank War* (London: Little, Brown, 2013).
Verney, G.L., *The Desert Rats, A History of the 7th Armoured Division 1938–45* (London: Hutchinson, 1954).
Warner, P., *Horrocks, the General who Led from the Front* (London: Hamish Hamilton, 1984).
Warner, P., *The D-Day Landings* (London: William Kimber, 1980).
Watkins, G.J., *From Normandy to the Weser, the War History of the 4th Battalion Dorsetshire Regiment, June 1944 to May 1945* (East Sussex: Naval and Military Press, 2015).
Watson, D.Y., *The 1st Battalion Worcestershire Regiment in North-west Europe* (London: privately published, 1946).
Whitehouse, S., *Fear is the Foe, A Footslogger from Normandy to the Rhine* (London: Robert Hale, 1988).
Whiting, C., *The Poor Bloody Infantry* (London: Paul, 1987).
Williams, A., *D-Day to Berlin* (London: Hodder & Stoughton, 2004).
Williamson, G., *Loyalty is my Honour* (London: Motorbooks, 1997).

Index

General

Aitken, Trooper Don 297, 322
Atlantic Wall 13, 15–17, 55, 96, 110,135, 151, 197, 222, 515
Audrieu 247, 249-251, 253, 256, 300, 321, 346, 349, 374, 394, 421

Backhouse, Major John Edmund 574
Bailey bridges 491, 518, 553-555
Baker, Trooper Austin 67, 158-159, 271, 353, 355, 374, 591
Balleroy Road 319, 340
Barbee Farm 349, 357–3p59, 362–363, 366
Bayerlein *Generalleutnant* Fritz 216–218, 331
Bayeux 25, 54, 97, 125, 141, 143-144, 150, 192, 195-197, 200, 211, 213-214, 230-233, 235, 252, 258, 286, 298-300, 302, 320, 338, 345, 418, 586
Bean, Lieutenant Donald Francis 485
Berjou 487-497
Bois-du-Homme 445–7, 449
Bois Jerome 548, 562, 572–574, 578–579
Bretteville 286, 321, 349, 384-385, 388, 395, 399-400, 428
Briquessard 286, 436, 438–439, 441

Caen 46, 67, 97, 143-144, 214-215, 218, 222, 225, 243, 252, 258, 274-275, 278. 280, 292, 294, 300, 346, 349, 367, 422-426, 429, 431, 438, 476, 511,
Cahagnes 436, 438, 440–442, 444, 586
Caumont 217, 269, 275–276, 286, 290-291, 294, 426, 437-438
Centaur tanks 84, 94
Churchill tanks 84–86, 106, 158, 356

Conde-sur-Noireau 425, 436, 476– 477, 486, 488
Creully 125, 128, 131, 181
Cristot 120, 253, 255-256, 258-259, 286, 321, 327-330, 349, 426
Crocodile flamethrower tanks 142, 164, 213, 318, 333, 340, 402, 409, 413, 430-431
Cromwell tanks 159, 270-271, 275-277, 280-283, 285, 287, 291-292, 337, 577

Dring, Sergeant George 252, 377
DUKWs 214, 518, 525, 531, 533, 535, 542

Essame, Brigadier Hubert 269, 443, 473, 490, 493–494, 513, 559–560, 584

FFI (French Forces of the Interior) 513-515, 517, 523, 525
Firefly tanks 275, 282, 311–313, 377, 570
Flower, Sergeant Rex 328-329, 362, 364-366
Francs, Trooper Sydney 355
Fontenay-le-Pesnel 247, 286, 299, 346-352, 355–357, 362, 367–371, 373, 375–376, 380, 384, 406
Franks, Lieutenant Hugh 470

Gold Beach 16-17, 19, 25, 32, 62, 66, 68, 77, 80-84, 86, 88, 91, 101-112, 115, 117, 124, 126, 134, 136-140, 146, 148, 150, 152, 157, 161, 164-165, 167, 170-171, 179; 185, 187, 189-191, 197-198, 211, 214, 223, 234, 320, 586

Hardy, Private Norman 77, 239, 265, 512, 545
Harris, Sergeant Wilfred 311-313, 372

627

Hawker Typhoon fighter-bombers 73, 82, 91, 145, 158, 195, 219-222, 235, 243,289, 302, 315, 317, 348, 379, 413-414, 416, 431-432, 449-450, 485, 503-505
Hedgehogs 89–90, 97, 167
Hergest, Brigadier James 236-237, 242
Hills, Lieutenant Stuart 41, 115-116, 353, 356, 371, 376, 380, 383, 416, 439, 442, 448-450, 452, 454-455, 491, 494-495, 588
Hinde, Brigadier Robert 575, 580
Hitler, Adolf 13, 15-16, 18-19, 22, 93, 148, 224, 241, 436, 476, 501-502, 515-516
HMS *Orion* 129, 136
Honey tanks *see* Stuart light tanks
Horrocks, Major-General Brian 435, 470, 472-473, 487, 513, 517, 582
Hottot- Le-Bagues 269, 286, 294-295, 301, 321-322, 339-345, 407-408, 410, 412-417, 419-420, 586

Johnson, Sergeant Clifford 434
Jurques-du-Fresne 438, 447–451

La Rivière 16, 23, 25, 54, 67, 77, 85, 96-97, 100, 102, 112-113, 125, 477, 479, 488
La Variniere 460, 465–467, 473
LCAs 70, 74, 78–79, 88, 115, 123, 153, 156, 164, 172, 177–178, 183–186
LCTs 26, 47, 52, 54, 58-59, 64-68, 71, 76-79, 81-82, 84, 88, 90, 92, 96, 103-105, 115, 152, 155, 156-159, 161-162, 164-165, 173, 179
Le-Plessis-Grimoult 473–474, 476–478, 483
Lingèvres 301-3, 305, 307, 309-312, 314-316, 321-322, 330, 481

Mayo, Trooper Kenneth 66, 84, 162, 192, 440
Minogue, Trooper Joe 149, 161, 175
Mole, Brigadier George Herbert Leo 536, 538, 551, 574
Montgomery, General Bernard (Monty) 19-20, 30-32, 37-38, 43, 45-46, 50, 53, 67-68, 249, 167, 199-200, 224-225, 230, 257, 274, 296, 316, 346, 379, 404, 407, 421-422, 431, 433, 498, 501, 525, 583, 585-586
Mont Pinçon, 286, 436, 444-447, 453, 456, 458, 460, 462-4, 468-474, 476-48, 488, 586
Mortain 436, 501–2

Noireau (River) 486-90, 492, 496, 511

Noyers 286, 321, 426, 428-431, 586

Oldfield, Private Ronald 472
Ondefontaine 444–446, 449, 452–453, 455

Panther tanks 128, 272, 275, 281, 285, 310, 314, 342, 414
Postles, Trooper Eric 322, 338
Port-en-Bessin 25, 150, 153, 183, 187–189, 213, 234–236, 238, 240–243
Pressagny 552, 557, 560–561

Queudeville, 395, 399–400, 402, 428–429

Render, Lieutenant David 152, 155, 162-163, 166, 198, 249, 258, 263, 265-267, 269, 350-352, 368, 370, 376, 378, 410-415, 435, 439-440, 442, 444,451, 454-455, 486, 492, 510, 588
Rommel, *Generalfeldmarschall* Erwin 13, 16-20, 22-23, 75, 93, 149, 219, 269, 296, 379, 422, 585
Roucamps 457

Scissors bridge 489
Seulles (River) 128, 243, 247, 277, 298
Sherman tanks 43, 84, 105-106, 128, 131, 141-142, 145, 152, 155, 160, 163-166, 192-193, 198, 200-201, 205, 213, 250-251, 253, 255, 258-259, 265-267, 270-271, 275, 280, 282-284, 299, 302, 306, 310-311, 313-314, 328-329, 333-334, 336-367, 340, 342, 353-354, 355-356, 361, 371-373, 376-377, 379-381, 384-385, 388, 390, 392, 399, 402, 411-412, 415, 423, 426, 428-431, 435, 438-441, 444, 447-452, 455-456, 460, 465, 467-468, 471-472, 474, 480, 486, 489, 492, 494, 497, 510, 560-562, 563, 570, 588
Smith, Trooper Norman 159
Southampton Water 65, 68–69
Stanier, Brigadier Alexander 153, 163
St Pierre 247, 250, 252, 259–267, 346, 350
St Pierre-du-Fresne 436, 438, 443–445
St Pierre-la-Vieille 476, 479–482
Stuart light tanks 275, 282, 288

Taylor, Lieutenant-Colonel George 494, 552-553, 557-558, 560-561, 582
Tessel-Brettevillette 346, 371–372, 384–385, 387, 390

Tessel Wood 300, 321, 347–350, 355, 357–359, 361, 363–364, 366, 371–733, 384-385, 387, 390, 586
Tiger tanks 182, 251, 261, 266, 274-275, 277, 279-288, 291, 293, 308, 312-313, 330, 333, 340, 342, 347, 361, 369, 374, 376, 377, 383, 396, 408, 429, 431, 443, 448-450, 475-478, 557, 562-564, 566-581, 588
Tilly-sur-Seulles 247, 250, 253, 268–269, 274, 276, 293, 295, 299, 321–322, 330–331, 334, 337–339
Trasenster, Lietenant David 128-129
Trasenster, Lieutenant Michael 164, 166, 313, 406, 560-561
Treloar, Trooper George 468, 472

Utah Beach 18, 62

Verity, Major Jack 27, 29, 124, 126–27, 131, 149, 327, 482

Vernon 513–527, 529–582, 586–588
Vernonnet 515–516, 519, 531, 533, 535–536, 538, 540–541, 543–546, 548-549, 552-553, 556–557, 559, 563–564, 588
Verrières 301-303, 308-311, 316, 321-322, 483
Villers Bocage 217, 222, 225-226, 247, 249, 269, 274-294, 312, 321, 330, 340, 346, 367, 393, 426, 429, 432-437, 476, 587

Warters, Company Sergeant Major George 32, 124
Watson, Sergeant David 396-367
Williams, Lieutenant Jack 302, 305-7
Wittmann, *SS-Obersturmführer* Michael 278–83, 292–93
Woods, Lieutenant Colonel Humphrey Reginald 301, 305-309

Index of Military Formations & Units

British
55th Anti-Tank Regiment 328, 350, 365, 392, 395
68th Anti-Tank Regiment 366
73rd Anti-Tank Regiment 106-107
217th Anti-Tank Regiment 390
288th Anti-Tank Regiment 261

County of London Yeomanry 270, 274-278, 280-281, 283

Devonshire Regiment 51, 70-71, 97, 176-181, 187, 201, 214, 236, 238, 243, 264, 317, 322, 340, 342-343, 410, 416, 480-481
Dorsetshire Regiment 44, 61, 66, 97, 100, 152, 170-173, 176-177, 247-252, 264, 266-268, 301, 317, 319-320, 340, 417, 420, 434, 439-440, 447, 450-456, 463, 481-482, 486, 585
Duke of Cornwall's Light Infantry 444-445, 450, 473, 475, 490, 552, 557-559, 561
Duke of Wellington's Regiment 330, 348, 367, 369-371, 376, 378, 404-407, 444-445, 450, 473, 475, 490, 552, 557-558
Durham Light Infantry 30-32, 52, 54, 58, 63-64, 69, 75, 80, 136-147, 243, 245-247, 252, 259-264, 267, 301-316, 332, 334, 336, 344, 370, 379-380, 382, 388, 390-392, 394, 397, 402, 418-421, 435, 477-479, 481, 483, 498, 508

East Yorkshire Regiment 28-30, 46, 51, 60, 71, 73, 75, 97, 100-101, 104-114, 124, 126-127, 133-135, 148-149, 264, 268, 322, 326-327, 423, 434, 479-480, 504, 512, 588-589
East Lancashire Regiment 426-427
Essex Regiment 49, 59, 68, 189-191, 193-195, 230-232, 272-273, 332-339, 407-409, 432
Essex Yeomanry 80-81, 88, 156-157, 168, 175, 198, 200, 208, 235, 247, 253, 259, 494

Gloucestershire Regiment 42, 48, 52, 67, 189, 192-195, 231-232, 273, 332, 432
Green Howards 32, 35-36, 40, 42, 44-45, 57-58, 65, 70, 72, 78, 89, 97, 100, 104, 113-133, 135, 225, 227, 243, 253-258, 297-299, 320, 322-327, 340, 479, 482

Hampshire Regiment 37-39, 41, 49, 54, 65, 70, 76, 84, 88, 97, 150, 152, 155-157, 159, 161-162, 164, 166-170, 198-212, 301, 317-320, 326, 340-345, 410, 412-417, 421, 433, 439-440, 448, 450, 452, 455, 464, 471, 477, 480-482, 486, 497, 518, 587

King's Royal Rifle Corps (KRRC) 248, 371, 373-375, 588

Lincolnshire Regiment 300

50th (Northumbrian) Division 23, 25, 28-29, 31-32, 34, 37-38, 42, 44, 71, 77, 80, 92-94, 125, 197, 213, 220, 223, 234, 247, 252, 269, 272, 290-291, 294, 298, 301, 339, 344-345, 390, 418, 420, 431, 436, 438, 476, 484, 487, 498, 506, 518, 582

Rifle Brigade 275-276, 282, 584
Royal Army Service Corps (RASC) 214, 235-237, 242, 446, 526, 533, 551
Royal Dragoon Guards 67, 105, 120, 128-129, 142, 158, 164, 166, 213, 225, 227-228, 247, 253-256, 271, 296, 302, 305, 308, 310-316, 353, 356, 371-372, 374, 388, 406, 438, 441-442, 446, 473-474, 559-561, 563, 570-571, 580-581
Royal Engineers 84, 491, 518, 526, 539, 55-551, 553
Royal Marine Commando 25, 67, 78-79, 82, 91, 97, 111, 150, 159, 173, 175, 183-189, 234-239, 241-243, 391, 571
Royal Norfolk Regiment 427
Royal Scots Fusiliers 328, 350, 352-355, 367-368, 371-372, 390

59th (Staffordshire) Division 426-427, 431
Somerset Light Infantry 438-441, 443-444, 449, 463-465, 468-472, 485, 489, 463-465, 468-472, 485, 489, 490, 496, 498, 519-520, 525, 531, 533-536, 538, 548, 551-552, 559-563, 572-575, 578, 577

43rd (Wessex) Division 431, 436, 438, 440-442, 444, 446, 450, 453, 456, 463, 473, 476-477, 484-485, 487, 489-490, 494, 498, 513, 519, 522, 536, 541, 556-557, 561-562, 578, 580-582, 588
49th (West Riding) Division 298-300, 327, 346, 349, 367, 372, 379, 388-390, 394, 396, 402, 404, 431, 434
Wiltshire Regiment 445, 448, 456, 458, 471, 473, 486, 496-497, 519-520, 523, 525-527, 529-532, 536, 538-539, 541-542, 546, 548-550, 575-577
Worcestershire Regiment 441, 444, 446, 471, 473, 475-476, 490-491, 493, 494-497, 519-520, 536-538, 542-549, 552, 559, 562-565, 567, 569-572, 579-581

York & Lancaster Regiment (Hallamshire Battalion) 300, 347, 355

German
12th SS Panzer Division *Hitlerjugend* 150-151, 218, 220, 264–266, 268, 300, 351, 355–6, 364–365, 367, 369, 375–376, 379–380, 406–407, 423–424
Kampfgruppe Schrader 557, 561–563, 565, 570–573, 575, 579
Panzer-Lehr-Division, 216, 218, 267–268, 281, 283, 285, 287, 293–295, 331, 341, 343, 345, 366–367, 416, 418
I SS-Panzerkorps 274, 292–293, 388, 422